Exploration and Contestation in the Study of World Politics

EXPLORATION AND CONTESTATION IN THE STUDY OF WORLD POLITICS

edited by
Peter J. Katzenstein, Robert O. Keohane,
and Stephen D. Krasner

The MIT Press

Cambridge, Massachusetts and London, England

Second printing, 2000

© 1999 Massachusetts Institute of Technology and the IO Foundation

Library of Congress Cataloging-in-Publication Data

Exploration and contestation in the study of world politics / edited
   by Peter J. Katzenstein, Robert O. Keohane, Stephen D. Krasner.
      p.   cm.—(*International organization* reader)
   Originally published in *International organization,* v. 52, no. 4
   (autumn 1998).
   Includes bibliographical references.
   ISBN 0-262-11242-6 (hc : alk. paper).—ISBN 0-262-61144-9 (pbk. : alk. paper)
   1. International relations. 2. International cooperation. 3. World politics.
   I. Katzenstein, Peter J. II. Keohane, Robert O. (Robert Owen), 1941–   .
   III. Krasner, Stephen D., 1942–   . IV. Series.
JZ1242.E98   1999
   327.1′01—dc21   98-50302
                                                                      CIP

Contents

Contributors

Barry Eichengreen is John L. Simpson Professor of Economics and Political Science at the University of California, Berkeley.

Martha Finnemore is Associate Professor of Political Science and International Affairs at George Washington University, Washington, D. C.

Geoffrey Garrett is Professor of Political Science at Yale University, New Haven, Connecticut.

Robert Jervis is Adlai E. Stevenson Professor of International Politics, Columbia University, New York, New York.

Miles Kahler is Rohr Professor of Pacific International Relations at the Graduate School of International Relations and Pacific Studies, University of California, San Diego.

Peter J. Katzenstein is Walter S. Carpenter, Jr. Professor of International Studies at Cornell University, Ithaca, New York.

Robert O. Keohane is James B. Duke Professor of Political Science at Duke University, Durham, North Carolina.

Stephen D. Krasner is Graham H. Stuart Professor of International Relations and Senior Fellow in the Institute for International Studies at Stanford University, Stanford, California.

James G. March is Professor Emeritus of Management, Political Science, Sociology, and Education at Stanford University, Stanford, California.

Lisa L. Martin is Professor of Government at Harvard University, Cambridge, Massachusetts.

Michael Mastanduno is Professor of Government and Director of the John Sloan Dickey Center for International Understanding at Dartmouth College, Hanover, New Hampshire.

Helen V. Milner is Professor of Political Science at Columbia University, New York, New York.

Johan P. Olsen is Director of a research programme on the Europeanization of the nation state financed by the Norwegian Research Council and Adjunct Professor of Political Science at the University of Oslo, Oslo, Norway.

John Gerard Ruggie currently serves as chief adviser for strategic planning to United Nations Secretary-General Kofi Annan, at the rank of Assistant Secretary-General. He is on leave as Burgess Professor of Political Science and International Affairs at Columbia University, where he was Dean of the School of International and Public Affairs from 1991–96.

Kathryn Sikkink is Professor of Political Science at the University of Minnesota, Minneapolis, Minnesota.

Beth Simmons is Associate Professor of Political Science at the University of California, Berkeley.

Ole Wæver is Senior Research Fellow at the Copenhagen Peace Research Institute in Denmark.

Abstracts

International Organization and the Study of World Politics
by Peter J. Katzenstein, Robert O. Keohane, and Stephen D. Krasner

A distinct subfield of international relations, IPE, has emerged over the last thirty years, largely in the pages of *International Organization.* IPE began with the study of international political economy, but over time its boundaries have been set more by a series of theoretical debates than by subject matter. These debates have been organized around points of contestation between specific research programs, reflecting fundamental differences among the generic theoretical orientations in which these research programs are embedded. The fate of specific research programs has depended on their ability to specify cause and effect relationships and to operationalize relevant variables. Scholarship in IPE has become more sophisticated both methodologically and theoretically, and many of its insights have been incorporated into policy discussions. Past points of contestation, including those between realism and its liberal challengers and between various conceptions of domestic structure and international relations, help us to understand recent debates between rationalism and constructivism.

The Sociology of a Not So International Discipline: American and European Developments in International Relations
by Ole Wæver

The international relations (IR) discipline is dominated by the American research community. Data about publication patterns in leading journals document this situation as well as a variance in theoretical orientations. IR is conducted differently in different places. The main patterns are explained through a sociology of science model that emphasizes the different nineteenth-century histories of the state, the early format of social science, and the institutionalized delineation among the different social sciences. The internal social and intellectual structure of American IR is two-tiered, with relatively independent subfields and a top layer defined by access to the leading journals (on which IR, in contrast to some social sciences, has a high consensus). The famous successive "great debates" serve an important function by letting lead theorists focus and structure the whole discipline. IR in France, Germany, and the United Kingdom has historically been structured differently, often with power vested more locally. American IR now moves in a direction that undermines its global hegemony. The widespread turn to rational choice privileges a reintegration (and status-wise rehabilitation) with the rest of political science over attention to IR practices elsewhere. This rationalistic turn is alien to Europeans, both because their IR is generally closer to sociology, philosophy, and anthropology, and because the liberal ontological premises of rational choice are less fitting to European societies. Simultaneously, European IR is beginning to break the local power bastions and establish independent research communities at a national or, increasingly, a European level. As American IR turns from global hegemony to national professionalization, IR becomes more pluralistic.

Theories and Empirical Studies of International Institutions
by Lisa L. Martin and Beth Simmons

Studies of international institutions, organizations, and regimes have consistently appeared in the pages of *International Organization*. We review the theoretical and empirical work on international institutions and identify promising directions for the institutionalist research program. Early studies of international institutions were rich with empirical insights and often influenced by theoretical developments in other fields of political science, but lacking an overarching analytical framework they failed to produce a coherent body of scholarship. Current efforts to reinvigorate the study of international institutions draw on a new body of theory about domestic institutions. We argue that the assumptions of this new approach to institutions are more appropriate to international studies than those of earlier attempts to transfer theories across levels of analysis. We suggest that the most productive questions for future research will focus on specifying alternative mechanisms by which institutions can influence outcomes and identify particular sets of questions within this agenda that are especially promising.

Rationalizing Politics: The Emerging Synthesis Among International, American, and Comparative Politics
by Helen V. Milner

International relations has often been treated as a separate discipline distinct from the other major fields in political science, namely American and comparative politics. A main reason for this distinction has been the claim that politics in the international system is radically different from politics domestically. The degree of divergence between international relations (IR) and the rest of political science has waxed and waned over the years; however, in the past decade it seems to have lessened. This process has occurred mainly in the "rationalist research paradigm," and there it has both substantive and methodological components. Scholars in this paradigm have increasingly appreciated that politics in the international realm is not so different from that internal to states, and vice versa. This rationalist institutionalist research agenda thus challenges two of the main assumptions in IR theory. Moreover, scholars across the three fields now tend to employ the same methods. The last decade has seen increasing cross-fertilization of the fields around the importance of institutional analysis. Such analysis implies a particular concern with the mechanisms of collective choice in situations of strategic interaction. Some of the new tools in American and comparative politics allow the complex, strategic interactions among domestic and international agents to be understood in a more systematic and cumulative way.

Global Markets and National Politics: Collision Course or Virtuous Circle?
by Geoffrey Garrett

Increasing exposure to trade, foreign direct investment, and liquid capital mobility have not prompted a pervasive policy race to the neoliberal bottom among the OECD countries. One reason is that there are strong political incentives for governments to cushion the dislocations and risk generated by openness. Moreover, countries with large and expanding public economies (when balanced with increased revenues, even from capital taxes) have not suffered from capital flight or higher interest rates. This is because the modern welfare state, comprising income transfer programs and publicly provided social services, generates economically important collective goods that are undersupplied by markets and that actors are interested in productivity value. These range from the accumulation of human and physical capital to social stability under conditions of high market uncertainty to popular support for the market economy itself. As a result, arguments about the demise of national autonomy in the global economy are considerably overdrawn.

Economics and Security in Statecraft and Scholarship
by Michael Mastanduno

This article traces and explains how U.S. policy officials and IR scholars have conceived of the relationship between economics and security over the past half-century. During the interwar years, economics and security were integrated in both scholarship and statecraft. During the Cold War, scholars treated the two issues as separate areas of inquiry. U.S. policymakers integrated economics and security during the early Cold War, but by the 1970s the two components of U.S. foreign policy had drifted apart. After the Cold War, a renewed emphasis has emerged in both U.S. statecraft and IR scholarship on the integration of economics and security. Three factors explain these patterns: (1) the international distribution of material capabilities, (2) perceptions of the strategic environment, and (3) perceptions of the position of the United States in international economic competition.

What Makes the World Hang Together? Neo-Utilitarianism and the Social Constructivist Challenge
By John Gerard Ruggie

Social constructivism in international relations has come into its own during the past decade, not only as a metatheoretical critique of currently dominant neo-utilitarian approaches (neo-realism and neoliberal institutionalism) but increasingly in the form of detailed empirical findings and theoretical insights. Constructivism addresses many of the same issues addressed by neo-utilitarianism, though from a different vantage and, therefore, with different effect. It also concerns itself with issues that neo-utilitarianism treats by assumption, discounts, ignores, or simply cannot apprehend within its characteristic ontology and/or epistemology. The constructivist project has sought to open up the relatively narrow theoretical confines of conventional approaches—by pushing them back to problematize the interests and identities of actors; deeper to incorporate the intersubjective bases of social action and social order; and into the dimensions of space and time to establish international structure as contingent practice, constraining social action but also being (re)created and, therefore, potentially transformed by it.

International Norm Dynamics and Political Change
by Martha Finnemore and Kathryn Sikkink

Norms have never been absent from the study of international politics, but the sweeping "ideational turn" in the 1980s and 1990s brought them back as a central theoretical concern in the field. Much theorizing about norms has focused on how they create social structure, standards of appropriateness, and stability in international politics. Recent empirical research on norms, in contrast, has examined their role in creating political change, but change processes have been less well-theorized. We induce from this research a variety of theoretical arguments and testable hypotheses about the role of norms in political change. We argue that norms evolve in a three-stage "life cycle" of emergence, "norm cascades," and internalization, and that each stage is governed by different motives, mechanisms, and behavioral logics. We also highlight the rational and strategic nature of many social construction processes and argue that theoretical progress will only be made by placing attention on the connections between norms and rationality rather than by opposing the two.

Rationality in International Relations
by Miles Kahler

Rationalist models have faced four persistent sets of critics as the research program of international relations has evolved. Under neorealism's structural constraints of international competition and selection, agents' rationality may appear superfluous. Psychological critics have presented neither a single theoretical alternative to rational choice nor contingent hypotheses that specify when psychological distortions of rational decision making are most likely. Both rational choice and psychological approaches must construct models of action for social entities that aggregate individuals. The rationality and individualism of beliefs is questioned by theorists who stress culture, identity, and norms as independent sources of action. Careful stipulation of scope, acknowledgment of methodological shortcomings, and precise definition of differences can serve to bridge the theoretical divide between rational choice models and their critics. Problem-centered research provides a level playing field on which theoretical competition can be established.

The Institutional Dynamics of International Political Orders
by James G. March and Johan P. Olsen

The history of international political orders is written in terms of continuity and change in domestic and international political relations. As a step toward understanding such continuity and change, we explore some ideas drawn from an institutional perspective. An institutional perspective is characterized in terms of two grand issues that divide students of international relations and other organized systems. The first issue concerns the basic logic of action by which human behavior is shaped. On the one side are those who see action as driven by a logic of anticipated consequences and prior preferences. On the other side are those who see action as driven by a logic of appropriateness and a sense of identity. The second issue concerns the efficiency of history. On the one side are those who see history as efficient in the sense that it follows a course leading to a unique equilibrium dictated by exogenously determined interests, identities, and resources. On the other side are those who see history as inefficient in the sense that it follows a meandering, path-dependent course distinguished by multiple equilibria and endogenous transformations of interests, identities, and resources. We argue that the tendency of students of international political order to emphasize efficient histories and consequential bases for action leads them to underestimate the significance of rule- and identity-based action and inefficient histories. We illustrate such an institutional perspective by considering some features of the coevolution of politics and institutions, particularly the ways in which engagement in political activities affects the definition and elaboration of political identities and the development of competence in politics and the capabilities of political institutions.

Realism in the Study of World Politics
by Robert Jervis

The popularity of alternative approaches to international politics cannot be explained entirely by their scholarly virtues. Among the other factors at work are fashions and normative and political preferences. This in part explains the increasing role of rationalism and constructivism. Important as they are, these approaches are necessarily less complete than liberalism, Marxism, and realism. Indeed, they fit better with the latter than is often realized. Realism, then, continues to play a major role in IR scholarship. It can elucidate the conditions and strategies that are conducive to cooperation and can account for significant international change, including a greatly decreased tolerance for force among developed countries, which appears to be currently the case. But neither it nor other approaches have as yet proved to be reliable guides to this new world.

Dental Hygiene and Nuclear War: How International Relations Looks from Economics
by Barry Eichengreen

This article adopts economics as a perspective from which to view recent research in international relations. The most telling difference between international relations and economics, it argues, is in the connection between theory and empirical work. The strength of economics is the complementary and mutually supporting character of theoretical and empirical work. In international relations, in contrast, the connections between theory and empirics are looser. As a consequence, research in international relations has not converged to a core of common theoretical assumptions and an arsenal of commonly accepted empirical techniques.

Preface: *International Organization* at Its Golden Anniversary

Peter J. Katzenstein, Robert O. Keohane, and Stephen D. Krasner

This special issue of *International Organization* looks back on the first fifty years, and especially the last thirty, of this journal. As former editors, we were asked by the editorial board in 1996 to create a special fiftieth anniversary issue. In good academic style, the thought came late and the issue is tardy: you will notice that this is volume 52 of *International Organization* (founded in 1947). Like many a graduate student over these decades, we hope that the quality of our product will compensate for our long-standing "incomplete."

In its recent history, *IO* has emphasized certain themes: international political economy—a field pioneered largely in these pages during the 1970s; the connections between domestic and international political economy; how international institutions operate and change. But *IO* has not enunciated an orthodoxy. Controversy has flourished on issues ranging from the relative merits of approaches such as realism, rational institutionalism, and constructivism to the interaction between the pressures of an increasingly globalized world economy and the diverse institutions of domestic politics or the connections between security issues and political economy.

In this issue we try to capture this combination of thematic coherence and theoretical controversy. We emphasize the themes that have been most important to *IO* over the years. We do not pretend to survey "the field" of international politics, much less to pass judgment on the relative importance of all the research programs that have flourished, or atrophied, over the last thirty years. We have deliberately overlooked major areas of study that have not been prominent in these pages, such as issues of rationality and war, the "democratic peace," the success and failure of deterrence strategies, foreign policy decision making, and quantitative methodology and modeling in international relations. These literatures are all large and contain illustrious, important work, but little of that work first appeared in *IO*. Likewise, in our own article we have not surveyed the large body of work by scholars outside the United States that did not find an outlet in *IO*. However, we regarded this work as sufficiently important, and U.S. scholarship as sufficiently parochial, to commission an article by Ole Waever that would critically review U.S. work in light of European

International Organization 52, 4, Autumn 1998, pp. xv–xviii traditions. For better or worse, we have circumscribed our subject by the themes that *IO* has stressed.

In our article in this issue we speak with our own "voice"—not as editors, but as scholars in the field looking back especially on the thirty or so years during which we have been active in it. While preparing the article we encountered a dilemma that we were unable to fully resolve. We tried to write candidly and forcefully about how international political economy has evolved and also to represent a variety of research traditions fairly. Yet we know that we are not neutral external observers. We have been participants in the process, with our own axes to grind. Our views are clear on some debates because we were protagonists in them; other debates—equally important in generating interesting scholarship and enhancing our knowledge of the world—are more opaque to us because we were not so directly involved in them. Judging from reactions to earlier drafts, the article will encounter more debate than assent. No one else would tell the story just as we have; indeed, each of us individually would tell it somewhat differently. We hope, at least, that it is interesting and thought provoking.

The purpose of this issue is to illuminate past pathways and to open vistas on future directions for research. The articles explore major lines of research in the field of international political economy (IPE) broadly defined, demonstrate how they have evolved over time, show how they have interrogated one another, and illustrate how the engagement of scholars writing from many different orientations has illuminated an extraordinarily complex range of phenomena, encompassing international and domestic politics, power and wealth, and ideas and material concerns. As students of politics we know that power matters also in academia. Nevertheless, we hope that we have given open expression to diverse perspectives.

This issue is organized around three clusters of work. We built the core of the issue by commissioning articles that would develop arguments about the "state of the art" on different substantive or theoretical questions that have been important in the pages of *IO*. We began by asking for proposals from more than twenty distinguished scholars who have made contributions to *IO* over the years. We received sixteen proposals from which we made a selection in an attempt to publish an innovative but coherent set of final articles. In an effort to reach beyond the set of scholars who regularly publish in *IO*, we commissioned the articles by Ole Waever, James March and Johan Olsen, Barry Eichengreen, and Robert Jervis.

The articles are grouped into five parts. Part I offers a historical overview, with the first article written from the perspective of the United States and the second from the critical distance of Europe. In our own article we seek to weave together the major strands of work published in *IO* over the years; we also seek to make a dialectical argument about how the field has evolved through various points of contestation that, though never reaching definitive resolutions of the conflicts between generic analytical orientations, have enriched our knowledge of world politics. The second article, by Ole Waever, looks at the whole debate from a European perspective, helping us to understand the implicit assumptions and biases that have shaped this "American social science."[1]

The four articles in Part II reflect a "rationalist" orientation, as understood broadly. Two of the articles explore issues that have been prominent in *IO*: the study of international institutions, discussed by Lisa L. Martin and Beth Simmons; and international and domestic political economy, analyzed by Helen V. Milner. In the other two articles Geoffrey Garrett examines how global markets relate to national policies, and Michael Mastanduno reviews the connections between economics and security.

The articles in Part III are written from a "constructivist" orientation. In the articles by John Ruggie and by Martha Finnemore and Kathryn Sikkink, the authors differentiate their arguments from rationalism and seek to show why rationalism insufficiently accounts for a range of important issues in world politics.

The two articles in Part IV juxtapose in different ways rationalist and constructivist perspectives. Miles Kahler reflects on the role of reason in the study of international relations—the key point of contestation between contemporary rationalism and constructivism. James March and Johan Olsen emphasize the "logic of appropriateness" and the "logic of consequences" and question the equilibrium-oriented assumption of historical efficiency.

Finally, in Part V two critical commentaries are offered from the perspectives of realism and economics. Robert Jervis discusses the continuing relevance of realism in the study of world politics, counterbalancing the argument we develop in our article, which gives realism a lower profile. Barry Eichengreen compares his own discipline of economics to our field, much to the advantage of the former.

As this brief preview suggests, this special issue seeks to combine thematic coherence with intellectual pluralism. The pluralism may be more obvious than the themes. Yet common themes do exist as authors highlight recurring questions about theory, method, substantive knowledge, and different generic theoretical orientations and specific research programs. A set of issues recurs throughout this issue, including topics such as the role of reason, the impact of power asymmetries on international relations, the connections between economics and politics and between global and domestic political economy, and the processes characteristic of domestic and international institutions. We hope and expect that some of our readers, particularly graduate students, will see new connections among these themes and will develop new criticisms of specific arguments in this issue.

One of our aspirations when we began working on this issue was to link the world of *IO* with the world of policy. Few such connections, however, have been made here. Although one of our authors, John Ruggie, is currently a high official of the United Nations, he does not seek to draw a connection between his theoretical work (which he synthesizes in his article in Part III) and his role as an actor in world politics. As work published in *IO* has become more theoretically and methodologi-

---

1. Hoffmann 1977.

cally self-conscious, the connections prominent during the first years of the journal between academic analysis and policy have been stretched thin or even broken. Policy relevant articles have become few and far between. Nevertheless, the same cleavages have been at the center of both scholarly and policy discussions: power politics versus the opportunities for mutual gain; the possibilities for altering beliefs and objectives versus a focus on material gains or greater security. This might simply reflect parallel developments in both arenas, or scholars might even be following the lead of policymakers. But it is more likely that decision makers, confronted with multiple demands and short time horizons, draw on intellectual capital that has been generated in universities, often through discussions that are far removed from immediate policy concerns.

First drafts of most of the articles were discussed at an authors' conference held in August 1997. We, as editors, commented on all of the articles. The two other members of the *IO* review committee, Judith Goldstein and Arthur Stein, provided valuable comments on a number of drafts during the winter of 1997–98. We are also grateful to the many colleagues who commented on our own article, and they are individually acknowledged in the authors' note to that article.

For us this process has been a great learning experience. Commenting on the articles—and commenting on each others' comments on the articles—has been fascinating. Writing our own synthesis in a way that seems intelligible was a challenge, and our success is best judged by our readers. We can attest, however, that our friendship not only survived but grew stronger in the process. Nevertheless, it is humbling to recognize how incompletely the three of us understand a subject to which we have devoted, collectively, a century of our intellectual and professional lives.

International Organization
and the Study of World Politics

Peter J. Katzenstein, Robert O. Keohane, and Stephen D. Krasner

In this article we tell the story of the creation and evolution of a subfield, popularly known as "IPE," that has been closely associated with *International Organization (IO)* for almost thirty years. Initially, IPE was defined by the topics that it investigated, such as trade, finance, raw materials politics, and multinational corporations. Scholars associated with the field drew on economics and on a variety of existing theoretical orientations, notably realism, liberalism, and Marxism at the systemic level, and Marxism, statism, and pluralism at the domestic level.

Over time the boundaries of this subfield, as we define it, have been set less by subject matter than by theoretical perspectives. Whereas some research programs have relied heavily on economics, others have distanced themselves both from the substantive concerns of that discipline and the rationalism it represents. Since we are seeking in this article to describe how theorizing about world politics as represented in *IO* evolved, we focus on IPE, rather than on the substantive issues of international political economy with which it began. We use the term *international political economy* when we refer to real-world connections between politics and economics; we use the term *IPE* when we refer to the subfield of work, centered in *IO* since 1971, that evolved from the study of international political economy to analyze a variety of aspects of world politics.

Like any narrative, our story reflects the viewpoints of its authors; and since we played a role in these events, it inevitably reflects our own experiences and biases. As noted in the preface, we put our account forward as a perspective, not as a canonical representation of what is most important. Furthermore, we make no claim that the

During the writing of this article we received long, thoughtful, and detailed comments on previous drafts. They were enormously helpful in clarifying and equilibrating the historical narrative that we are offering here. Several colleagues offered valuable oral comments as well. We would like to thank Emanuel Adler, David Baldwin, Marc L. Busch, Benjamin J. Cohen, David Dessler, Judith Goldstein, Peter Gourevitch, Stephan Haggard, Ernst B. Haas, Peter Hall, Robert Jervis, Miles Kahler, Charles Kupchan, David Lake, Robert Lieber, Henry Nau, Joseph Nye, M. J. Peterson, Simon Reich, Thomas Risse, John Gerard Ruggie, Bruce Russett, Kiron Skinner, Arthur Stein, Janice Stein, Alexander E. Wendt, and Oran R. Young.

evolving subfield of IPE encompasses the most important work that has been done in international politics over the last thirty years. Major research has been carried out on subjects such as war initiation, the "democratic peace," and alliance politics, to mention only a few. Some theoretical orientations that have been highly salient for the study of security, especially organization theory and cognitive psychology, have been much less consequential for IPE. Studies generated by large-N statistical research programs such as the Correlates of War project have not been prominent in the pages of *IO*. Since this article was written for an anniversary issue of *IO*, it seems appropriate to ground it in the major lines of work for which the journal became known.

Theory in our field has been thought of in a variety of ways. In this article we focus on two of its meanings: general theoretical orientations and specific research programs. *General theoretical orientations* provide heuristics—they suggest relevant variables and causal patterns that provide guidelines for developing specific research programs. Political science is an eclectic discipline that finds many of its most fruitful ideas elsewhere, and many of the general theoretical orientations that have been relevant for IPE were borrowed from other disciplines, especially economics and sociology. Rationalist theories derived from economics, for instance, offer the following heuristic: if you have a puzzle, formulate it as a problem for rational actors with unproblematically specified interests, competing in a situation characterized by scarce resources. Constructivist theories, in contrast, look to the humanities and sociology for insights into how "reality," including the interests that partially constitute the identity of actors, is socially constructed. We argue in the fourth section of the article that rationalism (encompassing both liberal arguments grounded in economics that emphasize voluntary agreement and realist arguments that focus on power and coercion) and constructivism now provide the major points of contestation for international relations scholarship.

Specific research programs link explanatory variables to a set of outcomes, or dependent variables. What are the effects of various distributions of power, or of democracy, on the propensity of states to fight wars? Under what conditions do international institutions actually promote cooperation? What institutional features of state–society relationships explain variations in the effectiveness of foreign economic policy? When such theories are tested with evidence, answers are proposed— answers that are virtually always contested because of the difficulties of theory specification, testing, and controlled statistical analysis that bedevil the nonexperimental sciences in general, and fields such as ours in particular.

General theoretical orientations—such as realism, Marxism, liberalism, statism, pluralism, historical institutionalism, rational choice institutionalism, and constructivism—have been particularly prominent in the study of international relations. IPE is no exception. Such generic approaches do not disappear easily. They provide suggestions about relevant variables and their possible interrelationships but are consistent with many specific research tasks and clusters of testable hypotheses. We refer to these sets of tasks and hypotheses as *specific research programs,* without necessarily accepting Imre Lakatos's philosophy of science as applicable to our field.[1] The connection between generic orientations and research programs means that the intellectual standing of generic orientations is affected, though not entirely determined, by empirical evidence. As a result of confrontation with evidence, and also due to shifts in world politics itself, some hypotheses, and the research programs in which they were embedded, have received more support than others. Generic orientations that sheltered productive programs benefited at the expense of competitors; those that seemed to illuminate new developments in the world also gained adherents. Dissatisfaction with existing orientations and research programs, coupled with changes in the world, has created openings for alternative conceptualizations. This evolutionary process is often indirect and imperfect: there are no "decisive experiments" in international relations that discredit a research program much less a generic approach that has spawned research programs.

From its inception IPE has evolved two related though distinctive sites for research: the international system and the interactions between domestic politics and international political economy. The first site focuses at the level of the international system. In the 1970s systemic scholarship on the international political economy drew on realist arguments about the importance of the distribution of power among states, then the prevailing general theoretical orientation in international relations. IPE scholars also developed a variety of liberal research programs that were reflected in discussions of European integration, the growing role of multinational corporations, and increases in international interdependence. In the 1980s the differences between realism and liberalism were sharpened as neorealists and neoliberals debated the relative merits of their contrasting analytical programs.

Our story about the systemic variant of IPE goes as follows. In the late 1960s and mid-1970s some young political scientists studying international relations seized an opening created both by events in the world and in the social sciences. Growing levels of international interdependence pointed to by a few economists helped in the conceptualization of transnational relations theory. This analytical approach provided an alternative to the state-centric, realist approach then dominating the study of international relations more generally. It was the first analytical formulation that one could clearly associate with IPE as a distinct field. Transnationalism was challenged by hegemonic stability theory, which had both liberal and realist variants. These initial research programs were reformulated as a result of their interaction with each other and with some variants of Marxism. Hegemonic stability theory encountered both logical and empirical anomalies. Transnational relations theory was difficult to operationalize. In the 1980s neoliberal institutionalism and a specific realist formulation known as neorealism became the principal interlocutors—institutionalists emphasized the potential for interstate cooperation, whereas realists stressed the importance of state power. Since the late 1980s a new debate between constructivism and rationalism (including both realism and liberalism) has become more prominent as con-

1. Lakatos 1970.

tructivists have built on epistemological challenges rooted in sociological perspectives emphasizing shared norms and values.

The second site for research has been the linkage between domestic politics and the international political economy. Scholars working on these issues inquired into the determinants of the foreign economic policies of states and corporate strategies, which they have investigated with close attention to empirical detail. The questions asked in this line of research focused on the relative influence and autonomy of social forces and political institutions. Research was in general more empirically oriented. Metatheoretical concerns loomed less large for scholars in this area than for those working with systemic level theories, although in domestic as well as systemic analyses general research orientations—such as pluralism, statism, Marxism, rational choice institutionalism, and historical institutionalism—informed specific research programs. Empirically, the focus on state–society relations started with concrete analyses of the OECD countries and Latin American states. It spread from there to encompass the political economy of states in other world regions, specifically the analysis of varieties of state-led development in Asia and the transition out of socialism in eastern Europe and the states of the former Soviet Union.

Scholars of comparative politics insisted that systemic arguments were at best incomplete; variations in domestic structures (defined in terms of social structure as well as group and party alignments) would lead to different national and corporate responses to the same external pressures and opportunities. Some of the earliest domestic politics formulations associated with IPE drew on pluralism, then the prevailing approach to U.S. politics. Over time, a variety of approaches, including historical institutionalism and, more recently, rational choice institutionalism, were applied to a growing number of political economies worldwide.

There was a close interaction between comparative and international relations scholars; indeed, some individuals transcended the boundaries between these two fields. But during the 1970s and 1980s the difference between the international and domestic strands of the IPE field remained salient. That distinction has blurred somewhat in the 1990s because, as we argue later, rationalism (incorporating both realism and liberalism) and constructivism have established a new point of contestation. Some of the specific research programs generated by general theoretical orientations, such as rational choice institutionalism, are more readily applicable across different levels of analysis than was the case for most of the systemic and domestic orientations, such as realism and pluralism, that were prominent in earlier periods.

The difference between international and domestic perspectives does not overshadow, however, a common research practice that has marked empirical work in both of the main branches of IPE. Scholars have specified research problems in a way that was empirically tractable, intellectually interesting, and politically significant. They embedded explanatory variables in causal mechanisms through which outcomes seemed to take place. They conducted research that sought to control for some other explanatory factors. And they sought to determine whether the selected explanatory variable exerted a discernible effect on specified outcomes. Fruitful research programs combined deductive and inductive work in different proportions. But in the final analysis, any productive research program had to suggest ways in which variables or concepts could be operationalized; and its propositions had to be, at least in principle, empirically falsifiable.

General orientations and their associated specific research programs typically enter into complex mutual interrogations with their previously established counterparts. As a result of such dialogues, orientations are reconfigured or merged; or they remain separate, with one approach losing adherents; or they coexist, competing on relatively equal terms. Thomas Kuhn does not provide an accurate description of the study of IPE or, for that matter, international relations more generally.[2] IPE has not been characterized by scientific revolutions succeeded by a period of normal science in which a particular general theoretical orientation is uncontested. There has always been vigorous debate between competing general theoretical orientations and associated research programs.

The lines of thinking originally nurtured in *IO*, and largely limited to international political economy and its intersections with comparative politics and international institutions, seem in the 1990s to be merging into a broader and richly reconfigured field of world politics. Insights originally generated in studying the international political economy have been extended to other issue areas, such as environmental or security affairs. Linkages among issues mean that many important phenomena in world politics can no longer be neatly classified by issue area, such as economics or security affairs. And old boundaries between international relations and comparative politics, or between IPE and the rest of international relations, have become increasingly fluid. Responding to these changes, scholars have modified existing lines of research and initiated new ones. They have sharpened some analytical distinctions and erased others. They have sought to advance reformulated synthetic interpretations and focused on new points of intellectual contestation.

Since the mid-1980s a new debate between constructivism and rationalism (including both realism and liberalism) has become more prominent. New theoretical developments in rationalist institutional theory, open-economy economics, and comparative politics provided scholars with new intellectual openings as the Cold War ended. Conventional and critical contructivists, influenced by new trends in the humanities, put forward sociological perspectives that emphasized shared norms and values but which were in epistemological terms sharply differentiated from postmodernism. In the field of national security the discussion between rationalism (in its realist and liberal variants) and constructivism has been more fully joined than in the field of IPE.

We do not presume to predict the future of either world politics or international relations theory. But we do insist on two points. First, the evolution of the subfield of IPE is better described in terms of focal points of contestation and hypothesis testing than as an all-out war leading to the victory of one general orientation over another. Second, current intellectual developments in IPE can be made more comprehensible by comparing them with the last cycle—from the intellectual and political openings

2. Kuhn 1962.

of the 1970s to the relative syntheses of the late 1980s, which presaged another political and intellectual upheaval beginning around 1990. Thus, we interpret the past in order to understand the present.

In the first section of the article we briefly review some aspects of the field in the years between the late 1940s (when *IO* was founded) and 1968. We then discuss the intellectual opening for IPE, beginning in the late 1960s. In the second section we analyze the symbiotic yet contested relationship between realism and liberalism during the last thirty years. In the third section we trace the evolution of domestic politics research and its eventual differentiation into historical-institutionalist and rationalist styles of research. In the fourth section we analyze the new intellectual opening created by the end of the Cold War and argue that efforts from various quarters to understand actor preferences are creating new points of contestation in the study of world politics while blurring some established fault lines. In the conclusion we argue that current scholarship is integrating IPE even more fully into the broader discipline of international relations and into overarching debates in the natural and social sciences and in the humanities.

An Intellectual Opening, 1968–78

IO existed for two decades before 1968, representing an established tradition in the study of international organizations. During the 1960s *IO* published some of the leading work on European integration, work that challenged realism and provided concepts for the analysis of the politics of economic interdependence. As discussed in this section, after 1968 an intellectual opening for the study of international political economy emerged.

IO's First Two Decades, 1947–67

IO was founded at a time of profound and rapid change in international relations. An extensive and untried set of international organizations had been established during and just after World War II. Seeking not only to describe their activities, but also to promote "a comparative study of international organizations and why they have or have not worked in varying circumstances," the trustees of the World Peace Foundation decided in the spring of 1946 to establish this journal, whose first issue appeared in February 1947.[3] By that time, relations between the Soviet Union and its former Western allies had become highly strained, and what later became known as the Cold War was beginning, marked by crises in Iran and Greece and, in the spring of 1947, by the Truman Doctrine and the Marshall Plan.

IO had the task of analyzing both the formation of new international organizations and the superpower rivalry that threatened to kill or maim them at birth. In the lead

---

3. The World Peace Foundation was established in 1910 by Edwin Ginn, head of the publishing company bearing his name.

article in the first issue, Leland M. Goodrich argued that the nascent UN was uncomfortably similar to the League of Nations in its design: "Like the League, but for somewhat different technical reasons, the United Nations, in so far as its enforcement activities are concerned, is an organization for the enforcement of peace among the smaller states."[4] Other articles in the first three years of the journal's existence offered general arguments on the role of international organizations in world politics as well as articles on specific topics such as the politics of international air transport and the operation of the UN Security Council.[5] Later the journal published trenchant analyses of the UN's adaptation to the Cold War. Some of the outstanding work in this vein, by scholars such as Inis L. Claude, Jr., and Stanley Hoffmann, shrewdly commented on the politics of international organizations and the consequent limits on their potential range of successful operation. UN peacekeeping operations in Suez and the Congo were a particular focus of attention.

This work was not naive. Neither legalism nor moralism—those alleged bugaboos of Americans—obscured the authors' recognition that international organizations are profoundly affected by world politics, and that these organizations' transformative potential is modest, at least in the short run. However, despite its emphasis on realistic descriptive analysis, research was not particularly informed by general social science theory, and it was less concerned with testing alternative arguments than was the case for subsequent work such as Robert Cox and Harold Jacobson's analysis of decision making in international organizations.[6] Perhaps for these reasons, work published in *IO* in the 1950s and 1960s was closer to policy analysis and commentary than work published in the journal since the mid-1970s. The journal remained sharply focused on formal international organization, with substantial space devoted to summaries of activities in various UN agencies until the late 1960s. Even when behavioralism entered the pages of the journal, it took the form of statistical analysis of General Assembly voting.

If the UN had continued to be as significant in world politics as it briefly became under Secretary-General Dag Hammerskjöld (1953–61), both the shrewd political analysis and the more systematic behavioral study of politics—within the UN and in comparison to other intergovernmental organizations—might have continued to command a significant audience. But Hammerskjöld's death in a plane crash was followed by the collapse of the UN operation in the Congo and by the "Article 19 Crisis" over whether the Soviet Union could be deprived of its vote in the General Assembly in response to its nonpayment of assessments for UN peacekeeping operations. U.S. intervention in Vietnam took place without significant UN involvement. And in 1967 the UN peacekeeping force was withdrawn from Suez right before the June War. Actions against Israel, including the notorious "Zionism as Racism" resolution, drastically reduced U.S. support for the UN, including several of the specialized agencies. As the UN became increasingly irrelevant to major questions of world politics, students of world politics lost interest in it.

---

4. Goodrich 1947, 17.
5. See Rothwell 1949; Little 1949; and Dennett 1949.
6. Cox and Jacobson 1973.

The Intellectual Roots of IPE

Realism has been at the center of the theoretical debates of U.S. international relations scholarship for a long time. Historically, realism was a breed alien to the liberal
and progressive intellectual and political sensibilities of the United States. At its
inception in the early twentieth century, the discipline of international relations was
part of the progressive movement that sought to build a systematic social science for
the betterment of mankind in the United States and, by implication, worldwide. World
War II and the Holocaust, experienced and interpreted by a generation of brilliant
intellectuals closely linked to Europe, changed this. And so did the protracted Cold
War that held the world in its grip for four decades. Prudent statecraft, realism argued, required a space for diplomacy and strategy that was uncontested by normal
domestic politics. The grand debates in the field—idealism and realism in the 1930s,
neoliberalism and neorealism in the 1980s—are products of this distinctive historical
legacy.

No independently recognized field for studying the international political economy
existed in the 1950s and 1960s. Specialists of international relations paid little systematic attention to the political analysis of economic issues. For public policy as
well as for the academy, the focus was on security issues and "high politics." Communism was seen as an omnipresent threat. The Soviet Union, armed with nuclear
weapons and rockets—as the successful launch of Sputnik in 1957 indicated—was
perceived as a serious military, technological, economic, and ideological rival of the
United States. Leading students of world politics analyzed the role of nuclear weapons, techniques of deterrence, and the operation of U.S.-led alliances such as NATO.
Thomas Schelling introduced rational choice analysis to international affairs; Henry
Kissinger wrote about European statecraft and U.S. nuclear and alliance strategies in
Europe; Graham Allison used the Cuban Missile Crisis as a case study to sharpen the
theoretical lenses of the discipline.[7] Innovative analyses also dealt with issues of war
and peace, including major conceptual contributions by Kenneth N. Waltz and the
development of an impressive data set by the Correlates of War Project led by J. David
Singer.[8]

For the study of the international political economy a substantial stock of intellectual capital came from classic works on political economy, such as those of Albert
Hirschman, Eugene Staley, Charles Kindleberger, and Jacob Viner.[9] Hirschman, for
example, explained how foreign trade was used as an instrument of political pressure
through which Germany built its political sphere of influence in central-eastern Europe. Viner and Kindleberger illuminated the complementarity of power and wealth
in the seventeenth and eighteenth centuries and in the international monetary and
financial system. Staley examined how barriers against trade with states such as
Japan created conditions for political-military conflict. These authors offered

---

7. See Schelling 1960, 1966; Kissinger 1957a,b, 1965; and Allison 1971.
8. See Waltz 1959; and Singer 1972.
9. See Hirschman [1945] 1980; Staley 1939; Viner 1948; and Kindleberger 1973. See also D. Baldwin
1985.

insights into the way power provided the foundations for the international economy. Within the field of international relations, Edward Hallett Carr used his blend of Marxism and realism to analyze the collapse of the international order, including the international economy, in the interwar period.[10] The analytical focus of these books on material capabilities and asymmetric bargaining power provided the basis for parsimonious accounts of developments in the international economy that had a profound effect on the study of the international political economy in the 1970s.

Students of comparative politics who sought to link their work to international relations drew on a rich tradition of work that emphasized the importance of institutional factors in the shaping of political regimes, notably, in the 1960s, J. P. Nettl's article on the state and Samuel Huntington's analysis of political decay.[11] They also drew on economics and economic history, such as works on technology by David Landes and on tariffs by Charles Kindleberger.[12] Some books on U.S. politics were widely read by scholars of comparative politics.[13] Furthermore, the domestic determinants of foreign policy received extended attention by international relations scholars in the 1960s, a fact that received more than passing notice by comparative politics specialists who were interested in institutions. In 1959 Kenneth Waltz insisted on the primacy of the international system in shaping state policy, foreshadowing his *Theory of International Politics* published twenty years later.[14] A decade later, however, in a brilliant book on democratic foreign policy he offered a theory of foreign policy.[15] In the 1960s and early 1970s Waltz was not alone in pointing to the importance of the domestic determinants (such as political leadership, institutions, and bureaucratic organizations) of state action. Henry Kissinger, Graham Allison, Morton Halperin, and John Steinbruner, among others, published important articles and books on the subject that were widely read, discussed, and cited.[16]

Yet, the main source of inspiration for students seeking to connect international relations with domestic politics arose from within the field of comparative politics. In the 1960s discussions in comparative analysis revolved around efforts to explain differences in the paths taken by modern states—toward liberal democracy, fascism, or state socialism, for example. Interactions between international and domestic factors had been largely ignored by the structural-functional approach, which was the focal point of work in comparative politics during the 1960s. But for scholars such as Barrington Moore, Reinhard Bendix, Alexander Gerschenkron, and subsequently Charles Tilly and Theda Skocpol, these trajectories were the result not only of a polity's internal characteristics but also of how it was inserted into the international system both economically and politically.[17] A younger generation of comparative

10. Carr [1946] 1962.
11. See Nettl 1968; and Huntington 1968.
12. See Kindleberger 1962, 1978; and Landes 1969.
13. Bauer, Pool, and Dexter 1972.
14. Waltz 1959.
15. Waltz 1967.
16. See Kissinger 1969; Allison 1971; Halperin 1974; and Steinbruner 1974.
17. See Bendix 1964; Gerschenkron 1962; Moore 1966; Tilly 1975, 1990; and Skocpol 1979.

scholars would soon adapt the insights of these seminal studies to the analysis of the domestic determinants of the international political economy.

Despite this rich intellectual legacy, the 1960s lacked a coherent body of political-economy literature in international relations, and the scattered works that existed were far from the mainstream of international relations. Graduate students could go through international relations programs at major American universities, focusing on diplomatic history, theories of war and peace, and policy issues revolving around deterrence, and remain largely innocent of economics or its links to world politics. It did not help that economists were paying little attention to how political and institutional contexts affected their subject of study. Economics Ph.D. students were increasingly rewarded for their mathematical acumen rather than their analysis of how organizations actually operated; economists could not fashion successful careers by investigating the lending practices of the International Monetary Fund. Hence, in the analysis of international relations neither political science nor economics were conducting sustained research on subjects that would later be termed IPE.

European Integration as an Intellectual Opening

From the early 1960s until the early 1970s, the liveliest debates on international organizations focused on the significance of political integration for the nation-state: "obstinate or obsolete?" as Stanley Hoffmann put it in a famous debate with Ernst Haas.[18] Haas and some younger students and colleagues developed a specific research program about political integration, drawing on modernization theory and on the theory of functionalism as articulated by David Mitrany.[19] This research program reflected a general liberal theoretical orientation that pointed to the possibility of multiple actors in the international system and the importance of voluntary agreement. Their work complemented the analysis of national and supranational community formation that Karl Deutsch and his students had pioneered in the 1950s and 1960s, a research program that foreshadowed what later came to be labeled constructivism. It highlighted the importance of identity formation measured by social transactions and communications.[20] By 1970 integration theory had specified a substantial number of economic and social background factors that conditioned a series of political processes. These, in turn, shaped how political actors defined their interests and thus the policy strategies that elites adopted in different states. A nascent field of comparative regional integration studies was formed, based on fieldwork by scholars who went to East Africa and Latin America as well as to Europe.[21] In 1970 *IO* published a special issue on regional integration edited by Leon Lindberg and Stuart Scheingold. The articles in this volume represented attempts to use behavioral social science to account for variation in the success of efforts at regional integration.[22]

18. Hoffmann 1966.
19. See Haas 1958, 1961, 1964b; and Mitrany 1966.
20. See Deutsch 1953; Deutsch et al. 1957; Russett 1963; and Merritt 1966.
21. Outstanding books synthesizing this literature and presenting new findings include Lindberg and Scheingold 1970; and Nye 1971.
22. Lindberg and Scheingold 1971.

Comparative regional integration studies foundered on the overly optimistic assumption of neofunctionalism that such efforts would succeed around the world. Non-European efforts at regional integration in the 1960s failed, and the European effort stagnated after Charles De Gaulle's maneuvers of the mid-1960s and the Luxembourg Compromise of 1966. The field of integration studies atrophied. Formerly optimistic theorists became pessimistic. Their arguments became more indeterminate as an increasing number of explanatory variables was needed to account for the acceleration and retardation of integration processes.

The difficulty encountered after 1966 by neofunctionalism was ironically similar to that faced by neorealism (whose error was excessive pessimism) after 1989. Both approaches involved specific research programs with testable propositions, some of which were invalidated by events. Their arguments were formulated in ways that could be falsified. When disillusionment with integration theory set in, many younger scholars turned to newer themes such as those of international and comparative political economy. Integration theory, however, provided much of the existing analytical capital for investigating the connections between politics and economics. Several years later, Ernst B. Haas published an article on the "obsolescence" of regional integration theory.[23] However, empirical work on the European Community continued in Europe, and when U.S. scholars regained interest in the subject in the late 1980s, they relied heavily on this European work and were less inclined to put forward a general theory of integration processes.[24]

The Emergence of IPE

As long as security concerns dominated the attention of academics and policymakers, the intellectual vacuum in the study of the international political economy could be ignored. Beginning in the late 1960s, however, a series of developments brought political salience to international economic issues: the revival of the European and Japanese economies, inflationary pressures in the United States, the abandonment of Bretton Woods in 1971, and the OPEC oil embargo in 1973–74 all combined to end the era of overwhelming U.S. dominance of the world economy and the regime constructed in the late 1940s.

A few political scientists began at the end of the 1960s to observe these changes in the international political economy, stimulated especially by work on economic interdependence by Richard Cooper and on multinational enterprises by Raymond Vernon.[25] In 1971 *IO* published a special issue on transnational relations.[26] This volume was inspired by the work on multinational enterprises done by Vernon and others: over a third of the thirty-one scholarly works referenced in the editors' introduction pertained to the activities of these firms. The editors sought to broaden the study of

23. Haas 1975, 1976.
24. See Moravcsik 1991, 1998; and the collections edited by Wallace 1990; Keohane and Hoffmann 1991; and Sbragia 1992.
25. See Cooper 1968; and Vernon 1971.
26. Keohane and Nye 1972. For a review of the subsequent literature with a twenty-year perspective, see Risse-Kappen 1995b.

world politics to include "transnational relations," involving the activities of non-state actors, and "transgovernmental relations," in which subunits of governments dealt directly with their counterparts abroad.[27] The transnational relations special issue was chiefly a pointing exercise that made clear how much interesting activity had escaped the attention of analysts imprisoned in the "state-centric" paradigm. No testable theory was presented. The editors focused on the impact of changing economic and technological forces on politics. Their fundamental assumptions were borrowed from pluralism, which was the reigning theoretical orientation on domestic politics, at least in the United States. Actors were the starting point; their preferences were not explained. The fact that actors had different preferences created opportunities for mutually beneficial trade-offs. Beginning with the perceived reality of transnational relations, Robert O. Keohane and Joseph S. Nye discussed interstate dependence, and they highlighted the trade-offs between the economic benefits and political costs of interdependence. By considering the implications of transnational relations for state autonomy, they linked the study of interdependence to classic issues in political science.

Robert Gilpin challenged the editors' liberal orientation with a powerful essay published in the same volume.[28] Gilpin argued that transnational relations could only be understood within the context of interstate politics. A central and continuing issue—the interactions between transnational economic changes, on the one hand, and state power, on the other—was embedded in the international political economy debate from the outset. In a subsequent book on multinational corporations, Gilpin developed, systematically and self-consciously, a realist analysis of the international political economy. His trenchant analysis of the role of multinational corporations and U.S. foreign policy fused realism's analytical, historical, and policy concerns into a powerful synthesis.[29] Gilpin showed how realism's emphasis on power could provide both a political explanation of the emergence of liberal principles and practices in U.S. foreign economic policy and a parsimonious critique of liberal scholarship. His dynamic model of change paralleled some Marxist writings, which interpreted the Vietnam War as a reflection of economic contradictions that drove power-seeking elites to devise, under the flag of international liberalism, a counterrevolutionary imperialist strategy.[30]

Gilpin's work helped crystallize a debate about the role of states and markets in the international political economy, which became a major theme during the next decade. Scholars began to conceptualize what they meant by interdependence and to try

27. Keohane and Nye did not invent the phrase "transnational relations." They quote Arnold Wolfers as using it in an essay first published in 1959. See Keohane and Nye 1972, x. Wolfers treats the "transnational" terminology as conventional, stating that "there is no lack of a suitable vocabulary to identify a set of non-state corporate actors, but it is not without significance that all the terms refer to something called 'national,' which is the characteristic feature of the nation-state." Wolfers 1962, 20.

28. Gilpin 1972.

29. Gilpin 1975. For other outstanding work with a realist cast, albeit not so systematic or powerful as Gilpin's, see Knorr 1975; and Strange 1976.

30. See Baran and Sweezy 1966; Magdoff 1969; Mandel 1976; and Gilpin 1975, 1981.

to measure it.[31] The writings of Susan Strange were particularly important in focusing attention on markets and how states interacted with them.[32] On one side of the debate in the 1970s were liberal analyses that emphasized economic processes and technological change in the process of modernization.[33] These arguments have their counterparts in some contemporary work on globalization, which, in the words of Strange, contends that "the authority of the governments of all states, large and small, strong and weak, has been weakened as a result of technological and financial change and of the accelerated integration of national economies into one single global market economy."[34] In contrast to these market-oriented arguments is the state-structural orientation of Gilpin or of Stephen Krasner, who argued in 1976 that variations in the degree of openness or closure in foreign trade were inexplicable without understanding configurations of state interests and power. "In recent years," he declared, "students of international relations have multinationalized, transnationalized, bureaucratized, and transgovernmentalized the state until it has virtually ceased to exist as an analytic construct . . . This perspective is at best profoundly misleading."[35]

Whether one emphasized the role of markets or of states, it became clear during the 1970s that neither phenomenon could be adequately analyzed without accounting for the other. As Keohane and Nye explicitly recognized in their book published in 1977, power and interdependence would have to be analyzed together.[36]

IPE: Liberal Challenges to Realism

During the decade after the publication of Gilpin's book the various approaches to problems of bargaining and cooperation drew their inspiration from long-standing generic orientations, notably realism, liberalism, and Marxism. Each perspective gave pride of place to a different explanatory variable: the distribution of power for realists, the interests of different groups for liberals, the structure of the economy or, more simplistically, the interests of capitalists for Marxists. Each perspective emphasized different causal relations: power and coercion for realism, mutual agreement and contracting for liberalism, mechanisms of exploitation for Marxism. These generic orientations created specific research programs that were subject to empirical verification, including hegemonic stability theory, liberal regime theory, and dependency theory. The most prominent debates were those between different variants of realism and liberalism, and increasingly between systemic-level analysis (particularly neoliberal institutionalism) and analysis rooted in domestic-level interests and

---

31. See Waltz 1970; Rosecrance and Stein 1973; and Katzenstein 1975.
32. Strange 1979, 1988.
33. Morse 1970 and 1976. In an investigation of war, Gilpin further explored the relationships between technological change and world politics. Gilpin 1981.
34. Strange 1996, 14.
35. Krasner 1976, 317.
36. See Keohane and Nye 1977; and Baldwin 1979.

institutions, which sought to understand "state interests," rather than taking them for granted.

Realism and Its Critics in the 1970s

For most American students of international politics, at least through the 1980s, realism was the perspective against which new ideas had to be tested; and during the 1960s, when IPE emerged as an independent field of study, realism was intellectually hegemonic. Hans Morgenthau's *Politics Among Nations* was the most important text.[37] Kenneth Waltz had published his first book in 1959 in which he initiated the intellectual project that culminated in his influential exposition of what came to be termed neorealism twenty years later.[38] Systems theory was guided by a realist rhetoric, although, as Waltz later pointed out, these studies were more reductionist than either their authors or readers realized.[39]

But realism has always been vulnerable, because some of its core assumptions were problematic, and because its empirical validation was never compelling. Realism's core assumptions can be variously classified, but four are particularly important: (1) states are the key actors in world politics; (2) states can be treated as homogeneous units acting on the basis of self-interest; (3) analysis can proceed on the basis of the assumption that states act as if they were rational; and (4) international anarchy—the absence of any legitimate authority in the international system—means that conflict between self-interested states entails the danger of war and the possibility of coercion. The state-centric assumption was challenged by work on transnational relations, the homogeneity assumption by students of domestic structure and bureaucratic politics, the rationality assumption by analysts of cognitive psychology and group decision making, and the anarchy assumption by theorists of international society and institutions.

During the 1960s and 1970s three major liberal challenges to realism directed their fire at the assumption that states could be treated as unified rational actors: neofunctionalism, bureaucratic politics, and transnational relations and linkage politics.[40] All three were grounded in a pluralist conception of civil society and the state. Public policy was the result of clashes among different groups with conflicting interests. Groups could often only succeed by building coalitions, which would vary from one issue area to another. Robert Dahl, the most influential American exponent of pluralism, emphasized that these cross-cutting cleavages would preclude the dominance of any one specific group, an observation designed to rebut Marxist arguments about the ability of major capitalists to dominate the formulation of public policy.[41]

Neofunctionalism stipulated that institutional change would alter the incentives of groups in civil society, leading them to support policies that would promote still

---

37. Morgenthau 1948.
38. Waltz 1959, 1979.
39. See Kaplan 1957; Rosecrance 1963; and Waltz 1979, 1986.
40. See Haas 1958, 1964a,b; Allison 1971; Keohane and Nye 1972; and Rosenau 1969a.
41. Dahl 1961.

more integration in a process that would spill over from one issue area to another. But as we have seen, this argument apparently failed to predict or explain the direction taken by the European Community after 1966.[42] Bureaucratic politics extended pluralist interest group arguments into the government itself: "where you stand depends upon where you sit."[43] Policy, including foreign policy, is a product of compromise among different bureaucratic actors, reflecting the power and intensity of interest of bureaus, which vary from one issue area to another. Coherent foreign policy is elusive, since decisions in different issue areas are being taken by different actors with different preferences. Theories about transnational relations, which were central when IPE emerged as a distinct field in the 1970s, carried the pluralist argument one step further: there could be many different actors in the international environment, including groups from civil society. These nongovernmental actors could be directly linked with their counterparts in other countries, in ties that would not necessarily be controlled by states. Transgovernmental relations were also possible: situations in which there would be direct relations among interested bureaucracies in different countries.[44]

For IPE, bureaucratic politics and transnational relations oriented early work in the field, but these research programs faltered despite the fact that their political ontology, a nuanced landscape composed of many different elements, was much richer than the black-box view of the state provided by realism. Transnational relations posited a world composed of many different actors with different interests and capabilities. Such a model can provide a rich description. But the operationalization of cause and effect relationships is complex because it is difficult to specify interests and capabilities ex ante. The larger the number of actors, the greater the diversity of their resources (ideas, money, access, organization); and the wider the number of possible alliances, the more difficult such specification becomes, especially if there are interaction effects among different groups.

Bureaucratic politics captured the complexity involved in policy formulation and implementation in any advanced polity—complexity that eluded realism with its radically simplifying assumptions about the nature of the state. In some instances the interests of bureaucracies were clear, but in others they were more elusive. Some of the initial proponents of bureaucratic politics recognized that the most obvious specification of bureaucratic interests, maximizing budget size, did not always work. For example, the U.S. Army after World War II did not try to keep control of the air force but rather supported the creation of a third independent service that would be coequal with the army and the navy.[45] Army leaders rejected keeping the air force as part of the army (it was the U.S. Army Air Force during World War II) because it would have changed the "bureaucratic essence," or what would be called today the collective identity of the army, which was rooted in land warfare and the infantry. Bureaucratic

42. Burley and Mattli suggested that spillover continued through the European judicial process, overlooked by many analysts. Burley and Mattli 1993.

43. Allison attributes this aphorism to Don K. Price. Allison 1971, 316, n. 71.

44. Keohane and Nye 1974. See also Rosenau 1969a.

45. Halperin 1974.

politics, like transnational relations, had great difficulties in operationalizing variables. It did not become a compelling alternative to realist perspectives.

In the mid-1970s a new liberal challenge to realism began to emerge. This challenge focused on the concept of "international regime," drawn from a long-standing tradition of international law and first used in the political science literature by John Ruggie and subsequently elaborated by Keohane and Nye. Ruggie defined regimes as sets of "mutual expectations, rules and regulations, plans, organizational energies and financial commitments, which have been accepted by a group of states." Keohane and Nye treated them simply as "governing arrangements that affect relationships of interdependence."[46] Ruggie's understanding was sociological or constructivist, emphasizing the importance of intersubjective, shared understanding that defines rather than just reflects the preferences of actors; Keohane and Nye understood regimes as devices for enhancing the utility of actors whose interests were taken as given. Students of international regimes did not challenge one of the meanings of "anarchy": that no institutional hierarchy capable of enforcing rules exists in world politics. They did question the frequent implication that anarchy in this sense implied the absence of institutions based on rules.

However, regimes could also be explained in realist terms—as Gilpin and Krasner had, in effect, sought to do. By the end of the 1970s students of international regimes had introduced a potentially important new dependent variable into the analysis of world politics. At that time, however, this new dependent variable was not linked with a distinctive set of explanatory variables through an articulated causal mechanism and, therefore, did not seriously threaten the well-articulated explanatory project of realism based on interests, power, and anarchy.

Support for realist theory was enhanced by the fact that the best-operationalized new research program of these years, hegemonic stability theory, was entirely consistent with realist premises—although, ironically, its first articulation (with somewhat different terminology) was by a liberal economist, Kindleberger.[47] Hegemonic stability theory maintained that an open international system was most likely to occur when there was a single dominant power in the international economic system. Kindleberger argued that the Great Depression, a market failure of monumental proportions, was caused by the absence of a lender of last resort in the international financial system. There could only be a lender of last resort if there were a single dominant power in the international system. Only a hegemon would have the capacity and interest to provide the public good of financial stability. Thus, Kindleberger used a realist ontology (the actors were states) and a half realist causality (the outcome was determined by the distribution of power among states, although through the voluntary choice of the hegemon not coercion) to analyze a liberal problem, the provision of collective goods in the international system.

Gilpin and Krasner suggested that a similar analysis could be applied to multinational corporations and trade.[48] Not only were the ontology and causality fully realist,

---

46. See Ruggie 1975, 570; and Keohane and Nye 1977, 19.
47. Kindleberger 1973.
48. See Gilpin 1975; and Krasner 1976.

but so was the fundamental problem. States were interested in maximizing their own interests. And the promotion of these interests could involve relative gains and distributional conflicts. In their analyses, the distribution of power was the key explanatory variable, accounting for the rules governing multinational corporations, and for trade openness or closure. All states had a few simple goals that they sought to promote in the international economic system—economic utility, growth, social stability, and political leverage. Because it provided economic utility with limited social instability and enhanced the political leverage of the dominant power, for a hegemonic state an open system was the most attractive way to secure these objectives. The firms of the hegemonic power would most benefit from an open system, since they were the most competitive and had the easiest access to capital.

Hegemonic stability theory—or, more generally, arguments about the relationship between the distribution of power and the characteristics of international economic behavior—operationalized the explanatory variable, state power, in terms of some overall measure of size (such as GNP or share of world trade) and the dependent variable, international economic behavior, in terms of openness in the world economy as indicated both by rules and the pattern of exchange. These systemic theories could be proven wrong: either the pattern of international economic behavior changed with the distribution of power among states or it did not. The operationalization of variables, specification of causal relationships, and falsifiability made systemic power theory a fruitful research program. Its findings could be elaborated and systematically criticized.

However, the very clarity of hegemonic stability theory and its ease of operationalization made it vulnerable to persuasive critiques. Timothy McKeown showed that Great Britain's behavior in the nineteenth century was inconsistent with the theory, and Arthur Stein argued that the trade liberalization measures of that century did not emerge from hegemonic policy but from asymmetric bargains that permitted discrimination against the hegemon.[49] David Lake and Duncan Snidal demonstrated that a hegemonic distribution of power was not the only one that was consistent with an open economic system. Reasoning from ontological and epistemological premises that were entirely consistent with hegemonic stability theory, they demonstrated that a small number of leading states would have the interest and capability to support an open system.[50] Even though some arresting reconceptualizations of a realist approach to international trade were later put forward,[51] by the middle of the 1980s the general assumption of the field was that hegemonic stability theory had been seriously undermined.

At the end of the 1970s, these refutations to hegemonic stability theory lay in the future. When Ronald Reagan won the presidency, realist analysis still held pride of place in the United States; it was still the theory that had to be refuted before a convincing intellectual challenge could be offered. Realism maintained its dominant position despite alternative arguments that appeared more accurately to describe ac-

---

49. See McKeown 1983; and Stein 1984.
50. See Lake 1984; and Snidal 1985b. See also, on trade policy, Milner 1987, 1988; and Oye 1992.
51. Gowa 1989, 1994.

tors, and despite the fact that its empirical validation had always been problematic. Realism continued to be *primus inter pares* because liberalism did not offer an alternative research program that specified causality and operationalized variables clearly enough to be falsifiable. The renewal of the Cold War after the Soviet invasion of Afghanistan at the end of 1979 seemed to reinforce realism's intellectual triumph.

Neoliberal Institutionalism

The development of neoliberal institutionalism posed a serious challenge for realist analysis. A special issue of *IO* laid the foundations in 1982. In his introduction Stephen Krasner presented a definition of regimes, developed by the group of authors writing for this issue: "sets of implicit or explicit principles, norms, rules, and decision-making procedures around which actors' expectations converge in a given area of international relations."[52] This agreed definition was ambiguous; but it identified regimes as social institutions and avoided debilitating definitional struggles, as advocates of the regimes research program sought to show that their work could illuminate substantive issues of international relations.

In his article in that volume, and more comprehensively two years later in a book, Robert Keohane developed a rationalist argument to explain the existence of international institutions.[53] Drawing an analogy to problems of market failure in economics, he argued that high transaction costs and asymmetrical uncertainty could lead, under conditions such as those modeled by Prisoners' Dilemma (PD) games, to suboptimal outcomes. Chiefly by providing information to actors (not by enforcing rules in a centralized manner), institutions could enable states to achieve their own objectives more efficiently. Institutions would alter state strategies by changing the costs of alternatives; institutionalization could thus promote cooperation. Keohane argued that institutions mattered because they could provide information, monitor compliance, increase iterations, facilitate issue linkages, define cheating, and offer salient solutions. Keohane did not deny the importance of power, but within the constraints imposed by the absence of hierarchical global governance, states could reap gains from cooperation by designing appropriate institutions.

The initial inspiration for this line of argument came from new work in economics and from the renewed attention being paid to PD games. Economists had begun to recognize the importance of institutions.[54] Robert Axelrod suggested that PD could be resolved if the payoff matrix were not skewed too much in favor of the sucker's payoff, if games were iterated frequently and indefinitely, if the costs of monitoring others' behavior and of retaliating were sufficiently low, and if actors did not discount the future at too high a rate.[55] Institutions could, it was argued, affect the values of these parameters, for instance, by nesting particular games in durable rules, provid-

52. Krasner 1983b, 1.
53. See Keohane 1982 and 1984.
54. See Olson 1965; Akerlof 1970; North 1981 and 1990; and Williamson 1975.
55. See Axelrod 1981, 1984; and Oye 1986. See also Rapoport and Chamnah 1965. For a further development of this line of work, see Axelrod 1997; and Cederman 1997.

ing information about other states' activities, and furnishing standards for evaluating whether cheating was taking place. In the 1990s U.S. and European scholars developed a number of different though complementary approaches to analyzing international regimes.[56]

Where the neoliberal institutionalism research program differed with realist arguments was not on its assumptions about actors, but rather on the nature of the exemplary problem in the international system: were states primarily concerned with market failure or with relative gains and distributional conflicts? Could issues be resolved through the voluntary acceptance of institutions that left all actors better off, or would coercion and power be more important for determining outcomes? Krasner suggested that distributional conflicts rather than market failure or relative gains are the central concern for states in the international system. The issue is not just reaching the Pareto frontier, but the point on the frontier that is chosen; an issue that can be resolved only through bargaining and power, not just optimal institutional design.[57] Joseph Grieco argued that states were, in fact, concerned with relative gains even in the European Community, which seemed to be designed to enhance absolute well-being.[58] Robert Powell clarified this relative gains discussion, arguing that even within a realist logic relative gains only mattered if they compromised a state's future ability to secure absolute benefits.[59] A number of important studies in the early 1990s explored the connections between power and potential gains from political exchange.[60]

Neoliberal institutionalism has offered a set of heuristically powerful deductive arguments that could eventually be made more precise. Indeed, such arguments can be formalized using game theory, as Helen Milner argues in her article in this issue. Hypotheses generated by neoliberal institutionalism were applied to a wide range of empirical problems, such as bargaining between the United Kingdom and the other members of the European Community over the Falklands or the evolution of international regimes for debt rescheduling.[61] The appeal of neoliberal institutionalism was enhanced by its affinity with the reigning king of the social sciences in the United States—economics.

Domestic Politics and IPE

From the outset IPE blurred the boundaries between comparative and international politics. Even analysts who took the state-as-actor approach did so explicitly for convenience—to enable them to develop coherent theories—rather than on phenom-

56. See, for example, Young 1989, 1994, 1997; Lipson 1991; and Rittberger 1993.
57. Krasner 1991.
58. Grieco 1988, 1990.
59. Powell 1991, reprinted in Baldwin 1993. See also Keohane 1993. The relative gains discussion is an example of a controversy that began at the level of competing "isms"—the assumptions of neorealism and neoliberal institutionalism, respectively—that generated some empirical research and eventually yielded to an analytical solution.
60. See Stein 1990; Martin 1992a; and Oye 1992.
61. See Martin 1992c; and Aggarwal 1996.

enological grounds. In fact, realism and liberalism as general research orientations had specific domestic and systemic research programs: statism for realism, and pluralism and various theories of interest aggregation for liberalism. The actors were different at the domestic and international levels, but the causal mechanisms, voluntary exchange as opposed to power and coercion, remained the same. Using class analysis, Marxism offered an integrated view of international and domestic political economy. Analysts of the international political economy continued to emphasize how variations in domestic politics affected foreign policy and to suggest ways in which the international system could affect domestic political structures and interests. We begin this section by discussing what happened to Marxism; we then turn to statist arguments and to a variety of domestic structure approaches.

Marxism

For Marxists, the organization of capitalism determined political and economic outcomes at both the domestic and international levels. Marxism offered a structural or institutional rather than an actor-oriented argument, providing an integrated picture of both domestic and international politics.

Arguing that the state was simply the handmaiden of leading capitalists, instrumental Marxism offered clear causal statements that proved to be empirically problematic. Many of the major public policy initiatives of the twentieth century, such as social security and the recognition of labor unions, had been opposed by leading capitalists. Sophisticated Marxist analysts recognized this problem and proposed structural Marxism as a more persuasive framework that was more consistent with Marx's own formulations. Structural Marxists argued that capitalist states would act in the interest of preserving capitalism as a whole. The state was relatively autonomous from its own economy and society. However, specifying this orientation in an empirically tractable way was difficult. If the state were relatively autonomous, exactly how autonomous could it be? What policy would be inconsistent with this perspective? Both policies that reflected the preferences of the capitalist class and those that did not could be accounted for by structural Marxist analyses.

Scholars influenced by Marxism also emphasized social forces and production relations, as in the work of Robert W. Cox.[62] One particularly influential research program based on a generic Marxist orientation was dependency theory. In the late 1940s Raoul Prebisch, an Argentinian economist working at the UN Economic Commission for Latin America, argued that the world economy enmeshed poorer countries exporting raw materials in relationships of unequal exchange. Prebisch's arguments, and older ones about imperialism, were developed by social scientists from developing areas, especially Latin America, as well as from North America and Europe, into a research program that explained the poverty of the states of the south in terms of their position in the world economy.[63] The world systems research program elaborated by Immanuel Wallerstein and his colleagues presented a similar

---

62. R. Cox 1981, 1987.
63. See Prebisch 1959; Cohen 1973; and Cardoso and Falleto 1979.

analysis for a much longer time period.[64] In a 1978 special issue of *IO* James Caporaso emphasized the distinction between dependence and dependency. In contrast to the internationalism of traditional Marxism, dependency theory offered a disguised form of nationalism in which the role of the state loomed large, especially for weak polities. It was not just that the polities of the south were dependent and weak, but that they were in a relationship of dependency that undermined their autonomy and exploited their wealth. These mechanisms of exploitation included both specific economic arrangements and the general penetration of developing states by more powerful and better organized capitalist states of the north.[65]

As the experience of the developing world became more differentiated and as some states and world regions did better than others, dependency theorists suggested that there could be a pattern of dependent development. Some groups within developing states, such as larger capitalists and the military, would ally themselves with powerful actors from the north, such as multinational corporations and northern militaries. States in the south could prosper, but their options would always be truncated by the way in which they were inserted into the world capitalist system.[66]

From the early 1980s onward, dependency theory encountered serious criticism and anomalies. It was criticized for failing to clearly spell out causal regularities that could be empirically supported or falsified.[67] Furthermore, it had great difficulty explaining the uneven rates of growth in what was known as the Third World, especially the stunning economic development of a number of East Asian countries. Cross-national variations in endowments, institutions, and policies seemed to provide more promising explanations. Political economy work on developing countries increasingly relied on a combination of economics and comparative politics rather than on dependency theory.[68] One of the leading exponents of dependent development, Fernando Henrique Cardoso, even became the liberal reformist president of Brazil.

The collapse of the Soviet empire and, more importantly, the profound corruption revealed by its demise dealt a heavy blow to the research programs that drew on Marxism for their theoretical orientation. However, Marxism as a theoretical orientation did not disappear. Marxists have grappled with some of the same issues that have engaged liberal scholars. A neo-Gramscian strand of Marxist scholarship has built on a tradition of analysis that emphasizes the importance and sources of legitimating ideas and ideologies.[69] This scholarship is therefore more consistent with constructivist work (reviewed in the fourth section of this article) that stresses the importance of ideas and culture than are materialist versions of Marxism.

It would be a mistake to judge the insights of Marxist analyses simply in terms of any one specific research program. Marxist analysis poses probing questions about

---

64. See Wallerstein 1974, 1979, 1991; and Arrighi 1994.
65. Caporaso 1978a.
66. Evans 1979.
67. Packenham 1992.
68. See, for example, Haggard 1990; Wade 1990; Evans 1995; and Haggard and Kaufman 1992, 1995.
69. For a collection of essays on Gramsci and international relations, see Gill 1993, which reprints the seminal essay by Cox 1983.

the relationship between power and wealth. It offers a conceptual apparatus that can be applied both to international and domestic developments and to their connections. And it addresses enduring moral concerns concerning equality and justice. Specific research programs generated by a generic Marxist orientation can, like specific liberal and realist research programs, be called into question by problems of variable specification and empirical evidence. This does not mean, however, that Marxism as a general orientation will necessarily be discarded. Rather, it is precisely the heuristic richness of the major general research orientations that allows them to be reformulated to address changed empirical and political contexts. The fate of a general theoretical orientation does not depend on the success of any one specific research program.

Statism: Reaction Against Liberalism and Marxism

Statism is a general theoretical orientation that has generated several specific research programs, all of which assert the autonomy of state institutions. Statism thus stands in contrast to the societally oriented domestic political perspectives that dominated much of liberal and Marxist political analysis in the 1970s. Statism gave greater attention to state institutions, especially those charged with maintaining the stability and well-being of the polity as a whole. The state could be conceived of as an actor, not simply an arena in which conflicting societal interests struggled to secure their preferred policy objectives. States could be strong or weak, relative to their own societies.[70]

Statist arguments did not have a particularly sophisticated conceptualization of the relationship among state institutions. States could be strong in some issue areas but weak in others. Specifying the trade-off among different issue areas was problematic. Statism had difficulty capturing the nuances of state–society relations. It detached the state not only from particular group pressures but also from the larger polity in which it was embedded.[71]

These empirical difficulties led not to the disappearance of statism as a general theoretical orientation but to the reformulation of specific research programs. Instead of a narrow focus on the state, which was itself a reaction to an overly societal perspective, additional work analyzed interactions between different components of the polity. In 1988 John Ikenberry, David Lake, and Michael Mastanduno edited a special issue of *IO* in which authors investigated the effect on U.S. foreign economic policy of different configurations of interest, the ability of state leaders to mobilize societal support, and the consequences of ideas, as well as the discretionary power of the executive.[72] More recently, discussions of state–society relations employing a

---

70. Krasner 1977, 1978. See also Katzenstein 1976; Evans, Rueschemeyer, and Skocpol 1985; and Evans 1995.

71. In a prescient article that drew on discourse theory, Bruce Andrews suggested that the state could be seen as a rule-governed social actor. This line of analysis lay dormant for more than a decade. Andrews 1975.

72. Ikenberry, Lake, and Mastanduno 1988.

rational choice perspective on institutions, especially the importance of commitment, have shown that some of the factors that statism identified as weaknesses were, in fact, sources of strength. Democratic states are often able to extract more resources from their own societies than are autocratic states, precisely because members of civil society believe that what would have been considered a weak state will keep its promises. In this analytic jujitsu, the notion that states were strong because they were independent of their societies is turned on its head. States can secure resources from their own societies only if they are constrained.[73] Reformulated versions of statism focus on state guidance of the economy, the links between political parties and state bureaucracies, how state institutions relate to social movements, and the role of law. As a general theoretical orientation, statism has been refurbished but not abandoned as some of its research programs encountered empirical anomalies.

Domestic Structures and Their Relation to the International System

Students of comparative politics focused their attention on the connections between domestic structures and international relations, which were bracketed by neoliberalism and realism. Katzenstein, for example, relied on a historically informed taxonomy that emphasized different constellations of state and society in different political settings. Drawing insights from Gerschenkron and Moore, Katzenstein argued that early industrializers like Britain differed systematically from late industrializers like Japan in the character of the dominant social coalition and in the degree of centralization and differentiation of state and society.[74] In sharp contrast to the statist literature that viewed states as actors, the analysis of domestic structures privileged state–society relationships. Different social coalitions define the content of policy. And differences in domestic policy networks have discernible effects on the formulation and implementation of foreign economic policies in different economic issues such as money and trade. John Zysman extended this perspective to the politics of industry and finance.[75]

In various policy domains, both foreign and domestic, scholars analyzed contrasts between the liberal market brand of Anglo-American capitalism, welfare state capitalism on the European continent, and developmental state capitalism in Japan and East Asia. Ellen Comisso and Laura Tyson edited a special issue of *IO* on comparative socialism.[76] Subsequently, comparative political economy spread to encompass Latin America, the transitions from socialism in the successor states of the Soviet Union and east-central Europe, and even the Leninist capitalism emerging in the People's Republic of China.[77] This body of research specified, in contextual and

---

73. See North and Weingast 1989; Fearon 1994b; and Schultz 1996.
74. Katzenstein 1978.
75. Zysman 1977, 1983.
76. Comisso and Tyson 1986.
77. The literature is too large to be listed here. Since the early 1980s, *Cornell Studies in Political Economy,* for example, comprise more than seventy volumes on this subject.

historical detail, incentives for states, governments, or corporate actors to choose specific strategies.

Peter Gourevitch emphasized the pervasive influences that the international state system and the international political economy can have on domestic structures and the policy preferences of groups.[78] Following Gourevitch's lead, analysts pointed to two different ways in which enmeshment in the world economy could affect different polities: first, involvement could influence the basic institutional structures of polities, including their governing norms; second, it could affect the capabilities and strategic opportunities of different interest groups. This research program included analyses of the effects of the international system on the democratic corporatism of the small European welfare states, on societal groups or economic sectors, and on coalitions, institutions, ideologies, and economic structures.[79]

The concept of two-level games elaborated by Robert Putnam was one effort to systematically integrate domestic structures, systemic opportunities and constraints, and foreign economic policy.[80] Any international agreements must satisfy both other states and domestic constituencies. The bargaining power of a state could be enhanced if its rulers can demonstrate that their domestic supporters would only accept a narrow range of outcomes. In more recent work, Andrew Moravcsik has elaborated a related perspective on domestic-international interactions that emphasizes how societal interests shape the policies of states.[81]

One difficulty encountered with this line of research was the absence of a general and systematic taxonomy for classifying domestic structures. In a bold and imaginative book Ronald Rogowski offered one answer to this taxonomic issue. He applied the elegant reasoning of the Stolper-Samuelson model of international trade to show how, in general, trade policies and practices would affect social cleavages. Export-oriented goods used intensively the factors of production with which a country was relatively well-endowed. If trade became more open, the abundant factor would benefit. If it became more closed, the relatively scarce factor would be advantaged. In general a more open international trading system would be supported by, and would strengthen, the relatively abundant factor in different states. These changes in the domestic position of different factors, such as labor and the ownership of land and capital, could influence policy.[82] Using basically the same logic, Jeffry Frieden emphasized the importance of factor specificity; factors of production such as labor were not homogenous but rather were associated with specific economic sectors. Moreover, macroeconomic policy, not just trade policy, could affect and be affected by a country's openness to the world economy.[83]

78. Gourevitch 1978.
79. See Cameron 1978; Kurth 1979; Katzenstein 1984, 1985; Snyder 1991; Kupchan 1994; and Simmons 1994.
80. See Putnam 1988; and Evans, Jacobson, and Putnam 1993.
81. Moravcsik 1997.
82. Rogowski 1989.
83. Frieden 1991.

Rogowski, Frieden, and others who followed their lead were fully aware that their perspective offered no easy way of incorporating variations in institutional arrangements, a shortcoming that Helen Milner and David Lake, among others, have sought to correct.[84] But they provided a parsimonious, general explanation that links the world economy to domestic interests and policies. Their analytic framework requires no specific knowledge about context. It can be applied to any political system. In the framework's sparse formulation the preferences of actors can be read directly off material structures, bypassing the analysis of political processes and ideational phenomena. Although it required information about which factors were relatively abundant, it did not require any institutional knowledge about specific polities. However, such general structural theories encounter numerous empirical anomalies, as Rogowski's historical discussion revealed.

Globalization and Domestic Politics

Increasing levels of transboundary movements and their associated effects, what has come to be termed globalization, encourage a more intimate analytic relationship between international and domestic politics. High levels of cross-border flows are not an unprecedented development. Labor migration reached its highest levels in the nineteenth century. By some measures international capital markets were more integrated at the end of the nineteenth century than they are now, since financial flows fell dramatically with the two world wars and the Great Depression. Trade flows have followed a similar pattern, increasing sharply during the nineteenth century, then falling in the first part of the twentieth, and reaching unprecedented levels for some countries, most notably the United States, in the last two decades of the twentieth century. Technology has dramatically reduced the costs of communications. Social movements have been mobilized in specific locales for global issues such as the environment, human rights, and feminism. Illicit activities including organized crime and trade in drugs have become more salient. All of these developments, lumped under the label of globalization, have affected both national polities and the international system.[85]

Globalization draws our attention to the increasing political salience of transboundary activities. Is the growing enmeshment of polities in the international political economy making institutions and policies, groups and individuals more alike, or are they retaining most of their differences? Is globalization altering ''inter''national relations marginally, or is it fundamentally transforming them to ''trans''national relations? Those who emphasize how globalization is remaking world politics stress how policy preferences and political coalitions at home change as a result of changing international pressures. Conversely, analyses, including Geoffrey Garrett' s contribution to this issue, that emphasize the persistence of distinctive national practices

---

84. See Frieden and Rogowski 1996, 42–47; Milner 1997; and Lake 1996 and forthcoming.
85. See Keohane and Milner 1996, 10–14; Feldstein and Horioka 1980; Oman 1994; Shaw 1994; Jones 1995; Rodrik 1997; and Obstfeld and Taylor 1997.

have shown how domestic institutions block price signals, freeze existing political coalitions and policies, and shape the national response to global change.[86]

Both of these arguments focus on domestic political institutions, firms, interests groups, and economic sectors as units of analyses. An alternative conceptualization focuses not on the units themselves, but rather on the relationships among them and makes problematic the nature of these units in the first place. Households, communities, regions, and social movements, among others, reconstitute themselves in a global setting. This conceptualization points to processes of "glocalization" that are transforming the identities, interests, and strategies of actors through a combination of global and local processes and are thus adding new political actors and processes to an increasingly global politics.[87]

Globalization, however conceived, is a reflection of a phenomenon that scholars associated with IPE have recognized since the inception of the field: international and domestic politics cannot be isolated from each other. Neorealists and neoliberals did not incorporate domestic politics into their theoretical formulations, but they never denied its importance. States did not all respond in the same way to the opportunities and constraints presented by the international system. Studies of domestic politics enhanced our understanding of what neorealists and neoliberals took for granted in their theories in the 1980s: "state preferences." Domestic structure analysis suggested that preferences could be understood in two possibly complementary ways: either as the result of institutionalized norms or as the aggregations of the preferences of individuals, firms, and groups. Historical-institutional research on the reciprocal effects of domestic structures and the international political economy has been complemented by a decidedly economic and materialist variant that pays virtually no attention to the role of ideas, norms, and institutions. Different interpretations of the process of globalization reflect this difference in orientation.

A Post–Cold War Opening: Rationalism and Sociology Revisited

Even during the Cold War, there was substantial dissatisfaction with reigning realist and liberal approaches to international relations, especially outside the United States and in the related field of comparative politics. The end of the Cold War was a catalyst in several ways. It raised new issues for the ongoing rationalist debate, which pitted realists, who stressed the role of coercion, against liberals, who emphasized contractual relationships. The end of the Cold War also opened up space for cultural and sociological perspectives, often referred to as "constructivist," that had been neglected by both realists and liberals. And the discussions that ensued highlighted conceptual differences between possible points of complementarity of rationalism and constructivism.

---

86. See Keohane and Milner 1996; Garrett and Lange 1995 (reprinted in Keohane and Milner 1996); Pauly and Reich 1997; and Samuels 1994.
87. See Rosenau 1990, 1997; and Appadurai 1996.

Rationalism: Realism and Liberalism After the Cold War

Realism has been not only a salient general theoretical orientation but also part of a more enduring normative discourse, like liberalism and constructivism, about the most appropriate way to secure peace, stability, and justice in human society. Its self-conscious intellectual pedigree is long and impressive. It will not disappear.

However, recent developments in world politics and within specific research programs have confronted realism with much greater challenges than it has faced since the founding of *IO*. For realism, power and conflict are inherent aspects of international politics. The interests of states will differ. Force and coercion are always available options. The astonishingly peaceful end of the Cold War and the collapse of the Soviet Union are not what a realist would have expected.[88] Realism has not been silent, of course. The simplest explanation for the end of the Cold War is that Soviet power declined; the Soviet Union was a challenger that could no longer challenge. Predictions about relative changes in state capability have rarely been incorporated into realist research programs, and realism did not predict this decline.[89] Realists, especially Waltz, have emphasized the importance of nuclear weapons in altering the likelihood of war. With secure second-strike capability, it is more evident now than at any other time in human history that a conflict among the major powers would reduce the well-being of all states. At least some observers view this situation as a change in the nature of the international system itself, not just an alteration in the characteristics of individual states.[90] From a realist perspective, in a nonnuclear world it would have been much riskier for the Soviet Union to abandon its empire in eastern Europe and for any leader to break up the Soviet Union itself, acts that would have left even Russia's core territory more vulnerable to invasion.

Nevertheless, in the 1980s analysts working within a realist framework were arguing that bipolarity would continue. And they assumed that neither pole could disappear peacefully. When the Soviet Union did collapse, realists were skeptical about the robustness of international institutions, especially those related to international security, such as NATO, and the prospects for continued cooperation in the international economy. Over the last decade things have turned out much better than realists had any right to expect.[91]

The challenges to realism presented by the peaceful end of the Cold War were aggravated by the intellectual salience of neorealism as a specific research program. Waltz's most important contribution was to force analysts to make a fundamental distinction between what he called structural and reductionist arguments. Waltz was, of course, aware of the importance of domestic political factors, but he insisted that neorealism was concerned only with the distribution of power among states. States

---

88. See Lebow 1994; and Stein 1994.
89. Wohlforth 1994.
90. See Waltz 1990; and Snyder 1996.
91. See Mearsheimer 1990; and Waltz 1993. See also Mearsheimer 1994 and the subsequent exchange in *International Security*.

were interested in security, not in expanding their power. Treating all states as if the international relations goals were the same was a departure from earlier realist discussion, much of which had been based on the assertion that it was necessary to distinguish between revisionist and status quo states.[92] The conflict between the Soviet Union and the United States was consistent with both a strictly neorealist analysis (the poles in a bipolar world would be in conflict) and with realist arguments that posited the importance of exogenously given variations in state objectives (a revisionist Soviet Union would be in conflict with a status quo United States).

With the end of the Cold War, neorealism offered less purchase on international conflict that appeared to be embedded primarily in variations in the goals of states or, in the case of ethnic conflict, substate actors. Many scholars argued that the materialist assumptions of neorealist analysis prevented it from explaining the rapid changes observed in core national security issues. According to these authors, historically constructed norms, ideas, and discourses needed to be analyzed before one could make sense of patterns of stability and change in world politics.[93] Some realists responded to this challenge by rejecting the sparse assumption of neorealism that all states would seek security and embracing instead the recognition that state objectives could vary because of domestic, not systemic factors. States' goals could be aggressive or passive, revolutionary or status quo, ethnonationalist or tolerant. The extent to which the presence of revisionist states would result in confrontations, especially war, would still depend on the distribution of material power in the international system. The rulers of greedy states would not commit suicide by attacking a manifestly stronger enemy. But knowledge of the distribution of power alone would not allow analysts to understand patterns of international conflict and cooperation.[94]

The burgeoning of ethnic conflict in the last decade has presented the kinds of problems that realist perspectives were designed to analyze, although not necessarily with states as the most salient actors. Ethnic conflicts have arisen between states and among groups within states, albeit groups operating in environments where authority structures have eroded or disappeared and where security dilemmas operate at the substate level.[95] However, this return to a focus on the importance of variations in state objectives (of which ethnic conflict is only one example), as a result of factors exogenous to the distribution of power in the system as a whole, confronts realist analysis with the challenge of explaining why such variations should exist—a challenge that can only be met through a more systematic integration of realism with domestic politics.

In international political economy the specific research programs that reflect a general realist theoretical orientation have focused on the possibility of coercion that can leave some actors worse off, on the consequences of bargaining asymmetries, and on the problems of commitment in an anarchic environment. Some of these specific projects reflect the influence of constructivist or liberal perspectives. More

92. See Morgenthau 1948, chap. 2, 3; and Schweller 1996.
93. See Katzenstein 1996b; and Lapid and Kratochwil 1996.
94. For example, Frankel 1996.
95. See Fearon and Laitin 1996; and Posen 1993a.

powerful states may be in a position to alter the conceptions that weaker actors have of their own self-interest, especially when economic and military power has delegitimated ideological convictions in weaker or defeated polities. The United States, for instance, pressed for a particular vision of how international society should be ordered after World War II and renewed and reinvigorated this project after the end of the Cold War. The goal was not simply to promote a particular set of objectives, but to alter how other societies conceived of their own goals. This emphasis on what Nye has called soft power engages both conventional realist concerns about relative capabilities and constructivism's focus on beliefs and identity.[96]

Powerful states can also alter strategic options in ways that skew payoffs in some cases by unilaterally changing their own policies.[97] They may be able to establish institutional arrangements that preclude certain initiatives or facilitate the strategic use of information.[98] Commitment problems may make states reluctant to engage in arrangements that provide them with absolute benefits in the short term, especially if they may be relatively worse off in the long term. If a state's future bargaining leverage would be compromised, it might reject immediate gains because of its anxiety about potential future losses.[99] Arguments emphasizing the importance of agenda setting, uncertainty, and strategic manipulation are based on the same game-theoretic formulations that have guided much recent work from more liberal perspectives emphasizing the mutual benefits of cooperation. In the post–Cold War world realist projects have become more sensitive to variations in state objectives and to a more complicated set of relationships between absolute gains and distributional conflicts.

Neoliberal institutionalism correctly anticipated that the end of the Cold War would not undermine such institutions as NATO and the European Union, so it did not go through an "agonizing reappraisal" such as that experienced by some realists. Indeed, institutionalists began to apply their theory to security institutions such as alliances and to interpret post–Cold War politics in institutionalist terms.[100] And, as the articles in this issue by Lisa Martin and Beth Simmons and by Helen Milner indicate, institutionalist work drew heavily on scholarship from other fields, notably U.S. politics, to become theoretically more rigorous. Since institutionalist work is so well discussed in these two articles, there is no need for us to review it in detail here. Brevity should not be interpreted as indicating insignificance.

Institutionalist thinking has made a big impact on IPE during the last fifteen years, stimulating a set of research programs that have illuminated relationships among interests, power, and institutions. But it was of less value in understanding shifting identity politics afterwards. Advocates of domestic structure approaches had for several decades criticized international relations research, including neoliberal institutionalism, for taking for granted the preferences or identities of the actors whom it studied. Neoliberal institutionalism paid virtually no attention, for example, to the

---

96. See Nye 1990; and Ikenberry and Kupchan 1990.
97. See Scott and Lake 1989; and Nau 1990.
98. Morrow 1994b.
99. Fearon 1995.
100. See Keohane, Nye, and Hoffmann 1993; and Wallander 1998.

phenomenon of nationalism. And it could not capture the fact that during the 1980s increased interest in human rights and environmental issues seemed driven largely by normative concerns. After 1989, some rationalists began to think of ideas as variables that affected the solutions to games—for instance, by reducing uncertainty or providing focal points.[101] Ideas could be incorporated into an institutional framework by emphasizing how particular conceptions become institutionalized and, therefore, persist over time.[102] Since it was not wedded exclusively to a materialist conception of structure, neoliberalism could engage some of the issues of changing beliefs or identities posed by end of the Cold War.

The Revival of Sociological and Cultural Perspectives

Sociological perspectives have always been important for comparative politics and have never been completely absent from international studies. In Europe, where the boundary between international and domestic politics was never particularly salient, the sociological bent of scholarship differed from prevailing American perspectives. This was true, for example, of Scandinavian and German peace research, which remained largely unnoticed in the United States and was often regarded as politically suspect when read. The theoretical contributions of the French School, represented by Stanley Hoffmann's writings and those of Raymond Aron, especially in the 1950s and 1960s, and of the British School, clustering in the 1970s and 1980s around the writings of Hedley Bull and Martin Wight, remained uninterested in the debates between the general theoretical orientations that dominated American scholarship, such as realism and liberalism.[103] These schools of thought were at odds with the emphasis in American international relations scholarship on clearly stated causal propositions and their systematic exploration in methodologically rigorous ways.

In the United States Ruggie published a series of papers demonstrating the value of a sociological orientation. He argued that the postwar international economic regime reflected what he termed embedded liberalism, identified by a shared intersubjective understanding that open international markets would be tempered by the need to maintain social stability. He criticized Waltz's theory for its lack of sociological content and for failing to explain systemic change.[104] And, together with Friedrich Kratochwil, he pointed out that analysts had failed to investigate the shared understandings that led to the convergence of actor expectations on which, by some accounts, regime stability depended. They argued also that the treatment of principles and norms as "independent" or "intervening" variables, linking material structures to outcomes, was not easily accommodated within the epistemological foundations of institutional and normative analysis. Subsequently, Kratochwil and Nicholas Onuf

---

101. See Goldstein and Keohane 1993b; and Garrett and Weingast 1993.
102. Goldstein 1993, 1996. See also Hall 1989b; and Sikkink 1991, 1993a,b.
103. Raymond Aron's massive sociological study of war and peace did not play a major role in graduate training in the United States, and Hedley Bull's major book on international society had little impact until about a decade after its publication. See Aron 1966; Bull 1977; and Hoffmann 1986, 1987.
104. Ruggie 1983a,b, 1998.

put forward a conception of rules informed by, among others, philosophy, linguistics, and sociology.[105] And in several papers Wendt suggested a social theory of international relations that engaged the claims of neorealism head on.[106]

This sociological turn was intellectually deeply indebted to fields of scholarship well beyond the confines of IPE. Philosophy, structural linguistics, critical theory, geography, science and technology studies, postmodern political theory, anthropology, media studies, and literary criticism, among others, all had, in different though related ways, grappled with the project of modernity gone awry in the twentieth century.[107] There is a growing body of work in international relations and in security studies but, significantly, not yet in IPE that is self-conscious in conducting empirical research from a constructivist perspective. Sociological work falls into three broad clusters: conventional, critical, and postmodern.[108]

Conventional constructivists insist that sociological perspectives offer a general theoretical orientation and specific research programs that can rival or complement rationalism. In this view a full understanding of preferences requires an analysis of the social processes by which norms evolve and identities are constituted. Since they emphasize how ideational or normative structures constitute agents and their interests, conventional constructivists differ sharply from rationalists on questions of ontology. Furthermore, constructivists insist that agents and structure are mutually constitutive and thus hope to give social science a more dynamic conception of change of system structures. On issues of epistemology and methodology, however, no great differences divide conventional constructivists from rationalists.

Outstanding among constructivist contributions is the research program of the sociologist John Meyer and his colleagues. Informed by a cognitive approach to world culture, this research program demonstrated an astonishing degree of similarity in formal national practices relating to issues as diverse as censuses, social security, education, and science despite great variations in national socioeconomic and ideological characteristics. For Meyer and his associates, the key to understanding this story is the script of modernity, often presented by international organizations, which suggested to national leaders what policies they ought to adopt if they wanted to appear, to themselves and others, to be modern and progressive.[109]

Sociologically inclined scholars have in recent years analyzed empirically a number of cases to bolster this research program in international relations and security studies. Slavery and child labor, for example, were accepted for millennia as acceptable social practices; in the course of barely a century they became incompatible with

105. See Kratochwil and Ruggie 1986; Onuf 1989; and Kratochwil 1989, especially chap. 4.
106. Wendt 1992 and forthcoming.
107. For a brilliant discussion of the constructivist perspective from a philosophical standpoint, see Searle 1995.
108. We choose the three categories here for heuristic purposes and in full awareness of the fact that considerable differences exist within each of these clusters, borders between clusters are porous, and scholars may change positions in different publications. Our discussion is influenced by Price and Reus-Smit 1998; and Hopf 1998.
109. See Meyer 1980; Thomas, Meyer, Ramirez, and Boli 1987; Strang 1991; and Finnemore 1996a,b.

civilized society.[110] International war may possibly be relegated to a similar status.[111] Half a century ago it was normal and appropriate for Japanese and German young men to volunteer to die for emperor and fatherland. By the 1990s the institutionalization of identities and norms that have marked Japanese and German politics since 1945 make such individual choices and social practices a rare exception.[112] In national security studies a growing number of mostly younger scholars addressed conventional topics—such as the spread of weapons of mass destruction, deterrence, arms races, strategic culture, or alliance politics—with unconventional sociological and cultural approaches.[113] And during the last two decades feminists have been successfully redefining the meaning of human rights to encompass gender identities.[114]

Conventional constructivist studies have focused both on critical historical junctures from which new structural arrangements emerge and on interactions between existing structures and agents. Ruggie's historical arguments about the replacement of feudalism by the modern state system have made a major impact on international relations theory.[115] Recent analyses of how actors and structures are reproduced in contemporary world politics include studies on Japanese norms indicating that drastic changes in Japan's security policies are highly unlikely and studies on changes in norms about weapons indicating that some classes of weapons may be seen as illegitimate, regardless of their strategic usefulness.[116]

As a general theoretical orientation constructivist research illuminates the sources of both conflict and cooperation. Iain Johnston, for example, has formulated a constructivist argument that seeks to account for China's consistently militant security strategy. The balance of material capabilities in the international system changed greatly over the last decades and centuries; China's parabellum strategic culture did not. Hence it is the latter that offers a compelling explanation of security policy.[117] Similarly, Henry Nau has combined constructivist and realist insights in his writing to address central elements in U.S. foreign policy.[118]

In rejecting rationalist conceptions of human nature, critical constructivists agree with conventional constructivists on the issue of ontology. Like conventional constructivists, they are interested in how actors and systems are constituted and coevolve. Their research program focuses on identity issues that include, besides nationalism, subjects such as race, ethnicity, religion, and sexuality. Critical constructivists also accept the possibility of social scientific knowledge based on empirical research. They are, however, deeply skeptical of the possibility of formulating general covering laws, and they are pluralistic about appropriate research methodologies. Institu-

110. Keck and Sikkink 1998.
111. Mueller 1989.
112. See Katzenstein 1996a; and Berger 1996.
113. See the contributions in Katzenstein 1996b. See also Kier 1997.
114. See Tickner 1992; and Keck and Sikkink 1998.
115. Ruggie 1983a.
116. See Katzenstein 1996a; and Price 1997.
117. Johnston 1995a.
118. Nau 1990, 1997.

tional arrangements, norms, and identities are embedded in specific historical contexts that can vary so dramatically that they can only be investigated through an ideographic rather than a nomothetic approach. Emphasis is placed on the detailed study of texts to understand the symbolic systems that govern actors' discourses, rather than on an analysis of a large number of cases.[119]

Critical constructivists insist that scholars' work has normative consequences. A scientist may try to find a cure for cancer or instead develop a more virulent strain of anthrax. This choice, however, does not alter the mechanisms that cause cancer or anthrax. Critical constructivists, however, understand their project not simply as revealing relationships that exist independent of the investigator, but also as having the potential to alter these relationships themselves.

Critical constructivists are developing a research program that is generating new and significant insights on important issues in world politics for which rationalist analysis has lacked compelling answers. For example, constructivists offer analyses of the transformative shift from the medieval to the modern state system; of the end of the Cold War as a recent, significant change within that system; and effects on the international system of variations in the moral purposes of states and different systems of procedural justice.[120] Constructivist arguments about issues ranging from the role of norms in sanctions against South Africa to why chemical weapons are viewed as "weapons of mass destruction" even when their destructive power may be smaller than that of "conventional" weapons both complement and challenge rationalist accounts.[121]

This research program is open to rationalist critiques on the use of evidence and the limits of interpretation, the possibility and the status of generalizations, the use of alternative explanations, and problems of variability and comparability. Rationalists may view critical constructivists working closely with texts as postmodernists. This is a mistaken impression. What separates critical constructivism and postmodernism is not the shared focus on discourse, but the acknowledgment by critical constructivists of the possibility of a social science and a willingness to engage openly in scholarly debate with rationalism.

On both scores postmodernists differ sharply from critical constructivists, whom postmodernists charge with bringing in rationalism and positivism through the backdoor.[122] Postmodernists insist that there is no firm foundation for any knowledge. Since there is no position from which to pass scientific or ethical judgments, postmodernist analysis is restricted to the task of unmasking the power relations that are concealed in all knowledge claims, including their own, and all forms of communicative rationality. Through a close analysis of language, postmodernism points our attention to the inherent instability of all symbolic and political orders. Since subjects only understand the world through language, and control of language implies power,

119. See Risse 1997; and Adler and Barnett 1998.
120. See Ruggie 1983a, 1992, 1998; Koslowski and Kratochwil 1994; Risse-Kappen 1994; and Reus-Smit forthcoming.
121. See Klotz 1995c; and Price 1997.
122. George 1994.

linguistic presentations are always open to cognitive and political processes of destabilization. Postmodernist analysis seeks out these sources of potential instability. It is interested in decentering established discourse, including its own, by paying attention to what is marginal or silent.

Since the mid-1980s, postmodernist analysis has grown substantially both inside and outside of the United States, although primarily in the humanities. Richard Ashley was one of the first in international relations who suggested that neorealism's totalizing vision determined not only international relations research but also diplomacy. Thus, it obscured issues of human agency to which realism had remained responsive.[123] For postmodernism, reality is a creation of the analytical and ideological categories through which that theory perceives the world and in the name of which it exercises a coercive power that precludes the emergence of communicative rationality.

Little of this debate was published in *IO*, since *IO* has been committed to an enterprise that postmodernism denies: the use of evidence to adjudicate between truth claims. In contrast to conventional and critical constructivism, postmodernism falls clearly outside of the social science enterprise, and in international relations research it risks becoming self-referential and disengaged from the world, protests to the contrary notwithstanding.

Yet it is easy to underestimate the direct importance and indirect influence of this intellectual current. Postmodernism has found many adherents both in the broader international studies field in the United States and in Europe where major journals and book series are dedicated to publishing the results of this work. Especially younger scholars of constructivist persuasion have experienced not so much a "turn" but an evolution of views that was rooted in the postmodernist challenge. The power of the rationalist and empiricist currents of social science research in the United States makes critical engagement with rationalism more compelling than isolation. Hence, in different ways both conventional and critical constructivists have positioned themselves quite self-consciously between rationalist theoretical orientations, such as realism or liberalism, and postmodernist orientations.[124]

Terminological Differences and Research Complementarities

Both the differences and complementarities between constructivism and rationalism promise to make the interaction between these two theoretical orientations a productive point of contestation. Both are concerned with what in ordinary language are called beliefs, but they understand this concept in different ways and use different terms in their analyses. The key terms for rationalists are preferences, information, strategies, and common knowledge. The key terms for constructivists are identities, norms, knowledge, and interests. Rationalist orientations do not offer a way to understand common knowledge. Constructivist arguments do not provide a way to analyze

---

123. Ashley 1984.
124. See Katzenstein 1996a,b; and Adler 1997.

strategies. Yet both strategy and common knowledge are usually necessary to under-stand political outcomes. We first discuss terminology, then turn to some differences and complementarities in how rationalists and constructivists analyze the role of beliefs.

Terminology.   All rationalists rely on the assumption of instrumental rationality to provide the crucial link between the environment and actor behavior. Game theory provides a useful language for rationalist analysis more generally. For game theory to offer a tractable analytic framework it must assume that actors have common knowl-edge. They all share the same view of the game, including the payoff matrix, the strategic choice points, the types of actors they are playing against, and the probabil-ity of each type. Players know the options from which they can choose. If they are uncertain about the nature of their opponent, they may have the opportunity to update their probability assessments as the game progresses because of information that is revealed by the moves taken in the game. Given preferences, probabilities, and choice points, it is possible to derive a complete set of strategies, choices that players will make at every node in the game, and equilibrium outcomes, of which there may be many.

All rationalists use the assumption of rationality to provide the crucial link be-tween features of the environment—power, interests, and institutional rules—and actor behavior. But on the issue of the importance of information, they are divided. Rationalists who subscribe to a materialist view of how to study the international political economy, such as Rogowski and Frieden, assume preferences for more wealth and infer strategies from structure, especially the competitive positions of factors, sectors, or firms in the world political economy.[125] Variations in information are unimportant in their analysis. These authors expect actors to understand the world accurately, and they do not conceptualize actors' choices in terms of game theory involving interdependent decisions.

In contrast, rationalists whose thinking is more indebted to game theory empha-size the importance of imperfect information and strategic interaction. They stress how changes in information can account for variations in strategies, even if the pref-erences of actors remain unchanged. Small changes in information can have a pro-found impact on equilibrium outcomes. Institutions or rules can be consequential because they can alter information and empower players to set the agenda, make amendments, and accept or reject the final package.[126]

Constructivists insist on the primacy of intersubjective structures that give the material world meaning.[127] These structures have different components that help in specifying the interests that motivate action: norms, identity, knowledge, and culture. Norms typically describe collective expectations with "regulative" effects on the

125. See Rogowski 1989; and Frieden 1991.
126. See Shepsle 1986; Morrow 1994b; and Fearon 1995. It should be noted, however, that game-theoretic rationalism typically shows that multiple equilibria exist, which undermines any deterministic predictions of behavior.
127. Katzenstein 1996b.

proper behavior of actors with a given identity. In some situations norms operate like rules that define the identity of actors; they have "constitutive" effects that specify the actions that will cause relevant others to recognize a particular identity. Epistemic knowledge is also part of a social process by which the material world acquires meaning. Finally, culture is a broad label that denotes collective models of authority or identity, carried by custom or law. Culture refers to both evaluative standards (such as norms and values) and cognitive standards (such as rules and models) that define the social actors that exist in a system, how they operate, and how they relate to one another.

Constructivist research is not cut from one cloth, as Finnemore and Sikkink argue in this issue. Conventional and critical constructivist analyses often focus on different components of a common constructivist research program—norms, identity, knowledge, and culture—and, in empirical research, accord different weights to each of them. And they are divided on whether the relationship between these components is definitional, conceptual, causal, or empirical. These disagreements are reflected also in the inevitable tensions that accompany their joint effort to engage rationalism, despite some differences in the approach each takes to issues of epistemology and methodology.

Common knowledge: A point of complementarity.   Rationalism and constructivism are generic theoretical orientations that are complementary on some crucial points. Game-theoretic rationalists typically assume the existence of actors, who have preexisting preferences and who share common knowledge of the game, which enables them to engage in strategic bargaining. Constructivist research focuses on the sources of actors' identities—in game-theoretic terms, their preferences—and of their interpretations of the context of their action: common knowledge. Hence, rationalism and constructivism share an interest in beliefs or knowledge.

Game theory provides a vocabulary and a visual image that highlight not only where rationalist and constructivist arguments part ways but also where they might come together. Any rationalist analysis must stipulate the nature of the actors in the sense of specifying their preferences and their capabilities. What do actors desire? What moves can they make? Moreover, for any formal game theoretic analysis to work, it is necessary to assume common knowledge. The players have to share the same knowledge about the game. They must know what they do not know because of imperfect information, and they must share the same view of the payoff matrix and the available set of strategies. Rationalist accounts make very limited claims about the insights they can offer into the origins of such common knowledge.

Some rationalist accounts suggest that normative structures can be generated from institutions that have been created to promote material interests. David Kreps, for instance, has argued that what he terms corporate culture is developed because it is impossible to fully specify the duties of employees in any complex environment. The world is too complicated for complete contracts to be written. Corporate culture provides a set of norms or guidelines that can guide behavior in situations not covered by formal arrangements.[128] Following David Hume and Blaise Pascal, Robert Sugden points out that practices initially developed to promote specific interests can acquire a normative element if they are widely understood and practiced within a given social setting.[129] An actor who violates existing practices will be normatively sanctioned by other members of the community. This is a line of analysis that puts rationalists at the border of constructivism. Norms are based on material interests, but they can take on an aura of authority that transcends their initial purpose.

Norms can also be consequential, because they can provide focal points in situations of multiple equilibria; that is, where there are many possible solutions to the game. Game theory has shown that such situations are very common in games of incomplete information. A rationalist analysis can stipulate that one of these outcomes can be chosen, but it does not tell us which one it will be. Shared cultural norms offer one way of selecting which equilibrium will be salient for the players.[130] In the late 1950s Thomas Schelling, then teaching at Yale, asked about forty acquaintances where and when they would meet a friend in New York City; more than half coordinated on the information booth at Grand Central Station (where the trains arrived from New Haven) at noon.[131] For professors at Columbia University in 1959, the time might have been the same, but Grand Central Station would hardly have been as salient. Common knowledge is contextualized within a specific social setting.

Not all common knowledge can be explained by practices and institutions designed to maximize material interests, for example, by resolving problems of multiple equilibria. Norms that define the options available to players, and that shape their preferences, are often prior to these instrumental practices and institutions. For example, slavery was a conventional option for securing the labor of conquered lands in earlier periods; it is not an option for contemporary states. Capturing slaves as spoils of war is no longer an available move. The medieval guilds, the holders of English capital in the late seventeenth century, the burghers of Amsterdam, and Michael Milken were all concerned about enhancing their material wealth, but the options available to them (the moves they could make) were hardly the same.

Constructivists seek to understand how preferences are formed and knowledge is generated, prior to the exercise of instrumental rationality. Constructivism analyzes discourses and practices that continuously recreate what rationalists refer to as common knowledge. Constructivists do not emphasize misperception: cognitive or emotional biases that distort rationality and can be corrected through the analysis of new information.[132] They are more interested in the collective processes that students of social psychology have identified.[133] Constructivists focus on discursive and social

---

128. Kreps 1990a.
129. Sugden 1989. Sugden mentions Hume's argument in the eighteenth century. Pascal made a similar argument a century earlier; see N. Keohane 1980, 278–81.
130. Ferejohn 1991.
131. Schelling 1960, 55–56.
132. Jervis 1976.
133. Janis 1983.

practices that define the identity of actors and the normative order within which they make their moves. We can think of these processes in two different ways: in terms of ideas about cause–effect relations and regulatory norms[134] or as more or less contested processes of identity formation.[135]

The differences and complementarities between rationalism and constructivism are illustrated by their treatments of persuasion.[136] Rationalists interpret persuasion in the language of incentives, strategic bargaining, and information. They analyze the provision of new information, sometimes through costly signaling, and appeals to audiences. For a consistent rationalist, it would be anomalous to think of persuasion in terms of changing others' deepest preferences. Constructivists, by contrast, insist on the importance of social processes that generate changes in normative beliefs, such as those prompted by the antislavery movement of the nineteenth century, the contemporary campaign for women's rights as human rights, or nationalist propaganda. For constructivists, persuasion involves changing preferences by appealing to identities, moral obligations, and norms conceived of as standards of appropriate behavior.

The different styles of analysis—"thin" information for rationalists versus "thick" norms and identities for constructivists—to some extent reflect the familiar contest in social science between economic and sociological traditions.[137] Constructivism is ideographic, whereas rationalism is nomothetic. Neither perspective is adequate to cover all aspects of social reality. But at one critical point they are joined. Both recognize—constructivism as a central research project and rationalism as a background condition—that human beings operate in a socially constructed environment, which changes over time. Hence, both analytical perspectives focus in one way or another on common knowledge—constructivism on how it is created, rationalism on how it affects strategic decision making. The core of the constructivist project is to explicate variations in preferences, available strategies, and the nature of the players, across space and time. The core of the rationalist project is to explain strategies, given preferences, information, and common knowledge. Neither project can be complete without the other.

Conclusion

The history of *IO* and the emergence of IPE as a field were built on a rich intellectual tradition that developed in the 1940s, 1950s, and 1960s. Many of the major lines of arguments that have preoccupied scholars of IPE and international relations for the

---

134. See Goldstein and Keohane 1993b; Haas 1993, 1997; Sikkink 1993a,b; Adler and Haas 1992; Adler 1987; and Haas 1992c.

135. Wendt 1987, 1992, forthcoming. See also March and Olsen 1989; Powell and DiMaggio 1991; and Jepperson, Wendt, and Katzenstein 1996.

136. On persuasion, see Finnemore 1996a; and a long tradition of legal scholarship, including Franck 1990; and Chayes and Chayes 1995.

137. Swedberg 1991.

last three decades were developed during these years. Then as now scholars continue to analyze the interaction between power, wealth, and social purpose.

The history of *IO* and the emergence of IPE have been part of the elaboration of more complex and self-consciously analytical formulations with which scholars have analyzed enduring problems of world politics. No historical narrative can reproduce the complex and idiosyncratic evolution of scholarship. For ease of presentation and because it reflects important aspects of our own intellectual autobiographies, our story has followed two distinctive strands: the interplay between realist and liberal currents of theory in the evolution of the analysis of IPE and the analysis of domestic politics and IPE.

We have argued that in the 1990s some of the major points of contestation shifted. Influenced by strong currents in economics and cultural studies, debates between rationalism and constructivism are becoming more important. They offer contrasting analytical orientations for research in the social sciences at large and in international relations and IPE. The greatest promise in the intellectual debate between proponents of rationalism and constructivism does not lie in the insistence that reality can only be analyzed in one conceptual language—the one preferred by the analyst. Insisting on one's own language is a sterile intellectual exercise. Knowledge and understanding are promoted by debates among the proponents of different research orientations and research programs. But one should never forget that at the end of the day orientations and programs are only useful if they are deployed to specify intellectually tractable and substantively important questions.

Analytical progress in the study of IPE is possible in research programs despite continuing contestations between general theoretical orientations. We believe that the field has become increasingly sophisticated; we have better conceptual tools and richer interpretations than we had in the 1970s. Our substantive findings, however, remain meager: counterintuitive, well-documented causal arguments are rare. And some analytical advances have told us why we cannot make strong predictions rather than how to go about doing so, as is the case for the revelation from game theory of the frequency of multiple equilibria. Nevertheless, we know a great deal more than we did thirty years ago about a number of processes that are central to how the world political economy works, such as how power is deployed under various conditions of vulnerability, how international regimes affect government policies, and how domestic institutions and world politics affect each other through institutional processes. Many of the articles in this issue could not have been written without the accumulation of substantive research findings in issues ranging from trade and industry, money and energy, and finance and investment to, among others, the environment and human rights.

In international politics and in the world of scholarship well-established boundaries are being blurred and new ones are being created. World politics is witnessing enormous change in the wake of the collapse of the Berlin Wall, the end of strategic bipolarity, and the peaceful disintegration of the Soviet Union. We are observing different types of democratization processes in different world regions, ethnic conflicts over the control of territory, and growing conflicts over the spread of weapons of mass destruction to regional powers. We are also seeing far-reaching experiments with economic integration in some world regions and continuing marginalization in others, expanded trade under the auspices of a revamped World Trade Organization, and the redefinition of the role of the International Monetary Fund and other governance mechanisms in the wake of Asia's financial crisis. At the same time, religious fundamentalism is gaining ground in much of the Muslim world. And strong secular social movements championing environmentalism, feminism, and human rights are active worldwide. Many opportunities exist for building innovative links across disciplinary and subdisciplinary boundaries. All of these developments illustrate the complexity of contemporary world politics and the opportunity to draw new connections across generic theoretical orientations and between specific research programs.

The rubric for this era of increasing transboundary activity is variously called "internationalization" or "globalization." This is not an unprecedented development. International financial markets were highly integrated at the end of the nineteenth century—perhaps even more so than they have been since, at least until very recently. Trade flows were also much higher at this time than for most of the twentieth century. New technologies have opened new opportunities, but it is not evident how they will affect the control and authority structures in state and society. How extensively national policies and practices will be reshaped by globalization—and how effectively institutions will resist such pressures—remains to be seen. Such research will focus again on issues of the relationships that have been central to the literature of the last thirty years: between wealth and power, states and markets, interests and institutions, the international political economy and domestic politics. Constraints and opportunities will change and so may the identity of the key actors and the norms they accept. But observers of this new reality will still be able to learn from the accomplishments, and the mistakes, of previous generations of IPE scholars.

The sophistication of work in IPE has not made it directly applicable to policy. As noted earlier, we cannot point to clear scientific "findings" about cause and effect that policymakers can readily apply. At the same time, the application of more rigorous social scientific standards by referees for *IO* seems to have discouraged policy commentary: policy-relevant articles have become few and far between. Hence, the pages of *IO* reflect the gulf that has developed between scholarship and practice in international relations.

Yet even if the links between scholarship and policy are not close, connections can be made. More significant than the specific debates or even findings in the literature are the interpretations of changing reality that have been put forward by analysts: concepts and broad "theorizing" in which the field has engaged. A number of ideas originally formulated in the literature are being taken for granted in policy discussions. Whether this reflects an *effect* of the international relations literature or simply parallel understandings in the policy and academic worlds is not clear. At any rate, it is conventional wisdom now that interdependence has implications for power as well as for wealth, that international institutions constitute a valuable set of instruments for promoting the interests of states through cooperation, and that understanding domestic political economy requires not just examining domestic interests but also taking into consideration domestic and international institutions as well as the structure of the world political economy. The significance of interactions between nonstate and state actors is also increasingly understood in the policy world.

The specific approach that scholars choose to follow in their work will depend on whether they are principally committed to advancing a theoretical viewpoint or to solving specific empirical problems, their own analytical predispositions, their methodological tools, the data to which they have access, the resources at their disposal, and the values they hold. None of us should be too sure that our own choices will be intellectually productive. Even though we build on works of earlier generations of outstanding social scientists, our vision is limited. Our nearsightedness should make us skeptical that the latest turn of the screw of a particular methodological, theoretical, or epistemological debate will magically bring our analytical binoculars into sharper focus. Yet new intellectual debates about aspects of world politics that change, and those that do not, point to high returns from an increasing integration of IPE scholarship into broader social science debates. This is a welcome opportunity for any author and an intellectually exciting prospect for the editors and readers of *IO*.

The Sociology of a Not So International Discipline: American and European Developments in International Relations

Ole Wæver

> You wish me to speak about "Science as a Vocation." Now, we political econo-
> mists have a pedantic custom, which I should like to follow, of always beginning
> with the external conditions. In this case, we begin with the question: What are
> the conditions of science as a vocation in the material sense of the term? Today
> this question means, practically and essentially: What are the prospects of a
> graduate student who is resolved to dedicate himself professionally to science in
> university life? In order to understand the peculiarities of German conditions it is
> expedient to proceed by comparison and to realize the conditions abroad. In this
> respect, the United States stands in the deepest contrast with Germany, so we
> shall focus upon that country.
> —Max Weber, "Science as a Vocation," speech at Munich University, 1918

Introduction

This special issue of *International Organization (IO)* exhibits a consistent ambivalence about whether it reports on the development of international relations (IR) or
American IR. Maybe this should be expected. IR is and has been "an American
social science".[1] The incident in the late 1980s when the International Studies Association (ISA) approached (other?) national associations (such as the British International Studies Association, BISA, and the Japan Association of International Relations, JAIR) in the mantle of the global meta-organization of international studies

I thank Michael Barnett, Barry Buzan, Thomas Diez, Klaus-Gerd Giesen, Nils Petter Gleditsch, Kjell
Goldmann, Stefano Guzzini, Lene Hansen, Pierre Hassner, Markus Jachtenfuchs, Pertti Joenniemi, Pirjo
Jukarainen, Thomas Risse, Marie-Claude Smouts, Arthur Stein, Jaap de Wilde, Michael Williams, and the
editors for commenting on drafts; Heine Andersen for guiding me to the relevant literature in the sociology
of science; and Karen Lund Petersen for her untiring work on statistics and figures. I gratefully acknowledge the financial support provided by an SSRC-MacArthur Foundation Fellowship on Peace and Security
in a Changing World.
   1. Hoffmann 1977.

International Organization 52, 4, Autumn 1998, pp. 687–727

asking for their annual report nicely illustrated this.[2] The ambivalence of some toward the organization's name was eventually resolved in favor of the ISA presenting itself as a regional organization cooperating on equal terms with the Japanese and European associations, but in some respects the opposite—less politically correct—resolution would have been more accurate: to acknowledge how small the difference was between American IR and the "global" discipline.

Movement toward a more pluralistic or balanced situation is widely expected, and several signs have appeared—from increased European self-assuredness and collaboration (with a new European journal and an emerging European association) and a successful, new, theoretical German-language journal to a growing interest in "non-Western" approaches. Dramatic change has not materialized so far, and the novelty is rather an expectation that "real world" developments will eventually be reflected in the discipline, and thus a more regionalized post–Cold War order, European integration, and Asian values will lead to the emergence of distinct IR voices.

Many scholars, however, argue that there is no such thing as national perspectives on international relations ("What do Kenneth Waltz, Richard Ashley, Cynthia Enloe, and Craig Murphy have in common?"[3]). Distribution among competing theories or "paradigms" is more important than national distinctions. If more Americans are participating in the networks of our globalized discipline, this is of no relevance to the content, to our theorizing. In this article I show that an American hegemony exists and that it influences the theoretical profile of the discipline, and I explain where it comes from.

Broadly, this article asks why IR develops as it does in different societies. More narrowly, it investigates American dominance in the field: what does it rest on and what are its effects? More specifically, why do some American theories travel and others do not? Behavioralism was absolutely central to American political science for two decades, and scholars often argue that its reverberations shaped the next two decades in the form of postbehavioralism.[4] Its importance in Europe was not comparable. Today, a similar question emerges in relation to rational choice: will it become as dominant in Europe as it has in the United States? So far this has not been the case, and there might be reasons to expect that it never will.

The prognosis is "American IR: from global hegemony to national professionalization." The American mainstream turns overwhelmingly toward rational choice approaches (noncooperative game theory in particular). Because this current wave is inspired from the other parts of political science as taught in the United States—comparative politics and American politics—this turn is accompanied by great hopes of establishing IR on a more solid theoretical foundation as part of a general scientific breakthrough in political science and in the social sciences in general. Maximizing its integration into political science as a unitary discipline weakens the basis for continued global hegemony. Mainstream IR enthusiastically integrates with theories

---

2. Strange 1995.
3. Porter forthcoming; for similar arguments see Palmer 1980.
4. Farr, Dryzek, and Leonard 1995.

peculiar to the United States (for example, those based on the logic of committees in the U.S. Congress), which are furthermore attractive due to the distinctively American ideals of social science. Therefore, the rest of the world increasingly sees the back of American IR.

I first show that the way the discipline usually reflects on its own development falls embarrassingly behind standards developed in sociology of science and historiography; I then turn to the sociology of science to establish an explanatory model to account for the national variations discovered. The main factors are organized at three levels: societal-political features of the country, the standing and structure of social science in general in that country, and the internal intellectual and social structures of the IR discipline, including its theories and forms of debate. I offer some data on the issue of dominance: who publishes what and where? I then follow the structure of the model based on the sociology of science and address these questions to German, French, British, and American IR. A central explanation for the lack of congruity between American and European IR at present is the gradual de-Europeanization of American IR. American IR is cutting itself off from those of its roots that are continental European and is building increasingly on a "liberal," Anglo-American philosophical tradition. There was always a strong European component in American IR, and when the U.S. community, for various reasons, became the largest and most innovative, it produced theory that was basically (re-)exportable to Europe. Current theory is shifting toward an American liberal format much less applicable to continental Europe and most other parts of the world. Finally, I explain causes and effects of the strange combination of American insularity and hegemony. What potentially useful forms of theory does American IR cut itself off from, and what are the effects on European IR?

One major line of argument starts by comparing IR to the ideal of a global discipline. "An ideal model of a community of scholars," Kal Holsti has written, "would suggest reasonably symmetrical flows of communication, with 'exporters' of knowledge also being 'importers' from other sources."[5] Later in the article, I outline the unbalanced relationship between American and non-American IR in terms of patterns of publication, citation, and, especially, theory borrowing. All other national IR communities are running huge balance-of-trade deficits against the United States. Although unpleasant for individual non-Americans in career terms, the situation need not have an impact on the content of the science. Maybe Americans and non-Americans do the same things, only the Americans better, and so they get published everywhere? However, the dominant approaches on the two sides of the Atlantic differ systematically, here documented along the current main axis of metatheoretical disagreement, rationalism versus reflectivism (compare the article in this issue by Peter Katzenstein, Robert Keohane, and Stephen Krasner). Judging from the tone of much rationalist scholarship, a likely counterargument could be that this difference is only a matter of time: American IR is ahead (due, for example, to the better training

5. Holsti 1985, 13. His own conclusion is "that patterns of international exchange of scholarly knowledge in our field remain far from an ideal model of an international community of scholars." Ibid., 148.

of students in methodology), and eventually Europeans and others will catch up and become equally rational choice. The discipline could be consoled: there is no distortion effected by an American dominance, only an acceleration of progress. I later show why this projection is unlikely to come about. Consistent and explainable differences exist between American and European IR. Although I do not offer a full sociological explanation of the history of IR, I do begin to sketch one because it is necessary for answering the American–European question.

Explaining How We Got Here

How (Not) to Depict Disciplinary Developments

Most of the articles in this issue take a characteristic form: a field is presented, previous attempts and contributions are critically evaluated, and an explanation is offered about why current approaches (most strongly articulated in the case of rational choice) have started to solve previous problems. According to almost all the authors, their subfields currently rest on sound footing.

Naturally, a field looks like this to its current practitioners. Typically, we are doing what we are doing because we believe it is the right thing to do, and this appears to us as superior to previous efforts. To a historian or sociologist of science, however, this will appear a naive approach. As typical "Whig" history writing it assumes a progress where the winning line is necessarily also the best, and the past should be measured on the standards of the present.[6] To assume that these previous studies were attempting to do what we are doing today, only less successfully, ignores their contemporary context (replacing it with allegedly eternal questions with which mankind grapples). Also, present theoretical contributions need to be placed in context and not read purely as relationships between disembodied academics and abstract issues. We need to not only explain past "mistakes" but also accept that what we do today can hardly be a result of the discipline having freed itself of all extra-scientific impulses and achieved some kind of purity. More likely, there are also social and contextual reasons why we do what we do. In no way should this imply that our efforts are disqualified as scientific, objective, or valuable. Only by assuming that true science purely reflects subject matter on a passive, receiving level would sociological explanation and scientific value be necessary opposites. More realistically, the theories of all eras should in like manner be submitted to sociological explanation at the same time that we conduct our usual discussions within the discipline to establish what theories we find most convincing, valid, or truthful. In the words of Theodore J. Lowi: "even assuming that we are all sincerely searching for the truth (and it is more interesting to assume that), there are reasons other than the search for truth why we do the kinds of political science we do."[7]

---

6. Butterfield coined the term, and it has been developed into a more general characteristic by the new historians of ideas in the Cambridge school: Pocock, Skinner, Dunn. See Butterfield 1959; compare Tully 1988.

7. Lowi 1992, 1.

The relationship between IR and sociology of science is virtually nonexistent.[8] Sociology of science has concentrated on the natural sciences, with most of the remaining attention reserved for medicine and law. Of the fraction left for social science[9] and humanities, most of the attention goes to economics and sociology. A subdiscipline (IR) within one of the least studied disciplines (political science), therefore gets no attention from "professional" sociology of science. If sociology of science were to be applied to IR, a combination of the two could come from the opposite side, but IR scholars usually write about the discipline without any theoretical framework whatsoever.[10] Usually they write about the past as part of one of the debates about who is right and who is wrong, what mistakes were made in the past, and why everyone should follow me now.

Explanations With or Without Sociology of Science

In the history and sociology of science, internal explanations originally referred to explanations based on the allegedly inherent telos of science (and therefore it produced linear, progressive stories), whereas external accounts introduced various political, economic, social, and intellectual causes. In IR, however, this setup has been curiously reversed. The most popular explanations are "external" in a particular sense: the impact of developments in real-world international relations on developments within the discipline of IR. Thus, paradoxically, external explanations reinstall receptiveness toward the empirical stuff the discipline is supposed to react to, assisting a quasi-positivist, progressivist self-understanding. This is paradoxical because "external" explanations in normal sociology of science debates mean external both to the academic universe of the discipline and to its subject matter—they mean developments in the surrounding society.

Often, IR's external stories seem convincing. The partial change from realism to transnationalism and interdependence surely had something to do with Vietnam, the oil crisis, post–Bretton Woods global finance, and détente. In several other cases, it sounds easier than it is: idealism was replaced by realism because of World War II. Maybe causality operates in reverse: the history of the interwar period is told with the idealists responsible for the war because realism won the battle. The general pattern could be that each major rupture in the international system triggers a swing away from whatever theory dominates. Currently, the end of the Cold War reads time to

8. One surprising—but then also systematically ignored—exception is Crawford and Biderman 1969, financed by the Behavioral Sciences Division of the Air Force Office of Scientific Research. It concentrates on "the relationship between social scientists and the activities of the United States Government in the international field since the beginning of World War II." (1969, v) But in this more limited task, it draws on and discusses developments within the sociology of social science.

9. "The hesitancy of social scientists to apply to themselves even a fraction of the energies that they have used in scrutinizing the behaviors of others may account for the slow development of the sociology of social science as a field of empirical research"; see Crawford and Biderman 1969, vi. A notable recent exception is the emerging body of work around Wagner, Whitley, and Wittrock discussed in a later section.

10. Whitley notices the same for economics. Whitley 1986. Partial IR exceptions are Giesen 1995; and Guzzini 1998.

leave neorealism. It is not evident why neorealism should be more troubled by this event than any of the other theories that cannot explain it. The causal connection between external events and developments in theory is, as usual, vague.[11]

The articles on the history of the discipline,[12] slowly growing in number, are usually not based on systematic research or clear methods. They are, at best, elegant restatements of "common knowledge" of our past, implicitly assuming that any good practitioner can tell the history of the discipline. However, without looking systematically at the past, we tend to reproduce myths such as the nature of the idealists in the (alleged) first debate.[13] For instance, without reading through all articles of *IO*, we assume that IR in the 1960s was generally centered around the Kaplan-Bull debate because it has come to represent that period. Reading the old issues brings lots of surprises (for example, see Lisa Martin and Beth Simmons' article in this issue) and makes one think about how the discipline looked to people writing at the time. This phenomenon is, of course, even more pressing for the periods that fewer current participants remember personally. How many scholars have reread the textbooks of the 1930s before speaking about typical IR in the interwar period? If they have, how can they ignore, for instance, the strong geopolitical component and continue with the story about dominant "idealism"?

Within the genre of self-reflections of the discipline and especially those scholars who discuss national perspectives, one contribution stands out (and most of the rest build on it): Stanley Hoffmann's article "An American Social Science: International Relations."[14] It contains many brilliant insights and is generally very convincing about why IR emerged as a full-size discipline in the United States, why it took the form it did, and what the peculiar problems of the American condition are. However, it is all very ad hoc. The factors and the framework are tailor-made for the American case. It is, of course, possible to transfer it to other cases, as Christer Jönsson, for example, has done very elegantly by comparing it to Scandinavian IR on exactly those points Hoffmann pointed to as typically American.[15] However, if the debate on the discipline evolves in this way, it paradoxically creates a kind of second-order Americanization. Also, the debate on the discipline and its Americanization is conducted in an America-shaped framework! One must be more deductive, guided by theory developments within the sociology of science, and set up a general framework for explaining evolutions within IR theory.

11. Compare Wæver 1992, vi–viii; and Schmidt 1998, 32–38.
12. For example, Alker and Biersteker 1984; Banks 1984; Bull 1972; Donnelly 1995; Gareau 1981; Hoffmann 1977; Holsti 1985; Kahler 1993; Katzenstein, Keohane, and Krasner, this issue; Knutsen 1992; Meyers 1990; Olson 1972; Olson and Groom 1991; Olson and Onuf 1985; Smith 1985, 1987, 1995; and Wæver 1992, 1996.
13. Schmidt made the first major attempt at serious historical scholarship like this (beyond more or less single-author or single-episode focused work). Schmidt 1998. Unfortunately, he only covers American (political science based) IR from the mid-1800s to 1940 and only with internal discursive explanations. He effectively shows the problems of posterity's dominant construction of this period; compare de Wilde 1991. However, he does not explore why and with what effects this myth has been established and thus misses how it has become socially real even if historically false.
14. Hoffmann 1977.
15. Jönsson 1993. Lyons builds parts of his discussion of French IR on the Hoffmann list. Lyons 1982.

Many will undoubtedly object that IR and the sociology of science have met often through Thomas Kuhn and Imre Lakatos. Surely, there was widespread reference to Kuhn during the late 1970s and early 1980s,[16] and the last ten years have seen declarations of allegiance to Lakatos and some attempts to apply his principles systematically.[17] However, this is not sociology of science. Kuhn's importance was primarily as a historically based intervention into the philosophy of science, and Lakatos had a constructive agenda of defining procedures that would reinstall a modified falsificationist methodology. More importantly, their IR applications were not empirical sociology or history of science, but a kind of metamethodology. A slightly sociologized philosophy of science retains the form of "rules" for appropriate behavior necessary (and guaranteed!?) to ensure scientific progress. As noted by Donald McCloskey, Karl Popper and Lakatos "do not pretend to give persuasive histories of how science actually did progress. Theirs is rational not historical reconstruction."[18] Whatever merits Kuhn's and Lakatos' approaches might have as schemes for measuring progress in the discipline, they have not proven useful for generating sociologically informed studies of the development of IR.

In the discipline of political science at large (and the subdiscipline of political theory in particular), a lively debate and growing literature has emerged on how to write its history.[19] In IR this has not been the case.[20] Therefore, I will establish an explanatory model based on general sociology of science, specific sociology of the social sciences, the literature on the history of political science, and the few existing essays on the history of IR.

The sociology of science developed in roughly three phases.[21] In the first phase, the original midcentury sociology of science focused on the ethos of science.[22] True science needs no social explanation—it reflects reality. A sociology of science should therefore, on the one hand, explain deviation (for example, Lysenkoism) and, on the other, study social conditions conducive for the development of science.

In the second phase, the so-called new sociology of science (or the sociology of scientific knowledge) explained knowledge purely from the social context, excluding any role for its cognitive validity (such as compatibility with empirical observations). It fought its main battle in relation to the natural sciences and technology to

16. For example, Mansbach and Vasquez 1981; and Banks 1984. For a convincing exception that brings Kuhn to constructive usage, see Guzzini 1998.

17. Most noticed, probably Keohane 1983b, 1986a; most recently Vasquez 1997.

18. McCloskey 1994, 92.

19. For example, Collini et al. 1983; Easton et al. 1991; Farr 1988; Farr et al. 1990; Farr et al. 1995; Farr and Seidelman 1993; Gunnell 1993; and Wittrock 1992.

20. Again, Schmidt seems to be the lonely exception. Schmidt 1998. A critical literature argues how *not* to use the classics and thus criticizes the mythic tradition(s), not least realism; works by Daniel Garst, Rob Walker, Steven Forde, Michael C. Williams, and Laurie M. Johnson mostly on Thucydides, Machiavelli, and Hobbes.

21. For general overviews of the development of the sociology of science, see Whitley 1984; Nowotny and Taschwer 1996; Zuckerman 1989; Restivo 1994; and Andersen 1997, chap. 1.

22. According to Merton, the ethos of modern science is communism (scientific knowledge is collective property for society), universalism, disinterestedness, and organized skepticism, CUDOS. Merton 1942.

show that even they had no neutral core. Case studies demonstrated how new theories and crucial experiments were socially conditioned. The main problem with this approach—beyond its neglect of the social sciences—was that science became indistinguishable from any other social form of knowledge. It ignored science as a specific social institution in a wider institutional setting.[23]

Explanatory Model—Toward a Comparative Sociology of IR

In the sociology of the social sciences, in particular, a third phase of analysis is emerging in which scholars are attempting a nonreductionist combination of social and cognitive explanations. With different irreducible layers, actors must forge "discourse coalitions" so that scholarly programs and policy programs become compatible or even mutually reinforcing. Within this "political sociology of the social sciences,"[24] Peter Wagner, in *Sozialwissenschaften und Staat,* works with three layers: the intellectual traditions, the scientific institutions, and the political structures.[25] For our specific purpose, this should be broadened a little. IR is specifically influenced by the foreign policy orientation of a country, for instance, and therefore the model must be extended while keeping the three layers intact. The result is a more elaborate typology (see Table 1) that retains the division into "intellectual, institutional, and political constellations."[26]

The first layer of the model is society and polity. Within this layer, four dimensions can be distinguished: cultural–linguistic, political ideology, political institutions, and foreign policy.

Regarding the cultural–intellectual dimension, Johan Galtung once made an elegant, provocative, and problematic characterization of Gallic, Nipponic, Teutonic, and Saxonic intellectual styles.[27] At one level, we all recognize the phenomenon, at another we have difficulty dealing with it. It will here not appear as an independent causal factor (leading into "national character" speculations). However, this variation becomes an important "instrument" when one country or region dominates. Today, because dominance is American, the stylistic criteria are those of the American brand of the Anglo-Saxon intellectual style, with brief, straightforward statements and linear progression of an argument (not simultaneous attached provisos as in German grammar). In American self-understanding this simply spells clarity, but it is experienced by some Germans, for example, as a barrier to expressing real complexity and thus introduces an increased distance between intention and text, that is,

23. See Wagner and Wittrock 1991, 331; and Whitley 1984, 5–7.

24. Wagner 1990a, 24. See also works by, especially, Björn Wittrock and Richard Whitley; and Wagner et al. 1991.

25. Wagner 1990a, 23. See also Wagner 1989.

26. Wagner and Wittrock 1991, 7. These three sound almost identical to Hoffmann's three factors: "intellectual predispositions, political circumstances, and institutional opportunities"; Hoffmann 1977, 45. His political factor, however, only contains foreign policy (Figure 1, 1d); his intellectual factors concentrate on dominant views of science (which is a subset of Figure 1, 2a, and possibly 1b; and his "institutional" factor mainly covers some ad hoc peculiarities, not the general setup (my second layer). The similarity, however, simplifies a merger of these independently generated works.

27. Galtung 1981.

TABLE 1. *Explanatory model*

Layer 1: Society and polity
   a. Cultural, intellectual styles
   b. "Ideologies" or traditions of political thought
   c. Form of state; state–society relations
   d. Foreign policy
Layer 2: Social sciences
   a. General conditions and definitions of social science
   b. Disciplinary patterning: disciplines and subdisciplines
Layer 3: Intellectual activities in IR
   a. Social and intellectual structure of the discipline
   b. Theoretical traditions

---

less clarity. Had the discipline a German hegemony, Americans not only would have to struggle with expressing themselves in the German language but also would experience the challenge of adapting to an alien ideal of intellectual style.

The other dimensions in the first layer of the model can be introduced more briefly because they will be covered later in the four national cases. Characteristically, the studies by Peter Wagner, Björn Wittrock, and their colleagues concentrate on parallel histories of state and social science. Changing forms of state and state intervention raise a need for social scientific knowledge, and thus political developments are shaped by whether and how social scientists supply this, and the social sciences are structured by these roles. State–society relations (Table 1, 1c) are therefore central, but national traditions of thought about state and society (1b) are an independent factor influencing the social sciences through different channels (modes of thinking versus political constellations) and are often more inert than political structures. That a country's foreign policy situation (1d) can influence the development of IR theory is probably the least controversial element in the model.

The second layer of the model is partly about the emergence of "social science" as such (2a) and partly about the division into disciplines (2b) that emerged at different times and in different ways in different countries. To become an accepted science depended both on the links that a discipline could make to societal interests (discourse coalitions) and on the formulation of an organizing concept and from that a scientific language.

The third layer deals with internal developments in IR. Third-generation sociology of science categorizes disciplines and subdisciplines according to their intellectual and social structure; according to factors such as degrees of formalization, unity, and stability of paradigms; and according to social hierarchy. In this context I investigate the role and meaning of the famous "great debates" of IR: Are these an IR peculiarity, and, if so, why? The second major element of the third layer is "content," that is, the main theoretical traditions in different countries.

This model will be implemented using a two-step process. In the fourth section I explain and characterize the second layer—the general situation and subdivisions of social sciences in the different countries and the overall orientation of IR. I draw mainly on 1c in Table 1 and, for the IR-specific part, 1d. As patterns form in the second layer, these become causes for their own reproduction and influence later transformations. I address the third layer in the fifth section. The structural characteristics of IR are discussed both generally for the discipline and in terms of national variations. In addition to explanations from the second layer, I discuss how the specific development of different traditions of IR thinking has been influenced by 1b (national ideological and philosophical traditions) as well as by 1d (foreign policy).

Before applying this model to the United States and the major European countries, we need a clearer picture of what it will explain. How does the current more or less global discipline look? Can the widely assumed U.S. dominance in IR actually be documented, and is it decreasing or increasing? Does such dominance have implications for content—that is, do Americans and Europeans publish the same kinds of articles, only the Americans do so more successfully?

IR: A Global Discipline?

Anglo-American, Western, Global

This article concentrates on IR in North America and Europe. But what about the rest of the world? Some surveys claim that not much research is to be found elsewhere— the next largest community is the Japanese, which produces very little theory in general and much less that is not based on American inspiration. The most obvious candidate for an independent IR tradition based on a unique philosophical tradition is China, though very little independent theorizing has taken place.[28] Even a sympathetic pro-non-Western observer like Stephen Chan concludes that for most of the non-Western world strategic studies overshadows IR theory.[29]

Still, this is not my line—quite the contrary. There is much to be learned from many non-Western writings, even if not yet well-established. However, I intend to present data to describe the situation and sociology of science to explain it. This can only be done systematically with fewer countries, especially those where many variables vary little. Finally, Europe and the United States not only are compared; they also have interacted in important ways, which makes a study focused on these two most fruitful—for a start. In the future, it will be important to investigate non-Western cases equally systematically.

How American? Patterns of Publishing in Journals

To look for patterns in IR, one could examine three types of sources: textbooks (used by Holsti in *The Dividing Discipline*), curricula (such as by Hayward Alker and

---

28. G. Chan 1997.
29. Chan 1994, 248; in this extensive survey, Chan finds that policy work of a relatively realist orientation dominates in India, Pakistan, Bangladesh, Japan, China (with some exceptions), and all of Africa; the most important area of original theory was Iran. For similar conclusions, see Holsti 1985.

Thomas Biersteker and in a small survey of national distribution by Alfredo Robles),[30] and, finally, journals. Journals are the most direct measure of the discipline itself. The sociology of science from Merton to Whitley has pointed to journals as the crucial institution of modern sciences. Textbooks are important because they introduce newcomers, but though they might affect the discipline, they are not the discipline itself. For practitioners, the field exists mostly in the journals.

Table 2 compares the distribution of authors'country of residence in the leading journals in North America and Europe.[31] In all four North American journals for all investigated years (1970–95), Americans account for between 66 and 100 percent of the authors, with an average of 88.1 percent. The European journals are relatively balanced, with Americans and Britons equally represented at around 40 percent in the *Review of International Studies* and *Millennium* (though with a clear majority of Britons in 1975), and with Americans and "the rest of Europe" (meaning, in this case, primarily Scandinavians[32]) equally represented at about 40 percent in the *Journal of Peace Research*. This difference between American "concentration" and European variety (or asymmetric penetration) in 1995 is shown in Figure 1. (Note that this analysis is not a claim about discrimination, gate keeping, or closedness—we cannot know what stems from patterns of submissions, evaluation, or quality. Relevant is simply the fact of this pattern.) There seems to be no strong change over time, as shown for the case of *IO* in Figure 2.

How does this situation compare with other disciplines? A recent comparison of thirty-eight leading journals from different fields found that in the natural sciences, the percentage of American authors in U.S.-published journals was typically 40–50 percent, whereas almost all the social science journals have a score of more than 80 percent for American authors. The two journals publishing the highest percentage of American authors are the two American political science journals in the survey: *American Political Science Review* (97 percent American authors) and *American Journal of Political Science* (96.8 percent American authors).[33]

Knowing the authors'countries of residence may be useful for showing the relative "power" of the different IR communities. However, it tells us little about what they write; and given the increasing importance of European journals, knowing whether they still work from American theories or develop independent theories and debates

---

30. See Holsti 1985; Alker and Biersteker 1984; and Robles 1993.

31. One might discuss whether country of residence or country of origin is most interesting. Besides the former being much easier to register, it could also be argued that because of the way the American metropole works, ambitious scholars from other regions are drawn to it as the only way to register on the main screen whereby the dominance of the American environment is reinforced. Thus, country of residence captures more accurately the actual dominance of North America as the leading academic community, whereas the other measure might be more relevant if our interest were relative career opportunities for IR scholars born in different countries.

32. According to similar statistics in Goldmann 1995, 252—and nonquantified impressions from my own data.

33. Andersen and Frederiksen 1995, 20, tab. 2. Two more political science journals are included, the *British Journal of Political Science,* with 25.5 percent for country of publication, and *Politische Vierteljahresschrift* (Germany), with 90.2 percent for own country.

TABLE 2. *Distribution of authors by geographical residence in American and European journals, 1970–95*

Journal/Origin		North American (%)	British (%)	Rest of Europe (%)	Rest of the world (%)
International	1970	92.3 (24)	0	3.8 (1)	3.8 (1)
Organization	1975	100 (25)	0	0	0
	1980	66.7 (14)	14.3 (3)	4.8 (1)	14.3 (3)
	1985	80 (16)	10 (2)	5 (1)	5 (1)
	1990	78.1 (12.5)	0	18.8 (3)	3.1 (0.5)
	1995	85.7 (18)	4.8 (1)	9.5 (2)	0
International	1970	95.5 (21)	4.5 (1)	0	0
Studies	1975	92.9 (19.5)	0	0	7.1 (1.5)
Quarterly	1980	88.5 (23)	0	7.7 (2)	3.8 (1)
	1985	88.5 (23)	0	7.7 (2)	3.8 (1)
	1990	90.9 (20)	0	9.1 (2)	0
	1995	83.3 (20)	8.3 (2)	8.3 (2)	0
International	1980	68.75 (22)	18.75 (6)	0	12.5 (4)
Security (1975)	1985	100 (28)	0	0	0
	1990	86.4 (19)	9.1 (2)	0	4.5 (1)
	1995	96 (24)	0	4 (1)	0
World Politics	1970	100 (20)	0	0	0
	1975	79.3 (18.25)	15.2 (3.5)	4.3 (1)	1.1 (0.25)
	1980	81.8 (9)	0	9.1 (1)	9.1 (1)
	1985	100 (22)	0	0	0
	1990	89.5 (17)	0	0	10.5 (2)
	1995	91.7 (11)	0	0	8.3 (1)
Review of	1975	0	100 (20)	0	0
International	1980	40 (6)	40 (6)	6.7 (1)	13.3 (2)
Studies, formerly	1985	26.1 (6)	65.2 (15)	0	8.7 (2)
British Journal (1976)	1990	14.7 (2.5)	73.5 (12.5)	5.9 (1)	5.9 (1)
	1995	43.3 (8.66)	40 (8)	5 (1)	11.7 (1.33)
European Journal (1995)	1995	30.8 (6.16)	30 (6)	39.2 (7.83)	0
Millennium (1972)	1975	28.6 (6)	71.4 (15)	0	0
	1980	15.4 (2)	52.3 (6.8)	23.1 (3)	9.2 (1.2)
	1985	34.4 (5.5)	43.8 (7)	12.5 (2)	9.4 (1.5)
	1990	61.1 (11)	38.9 (7)	0	0
	1995	46.7 (7)	33.3 (5)	13.3 (3)	6.7 (1)
Journal of Peace	1970	28.6 (6)	0	71.4 (15)	0
Research	1975	18.8 (3)	6.3 (1)	75 (12)	0
	1980	50 (12)	12.5 (3)	33.3 (8)	4.2 (1)
	1985	43.5 (10)	4.3 (1)	43.5 (10)	8.7 (2)
	1990	50 (16)	9.4 (3)	34.4 (11)	6.2 (2)
	1995	43.8 (14)	12.5 (4)	39.1 (12.5)	4.9 (1.5)

Note: Actual numbers are shown in parentheses. Fractions occur because co-authored articles are divided among the authors. For example, an article with two authors is counted as .5 to each.
   Years in parentheses are first year of publication for journals founded after 1970.

is crucial. One way of approximating this would be to compare the relative distribution, by country of publication, of sources cited in reference lists in different journals. This method, however, is often very difficult, especially for books (due to copublishing) and minor journals. A more manageable and reliable coding is the method chosen by Kjell Goldmann, which looks for the most cited journals in the different

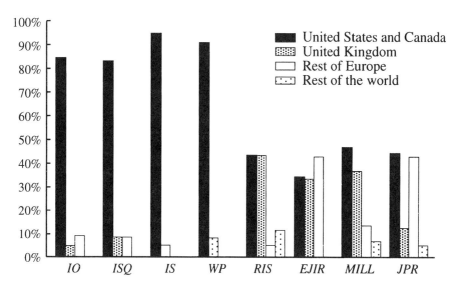

IO = International Organization
ISQ = International Studies Quarterly
IS = International Security
WP = World Politics

RIS = Review of International Studies
EJIR = European Journal of International Relations
MILL = Millennium
JPR = Journal of Peace Research

FIGURE 1. *Distribution of authors by country of residence in international journals, 1995*

journals.[34] If anything, Goldmann found a modest increase in American sources in the European journals; in both 1972 and 1992 the only journals cited in large numbers by authors in the American journals were American journals.

All such citation and publication habits must be measured against the relative size of the different research environments. Not that one should expect a proportional representation, but some sense of size is still necessary—fewer citations to Estonian IR, for example, than to Canadian IR most likely reflects the difference in numbers of IR scholars in the respective countries. American IR is the largest community, whether one counts membership in associations,[35] attendance at annual conferences,[36] or (the

34. Goldmann 1995, 254, tab. 7. For seven major journals, Goldmann measured which other journals accounted for 3 percent or more of the references to journals.

35. Membership at the end of 1997 was about 3,200 in ISA (founded in 1959), 920 in BISA (founded in 1975), 1,987 in JAIR (founded in 1956), 120 in the Scandinavian "Nordic International Studies Association" (NISA, founded in 1993), and no individual members yet in the young Central and East European International Studies Association (CEEISA, founded in 1996). It is not easy to compare the United States and Europe directly, because the all-European emerging organization does not have individual memberships, and countries like Germany and France do not have separate national IR organizations, only sections within the Political Science Association. At the European meetings, however, the biggest contingency is the British, with Scandinavians second, Germans third, and the French as well as various East Central and Southern Europeans making up small groups that add up to a third of the attendance. Therefore, had there been a European membership organization, it probably would have numbered some 2,000 members.

36. During 1995–97, the annual conference of ISA drew an attendance averaging 1,800, BISA somewhere around 350, and JAIR approximately 500. The triennial "European" conference organized by the

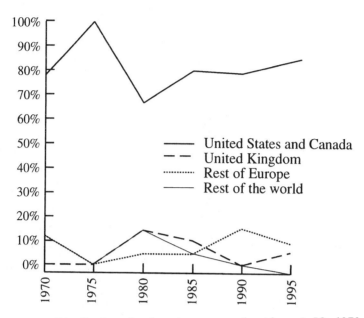

FIGURE 2. *Distribution of authors by country of residence in* IO, *1970–95*

very tricky figure of) academic posts under an IR label. However, the numbers are probably only slightly larger than the aggregate figure for Europe (which weighs less by not actually being a category of its own), and certainly less than a total "non-American" category.[37] Thus, there is a quite significant American dominance in sheer numbers. But the dominance in the journals is still much higher than it should be if all appeared proportionally.

Probably in contrast to some expectations, American journals are not becoming more "global" —that is, densely populated by non-American authors. The American dominance of American journals—both in terms of authors and sources—is overwhelming. The American presence in European journals is, if anything, increasing slightly. How this latter finding is to be interpreted is, however, an open question. It could be a sign of increased dominance regarding the production of theory, or it might reflect a shift in the European journals toward more theory[38] and possibly an emergence of the European journals as respectable outlets for Americans.

---

elegantly named "Standing Group on International Relations of the European Consortium for Political Research" attracted 460 at the first conference in 1992 and 480 in 1995.

37. Approximately 25 percent of the members of ISA are non-North American. On the one hand, we could correct for this without changing the overall result. On the other hand, we probably should not: That others join the ISA simply means that the America-centered IR research community has more members (including extraterritorial ones), whereas some of the other communities are unable even to attract their natural clientele, who then obviously do not define themselves as members of say a "Scandinavian" IR community.

38. Documented by Goldmann 1995.

Not much more can be said about hegemony without including questions about content. How strong are different theories in different places?

Content—Metatheoretical Orientations

This investigation concentrated on two leading journals from each side of the Atlantic (*IO, International Studies Quarterly, European Journal of International Relations,* and *Review of International Studies*).[39] All articles appearing in these journals for the last three years have been sorted into five main categories along the axis that seems most decisive for these decades: rationalist-reflectivist.[40] The categories, as shown in Figure 3, are (1) formalized rational choice, game theory, and modeling; (2) quantitative studies;[41] (3) nonformalized rationalism, that is, "soft rational choice," which includes most neorealism, all neoliberal institutionalism, and a few "independents;" (4) non-postmodern constructivism; and (5) the "radicals," be they poststructuralists, Marxists, or feminists. Finally, "other" typically means purely historical or policy articles (without theory), articles on authors (ancient or current), or articles that drew on theories from other fields (for example, organization theory). (These five categories are rough and combine approaches that differ in other respects. Therefore, each was subdivided in order both to see whether the journals varied strongly within the categories and to be able to count along other axes for specific questions.[42]) Although some classifications involve difficult judgments, the result is striking enough to rule out any decisive impact of any minor border problems. Actually, the most complicated and recurrent border problem was a genre of alleged "constructivism" that uses rationalist methods and assumptions. These are a growing presence in *IO,* and thus, with a slightly more restrictive criteria for constructivism, the contrast would have been stronger. (To become aware of this genre, which is in itself an interesting trend, was an additional benefit of the coding effort.)

Formalized rational choice arguments make up 22.1 percent of the articles in the one American journal and 16.7 percent in the other, whereas in the two European journals they make up 9.6 and 0 percent. The three rationalisms (quantitative plus formalized and nonformalized rational choice) add up to 77.9 percent in *Interna-*

39. No specific bias has been introduced by choosing a European journal with a particularly radical profile like *Millennium* (although many Europeans would undoubtedly count it as one of the two or three leading journals) or an American journal that has specialized in game theory and quantitative methods for decades, *Journal of Conflict Resolution. International Studies Quarterly* has recently become almost as specialized, but it after all remains the official journal of ISA, with both the status and circulation this involves, and *IO* is clearly the leading American journal. In terms of impact factor, according to *Journal Citation Reports* from the Social Science Citation Index, *Journal of Peace Research* is actually the highest scoring European journal in the field of IR, but since it is not a strictly IR journal, including it would create problems of interpretation.
40. Compare Keohane 1988; Katzenstein, Keohane, and Krasner, this issue; and Wæver 1996.
41. Quantitative studies are, of course, not necessarily rational choice. They are listed on the same "side" in order to catch the axis of formalization irrespective of whether it follows "second debate" (quantitative vs. traditional) or fourth debate (rationalist–reflectivist) patterns.
42. The data for the categories and subcategories are presented in the appendix; the total documentation, including the coding of each specific article, can be viewed at *http://www.copri.dk/staff/owaever/htm*

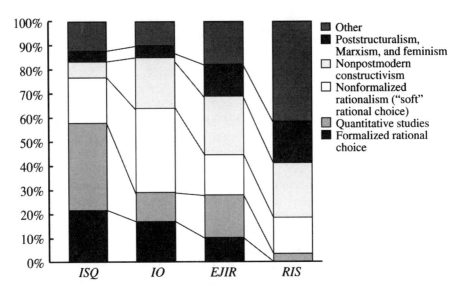

ISQ = International Studies Quarterly   *EJIR = European Journal of International Relations*
IO = International Organization   *RIS = Review of International Studies*

FIGURE 3. *Theoretical position of articles in four international journals, 1995–97*

tional Studies Quarterly and 63.9 percent in *IO,* compared with 42.3 percent in *European Journal* and only 17.4 percent in *Review of International Studies.* Conversely, the two forms of "reflectivism" add up to 7.8 and 25.0 percent in the two American journals; and 40.6 percent in the *Review of International Studies* and 40.4 percent in the *European Journal*—postmodernism varied from 2.6 percent in *International Studies Quarterly* to more than 15 percent in both European journals.[43] The contrast is overwhelmingly clear.

If one re-counts the articles on the basis of country of residence, Americans who publish in European journals are more rationalist than the Europeans but clearly more constructivist than Americans publishing in American journals.[44] Thus, what

43. It might be objected that the "other" category should be subtracted from these numbers and from those in Figure 3. This would have been convincing had it been a simple "error" or "don't know" category. However, the contributions in "other" have an equally clear identity to those that are classified in the other categories (only not any of the dominant ones in the self-categorizations of the discipline), and thus they are part of the diversity of especially the *Review of International Studies.* Excluding them, of course, boosts the numbers for the two European journals and for the *Review of International Studies* in particular. This would narrow the gap on rationalism a little but far from close it (*International Studies Quarterly,* 90.9; *IO,* 71.9; *European Journal of International Relations,* 51.2; *Review of International Studies,* 30 on the three rationalisms combined), and the gap on reflectivism would grow (*International Studies Quarterly,* 9.1; *IO,* 28.1; and *European Journal of International Relations,* 48.8; and *Review of International Studies,* 70 on the two reflectivisms combined).

44. Aggregate numbers for hard rational plus soft rational plus quantitative studies versus hard constructivist plus soft constructivist are (the remaining percentage up to 100 is in the "other" category): Americans in American journals, 68.3 percent and 17.4 percent, respectively; Americans in European journals, 39.1 percent and 38 percent, respectively; Europeans in American journals, 46.9 percent and 23.4 percent, respectively; Europeans in European journals, 21.9 percent and 41.1 percent, respectively.

Europeans publish differs from what Americans publish.[45] The difference between what Americans publish in America and in Europe underlines that the general intellectual environment must be different in a way that influences acceptance rates and/or motivation for submitting to one journal rather than another. All four journals are sufficiently embedded in their own academic establishments on the respective sides of the Atlantic that systematic variation among the journals can be seen as expressions of differences between "American" and "European" IR.

Could it be that a specialization among journals is self-reproducing, so that if you have a test of neoliberal institutionalism on a trade negotiation you send it to *IO,* whereas if it is a constructivist analysis of the European Union you send it to *European Journal of International Relations?* Even allowing for this specialization, it would be indefensible to treat the different journals simply as transnational issue- or school-specific specializations within one deterritorialized discipline. We have looked at central institutions—the leading journals—on each side. Two journals are published in Europe, mainly edited by Europeans, refereed by Europeans, and thus partly reflecting, partly constituting the definition of what is good IR in Europe. Two are published in the United States, edited mainly by Americans, refereed mainly by Americans, and, in contrast to the European journals, adding a fourth factor, predominantly written by Americans—and they show a different profile, which is then likely to mean a different ideal of IR scholarship. Of course, it is possible to move down the ranks and find journals in the United States with a theoretical profile more like the European journals, but the four journals discussed here are, or are clearly among, the leading journals.

There is one IR discipline, not several. Lots of interaction and transatlantic publishing takes place—especially in the one direction. Theories are mainly produced in the United States. Metatheoretical orientations differ on the two sides of the Atlantic, with much more U.S. interest in (more or less formalized) rational choice approaches versus more European interest in constructivism and postmodernism.

This could all be explained away by the suggestion that there is a European "delay" in coming to rational choice (which would seem most in line with several of the most programmatic articles in this issue of *IO*). Only the future can answer this definitively, but we might as a preliminary answer look for a causal explanation of the current differences. If a sociology of IR can explain this pattern, maybe it rests on more solid pillars and will therefore continue.

The Evolution of IR as a Social Science in Four National Contexts

I will briefly discuss the evolution of IR in four cases: Germany, France, the United Kingdom, and the United States. Other interesting cases within the European context are Italy and Russia, with unique state histories, and Scandinavia, the second or third largest IR community in Europe today.

45. "Europeans" and "Americans" here still refer to institutional setting, not nationality.

Each country section follows the same format. The modern social sciences were born in the mid-nineteenth century in the context of two important institutional transformations: the nation-state underwent dramatic changes (national unification in Germany and Italy, modernization in France, and the beginning of state building in the United States), and the universities went through intensive reform, moving toward the modern research-oriented university. After considering the general constitution of social science, I address the struggles among the social sciences: what pattern and especially what kind of political science? Since IR is in most places a subdiscipline in political science, and political science emerged as a distinct discipline before IR—but usually after the other social sciences—the other social sciences are dealt with mainly during the nineteenth century and political science during the late nineteenth to the early twentieth century. I then trace the development of IR through the interwar, immediate postwar, and later periods. Did an independent IR evolve—and if so, with what borders, core, and characteristics?

Germany

Compared with France and Italy, fewer attempts were made to develop political science in Germany after 1870 "perhaps because the state was least challenged by the contemporary social transformations. On the contrary, in the eyes of many of the "Mandarins," university professors in the state service . . . , the idea of the state had ultimately come to realize itself in imperial Germany, and if there was anything to do for policy intellectuals, it was not to scrutinize the structures and workings of this state but to serve to enhance its fulfilling its functions."[46] Political institutions could be excluded from analysis because of a basic complementarity to the legal theory of the state, as formulated in legal positivism. With its systematic body of concepts and knowledge, it promised a doctrine for lawyers, judges, and state officials to act from and allowed law to form as a modern discipline with specific methods and concepts.[47] This discourse coalition between actors in the scientific and political fields was more efficient in Germany than elsewhere because of the state-building process.

The famous early nineteenth century university reforms by Prussian minister of education Wilhelm von Humboldt had three major effects, two of which were intended. First, Humboldt intended a strong role for professors—appointed by the state, not the university—and entrenched the single professor system (in contrast to the American multiprofessor department). Second, the discipline-divided university was contrary to Humboldt's intention of *allgemeine Bildung*, though partly a result of his third effect. Third, the research-oriented university with unity of research and higher education created a dynamism demanding eventual specialization. Compared to a more pragmatic process in the United States, specialization in Germany went through extreme theoretical purification to pure economy, law, and sociology.[48] The threshold

---

46. See Wagner 1990b, 269; and Kastendiek 1991, 110.
47. See Wagner 1990b, 271–76; Dyson 1980, 107–17; and Wittrock 1992.
48. Wagner and Wittrock 1991, 345–48.

for disciplinary status was high, and the cognitive demands difficult to meet for political science. Implications of lasting importance for our subject were, first, the development of a weak political science, not in control of professional training (which law has largely kept to this day); and, second, the establishment of a hierarchical structure within departments.

Paradoxically, a conceptual core formed in the nineteenth century for what could have been—and in a sense later became in the United States—a discipline of IR. In this place and time this set of ideas was seen as the core of history, so it did not trigger attempts to construct a separate discipline of IR. Historicism or the "power school" in German history constructed from the idealist, strong concept of the state a general and strict power theory with states as units.[49]

All such links, including developments of IR in the interwar period, are, however, in the German case less important than elsewhere because of the rupture in Germany in 1945. Institutional features rather than content were carried over and achieved importance for postwar developments. IR developed solidly within political science (no separate organization, and a separate theoretical journal only since 1994). Content was shaped by the impossibility of continuing with realism (not to speak of geopolitics). Paradoxically, at a time when the mainly German-bred tradition of realism became the official theory of the dominant, American IR community, it had a very hard time in American-dominated Germany.[50] This turn of events led to several peculiarities in German IR. In the 1960s to 1980s much of the theoretically innovative work took place within peace research. Although some of it was more sociological than political science–inspired (like the Galtung-type Scandinavian peace research with which it was closely integrated), much of it engaged directly with the IR literature, such as Dieter Senghaas's path-breaking works on deterrence.[51] Much of the critical theory that emerged in the Anglo-American world in the 1980s and 1990s must have looked strangely familiar to a middle-aged German peace researcher.

In the 1970s the median point in German IR leaned more toward transnational–interdependence than was the case in the United States or even more clearly in the United Kingdom. Most of this "liberal" IR literature leaned on American IR and contributed little original theory. For a number of reasons, German IR in the 1990s seems to have both developed more independent theory and, to a lesser extent, oriented these theories toward an international audience. Should this continue, German scholars have a number of comparative advantages, both theoretical and contextual.[52] For instance, one has a Habermas at hand (in the original language). Therefore, the whole discussion about rational choice, which at first looks like the U.S.

---

49. Meinecke [1924] 1976, especially 409–21.

50. The "Munich school" of "neorealism" was the lonely exception and did not catch on beyond Munich; compare Meier-Walser 1994. Several of the German-speaking "Americans" had their works translated "back" into German: Morgenthau, Herz, Kissinger, and the German-speaking Czechoslovak Deutsch. Only the latter seems to have retained a continuous engagement with German academic circles.

51. Senghaas 1969.

52. *Zeitschrift für internationale Beziehungen* hosted a much noticed debate among primarily Gunther Hellmann (1994) and Michael Zürn (1994) on the state of IR in Germany compared to the United States and whether one *should* compare to (and then copy from) the United States.

debate, is couched in different terms because the alternative to strategic rationality is not mainly norm-regulated but communicative rationality.[53] The linguistic advantage might become even more pronounced when the systems theory of Niklas Luhmann finally reaches IR.[54] A major contextual advantage stems from Germany being in important ways the most deeply Europeanized country,[55] and, therefore, from German scholars being prone to the most radical postsovereign interpretations of integration (compare the discussion in the section titled "Status and Outlook" and footnote 126).

Still, most of the mainstream scholars—not least, the still very important lead professors at the large universities—are mainly engaged in elaborations on American theories. Characteristic are the works that are probably best known to an English-speaking audience, the regime theory of the Tübingen team headed by Volker Rittberger.[56] A theory that is already too complex and open-ended is exposed to German *Gründlichkeit,* and the result is a complicated model that might be more "correct" but certainly misses the American call of the day for "parsimony." Under the pressure from an increasingly mobilized lower level—vindicated by the successful journal *ZIB*, which has not been dominated by the mandarins[57]—and a transnationalization of European IR, things might start to happen in German IR. At last, some might add. But the conditions are probably better here than anywhere else for an independent dynamism, drawing on national traditions while fully keeping up with American developments.

France

Observers of the French scene often notice the creative and societally influential sociology, "the administration-oriented, professional character of political science, and the mixture of neoclassical and engineering thinking in economics."[58] Institutional cleavages dating back to the seventeenth and eighteenth centuries explain the present tripartite structure of French social science. Transformations of the French state had a decisive impact on the cognitive identity of the social sciences.

Whereas the social sciences in some other countries evolved together and were only reluctantly differentiated (as from one Ur-social science), they grew quite separately in France. During the eighteenth century the human sciences came to include different forms of social theory; and in the nineteenth century disciplines like philosophy, psychology, and sociology were institutionalized in a "faculty of letters." Simultaneously, economics was incorporated into the faculty of law. Political science had for a long time no institutional home, and when it got one in 1871 it was in the form

53. Müller 1994 and 1995; Keck 1995; Risse-Kappen 1995a; Schmalz-Bruns 1995; and several more interventions. For an excellent discussion (in English) of this German debate in relation to the American one, see Risse 1997.
54. Watch for future publications by Mathias Albert.
55. Katzenstein 1997.
56. See Rittberger 1993; and Hasenclever et al. 1997.
57. Off the record, this is widely ascribed to a healthy institutional Americanization: the introduction of the—in Germany relatively rare—system of anonymous peer reviews.
58. Wagner and Wittrock 1991, 7.

of a professional school primarily for training upper-level civil servants (Ecole libre des sciences politiques, today's Institut d'études politiques). In the early postwar period, all of the disciplines achieved professional organizations, journals, a university degree, and thus became full-fledged disciplines, but they remained in their separate contexts. A "faculty for the social sciences" is not the normal format in France.[59]

Two important sources for this development are the absolutist state and the decline of the university. In contrast to Germany, for example, the universities did not remain important centers of learning in the seventeenth and eighteenth centuries. New institutions became more dynamic—the Collège de France (1530) and the academies. Independence from the church and dependence on the state influenced different proto-disciplines differently. The humanities achieved an unusual degree of freedom and prestige, creating the French tradition for "intellectuals." "The one domain for which no academic rights were granted was that of politics, law, and administration. . . . In absolutist France, politics was a state monopoly and was not recognized as being a legitimate subject for intellectual consideration."[60]

Within the contemporary fragmentation between teaching, research, and professional education (each entrusted to separate institutions), the grandes écoles embody the Napoleonic ideal of the "engineer-administrator."[61] Taking the latter route, political science gained full intellectual recognition but at the cost of becoming "a profession without a cognitive core."[62] Emile Boutmy, who founded the Ecole libre, gave institution building priority over his own (political psychology inspired) program for a political science. A training institute was thus established but without any clear profile for a political science within it. Today political science can be found in all three parts of the academic system: research within Centre National de la Recherche Scientifique (CNRS), in the case of IR mainly in Centre d'Etudes et de Recherches Internationales (CERI); elite training in the Grandes Ecoles; and mass teaching in the universities, where a few have politics departments and the others position politics as the junior partner of law. However, the early history, with political science primarily institutionalized in the elite training function, left its mark.

Many themes that are elsewhere political science went in France to political economy or sociology. In the practical field, however, French political science was for a while strong compared with, especially, Germany because it supplied many of the civil servants. However, when de Gaulle created Ecole Nationale d'Administration (ENA) in 1945, the training role of political science was weakened. Still, it remained practical, which orients IR toward practical knowledge such as international law rather than toward theory. Where the ideal for political scientists in the United States is economics (and ultimately the natural sciences), French political science is torn between administration and the humanities.

59. This and the following paragraph are mainly based on Heilbron 1991.
60. Heilbron 1991, 78.
61. Hayward 1983, 214.
62. Wagner and Wittrock 1991, 10.

Because French state institutions were more consolidated than those in Germany and Italy, sociology became more central to cohesion than law. The new nation-states imposed in the 1860s–70s on heterogeneous societies in Germany and Italy had to rely on legal thinking. "In France, in contrast, the understanding of societal solidarity, as advanced in Durkheimian sociology, became an important element of the self-understanding of a republican state."[63] Thus, when political science turns theoretical, it is most obvious to borrow from a theoretical, society-centered sociology.

Three other general effects on IR are that no separate IR discipline exists, most IR is practical and lacks theory, and, finally, single intellectuals can range widely across fields. Leading sociologists like Alain Touraine or Pierre Bourdieu publish on IR as do philosophers like André Glucksmann and Alain Finkielkraut. And IR scholars regularly appear side by side with other intellectuals in journals like *Esprit* and *Le Débat*, as did Hans Morgenthau and a few others in the first postwar decades in similar American publications. (Today, the leading American IR theorists are not public intellectuals.[64])

French IR did not have a heated realism–idealism debate in the interwar years, much less the following debates. As Marie-Claude Smouts suggests: "Impervious to the systems theory of M. Kaplan, indifferent to K. Waltz, skeptical of the successive versions of 'transnationalism' (functionalism, integration, interdependence, etc.), the fellow countrymen of General de Gaulle probably felt American imperialism over the discipline a good deal less than their German and Scandinavian counterparts."[65]

Where the Germans, for example, have been concerned about measuring up to the Americans,[66] the French have not been terribly interested in comparing themselves, neither in having a national tradition nor in making it in some global discipline.[67] As noted by John Groom, French scholars have played a surprisingly minor role internationally, but "the relative isolation of the French academic world does have advantages. It gives the subject of International Relations an element of diversity and an independent academic discourse. It gives the outsider the shock of the new and of the different, and this is, or can be, salutary. It is not a question of center-periphery but of a separate, autonomous, intellectual agenda and academic discourse. By simply existing, it serves a purpose."[68]

Raymond Aron is by far the best-known figure outside France, but he was atypical in taking a strong interest in American IR (Morgenthau in particular) and thus phrasing his work in ways recognizable (if still different) to Americans. (Different, primarily because he strove to integrate history, sociology, and "praxeology.") The other main tradition in postwar French IR, the historical school, was more idiosyncratic, not least as diplomatic history was increasingly merged with inspiration from the

---

63. Wagner and Wittrock 1991, 344; also see Wagner 1990a, 73ff.
64. Neumann 1997, 364–67.
65. Smouts 1987, 283.
66. See Hellmann 1994; Zürn 1994; and Rittberger and Hummel 1990.
67. See Leander 1997, 162; Groom n.d.; and Giesen 1995.
68. See Groom n.d.; compare Groom 1994, 223.

Annales school.[69] In the last decades, Annales has mainly been important through its influence on Marcel Merle. Merle, Badie, and Smouts stress the importance of cultural specificity versus American universalist theorizing, and—in stark contrast to Aron—the basic idea of a uniform state unit is given up.[70] The result is a surprisingly radical transnationalism, which does not seem to correspond well with the dominant conception in French policy circles. This probably has to be understood on the basis of the weak link between theoretical and empirical work in French IR and the lower status of theory. Most French IR scholars do empirical or policy work without the obligation felt by American scholars to locate themselves theoretically or to justify an article by referring to theory implications. Consequently, many write in the old, state-centric tradition, more or less influenced by Aron. Since theory is superfluous, it can develop independently and takes the role of opposing conventional wisdom.[71] What counts in both theory and policy work is firm conceptualization and a proper use of the concepts, not a constant positioning vis-à-vis one general debate.

Area studies is widely recognized as one of the strengths of French IR and influences theory development.[72] In a process that has almost disappeared in other IR communities, some, like Bertrand Badie, began work in another discipline and developed quite late into international relationists.[73] Those working in IR in a more strict sense have had almost no design for claiming autonomy for the subject—according to Smouts, because it seemed unrealistic given the difficulty political science had in being established.[74] More maliciously, Klaus-Gerd Giesen has suggested that a dominance on the home market is secured by decoupling from the world market, and therefore a clear disciplinary identity as IR is unattractive to the leaders.[75] The most benign explanation would be that it serves to preserve the main strength of French IR: the close relationship to sociology, philosophy, and anthropology, one of its main characteristics from Aron to the current, innovative literature on the post-Westphalian system.

United Kingdom

The case of the United Kingdom is comparatively simple because it has one major thematic string, which, though multidimensional, explains most of the current situation. The old tradition of a liberal education as "gentlemen's knowledge" was continued and aligned with the new roles of university education. Rather than transmit-

69. Renouvin and Duroselle 1964 (traditional diplomatic history) and Renouvin 1954 (more Annales school). For an excellent discussion of the main traditions in French IR, see Giesen 1995.

70. See Merle 1987; and Badie and Smouts 1992. For an introduction to Badie—in English—see Leander 1997. For a state-of-the-art overview on French IR as conducted mostly by the CERI people, see Smouts 1998.

71. Ulla Holm suggested this interpretation.

72. See Smouts 1987; Giesen 1995; and Groom 1994 and n.d.

73. Leander 1997.

74. Smouts 1987, 282.

75. Giesen 1995, 160.

ting knowledge, the colleges of the old British universities aimed to form the characters and minds of very young students and produced in the nineteenth century a homogeneous governing class for the empire.[76] This "reflected the well-entrenched position of a landed aristocracy, hostile towards efforts at formalized, central control and rule. . . . [R]elatively non-formalized state institutions . . . were ultimately sustained by an elite culture. To some important extent that elite culture was reproduced and modified in academic institutions, which then may be better described as seats of elite socialization rather than of formal training for particular professions."[77]

This traditional core was supplemented even at Oxford and Cambridge by more professional medicine and engineering and also at the end of the nineteenth century by a number of new universities. The old role was, however, never displaced by the new elements. Civil servants still often have their training in quite classical and "unpractical" subjects.

Political science therefore remained centered on political philosophy, especially at the elite institutions, until the mid-twentieth century. The war experience of involvement and the postwar demands of regional development and the welfare state created an agenda of planning and administration that was met not least in the newly established politics departments in the younger universities (beyond London, Oxford, and Cambridge). The subject shifted from law and history to sociology, economics, and psychology. However, in the 1950s—under Michael Oakeshott—at the leading political science department, the London School of Economics, "The study of politics was in effect political theory and the history of political ideas, and the rest of the curriculum was public administration or what an Oakeshottian would call the 'plumbing' side of political inquiry."[78]

IR was originally seen not as part of political science, but as a new field drawing on many disciplines. Even when it became institutionalized within political science, this discipline was itself not closed to other disciplines. IR could therefore continue to cultivate its links to especially history, international law, political philosophy, and sociology.[79] IR is much less one-dimensionally defined as political science than is the case in the United States.

The leading role of the United Kingdom in the early history of IR is explained primarily by the foreign policy situation. The policy- (that is, peace-) oriented study of international affairs that emerged after Versailles was ideationally and institutionally linked to the League of Nations and thus naturally headed by the status quo powers (and specific circles in Germany). Additionally, Arnold Wolfers' classical argument about the Anglo-American tradition in foreign affairs offers a paradoxical explanation. Continental theories of international relations center on "necessity of state," due to experiences of being exposed to forces beyond their control. With insular security, England and America experienced a choice of how to apply prin-

76. Wittrock 1993, 324–27.
77. Wagner and Wittrock 1991, 343. See also Hayward 1991.
78. Vout 1991, 166.
79. Hill 1987, 305ff.

ciples of morality to foreign policy.[80] Choice stimulated a search for new solutions and thus a new discipline.

Most noticed about British IR is its one distinct contribution to "grand theory," the English school or "the international society tradition." However, only a minority of British IR scholars are involved in this "school." The British community is uniquely diverse and ranges from the "very American" to the type that Steve Smith depicts as critical of recent overly theoretical approaches like Morgenthau, that is, believes diplomatic history really is what IR should be.[81]

The English school itself was—as argued by its primary chronicler, Tim Dunne—created by reformist realists. British and American IR share the foundational event of the realist-idealist (pseudo-)debate, but whereas in the United States it was mostly kept as a mobilizable rhetorical blackmail, in the United Kingdom it was soon taken for decided (won by the realists), and both E. H. Carr and those influenced by him wanted to explore the societal elements of international relations.[82] The policy context thus plays an important role: Without the specific educational need felt by American postwar realists, it was absurd for realists to just stick to cultivating the bottom line lesson. Furthermore, the idea of international society derives from experiences in European, maybe particularly British, history.[83] Americans who thought about history usually meant post-1945, not imagining that much earlier history could be relevant to the problems of this unique, nuclear superpower.[84] In the British case, continuation of the Eurocentric diplomatic system meant a link to the part of history where Britain played a significant role and possibly implied a continued British role.

The international society tradition offers an organizing core for IR because it argues that international relations should be studied as a society in its own right, not assimilated through "domestic analogy" into either polar opposite or delayed replica of domestic society.[85] This probably contributes to the reluctance among British IR scholars to see IR as a subset of political science.

The American image of British IR remains shaped by the fact that from here Bull led the counterattack in the second debate against "scientific approaches." British "traditionalism" has thereby become a cliché. However, the hard scientific approaches never did find many followers in Britain and neither does rational choice today. The main explanation remains the embeddedness of IR in liberal education and the relationship to history and philosophy. However, a strategic factor should not be underestimated. Britain is the second strongest IR community (compare Figure 1 and Table 2), and thus the natural challenger for the United States. Thus, surprisingly, in light of British attitudes to (other) European integration but not surprising to balance-of-power theory, the British lead the attempt to form a European IR organization aiming at a stronger stand in relation to the United States.

80. Wolfers 1956.
81. Smith 1993.
82. Dunne 1994.
83. Lyons 1986, 642.
84. Isaacson 1992, 74–75.
85. Bull 1977.

Whereas prognoses for French and German IR revolve around the question of forming a more coherent national community, the prospects for British IR are different because it shares a language with the dominant community. This situation makes it more realistic for individuals to enter the U.S.–global arena (although there are still surprisingly few Britons who make it in the general discipline; hardly more than one or two would be included in a top-twenty-five list based on the Social Science Citation Index, which is still better than the likely zero for continental Europeans). This British participation in the global, English-speaking discipline is supplemented in some fields by a U.K.-centered (but open) community, and British international relationists are very active in the emerging European community (which is predominantly English speaking). A more distinct and self-conscious national community is therefore a less likely option in the United Kingdom than in France and Germany. Rather, Britons are likely to continue to play important roles in several overlapping transnational systems.

United States

Modeled on (an often idealized image of) German universities, the new nineteenth century American universities soon both developed unique features and overtook the Germans on those they shared. Already at the turn of the century, the number of students enrolled in American universities was six times larger than in the celebrated German universities.[86] The American universities were more adaptive, less dependent on the state, and had strong presidential leadership instead. Due to less ingrained vested interests, specialization into disciplines occurred more easily and fully here.[87]

In the late nineteenth century when the separate organizations split out from the American Social Science Association, they shared "a commitment to an empirical, often and increasingly quantitative, methodology and to some conception of the usefulness of scientific knowledge for the allegedly neutral solution of social problems."[88] The atheoretical and empirical work fit the progressive agenda, not critical of the state, rather of the lack of state.[89] Dorothy Ross has shown the importance of American historical consciousness. The millennial belief in American exceptionalism exempted the United States from qualitative change, and the historicist threat to this ideology was kept at bay with the assistance of a naturalistic social science containing change within the categories of progress, law, and reason. This historical consciousness adapted and survived dramatic challenges and thus sustained—very differently from Europe with its historicist consciousness—a more abstract and "scientific" social science, divorced from history.[90]

As already noticed by Thorstein Veblen in 1906, American social science had become empiricist, abstaining from studying underlying (allegedly "metaphysical")

86. Wittrock 1993, 330.
87. Ibid., 331.
88. Wagner and Wittrock 1991, 347.
89. Lowi 1992, 1–2.
90. Ross 1991.

causes and searching for prediction and control. This fit with both ameliorist ambitions and universities controlled by businessmen. Searching for complex "underlying" causal determinants of, for instance, poverty could be dangerous, whereas empiricism apologetically conserves the framework of givens and points to conformist remedies.[91] World War I secured decisive victory for positivism. The competing, older German tradition of "metaphysical," statist, historical, and holistic social science was delegitimized, as was everything German. Furthermore, support for the war effort entrenched the practical role.

Although American universities were generally created with great German inspiration, political science borrowed content in a particularly striking way because it went against dominant conceptions in American society. The concept of "the state" was made the organizing center of political science. The American classics did not use that concept much (preferring, instead, terms like "government," "civil polity," "civil society," and "nation").[92] Introducing a concept of the state in mid- and late nineteenth century America did have societal, political functions—the northern side in the Civil War, nationalism, state building—but political scientists pressed it with unusual force because it gave coherence to the emerging discipline.

John Gunnell speaks of a Germanization of the discipline. He convincingly argues both against seeing these concepts as ordinary ideas in the United States and against seeing them as completely alien and un-American—otherwise they would not have had a chance. They had political functions, but their general philosophical inspiration, and thus their ideational import, clearly meant a sudden pipeline to German idealism and organicism, which were basically at odds with the liberalism embedded at the heart of American self-understanding and political lexicon. Political science was founded in the United States on a continental European (German) philosophical tradition, which could make some relevant interventions in the United States but basically deviated from the mainstream. The counterattack by Harold Laski and other pluralists was generally in better conformity with the American conceptions of state, society, and individual; but it left political science without a focus. The state had been it. This led generations from Charles E. Merriam to the present to seek "the identity and authority of political science more in its method rather than its subject matter."[93]

Hoffmann offers two criteria for the emergence of IR: (1) the democratization of foreign policy, and (2) a country actually involved in real foreign policy—that is, one neither standing aloof (as with the United States in relation to Europe before the 1930s) nor simply dominating weak neighbors (as the United States did in the Western Hemisphere); ideally, the country should be so involved that studying its foreign policy becomes synonymous with studying the system. After 1945, the United States fulfilled these criteria best, and accordingly it was here that IR became a discipline.[94] Scholars have often noted about the rigid formulation of postwar realism that it came

91. Manicas 1991, 50–51. The discussion refers to Veblen's 1906 essay "The Place of Science in Modern Civilization."
92. Gunnell 1991, 126.
93. Gunnell 1995, 29.
94. Hoffmann 1977, 42–43, 48–49.

close to caricature because its protagonists felt that this stance was necessary to teach a people inclined to go the opposite way. This observation might be said of IR in general: to get the message through, it was formulated as general propositions—an empirical science of laws or regularities of state behavior.

Hoffmann points to the American conviction that problems can be resolved and science will find the master key, issue by issue. The resulting prestige of the "exact sciences" (and the quest for certainty and the belief in progress) was, at the end of the war, bestowed on economics. Actually, one of the most striking features of American political science for an outside observer is this role model of economics, which seems self-evident to most American political scientists but needs explanation exactly as given by Hoffmann. It follows from a two-step development: first, the natural sciences were elevated to a much higher plane than the social sciences (in contrast to the situation in France or the United Kingdom, for example); and, second, economics is seen as making the jump. Political science has been shaped broadly by the drive for scientization stimulated by the image that a bar existed that could actually be surpassed and, more specifically, by imports of theory and methodology from economics.[95]

Despite the interest in linking to economics, American IR scholars generally take it for granted that IR is a subdiscipline of political science—in contrast to a widespread British wish to see IR as a separate discipline and its relationship to political science on par with that to other relevant disciplines. This finds expression in BISA being clearly the forum for IR scholars, whereas in the United States the ISA is hard pressed from the American Political Science Association (APSA) for the status as the most prestigious forum for IR. *IO's* editorial board meets at APSA's annual meeting, not ISA's.

In the United States (1930s–1940s) and later in Western Europe (1960s–1970s) and in contrast to most other parts of the world, university-based research, rather than the more policy-oriented research centers and think tanks, came to dominate the field.[96] Consequently, the influence of policy concerns decreased, and a social scientific approach won out against the earlier conception based on law, history, and geography.

After 1945, the U.S. led in channeling increased funds to research (inspired by the applicability of research during the war). Although maintaining academic control in the National Science Foundation and even some of the private foundations, the new money stimulated practical, useful knowledge and thereby "behavioral sciences" and "policy sciences."[97] (Due to the dominance of university-based research, these monies led to theory and research programs that promised policy relevance, not primarily to simple policy articles.)

In the postbehavioral period, economic methodology has increasingly replaced behaviorism as the method that organizes the discipline. This development occurred

95. Suhr 1997.
96. Kahler 1993, 398–402.
97. Wittrock 1993, 331–36.

for three reasons: (1) for IR to become more scientific, scholars have generally used economics as the most relevant model to emulate; (2) scholars needed methodology to replace the state as the conceptual core of the discipline, and (3) scholars thereby established correspondence with the political level, where, as argued by Lowi, "economics has replaced law as the language of the state. . . . Quite aside from whatever merits it may have as a method and however true its truths may be, public choice is hegemonic today for political reasons or (to be more dignified about it) for reasons of state."[98] Also, constructivism developed in the United States as a method, whereas in Europe it was more often defined as substance, as historically constituted political questions with which one must engage.[99]

There is no need to rehash the detailed development of American IR given the rest of this issue. The question of the conceptual core for IR in different periods will be discussed in the next section.

The Form and Content of IR

The third layer of a sociology of social sciences is the intellectual layer. It consists of two dimensions: first, the discipline as social and intellectual structure and, second, its main intellectual traditions. The first dimension will be discussed in relation to the common observation of IR's peculiar obsession with "great debates" —is it true, is it really unusual, and, if so, what causes it and what are its most important effects? The second dimension will be explored by summarizing some large patterns in intellectual traditions in IR to explain why some theoretical developments are more appreciated in the United States or Europe.

Great Debates and Other Ways of Organizing Disciplines

Observers often note that IR is peculiar among the social sciences for a series of "great debates." Ask an IR scholar to present the discipline in fifteen minutes, and most likely you will get a story of three great debates. There is no other established means of telling the history of the discipline. Even presenting in a positive, operational way what the discipline is and can do today seems to be difficult. Our perception of where we are in the development of knowledge about international relations is deeply shaped by the idea of these great debates.[100] Although this feature of IR is a common topic of conversation among IR scholars, no good explanations have yet been offered for its existence. Before attempting to explain it, we need to get the question right. Two implicit assumptions in the existing IR interpretation of the discipline's proclivity toward debates must be corrected.

98. Lowi 1992, 3–4 (see also 5).

99. Of course, many American constructivists use this approach to address important substantial issues, but it has become established as an increasingly respectable program due to its principled ideas and consciousness about what kind of questions constructivism can and cannot answer compared to the limitations of rationalism.

100. The role of debates shows in the tendency for labels to be coined by critics: "neorealism" (Cox, Ashley), "neoliberal institutionalism" (Grieco), and "reflectivists" (Keohane).

Both those who deplore the situation as fragmentation of the discipline and those (fewer) who celebrate it as pluralism assume that the alternative is a more coherent discipline—that is, agreement on a basic paradigm. However, debates are also expressions of coherence. Many of the social and human sciences are far more fragmented and therefore unable to agree on major debates. In comparative politics, for instance, there are often debates, but they are more fragmented than those in IR: which debates you believe to be currently central depends on what you study, and the various debates cannot be reduced to a common denominator as local versions of the same debate, for example, rationalism versus reflectivism. In IR, in contrast, the major debates orient the minor ones, and there is translatability across issues. A debate produces a shared frame of reference and expresses a less than totally fragmented discipline.

Additionally, other disciplines or subdisciplines that have roughly the same degree of fragmentation do not exhibit this particular pattern. Thus, we need both to explain this IR particularity and to ask systematically about its effects.

The usual masochistic contrast between natural and social sciences can be replaced by a more differentiated picture by drawing on Richard Whitley's *The Intellectual and Social Organization of the Sciences*.[101] Whitley argues that "scientific fields are a particular work organization which structures and controls the production of intellectual novelty through competition for reputations from national and international audiences for contributions to collective goals."[102] "They reward intellectual innovation—only new knowledge is publishable—and yet contributions have to conform to collective standards and priorities if they are to be regarded as competent and scientific."[103] This paradoxical combination of novelty and conformity creates a high level of task uncertainty, one of Whitley's two master variables (subdivided as technical and strategic task uncertainty).

"The more limited access to the necessary means of intellectual production and distribution, the more dependent do scientists become upon the controllers of such channels and the more connected and competitive are their research strategies likely to be."[104] The second variable is degree of mutual dependence, which "refers to scientists'dependence upon particular groups of colleagues to make competent contributions to collective intellectual goals and acquire prestigious reputations which lead to material rewards."[105] Through journals and conferences, scientists try to persuade influential colleagues of the correctness and importance of their work. Researchers are therefore "quite dependent upon certain groups of colleagues who dominate reputational organizations and set standards of competence and significance."[106] In fields where you can contribute to a number of distinct problem areas and seek reputations from different audiences by publishing results in different journals, this

101. Whitley 1984.
102. Ibid., 81.
103. Whitley 1986, 187.
104. Whitley 1984, 84ff.
105. Ibid., 87.
106. Ibid., 86.

dependence is much lower than in disciplines like particle physics, where journals form a clear hierarchy and audiences are clearly defined.

Functional dependence refers to the extent to which researchers depend on results, ideas, and procedures of fellow specialists to make contributions. Strategic dependence is the extent to which researchers have to persuade colleagues of the importance of their problem and approach to obtain a high reputation from them. This is about coordination of research strategies where functional dependence produces coordination through technique.[107] These basic patterns are not given features of the subject matter. For instance, increased state funding of biomedical research in the United States, especially for cancer and heart diseases, led to a decline of traditional disciplinary elites and boundaries, reduced strategic dependence, and thereby changed the dominant patterns in the field.[108]

Regarding IR, I will begin with the American-partly-turned-global discipline and then briefly compare the other three national situations. Within most subfields of IR, task uncertainty is relatively low: one knows which methods, approaches, and even questions count as appropriate. A student trained at one university and specializing in foreign policy analysis can go to another university and pass exams or get a job. Across subfields there is very high task uncertainty. A specialist in strategic studies who suddenly decides to write a feminist analysis of immigration policy—or vice versa—might have learned the techniques of this type of analysis in a general sense, but their application is sufficiently conventional to disable the writer from using the appropriate style and making the expected inferences.

In such a varied discipline, the crucial question is whether a hierarchy exists among fields. (Whitley points to a variation at equally low task uncertainty between chemistry and physics where only the latter has a hierarchy of fields, a privileging of theory, and thereby an integrative ordering of subfields.) Crucially, IR has a hierarchy of journals. The United States is a big job market with high circulation, and although a hierarchy exists among universities, the way up is through publications, so the leading journals are the most important bottleneck. In the natural sciences, the leading journals have high acceptance rates (65–83 percent) compared to 11–18 percent in economics, sociology, political science, and anthropology.[109] In the natural sciences, the norm seems to be that if nothing is wrong with an article, it should be printed, whereas leading journals in the social sciences assume that only the very best articles should be printed. Conversely, a scarce resource in the natural sciences is often access to expensive equipment, which makes being evaluated by foundations and being hired by leading institutions relatively more central to one's success than being published in journals, which take absolute priority in most social sciences. In most human sciences and some social sciences journals abound, and getting published is

107. Whitley combines these four times four possibilities to produce sixteen forms (summarized in Whitley 1984, 155, tab. 5.1) of which nine are unlikely or unstable, leaving a typology of seven. I will not, however, go through these, since IR does not fit comfortably into any of the forms. Instead, I focus on which dimensions vary among countries and which might explain the "debates."

108. Whitley 1984, 165.

109. See Hargens 1988, 150; and Andersen and Frederiksen 1995, 17–18.

easy. (Reaching the pinnacle in parts of sociology, for example, is defined by publishing books rather than articles.) In IR, too, almost any article can be published, but there is a relatively clear intersubjective understanding of the value of different outlets. Leading journals thus become absolutely central.

Here enters mutual dependence crucially. Functionally, scholars primarily rely and draw upon their fellow specialists, but the demands regarding form for an article to be accepted by a leading journal constitutes a metafunctional dependence. The exact pattern is shaped by the relationship between theorists and specialists. Whitley has shown how economics has a unique partitioned structure with a strong hierarchy headed by theorists.[110] Training is highly standardized based on formal, analytical theory that forms a stable core of the discipline with low task uncertainty. However, most economists do applications, which are much less certain and formal but publicly draw prestige from the theoretical nature of the core. The core, in turn, is closed to results from the applications because of its nature as formal theory and model building. This dualistic system has shown a paradoxical stability. For the most part, only the theory articles make it to the leading journals; the subfields are largely left on their own, free to draw on the core as they wish.

IR is much less segregated due to the nature of the lead journals and the relationship between theory and "applied" articles. Theory articles do not as such rank higher than empirical, applied ones. On the contrary, there is a fatigue with new theories or metatheories and a premium (not least, for *IO*) on good tests that assist development of existing theories. However, the journals are mainly defined, structured, and to a certain extent controlled by theorists. You only become a star by doing theory. The highest citation index scores all belong to theorists. Thus, the battle among theories/theorists defines the structure of the field, but it stimulates competition among the subfields to make it into the leading journals.

The result is a two-tiered discipline. To get into the lower tier, scholars have to manage the functional dependence within a subfield and become accepted as competent in it. Most subfields are relatively tolerant, welcome new members, and are not terribly competitive. They are hierarchical, but the hierarchy is not settled internally, so there is not much to fight over. Scholars gain top positions by making it into the upper tier, that is, by publishing in the leading, all-round journals, which means convincing those at the center about relevance and quality (they still have to prove technical competence to their fellow specialists because some of them will most likely be reviewers).

This specific structure explains the debates in IR. Debates ensure that theorists remain central but empirical studies important (in contrast to economics). (As illustrated in Figure 3, this shows up in the high proportion of articles in American journals that fit into the dominant categories compared with, especially, the British journals.) Without recurrent debates, empirical work would break off, and scholars would simply apply the accepted theory without a continuous need for following developments among theorists. Most other disciplines with a clear hierarchy have lower task

110. Whitley 1986 and 1984, 181–87.

uncertainty and therefore also direct translatability among subfields. In IR the sub-fields only meet through the theorists and only in the arena of central competition. The combination of hierarchy and medium-high task uncertainty makes debates ever possible, but they do not multiply across fields—they typically get organized into one lead debate at the center.

Debates are possible in the United States because the discipline is more unified there than in Europe. With the benefit of one big national "market," strategic dependence is higher and the discipline has broken local control. In the United States it is possible to compete for definition of the whole field; in Europe maintaining local peculiarities is easier.

As argued earlier, theory does not have the guiding role in France that it does in the United States. The French academic world is quite hierarchical, but the hierarchies play out within specializations, and general theory does not play the role of prioritizing and systematizing these different specialties.

German IR has traditionally been localized, with power still largely vested in professors, and, for example, until *ZIB,* there were no peer-reviewed journals, and a decisive premium on international publications did not necessarily exist. One's career depends more on one's relationship to the local professor (or local faculty for acceptance of the *Habilitationsschrift*) than on some national competition. This is beginning to change.

British IR is uniquely varied. Until recently, the theory debates were not central, and still the community managed to run journals that published across subfields. However, the journals often looked like many of those in the more fragmented human and social sciences: without any line or clear selection criteria. Also, the community was much smaller until recently and perhaps was managed as a less formalized social system. With growth and internationalization, British IR scholars are today primarily competitors in the global arena—which also means they are the ones complaining most consistently about the barriers and biases of American IR, the center of the global discipline.

These different structures explain some of the data discussed earlier—for example, the over-representation of American authors in American journals. This is explained not only by American journals metatheoretically privileging the kinds of theory that are dominant in the United States, not in Europe. The structure just uncovered also suggests that a much higher motive exists for Americans to make the effort to get into these journals. The reward structures in European settings generally do not convince European scholars of the rationality of spending the time necessary to meet the very specific demands of a leading journal.

The structure of different IR communities is reinforced by their convergence with different academic styles, confrontational versus balanced. European, and especially British, academic culture rewards balanced and civilized behavior. American culture is more oriented toward visibility, quotations (whether for something absurd or convincing), "originality" (the "I have a new theory" syndrome), and combativeness. Knowing now the function of debates in the structure of American–global IR, the emerging European IR community will need to stage some debates. Major debate among non-Americans—along lines not already defined by Americans—have been few. Most important were probably the Hoffman-Rengger debate in *Millennium* and *ZiB's* debates in German.[111]

Considering briefly a large field excluded by this article's focus on "national" characteristics, we might start an investigation of internal American hierarchies and differentiation. Asking for the percentage of articles where at least one author is from one of the ten highest ranking universities in the United States,[112] the aggregate figure for 1995–97 for *International Studies Quarterly* is 16 percent, for *IO* 40 percent. Combining this with the strong correlation between quantitative studies in *International Studies Quarterly* and soft and hard rational choice in *IO*, it seems that some hierarchies reach higher than others. If we can assume that the most successful and "high-scoring" authors will as a rule become located at the leading universities, the hierarchy affiliated with *IO* seems to reflect more closely the supreme reward structure, and its favored theories are dominant in the discipline.

Continental and American Traditions in International Thought

I noted earlier the instances when attempts were made to define a distinct discipline of IR on the basis of some core concept. Two main intellectual traditions have supplied candidates: classical, historicist realism and "liberalism" in an ontological sense. The former leads to substantial definitions about the nature of the subject matter, the latter usually finds expression in definitions based on methodology. IR in the United States has moved from the former—statist, historicist definitions—to methodology.

In the Anglo-American world there is a preference for seeing realism as "Hobbesian," but the realism that was installed in the 1940s by Carr, Morgenthau, Wolfers, and Aron had roots that were much more German. Postwar "realism" often hides a tension between continental, historicist, and British liberal roots. To the former, states exist because they do—due to history and to their own will. They are their own justification, and they clash and struggle for numerous more or less rational reasons. To the latter, states exist because they fulfill functions for individuals (contract theory for security plus collective goods), and their relationship to other states is anarchical, which complicates cooperation.

In the 1940s, most of the inspiration came from the former source. Therefore, the rationalist, "six principles" reading of Morgenthau is misleading. In the classical realist world, conflicts were unavoidable because of the tragic nature of human interaction and the impossibility of fully rational decisions. Drawing on the long continental tradition of diplomacy and statesmanship, the realists advised on how to act even in situations that could not be fully known—based on a sense of history, the true

---

111. Mark Hoffman and Nick Rengger discussed different kinds of critical theory (Hoffman 1987; Rengger 1988). *ZiB* has consciously stimulated debates through its "Forum" section. Important examples are those introduced earlier in this article—for one on German IR in relation to American IR, see Hellmann 1994; and Zürn 1994; and one on rational choice, see Risse 1997.

112. "Ranking of IR Ph.D. programs in 1998," *U.S. News and World Report* web page, *http://www.usnews.com*.

statesman would know how to shape reality.[113] (Most of this is erased from today's textbook presentations of realism that define it in terms of state-centrism and, paradoxically, rational actors.) This continental tradition was specifically colored by nineteenth century *Machtschule,* the state as a strong abstraction, and romanticism.[114]

The other main root of thinking is liberalism—less specifically liberal conceptions of international relations than liberalism as deep political ontology: a contract theory of the state, individualism, and rational calculation of interest. Whereas thinking about "power politics" can be traced back to ancient times, the conceptualization of the state of nature and of anarchy only emerged in the seventeenth century. From Hobbes stems the "liberal" problematique of order, an individualistic–atomistic social-contract perspective on society.

> How any collection of self-interested agents might be capable of coexistence is one of the central substantive questions for social science paradigms in the positivist ontological mode. As the problem of individualism versus collectivism, it is the one procedural problem they all share. For there to be a problem, one must grant its terms. Agents are free; cooperative undertakings are calculated, and they are difficult. These are the terms of liberalism.[115]

Many contemporary Anglo-American realists are difficult to decipher exactly because their methodological and political approach is based on liberalism, while they qua their "tradition" have taken over a view of the state and politics deeply influenced by the continental tradition.

Despite the peculiar and idiosyncratic development of terminology in the United States, where "liberal" today means almost the opposite of what it has traditionally meant—state-loving and anti-individualist[116] —liberalism (in the classical sense) in the United States is not one side of a divide; rather, it is the consensus inside which people disagree. Almost all American political actors are "liberal" in this sense of individualism and basic concepts of politics, society, and economy.[117]

> In epistemological terms, it is much easier to characterize American political science than European. Broadly speaking, American scholarship has been dominated by the liberal intellectual tradition. In the original legal and constitutionalist approach, during the behavioral revolution, and now with rational choice analysis, the individual has been and remains the basic unit of analysis. . . . Historically, no single tradition has dominated European political science, and even today a complex mix of liberal, structural, and collectivist approaches coexist.[118]

In IR, the basic unit is not necessarily "the individual," but an individualistic and choice-theoretical ontology is transferred to other "primitive units" or ontologi-

113. For example, Kissinger 1957a, 329; and Morgenthau 1962.
114. The critical literature has an unfortunate tendency to make one monolithic problem out of positivism, realism, and Americans! Compare George, who seriously distorts the picture of realism by only pointing to the positivist elements; George 1994.
115. Onuf 1989, 163
116. Lakoff 1996.
117. Hartz 1955.
118. McKay 1988, 1054; compare Ross 1991.

cal givens who become the instrumental calculators, be they states, rulers, or firms.[119]

European postwar IR is more sociological—from Aron's "historical sociology" of international relations to the British "international society" tradition. Europeans did not generally continue the *Machtschule* tradition but made other historicist attempts to constitute a distinct field.

The émigré generation meant a Europeanization of American IR after World War II (to political science, a second Europeanization).[120] Postwar IR was a mixture of substantial ideas of international relations drawn from the classical, continental tradition and attempts to reconstitute the field from more minimalist, methodological premises. The long-term story is thus one of a gradual de-Europeanization of American IR. Although the *Realpolitik* tradition was the main import from Europe, this is not simply the story of "the fall of realism": Waltz's realism is (in this sense) liberal realism and very much an Americanized form of theory. Neorealism's microeconomic reformulation of realism is probably the clearest example of de-Europeanization.[121] Liberalism has become the shared premise of American mainstream rationalism. Therefore, "selling" American IR to societies that are less extremely liberalized has become more and more difficult. (The opposite, of course, is true for the—currently less dominant—"sociological turn" of American constructivists. Drawing on European inspiration like Durkheim, Weber, Giddens, and Habermas, it certainly sells well in Europe— compare, for example, Ruggie's article in this issue of *IO*.)

Another reason why American IR is becoming American is the trivial fact that most of the leading figures now are "natives," not immigrants. Almost twenty years ago, Norman D. Palmer rightly commented

> If international relations is "an American social science," this is due to a large extent to the contributions of European-born and European-educated scholars, including the author of "An American Social Science" himself. If asked to name the truly great figures in the academic field of international relations, I would mention Sir Alfred Zimmern, E. H. Carr, Quincy Wright, Hans J. Morgenthau, Karl Deutsch, and possibly also Arnold Toynbee, Arnold Wolfers, and Raymond Aron. Only one of them was born and educated in the United States. (Three of the others, to be sure, did much of their most significant work while living in the United States and made major contributions to the development of this "American social science.")[122]

---

119. Compare, for example, Krasner forthcoming; and Milner 1997.
120. Gunnell 1993.
121. Theory that is liberal also in the sense of drawing on classical liberal thoughts about IR has undergone a similar minimalist, microeconomic reformulation—even twice. First, an institutional theory was developed by Keohane and others, and more recently Andrew Moravcsik has formulated a theory about domestic interests and state–society relations. Moravcsik 1997. As neorealism, both of these theories downplay ethics, history, and praxis in order to create empirical social science theory in the liberal epistemological tradition. On these minimalist reformulations and their effects, see Wæver 1992, 125–51; 1996.
122. Palmer 1980, 347ff.

The reader might try to draw up a similar list today, and I guess most would end up with a list dominated by Americans born and educated in the United States.[123]

Status and Outlook

There is a global discipline of IR, since most national IR communities follow the American debates, teach American theories, and Americans publish in European journals. Still, IR is quite different in different places. Some American theories travel well, others—typically those most rationalist and methodology-based, such as behavioralism and rational choice—do not. Traffic into the United States is only possible by individuals migrating and Americanizing themselves.

What is the price of this pattern to Americans, Europeans, and the discipline at large? Systematic variations in theoretical development mean that both Americans and Europeans miss out on potentially interesting contributions. To both sides, this is an intellectual loss. The price, however, due to the asymmetrical setup in IR, is not distributed equally. Europeans will typically be aware of developments in the United States, but the opposite is far from always the case (variously caused by lack of attention or language skills). Europeans at least have the theoretical choice that to Americans appears nonexistent. Personally, in terms of careers, the price is skewed the opposite way, that is, to the advantage of Americans, because their approaches typically will be better rewarded, offer access to more prestigious journals, and thus result in materially superior jobs. This reinforces a situation in which European IR can be criticized for insufficient professionalism and too much local control, whereas American IR is threatened by parochialism and sequences of fads. The result for the discipline is lower standards, less exchange, and fewer challenges to think in new ways. Global orientation could help to break exceedingly local bastions, especially in Europe, while overcoming the structural narrow-mindedness of much of American IR.

Two examples from the last decade illustrate how the differences materialize on specific issues. The first example relates to EU studies. Since the new dynamism in Europe stemming from the mid-1980s launch of the 1992 program for the single market of the EU and the 1989–90 end of the Cold War and of Europe's division, the study of European integration has received an upsurge of interest. Theoretical developments in the United States and Europe have already gone through several phases in which the two sides of the Atlantic were simultaneously markedly different, yet closely connected.

The first phase showed (once again) disappointingly low levels of theorizing in European IR. For all the complaints from European scholars about American hegemony and the difficulties of being heard, it must be noticed that even when a tempt-

---

123. A recent (European) attempt to, problematically, single out twelve "masters in the making" contained ten North Americans (of which two—Ruggie and Walker—were born in Europe but trained in North America, and one—Der Derian—did his Ph.D. in Britain), one Briton, and one Frenchman; Neumann and Wæver 1997. See also Lyons 1982, 138.

ing new agenda was served right in front of Europeans, little impressive theoretical work was done. Most work was atheoretical, and at best old neofunctionalism was dusted off without answering the criticisms that brought it down the first time around. Filling this void, Andrew Moravcsik's *IO* article in 1991 had an extraordinary reception in Europe.[124] Here was an effort that both made sense in relation to existing categories—neofunctionalism and general IR schools—and offered clear theoretical propositions. Only an American seemed to have the courage to simplify and put forward new theory in contrast to European elaborate explanatory schemes built on dated American theories.[125] If microphones had been installed to generate an oral citation index at the second all-European IR conference in Paris in 1995, Moravcsik's name would have, undoubtedly, been the one most frequently heard—most likely not primarily because of support but rather as the Waltz of integration studies—the one clear theoretical position to define oneself against. This signaled the move into the second phase.

Recently, a new literature on each side has begun to emerge. One literature, mainly European (with important American contributions), is organized around the idea of multilevel governance;[126] the other, mainly American (with some Europeans), applies rational choice approaches to the European institutions.[127] Both are promising, but their contrast is striking. The European literature is a historicist attempt to capture an epochal transformation of the European order and its corresponding political lexicon; the American literature is driven by methodology and general theory.

The second example of the differences between American and European IR relates to identity and security. After the Cold War, security studies confronted the challenge of nationalism and ethnic identity, especially in Europe. American security studies has a clearly focused and hierarchical structure led by the journal *International Security*. In security studies neorealism actually is hegemonic (in contrast to general IR, where numerous articles are legitimized as critiques of the allegedly hegemonic neorealism, and critiques far out-number the purported hegemon). The reaction to identity was therefore largely a question of how to reconcile it with neorealism. As noticed by Yosef Lapid and Friedrich Kratochwil, the result was a very constrained process where "nations" were reinterpreted as protostates to be re-entered into the existing and thereby unchanged theory.[128]

124. Moravcsik 1991.

125. For a rather depressing picture of the state of European efforts in the early 1990s, see the proceedings from the first in the series of European IR conferences held every third year by the Standing Group on International Relations under the European Consortium for Political Research: Pfetsch 1993.

126. For instance, Jachtenfuchs and Kohler-Koch 1996; Hix 1998; Marks 1993; Majone 1996; and more radical contributions like Diez 1997. In the words of one of the leading exponents, Markus Jachtenfuchs, "the governance approach to European integration is mainly a European one. It simply has to do with the fact that Europeans are exposed to the actions of the EU on a day-to-day basis and are thus highly sensitive to questions of effective and democratic governance in the European multi-level system. They are much less interested in U.S.-style reasoning about the true motives for and the decisive actors behind European integration." Jachtenfuchs, personal correspondence with the author, 18 April 1998.

127. Notably, Tsebelis 1994; Garrett and Weingast 1993; Milner 1997, chap. 7–8; and Schneider et al. 1995.

128. Lapid and Kratochwil 1996. See this article for a list of the most important contributions by the *International Security* school—authors like Posen, Mearsheimer, and van Evera.

A number of French contributions draw much more intensively on sociological, philosophical, and anthropological literature while, in some cases, also staying close to policy concerns. Suddenly it pays off for individuals strong in IR and strategic studies to also be cognizant of general developments in social theory and philosophy (due to the all-round nature of Parisian intellectuals).[129] Pathbreaking works by Didier Bigo on the merger of internal and external security draws on Foucault and Bourdieu while doing detailed empirical work on European police cooperation.[130] Pierre Hassner, who has been at the forefront so often in the study of European changes, has increasingly linked back to his original interests in philosophy and general social theory.[131]

In-between these two is the so-called Copenhagen school.[132] Those working from this perspective are more traditional than the French in striving for interoperability with mainstream IR and strategic studies while modifying even central features of neorealism. The price is a more problematic treatment of concepts like identity and society. Finding a Scandinavian–British cooperation in-between the French and the American is hardly surprising: research in Scandinavia is often oriented toward the American mainstream. Although having distance and freedom enough to operate differently from the mainstream, usually the aim is ultimately to make an impact in the heartland of security studies/IR. Criteria of validation and reward are not as independent as those in France; they are rather those of a relatively independent periphery.

Recently, a second American wave of literature under the heading "security and identity," this time by constructivists, was epitomized by the monumental *The Culture of National Security*.[133] Structured more by the theory- (or even "school-") driven debate among constructivists and rationalists, constructivists have joined efforts to show, in an important field like security, what significant results their approach can yield. This is not the policy-guided "security studies" question of how to deal with these new challenges, but in characteristic American fashion a theory-driven agenda, the current great debate.

These two examples illustrate how characteristic patterns reproduce on new agendas. How issues in international affairs are theorized follows not only from the influence of international events on the learning processes of a deterritorialized discipline, but also from the process being very much a product of national, academic culture.

Conclusion: American IR—from Global Hegemony to National Professionalization?

Differences in how—and how much—IR has developed in different countries is not just a matter of national idiosyncrasies or unnamable national character. Political,

---

129. See, for instance, several of the contributions to Le Gloannec 1998.
130. Bigo 1996.
131. Hassner 1997.
132. Discussed by McSweeney 1996; Huysmans 1998; and Lapid and Kratochwil 1996. Most recent work from the school is Buzan et al. 1997.
133. Katzenstein 1996c.

institutional history explains different definitions, relationship to neighboring disciplines, and scientific ideals. Widespread American expectations that others will follow their current development are therefore likely to be frustrated. As often pointed out by French scholars, American IR scholars are prone to thinking in universalistic categories, but they are likely to be reminded of the cultural specificity of these categories.

The internal intellectual structure of American IR explains both the recurring great debates and why American IR generates global leadership. It has a hierarchy centered on theoretical journals, and scholars must compete for access to these. This they have not had to do in Europe, where power historically rested either in subfields or in local universities, not in a disciplinary elite. American IR alone generates an apex that therefore comes to serve as the global core of the discipline.

American IR is heading for national professionalization, but since it happens on the basis of a liberal ontology through rational choice methods, it will not be easily exportable and therefore entails a de-Americanization of IR elsewhere. The best hope for a more global, less asymmetrical discipline lies in the American turn to rational choice, which is not going to be copied in Europe.

European IR simultaneously shows signs of increasing professionalization, but not necessarily Americanization.[134] IR in Germany, France, and the United Kingdom has started to break the very local (single university, subdisciplinary, or informal, personal) power structures and is heading toward a larger academic market—national, or maybe more often defined by language area (French-speaking, German-speaking[135]), and occasionally European.

The result is likely to be a slow shift from a pattern with only one professional and coherent national market—the United States, and the rest of the world more or less peripheral or disconnected—toward a relative American abdication and larger academic communities forming around their own independent cores in Europe. When and to what extent this increasing pluralism will include sizable independent IR communities beyond the West are among the important questions remaining for a future sociology of the IR discipline.

134. This in contrast to the true periphery, where the aim is to reach America. To get tenure in Israel, you have to be published in an American journal and complete training outside the country (personal communication from Michael Barnett, 18 March 1998), and even the relatively large Scandinavian research community uses the revealing language of "publishing internationally" (meaning in the United States). As noted by Andersen and Frederiksen, the term is small-state language; Andersen and Frederiksen 1995, 18. "An American researcher would hardly say he has "published internationally," if he, for once, had an article printed in a foreign journal in another language than English. Sivertsen 1994, 42. In such places, professionalization is likely to mean increased Americanization.

135. Compare Giesen 1995; and Rittberger and Hummel 1990. The role of language areas would justify treating Scandinavian IR as a unit rather than as national communities— in the event of a future extended analysis.

Appendix

TABLE A.1. *Theoretical position of articles in four international journals, 1995–97*

Metatheoretical Position	European Journal of International Relations (%)				Review of International Studies (%)				International Studies Quarterly (%)				International Organization (%)			
	1995	1996	1997	Total	1995	1996	1997	Total	1995	1996	1997	Total	1995	1996	1997	Total
Formalized rational choice	14.3 (3)	6.25 (1)	6.7 (1)	9.6 (5)	0 (0)	0 (0)	0 (0)	0 (0)	20.8 (5)	26.1 (6)	20.0 (6)	22.1 (17)	19.2 (5)	26.1 (6)	4.3 (1)	16.7 (12)
Quantitative studies	19.0 (4)	12.5 (2)	13.3 (2)	15.4 (8)	4.5 (1)	0 (0)	4.0 (1)	2.9 (2)	37.5 (9)	30.4 (7)	40.0 (12)	36.4 (28)	7.7 (2)	17.4 (4)	8.7 (2)	11.1 (8)
Nonformalized rationalism ("soft" rational choice)	23.8 (5)	6.25 (1)	20.0 (3)	17.3 (9)	13.6 (3)	9.1 (2)	20.0 (5)	14.5 (10)	16.7 (4)	17.4 (4)	23.3 (7)	19.5 (15)	38.5 (10)	30.4 (7)	39.1 (9)	36.1 (26)
Nonpostmodern constructivism	28.6 (6)	18.8 (3)	26.7 (4)	25.0 (13)	18.2 (4)	27.3 (6)	20.0 (5)	21.7 (15)	4.2 (1)	8.7 (2)	3.3 (1)	5.2 (4)	19.2 (5)	8.7 (2)	34.8 (8)	20.8 (15)
Post-structuralism, Marxism, and feminism	0 (0)	31.25 (5)	20.0 (3)	15.4 (8)	13.6 (3)	27.3 (6)	16.0 (4)	18.8 (13)	4.2 (1)	0 (0)	3.3 (1)	2.6 (2)	3.8 (1)	8.7 (2)	0 (0)	4.2 (3)
Other	14.3 (3)	25.0 (4)	13.3 (2)	17.3 (9)	50.0 (11)	36.4 (8)	40.0 (10)	42.0 (29)	16.7 (4)	17.4 (4)	10.0 (3)	14.3 (11)	11.5 (3)	8.7 (2)	13.0 (3)	11.1 (8)
Number of articles	100.0 (21)	100.1 (16)	100.0 (15)	100.0 (52)	99.9 (22)	100.1 (22)	100.0 (25)	99.9 (69)	100.1 (24)	100.0 (23)	99.9 (30)	100.1 (77)	99.9 (26)	100.0 (23)	99.9 (23)	100.0 (72)

Note: Actual numbers are shown in parentheses.

Theories and Empirical Studies
of International Institutions
Lisa L. Martin and Beth A. Simmons

The role of international institutions has been central to the study of world politics at least since the conclusion of World War II. Much of this research was, and continues to be, pioneered in the pages of *International Organization*. In this article we take stock of past work on international institutions, trace the evolution of major themes in scholarship over time, and highlight areas for productive new research. Our central argument is that research should increasingly turn to the question of how institutions matter in shaping the behavior of important actors in world politics. New research efforts should emphasize observable implications of alternative theories of institutions. We advocate approaching international institutions as both the object of strategic choice and a constraint on actors' behavior, an idea that is familiar to scholars of domestic institutions but has been neglected in much of the debate between realist and institutionalist scholars of international relations.

The article is organized into three major sections. The first section provides an analytical review of the development of studies of international institutions. From the beginning, the pages of *IO* have been filled with insightful studies of institutions, in some cases asking questions consistent with the research agenda we propose in this essay. But the lack of a disciplinary foundation in the early years meant that many good insights were simply lost, not integrated into other scholars' research. With the professionalization of the discipline since the late 1950s, scholarship on international institutions has become more theoretically informed, and empirical research has begun more often to conform to social-scientific standards of evidence, with results that provide both caution and inspiration for future research. One of the most consequential developments for our understanding of international institutions came in the early 1970s, when a new generation of scholars developed insights that opened up inquiry beyond that of formal organizations, providing intellectual bridgeheads to the study of institutions more generally.

Our thanks for comments on previous versions go to Marc Busch, Peter Katzenstein, Bob Keohane, Steve Krasner, and participants in the *IO* fiftieth anniversary issue conference.

International Organization 52, 4, Autumn 1998, pp. 729–757

The second section explicitly addresses a theme that arises from the review of scholarship on institutions: whether international politics needs to be treated as *sui generis,* with its own theories and approaches that are distinct from other fields of political science, or whether it fruitfully can draw on theories of domestic politics. As our review shows, developments in studies of American politics, such as studies of voting and coalitional behavior, have often influenced the way that scholars approached international institutions. Most of these efforts did not pay off with major insights. The functionalist approach to institutions adopted in the 1980s owed little to theories of domestic politics, drawing more on economic models. Today, we see the pendulum swinging back, as more scholars turn to modern theories initially developed to study domestic political phenomena (see Helen Milner's article in this issue). Here, we assess whether these new attempts are likely to be any more successful than previous efforts.

The third section turns to the problem of research agendas. Where does scholarship on international institutions go next? Our primary argument in this section is that attention needs to focus on *how*, not just *whether*, international institutions matter for world politics. Too often over the last decade and a half the focal point of debate has been crudely dichotomous: institutions matter, or they do not. This shaping of the agenda has obscured more productive and interesting questions about variation in the types and degree of institutional effects, variations that were in fact well documented in the less theoretical but well-researched case studies of the journal's earliest years. Of course, we do not suggest a return to idiographic institutional analysis. Rather, we suggest a number of lines of theoretically informed analysis that may lead to research that both asks better questions and is more subject to empirical testing. These paths include more serious analysis of the distributional effects of institutions, the relation between international institutions and domestic politics, the problem of unanticipated consequences, and a typology of institutional effects.

The Evolution of an Idea:
Institutions in International Politics

Early Studies of the Institutionalization of the Postwar World

The "poles" of realism and idealism—of which much is made in graduate seminars— had little to do with the highly practical organizational analysis that dominated the pages of *IO* in the first decades after the war. The focus of attention was on how well these newly established institutions met the problems that they were designed to solve. On this score, few scholarly accounts were overly optimistic. Overwhelmed by the magnitude of the political and economic reconstruction effort, few judged postwar organizations as up to the task. Central to this debate was a highly realistic understanding that international politics would shape and limit the effectiveness of postwar institutions; virtually no one predicted that these would triumph over politics. The UN,[1] the General Agreement on Tariffs and Trade (GATT),[2] the International Monetary Fund[3] —all were the subject of highly critical review.

A number of important studies grappled explicitly with the impact of these institutions on the policies of the major powers and the outcomes for the central political and military competition between them. The answers, predictably, were derived from little more than informed counterfactual reasoning, but they displayed a sensitivity to the broad range of possible impacts that institutions such as the League and the UN could have on the major powers. In their examination of the ideal of collective security, Howard C. Johnson and Gerhart Niemeyer squarely inquired into the role that norms, backed by organizations such as the UN, play in affecting states' behavior. They asked whether states were "prepared to use force or the threat of force for the sake of public law and order rather than for the sake of their national advantage in relation to that of other states. . . . How has the behavior of states been affected by these standards?"[4] Though ultimately more confident in the balance of power than in norms embodied in the rule of law, these scholars were correct to push for a mechanism that might explain the effects of institutions on behavior: "We cannot claim to have learned much about the League experiment until we know *how* it has affected the problem of harnessing and controlling the factors of force and their role in the relations of power."[5]

A flurry of studies in the early 1950s suggested possible answers. Pointing to the U.S. role in decolonization and military aid for Korea, collective institutions were said to raise U.S. "consciousness of broader issues" that might affect American interests and thereby make the U.S. more responsive to world opinion.[6] By subjecting policies to global scrutiny—a mechanism not unlike those of transparency and reputation central to the literature in the 1980s—the UN was viewed as having had an (admittedly marginal) effect on some of the most central issues of world politics.

Though lacking the elaborate theoretical apparatus of current research, early studies of postwar organizations had many of the same insights that have informed "modern" institutionalism. Paralleling much contemporary argument on the form of cooperation,[7] one study as early as 1949 argued that multilateralism was precluded in cases where there were significant bargaining advantages and discrimination advantages of proceeding bilaterally.[8] Foreshadowing more theoretically sophisticated treatments of informal versus formal agreements,[9] studies of GATT as early as 1954 recognized that some agreements gain strength through their informal nature, and

---

1. See Goodrich 1947, 18; Fox 1951; Hoffmann 1956; Claude 1963; and Malin 1947. But for the optimistic view, see Bloomfield 1960.
2. Gorter 1954.
3. See Knorr 1948; and Kindleberger 1951a.
4. Johnson and Niemeyer 1954, 27.
5. Niemeyer 1952, 558 (italics added).
6. Cohen 1951. For a parallel analysis of institutional effects on Soviet behavior, see Rudzinski 1951.
7. See Oye 1992; and Martin 1992b.
8. Little 1949.
9. Lipson 1991.

prescient of the regimes literature viewed the value of GATT as "a focal point on which many divergent views on appropriate commercial policy converge."[10] Lacking a theoretical hook on which to hang these observations, and without a professionalized critical mass of scholars to develop these insights, many important findings were only rediscovered and advanced more than two decades later.

Nowhere is this more true than in the rediscovery of the relationship between international institutions and domestic politics. The idea that international institutions can influence state behavior by acting through domestic political channels was recognized by scholars writing in the mid-1950s. Referring to the example of the International Finance Corporation, B. E. Matecki wrote that international organizations could be "idea generating centers" with the ability to set in motion national forces that directly influence the making of national policy.[11] Reflecting on the efforts of the Council of Europe to gain acceptance of its vision for Europe in national capitals, an early study by A. Glenn Mowers pointed out the conscious strategy of direct lobbying of national governments through national parliaments.[12] And in a fascinating study of the role of the Security Council in influencing Dutch colonial policy, Whitney Perkins pointed to the crucial interaction between authoritative international decisions and democratic politics: "By defiance of the Security Council the Dutch alerted powerful monitors who allied their strength with domestic forces in requiring them to live up to principles [of decolonization]."[13] "In this type of interaction between democratic governments and the UN emerge some of the essential elements of a world political process."[14] Anticipating a mechanism for institutional effects that have recently resurfaced in contemporary studies, he concluded that "The role of the UN is to exert pressures designed to enable the loser in public sentiment to accept the consequences of its loss."[15] This research approach reflected an effort to flesh out the mechanisms by which the policies and perspectives of international institutions could work through national politics.

In short, the early postwar literature on international institutions, while highly focused on formal organizations, was far less naive and legalistic, more politically sensitive and insightful than it is often given credit for being. Early insights included the recognition that the nature of the international political system provided a context for the effectiveness of international institutions, that institutional effectiveness should be subject to empirical investigation, and that elaborate organizational structure is not always the best approach to achieving international cooperation. Moreover, the best of this early literature was concerned not merely with *whether* international institutions had an impact, but *how* one might think about a mechanism for their effects. Transparency, reputation, and legitimacy as well as domestic political pressures were suggested in various strands of thought. But there was no conceptual

10. Gorter 1954, 1, 8.
11. Matecki 1956.
12. Mowers 1964.
13. Perkins 1958, 40.
14. Ibid., 26.
15. Ibid., 42

framework that could tie these insights together; nor was there a systematic compara- tive enterprise to check for their regularity. Rather, another research agenda, replete with fancy methodological tools imported from American politics, was to demote these questions in favor of an only partially fruitful examination of the internal poli- tics of international organizations.

The Influence of Behavioralism:
Politics Within International Institutions

If few thought international organization would liberate the world from politics, it arguably became important to understand who has power in these organizations and how that power was being exercised. Especially since the use of the veto had appar- ently rendered the Security Council toothless, concern began to focus on the develop- ment of rules and norms in the General Assembly. The supposed "specter" of bloc voting in that forum—increasingly of concern to American scholars and policymak- ers as the Cold War extended its gelid reach—became a central concern.[16]

This debate took what appears today to be an odd early direction. Perhaps due to new and exciting work in U.S. legislative behavior, the research program quickly became focused on how to describe patterns of voting in the General Assembly, without a systematic attempt to sort out the usefulness of the voting behavior ap- proach. Despite warnings that the international system was fundamentally different from domestic political systems,[17] this research program easily accepted that voting in the UN was a proxy for power in that institution. Certainly there were skeptics: Rupert Emerson and Inis L. Claude, for example, cautioned that voting in an interna- tional body does not have the same function as in a democratically elected parlia- ment; an international conference is a negotiating rather than a legislative body. Voting in such a situation, they noted, was unlikely to play a deliberative role, since such votes were no more than propaganda efforts.[18] Few of these studies explicitly defended their assumption that General Assembly resolutions somehow mattered to the conduct of world politics. But the fascination with the method for analyzing voting behavior overcame fairly readily the caution that the domestic–international logic should be subject to close scrutiny. Moreover, the hope of providing an explic- itly political (legislative) model inspired by American politics may have been a reac- tion against the overly "anarchic" systems analysis of the late 1950s.[19]

Much of this work can be traced directly to developments in the study of American politics. Hayward Alker and Bruce Russett's study *International Politics in the Gen-*

16. For one of the earliest studies of bloc voting, see Ball 1951. For a study focusing primarily on the behavior of the Commonwealth countries, see Carter 1950. Concern with the influence of the Common- wealth grew as former British colonies gained independence and membership in the early 1960s. See Millar 1962.

17. Hoffmann 1960, 1–4.

18. Emerson and Claude 1952. See also Jebb 1952.

19. Alker and Russett 1965, 145, explicitly refer to Liska 1957 and Kaplan 1957. They argue that "[i]t is simply erroneous to think of international politics as anarchic, chaotic, and utterly unlike national politics." Alker and Russett 1965, 147.

eral Assembly, for example, acknowledged "that studies of the American political process by Robert Dahl, Duncan Macrae,[20] and David Truman were theoretically and methodologically suggestive of ways in which roll-call data could be used to test for the existence of a pluralistic political process in a quasi-legislative international organization."[21] Influenced by James March[22] and Robert Dahl, this study sought to understand various influences on UN voting behavior across issue areas in which the dimensions of power and influence were likely to differ. Certainly, one factor influencing this research agenda was the priority given to reproducible and "objective" forms of social science; the focus on General Assembly voting was acknowledged to be an artifact of the availability of fairly complete voting records.[23]

Largely related to the ferment in American voting studies, politics within the UN dominated the research agenda for most of the decade from the mid-1960s. Central was the concern to explain why certain countries had a tendency to vote together, to vote in blocs, or to form "legislative coalitions."[24] Also obviously inspired by American politics, another branch of inquiry focused on the determinants of successfully running for elective UN office.[25] Much of this literature was methodologically rather than conceptually driven and highly inductive with respect to its major empirical findings.[26] Little effort was made to explore the extent to which the concept of representation or the winning of elections in the domestic setting could travel meaningfully to an international institution. The research program lost steam under heavy fire from scholars who demanded a stronger justification for focusing on the General Assembly as a microcosm for world politics.[27]

Partially in response to the critique that the General Assembly was hardly the center of world politics, and partially influenced by another trend in American politics growing out of the study of bureaucratic politics and political systems, another research path was taken by Robert Cox and Harold Jacobson's study of eight specialized agencies within the UN.[28] In their edited volume, the focus was on the structure and process of influence associated with these institutions and their outputs, rather than on their formal character. Reflecting once again a major thread in American politics, the underlying assumption was that international organizations could be fruitfully analyzed as distinct political systems in which one could trace out patterns of influence: "The legal and formal character and the content of the decision is less important than the balance of forces that it expresses and the inclination that it gives to the further direction of events."[29]

20. MacRae 1958.
21. Alker and Russett 1965, vii.
22. March 1955.
23. On objectivity, see Alker and Russett 1965, 2–3; on availability of data see p. 19.
24. See Riggs 1958; Hovet 1958; Keohane 1967, 1969; Weigert and Riggs 1969; Gareau 1970; Alker 1970; Volgy 1973; and Harbert 1976.
25. See Volgy and Quistgard 1974; and Singer and Sensenig 1963.
26. See, for example, Rieselbach 1960.
27. For two systematic reviews of the quantitative research on the UN and international organizations, see Riggs et al. 1970; and Alger 1970.
28. Cox and Jacobson 1973.
29. Ibid.

The work of Cox and Jacobson also encouraged the study of international organizations to consider a more transgovernmental model of their influences. Whereas other research inspired by behavioralism typically assumed a unified model of state interests and actors, this work focused on transgovernmental coalitions involving parts of governments and parts of international organizations. One of the most important insights generated was highly consonant with developments in transgovernmental relations that had come on the intellectual scene in the 1970s:[30] the observation that one channel through which international organizations could affect state policies was through the potential alliances that could form between international bureaucracies and domestic pressure groups at the national level.[31] Although this was an interesting insight, and case studies tended to confirm the importance of such "transnational coalitions" for policy implementation, their effect on policy formulation remains unclear.[32] Meanwhile, the issues facing the international community changed drastically in the early 1970s, giving rise to a new approach to the study of international institutions, discussed in the following section.

Finally, a strand of research stimulated by Ernst Haas's "neofunctional approach" to integration also left a telling mark on the study of empirical effects of international institutions in the 1970s. Neofunctionalism ascribed a dynamic role to individuals and interest groups in the process of integrating pluralist communities.[33] By virtue of their participation in the policymaking process of an integrating community, interest groups and other participants were hypothesized to "learn" about the rewards of such involvement and undergo attitudinal changes inclining them favorably toward the integrative system. According to Haas, "political integration is the process whereby actors shift their loyalties, expectations, and political activities toward a new center, whose institutions possess or demand jurisdiction over preexisting national states."[34] The implications for empirical research on such institutions were readily drawn: those who participate in international organizations should exhibit altered attitudes toward their usefulness and effectiveness.

American politics provided yet another methodological instrument that dovetailed nicely with what was thought to be an empirically testable proposition of Haas's theory: survey research! From the late 1950s into the early 1980s, a plethora of studies tried to establish whether international organizations could contribute to "learning," whether cognitive or affective.[35] The attitudes of civil servants,[36] political appointees, and even national legislators[37] were scrutinized for evidence that the length or nature of their association with various kinds of international organizations had induced attitudinal change. The impact of methods from American politics was obvi-

---

30. Keohane and Nye 1974.
31. See Cox 1969, 225; and Cox and Jacobson 1973, 214.
32. See, for example, Russell 1973; and Keohane 1978.
33. See Haas 1958; and Pentland 1973.
34. Haas 1958, 10.
35. See Kelman 1962; Alger 1965; and Jacobson 1967. See also Wolf 1974, 352–53; and Volgy and Quistgard 1975.
36. See Ernst 1978; and Peck 1979.
37. See Bonham 1970; Kerr 1973; Riggs 1977; and Karns 1977.

ous: in some cases, indicators were used that precisely paralleled the "thermometers" used by the National Opinion Survey Research project.

Three problems bedeviled this research approach for years. First, it failed to produce consensus on the effect of international institutions on attitudes.[38] Second, attitudes were never reconnected with outcomes, policies, or actions.[39] Third, researchers were never able to overcome the problem of recruitment bias, which itself accounted for most of the positive attitudes held by personnel associated with international institutions. As neofunctionalism as a theoretical orientation lost favor over the course of the 1970s and integrative international organizations such as the European Community and the UN seemed to stagnate in the face of growing world problems beyond their purview, this research program declined, though today a version is pursued primarily in studies that attempt to document mass attitudes toward the European Union.

Politics Beyond Formal Organizations:
The Rise of International Regimes

As the study of international institutions progressed over the post–World War II years, the gulf between international politics and formal organization arrangements began to open in ways that were not easy to reconcile. The major international conflict for a rising generation of scholars—the Vietnam War—raged beyond the formal declarations of the UN. Two decades of predictable monetary relations under the Bretton Woods institutions were shattered by a unilateral decision by the United States in 1971 to close the gold window and later to float the dollar. The rise of the Organization of Petroleum Exporting Countries and their apparent power to upset previously understood arrangements with respect to oil pricing and availability took place outside the structure of traditional international organizations, as did consumers' response later in the decade. For some, the proper normative response seemed to be to strengthen international organizations to deal with rising problems of interdependence.[40] Others more familiar with the public choice literature argued that a proper extension of property rights, largely underway in areas such as environmental protection, rather than a formal extension of supranational authority per se, was the answer to solving problems of collective action.[41] Overall, few doubted that international life was "organized," but, increasingly, it became apparent that much of the earlier focus

---

38. Studies that failed to confirm expectations of attitudinal change include Siverson 1973; and Bonham 1970. A few studies even found negative impacts on attitudes due to association with international organizations: Smith 1973; and Pendergast 1976.

39. To the extent that such associations affected outcomes, the results were generally innocuous. See, for example, Mathiason 1972.

40. Brown and Fabian, for example, modestly call for "a comprehensive ocean authority, an outer space projects agency, a global weather and climate organization, and an international scientific commission on global resources and technologies." See Brown and Fabian 1975. See also Ruggie 1972, 890, 891; and Gosovic and Ruggie 1976.

41. Conybeare 1980.

on formal structures and multilateral treaty-based agreements, especially the UN, had been overdrawn.[42]

The events of the early 1970s gave rise to the study of "international regimes," defined as rules, norms, principles, and procedures that focus expectations regarding international behavior. Clearly, the regimes movement represented an effort to substitute an understanding of international organization with an understanding of international governance more broadly.[43] It also demoted the study of international organizations as actors: prior to the study of international regimes an inquiry into the effects of international institutions meant inquiring into how effectively a particular agency performed its job, for example, the efficiency with which the World Health Organization vaccinated the world's needy children.[44] When regimes analysts looked for effects, these were understood to be outcomes influenced by a constellation of rules rather than tasks performed by a collective international agency.

But just what effects regimes analysis sought to uncover has changed as the research program has unfolded.[45] A first collective effort by the scholarly community to address regime effects was primarily interested in the distributive consequences of the norms of the international food regime, arguing that it is important to consider the "ways in which the global food regime affects . . . wealth, power, autonomy, community, nutritional well-being, . . . and sometimes physical survival."[46] In this view, regime "effects" were to be reckoned in terms of the distributive consequences of the behavior of a myriad of producers, distributors, and consumers, and, in a minor way, by international organizations and state bureaucracies. Certainly, there was in this early volume little thought that regimes were somehow efficient or efficiency-improving outcomes, as later theorizing would imply; rather, the food regime was characterized by "broad and endemic inadequacies," which are the result of national policies that are "internationally bargained and coordinated . . . by multilateral agreement or unilateral dictate."[47]

Further research on international regimes moved thinking in three important directions. First, distributive consequences soon fell from the center of consideration as research began to focus on how international regimes are created and transformed in the first place as well as the behavioral consequences of norms or rules,[48] rather than the distributive consequences of behavior itself. (We argue later that attention to distributive issues ought to be restored.) Second, in one (though not dominant) strand

---

42. On skepticism regarding the centrality of the GATT regime, see Strange 1988. On the declining importance of "public international agencies" in general and the FAO in particular, see McLin 1979.

43. See, for example, Hopkins and Puchala 1978, especially 598.

44. Hoole 1977. The focus on international organizations as actors providing collective or redistributive goods has a long history. See Kindleberger 1951a; Ascher 1952; Wood 1952; Loveday 1953; Sharp 1953; and Gregg 1966.

45. We focus here on effects of international regimes because, as argued later, we think this is the question on which future research should concentrate. For a review of theories that purport to explain international regimes, see Haggard and Simmons 1987.

46. Hopkins and Puchala 1978, 598.

47. Ibid., 615–16.

48. Krasner 1983b, introduction and conclusion.

of research, attention to the normative aspects of international regimes led naturally to consideration of the subjective meaning of such norms and to a research paradigm that was in sympathy with developments in constructivist schools of thought.[49] (See the essay by Martha Finnemore and Kathryn Sikkink in this issue of *IO*.)

Third, by the mid-1980s explanations of international regimes became intertwined with explanations of international cooperation more generally. The work of Robert Keohane especially drew from functionalist approaches that emphasized the efficiency reasons for rules and agreements among regime participants.[50] Based on rationality assumptions shared by a growing literature in political economy, this research sought to show that international institutions provided a way for states to overcome problems of collective action, high transaction costs, and information deficits or asymmetries. This approach has produced a number of insights, which we will discuss and extend later. But its analytical bite—derived from its focus on states as unified rational actors—was purchased at the expense of earlier insights relating to transnational coalitions and, especially, domestic politics. Furthermore, the strength of this approach has largely been its ability to explain the creation and maintenance of international institutions. It has been weaker in delineating their effects on state behavior and other significant outcomes, an issue to which we will return.

This weakness opened the way for an important realist counterthrust in the late 1980s: the challenge to show that international institutions affect state behavior in any significant way. Some realists, particularly neorealists, raised logical and empirical objections to the institutionalist research agenda. On the logical side, Joseph Grieco[51] and John Mearsheimer argued that relative-gains concerns prevent states from intensive cooperation. The essence of their argument was that since the benefits of cooperation could be translated into military advantages, states would be fearful that such benefits would disproportionately flow to potential adversaries and therefore would be reluctant to cooperate in substantial, sustained ways. Responses by Duncan Snidal and Robert Powell showed that, even if states did put substantial weight on such relative-gains concerns, the circumstances under which they would greatly inhibit cooperation were quite limited. Mearsheimer, in his extensive challenge to institutionalism, also argued that the empirical evidence showing that institutions changed patterns of state behavior was weak, especially in the area of security affairs. While we might dispute the extreme conclusions drawn by Mearsheimer, we take seriously his challenge to provide stronger empirical evidence. In the third section of this article we suggest lines of institutionalist analysis that should lend themselves to rigorous empirical testing, avoiding some of the inferential traps and fallacies that Mearsheimer and other realists have identified.[52]

49. See Haas 1983; and Ruggie 1972.
50. Keohane 1984.
51. See Grieco 1988; and Mearsheimer 1994.
52. See Snidal 1991; and Powell 1991. See also Baldwin 1993.

Institutions Across the Level-of-Analysis Divide:
Insights from Domestic Politics

Early studies of international institutions were often motivated by the attempt to apply new methods used in the study of domestic politics. As just reviewed, studies of voting behavior in the General Assembly, electoral success in the UN governing structure, and surveys regarding attitudinal change as a result of international organization experience are all prime examples. Similar studies continue today, for example, in calculations of power indexes for member states of the European Union.[53] These approaches have not, however, been widely influential recently and have been subject to trenchant criticisms.[54] In spite of this less-than-promising experience, scholars today are turning once again to models of domestic politics to suggest new questions and approaches to the study of international institutions. In this section, we briefly consider whether these new approaches are more likely to bear fruit.

We find reasons to be relatively optimistic about today's attempts to transport models across levels of analysis, as long as such attempts are undertaken with some caution. In particular, we see substantial potential in looking at theories of domestic institutions that are rooted in noncooperative game theory. Rationalist theories of institutions that fall into the category of the "new institutionalism" have applicability at both the domestic and international levels. Virtually all the early attempts to apply techniques and research strategies from domestic politics to the international level were implicitly based on the assumption that agreements among actors are enforceable. Indeed, this was the *only* assumption under which it made sense to look at the politics that underlay voting and decision making in international institutions at all. Models that assume that agreements will be enforced by a neutral third party are especially inappropriate for the international setting; calculating voting power in the General Assembly in a world of unenforceable agreements may have more than a passing resemblance to arranging deck chairs on the Titanic. Thus, it is not surprising that these models have not had great influence when transported to the international level.

However, recent models of domestic institutions as a rule draw, often explicitly, on noncooperative game theory. The basic assumptions of noncooperative game theory are that actors are rational, strategic, and opportunistic, and that no outside actor will step in to enforce agreements. Therefore, agreements that will make a difference must be self-enforcing. These conditions are remarkably similar to the usual characterization of international politics as a situation of anarchy and self-help.[55] As long as models use the same basic assumptions about the nature of actors and their environment, the potential for learning across the level-of-analysis divide could be enormous.

53. Hosli 1993.
54. Garrett and Tsebelis 1996.
55. Waltz 1979.

As one example, consider what international relations scholars might learn from looking at current debates on the nature of legislative institutions.[56] Analogously to how realist theory portrays states with a mixture of common and conflicting interests but without supranational enforcement, these models treat legislators as self-interested, individualistic actors in a situation where they must cooperate with one another to achieve mutual benefits.[57] They ask how legislators under these conditions might construct institutions—such as committees or parties—that will allow them to reach goals such as reelection.[58] Similarly, international relations scholars are interested in how states or other entities design institutional forms (organizations, procedures, informal cooperative arrangements, treaty arrangements) that assist in the realization of their objectives. The point is *not*, as much of the earlier literature assumed, that "legislative activity" at the international level is interesting per se. The power of the analogy rests solely on how actors choose strategies to cope with similar strategic environments. In general, we suggest that more progress can be made by drawing out the aspects of domestic politics that are characterized by attempts to cooperate by actors with mixed motives, who cannot turn easily to external enforcement, and applying them selectively to the study of international relations.

The debate about legislative organization, which we argue may provide insights into international institutions more generally, has been roughly organized into a contrast between informational and distributional models. Informational models concentrate on the ways in which legislative structures allow legislators to learn about the policies they are adopting, thus avoiding inefficient outcomes.[59] Researchers have argued that properly structured legislative committees can efficiently signal information about the effects of proposed policies to the floor, and that informational concerns can explain both the pattern of appointment of legislators to committees and the decision making rules under which committees operate. All of these claims have stimulated intense empirical investigation, which has been challenged by the distributional perspective discussed later. Informational models can be used to extend and clarify arguments in the international literature that stress the role of institutions in the provision of information, as Keohane has argued, and in the learning process, as Ernst and Peter Haas have emphasized. They can lead to predictions about the conditions under which international institutions can effectively provide policy-relevant information to states, about the kinds of institutions that can provide credible information, and about the effects of such information provision on patterns of state behavior. An example of an issue area where these effects might be prominent is environ-

---

56. The work on legislative institutions is just one example of the application of noncooperative game theory to domestic institutions. But since it is a particularly well-developed literature, we concentrate on it here, without wishing to imply that this is the only branch of research on domestic institutions that may have interesting analogies to international institutions.

57. Shepsle and Weingast 1995.

58. Although much of the work on legislative organization concentrates on the American context, in recent years creative efforts have been made to develop such models in non-U.S. settings. See Huber 1996b; Tsebelis and Money 1995; Ramseyer and Rosenbluth 1993; G. Cox 1987; and Shugart and Carey 1992.

59. See Gilligan and Krehbiel 1990; and Krehbiel 1991.

mental institutions, where it is highly likely that the ability of organizations to provide reliable, credible information about the effects of human activities on the environment is a key factor in explaining the success or failure of negotiations on environmental treaties. Another possible application might be the creation of international financial institutions, such as the Bank for International Settlements, an original function of which was to provide credible information to markets on German creditworthiness.[60] Within the European Union, the Commission's role as a relatively independent collector of policy-relevant information is a plausible explanation for its ability to exercise considerable influence over policy outcomes.[61]

Distributional models, on the other hand, assume that information is not all that problematic. Instead, they concentrate on the fact that legislators are heterogeneous in their tastes, caring differentially about various issues.[62] Achieving mutual gains, in this framework, means cutting deals that will stick across different issues. Since exchanges of votes cannot always be simultaneous, legislators have developed structures such as committees and agenda-setting rules that allow them to put together majorities on the issues of most intense particularistic interest to them. This structure provides predictions about the distribution of benefits to individual legislators. Distributional benefits flow through appointment to powerful legislative committees. Like researchers in the informational tradition, those in the distributional tradition have used such models to explain and predict various aspects of legislative organization. For example, they argue that committees will be composed of preference outliers—those legislators who care most intensely about particular issues—and that such committees will be granted agenda-setting power, which is necessary to keep cross-issue deals from unraveling on the floor. Distributional models may be especially useful in exploring in a rigorous fashion the role of international institutions in facilitating or hampering mutually beneficial issue linkages that have been an important research agenda in international relations.[63]

The debate between informational and distributional models of legislative organization has been highly productive, in both theoretical and empirical terms. It has provided new insights into the types of problems confronted by legislators, the types of solutions available to them, and the role of institutions in democracies. On the empirical side, it has generated a plethora of alternative observable implications, for example, about the composition of congressional committees or the conditions under which actors gain gatekeeping or amendment power. Empirical research on both sides has led to deep insights about how the structure of institutions, such as legislative committees, influences their ability to help individuals overcome collective-action problems, and the conditions under which individuals will be willing to delegate substantial decision-making authority to such institutions. Both types of questions are highly relevant and essential to an understanding of the role of institutions in international politics as well. For example, the informational model suggests

---

60. Simmons 1993.
61. See Haas 1989; and Bernauer 1995.
62. Weingast and Marshall 1988.
63. On issue linkage, see Stein 1980; and Martin 1992c.

that institutions should be most influential in promoting cooperation when they are relatively independent, "expert" sources of information and when such information is scarce and valuable to states. We should expect this model to be most useful in international issue areas characterized by information asymmetries or in the development of expert knowledge (such as financial and banking regulation). The distributional model predicts that institutions will be most successful in allowing for credible cross-issue deals between states when those with the most intense interest in any particular issue dominate policymaking on that dimension and when institutional mechanisms inhibit states from reneging on cross-issue deals, even if performance on different dimensions is not simultaneous. Institutions that try to cope with environmental protection and development needs in the same package (such as UNCED and the Agenda 21 program) provide a plausible example. For our interests, another striking analogy between the international arena and the legislative literature is the degree to which the terms of the debate—information versus distribution—reflect the emerging debate about the significance of international institutions.

In many essential respects the problems faced by individual legislators mirror those faced by individual states in the international system. Individual actors face situations in which they must cooperate in order to achieve benefits but also face temptations to defect from cooperative arrangements. No external authority exists to enforce cooperative agreements; they must be self-enforcing. Self-enforcement takes the form of exclusion from the benefits of cooperation, a coercive measure. Given these analogies, there is every reason to expect that some of the methods, insights, and results of these new studies of legislators could usefully inform new studies of international institutions, *in spite of the fact that legislators (usually) operate in a more densely institutionalized environment.*[64] More generally, rationalist models of institutions that have been developed in domestic settings have the potential to be translated to the international level. As long as we are considering mixed-motive situations in which actors must cooperate in order to pursue their objectives, the incentives to construct institutions to structure and encourage cooperation are similar.

How Institutions Matter

Since the 1980s, work on international institutions has been defined for the most part by the demand that scholars respond to a realist agenda: to prove that institutions have a significant effect on state behavior. While structuring the debate in this manner may have stimulated direct theoretical confrontation, it has also obscured some important and tractable research paths. Allowing realism to set the research agenda has meant that models of international institutions have rarely taken domestic poli-

---

64. One could make a similar argument about domestic theories of delegation. See Epstein and O'Halloran 1997; Lohmann and O'Halloran 1994; and Lupia and McCubbins 1994. The analogy between politicians deciding to delegate authority to bureaucrats or committees and states delegating authority to international institutions is strong.

tics seriously, treating the state as a unit. The debate has also been reduced to a dichotomy: either institutions matter or they do not. Insufficient attention has been given to the mechanisms through which we might expect institutional effects to work. Institutionalists, in response to realism, have treated institutions largely as independent variables, while playing down earlier insights that international institutions are themselves the objects of strategic state choice. Treating institutions as dependent variables has mistakenly been understood as an implicit admission that they are epiphenomenal, with no independent effect on patterns of behavior.[65]

Although it has been important to go beyond merely explaining the existence of international institutions, productive new lines of research emerge if we accept that institutions are *simultaneously causes and effects*; that is, institutions are both the objects of state choice and consequential. In a rationalist, equilibrium framework, this statement is obvious and unexceptionable: states choose and design institutions. States do so because they face certain problems that can be resolved through institutional mechanisms. They choose institutions because of their intended effects. Once constructed, institutions will constrain and shape behavior, even as they are constantly challenged and reformed by their member states. In this section, we outline a number of lines of research that show promise to take us beyond the "do they matter or don't they" structure of research on international institutions.

The following research agenda is firmly in the rationalist tradition. Although this approach allows for substantial variation in patterns of preferences over outcomes, and indeed provides predictions about outcomes based on exogenous change in such preferences, it provides relatively little explanatory leverage with respect to the sources of change in such preferences. A few words on how this agenda is related to the constructivist research program may be in order. To the degree that constructivist approaches prove powerful at making changes in actors' fundamental goals endogenous, providing refutable hypotheses about the conditions for such change, the constructivist and rationalist approaches will be complementary. Although rationalist approaches are generally powerful for explaining how policy preferences change when external constraints or information conditions change, alternative approaches, such as constructivism, are necessary for explaining more fundamental, internal changes in actors' goals. However, the rationalist research program has much to contribute even without strong theories about the reasons for change in actors' goals. One of the core insights of theories of strategic interaction is that, regardless of actors' specific preferences, they will tend to face generic types of cooperation problems over and over again. Many situations give rise to incentives to renege on deals or to behave in time-inconsistent ways that make actors happy in the short run but regretful in the long run. Likewise, many situations of strategic interaction give rise to benefits from cooperation, and conflicts over how to divide up this surplus will plague cooperative efforts. Thus, considerations of how to prevent cheating and how to resolve distributional conflict, to give two prominent examples, are central to theories of cooperation regardless of the specific goals of actors. Rationalist ap-

65. Mearsheimer 1994.

proaches are powerful because they suggest observable implications about patterns of cooperation in the face of such dilemmas, even absent the kind of precise information about preferences that scholars desire. It is to such dilemmas that we now turn our attention.

Collaboration Versus Coordination Problems

The most productive institutionalist research agenda thus far in international relations has been the rationalist–functionalist agenda, originating with Keohane's *After Hegemony* and Steve Krasner's edited volume on international regimes.[66] This work was informed by a fundamentally important insight, inspired by the metaphor of the Prisoners'Dilemma (PD). Individually rational action by states could impede mutually beneficial cooperation. Institutions would be effective to the degree that they allowed states to avoid short-term temptations to renege, thus realizing available mutual benefits.

Some authors, recognizing that PD was only one type of collective-action problem, drew a distinction between collaboration and coordination problems.[67] Collaboration problems, like PD, are characterized by individual incentives to defect and the existence of equilibria that are not Pareto optimal. Thus, the problem states face in this situation is finding ways to bind themselves and others in order to reach the Pareto frontier. In contrast, coordination games are characterized by the existence of multiple Pareto-optimal equilibria. The problem states face in this situation is not to avoid temptations to defect, but to choose among these equilibria. Such choice may be relatively simple and resolved by identification of a focal point, if the equilibria are not sharply differentiated from one another in terms of the distribution of benefits.[68] But some coordination games, like the paradigmatic Battle of the Sexes, involve multiple equilibria over which the actors have strongly divergent preferences. Initially, most authors argued that institutions would have little effect on patterns of state behavior in coordination games, predicting substantial institutional effects only in collaboration situations. Interestingly, these arguments led both to expectations about institutional effects on state behavior and to state incentives to delegate authority to institutions, consistent with the kind of equilibrium analysis we find most promising for future research.

As the logic of modern game theory has become more deeply integrated into international relations theory, and as authors have recognized the limitations of the collaboration–coordination distinction, we have begun to see work that integrates the efficiency concerns associated with collaboration and the distributional concerns associated with coordination. Krasner made a seminal contribution to this line of analysis.[69] He argued that when states are attempting to cooperate with one another, achieving efficiency gains—reaching the Pareto frontier—is only one of the challenges they

---

66. See Keohane 1984; and Krasner 1983b.
67. See Snidal 1985a; Stein 1983; and Martin 1992b.
68. Garrett and Weingast 1993.
69. Krasner 1991.

face and often not the most difficult one. Many equilibria may exist along the Pareto frontier, and specifying one of these as the locus of cooperation, through bargaining and the exercise of state power, dominates empirical examples of international cooperation. Krasner's insight is perfectly compatible with the folk theorems of noncooperative game theory that show that repeated play of a PD-type game gives rise to many—in fact, infinite—equilibria. Thus, repetition transforms collaboration problems into coordination problems. In most circumstances, states have simultaneously to worry about reaching efficient outcomes and resolving distributional conflict.

Once we recognize this fact, our approach to international institutions becomes both more complex and more closely related to traditional international relations concerns about power and bargaining. To be effective, institutions cannot merely resolve collaboration problems through monitoring and other informational functions. They must also provide a mechanism for resolving distributional conflict. For example, institutions may construct focal points, identifying one possible equilibrium as the default or "obvious" one, thus reducing state-to-state bargaining about the choice of a particular pattern of outcomes. The role of the European Court of Justice (ECJ), discussed elsewhere in this article, is captured in part by this type of constructed focal-point analysis. The Basle Banking Committee's role in devising international standards for prudential banking practices similarly helped to coordinate national regulations where a number of plausible solutions were available.[70] Where states fear that the benefits of cooperation are disproportionately flowing to others, institutions can provide reliable information about state behavior and the realized benefits of cooperation to allay such fears. Trade institutions perform many functions; one function that could stand more analytical scrutiny is the provision of such information about the distribution of benefits among members. Another way institutions could mitigate distributional conflict is to "keep account" of deals struck, compromises made, and gains achieved, particularly in complex multi-issue institutions. The networks created within the supranational institutions of the European Union, for example, provide the necessary scope for issue-linkage and institutional memory to perform the function of assuring that all members, over time, achieve a reasonably fair share of the benefits of cooperation.[71] Unless the problem of equilibrium selection is resolved, all the third-party monitoring in the world will not allow for stable international cooperation.

Thus, a promising line of research will involve bringing distributional issues back into the study of international institutions, issues that were in fact the focus of some of the early regimes literature discussed earlier. Institutions may interact with distributional conflict in a number of ways. Most simply, they reflect and solidify settlements of distributional conflict that have been established through more traditional means. These means include the exercise of state power, which Krasner emphasizes, market dominance, and alternative methods of bargaining such as making trades across issues.[72] In this perspective, institutions can make a difference if they lock in a

70. Simmons 1998.
71. Pollack 1997.
72. Fearon 1994a.

particular equilibrium, providing stability. But rather than merely reflecting power in an epiphenomenal fashion, as realists would have it, institutions in this formulation prevent potential challengers from undermining existing patterns of cooperation, explaining why powerful states may choose to institutionalize these patterns rather than relying solely on ad hoc cooperation.

Institutions may also serve a less controversial signaling function, therefore minimizing bargaining costs. This would be the case if institutions construct focal points or if they primarily keep account of the pattern of benefits over time, as discussed earlier. In either case, they effectively increase path dependence. Once a particular equilibrium is chosen, institutions lock it in. Researching the ways in which institutions do this—how do they enhance path dependence, and under what conditions?—would be intriguing. Normative questions also rise to the top of the agenda once we recognize the lock-in role of institutions. If they do in fact solidify a pattern of cooperation preferred by the most powerful, we should question the ethical status of institutions, turning our attention to equity, as well as efficiency, questions.

In the most traditional, state-centric terms, institutions reflect and enhance state power; in Tony Evans and Peter Wilson's words, they are "arenas for acting out power relations."[73] On the other end of the spectrum, we may want to ask about situations in which institutions play a more active role in resolving distributional conflict. Perhaps institutions sometimes do more than lock in equilibria chosen through the exercise of state power, having an independent part in the selection of equilibria. Such an argument has been made most clearly in the case of the ECJ. Here, Geoffrey Garrett and Barry R. Weingast find that there are a number of ways in which the European Community could have realized its goal of completing the internal market.[74] The ECJ made a big difference in the course of European integration because it was able to construct a focal point by choosing one of these mechanisms, that of mutual recognition. This choice had clear distributional implications but was accepted by member states because it was a Pareto improvement over the reversion point of failing to complete the internal market. A distinct research tradition emphasizes the legitimizing role that international institutions can play in focal-point selection. Some scholars point out that institutionally and legally enshrined focal points can gain a high degree of legitimacy both internationally and domestically.[75] This legitimacy, in turn, has important political consequences.[76]

To develop a research agenda on how institutions resolve problems of multiple equilibria and distribution, we would have to build on these insights to ask conditional questions. When are states, particularly the powerful, willing to turn the problem of equilibrium selection over to an institution? What kinds of institutions are most likely to perform this function effectively—those that are strategic or those that

---

73. Evans and Wilson 1992.

74. Garrett and Weingast 1993. They also argue that the multiple equilibria were not sharply distinguished from one another in terms of efficiency and do not concentrate on distributional conflict among equilibria. They have been criticized on these points. See Burley and Mattli 1993.

75. See Franck 1990; and Peck 1996, 237.

76. Claude 1966, 367.

are naive; those that rely on political decision making or those that rely heavily on relatively independent experts and/or judicial processes; those that broadly reflect the membership of the institution or those that are dominated by the powerful? Under what conditions are constructed focal points likely to gain international recognition and acceptance? Overall, bringing the traditional international relations focus on distributional conflict back into the study of international institutions holds the potential for generating researchable questions that are both positive and normative in nature.

International Institutions and Domestic Politics

In allowing their agenda to be defined by responding to the realist challenge, institutionalists have generally neglected the role of domestic politics. States have been treated as rational unitary actors and assigned preferences and beliefs. This framework has been productive in allowing us to outline the broad ways in which institutions can change patterns of behavior. But in privileging the state as an actor, we have neglected the ways in which other actors in international politics might use institutions (a central insight of earlier studies of transgovernmental organization) and the ways in which the nature or interests of the state itself are potentially changed by the actions of institutions (an implication of the early neofunctionalist literature). Here we outline a few lines of analysis that should be fruitful for integrating domestic politics and international institutions in a systematic manner, rather than treating domestic politics as a residual category of explanation. Because the lines of analysis here have foundations in specific analytical frameworks with explicit assumptions, applying them to the problem of international institutions should result in productive research paths, rather than merely the proliferation of possible "explanatory variables" that has characterized many attempts to integrate domestic politics and international relations. We should note that bringing domestic politics back into the study of international institutions is an agenda that should be understood as analytically distinct from that of applying institutionalist models developed in the domestic setting to the international level, an agenda addressed elsewhere in this article.

As we will argue, one of the more fundamental ways in which international institutions can change state behavior is by substituting for domestic practices. If policies formerly made by domestic institutions are now made on the international level, it is reasonable to expect substantial changes in the patterns of world politics. Three related questions are central to understanding the relations between domestic and international institutions. First, under what conditions might domestic actors be willing to substitute international for domestic institutions? Second, are particular domestic actors regularly advantaged by the ability to transfer policymaking authority to the international level? Third, to what extent can international institutional decisions and rules be enforced by domestic institutions, and what are the implications for compliance? These questions are tied together by the assumption that domestic actors intentionally delegate policymaking authority to the international level when this action furthers pursuit of their interests.

Domestic institutions can at times be a barrier to the realization of benefits for society as a whole. Failures of domestic institutions can arise through a number of mechanisms. Perhaps most obviously, domestic institutions can be captured by preference outliers who hold policy hostage to their demands. Recent research suggests that this may be the case with respect to the settlement of territorial disputes between bordering states in some regions: repeated failure to ratify border agreements in the legislature is one of the most important domestic political conditions associated with the willingness of states to submit their disputes to international arbitration.[77] More generally, this situation is likely to arise when some actors, such as those looking for particularistic benefits, find it easier to organize than do actors more concerned with the welfare of the average citizen. Such is the story often told about trade policy. Import-competing producers and others with an interest in protectionist policies may find it easier to organize than those who favor free trade, a coalition of exporters and consumers. This differential ability to organize will bias policy in favor of protection, decreasing overall welfare. Transferring the policymaking process to the international level, where exporters can see that they have a stake in organization in order to gain the opening of foreign markets, can facilitate a more evenhanded representation of interests. Those actors who have the most to gain from pursuit of general welfare— such as executives elected by a national constituency—will show the most interest in turning to international institutions under such circumstances. Judith Goldstein provides an analysis along these lines when she explains the paradox of the U.S. president agreeing to bilateral dispute-resolution panels in the U.S.–Canada Free Trade Act (FTA), in spite of the fact that these panels predictably decide cases in a way that tends to deny protection to U.S. producers.[78]

We can identify other incentives for domestic actors to transfer policymaking to the international level. One common problem with institutions that are under the control of political actors is that of time-inconsistent preferences. Although running an unexpectedly high level of inflation today may bring immediate benefits to politicians up for reelection, for example, allowing monetary policy to be made by politicians will introduce a welfare-decreasing inflationary bias to the economy. Putting additional constraints on policy, for example, by joining a system of fixed exchange rates or a common currency area, can provide a mechanism to overcome this time-inconsistency problem, as argued by proponents of a single European currency. In general, if pursuit of gains over time involves short-term sacrifices, turning to international institutions can be an attractive option for domestic policymakers.

A second and related question about domestic politics is whether particular kinds of actors will regularly see an advantage in turning to the international level. At the simplest level, it seems likely that "internationalist" actors—those heavily engaged in international transactions,[79] those who share the norms of international society,[80]

---

77. Simmons 1998.
78. See Goldstein 1996; and Gilligan 1997.
79. Frieden 1991.
80. Sikkink 1993a.

or those who have a stake in a transnational or global resource[81] —will have an interest in turning to the international level. This may especially be the case when such groups or parties are consistently in a minority position in domestic politics. Drawing on these ideas, we could begin to develop hypotheses about the kinds of domestic interest groups that will most favor transferring some authority to the international level.

Certain domestic institutional actors may also have a tendency to benefit from international-level policymaking. One such actor, which is just beginning to enter political scientists'analysis of international institutions, is the judiciary. Increasingly, international agreements are legal in form. This means that they often are interpreted by domestic courts, and that judges can use international law as a basis on which to make judgments.[82] Because international law provides this particular actor with an additional resource by which to pursue agendas, whether bureaucratic or ideological, we might expect that the judiciary in general tends to be sympathetic to international institutions.

Overall, as we work toward more sophisticated specification of the causal mechanisms through which institutions can influence behavior, we will have to pay much more attention to domestic politics than studies of international institutions have thus far. The development of general theories of domestic politics provides an opening for systematic development of propositions about domestic actors. We no longer need to treat the domestic level as merely the source of state preferences, nor as a residual category to explain anomalies or patterns of variation that cannot be explained by international factors. Instead, we can move toward genuinely interactive theories of domestic politics and international institutions, specifying the conditions under which certain actors are likely to prefer that policy be made on the international level. This focus allows us to specify conditions likely to lead to the delegation of policymaking authority to the international level, some of which we have outlined here.

Unanticipated Consequences

In a rationalist framework, institutions are both the object of state choice and consequential. The link that ties these two aspects of institutions together, and allows the analyst to develop refutable propositions about institutions within an equilibrium framework, is the ability of actors to anticipate the consequences of particular types of institutions. For example, in the preceding discussion of domestic politics, we assumed consistently that domestic actors were able to gauge with some degree of accuracy the ways in which working within international institutions would affect their ability to pursue their material or ideational goals.

The rationalist approach stands in distinction to a historical or sociological approach to institutions.[83] These approaches see institutions as more deeply rooted and

---

81. Young 1979.
82. See Alter 1996; and Conforti 1993.
83. See Steinmo, Thelen, and Longstreth 1992; and Pierson 1996b. Historical institutionalism stresses the path-dependent nature of institutions, explaining why apparently inefficient institutions persist. Socio-

draw attention to their unanticipated consequences. Although we may question whether many international institutions reach the same degree of "taken-for-grantedness" that we see in domestic politics or smaller-scale social relations, it seems undeniable that they sometimes have effects that surprise their member states. It is important to differentiate between unintended and unanticipated effects. Effects may be anticipated but unintended. For example, it is generally expected that arrangements to lower the rate of inflation will lead to somewhat higher levels of unemployment. Thus, higher unemployment is an anticipated, although unintended, consequence of stringent monetary policies. It is best understood as a price actors are sometimes willing to bear to gain the benefits of low inflation. Such unintended but anticipated consequences of institutions present little challenge to a rationalist approach, since they fit neatly into a typical cost-benefit analysis. Genuinely unanticipated effects, however, present a larger challenge.

Specific examples of apparently unanticipated consequences of international institutions are not difficult to find. States that believed that human-rights accords were nothing but meaningless scraps of paper found themselves surprised by the ability of transnational actors to use these commitments to force governments to change their policies.[84] In the European Community, few anticipated that the ECJ would have the widespread influence on policy that it has.[85] Prime Minister Margaret Thatcher was apparently quite surprised at the results of agreeing to change voting rules within the European Community, such as the adoption of qualified-majority voting, which she accepted in the Single European Act.[86]

How might a rationalist approach deal with these events? One productive approach might be to attempt to specify the conditions under which unanticipated consequences are most likely. This specification would at least allow us to suggest when a simple rationalist model will provide substantial explanatory leverage and when it might become necessary to integrate the insights of other schools of thought. If unanticipated consequences dominate political outcomes, we would have to draw on alternatives to rationalist models in a way that goes far beyond using them as a way to specify preferences and goals. Here, we begin specifying when unanticipated consequences are most likely to confound patterns of international cooperation.

Inductively, it appears that changes in secondary rules—that is, rules about rules—are the changes most likely to work in unexpected ways. Changes in voting rules within an institution, for example, can give rise to new coalitions and previously suppressed expressions of interest, leading to unpredicted policy outcomes. Changes in decision-making procedures can have even more widespread and unexpected effects if they open the policy process to input from new actors. Many examples of unanticipated consequences arise from decision-making procedures that provide access to nongovernmental and transnational actors, as, for example, Kathryn Sik-

---

logical institutionalism emphasizes the social nature of institutions, stressing their role in defining individuals' identities and the fact that many important institutions come to be taken for granted and therefore not seen as susceptible to reform.

84. Sikkink 1993a.
85. Burley and Mattli 1993.
86. Moravcsik 1991.

kink's work has shown.[87] Both as sources of new information and as strategic actors in their own right, such groups are often able to use new points of access to gain unexpected leverage over policy. Changes in decision-making rules will have wide-spread effects on a variety of substantive rules and are thus more likely to have unanticipated effects on outcomes than changes in substantive rules themselves. If this observation is correct, we should see more unanticipated consequences in situations that have relatively complex and permutable secondary rules, such as legalized institutions. Traditional state-to-state bargaining with a unit veto, which has little secondary rule structure, should provide less opportunity for nonstate actors or coalitions of the weak to influence outcomes unexpectedly.

One question that often arises, especially in the international arena, is why governments are willing to live with unanticipated outcomes. After all, participation in international institutions is voluntary. If unpleasant and unexpected outcomes frequently occur, states as sovereign actors retain the right to pull out of institutions. Why might they choose to remain in? The trivial answer is that the benefits of remaining in are greater than the costs. But we can turn this answer into something nontrivial by thinking about the conditions when institutional membership is likely to provide the greatest benefits. Some of these have been spelled out in functionalist theory. Keohane argues that the demand for international institutions will be greatest under conditions of interdependence, when states face a dense network of relations with one another and where information is somewhat scarce.[88] We could generalize that states are least likely to be willing to withdraw from an institution in the face of unanticipated consequences when they are dealing with issues that exhibit increasing returns to scale, which, in turn, create conditions of path dependence. Consider the creation of regional trading arrangements in the 1990s. These arrangements provide their members with economic benefits, and those on the outside of the arrangements find themselves losing investment and trading opportunities. We therefore see eastern European, Caribbean, and other states clamoring to become members of the relevant regional trading arrangements. This is a good example of how increasing returns to scale create a high demand for institutional membership. Under these conditions, it seems likely that these states will be willing to put up with a high level of unexpected outcomes before they would seriously consider withdrawing from an institution. However, this example begs the question of whether trade agreements are likely to have substantial unanticipated effects. They are only likely to do so in the case of rapid technological change or large international economic shocks, such as the oil shocks of the 1970s.

Typology of Institutional Effects

As we turn our attention to the problem of how, not just whether, international institutions matter, it becomes essential to understand alternative mechanisms through which institutions might exert their effects. To prod our thinking in this direction, we

---

87. Sikkink 1993a.
88. Keohane 1983a.

introduce a preliminary typology of institutional effects. The reasoning behind this typology is that different institutions, or perhaps similar institutions in different settings, will have different types of effects. Specifying these effects will not only allow us to develop better insights into the causal mechanisms underlying the interaction between institutions and states or societies. It will also provide for more testable propositions about how and when we should expect institutions to exert substantial effects on behavior.

The typology we suggest is analytically informed but aims first to provide a language for describing patterns of change in state behavior after creation of an international institution. Here we spell out the typology and present some illustrative examples. The next step will be to link the typology to causal processes, and we suggest some preliminary ideas along these lines. We begin by suggesting two types of institutional effects: *convergence* and *divergence* effects. Of course, the null hypothesis is that institutions have no effect. Development of a clearer analytical framework may force us to consider situations in which we combine effects: for example, perhaps some types of states are subject to convergence effects and others to divergence effects.

We begin with convergence effects, since the logic of most rationalist, economistic, and functionalist theories of international institutions leads us to expect such effects. These models posit goals that states find it difficult to achieve on their own, whether for reasons of time-inconsistent preferences, collective-action problems, old-fashioned domestic political stalemate, or other failures of unilateral state action. In this functionalist logic, states turn to international institutions to resolve such problems; institutions allow them to achieve benefits unavailable through unilateral action of existing state structures. Functionalist analysis sees international institutions as important because they help states to solve problems. Many of these problems have their roots in the failures of domestic institutions, and their resolution involves turning some types of authority over to the international level. Once policy is delegated to an international institution, state behavior will converge: members will tend to adopt similar monetary, trade, or defense policies.

What has been missing from functionalist accounts of institutionalization is the systematic connection between domestic political conditions and incentives to construct and comply with international institutions. But once we recognize that international institutions may make a difference because they effectively substitute for domestic practices (making policy decisions, setting policy goals, or undertaking monitoring activities), our attention turns to the domestic political conditions that make such substitution a reasonable policy alternative. If domestic institutions are the source of persistent policy failure, if they somehow prevent the realization of societal preferences, or if they interfere with the pursuit of mutual benefits with other states, turning functions over to the international level can enhance national welfare.[89] Monetary policy is a prime example of this logic. Other examples might

---

89. Some would argue that this process is antidemocratic. See Vaubel 1986. However, such an argument rests on weak foundations. First, it assumes that domestic institutions are necessarily responsive to

include trade policy, if domestic trade policy institutions are captured by protectionists; or environmental policy, if domestic institutions encourage a short-term rather than a long-term perspective on the problem. Thinking about the logic of substitution requires much more attention to inefficient domestic politics than most functional theories have provided to date.

A classic example of international institutions acting as substitutes for domestic institutions and therefore having convergence effects lies in arguments about why high-inflation states such as Italy might choose to enter the European Monetary Union (EMU).[90] High inflation is a public bad, leading to lower overall welfare than low inflation. However, the short-term benefits to politicians from allowing spurts of unanticipated inflation make it difficult to achieve low rates of inflation unless institutions that set monetary policy are independent of political influence.[91] Thus, transferring authority to an institution that is relatively insulated from political influence, and that itself has a preference for low inflation, can provide overall welfare benefits for the country. This is the logic that leads a state like Italy to take the unusual step (for a relatively rich, developed country) of transferring a core aspect of sovereignty—control over the currency—to a European Central Bank.

Given this logic of delegation, states that become members of the EMU should see a convergence in their rates of inflation.[92] Although the debate rages among economists about whether the European Monetary System has in fact worked in this manner,[93] there is little doubt that one of the major motivations for monetary union is for high-inflation states to "import" low German rates of inflation, leading to similar inflation rates in all member states. If we looked at the variation in inflation rates prior to entry into monetary union (or into a monetary system more generally), and compared it to inflation rates after entry, we should see a decline in the level of variation.

Although monetary union is a prominent and intriguing example of convergence effects, we can imagine a similar dynamic in other issue areas as well. Environmental institutions should lead to convergence of environmental indicators, such as carbon dioxide emissions.[94] Human-rights institutions acting as substitutes should lead members to adopt increasingly similar human-rights practices. Even if full convergence does not occur, the major effect of an institution that is acting as a substitute will be to bring state practices more closely in line with one another.

A convergence effect could be measured and identified by decreased variation in relevant indicators of state practices, whether inflation rates, pollution, or human-

---

national preferences. For the kinds of reasons just discussed, such as time-inconsistent preferences, or institutional capture, this assumption is often false. Second, the argument assumes that international institutions are necessarily more difficult to monitor, constrain, and influence than domestic institutions. Although this may be a reasonable assumption for some kinds of societal actors and some states, it is not universally true.

90. For a contrasting argument on the logic of EMU, see Gruber 1996.
91. Rogoff 1985.
92. Fratianni and von Hagen 1992.
93. See Giavazzi and Giovannini 1989; and Weber 1991.
94. Levy 1993.

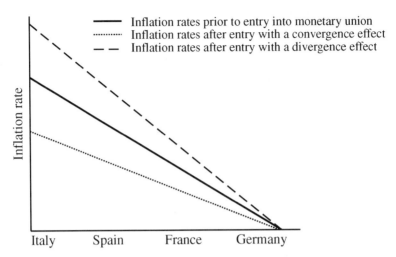

FIGURE 1. *International institutions with convergence or divergence effects*

rights abuses. The existence of a convergence effect could also be identified through graphical means. Figure 1 gives an example. On the *x*-axis, states are arrayed in order of their performance on the outcome dimension, say inflation rates. These rates are indicated on the *y*-axis. The solid line indicates inflation rates prior to entry into monetary union. Its steep slope indicates that the states exhibit substantial variation in inflation rates. The dotted line represents the outcome of monetary union acting as substitute, causing convergence in inflation rates. The more shallow slope indicates less variation than observed before entry into monetary union.

The notion that international institutions might substitute for domestic ones underlies functionalist theories of institutions. However, some empirical work on the effects of institutions has found a pattern quite different from the convergence of outcomes predicted by such a mechanism. Instead, some authors have found that the primary effect of institutions is to exaggerate preexisting patterns of behavior. For example, Andrew Moravcsik has found, in a regional comparison of human-rights institutions, that these institutions only led to an improvement in practices in those states that already exhibited a high level of respect for human rights.[95] Thus, West European states, through participation in institutions, have improved their already very good human-rights records, whereas Latin American states, according to his evidence, show little impact of institutional participation.

This pattern suggests that international institutions sometimes lead to divergence of state practices, in effect complementing and magnifying preexisting tendencies rather than overriding them. In this case, institutions will have a divergence effect. This effect results when states whose initial practice falls far from institutional guidelines will show little change from behavior, whereas those near the guidelines move

95. Moravcsik 1995.

even closer to them. In contrast, a convergence effect appears when institutions exert their greatest influence on precisely those states whose behavior deviates substantially from institutional norms. Divergence is likely to emerge when institutions exaggerate domestically generated tendencies of state behavior or when they primarily mimic domestic institutions. Anne-Marie Slaughter has argued something along these lines in pointing out that liberal states are the ones most likely to create and abide by relatively liberal international institutions.[96] According to this logic, liberal institutions will change the behavior of liberal states but not illiberal ones, leading to divergence of state behavior.

A divergence effect means that those states that already come close to institutional norms will move further toward them, whereas the behavior of those that deviate from such norms will remain unchanged. If we were to develop a measure of state behavior, we would see a divergence effect in increased variation of state behavior after institutional creation. We can also illustrate divergence effects graphically, as in Figure 1. Here, institutional effects result in a steeper line, indicating greater divergence in the relevant outcome variable. For ease of comparison, we continue to use the EMU-inflation example. Although such an outcome seems unlikely in practice, for the sake of argument we could imagine that monetary union that allowed for decentralized, unconstrained fiscal policymaking while providing additional resources to cover national debts could lead to such a perverse outcome. Another, perhaps more plausible, example of a divergence effect is in the area of overseas development aid. In the 1970s, OECD countries agreed to devote a set percentage of their GDP, 0.7 percent, to development assistance. Although some countries have come close to providing this level of aid and use the target figure as a tool in domestic debates, others have wholly neglected this target and instead decreased the percentage of their national income that they devote to foreign aid.

If this typology provides a useful way to describe alternative institutional effects, the next challenge is to begin to link up these patterns of behavior to alternative causal mechanisms. This project appears promising, and we outline preliminary ideas here. As suggested earlier, institutions that lead to convergence of state behavior link up nicely to the functionalist approach that has dominated studies of international institutions, regimes, and organizations over the last fifteen years. In this situation, the failure of domestic institutions or of unilateral state action creates incentives to rely on international mechanisms. The kinds of problems that would prompt states to use international institutions that lead to convergence of behavior are relatively well understood. They include time-inconsistency problems that create incentives for states to bind themselves and collective-action problems among states or within polities. When states turn to international institutions as the result of such problems, and when these institutions are operating as intended, we would expect to see convergence of state behavior.

The conditions that would prompt states to use institutions that lead to divergence of behavior are not as well understood. We can begin by noting that states facing

96. Slaughter 1995.

collective-action problems, such as a PD or a coordination game, would be unlikely to rely on an institution that exaggerated differences in state behavior. The fundamental problem in such cases is to create incentives for states to adopt similar policies: free trade, stringent fiscal policies, arms control, and so on.[97] In such a situation, an institution that led to increased divergence of state practice would quickly become irrelevant as states ignored its constraints. Thus, one initial expectation is that institutions should not lead to divergence in situations where incentives exist to adopt similar policies, as when strong externalities to divergent or unilateral state behavior exist. Perhaps this helps us understand why we appear to see some divergence effects in the human-rights issue area. Although human rights are a matter of concern around the globe, human-rights practices usually do not involve the kinds of externalities and incentives for strategic interaction that exist in issue areas such as the environment or monetary policy.[98]

However, lack of externalities does not provide a direct answer to why divergence would occur. To understand this effect, it is likely that we need to consider domestic politics, returning us to an argument made earlier in this article. International agreements, even those without enforcement mechanisms such as the OECD aid target, can provide "hooks" by which interest groups that favor the international agreement can increase their influence on the domestic agenda. For example, in Scandinavian countries the OECD target has become a potent arguing point in parliamentary debates. In states without a well-organized group to grab onto this hook, or in those with a more closed political process, agreements without enforcement mechanisms or substantial pressure from other states to comply are unlikely to have any effect. These contrasting domestic political dynamics are likely to give rise to divergence of state behavior among members of the institution.

A rationalist research agenda for the study of international institutions is rich and promising. This agenda begins by recognizing that, in equilibrium, institutions are both causes and effects, and that empirical researchers must begin to consider the question of how institutions matter, not just whether they do. Thinking in these terms turns our attention to the problem of how institutions might resolve bargaining and distributional conflict as well as the more recognized problems of cheating. It forces us to differentiate anticipated from unanticipated effects of institutions and to ask about the conditions under which unanticipated effects are most likely. Rationalist theories provide a mechanism for bringing domestic politics more systematically into the study of international institutions, an area of research that has been slighted by the development of the field thus far. Finally, a rationalist approach allows us to

---

97. There may be some coordination situations, for example, some discussed by Simmons, in which the solution to the coordination problem does not involve adoption of similar policies by all states but clear division of responsibilities among states. See Simmons 1994. The Bretton Woods systems, for example, coordinated state behavior by creating expectations that the United States would behave differently from other members of the system.

98. Donnelly surveys the landscape of human rights regimes. See Donnelly 1986. There may be exceptions to the generalization that international strategic interaction on human rights is minimal, for example, when severe human-rights abuses lead to massive refugee flows. This kind of logic could lead to testable propositions within the issue area, for example, that institutions should function differently when such externalities exist than under "normal" circumstances.

begin differentiating between different types of institutional effects and developing refutable propositions about the conditions under which we are most likely to observe such effects.

Conclusions

Studies of international institutions have varied in their theoretical sophistication and frequency over time but have remained a staple of international relations research and the pages of *IO* over the last fifty years. In this article we have examined the development of these studies and outlined some promising directions for future research on international institutions. Early studies of institutions were very much problem-driven, focusing on the problems of the postwar world that some hoped international organizations could solve. Although on balance realistic and insightful, the results of these studies failed to cumulate, likely due to the lack of a disciplinary or theoretical framework in which to situate the studies. A more scientific approach showed itself in a newer wave of work on institutions, drawing on methods and models of American politics. But because these models were in general poorly suited to the realities of international politics, they failed to generate substantial new insights. It was not until the 1980s, with the development of work on international regimes and functionalist theories, that a more progressive research program on institutions arose.

One failing of the current research program, however, has been its intense focus on proving that institutions matter, without sufficient attention to constructing well-delineated causal mechanisms or explaining variation in institutional effects. We consider two approaches that might move research beyond this impasse. First, we ask whether applying recent models of domestic politics might be more successful than have past attempts. We find scope for optimism here, since modern theories of domestic institutions typically draw on similar assumptions of unenforceable agreements and opportunistic behavior by individuals that characterize most work in international relations. Finally, we turn to some more specific research directions that are likely to give rise to important and testable propositions. These include more careful consideration of distributional issues, the role of domestic politics, unanticipated consequences, and a typology of institutional effects.

As we consider international institutions as both objects of strategic choice and consequential, allowing them to serve as both dependent and independent variables in our models, the potential for increasing our understanding of institutions and of international politics in general is substantial, as preliminary empirical work has begun to show. The earliest work on international institutions produced insights that failed to add up to much because of the lack of an analytical framework in which to situate these insights; the next generation of work had the benefit of such a framework, but one that was poorly suited to the task at hand. In this article, we hope to have identified lines of research that will combine the best of both worlds: theoretically grounded research on institutions that draws on assumptions that are appropriate for the persistent problems of international relations.

Rationalizing Politics: The Emerging Synthesis of International, American, and Comparative Politics

Helen V. Milner

> The distinction between international and domestic politics has become deeply embedded conceptually, pedagogically, and institutionally. . . . Blame is often placed on the lack of purposeful communication between specialists in international politics and specialists in comparative politics. In truth, many of us have imprisoned ourselves in conceptual jails of our own making where we remain incommunicado and deaf to the voices from next door.[1]

Introduction

International relations has often been treated as a separate discipline distinct from the other major fields in political science. A main reason for this distinction has been the claim that politics in the international system is radically different from politics domestically. Politics internationally has been seen frequently as sui generis. Both the type of actors and the role of institutions have been viewed as making international politics distinct from domestic politics. These substantive differences have, in the eyes of some, necessitated a distinct methodology for international relations as well.

This separation, and the reasons for it, have limited the field's ability to understand international relations even during the Cold War period, let alone since its passage. The central paradigms of the field of international relations (IR)—realism and neoliberal institutionalism—have ignored a key aspect of international relations: domestic politics. To understand the major issues in international politics, such as the likelihood of peace, the sources of conflict, and the possibility of cooperation among states, IR theorists must bring a systematic analysis of domestic politics into the field. The end of the Cold War would seem to drive home that merely assuming that

I would like to thank David Baldwin, Marc Busch, Peter Gourevitch, Robert Jervis, Peter Katzenstein, Robert Keohane, Steve Krasner, David Lake, Jack Snyder, and the participants in the seminar on international politics at the University of California at San Diego and Santa Barbara and Ohio State University for their helpful comments.
1. Hanrieder 1968, 482.

International Organization 52, 4, Autumn 1998, pp. 759–786

states—even superpowers—are stable, unitary actors is likely to be highly mislead-ing. Further, the spread of democratization—both its actual practice and claims for it—also seems to make an understanding of domestic politics a sine qua non for IR if it is to have either predictive ability or policy relevance. For example, if U.S.–Chinese relations become the fulcrum for world politics, assuming China (or the United States) is a unitary actor, focusing largely on their balance of military forces is likely to be insufficient. Greater understanding will arise from an analysis of both countries' domestic politics.

Attention only to their *interstate* relations may also be insufficient. For instance, although government-to-government contacts between the United States and China remain important, relations are also going to be affected by U.S. multinationals and other foreign investors, the International Monetary Fund, the UN, and human rights organizations. Governments are a central force in international politics, but exclusive attention to them risks overlooking the effects of international institutions on rela-tions among states. Can one, for instance, estimate the probability of war in Europe without discussing the role of the European Union (EU), NATO, or the UN? Integrat-ing IR with comparative and American politics holds out the possibility that the field will acquire a better understanding of both the domestic and international institutions that affect world politics. Although an interest in domestic and international institu-tions is not new, the particular form of this interest is: it involves closer attention to the strategic interaction among agents within these institutions.

The degree of divergence between IR and the rest of political science has waxed and waned over the years, but in the past decade it seems to have lessened. This process has occurred mainly in the "rationalist research paradigm," and there it has both substantive and methodological components. Scholars in this paradigm have increasingly appreciated that politics in the international realm is not so different from that internal to states, and vice versa. Anarchy within states threatens, whereas the institutionalization of international politics beckons. Moreover, scholars across the three fields now tend to employ the same methods, as several recent books make clear.[2] The move away from behavioralism in American and comparative politics has also coincided with changes in IR.

In addition, the last decade has seen increasing cross-fertilization of the fields around the importance of institutional analysis. Although a number of "new institu-tionalisms" exist, I focus on that developed within the rationalist framework follow-ing from the work on "structure-induced equilibria."[3] Such institutional analysis implies a particular concern with the mechanisms of collective choice in situations of strategic interaction. Institutions in this view are the means by which the diverse

---

2. See Morrow 1994a; and King, Keohane, and Verba 1994.

3. Shepsle 1979. This type of institutional analysis is different from the "new institutionalism" pio-neered by Coase 1937, 1960; Williamson 1985; and North 1981, 1990, which is more "the economics of institutions," Eggertsson 1996, 6. Institutions here are analyzed to see how they affect economic growth through attention to the problems of transaction costs and property rights. Some political scientists have followed in this tradition, but a central limitation has been the issue of efficiency in politics and political institutions.

preferences of individuals are aggregated into choices or outcomes for the collective. Institutions here both shape and reflect the strategic interaction among agents. Critical is the attention both to institutions and to strategic interaction among agents.

This rationalist institutionalist research agenda challenges two of the main assumptions in IR theory. A central assumption has been that states are unitary actors. Relaxing this assumption means bringing domestic politics back in. It implies moving away from using the state as the basic unit of analysis; instead, other domestic actors—such as the executive, the legislature, bureaucracies, political parties, and interest groups—become the primary units of analysis. These are the familiar actors from American and comparative politics, as well as from earlier foreign policy studies. Examining them gives IR scholars the ability to use the theories and tools of domestic politics to understand their complex, strategic interactions. Rationalist institutionalism can show how diverse domestic preferences are aggregated into collective choices (for example, foreign policy), given different political institutions. It provides a systematic way of showing how variations in preferences and in institutions affect policy choices. Domestic actors have been present in IR studies for many years, but the systematic analysis of domestic politics in IR has been less successful. Some of the new tools in American and comparative politics allow the complex, strategic interactions among domestic agents to be understood in a more systematic and cumulative way.

Relaxing another major assumption in IR theory is also part of this research agenda. That states are the most important, if not the sole, actors of consequence in international politics is a central tenet of realism and neorealism. Although this assumption commingles what are two distinct assumptions, scholars often move easily from assuming that states are the most important actors to acting as if they were the sole actors of consequence. Changing this assumption means focusing on a broader set of actors in international relations, including international institutions. Again, although this "new" focus is not new, applying rationalist institutional analysis to the international level is more novel. Institutional analysis of these actors, such as multinational corporations, international organizations, and nongovernmental organizations (NGOs), can then be used to examine their impact on other actors and on the international system. Such institutional analysis could be important for IR and could possibly enhance its policy relevance, especially if some evolution occurs in how international institutions are analyzed.

I argue that the spread of rationalist institutionalism is occurring along three dimensions: (1) the nature of actors, (2) the importance of institutions in situations of strategic interaction, and (3) the methodology of noncooperative game theory. First, the central actors in the fields are becoming more similar. In the past, IR theorists tended to focus on "the state" as the primary actor. In the other fields, actors that composed "the state" and those in society have been the most important. Although the state-centric approach has long been challenged in IR, a more coherent alternative now seems likely. This alternative emphasizes the strategic interaction among parties within the state as well as between state and societal actors; and it enables the systematic analysis of policy outcomes among strategic agents as their institutional contexts and preferences change.

Second, the fields have come to appreciate, once again, the importance of institutions in politics. The impact of the rules and norms that structure the environment of actors and shape how collective outcomes are reached has become a central focus of attention throughout political science lately. Again, this emphasis is not new, but its explicit attention to strategic interaction as shaped by institutions is. Furthermore, borrowing from IR, perhaps unwittingly, comparativists and Americanists have adopted a "noncooperative" view of actors and institutions, now much more sensitive to the role of power in institutions and the importance of credibility and commitment. Rationalist institutionalism thus brings with it a political understanding of institutions, viewing them as biasing outcomes in favor of certain groups as well as arenas for conflict and cooperation.[4]

Third, on the methodological front, use of the central ideas from noncooperative game theory has spread across the three fields. Within and across states, actors are now increasingly seen as playing strategic games in which they cannot make binding commitments. Some of the earliest uses of noncooperative game theory came from IR[5] and have moved into the other fields and then back into IR. Thus, it is not simply that IR has learned from the other fields; it is a more mutual synthesis.

I do not claim that all those in IR and American and comparative politics are adopting such a "rational institutionalist" approach. Each of the fields is too large and diverse to characterize this way. Moreover, within each are scholars who object to the rationalist approach. My argument is that a strain of such rationalist institutional work now exists in all three fields, and the scholars who are applying it are asking many of the same questions and using the same analytical tools. The point of this article is to examine what this research agenda means for the field and to suggest where it may lead.

Why Has IR Diverged?

IR has often seemed disconnected from the other fields in political science. Until the 1960s, many scholars desired to separate IR from political science. During the interwar and early post–World War II periods, scholars in Britain and the United States set up independent masters and Ph.D. programs in IR; prominent universities, such as Yale and Chicago, maintained separate Ph.D. programs in IR well into the 1960s, and the London School of Economics retains its own IR department to this day.[6] These academic programs reflected the conviction that IR was and should be a separate discipline from political science.

---

4. For example, Knight 1992.
5. For example, Schelling 1960.
6. See Fox and Fox 1961, 353; and Lyons 1986, 627.

In the 1950s a strong consensus existed among leading IR theorists about the autonomy of the field. As Frederick Dunn, a distinguished IR scholar, wrote,

> The questions which arise out of the relations among nations . . . possess their own coherence and uniqueness since they arise out of relations in a special kind of community, namely, one made up of autonomous units without a central authority having a monopoly of power. . . . Recent events have reinforced the growing conviction that the questions of international relations are too complex and dangerous to be dealt with any longer as sidelines of existing disciplines.[7]

This view is supported and amplified by many leading IR scholars of his generation. For instance, Stanley Hoffmann, in his seminal piece on IR theory, echoes Dunn by claiming that "the field *can* be sufficiently isolated for analytical purposes. International relations take place in a milieu which has its own 'coherence and uniqueness,' its rules of the game which differ sharply from the rules of domestic politics, its own perspective. . . . Since this prerequisite is met, the field *should* be treated as an autonomous discipline."[8]

Theorists tend to cite two reasons for the autonomy of IR. First, the field is broader than mere political science. IR, it is claimed, is truly interdisciplinary. As William Fox noted in a survey of the field in 1949, "the distinctive characteristic of international relations problems was that they tended to be interdisciplinary."[9] Scholars in IR have rightfully noted the importance of other fields such as economics, sociology, history, and law to their topic and sought to make the field inclusive. This interdisciplinary focus is reflected in the organization of curricula in programs that grant separate degrees in IR, whether at the undergraduate level (for example, Stanford), masters (for example, the School of International and Public Affairs) or Ph.D. (for example, the London School of Economics). The inclusiveness of IR as an interdisciplinary pursuit has been one of its strong points.[10]

Second, many scholars have felt that IR's unique subject matter makes it best approachable as an autonomous field, a position that has had less beneficial effects. Dunn again sets the tone for his generation: "The best current views tend to . . . look upon international relations as the particular set of questions that arise out of the division of the world into a number of autonomous political units. If there were no political divisions in the world, there would be no such questions and hence no international relations."[11] International relations involves the "special kind of power relationship that exist in a community lacking an overriding authority."[12] This ap-

---

7. Dunn 1948, 143.
8. Hoffmann 1959, 346–47.
9. See Fox 1949, 72. See also Dunn 1949, 86, 90; Snyder 1955, 465; and Fox and Fox 1961, 344, 348–49.
10. The interdisciplinary nature of IR, however, need not distinguish it from other fields in political science. Comparative politics, especially in its regional studies format, is as interdisciplinary as IR. American politics has been studied from many angles as well: historical, sociological, and economic.
11. Dunn 1949, 85.
12. Dunn 1948, 145.

proach to IR renders it a narrower specialty, one concerned with a specific type of power relationship among particular kinds of units. It also tends to make it more exclusive of other fields since it assumes that politics in the international arena is quite distinct from that within states.

The assumptions that helped turn IR into a narrower, separate discipline were common after the interwar period. The great debate then engaging scholars was that between "idealists and realists."[13] Notable about this debate is that scholars in it shared much common ground. They tended to share a set of assumptions about international politics: namely, that it involved primarily states that could be thought of as units operating in an anarchic environment. As one survey of the field recently noted, "For all their disagreements, the interwar idealists and postwar realists shared an essentially state-centric view of the world which assumed that the dominant feature of international relations was the decentralized Westphalian system of territorially based sovereign states; both schools identified the same problem, although they arrived at different solutions."[14] With these assumptions about the nature of the units and their interaction, IR could separate itself from political science. The role of institutions and ideas tended to drop out of IR as it focused ever more on the exercise of power by unitary states unconstrained by such factors.

Realist theory and its hegemony in IR helped to magnify the distinctions between domestic and international politics because it concretized these assumptions.[15] As Hoffmann noted, "The theory which has occupied the center of the scene in this country during the last ten years is Professor [Hans] Morgenthau's 'realist' theory of power politics. . . . The theory succeeds in focusing attention on the principal actors in world affairs: the states, and on the factors that account for the autonomy of international relations: the differences between domestic and world politics which thwart the operation in the latter of ideas and institutions that flourish in the former, the drastic imperatives of survival, self-preservation, and self-help which are both the causes and the products of such differences."[16] This view of realism and its principal assumptions has endured remarkably well.

Despite many challenges, realism has remained the dominant paradigm in IR. Harrison Wagner in his mid-1970s review entitled "Dissolving the State" points out that, although much attacked, the assumptions that states are unitary and the sole important actor in international politics "have been the most important starting points for serious analysis in the field, and that they underlie much, though certainly not all, of the empirical work done in it."[17] Writing in the 1970s, Robert Keohane and Joseph Nye also point out the continued dominance of realism and the starkness of its assumptions, which they see as profoundly shaping the way scholars approach IR:

13. Fox and Fox 1961, 343.
14. Rochester 1986, 793.
15. Realism has, of course, been attacked for other reasons as well. As Quincy Wright eloquently phrased it, "If the demand for 'realism' in international politics means to deny that words are weapons, that values and ideas have influence, and that ideas give power, it can find little to sustain it in modern social thought"; Wright 1952, 124.
16. Hoffmann 1959, 349–50.
17. Wagner 1974, 467.

We believe that the assumptions of political realists, whose theories dominated the postwar period, are often an inadequate basis for analyzing the politics of interdependence. The realist assumptions about world politics can be seen as defining an extreme set of conditions or *ideal type*. . . . For political realists, international politics, like all politics, is a struggle for power, but, unlike domestic politics, a struggle dominated by organized violence. . . . Three assumptions are integral to the realist vision. First, states as coherent units are the dominant actors in world politics. This is a double assumption: states are predominant; and they act as coherent units.[18]

Note that this critique of realism and its dominance occurred just before the publication of Kenneth Waltz's *Theory of International Politics* in 1979, which is widely thought to have fostered a resurgence of realism. The theory of "neorealism" proffered an even more tenacious defense of these assumptions about international politics. Thus, although challenges to realism proliferated in the late 1960s and 1970s, many scholars nevertheless claim that realism was still dominant even in the late 1970s.

For example, Rosenau et al. published an examination of the major texts used in IR courses in 1977, showing the continuing dominance of realism.[19] The key trends noted about these texts were the tendency to portray the world as centered around nation-states, the lack of attention to domestic politics, the relative neglect of international organizations, and the emphasis on conflict and force (as opposed to cooperation and bargaining). They note that the state-centric focus means that

> it is as if the role of subnational actors has yet to be adequately researched, and thus their activities and importance are understood only at the conceptual level, whereas the role of international organizations is historically clear but conceptually obscure. One "knows" that subnational actors exert influence on foreign policy, but it is an influence that is difficult to trace empirically, and few case studies that do so are available. On the other hand, one "sees" international organizations at work almost daily, but whether and how they perform a central role in the dynamics of world politics is hard to derive from the welter of observations.[20]

Their main point was that realism had remained dominant in IR and that its assumptions had focused studies in IR on specific factors such as states, conflict, and force to the neglect of other important factors such as international organizations, domestic politics, cooperation, and bargaining.

The outpouring of neorealist studies after Waltz's *Theory of International Politics* was published makes it even harder to argue that these assumptions about interna-

---

18. Keohane and Nye 1977, 23.

19. This review examined the major texts in IR; many of these were major research statements and not just textbooks. For example, the most cited works were by Morgenthau, Claude, Waltz, Carr, Schelling, Wolfers, Allison, Magdoff, Wright, Rosecrance, Kaplan, and Sprout. These works by major scholars reflected not only simplified versions of IR for undergraduates then but also key statements of the central theories in IR of the time.

20. Rosenau et al. 1977, 319.

tional politics have not dominated IR, as Keohane again bemoaned in the late 1980s.[21] Following Waltz, many of these studies reinforced the differences between international and domestic politics and refuted attempts to move beyond realist assumptions. These works are not a sideshow in the field either; they are written by the leading theorists in IR today.[22] More tellingly, even critics of neorealism often adopt these assumptions.[23]

The dominance of realism has not gone unchallenged, however. This article is in no way the first to critique or question realism's assumptions. There is a long tradition of such attempts to go beyond realism. Although I cannot mention all the scholars or movements seeking to challenge realism, let me point out some of the more notable ones. Attention to domestic politics has been a constant refrain in IR. From the initial days of the field, IR scholars have been aware of the importance of decision making. From the early work of Harold Lasswell, Nathan Leites, and Richard Snyder, H. W. Bruck and Burton Sapin to the more recent work of Robert Jervis and Ole Holsti, these authors have departed from the strict assumptions of realism and have seen individual decision makers, not states, as the primary units of analysis.[24] This has helped to connect them to a large literature in political science and elsewhere on the psychology of decision making. Others have also avoided the state-centrism pervading IR by focusing on domestic actors like the legislature,[25] public opinion,[26] bureaucratic politics,[27] and the interaction of domestic actors.[28] In addition, scholars have rejected the assumption that states are the most important or sole actors in international politics by focusing on international institutions and regimes and transnational organizations like multinational corporations.[29] Much of the work on foreign policy has also not shared the assumptions of realism. Various studies have all challenged the idea that the state is a unit that makes foreign policy alone.[30] In summary, challenges to the dominant assumptions of realism have been plentiful and powerful. However, despite all these critiques, realism has remained pervasive, and theories using alternate assumptions have failed to make much headway. In part, as I argue in more detail later, the lack of systematic theoretical underpinning and the inattention to strategic interaction among domestic agents in many of these studies

21. Keohane 1989b, 38–41.
22. For instance, Posen 1984; Van Evera 1984a; Walt 1987; Mearsheimer 1990 and 1994; Grieco 1990; Gowa 1994; Krasner 1976 and 1991; Gilpin 1975 and 1987; and even Powell 1990.
23. For example, Baldwin 1993.
24. See Lasswell 1930; Leites 1953; Snyder, Bruck, and Sapin 1962; Jervis 1976; and Holsti 1970.
25. Hilsman 1958.
26. Almond 1950.
27. See Allison 1971; and Allison and Halperin 1972.
28. For example, Rosenau 1969b.
29. On the former, see Goodrich 1956; Claude 1956; Keohane and Nye 1972, 1977; Haas 1958; Nye 1971; Keohane 1984; Krasner 1983b; and Ruggie 1983b. On the latter, see Keohane and Nye 1972; and Vernon 1971.
30. See, for example, Rosenau 1966; Katzenstein 1978, 1985; Snyder 1991, Rogowski 1989; and Milner 1988. Interestingly, one branch of foreign policy studies does share the state-as-unit assumption. The "statist" approach to foreign policy, typified by Krasner 1978; Zysman 1983; Lake 1988; and Ikenberry, Lake, and Mastanduno 1988, has retained the assumptions of realism in the study of foreign policy.

has retarded the development of a cumulative research paradigm focused on domestic politics in IR.

The major assumptions of realism then have cut off IR from important cross-currents in political science. For example, in his pathbreaking article on the "state as conceptual variable," J. P. Nettl basically rules out discussion of the state as conceived in international politics. He notes that the state is invariant in international politics and hence it can contribute nothing to the "rigorous comparative analysis" of the state that he is building.[31] This is because "the state represents a unit in the field of international relations. . . . Here the state is the basic, irreducible unit, equivalent to the individual person in a society. . . . In this international context the concept of state, in addition to being a unit, also generates the almost exclusive and acceptable locus of resource mobilization."[32]

Relaxing the core assumptions of a field may lead to new insights. For example, in economics the systematic relaxing of the strict assumptions of classical and neoclassical theories has produced major new developments in the field. In particular, the relaxation of classical assumptions about the relationship between demand and supply allowed John Maynard Keynes to develop a new theory of macroeconomics; changing assumptions about the rationality of economic actors created the new brand of rational expectations macroeconomics; and relaxing assumptions about perfect competition led to creation of new international trade policy models, termed strategic trade theory.[33] These new departures—whether one calls them progress or not—came from scholars understanding the assumptions of previous models and changing them to see the results.

Relaxing the Assumption that States Are Units

The assumption that the state acts as a unit in international politics has cut the field off from the other areas of political science. This assumption was often connected with the use of systemic theory. That is, those who wanted to explain IR as a function of the international system's pressures on its units tended to assume that the only way to do this was by employing states as their unit of analysis. This does not seem to be a logical necessity, however. The appropriate specification of the units does not necessarily depend on the level of analysis. One can use actors other than unitary states when employing the systemic level of analysis; one can ask how the international system affects actors like executives, legislatures, interest groups, and militaries, examining how it affects their interaction both with one another and across borders. Giving up the unitary state assumption does not foreclose systemic analysis.[34]

31. Nettl 1968, 562–64.
32. Ibid., 563.
33. Krugman 1986.
34. For systemic analysis that uses actors other than the state, see world systems theory (for example, Wallerstein 1974; and Strange 1988). Recent work on globalization has tended to adopt a systemic frame focused on actors like foreign investors and bond markets.

The issue posed then is not about the appropriate level of analysis, but about the appropriate designation of the actors or units. As Frederick Frey has observed, the problem of actor designation affects all forms of political inquiry, not just international politics. "Awareness of actor designation as a crucial form of social scientific conceptualization, rather than something simply given by 'the real world' or conceptually trivial, is a requisite for effective political inquiry."[35] According to him, two criteria determine the appropriate unit. One should use (1) the highest level of generality subject to (2) the ability of this collectivity to act as a coherent unit. The second criterion of coherence poses a problem for the unitary state. Do the actors within states display sufficient behavioral cohesion so that "knowledge of the relevant behavior of some few group members (leaders, spokesmen, representatives, etc.) permits prediction of the behavior of the rest"? Are the actors within the state "sufficiently cohesive . . . and irreducible so that their further analytical decomposition would not significantly improve the conclusions"?[36] Many scholars in IR seem to assume that the state meets this criteria, although few, if any, either argue this point or demonstrate it empirically. The rest of political science, in contrast, has rarely accepted this characterization.

Here I want to explore what this assumption means and how changing it can change our thinking about the field. Figure 1 shows the four distinct ways we can conceptualize the actors and their interactions in international politics. It illuminates how the choice of units and their interactions matter for our theories. My argument is that moving from the upper-left quadrant to the lower-right quadrant is likely to be fruitful for IR theory.

When you move across the top row of Figure 1, realist assumptions hold. Here the main actor in international politics is the "state" as a unit. In this formulation, the state can be thought of as the "representative actor" for all of its domestic politics. This implies that the state possesses a single set of preferences, which it attempts to forward in international politics. For realists, this set of preferences is termed the "national interest." This assumption implies that one of three conditions relating to the aggregation of preferences domestically necessarily holds:

1. Some internal political process selects one individual or group as the decision maker, and its preferences are what is being maximized; for example, one could imagine that the state represents the interests of the median voter. Or, as much of the "statist" literature presumes, the representative actor may simply be the executive (for example, the president, prime minister, or dictator).[37] Basically, one actor domestically, it is assumed, controls foreign policy.

2. On a particular issue, all individuals in the nation may have the same set of preferences; their preferences can then be represented as a single, identical function. For example, realists would claim that the preference for national survival is shared by all within the nation; hence, it is the "national interest."

35. Frey 1985, 136–37.
36. Ibid., 142.
37. See, for example, Krasner 1978; and Ikenberry, Lake, and Mastanduno 1988.

		Environment	
		Decision theoretic (small-country assumption)	*Strategic interaction (large-country assumption)*
Actors	*State as unit (representative actor)*	**Perfect markets** (Waltz 1979; Lake 1996; Krasner 1978)	**Game theory** (Jervis 1978; Axelrod 1984; Powell 1990)
	State as polyarchy (political economy)	**Domestic sources** (Allison 1971; Katzenstein 1985; Milner 1988; Rogowski 1989; Frieden 1991; Jervis 1976; Grossman and Helpman 1994)	**Two-level games** (Snyder and Diesing 1977; Putnam 1988; Fearon 1994; Milner and Rosendorff 1996, 1997; Grossman and Helpman 1995)

FIGURE 1. *Actors and their environments*

Because of the pressures and threats exerted by the international system, each and every actor domestically holds this preference.

3. All national politics can be summarized in the form of one utility function that no individual in the polity may actually have but that represents what results when the domestic game of politics is played. This process "black boxes" what occurs internally and only focuses ex post on the emergent preference. In a sense it follows the procedure of revealed preference used by economists. In this third variant, however, it is impossible to point to any actor in domestic politics who actually holds the preference revealed to be the national one, since it represents some aggregation of the domestic actors' preferences.

Holding one of these three positions seems to be a necessary condition for using the state-as-unitary-actor assumption. Each allows the theorist to derive the "state's" interests, which is a necessary step for establishing that it is indeed an actor.[38] The three methods avoid specifying or examining the ways in which domestic preferences are aggregated into the national one; this is how the unitary state assumption bypasses concerns for domestic politics. Simplifying assumptions are obviously necessary for any theory. Moreover, one could argue that the lack of realism of the first two assumptions should not trouble one either. But, as I argue in more detail later, the assumptions either that one group controls foreign policy or that all (important) domestic actors have the same preferences seem quite problematic. This leaves the third assumption, which treats the state "as if" it were a unit by black boxing domes-

38. All three of these positions assume that the construction of the national interest can be separated from the international game among states.

tic politics. Realists often adopt this position, emphasizing that it may not actually be true. The virtue of simplifying assumptions, however, is not just their simplicity but also their explanatory power; parsimony refers to both aspects. To evaluate the parsimony of two theories one must be able to compare their explanatory power. This immediately implies that relaxing the simplifying assumptions and testing the hypotheses that arise from these new models are necessary steps for judging the parsimony of any one theory.

Interestingly, after making the unitary state assumption, scholars often jump quickly to arguing that all states have the *same* set of preferences. For instance, "By focusing on the presumed common objective of maintaining the autonomy of governments against the danger of military defeat, it is an easy step to the assumption that all governments are internally united by a desire for military security and externally preoccupied by threats of it."[39] These two assumptions are distinct, however; assuming that states are unitary does not imply that they all have the same preferences.

If states are the main units in international politics, two types of interactions among them can be conceived. In the upper-left quadrant of Figure 1, each unitary state simply tries to maximize its own utility, acting in a nonstrategic fashion vis-à-vis other states. This decision-theoretic view is the traditional representation of how firms interact in competitive markets. Firms are so numerous or small that they are unable to affect each other, so they act as if they are maximizing their utility independently. The actors are "price-takers." Economists also call this the small-country assumption; that is, a country is small when its actions do not affect other actors and their actions do not influence the small-country's behavior.

This characterization of international politics is not uncommon, especially among realists. At times, this assumption seems to characterize Waltz's position in *Theory of International Politics*.[40] He defines the structure of the international system and describes its operation using an analogy to competitive markets in microeconomic theory, after noting that such "reasoning by analogy is permissible where different domains are structurally similar."[41] Thus, similar to firms in competitive markets maximizing their profits, all states balance in order to preserve themselves, no matter what other states are doing. Another example of this perspective is shown in the work of David Lake. He posits that a state's choice of grand strategy is "a function of the expected costs of opportunism and governance."[42] While he claims the theory is dyadic, each state is choosing its optimal strategy given the exogenously determined costs of governance and opportunism; the behavior of the other states is not strategic since they do not affect these variables. This characterization avoids a concern with institutions, whether domestic or international, since no method of aggregation of preferences at either level is explicitly proposed.

A second way to characterize the interaction among unitary states is as a game of strategic interaction, as in the upper-right quadrant of Figure 1. Here states as units

---

39. Wagner 1974, 438.
40. At other times, Waltz clearly understands that he is describing an oligopolistic system in which the few major powers exert much control over the system and interact strategically.
41. Waltz 1979, 89, 88–94.
42. Lake 1996, 29.

bargain with one another; they do not simply try to maximize their utility independently. Their optimal strategies depend on what other states are doing, and they can only achieve their goals to the extent that other states do not interfere with them. This form of interaction is similar to economists' depiction of oligopolistic markets. Firms in these markets are few and large enough that their behavior affects the others; they are interdependent because each one's ability to realize its preferences depends to an important extent on the behavior of the other players.[43] In these circumstances, tacit and explicit bargaining is the norm. This characterization of states allows for states, like domestic actors, to bargain with one another. The international game now has explicit mechanisms for arriving at collective outcomes and hence is no longer institutionless.

If one were wedded to the unitary state assumption, it would seem that more progress could be made by examining strategic interaction among states than by assuming they act independently. That is, even realism seems to presume a move from the upper-left quadrant of Figure 1 to the upper-right quadrant. Logical deductions about how states will interact with each other under different conditions could provide important hypotheses about state behavior and systemic stability. The body of theory that economists have built by developing increasingly complex models of oligopolistic competition testifies to the potential richness of such an endeavor.[44]

A particularly apt way to study such strategic environments is with game theory. And indeed most game theory in IR takes the form of unitary states bargaining with each other. For example, Jervis's "Cooperation Under the Security Dilemma," Robert Axelrod's Tit-for-Tat game in *The Evolution of Cooperation*, or work by Duncan Snidal, Robert Powell, Joanne Gowa, and Bruce Bueno de Mesquita and David Lalman, to name a few, all portray states as unitary actors but assume that they interact in a strategic environment, often characterized using game theory.[45]

This type of game theory is the same that many use for analyzing domestic politics. For example, Axelrod's work takes its inspiration from earlier studies done by Anatol Rapoport and Albert Chammah and by Michael Taylor that were used to discuss the evolution of cooperation within societies.[46] Moreover, James Fearon's "rationalist paradox of war" is a variant of the so-called Hick's paradox devised to explain the breakdown of bargaining in situations like labor strikes.[47] With the recent and increasing adoption of noncooperative game theory to explain domestic politics and the move to more strategic characterizations of states in international politics, the two fields have adopted a more similar view of politics, even without dropping the assumption of a unitary state.[48] As Oran Young predicted,

> There is no reason to suppose that the study of international relations will ultimately require the development of theories that are entirely new, in the sense that

43. Schelling 1960. See also Cohen 1990, 21.
44. Tirole 1989.
45. See Snidal 1985b; Powell 1990; Gowa 1994; and Bueno de Mesquita and Lalman 1992.
46. See Rapoport and Chammah 1965; and Taylor 1967.
47. Fearon 1995.
48. For a discussion of the increasing use of noncooperative game theory in American politics and its benefits, see Ferejohn 1995, xi–xii.

they bear no relationship to theories in other fields. On the contrary, it seems that viable theories of international relations . . . will often be special cases of more general theories for situations involving strategic interactions among collective entities. . . . There is good reason to believe that the basic form and structure of the resultant theories will be quite similar across a number of substantive fields. . . . [In particular,] any significant advances in the analysis of oligopolistic markets, party systems, and even intra-family interactions should have distinct relevance for students of international relations. And any important theoretical advances in the analysis of international relations should prove interesting to students in a number of other fields.[49]

But the more important change lies in relaxing the assumption about the state as a unit, as I will try to show.

In the lower quadrants of Figure 1, states are no longer assumed to be unitary. Rather, they are now composed of at least two actors. In economics, such an approach is often termed a "political economy" one since it implies that these actors have different preferences and any outcome will have to reflect these differences.[50] The "representative actor" approach is thus avoided by such political economists since they reject the idea of using a single utility function to represent all agents in society. In other words, the national interest is now a contested term.[51] This is not a new claim; it is very compatible with many studies of foreign policy as well as with much of the bureaucratic politics literature in IR. Actors domestically have distinct preferences, and fashioning some single national preference is dependent on the resources the actors possess and the institutions in which they operate. In this approach the national interest cannot just be assumed; it must be explained. In addition, this approach prompts a change in the designation of the main actors in international politics. No longer are states the actors; rather, governments composed of central decision makers, legislatures, bureaucracies, and other domestic groups become the agents. The "national interest" is the central variable in this approach, because it is the result of the strategic interactions among these groups.

The assumption that the state is unitary is thus highly consequential. It leads to a neglect of the differences in internal preferences and political institutions within states.[52] These differences among states in their internal characteristics have important effects on international politics. Indeed, if Holsti is correct, the central problem in IR theory—war—has more to do with domestic politics than with relations among states now. His data show that "since 1945 most wars have been within and about states. . . . Almost 77 percent of the 164 wars were internal, where armed combat was

49. Young 1972, 195.

50. For example, Grossman and Helpman 1994.

51. The term *national interest* has been a subject of debate for years. As Beard concluded over sixty years ago, "In studying thousands of actors justified by the appellation 'national interest,' I was tempted to conclude that the conception was simply a telling formula which politicians and private interests employed whenever they wished to accomplish any particular designs in the field of foreign affairs"; Beard 1935, v–vi.

52. In contrast to Moravcsik, who advocates a "liberal" theory of IR based on preferences, the claim here is for a theoretical approach that includes both preferences and institutions; Moravcsik 1997.

not against another state but against authorities within the state or between armed camps."[53] Holsti then argues that "the assumption that the problem of war is primarily a problem of relations *between* states has to be seriously questioned. . . . Security *between* states . . . has become increasingly dependent upon security *within* those states. . . . The problem of contemporary and future politics, it turns out, is essentially a problem of domestic politics."[54]

Moreover, his research shows that the *institutional* differences among states are a major factor in accounting for war. The strength of a state's domestic institutions is decisive, not its military capabilities.[55] "Regions of the world populated by weak and failing states are zones of war. Regions populated by strong and strengthening states are zones of peace. . . . The sources of wars [of the contemporary period lie] primarily in the domestic structures of states."[56] Similar to the argument here, his conclusion about the nature of future research is that "Realist and neo-realist approaches to the study of war offer little in the way of understanding these dynamics. . . . [Rather,] the comparative study of states—how they are formed, how they develop legitimacy and strength, and how they persist or fail—seem better avenues for future research on the study of war."[57]

But a major problem for theory building has been to develop a systematic way to explore which and how domestic factors affect international politics. A key problem with earlier work on the domestic politics in IR has been its tendency to produce lists of variables rather than theories. Such lists not only lack parsimony but also under-conceptualize domestic politics. As Charles Hermann concludes in his review of comparative foreign policy, "Research on the processes by which foreign policy is formed . . . has been hampered by the absence of theories, hypotheses, and between-country comparisons."[58] Later, R. Harrison Wagner, in his review of IR studies that "dissolve the state," concludes similarly, noting that both the transnational and bureaucratic politics literatures fail in the end to provide systematic models of domes-

53. Holsti 1996, 21.

54. Holsti 1996, 15. Much the same can be said for the notion of security. As a study by Scully showed, "democide, a Latin word meaning indiscriminate state killing, and genocide, the murder of minorities, have claimed the lives of 170 million people this century—four times as many as civil and international wars"; Gerald Scully, cited in *The Wall Street Journal*, 5 November 1997. Security for individuals may be more a function of domestic politics than of international relations.

Posen notes the similarity between domestic and international security, applying the "security dilemma" to domestic politics. "Realism . . . explicitly addresses the consequences of anarchy—the absence of a sovereign—for political relations among states. In areas such as the former Soviet Union and Yugoslavia, 'sovereigns' have disappeared. They leave in their wake a host of groups [who] must pay attention to the first thing that states have historically addressed—the problem of security. . . . The security dilemma affects relations among these groups, just as it affects relations among states"; Posen 1993a, 104, 105.

55. As Holsti defines it, "state strength . . . is not measured in military terms. It is, rather, in the capacity of the state to command loyalty—the right to rule—to extract the resources necessary to rule and provide services, to maintain that essential element of sovereignty, a monopoly over the legitimate use of force within defined territorial limits, and to operate within the context of a consensus-based political community"; Holsti 1996, 82–83.

56. Holsti 1996, 141.

57. Ibid., 206–207.

58. Hermann 1968, 534.

tic politics.[59] And even more recently Keohane concludes that "we need better theories of domestic politics . . . so that the gap between the external and internal environments can be bridged in a systematic way, rather than by simply adding catalogs of exogenously determined foreign policy facts to theoretically more rigorous [international] structural models."[60] More recent work has tried to overcome these problems by using theoretical conceptions of domestic politics drawn from the other fields of political science.

Often, domestic politics is viewed as organized hierarchically, with a single actor at the top making the final decisions. Power, or decision-making authority, is assumed to flow along a vertical hierarchy—from top to bottom. In contrast, international politics is characterized as anarchic, where in effect each player has a veto. As Waltz says in discussing the ordering principles of systems, "The parts of domestic political systems stand in relations of super- and subordination. Some are entitled to command; others are required to obey. Domestic systems are centralized and hierarchic. The parts of international-political systems stand in relations of coordination. Formally, each is the equal of all the others. None is entitled to command; none is required to obey. International systems are decentralized and anarchic."[61] Anarchy and hierarchy then define the opposite ends of a continuum showing the possible distributions of power among actors.

Most politics—domestic and international—however, lie in between the poles of anarchy and hierarchy, in the area I characterize as polyarchic.[62] Polyarchy is a more complex structure than either anarchy or hierarchy. There is no single group at the top; power, or authority, over decision making is shared, often unequally. In this situation, international politics and foreign policy are part of the domestic struggle for power over collective outcomes and the search for internal compromise. Domestic politics, and I would argue international politics as well, varies along a continuum from hierarchy to anarchy, with most politics resembling polyarchy, which lies in between these extremes.

Several factors are important in defining a state's placement in this continuum: the policy *preferences* of domestic actors and the *institutions* for power sharing among them. First, polyarchy assumes that actors' preferences differ. If all important domestic actors have the same preferences, then even if they share the ability to control outcomes, the situation will resemble that of the unitary state, as noted earlier. With the same preferences, no matter which domestic actors hold power, the same policies will be chosen. Second, decision making must be shared. If a single actor controls all decision making, one is back to the unitary actor model where hierarchy prevails. Indeed, the more control over policy choices one actor alone possesses—say, the

59. Wagner 1974, 451.
60. Keohane 1989b, 60.
61. Waltz 1979, 88. Elsewhere I, along with others, have talked about the consequences of relaxing the assumption that international politics is always pure anarchy. See Milner 1991; Ruggie 1983b; and Keohane 1984.
62. Robert Dahl coined this term to refer to the degree of democracy present in a country. Dahl 1984, 75–93. Here the term is used differently; it refers to the power-sharing arrangements among domestic groups; see Milner 1997.

executive (that is, the less the executive has to share decision-making power with others)—the more the situation resembles a unitary actor model or a strict hierarchy. Hence, domestic interests and institutions become key variables.

Even in nondemocratic systems domestic politics is rarely a pure hierarchy with a unitary decision maker. The support of the professional military, the landed oligarchy, big business, and/or a political party are usually necessary for even dictators to remain in power and implement their policies. These groups can often exercise veto power over the executive's proposals, and in other ways, such as setting the agenda, may share power with the executive. Even such autocratic leaders as Hitler and Stalin depended on the support of internal groups to retain their positions and make policy. As one study of Stalin notes, "Most revisionist accounts of the 'Cold War'. . . portray the Soviet leaders both as monolithic and essentially passive. . . . The Soviet decision-making process, however, was contingent as much upon developments in [internal] factional struggles within the Soviet Empire, as upon 'objective' Soviet interests abroad. . . . Thus, as in so many other instances, Soviet 'policy'. . . largely seems to have been a function of the ebb and flow of [domestic] factional conflict."[63]

Democratic systems are even more likely to be polyarchic. Like nondemocratic states, they vary in their principles of internal organization, some being more anarchic and others more hierarchical. In most cases at least two sets of actors vie for control over decision making. Usually both the legislature and the executive influence policymaking. Or sometimes two or more political parties may be in competition, the governing party or coalition and its opposition. In corporatist systems, at least three actors are important: the executive ("the state"), organized labor, and organized capital. These actors share control over the key elements of policymaking: setting the agenda, devising policy proposals, amending, ratifying, and implementing policies. How their diverse preferences are aggregated into collective outcomes depends on the nature of their political institutions. In polyarchies, strategic interaction among the players within certain political institutions is of central importance to policy choices.

The implications of polyarchy for international politics are central, since it changes the way that international politics is played. The bureaucratic politics literature recognized this years ago. "The actions of a nation result not from an agreed upon calculus of strategic interests, but rather from pulling and hauling among individuals with differing perceptions and stakes."[64] As Graham Allison and Morton Halperin concluded, "Decisions of a government seldom reflect a single, coherent, consistent set of calculations about national security interests. . . . Decisions typically reflect considerable compromise."[65] Policy choices—whether for domestic or foreign policy—are the result of a strategic game among the internal actors. The key point about this characterization of domestic politics is that by highlighting domestic interests and institutions, it (re)connects IR to other fields in political science.

63. Ra'anan 1983, 8.
64. Allison and Halperin 1972, 57.
65. Ibid., 53.

In polyarchic situations, actors can be characterized as interacting in one of two ways: independently or strategically. This dichotomy applies to both their domestic and external interactions. In the lower-left quadrant of Figure 1, for instance, each state is seen as a collection of domestic actors involved in the formation of policy outcomes. Internally, how their preferences are aggregated into a national policy choice is sometimes left unspecified, as in Jeffry Frieden or Helen Milner, or is assumed as the result of some process of bargaining among the actors, as in Snyder.[66] Ronald Rogowski's model of coalitions takes a similar tack: either denying that it reveals anything about collective outcomes or assuming that groups benefiting from increased trade are powerful enough to dominate outcomes.[67] Internationally, these studies tend to assume that once a collective national position is reached, the actors maximize their utility independently of the behavior of other states. Strategic interaction internationally is not central.

This characterization includes many different literatures in IR. For example, the bureaucratic politics literature, decision-making studies, as well as most of the so-called societal approaches to foreign policy share these assumptions about politics domestically and internationally. These studies often advance a new conception of the actors and their preferences in international politics, combined with a lack of understanding of how these preferences are aggregated internally and externally into collective outcomes—that is, of political institutions. The strength of these studies is that they illuminate the preferences of the actors. And, as noted earlier, understanding preferences is as important as understanding institutions. Scholars in IR should not make the same mistake for which Karen Remmer has recently chided the comparativists: "In bringing institutions back in, comparativists have too often pushed society out, defining the importance of institutions more in terms of their strength and autonomy vis-à-vis society than in terms of patterns of state–society interaction."[68]

Some recent studies in political economy have taken a different direction; these studies tend to have explicit models of domestic institutions but still neglect the international environment.[69]

In the lower-right quadrant of Figure 1, in contrast, the political economy approach is fully strategic; this is best represented by "two-level games" when conceived in strategic form.[70] Here actors internally bargain with one another, while they also bargain externally. Political institutions define how this bargaining results in collective outcomes taking into account strategic interaction at both levels. In this situation, one can use theories and institutional analysis from comparative and American politics to better understand these collective outcomes. These approaches examine how bargaining among executives, legislatures, bureaucracies, and interest groups or the public is structured by national political institutions to yield particular collec-

---

66. See Frieden 1990, 1991; Milner 1988; and Snyder 1991.
67. Rogowski 1989.
68. Remmer 1997, 57.
69. See, for example, Grossman and Helpman 1994; Lohmann and O'Halloran 1994; and O'Halloran 1994.
70. Putnam 1988.

tive outcomes, given certain preferences. Moreover, they usually embed this domestic game within an international one, so that only outcomes that lie within the acceptable range of both domestic and foreign actors will emerge.

How can this type of analysis advance the study of domestic politics in IR? Many earlier studies of domestic politics in IR failed to look at strategic interaction internally or they simply assumed some method of aggregating preferences into national policy choices. For example, the literature on bureaucratic politics stressed that actors located in different bureaucratic agencies were likely to hold different preferences about foreign policy and that these preferences could be derived from their bureaucratic position. How these preferences were aggregated into policy was left less clear. Indeed, the common wisdom, as cited earlier, was that "pulling and hauling" occurred until some group's preferences won out. This literature was criticized for lacking any coherent way of predicting this outcome and for assuming that bureaucrats operated in isolation from other governmental bodies. These two criticisms are exactly what a more strategic view of bureaucracies would take into account. For example, John Ferejohn and Charles Shipan show that legislatures can control bureaucracies even without actively checking on them or vetoing their policies.[71] They show how the interaction among bureaucracies and the legislature leads to certain policy choices and how changes in various conditions, such as the preferences of either of these groups or the institutional structure, alter the outcomes. This form of rationalist institutionalism then provides a way of understanding how policy results from the strategic interaction of bureaucrats and other governmental actors within specific institutions. It also allows for the development of testable hypotheses about how changes in preferences or institutions will lead to changes in national policy choices.

So-called statist arguments about foreign policy also are vulnerable to the same criticisms. Statist arguments point out that the executive can often be treated as a unitary actor when there exists a well-defined hierarchy within this branch and when other actors in society and the state are weak.[72] It is often unclear, however, in their arguments how the varied preferences even within the executive branch are aggregated into policy. And it is often widely debated whether one can assume that even if other actors do little they have no influence over the executive. Rationalist institutional arguments would suggest that this view of the executive neglects the strategic interaction that occurs within political institutions. For example, rational choice models of the most independent central banks—such as those in the United States and Germany, which can be treated as the state for purposes of monetary policy—have suggested that even central bankers must anticipate the reactions of other actors, lest they ultimately lose their independence.[73] Another example of such work suggesting that a strategic interaction approach leads to quite different interpretations of behav-

71. Ferejohn and Shipan 1990.
72. See, for example, Krasner 1978; and Zysman 1983.
73. See Wooley 1984. Lohmann 1998 and Clarida and Gertler 1996 also provide data showing this is likely.

ior is Mark Ramseyer and Frances Rosenbluth's study of Japan.[74] They explore the game between legislators representing political parties, bureaucrats, and interest groups and show that although bureaucrats may look dominant in Japan, as statists claim, when one considers the institutional and informational constraints on them, they are better seen as operating in a strategic environment constrained by other players. Again, their rational institutionalist model suggests a way of explicitly understanding preference aggregation and collective decision making in situations of strategic interaction.

Finally, the work on societal actors in foreign policy also tends to suffer from an inexplicit understanding of the aggregation mechanisms of politics and from a lack of attention to strategic interaction. Many of these models focus on societal groups and their preferences, often failing to account for how these diverse preferences are aggregated into policy and how competition among interest groups might affect this process.[75] Again, rational institutionalist approaches suggest that their results may be too simplistic. Work by such scholars as Gene Grossman and Elhanan Helpman, and David Austin-Smith and John Wright shows the conditions under which interest groups will become politically active, how competition among them will affect each one's influence, and what impact they will have given different political institutions.[76] They derive some striking results, many of which would be at odds with the societal arguments cited earlier. For example, Grossman and Helpman show that if every interest group lobbies over trade policy, then none may get what it wants (that is, protection); more interest group pressure may lead to more free trade, not less. The central point here is not that work on domestic politics is lacking in IR, but that one means for making this work more systematic and cumulative is through the use of rational institutionalist approaches, which can systemically explore the consequences of strategic interaction among actors with diverse preferences when facing differing political institutions. These approaches allow us to better understand the complex interaction among domestic actors and the effects of institutions on those interactions.

In addition to strategic interaction domestically, rational institutionalism can be useful at the international level to make it strategic too. Such "two-level" strategic games are evident, for example, in works by Glen Snyder, Paul Diesing, Fearon, Milner, B. Peter Rosendorff, Gerald Schneider, Cedric Dupont, George Downs, and David Rocke.[77] A number of these works cast light on the circumstances under which we can expect states to cooperate. For example, Schneider, Dupont, and Milner all explore the domestic conditions that make European integration more likely. Their conclusions diverge from both functionalist and realist explanations of such cooperation.[78] In addition, Fearon and Snyder and Diesing examine the conditions under which crises are more likely to escalate into war. Fearon, in particular, adds an impor-

74. Ramseyer and Rosenbluth 1993.
75. See, for example, Gourevitch 1986; Milner 1988; Frieden 1991; and Rogowski 1989.
76. See Grossman and Helpman 1994; Austin-Smith and Wright 1992; 1994; and Austin-Smith 1995.
77. See Snyder and Diesing 1977; Fearon 1994b; Milner and Rosendorff 1996, 1997; Schneider 1994; Dupont 1994; Milner 1997; and Downs and Rocke 1995.
78. Moravcsik 1991.

tant claim to the debate on the democratic peace. He suggests why domestic conditions in democracies may make crisis escalation less likely by making threats more credible. Thus, in at least two areas these types of two-level strategic games have produced interesting results.

Foreign policy in these studies is now a result of the explicit aggregation of diverse domestic preferences within political institutions, and the collective systemic outcome is a function of the explicit strategic interaction among these groups internationally. This change in the designation of the actors and their interaction is important. It promises greater empirical accuracy and perhaps greater parsimony than the other approaches. For example, it is not clear that in Bueno de Mesquita and Lalman's *War and Reason* the international politics model is any simpler than the domestic politics model, and the latter certainly seems to have greater explanatory power. Furthermore, the addition of imperfect information into models of strategic interaction among unitary states, which is often essential to improve their empirical accuracy, leaves such models with little claim to simplicity.[79] Thus, abandoning the assumption of a unitary state need not condemn one to hopeless complexity nor to a lack of parsimony. Once one leaves the world of states as unitary actors, one can use the concepts and theories from American and comparative politics, some of which provide powerful, parsimonious tools for understanding strategic interaction in different institutional environments.

Relaxing the Assumption that States Are the Main or Sole Actors in International Politics

A second critical assumption in IR has been that states are the most important or sole actors in international politics. In its weaker form this assumption implies that although other actors may exist internationally, they are not nearly as important as states. In its stronger formulation this assumption implies that states are the only actors worth examining. This form of the assumption rules out the study of other actors, since they are seen as epiphenomenal to states. That is, other international actors are not important because their existence and influence depend on states. As John Mearsheimer states most boldly, "realists maintain that [international] institutions are basically a reflection of the distribution of power in the world. They are based on the self-interested calculations of great powers, and they have no independent effect on state behavior."[80] This seems to hold for all other actors in international politics as well, including multinational corporations and NGOs.[81] Although many scholars claim the weaker version of this assumption, they often quickly slip into the stronger version of it. Combined with the earlier assumption that states are unitary, this assumption leaves little room for any kind of institutional analysis in international politics.

79. Such as Powell 1990 or 1996.
80. Mearsheimer 1994, 7.
81. For example, Gilpin 1975.

But how important are institutions in international politics? Or, to put it more bluntly, how much can we learn about IR from studying these institutions? This goes to the heart of a central debate raging in IR these days and one that will not be settled here.[82] My claim is that ignoring international institutions is likely to limit our understanding of IR; furthermore, using a systematic rationalist approach may help in understanding the role they play. Obviously, this does not mean ignoring states. After all, it is politics within the state that I argue is most important for understanding international relations.

Challenges to the assumption that states are the dominant players in IR have been widespread and long standing, as Garrett in this issue shows. I do not want to go into a detailed history of these challenges, in part because others in this issue are doing so (see, for instance, the article by Lisa Martin and Beth Simmons). The claims I want to make are two. First, recent studies that relax this assumption have profited from employing rationalist institutionalism prevalent in studies of domestic politics. A common language for thinking about institutions at both the domestic and international levels has emerged; such a common language is important because it allows one to make generalizations across diverse contexts. Second, further evolution in the study of international institutions is important. Two steps need to be considered: more comparative analysis of institutions and greater concern with the democratization of international institutions.

What can a "rationalist institutionalism" view of international institutions contribute to IR? Notable about some new IR studies is that they employ the same form of analysis that has been used to explore domestic institutions, such as the U.S. Congress,[83] presidential systems in general,[84] or various parliamentary systems.[85] Should we believe that an approach that tells us something about the U.S. House of Representatives or the French Parliament can tell us anything about international politics? Yes, if institutions function similarly in these areas, which is the claim of the rationalist paradigm. That is, institutions, whether domestic or not, act to aggregate diverse preferences into a collective outcome. How they do this depends much on their particular norms and rules of operation. The committee structure of the U.S. House is not similar to the decision-making apparatus of the World Trade Organization (WTO) or NATO. But, this approach claims, there are elements of the decision-making structure in each of these international institutions that are very important for shaping how outcomes are formed and can be studied in a rationalist institutionalist framework. The particular model used to study the U.S. House may not be relevant for any international institution, but the general idea that every institution has such aggregating mechanisms, which explain how diverse preferences are formed into a collective outcome, is applicable to every institution. Of course, this begs the question of how important institutions are overall in international politics.

82. See, for example, Baldwin 1993; Mearsheimer 1994; Keohane and Martin 1995; Ruggie 1995a; and Wendt 1995.
83. For example, Krehbiel 1991.
84. Shugart and Carey 1992.
85. See, for example, Huber 1992, 1996a; and Laver and Shepsle 1995.

Three recent studies of international institutions serve as exemplars of the rationalist approach. George Tsebelis and Geoffrey Garrett bring the new institutional analysis to bear on the EU.[86] They use game theoretical analysis of the legislative procedures for enacting policy in the community to show why integration occurs and how the diverse national preferences within Europe are aggregated into collective policy outcomes. As they note, intergovernmental approaches that ignore the institutional structure of the EU "come to mistaken conclusions regarding the effective influence of different countries, the likelihood of different outcomes, and the likelihood of coalitions that support these outcomes."[87] They instead demonstrate that "different [institutional] procedures, by giving the power to propose and the power to veto to different actors, systematically lead to different outcomes" and that this "conclusion cannot be reached without careful study of the EU's institutions."[88] Particularly notable about Garrett and Tsebelis is that they compare different institutional procedures to show how they aggregate preferences differently.

Downs and Rocke offer another game theoretical analysis focused on explaining international institutions.[89] They are concerned with explaining the enforcement rules of the GATT and in particular why they are so weak. In their analysis, uncertainty at home about future interest groups' demands for protection make a weak punishment strategy optimal from every state's perspective. Note that, like Garrett and Tsebelis, they include a comparative institutional framework, since they first ask what the optimal punishment rules would be in the absence of domestic uncertainty. Without domestic uncertainty, they show that a much stronger set of punishment rules would be chosen. The weaker GATT rules that we actually see then may result from domestic pressures for intervention, as Ruggie's idea of "embedded liberalism" predicts.[90] Downs and Rocke also bring out the strategic interaction between actors at the domestic and international levels in their explanation of the GATT, thus overcoming a shortcoming of earlier institutional analysis that Stephan Haggard and Simmons pointed out.[91]

Judith Goldstein demonstrates the reciprocal influence of international institutions and domestic politics using the new institutionalism.[92] Using models similar to that of Garrett and Tsebelis, she shows how the institutional procedures devised for dispute settlement (DSM) in NAFTA affected whose domestic preferences were chosen as policy. In turn, she shows why the U.S. executive would have negotiated such procedures in the first place. Although she does not conduct comparative analysis to show that these procedures work better than others, she does show why the existing procedures may be optimal for all the countries, given their domestic politics.

These three studies then bring the study of international institutions closer to comparative institutional analysis. Comparative analysis of institutions seems especially

---

86. See Tsebelis 1994; and Garrett and Tsebelis 1996.
87. Garrett and Tsebelis 1996, 294.
88. Ibid.
89. Downs and Rocke 1995.
90. Ruggie 1983b.
91. Haggard and Simmons 1987, 513–17.
92. Goldstein 1996.

important because it avoids the post hoc quality of some institutional research.[93] If one can show that different institutions result in different outcomes and the conditions under which those different institutions might be optimal, then both a positive and prescriptive perspective on institutions can be achieved. One would know when particular institutions were more likely to be created if one knew the conditions under which they were being established. And one could make assessments about which institutions might be optimal under different conditions. This might contribute to the policy relevance of such studies because one could then postulate that certain types of institutions would be better for particular situations.

Finally, a future step for institutional analysis beyond comparison involves the democratization of international institutions. If such institutions are to thrive, it seems likely that they will have to become more democratic. As the EU makes clear, one strong source of resistance to the growing role of international institutions is their lack of democracy. As international institutions are becoming more salient in people's lives—for example, the EU or even NAFTA—it seems unlikely that individuals will willingly relinquish control over their fates to international institutions less democratic than the states previously controlling these aspects of their lives. Can international institutions be democratized? What would this mean in terms of their structure? What would be the effects of this change? If being seen to adequately represent the diversity of domestic interests is necessary for international institutions to possess legitimacy and influence, then how can international institutions develop such mechanisms of representation? Addressing these issues calls out for use of the theories and tools developed in comparative and American politics to explore which democratic institutions would be most appropriate for particular international settings. Robert Dahl poses the question historically:

> Is democracy in the national state, then, destined to meet the fate of democracy in the city-state? . . . If so, just as democracy on the scale of the national state required a new and unique historical pattern of political institutions radically different from the ancient practices of assembly democracy that the small-scale of the city-state made possible, will democracy on the transnational scale require a new set of institutions that are different in some respects, perhaps radically different from familiar political institutions of modern representative democracy?[94]

Rational Institutionalism and Game Theory

Scholarship in the rationalist paradigm in IR is returning to its earlier attention to game theory, which suffused much of deterrence theory in the 1950s and 1960s. With various advances in game theory since then—especially in the handling of incom-

---

93. Note that this is exactly what Young called for in the 1980s to move regime analysis forward. "Taking a cue from the public choice movement, students of international regimes might well consider devising a series of controlled experiments to investigate the consequences of alternative institutional arrangements under conditions that simulate those prevailing in international society"; Young 1986, 117.

94. Dahl 1994, 27.

plete information—the reemergence of noncooperative game theory and its ideas is perhaps not surprising. What is interesting is that this trend is occurring in the field of American politics and to some extent in comparative politics.[95] This trend relates to the type of institutional analysis now being used in these fields.[96]

As noted earlier, rational institutionalist analysis has focused on *strategic interaction* among domestic players under particular institutional conditions. The focus on strategic interaction has led to the use of game theory, in particular noncooperative game theory.[97] Game theory is ideal for analyzing such situations since it provides a "theory of interdependent decisions—when the decisions of two or more individuals jointly determine the outcome of a situation. [Moreover, it] provides a way to formalize social structures and examine the effects of structure on individual decisions."[98]

The three examples discussed in the section on international institutions all employ the type of noncooperative game theory associated with institutional analysis in American and comparative politics. These models provide a way to see what outcomes will result when several players interact strategically in an environment structured by particular political institutions. They allow one to see how altering these institutions, while holding the actors' preferences constant, changes the outcomes; that is, they promote comparative institutional analysis. (They also demonstrate the results of altering the players' preferences while holding the institutions constant.)[99] This institutional analysis is useful because it can capture how institutions affect an

---

95. For a discussion of rational choice in comparative politics, see Bates 1997b. For examples in comparative politics, see Tsebelis 1990, 1995; Tsebelis and Money 1997; Laver and Shepsle 1995; G. Cox 1987, 1997; Huber 1996b; Shugart and Carey 1992; Carey 1996; Levy and Spiller 1996; Przeworski 1991; Rogowski 1987, forthcoming; Weingast 1995, 1997; Baron and Ferejohn 1989; Baron 1991; North and Weingast 1989; and Fearon and Laitin 1996.

96. Rational choice theory has been in use for many years now. Some early examples in IR include the essays by Schelling, Quandt, and Verba in Knorr and Rosenau 1961; Schelling 1960; Harsanyi 1969; and Frohlich, Oppenheimer, and Young 1971.

97. Noncooperative game theory does not imply that the actors cannot cooperate; they can at times, and the theory seeks to show when it is rational to do so. The difference between cooperative and noncooperative games is traditionally claimed to be that in the latter communication is not allowed among the players. But this distinction is no longer the most appropriate, since now noncooperative games do explicitly model certain types of communication. The central difference is that in cooperative games the players can coordinate their strategies through binding agreements. In noncooperative games, instead, the players must enforce any coordination of their strategies through the game itself, which means that coordination must result from the individual interests of the players; Morrow 1994a, 75–76. In noncooperative games, then, one must demonstrate how cooperation among the players is implemented and what incentives the players have for violating the agreements they make. Cooperative games allow players to bind themselves to agreements that may not be enforceable but conform to certain axioms of fairness; Fudenberg and Tirole 1991, xviii. Hence, they abstract from how and why players find and keep agreements in the first place.

In addition, in noncooperative games the units of analysis are the individual players, who try to do the best they can subject to the structures they face and the moves of the other players. In contrast, in cooperative games often the group or coalition is the unit of analysis; Kreps 1990b, 9. These differences in the nature of the two games are important because they make noncooperative game theory more suitable for exploring the interaction among individual players when cooperation is difficult and there are incentives to defect. These are conditions easily applicable to IR. The real change has been in their acceptance in the domestic politics arena.

98. Morrow 1994a, 1.

99. For other examples, see Milner and Rosendorff 1996, 1997; Milner 1997; and Martin 1997.

actor's power. Institutions are not viewed as neutral arenas for cooperation, rather they are political means to realize one's preferences.

The rise of noncooperative game theory to explore domestic politics combined with the adoption among IR scholars of institutional analysis and of domestic players as their unit of analysis has drawn the fields onto similar paths both substantively and methodologically. Will this be fruitful? Criticisms of the rationalist paradigm are legion. Without rehearsing these debates, let me discuss two major criticisms. Many have argued that rational choice only works when actors' preferences are already known. Related is the problem of the beliefs held by the actors. In complete information games, these beliefs are assumed to be the same across the players and known to all the players (the "common knowledge" assumption). In imperfect information games, these beliefs become all the more important, for in this case usually at least one player does not know something about the game or the other players. Another major problem with game theory is the indeterminacy resulting from many games.[100] In different classes of games, multiple equilibria are possible, as the chaos results from spatial models and the folk theorem from repeated games make evident. Although there are various equilibrium refinements to choose from among these equilibria, they tend to provoke more questions than they answer. Without imposing stronger assumptions, many game models yield no unique, robust equilibrium.

Rational choice theorists have tended to deal with these problems by assumption.[101] In the political arena, the most common assumption has been that political actors want to get or stay elected to office; office holding gives them power to obtain the goods they prefer: personal wealth, particular policies, the glory of the nation. This simple assumption has been used in widely different areas and has produced interesting results.[102] Other than by assumption, preferences have been identified through two methods. One method has been to deduce policy preferences from basic interests and to use these policy preferences to define the game's payoff structure.[103] This does not, however, avoid the problem, because the issue of defining "basic interests" ultimately arises.

The other method has been to borrow from research traditions that directly examine the sources of preferences and beliefs. Research on both ideas and on the social construction of identity can provide information about actors' preferences that rationalists can use. Recent work in the rationalist paradigm has tried to make use of these nonrationalist accounts of preferences and beliefs. For example, Garrett, Barry Weingast, and Ferejohn suggest that ideas and identities provide focal points that can be used to solve multiple equilibria problems in game theoretic analyses.[104] Weingast shows how a common set of beliefs is necessary to support a democratic form of

---

100. It is interesting to note that rational choice is often criticized for being deterministic. In games with a unique equilibrium, rather than being too indeterminate, the approach is often seen as too determinant.

101. Since rational choice derives from economics and liberal theory, the unwillingness to impose preferences on the actors is often seen as a plus.

102. See, for example, Downs 1957; and Carey 1996.

103. See Milner 1988, Rogowski 1989; and Frieden 1991, 1997a.

104. See Garrett and Weingast 1993; and Ferejohn 1993.

government: "To survive, the rule of law requires [that] limits on political officials be self-enforcing. As we have seen, self-enforcement of limits depends on the complementary combinations of attitudes and reactions of citizens as well as institutional restrictions."[105] This type of work holds out the promise of combining the advantages of game theory and its focus on strategic interaction with the knowledge of preferences and beliefs gained from other research paradigms. One of the earliest such combinations is Jervis' exquisite *The Logic of Images*, which blends Thomas Schelling's *Strategy of Conflict* and Erving Goffman's *The Presentation of Self in Everyday Life* and shows how ideas and beliefs affect strategic interaction and how strategic manipulation, in turn, can affect identity and beliefs.

Conclusions

Given that the field of international relations has not been very successful in predicting either the evolution of international politics during the Cold War or its conclusion, what can IR theory do to be able to better understand world politics in the future? I argue here that relaxing two of the central assumptions of IR theory can make a difference. Bringing domestic politics back in is a first step. Adopting the tools used in the fields of American and comparative politics to build a more systematic analysis of domestic politics is an important step. The rational institutionalist approach provides one way to do this and might generate some interesting ideas.

The applicability of this approach to IR might seem limited. But if institutions are seen as a means for aggregating diverse preferences into collective outcomes in situations of strategic interaction, then institutions are important in IR too. Moreover, the focus on domestic politics to see how diverse preferences are crafted into a national interest and how strategy is chosen also seems germane to all parts of IR. Even when external pressures are strong, these must be filtered through the domestic polity, and different groups within the state are likely to respond to them in different ways.

Being able to systematically explore domestic politics and its effects on international relations holds out the promise of more cumulative research. Understanding how preferences are aggregated to arrive at the "national interest" and how different political institutions will yield different outcomes are important steps.[106] For example, this type of institutional analysis allows one to synthesize both societal and statist approaches to foreign policy. One begins with an appreciation of actors' preferences and beliefs, which may come from outside the rationalist paradigm. But analysis cannot stop here: the policy chosen rarely reflects some single actor's interests. Instead, policy is likely to be the result of a complex strategic interaction among the players as structured by domestic institutions. Ideally, this understanding should be combined with a similar understanding on the international level in order to explain not only policy choices but also the outcomes of those choices.

105. Weingast 1997, 262.
106. See, for example, Garrett and Lange 1996; and Milner 1997.

Two further steps in institutional analysis could be fruitful as well. Following studies of domestic politics, IR might move toward more comparative institutional analysis at both the domestic and international levels. Scholars might explore the effects that different political institutions have on policy choices and how these policies are implemented. Some studies of the democratic peace have begun this process.[107] But more could be done on issues of both political economy and national security by exploring the effects of different institutions within democracies and autocracies. On the international level, comparative institutional analysis is only beginning. The analysis of different mechanisms for settling disputes and enforcing agreements seems to be a priority.[108] Such studies might also have important policy implications. Being able to show the ways in which different institutions shape how organizations like NATO can most effectively maintain peace and security or how the WTO can best promote freer trade could have major benefits.

Finally, if democracy is a value to be pursued domestically, one might want to extend that to the international level. Crafting more democratic institutions globally may be most important for their continued success. The EU has brought this issue to the fore. After centuries of struggle to achieve democracy, societies in Europe are likely to demand that the international institutions that hold sway over growing portions of their lives should be at least as democratic. If leaders do not heed such calls, international institutions are likely to remain brittle. Without popular representation and the legitimacy it accords, these institutions will not be able to create the commitment that their continuity demands. Publics when frustrated by the decisions of these institutions will simply elect to ignore or exit them. The democratization of international institutions is an important issue. Political scientists can contribute to it by using existing knowledge about the sources and means of democratization within countries.

International Organization, as a long-standing forum for the analysis of actors other than states in international politics, has been at the forefront of these changes. It has given voice to many of the challenges to realism since its inception. But lately it has taken up the challenges advocated here. Perusal of its pages shows that it was a leader in scrutinizing the UN; in pioneering the debate about regional integration and the EU; in making transnational politics a key research area; in initiating the study of international regimes; and lately in providing a forum for rational institutionalist analysis applied to both domestic and international institutions. Increasingly, *IO* has been the venue for publication of articles exemplifying the emerging synthesis in the study of American, comparative, and international politics.

---

107. See, for example, Russett 1993; and Fearon 1994b.
108. See, for example, Yarbrough and Yarbrough 1992.

Global Markets and National Politics: Collision Course or Virtuous Circle?

Geoffrey Garrett

The impersonal forces of world markets are now more powerful than the states to whom ultimate political authority over society and economy is supposed to belong. Where states were once the masters of markets, now it is the markets which, on many crucial issues, are the masters over the governments of states.[1]

Throughout the world today, politics lags behind economics, like a horse and buggy haplessly trailing a sports car. While politicians go through the motions of national elections—offering chimerical programs and slogans—world markets, the Internet, and the furious pace of trade involve people in a global game in which elected representatives figure as little more than bit players. Hence the prevailing sense, in America and Europe, that politicians and ideologies are either uninteresting or irrelevant.[2]

While the world stands at a critical time in postwar history, it has a group of leaders who appear unwilling, like their predecessors in the 1930s, to provide the international leadership to meet economic dislocations. . . . Like the German elite in Weimar, they dismiss mounting worker dissatisfaction, fringe political movements, and the plight of the unemployed and working poor as marginal concerns compared with the unquestioned importance of a sound currency and balanced budget. Leaders need to recognize the policy failures of the last 20 years and respond accordingly. If they do not, there are others waiting in the wings who will, perhaps on less pleasant terms.[3]

These three quotations reflect widely held beliefs about the fate of national autonomy in the global economy. The nation-state is purportedly an outmoded and beleaguered

I would like to thank Stephen Brooks, Benjamin Cohen, Jeffry Frieden, Robert Inman, Torben Iversen, Bruce Kogut, Peter Lange, Jonas Pontusson, Dennis Quinn, Jonathan Rodden, Dani Rodrik, Beth Simmons, Arthur Stein, and Duane Swank for helpful comments and discussions. Quinn and Swank graciously agreed to share unpublished data with me. Special thanks are due to Peter Katzenstein, Robert Keohane, and Stephen Krasner, not only for excellent comments on successive iterations of this article, but also for the manifold collective goods they have provided over the years to me and other students of international political economy.

1. Strange 1996, 4.
2. Roger Cohen, "Global Forces Batter Politics," *The New York Times Week in Review,* 17 November 1996, 1.
3. Kapstein 1996, 37.

International Organization 52, 4, Autumn 1998, pp. 787–824

institutional form, on a collision course with the ever more international scale of markets. Policy autonomy, if not de jure sovereignty, is considered the primary casualty.[4] Governments competing for mobile economic resources are thought to have little choice but to engage in a policy race to the neoliberal bottom,[5] imperiling the efficacy and legitimacy of the democratic process itself.[6]

This article puts under the analytic microscope the proposition that global markets trump national politics as social forces. I focus on the relationships between three dimensions of integration into international markets—trade in goods and services, the multinationalization of production, and financial capital mobility—and the macroeconomic policy choices of the advanced industrial countries up until the mid-1990s.

One can certainly point to examples where globalization constraints on national policy choices are readily apparent. The mobility of financial capital, for example, has tended to put downward pressure on budget deficits because of the interest rate premiums the capital markets attach to them. But it is hard to make the case that globalization constraints are pervasive, or even the norm. Indeed, there are numerous instances in which various facets of market integration have been associated with both more interventionist government policies and greater divergence in national trajectories over a range of policy areas—without precipitating damaging capital flight in countries that have eschewed the neoliberal path.

Trade and government spending is the classic relationship that goes against simplistic conceptions of the lowest common denominator effects of market integration—not only in the Organization for Economic Cooperation and Development (OECD)[7] but also in the developing world.[8] Other globalization myths, however, should also be exposed. For example, increasing liquid capital mobility has been associated with faster growth in government spending and even with increases in effective rates of capital taxation—without resulting in capital flight or higher interest rates. Moreover, there is no evidence that the multinationalization of production has reduced macroeconomic policy autonomy.

There are two basic reasons why globalization constraints on policy choice are weaker than much contemporary rhetoric suggests. First, market integration has not only increased the exit options of producers and investors; it has also heightened feelings of economic insecurity among broader segments of society. This situation

---

4. Others have analyzed the effects of globalization on phenomena as diverse as culture (Barber 1995; Meyer et al. 1997), ethnic nationalism (Huntington 1996), urban development (Sassen 1997), and inequality (Wood 1994).

5. See Andrews 1994; Cerny 1990; Gill and Law 1989; Kurzer 1993; McKenzie and Lee 1991; Moses 1994; Scharpf 1991; and Schwartz 1994. There are, of course, stronger and weaker versions of the argument, as some analysts have been careful to point out; see Hirst and Thompson 1996; and Pauly 1995.

6. Not everyone considers the consequences of diminished national autonomy bad. Fukuyama and Ohmae, for example, argue that the effective demise of the nation-state will make the world more peaceful and wealthier. See Fukuyama 1992; and Ohmae 1995.

7. Cameron 1978.

8. Rodrik 1997.

has strengthened political incentives for governments to use the policy instruments of the state to mitigate market dislocations by redistributing wealth and risk.

Second, although there are costs associated with interventionist government (the familiar refrain of neoclassical economics about tax distortions, crowding out, and regulatory rigidities), numerous government programs generate economic benefits that are attractive to mobile finance and production. Today it is not controversial to argue that good government entails protecting property rights and increasing human capital and physical infrastructure. But the logic should be extended further. Some economists have argued that reducing inequality stimulates growth by increasing social stability.[9] Prominent political scientists contend that economic policies redistributing wealth and risk also maintain popular support for the market.[10]

It should be a central objective of globalization research to see how these two sets of dynamics—capital's exit threats versus popular demands for redistribution, and the economic costs and benefits of interventionist government—play out in different contexts. In this article I point to two sources of variation. The first concerns differences among various facets of market integration and aspects of government policy choice (see the preceding examples). The second source of variation concerns domestic political conditions. Countries in which the balance of political power is tilted to the left continue to be more responsive to redistributive demands than those dominated by center-right parties. The existence of strong and centralized organizations of labor and business that coordinate economic activity reduces the economic costs of interventionist government by mitigating free-rider problems.

In summary, I do not believe that "collision course" is the correct metaphor to apply to the panoply of relationships between interventionist national economic policies and global markets. Peaceful coexistence is probably a better general image, as all agree it was during the golden age of capitalist democracy after World War II. One might go further to argue that, even in a world of capital mobility, there is still a virtuous circle between activist government and international openness. The government interventions emblematic of the modern welfare state provide buffers against the kinds of social and political backlashes that undermined openness in the first half of the twentieth century—protectionism, nationalism, and international conflict. At a time when Ethan Kapstein and others voice fears of the 1930s all over again, it is important that the economic benefits of government activism be better understood.

The remainder of the article is divided into seven sections. First, I sketch the contours of the globalization and national autonomy debate. Second, I trace the genealogy and details of arguments about globalization constraints. Third, I elaborate my critique of the conventional wisdom. Fourth, I assay the differences across countries and market segments concerning the extent of market integration in the OECD. Fifth, I analyze the effects of globalization on macroeconomic policy choice in these countries. Sixth, I explore the macroeconomic consequences of interventionist eco-

9. Alesina and Perotti 1996.
10. See Katzenstein 1985; Przeworski and Wallerstein 1982; and Ruggie 1983b.

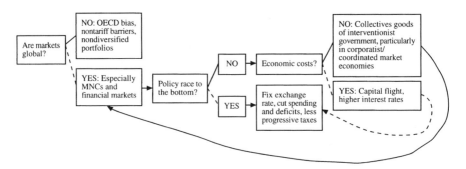

FIGURE 1. *Globalization and national autonomy*

nomic policies. The final section is a summary of my analysis of the opportunities for and constraints on governing in the global economy.

The Globalization–National Autonomy Debate

Figure 1 depicts the contemporary globalization debate. Three central questions must be answered. First, are markets global? For many analysts, international market integration is the definitive characteristic of the contemporary world political economy. The case can be made regarding the rapid growth of trade in goods and services, but most attention focuses on the multinationalization of production (through foreign direct investment [FDI], international mergers, and strategic alliances) and the integration of financial markets (in equities, bonds, currencies, and ever more exotic derivatives). In many instances growth rates are exponential and the dollar figures involved are staggering. To take the classic example, the Bank of International Settlements estimates that global currency transactions in 1992 were worth $1.2 trillion per day—almost double the 1989 figure and considerably larger than the currency reserves of the world's central banks.

Globalization skeptics, in contrast, voice numerous reservations about the extent of market integration. First, markets today are not much more internationally integrated on many dimensions than they were at the end of the nineteenth century.[11] From a longer historical perspective, the most important story about the twentieth century may well be the precipitous decline in globalization in the middle of the century, rather than the upswing in international activity in recent decades. Second, the bulk of international economic activity is still concentrated in the advanced industrial democracies, with growing linkages between East Asia and the OECD standing out as the most notable geographic extension of international markets.[12]

---

11. See Maddison 1995; and Obstfeld and Taylor 1997.
12. Wade 1996a.

Third, no international markets are nearly as integrated as they are within national borders. Domestic savings continue to constrain national patterns of investment,[13] and investors' portfolios are far from optimally diversified across countries.[14] The best estimates of multinationalized production indicate that such activity comprises less than 10 percent of output even in the world's most integrated economies.[15] Finally, notwithstanding the effects of the Uruguay Round of the GATT (General Agreement on Tariffs and Trade), substantial nontariff barriers continue to restrict trade.[16]

My intention is not to debate the merits of calling markets "global." Rather, I accept the more cautious proposition that markets have "globalized" in recent decades, allowing us to focus on the consequences of this process for national policy autonomy. This raises the second key question about globalization: does increased market integration exert lowest common denominator pressures on national economic policies? The conventional answer is unequivocal affirmation, based on the notion that internationally mobile capital (both financiers and multinational firms) can credibly threaten to exit national economies in which economic policies are not closely tailored to their preferences. Fixed exchange rates, balanced budgets, smaller government, regressive tax cuts, and deregulation are the likely result.

Globalization skeptics, however, note that this economic logic view does not take into account the fact that globalization increases economic insecurity among broad cross sections of society, strengthening political incentives for governments to redistribute market allocations of risk and wealth. This political logic of voice stands in marked contrast to the economic logic of exit.

The final question in the globalization debate is if policy regimes do not converge around a free market ideal type, does this have macroeconomic costs? The common answer to this question is again a resounding "yes." Productive and financial capital will hemorrhage, interest rates will rise, investment will decline, and economies will stagnate. The alternative view is that government may provide a range of collective goods that are valuable to firms and investors. These may at least balance the costs of interventionist government. Under certain conditions, the benefits of big government may even outweigh the costs.

Having sketched the contours of the globalization debate, the following two sections discuss in more detail the two contending views about the domestic effects of market integration.

Globalization Constraints

Three Globalization Mechanisms

Market integration is thought to affect national policy autonomy through three basic mechanisms. These are trade competitiveness pressures, the multinationalization of production, and the integration of financial markets.

13. Feldstein and Bacchetta 1991.
14. See French and Poterba 1991; and Gordon and Bovenberg 1996.
15. Lipsey 1998.
16. OECD 1996.

Increasing trade competition is the first component of the conventional globalization thesis. According to this view, big government is by definition uncompetitive.[17] Government spending crowds out private investment, is less efficient than market allocations, and cushions market disciplines on prices and wages. In turn, spending must be funded either by borrowing or by higher taxes. Taxes cut into firms' profits and depress entrepreneurial activity. Government borrowing increases interest rates. As a result of these effects, output and employment suffer from public sector expansion. Since no government can afford these consequences, trade competition must result in a rolling back of the public economy.

The second globalization mechanism concerns the multinationalization of production and the attendant credibility of firms' threats to move production from one country to another in search of higher rates of return. This was the "giant sucking sound" Ross Perot predicted the North American Free Trade Agreement would produce. Multinational exit has also been at the forefront of European debates in the 1990s. Indeed, for some, software engineers telecommuting from Bangalore to Seattle and Silicon Valley are the harbingers of the New World of the twenty-first century.[18] Robert Reich, for example, proclaimed in influential articles in the *Harvard Business Review* that the distinction between "us" and "them" in the global economy is not between countries, but rather between a nation's citizens and multinational firms operating in it, irrespective of where they are owned.[19]

As with trade, conventional arguments about the policy consequences of the multinationalization of production focus on the costs to business of interventionist government. The difference is that firms with production facilities in more than one country can evade these costs by exiting the national economy. Governments must thus embrace the free market if they are to compete for the investment and jobs provided by multinational firms.

The final argument made about globalization constraints focuses on the international integration of financial markets. Traders operating twenty-four hours a day can move mind-boggling amounts of money around the globe more or less instantaneously in ceaseless efforts to arbitrage profits. The potential for massive capital flight acts as the ultimate discipline on governments. In an already infamous aside, Clinton political strategist James Carville is said to have uttered "I used to think that if there was reincarnation, I wanted to come back as the president or the pope. But now I want to be the bond market: you can intimidate everyone." [20]

Scholarly analyses of the domestic effects of the integration of financial markets often are almost as strident, replete with evocative images such as "casino capitalism," [21] "quicksilver capital," [22] and "who elected the bankers?" [23] The central logic

17. See Pierson 1991; and Pfaller et al. 1991.
18. Greider 1997.
19. Reich 1990 and 1991.
20. "A Survey of the World Economy: Who's in the Driving Seat?" *The Economist*, 7 October 1995, 3.
21. Strange 1986.
22. McKenzie and Lee 1991.
23. Pauly 1997.

underpinning this research program is the power conferred on financial capital by the credibility of its exit threats. Governments are held to ransom by the markets, the price is high, and punishment for noncompliance is swift.[24] If the policies and institutions of which the markets approve are not found in a country, money will hemorrhage until they are.

Déjà Vu All Over Again?

The urgent tenor of the contemporary globalization debate would seem to imply that the besieged nation-state is a new phenomenon. But the implications of international integration for domestic policy have been of concern for more than two hundred years—basically since the birth of industrial capitalism. David Hume, Charles Louis Montesquieu, and Adam Smith all believed that capital mobility would restrain the growth of the state.[25] Indeed, Adam Smith's argument about capital taxation in *The Wealth of Nations* is remarkably similar to contemporary claims:

> The proprietor of stock is properly a citizen of the world, and is not necessarily attached to any particular county. He would be apt to abandon the country in which he was exposed to a vexatious inquisition, in order to be assessed a burdensome tax, and would remove his stock to some other country where he could either carry on his business, or enjoy his fortune more at ease A tax which tended to drive away stock from any particular country, would so far tend to dry up every ounce of revenue, both to the sovereign and to the society.[26]

In the twilight of the Victorian empire, Norman Angell thought that the effects of international economic integration were so pervasive that they had made the ultimate expression of sovereignty, war, virtually unthinkable.[27] The penultimate wave of concern about the future of the nation-state swelled in the late 1960s. Charles Kindleberger famously proclaimed that "the state is about through as an economic unit" as a result of the power of multinational firms.[28] Raymond Vernon entitled his influential book on the same subject *Sovereignty at Bay*.[29] In the first systematic analysis of domestic effects of interdependence, Richard Cooper argued that national economic policy autonomy was significantly constrained by the international integration of markets.[30]

In this subsection, I focus on two research themes spawned by the writings of Cooper, Kindleberger, and Vernon that occupied many pages in *IO* during the 1970s—transnational relations and interdependence, and dependency and underdevelopment. The 1971 special issue "Transnational Relations and World Politics," edited

---

24. For review articles, see Cohen 1996; and Andrews and Willett 1997.
25. I thank Arthur Stein for informing me about these arguments. See also Hirschman 1981; and Stein 1993.
26. Quoted in Hirschman 1981, 256.
27. Angell 1911.
28. Kindleberger 1969, 207.
29. Vernon 1971.
30. Cooper 1968.

by Robert Keohane and Joseph Nye, was the journal's first concerted foray into international political economy.[31] The issue's central claim was that realist models stressing conflict among unitary states could not take into account the contemporary international environment populated, in addition to nation-states, by nonstate actors (including, but not limited to, multinational firms and international financiers) with links cutting across territorial boundaries.[32] Subsequent work in this tradition emphasized the effects of differential sensitivity and vulnerability to international economic developments on power relations among states,[33] the nature of cooperation in the international system,[34] and the role of international institutions in fostering cooperation.[35]

The primary focus of the transnational relations–interdependence school was outward looking—to build a new paradigm of international politics. Nonetheless, the parallels are striking between the analytic foundations of interdependence scholarship and contemporary arguments about globalization. Consider the following quotation from Edward Morse that opens his article in the transnational relations special issue of *IO*:

> Changes in the structure of the global economy have resulted in a withering of governmental control of certain activities presumed to be de jure within the domain of governments. . . . [I]nternational monetary crises . . . have demonstrated the emergence of financial markets that seem to operate beyond the jurisdiction of even the most advanced industrial states of the West and outside their individual or collective control. The flourishing of multinational corporations has affected the . . . economic growth policies of highly developed and less developed states alike by restricting the freedom of those governments to establish social priorities. Tariff reductions . . . have similarly increased the number of nonmanipulable and unknown factors which must be accounted for in planning a wide spectrum of domestic and foreign economic policies—from regional development policy or anti-inflationary efforts on the domestic side to the international exchange rate of a state's currency.[36]

Morse thus argued that three (now familiar) facets of market integration posed a grave threat to national autonomy—trade, multinational firms, and international financial markets. Other authors in the transnational relations issue made similar claims. Louis Wells argued that "the enterprise with subsidiaries scattered around the globe clearly has the potential to evade the influence of many government policies."[37] Lawrence Krause asserted that "the integration of financial markets is of particular concern because private international financial activities have seriously infringed on

---

31. Reprinted as Keohane and Nye 1972.
32. The special issue also contained articles on a diverse array of noneconomic actors, including the Ford Foundation and the Roman Catholic Church.
33. Keohane and Nye 1977.
34. Krasner 1983b.
35. Keohane 1984.
36. Morse 1972, 23.
37. Wells 1972, 97.

governmental sovereignty."[38] Keohane and Nye concluded that "transnational relations create a 'control gap' between the aspirations for control over an extended range of matters and the capability to achieve it. The problem is not a loss of legal sovereignty but a loss of political and economic autonomy."[39]

Transnational relations–interdependence, however, was not the only market integration–nation-state research program to feature prominently in *IO* in the 1970s. Disillusioned with the failures of mainstream economists' policy prescriptions for development, Latin American scholars—beginning in the 1950s with the United Nations Economic Commission for Latin America headed by Raúl Prebisch—argued that international integration was not the path to prosperity, but rather the road to dependency and underdevelopment.

Only Peter Evans in the transnational relations issue squarely addressed development issues.[40] In 1978, however, *IO* devoted a special issue to the dependency thesis. The issue's editor, James Caporaso, captured the distinctiveness of this enterprise by noting that the antonym of dependency is autonomy, not interdependence.[41] The bulk of the articles in the issue were ambivalent about the merits of the claims made by the Latin American dependentistas. Richard Fagen was the one clear exception. He argued that "hardly anyone anymore suggests that 'the free play of market forces' will bring in its wake movement toward the eradication of poverty, more equitable distribution of life chances, and other valued goals of development."[42]

Fagen believed that developing countries could and should insulate themselves from damaging international economic ties, by nationalizing multinational firms and protecting domestic industry. This emphasis on multinationals and protectionism has subsequently been supplanted in development scholarship by a concentration on the domestic effects of financial integration.[43] Observers of the industrial democracies today, of course, share these fears about the consequences of capital mobility. The contemporary globalization debate thus blurs what was a clear distinction in the 1970s between interdependence and dependency.

Summary

In this section I have made two basic points. First, there are three different facets of globalization that many consider to constrain national autonomy—trade, the multinationalization of production, and the internationalization of financial markets. Second, contemporary arguments about these globalization pathways are nothing new. One could transplant much of the work published in *IO* in the 1970s on interdependence and dependency into the 1990s globalization literature without fearing for its rejec-

38. Krause 1972, 189.
39. Keohane and Nye 1972, 393.
40. Evans 1972.
41. Caporaso 1978b, 18.
42. Fagen 1978, 292–93.
43. See Maxfield 1997; and Winters 1996.

tion as outmoded. Indeed, with appropriate changes in lexicon, the same could be said for Adam Smith.

With hindsight we know that the nineteenth century was one of great state building and that the 1970s was a decade in which the scale and scope of government activism increased rapidly. Should one expect things to be different today, as contemporary rhetoric suggests?

Reassessing the Policy Consequences of Globalization

Trade, Compensation, and Embedded Liberalism

Arguments about the constraining effects of market integration on economic policy choice have a long and distinguished history. There is, however, a very different approach to the globalization–domestic politics relationship that also has an impressive pedigree. Karl Polanyi's analysis of the emergence of industrial democracy in the nineteenth century emphasized a "double movement" with two components.

> One component was the principle of economic liberalism, aiming at the establishment of a self-regulating market, relying on the support of the trading classes, and using largely laissez faire and free trade as its methods; the other was the principle of social protection, aiming at the conservation of man and nature as well as productive organization, relying on the varying support of those most immediately affected by the deleterious action of the market, and using instruments of intervention as its methods.[44]

Forty years later, John Gerard Ruggie made a similar argument about the post–World War II reconstruction of open markets and democratic politics.[45] He characterized the Bretton Woods system as sustaining an "embedded liberalism" compromise that coupled trade liberalization with domestic policies that cushioned market dislocations. At about the same time, Peter Katzenstein argued that the distinctive feature of the small European democracies was their willingness to adjust and adapt to international markets while compensating those adversely affected by this process.[46] Most recently, Dani Rodrik showed that the trade openness–domestic compensation nexus continues to hold throughout the world, not just in the industrial democracies.[47]

The embedded liberalism perspective did not question the core proposition of trade theory that liberalization, in the long run, is good for all segments of society. The distinctive feature of this scholarship was the recognition that the short-run political dynamics of exposure to trade (and to other international markets) are very different. Openness increases social dislocations and inequality and hence heightens political pressures for dampening these effects. If protectionism (and the disastrous spiral of economic decline, nationalism, and conflict with which it was associated in

44. Polanyi [1944] 1957a, 132.
45. Ruggie 1983b.
46. Katzenstein 1985.
47. Rodrik 1997.

the 1930s) is to be averted, government must redistribute market allocations of wealth and risk.

Bretton Woods facilitated the twin goals of trade liberalization and domestic compensation by combining fixed exchange rates with capital controls.[48] Fixed rates promoted trade by stabilizing expectations about future price movements. Capital controls gave governments the macroeconomic autonomy to smooth business cycles through countercyclical demand management.

The impact of capital controls on policy autonomy is best understood in terms of the Mundell-Fleming approach to open economy macroeconomics.[49] Only two of the following three conditions can obtain at once: a fixed exchange rate, monetary policy autonomy, and free movement of capital across borders. If Bretton Woods had committed countries to removing all restrictions on capital flows in addition to fixing their exchange rates, countries would have lost their monetary autonomy as well. National governments would have been unable to mitigate economic downturns by printing more money because capital would have exited unless and until interest rates rose to the world rate. But the final Articles of Agreement obviated this possibility by adopting John Maynard Keynes' recommendation that the imposition of capital controls be allowed, if not encouraged.[50]

Strategies of domestic compensation in response to trade liberalization, however, were not limited to demand management. Rather, analysts describe the domestic policy regimes that emerged during the Bretton Woods era as the "Keynesian welfare state." In addition to the Keynesianism described earlier, the term also implied the public provision of social insurance (through pensions, unemployment benefits, and other income transfer programs) and social services (most notably education and health care), all paid for by relatively high and progressive systems of taxation.[51]

It is easy to see why the welfare state component served the political purposes of embedded liberalism. Social insurance directly supports those adversely affected by market risk. The public provision of social services not only provides benefits to consumers irrespective of their ability to pay but also generates a source of employment that is less vulnerable to the vicissitudes of market competition. Progressive taxes take into account the ability of different segments of society to pay for government programs. The welfare state redistributes wealth and risk, thereby dampening popular opposition to free markets.

But what about the economic effects of the welfare state (that is, assuming spending and taxation are in balance)? Here, the ambit of macroeconomic policy must be

48. The Bretton Woods system also allowed for consensually agreed adjustments in exchange-rate parities to correct fundamental disequilibrium in the balance of payments and IMF lending to support exchange rates during temporary crises. For an excellent analytic history of Bretton Woods, see Eichengreen 1996.
49. Mundell 1962. For a systematic application to politics, see Frieden 1991.
50. Many of Keynes' prescriptions were unacceptable to the United States, but this was not the case for capital controls.
51. The seminal study is Shonfield 1965. Other important examples include Esping-Andersen 1985; Goldthorpe 1984; and Lindberg and Maier 1985.

extended beyond that analyzed in the Mundell-Fleming framework to focus on the costs and benefits of different aspects of the public economy. The contending arguments mirror closed economy analyses from public finance, made all the more important by trade liberalization, which renders national economies price takers in international markets. Claims about the uncompetitiveness of the welfare state concentrate on the costs of government provision of social insurance and social services. The welfare state lessens market disciplines and crowds out private sector entrepreneurship; taxes distort investment decisions in ways that reduce efficiency.

On the other hand, many people argue that interventionist government generates numerous economic benefits that may at least offset these costs. The key notion here is the public provision of collective goods that are undersupplied by markets. Even economists in the Chicago school tradition consider some government services to be essential to capitalism: the rule of law and securing of property rights.[52] For new growth theorists, public education and the government provision of human capital and physical infrastructure are also important drivers of development.[53]

The logic of politically correctable market failures can, however, be applied more broadly. For example, it is well established in development economics that material inequality is bad for growth. Alberto Alesina and Roberto Perotti have argued that this is because inequality leads to social conflict, which stability-seeking investors do not like.[54] Since the welfare state mitigates conflict by reducing market-generated inequalities of risk and wealth, it may have beneficial rather than deleterious consequences for business.[55] Government spending may thus stimulate investment via two channels–increasing productivity through improvements in human and physical capital and increasing stability through maintaining support for market openness.

In summary, the embedded liberalism compromise of the Bretton Woods period combined an international regime of trade openness, fixed exchange rates, and capital controls with the domestic political economy of the Keynesian welfare state. The final observation that should be made about this combination is that many analysts believe that embedded liberalism was most prominent and worked best in countries characterized by strong and centralized (corporatist) labor movements and powerful social democratic parties. Center-left parties are more likely to be sensitive to the political demands of short-term market losers. Corporatist labor movements have incentives to tailor wage growth to benefit the economy as a whole and hence not to take advantage of government compensation (in the form either of Keynesian demand management or welfare state expansion) with demands for less work at higher pay.[56]

52. The most influential proponent of this view today is North; North 1990. It has also become a central component of official development policy; World Bank 1997.
53. See Aschauer 1991; and Barro and Sala-I-Martin 1995.
54. Alesina and Perotti 1996.
55. Garrett 1998a. For an alternative view, see Persson and Tabellini 1994.
56. See Alvarez, Garrett, and Lange 1991; Garrett 1998a; and Lange and Garrett 1985. Some scholars argue that the successes of this regime type had as much to do with the organization of business as the organization of labor; see Soskice 1990; and Swenson 1991.

The Crisis of Embedded Liberalism?

Notwithstanding the manifest successes of embedded liberalism in the Bretton Woods period, it is widely believed today that the open markets–domestic compensation compromise is no longer viable. The most prominent causal agent in its purported demise is heightened mobility of productive and financial capital and the decline on restrictions on international flows with which it has been associated.[57] No one suggests that political demands for compensation or the need for government to mitigate anti-international pressures have declined.[58] Rather, the conventional view is that the ability of government to deliver its side of the embedded liberalism compromise has been dramatically reduced.

There are two different mechanisms by which increased capital mobility is thought to render domestic compensation infeasible.[59] The first concerns financial market integration and traditional Keynesianism. Ruggie and others argue that financial integration makes fixed exchange rates imperative, to increase the markets' confidence about the stability of national economic policy.[60] But following Mundell-Fleming, fixing the exchange rate under capital mobility vitiates macroeconomic policy autonomy.

The second mechanism concerns the multinationalization of production and the nature of the public economy. Rodrik argues that governments can no longer maintain, let alone expand, the generous welfare state–progressive taxation mix.[61] Mobile firms are deemed unwilling to pay the taxes to fund government programs. Rodrik claims that the future of the welfare state can only be secured by shifting the tax burden from mobile (firms and financiers) to immobile (labor) asset holders, emasculating its redistributive effects.

Thus, two of the most perceptive students of the contemporary international political economy both accept the core proposition of the conventional wisdom on globalization. A quantum leap in the exit threats of mobile producers and investors has tilted the balance of power strongly in favor of the market over politics at the national level. The following two subsections question this argument by exploring in more detail the domestic effects of the multinationalization of production and financial market integration.

57. Some scholars suggest that financial integration has been driven by developments in information technology over which governments have had little control; see Bryant 1987; and Goodman and Pauly 1993. Others argue that the removal of capital controls was an ideological choice that could be reversed; see Sobel 1994; and Banuri and Schor 1992. I take the intermediate position of Frieden and Rogowski that, even if theoretically still effective, the opportunities costs associated with capital controls have increased greatly in recent decades; Frieden and Rogowski 1996.

58. Pierson 1996a.

59. Scholars often argue that corporatist labor market institutions have eroded over time, particularly in Scandinavia. Iversen 1996; and Pontusson and Swenson 1996. But more broadly based studies suggest that the structure of organized labor movements has been remarkably stable; see Golden 1998; Lange and Scruggs 1997; and Lange, Wallerstein, and Golden 1995.

60. Ruggie 1996a. See also Scharpf 1991.

61. Rodrik 1997. For a similar argument, see Steinmo 1993.

The Multinationalization of Production and the Collective Goods of Government

Embedded liberalism, Bretton Woods style, comprised three elements—fixed exchange rates and capital controls, Keynesian demand management, and extensive government spending and redistributive taxation. How might we expect these to be affected by the multinationalization of production?

One could argue that multinationals favor fixed exchange rates because these lessen uncertainty about the consequences of internationally diversified production regimes.[62] If this were the case in a world of liquid capital mobility, governments that acceded to the demands of multinationals would also be giving up their monetary autonomy. But today there is arguably a better way than pressing for fixed exchange rates for multinational producers to insure against international price movements: hedging using financial instruments. The range of derivatives options available to investors is limited only by the imagination of market makers. And multinationals would probably prefer to control their own risk portfolios than to cede this right to governments. This is all the more likely given the difficulty of running stable pegged exchange rates in the contemporary era (see the next subsection). As a result, it seems unlikely that the multinationalization of production should significantly increase the incentives for governments to fix their exchange rates and hence tie their hands with respect to monetary policy.

The primary concern of the globalization literature with respect to the multinationalization of production, however, is the reaction of mobile producers to high levels of government spending and taxation (and to other production costs, most notably wages). The conventional view is that the decisional calculus of multinationals is simple: produce in the lowest cost location. If this were correct, increased exit options for firms would put considerable downward pressures on the size and scope of the public economy.

For those who study FDI decisions and corporate alliance strategies for a living, however, the behavior of multinational producers is more complex. First, the right metric of costs controls for productivity, and on this score small government–low-wage economies do not look nearly so attractive.[63] Second, the literature on international corporate strategy focuses primarily on accessing new technology, new distribution channels, and new markets as the drivers of FDI and strategic alliances.[64] Third, if a firm opens, acquires, or allies with a production facility in a foreign country, this does not necessarily imply that it reduces activity in its home country. Under many circumstances new foreign activities will go hand in hand with increased activity and employment at home—"upstream"—in portions of the productive, marketing, and distributive processes where more of the final value is added.

---

62. Moravcsik makes this argument, for example, with respect to European efforts to fix exchange rates since the end of Bretton Woods; Moravcsik 1998.

63. Krugman 1996. Nonetheless, many fear that the rapid dissemination of technology will soon dramatically reduce productivity differences among countries.

64. See Cantwell 1989; Caves 1996; Dunning 1988; and IMF 1991.

Finally, international diversification provides another way for firms to hedge against currency risk. Taken together, these considerations belie the notion of a lowest cost mantra in the location decisions of multinational producers.[65]

Why might multinationalized producers be willing to locate in countries with large public economies and high taxes? My answer is the same as that for trade. Multinational producers care about the real economy, and factors such as productivity and stability heavily influence their investment decisions. Activist governments can do something positive to influence these decisions, by increasing human and physical capital stocks and by promoting public support for open markets. Indeed, these collective goods may be even more important than was the case for trade as a result of the heightened feelings of economic insecurity among citizens generated by multinationalization.

There is an important objection to my argument, however, that was not germane to the trade discussion—tax competition among governments for mobile producers. Rodrik rightly argues that even if multinational producers benefit from government interventionism in the ways I have suggested, they nonetheless have incentives to try to free ride on these collective goods by not paying the taxes to fund them.[66] Multinationals can use threats of exit to force governments to shift the tax burden away from capital and onto labor. But before making such threats, firms must weigh the costs and benefits of helping finance the provision of collective goods from which they benefit in one country versus paying lower taxes but receiving fewer benefits in another.[67] It is an empirical, not a theoretical, matter whether the costs of big government outweigh the benefits I have outlined and hence whether multinationalization should put downward pressures on capital taxation.

In summary, there is little reason to expect that the multinationalization of production produces strong pressures for fixed exchange rates or constrains macroeconomic policy autonomy in the classical Keynesian sense. A better argument can be made about constraints on the spending, and particularly the taxing, policies of governments. But these constraints will be much less apparent if, as I argue is this case, large public economies generate numerous outcomes that are attractive to multinationals.

The Mobility of Financial Capital, Exchange Rate Regimes, and Fiscal Policy

Even if I am right to question common assumptions about the behavior of multinationalized producers, the debate could simply shift to policy constraints generated by the integration of financial markets. Here again, I wish to argue that the strictures

---

65. This is not to claim, however, that production costs are irrelevant. There are some sectors, such as textiles and apparel, where labor costs have a large bearing on location decisions. Leamer 1996. Moreover, there are temptations for governments to try to attract FDI by offering specific tax concessions and other monetary inducements; see Hines 1997.

66. Rodrik 1997.

67. Of course, multinational firms could still try to free ride on government services through tax evasion or accounting tricks.

imposed by global capital are not nearly so tight as is often presumed. Unpacking the likely policy effects of the international integration of financial markets should begin with its implications for the choice of exchange-rate regimes.

There is only one clear case where financial integration vitiates macroeconomic policy autonomy—monetary policy where there are no barriers to cross-border capital movements and where a country's exchange rate is fixed.[68] But this only raises the questions: why do countries choose to fix their exchange rates? How important is globalization to this choice?[69] European Union officials in the context of the monetary union debate have revived old arguments from Bretton Woods about the importance of currency stability to trade.[70] Empirical work, however, fails to show any strong positive impact of fixed rates on trade expansion, presumably because of the effectiveness of currency-hedging instruments under floating rate regimes.[71] The more common argument these days concerns the policy credibility of governments with the financial markets. By fixing the exchange rate, governments are supposed to be able to mitigate the damaging effects of capital flight or other policies that would be required to stop it.

Unlike exporters and multinational producers, financial market actors care much less about productivity and the real economy than they do about monetary phenomena that affect day-to-day returns on financial transactions. Inflation is the key variable. If the markets expect inflation to increase in the future, the price they are willing to pay for a national currency will decrease, and the interest rates they charge on loans will be higher. Thus, governments have incentives to establish reputations for price stability because inflationary expectations lead the financial markets to behave in ways that harm the real economy.

Few economists dispute the argument that inflation-fighting credibility is important to macroeconomic performance.[72] There is much less support, however, for the notion that fixing the exchange rate is a good way to achieve credibility under conditions of financial integration. The evidence is at best mixed as to whether participation in fixed exchange-rate regimes lowers inflation rates.[73] There may be better domestic ways to gain credibility with the financial markets, such as making the central bank more independent or enacting balanced budget laws.[74] Moreover, one should expect financial market actors to prefer floating exchange rates to fixed ones since they make money from arbitrage and commissions.[75]

On the other side of the equation, the costs of fixed exchange rates are often high. Although fiscal policy may be quite effective in a country that pegs its exchange rate,

68. Mundell 1962.
69. For a good precis of the various arguments about the determinants of exchange-rate regime choice, see Eichengreen 1994.
70. Commission of the European Communities 1990.
71. IMF 1983.
72. This is the core of the rational expectations revolution in macroeconomics. See Friedman 1968; and Lucas 1972.
73. Collins was the first to question the inflation-fighting properties of the EMS; Collins 1988.
74. Fratianni and von Hagen 1992.
75. Frieden 1991.

it cannot use monetary policy to adjust to any economic shock that affects it differently from the object of the peg (gold, a single currency, or a basket of currencies). Depreciating the nominal value of a currency remains a very effective way to increase the real competitiveness of an economy in recession—because domestic prices do not rise immediately in response to nominal depreciations.[76] But smooth depreciations are not possible for countries seeking to defend currency pegs. Rather, governments typically engage in desperate efforts to maintain a given exchange rate and are often vanquished by the markets in damaging waves of speculative attacks. In this context it should be noted that the headline currency crises of the 1990s—in Europe, Mexico, and East Asia—all involved countries seeking to sustain pegs that the markets deemed untenable.

For these reasons many economists today recommend that fixed exchange-rate regimes under conditions of financial integration should only extend to countries that constitute optimal currency areas. These areas comprise only those countries for whom there is little need to maintain domestic monetary autonomy—because their business cycles move together, wages adjust quickly to asymmetric shocks, labor is mobile across national borders, or fiscal arrangements transfer funds from boom to bust regions.

In the headline case of European monetary union, for example, most analysts believe that Europe's optimal currency area extends only to Austria, the Benelux countries, Germany, and perhaps France—but certainly not to Italy.[77] One could argue that Italy's fervent desire to participate in Europe's monetary union reflects its need to overcome long-standing credibility problems. Italy's economic history in the 1990s does not seem to lend much credence to this view. The lira was forced out of the exchange-rate mechanism of the European Monetary System (EMS) in 1992—an ignominious defeat for the Italian government at the hands of the foreign exchange markets. But the lira did not go into uncontrollable free fall, nor did instability and a lack of market confidence paralyze the Italian economy. On the contrary, the currency depreciated relatively smoothly to a level that could be easily sustained. Italian economic activity quickly picked up, against the continuing deep recession among the remaining EMS members. Thus, even in the Italian case, one probably must look beyond market credibility considerations to explain the government's desire to participate in monetary union.

In summary, the arguments in favor of the common globalization proposition that the integration of financial markets creates irresistible pressures for government to fix their exchange rates to increase market credibility are far from convincing. Fixed exchange rates may make sense for some highly interdependent economies. Countries that cannot gain market credibility with domestic policies (for example, some

---

76. Obstfeld 1997.

77. If this is correct, why would Germany want irrevocably to fix its exchange rate against Italy? Analyses of Germany's EMU position typically involve politics, specifically Helmut Kohl's ambitions concerning political union in Europe. For an accessible survey of the contending arguments and evidence, see Garrett 1998b.

unstable developing nations) may have little choice but to fix their exchange rates. But for many countries, and probably the bulk of the OECD, floating the exchange rate makes more sense under conditions of financial capital mobility.

Moving to fiscal policy, increasing public sector deficits clearly puts upward pressure on interest rates in a world of capital mobility (particularly if the exchange rate floats). But how large is this interest-rate premium? Financial integration reduces the costs of fiscal expansion by making available an immense size of potential lenders.[78] At some point, of course, higher debt burdens may trigger fears of governments' defaulting on their loans—resulting in dramatic reductions in the availability of credit and skyrocketing interest rates. This was the case during the Latin American debt crises of the 1980s, but this limit seems not yet to have been reached in any industrial democracy.[79]

Belgium is the clearest instance of the weakness of fiscal constraints under capital mobility. The Belgian franc has long been stably pegged against the deutsche mark, with very small interest-rate differentials between the two countries. This is despite the fact that Belgian public debt has been the highest in the OECD for most of the last decade, and more than twice as large as Germany's. To take a harder European case, public debt is also very high in Italy. Italian interest rates have sometimes during the past twenty years been as much as three or four points higher than German rates. But if this is the most brutal fiscal repression wrought by global finance among the industrial countries, the proclamations of many commentators would seem somewhat hyperbolic.

I have now discussed two conventional parts of macroeconomic policy—exchange-rate regime choice and the running of fiscal deficits—in the context of global finance. What about constraints on the size of government itself? Here a distinction should be drawn between the preferences of financial markets actors and those of multinationalized producers. The latter can and should pay predominant attention to the effect of government policy on productivity and real aggregates—and hence ask whether the costs of big government outweigh the benefits (as discussed in the previous subsection). Financial market participants, in contrast, focus almost exclusively on the effect of government policy on the supply of and demand for money.

The financial markets must ask a simple question: will a government raise new taxes to pay for higher spending, or will it seek to borrow money? If the answer is "tax," one should expect the markets to be relatively unconcerned—even if some of these revenues are raised by capital taxation. But if the answer is "borrow," the markets know that the government will have an incentive to inflate in the future to try to reduce the real cost of their debt. Higher interest rates must be charged if bond yields are to be maintained, the currency must depreciate if real exchange rates are to remain stable. Thus, the financial markets care much less about the size and scope of government interventions than about how they are paid for.

78. Corsetti and Roubini 1995.
79. Corsetti and Roubini 1991.

Summary

In this section I have made three basic points. First, contemporary claims about the dire consequences of globalization for national autonomy are nothing new. With respect to the industrial democracies at least, history proved wrong previous proclamations of the demise of the nation-state. Second, the policy constraints imposed by market integration are likely to be different for trade and the multinationalization of production, on the one hand, than for the integration of financial markets, on the other. For the former, the relationship between the public economy and productivity is most important. With respect to financial integration, issues affecting the value of monetary instruments are paramount. Third, there are good reasons to believe that the policy constraints generated by these relationships are weaker and less pervasive than is often presumed.

Market Integration in the OECD

In the remainder of the article I examine the empirical record for the OECD countries since the 1960s. I focus on these countries for pragmatic and methodological reasons. The data on both market integration and government policy are better for the OECD.[80] More importantly, the advanced industrial countries are more integrated into global markets than developing countries are; they are also presumably better equipped (in terms of political resources) to respond to the constraints globalization may generate. If the mixed economies of the OECD have not fared well under globalized markets, this cannot portend well for other countries.

Aggregate Trends over Time

The average exposure of the OECD countries to trade in goods and services (exports plus imports as a percentage of gross domestic product [GDP], unweighted by country size) increased consistently from less than 50 percent in 1960 to almost 70 percent by the mid-1980s, before stabilizing in the following decade (see Figure 2). Over the same period, the various GATT rounds reduced average tariff rates from around 25 percent to under 5 percent, although the use of nontariff barriers increased (at least until the Uruguay Round).[81] Rising trade, however, has not been accompanied by a secular increase in trade volatility. Volatility only increased markedly during the two oil shocks in the 1970s and with the halving of oil prices in the mid-1980s.

The aggregate data also suggest that the popular canard about the heightened importance of imports from low-wage economies should be qualified (see Figure 3). The oil shocks did result in a surge of non-OECD imports. But isolating OECD imports from low-wage economies (that is, excluding OPEC) shows that they have

---

80. For an analysis of available data for the developing world, see Garrett 1998d.
81. Wade 1996a, 69.

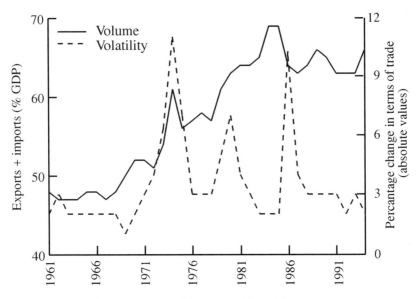

Source: OECD, Historical Statistics, 1960–94.

FIGURE 2. The volume and volatility of trade

consistently constituted over the period under analysis around 20 percent of all OECD imports. As Paul Krugman has argued with respect to the United States, it would be hard to blame rising low-wage imports for all economic problems in the industrial countries.[82]

Figure 4 presents data on intra-industry trade across the OECD from 1980 to 1992. The data measure the extent to which a country exports the same types of goods and services as it imports (based on two-digit SITC codes). A score of 0 would reflect pure inter-industry (Ricardian) trade; 1 would indicate that a country imported exactly the same types of products as it exported. Coupled with the stability in low-wage imports over time, high and rising intra-industry trade suggests that if competition has intensified, this has more to do with intra-OECD trade in the same sector (automobiles is a classic example) than with low wage competition from the developing world.

Turning to the globalization of capital, Figure 5 shows that (combined inflows and outflows of) FDI and international portfolio investments (assets and liabilities for bonds and equities) have grown much more rapidly than trade. These data underscore conventional views about the rise of footloose capital. The FDI numbers are particularly important since they represent the best available data on the multinationalization of production.

82. Krugman 1996.

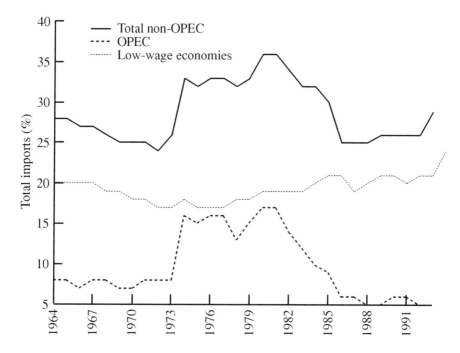

Note: Unweighted country averages.
Source: OECD, *Historical Statistics*, 1960–94.

FIGURE 3. *Imports from outside the OECD*

Economists are reticent to conclude, however, that the rapid growth of portfolio capital flows signifies a real increase in the mobility of financial capital. The dramatic upturn in flows since the early 1970s, for example, is no doubt in part the product of the end of the Bretton Woods fixed exchange-rate regime, necessitating international diversification to hedge against currency risk. In a seminal paper, Martin Feldstein and Charles Horioka argued that financial markets were, in fact, not very internationally integrated in the 1970s—because domestic investment was highly correlated with domestic savings.[83] Feldstein later reported similar results for the 1980s.[84] The Feldstein–Horioka approach, however, has been criticized on many grounds. Perhaps the most important is that anything that affects both savings and investment behavior will tend to inflate correlations between them and hence understate capital mobility.[85] As a result, I do not examine savings–investment correlations in the empirical analysis of globalization constraints on policy.

There are two measures of financial market integration that are arguably superior to savings–investment correlations. The first is based on official government restric-

83. Feldstein and Horioka 1980.
84. Feldstein and Bacchetta 1991.
85. Hallerberg and Clark 1997.

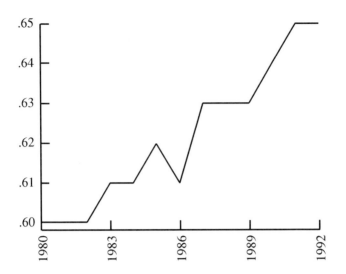

Source: OECD, *Trade Statistics*, various years, based on two-digit SITC. Definition from Grubel and Lloyd 1975, 36.

FIGURE 4. *Intra-industry trade*

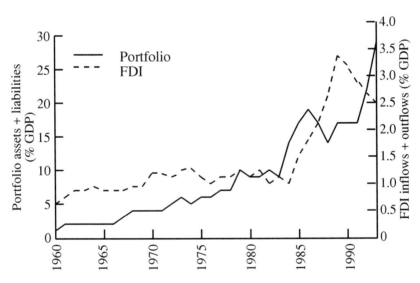

Source: IMF, *Balance of Payments Statistics*, various years.

FIGURE 5. *International capital flows*

tions on cross-border capital movements.[86] Capital controls, however, are not ideal instruments for assessing the independent effects of globalization constraints on policy autonomy because they are another aspect of government policy choice (even if one constrained by exogenous factors such as changes in information technology).

The second measure of financial market integration is based on differences in the costs of capital. Interest rates would converge in a truly global capital market. But when exchange rates float, one must first take into account expectations about future currency movements to isolate remaining differences in capital costs. This can be done using "covered" interest-rate differentials—the difference between interest rates on a given instrument in one country and those in an offshore benchmark (typically, the eurodollar market), controlling for the forward exchange rate against the dollar.[87] Remaining differentials reflect either sovereign risk or barriers to the movement of capital. Sovereign risk (the probability that governments will default on their debts) is generally thought to be low in the OECD, but in some cases (in the newer members of the rich nations' club, for example) it is surely not negligible. As a result, one cannot perfectly infer the magnitude of barriers to international financial flows from covered interest-rate differentials. Compared with capital controls, however, the advantage of this measure is that it is based on actual market behavior rather than on government policy.

I use both measures of financial market integration in this article, specifically Dennis Quinn's financial openness index (higher scores signify more integration) and the absolute value of covered interest rate differentials (higher differentials indicate less integration). Figure 6 plots cross-national averages for both variables over time. At this level of aggregation, the data on financial openness and interest rates are highly correlated (as they are with international portfolio flows). The story they tell is familiar, reflecting rapid increases in financial integration since the 1960s.

Variations Across Countries and Markets

Reading much of the globalization literature, one would assume that most industrial economies are similarly integrated into most international markets. Tables 1 and 2 show that this is manifestly not the case. I concentrate on two sets of summary statistics—the coefficients of variation within categories of market integration (the bottom row of Table 1) and Pearson's *r* correlations between pairs of categories (Table 2). The former provides a good measure of dispersion and convergence across countries; the latter is indicative of the extent to which different facets of market integration go together.

The coefficients of variation represent the standard deviation of the national observations divided by their mean. A score of zero would indicate complete cross-national convergence. There are only two coefficients of variation in Table 1 that could plausibly be interpreted as "near zero"–intra-industry trade and financial open-

---

86. See Quinn 1997; and Quinn and Inclan 1997.
87. See Frankel 1993; and Marston 1995.

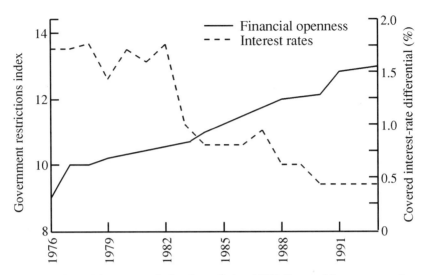

Source: Financial openness index from Quinn 1997. Covered interest rates from Shepherd 1994, 265–71.

FIGURE 6. *Capital mobility*

ness. Intra-industry trade does not feature prominently in many analyses of globalization. But the financial openness index coefficient is even lower, giving some support to the conventional wisdom.

Table 2 presents a matrix of correlations for the post-1985 period based on the same globalization data. Are economies that are globalized in one market highly integrated into other international markets as well? Not really. Consider the correlations between total trade and the other indicators of integration. Trade was positively (but not strongly) associated with more intra-industry trade, lower tariffs, and greater volumes of FDI and international portfolio flows. But bigger traders tended to be less dependent on low-wage imports, to have less volatile trade patterns, and to be more reliant on nontariff barriers. Moreover, there was no relationship between trade dependence and either measure of financial market integration. In turn the correlations between financial integration and other facets of globalization were generally not strong and positive. More financial openness and smaller covered interest-rate differentials were associated with more intra-industry trade and higher FDI flows but with less trade volatility and smaller portfolio investment flows.

Finally, one would expect Quinn's financial openness index to be highly correlated with covered interest-rate differentials. It certainly is over time for the OECD as a whole (as Figure 6 shows). At the cross-national level, the correlation is in the expected direction (more openness is associated with smaller differentials). But it is not very strong. This might suggest either that sovereign risk is quite significant in the OECD or, more plausibly, that important barriers to capital mobility are not captured

TABLE 1. *Market integration since 1985*

Country	Structure of trade				Trade policy		Multinationalization of production	Financial integration		
	Total trade (% GDP)	Low-wage imports (% total)[a]	Trade volatility[a]	Intra-industry trade	Tariffs[b]	NTBs[c]	FDI (% GDP)	Portfolio investment (% GDP)	Financial openness index	Covered interest-rate differentials
Australia	36.0	21.0	9.9	0.26	10.4	0.7	3.2	56.0	11.1	1.33
Austria	76.2	14.6	3.8	0.80	6.3	15.1	0.9	13.1	12.1	0.20
Belgium	140.7	11.0	2.5	0.81	4.6	22.1	6.0	45.7	11.8	0.46
Canada	54.6	14.0	1.9	0.70	5.7	8.3	1.5	8.7	13.5	0.16
Denmark	65.1	13.3	2.1	0.74	4.6	22.1	1.7	21.6	12.8	1.52
Finland	53.3	22.6	4.8	0.61	9.2	7.9	1.9	14.0	11.3	—
France	43.7	17.0	4.0	0.86	4.6	22.1	2.6	9.0	11.8	0.65
Germany	50.6	18.8	5.2	0.72	4.6	22.1	1.5	10.7	14.0	0.14
Greece	45.4	15.7	3.9	0.36	3.2	22.1	—	—	8.2	—
Iceland	67.7	—	—	—	4.2	3.0	—	—	—	—
Ireland	115.2	9.1	2.6	0.68	4.6	22.1	0.3	25.6	11.2	0.75
Italy	41.3	18.2	4.9	0.69	4.6	22.1	0.9	10.3	12.1	0.45
Japan	19.1	34.1	10.9	0.36	3.7	11.4	0.9	11.2	10.6	—
Luxembourg	191.1	—	—	—	4.6	22.1	—	—	—	—
Mexico	30.8	—	—	—	13.4	2.0	—	—	—	—
Netherlands	101.8	13.0	2.0	0.83	4.6	22.1	5.3	18.7	14.0	0.65
New Zealand	56.5	15.3	4.8	0.38	10.0	0.4	—	—	12.8	—
Norway	71.7	13.2	8.2	0.54	3.1	5.9	2.0	16.3	11.3	0.94
Portugal	66.6	11.7	—	0.49	4.6	22.1	—	—	9.9	—
Spain	39.5	16.7	5.1	0.71	4.6	22.1	—	—	11.7	—
Sweden	62.0	11.5	3.6	0.73	3.3	3.7	3.4	21.6	11.7	0.77
Switzerland	71.5	8.9	3.7	0.66	2.4	3.6	4.4	14.3	13.0	0.34
Turkey	33.6	—	—	0.47	9.8	0.2	—	—	13.0	—
United Kingdom	51.7	15.5	2.3	0.82	4.6	22.1	5.1	19.0	14.0	0.21
United States	20.6	34.0	2.2	0.64	4.5	23	1.3	2.5	13.7	0.11
Coefficient of variation[d]	0.60	0.41	0.58	0.28	0.49	0.66	0.69	0.72	0.12	0.75

Note: Country averages are for longest available period, 1985–present (see Figures 2–6). Dashes indicate that data are not available.
[a]Standard deviation of annual changes in the terms of trade, 1985–94.
[b]Post–Uruguay MFN (most-favored nation) tariff rates (binding on all merchandise trade) (Finger, Ingco, and Reincke 1996, 67).
[c]Percentage of all products subject to nontariff barriers in 1993 (OECD 1996, 52–55).
[d]Standard deviation/mean.

TABLE 2. *Correlations across market segments*

Correlation with:	Low-wage imports	Trade volatility	Intra-industry trade	Tariffs	NTBs	FDI	Portfolio investment	Financial openness	Covered interest rates
Total trade	−0.71	−0.44	0.44	−0.26	0.29	0.43	0.43	0.03	0.02
Low-wage imports		0.45	−0.35	0.17	0.02	−0.38	−0.29	0.01	−0.19
Trade volatility			−0.70	0.22	−0.46	−0.25	0.22	−0.44	0.30
Intra-industry trade				−0.41	0.52	0.30	−0.31	0.53	−0.33
Tariffs					−0.52	−0.10	0.44	0.10	0.29
NTBs						−0.02	−0.23	−0.02	−0.22
FDI							0.45	0.29	0.01
Portfolio investment								−0.36	0.51
Financial openness									−0.45

Note: Correlations are Pearson's *r*, based on the data in Table 1.

by formal government restrictions on capital flows. Either way, empirical analyses of the policy consequences of financial integration for national autonomy could differ considerably depending on which indicator of capital mobility is used. Reporting results for both is the prudent course.

Summary

In this section I have made two simple points about market integration in the OECD. First, the pace of globalization has varied considerably across different markets. Second, substantial cross-national differences in market integration endure. The OECD is not one giant seamless market. I now turn to the policy effects of globalization.

Macroeconomic Policy

In this section I examine the relationships between market integration and macroeconomic policy. I concentrate on three policy indicators: total government spending, public sector deficits, and capital taxation. Spending is a simple summary indicator of government involvement in the economy. Deficits measure overall budgetary stances. Capital taxation is the single part of tax systems that many believe to be most vulnerable to globalization constraints.[88]

---

88. These indicators exclude important facets of microeconomic reform that arguably have been driven by globalization in recent decades—deregulation and privatization, for example. The qualitative evidence on microeconomic reform, however, is not conclusive. For insightful analyses, see Berger and Dore 1996; and Vogel 1995.

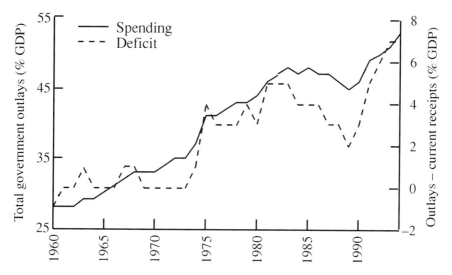

Source: OECD, *Historical Statistics*, 1960–94.

FIGURE 7. *Government spending and public sector deficits*

Over-Time Trends

Figures 7 and 8 present over-time policy trends for the OECD as a whole. Average government spending basically doubled as a portion of GDP from 1960 to the mid-1990s, when it comprised over half of total output. As might be expected, spending increased most during the deep recessions of the mid-1970s, early 1980s, and early 1990s. But the size of the public economy only decreased as a portion of GDP during one upturn in the business cycle—the mid-1980s. Given that this is the period on which many influential analyses of globalization constraints are based, this may explain the prominence of assertions about public sector rollback. Nonetheless, the history of government spending in the postwar OECD is predominantly one of sustained growth.

The expansion of the public economy has not been wholly matched by increased taxes. Budget deficits increased by about seven points from 1960 to 1994. It is often assumed that this revenue shortfall reflects the declining ability of governments to tax increasingly mobile capital. Changes in marginal rates of corporate income taxation are consistent with this view—they have declined considerably in most OECD countries in the past fifteen years.[89] But from the perspective of revenue-hungry governments, these marginal rates are not the whole story. Governments certainly have incentives to reduce taxes that impede growth-creating investment, of which marginal corporate tax rates are a clear example. But most cuts in marginal rates in the OECD have been accompanied by other reforms that have increased the tax

89. Cummins, Hassett, and Hubbard 1995.

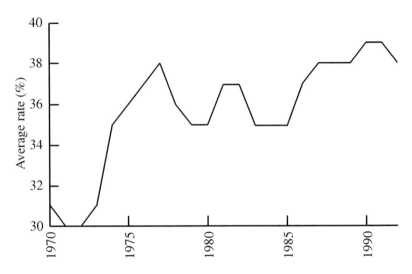

Note: See text for definition.
Source: Mendoza, Milesi-Ferreti, and Asea 1997.

FIGURE 8. *Capital taxation*

base—reductions in investment incentives, depreciation allowances, and other loop-
holes that pertain to capital taxation.[90]

Figure 8 presents data on average effective rates of capital taxation that take into
account both changes in marginal rates and in the tax base.[91] Notwithstanding the
short-term volatility of this measure resulting from variability in profits, the overall
trend in effective rates of capital taxation has been upward, quite strongly so. Rates in
the early 1990s averaged almost 40 percent, up from around 30 percent in the early
1970s. This is a long way from predictions of a free fall in capital taxation resulting
from the exit threats of multinational firms and financial speculators.

In summary, the trends over time in Figures 7 and 8 are hard to square with the
notion of pervasive globalization constraints on national economic policy autonomy.
Does one get a different picture by examining economic policy data on a country-by-
country basis?

Variations Across Countries and Market Segments

In this subsection I explore cross-national variations in economic policy and their
relationships with globalization. Three indicators of market integration are used—

90. Swank 1998.
91. These are calculated as government revenues from all sources of capital income—corporate profits,
capital gains, financial transactions, and property holdings—as a percentage of the gross operating surplus
(profits) in an economy. See Mendoza, Milesi-Ferreti, and Asea 1997.

total trade (a simple proxy for competitiveness pressures),[92] FDI flows (for the multi-nationalization of production),[93] and the financial openness index and covered interest-rate differentials (the integration of financial markets). These relationships are also compared with the associations between economic policy and a simple partisan politics variable (the combined power of left-wing parties and organized labor movements) that historically has had a marked impact on economic policy choice.

Table 3 presents data that allow us to answer a basic question: is it the case, as the conventional wisdom would suggest, that fiscal policy strategies have converged in the era of more globalized markets? The data in Table 3 are for the post-1985 period as well as for changes in policy from historic averages.

The coefficient of variation for total government spending since 1985 is quite small. One could debate whether OECD public economies have become "about the same size." After all, Switzerland's public economy is still only half the size of Sweden's. What is more interesting, however, is that national trajectories diverged considerably from historical averages (1960–84) to the post-1985 period. Taking the extreme cases, spending grew six times as much in Spain as in the United Kingdom. This divergence is precisely the opposite of the conventional wisdom about the effects of globalized markets.

The deficits data are even less supportive of the conventional view. There was considerable dispersion in budgetary stances in the post-1985 period as well as in terms of changes from historical averages. Some of the cross-national differences are dramatic. Switzerland ran surpluses of over 2 percent of GDP after the 1985 period, whereas deficits in neighboring Italy were over 10 percent. Deficits in Greece increased by more than six points from the pre- to post-1985 periods, but they declined by almost two points in Japan.

Perhaps most surprisingly of all, the capital tax coefficients of variation do not look much different from the spending and deficits numbers. In the post-1985 period, considerable dispersion in capital tax rates remained. But the divergence from pre- to post-1985 rates of capital taxation was even more marked. Capital tax rates declined by 2.7 points in the United States, but they increased by more than 10 points in Finland, Japan, and Sweden.

These descriptive data can only support one conclusion: fiscal policies among the OECD countries have not converged in recent years. Is there any more evidence of globalization constraints when one breaks market integration down into its components? Table 4 provides a reference set of hypotheses based on the conventional wisdom. Exposure to trade is thought to put downward pressures on government spending. But these effects should be stronger for the multinationalization of production and stronger still for financial integration. Moving across the table, the efficiency perspective would suggest that the downward pressures of each globalization vari-

92. Garrett and Mitchell show that the effects of total trade on welfare state expenditures are not significantly different from those of trade volatility or imports from low-wage economies; Garrett and Mitchell 1998.

93. Note that these flow numbers do not take into account the stock of foreign investment in a country, nor strategic alliances among multinational firms from different countries.

TABLE 3. *Fiscal policy since 1985*

Country	Total government spending		Public sector deficit		Effective rate of capital taxation	
	Level[a]	*Change[b]*	*Level*	*Change*	*Level*	*Change*
Australia	37.9	8.9	3.5	2.1	46.8	8.3
Austria	51.5	8.5	3.9	2.5	22.6	2.3
Belgium	57.9	10.7	7.4	2.1	36.7	2.9
Canada	47.9	11.9	6.7	3.8	41.4	0.7
Denmark	59.8	17.1	1.9	1.2	34.8	—
Finland	51.2	16.5	1.3	3.8	44.4	14.4
France	51.6	10.0	4.9	3.4	26.0	3.2
Germany	47.5	5.3	2.6	1.1	28.5	2.4
Greece	51.2	16.5	13.8	6.6	—	—
Iceland	39.6	8.1	3.7	4.3	—	—
Ireland	46.3	5.5	5.6	−1.4	—	—
Italy	52.8	14.3	10.9	4.5	28.1	—
Japan	32.6	8.2	−0.3	−1.8	48.8	19.4
Luxembourg	51.4	9.6	−3.1	−2.1	—	—
Mexico	—	—	—	—	—	—
Netherlands	59.0	10.9	5.1	2.4	30.5	—
New Zealand	—	—	—	—	36.7	—
Norway	52.4	10.7	−2.8	0.3	39.2	0.7
Portugal	43.2	15.6	5.8	3.6	—	—
Spain	43.7	18.4	6.1	4.7	—	—
Sweden	64.2	16.5	3.8	4.0	60.6	14.0
Switzerland	32.4	8.1	−2.4	1.7	28.2	6.2
Turkey	—	—	—	—	—	—
United Kingdom	43.7	3.1	4.3	1.0	57.5	1.9
United States	36.8	5.5	5.1	2.5	40.5	−2.7
Average	47.9	10.9	4.0	2.3	38.3	5.7
Coefficient of variation	0.18	0.41	1.02	0.96	0.28	1.15

Note: Dashes indicate that no data are available.

[a]Levels based on 1985–94 for spending and deficits; 1985–92 for capital taxation.

[b]Changes are 1985 averages minus 1960–84 for spending and deficits; 1965–84 (or first available year) for capital taxation.

able should be stronger on deficits than on spending and stronger still on the capital taxation. Finally, many commentators believe that the effects of partisan politics on policy have diminished considerably in recent years. This should be manifest in near zero correlations with economic policy in the contemporary era and negative associations in the change data (that is, larger reductions in activism in countries with stronger left-wing parties and trade unions).

The correlations for the post-1985 period in Table 5 send mixed signals. On the one hand, and consistent with my arguments, exposure to trade, FDI flows, and left-labor power were all associated with greater spending after 1985. On the other

TABLE 4. *The conventional wisdom about globalization and fiscal policy*

	Economic policy		
Globalization mechanism	*Government spending*	*Public sector deficit*	*Capital tax rate*
Exposure to trade	–	– –	– – –
Multinationalization of production	– –	– – –	– – – –
Capital mobility	– – –	– – – –	– – – – –
Left-labor power	0/–	0/– –	0/– – –

Note: Minus signs denote strength of the negative relationships.

TABLE 5. *Globalization, partisan politics, and fiscal policy since 1985*

	Economic policy		
Globalization mechanism	*Government spending*	*Public sector deficit*	*Capital tax rate*
Exports + imports/GDP (%)	.38	−.25	−.24
FDI inflows + outflows/GDP (%)	.18	−.01	.19
Financial openness index	.02	−.29	−.19
Covered interest rates[a]	−.34	.13	−.09
Left-labor power	.58	−.31	.27

Note: Figures are Pearson's *r* correlation coefficients. All data are averages for periods after 1984 to the latest available year, except left-labor power. Left-labor power is the standardized sum of cabinet portfolios held by left-wing parties, 1950–93 plus union density, 1960–89.

[a]Multiplied by −1 so that higher scores reflect more capital mobility.

hand, the covered interest rate–spending correlation implies a constraining effect of capital mobility on the public economy. One way to reconcile these findings would be to endogenize capital mobility, hypothesizing that strong left-labor regimes have chosen to protect their public economies by retaining significant controls on the mobility of capital.[94] This may have been the case in the past, but the correlation between the power of the left and the strength of trade unions and capital mobility all but evaporated by the latter half of the 1980s.[95]

An alternate explanation is that countries have reacted in very different ways to increasing capital mobility, based on the balance of partisan power within their borders. I have presented elsewhere more sophisticated analyses—using panel regressions with multiplicative interactions between globalization and partisan politics—

94. Quinn and Inclan 1997.
95. Garrett 1998a.

that support this view.[96] Strong left-labor regimes responded to financial market integration with ever-higher levels of public spending, whereas governments in countries with much weaker left parties and trade unions cut back the public economy.

Now consider the correlations for public sector deficits after 1985. Contra standard assumptions about left-labor power, deficits historically have been smaller in strong left-labor regimes than elsewhere.[97] Nonetheless, one should expect globalization—especially financial market integration—to have put downward pressures on deficits. The bivariate correlations do not strongly support this expectation. Financial openness and total trade were somewhat correlated with smaller deficits. But this was not the case for FDI or interest-rate differentials.

Finally and perhaps most surprisingly, the capital tax correlations for the post-1985 period were no more supportive of globalization conventional wisdom. Lower tax rates were correlated with greater exposure to trade, financial openness, and covered interest-rate differentials, but none of these associations was at all strong. In contrast, FDI flows were weakly associated with higher capital taxes. Finally, the association between left-labor power and capital tax rates was positive and larger than any of the globalization–taxation correlations were.

No great weight can be attached to these simple bivariate correlations. But even the most sophisticated existing research on taxation and globalization does not strongly support a race-to-the-bottom interpretation. Rodrik finds that capital mobility constrains capital taxation but only in countries with high levels of trade dependence and trade volatility.[98] Quinn and Swank report little or no relationship between capital mobility and corporate taxation.[99] Garrett argues that the effects of globalization on capital taxes, as was the case for spending, are contingent on the partisan balance of power.[100] Hallerberg and Basinger demonstrate that the number of veto players, not capital mobility, best explains changes in marginal corporate tax rates in the latter 1980s.[101]

Let us now turn to correlations based on changes in economic policy pre- and post-1985 (see Table 6). These data are no more indicative of a policy race to the bottom. Both measures of financial integration were quite strongly associated with faster increases in government spending (as was left-labor power). The financial integration–deficit correlations were much weaker and of contradictory signs.

Consistent with the over-time analysis, the bivariate correlations presented in this subsection belie common notions about strong and pervasive globalization constraints on national autonomy. These analyses are certainly not definitive, but they should prompt further research into what are undoubtedly complicated relationships between globalization and policy choice.

96. Garrett 1995.
97. Garrett and Lange 1991.
98. Rodrik 1997.
99. See Quinn 1997; and Swank 1998.
100. Garrett 1998c.
101. Hallerberg and Basinger 1998.

TABLE 6. *Changes in globalization and fiscal policy since 1985*

Globalization mechanism	Economic policy		
	Government spending	Public sector deficit	Capital tax rate
Exports + imports/GDP (%)	.00	−.14	−.22
FDI inflows + outflows/GDP (%)	.09	.23	.19
Financial openness index	.41	.10	.18
Covered interest rates[a]	.47	−.20	.03
Left-labor power	.51	.11	.22

Note: Figures are Pearson's *r* correlation coefficients. All data are averages for periods after 1984 minus historic averages (beginning in 1960 or first available year), except left-labor power (which is measured as in Table 5).

[a]Multiplied by −1 so that higher scores reflect more capital mobility.

Capital Flight

If the OECD countries have not converged around a less interventionist macroeconomic policy regime in recent years, have countries with larger public economies or bigger budget deficits suffered from debilitating capital flight? If the answer is "yes," one might reasonably suspect that globalization-induced convergence would soon become the norm. If not, continuing cross-national variations in policy regimes would seem more likely. This section examines the policy–capital flight relationship with respect to multinational exit, interest rate premiums, and currency depreciation.

The first column of Table 7 presents data on average annual net outflows (that is, outflows minus inflows) of FDI since 1985. These are correlated with the three policy variables from the last section—government spending, public sector deficits, and effective capital tax rates—over (as close as possible to) the same period. The spending and capital tax correlations were trivially small. Larger public sector deficits were associated with smaller, not larger, net outflows of FDI—reflecting the need for domestic debt to be funded by infusions of foreign capital. These correlations should give pause to purveyors of conventional globalization parables, for whom the loss of multinational investment as a result of interventionist government is a central theme.

Things were different, however, with respect to the behavior of the financial markets, measured by the long-term interest rates charged on government debt and the strength of currencies in foreign exchange markets. There was a clear correlation between a country's budgetary stance and the reaction of the financial markets. Bigger deficits were associated with higher interest rates and with greater depreciations against the dollar. Furthermore, interest rates were higher in countries with larger public economies, and depreciations were associated with higher rates of capital taxation.

TABLE 7. *Capital flight and fiscal policy*

Country	Net outflows of FDI[a]	Long-term interest rates[b]	Depreciation against the dollar[c]	Inflation[d]
Australia	0.7	11.8	3.3	4.7
Austria	−0.2	7.6	−5.2	3.3
Belgium	0.8	8.9	−4.9	3.5
Canada	−0.2	9.8	0.1	2.8
Denmark	−0.4	9.8	−4.4	3.2
Finland	−1.1	10.3	0.3	4.0
France	−0.6	9.5	−4.2	3.2
Germany	−0.9	7.2	−5.2	3.0
Greece	—	—	8.6	15.8
Iceland	—	7.0	9.6	15.1
Ireland	0.3	9.9	−2.8	3.1
Italy	−0.1	12.0	−0.3	6.3
Japan	−0.8	5.4	−7.5	1.2
Luxembourg	—	—	−4.9	4.6
Mexico[e]	—	17.1	46.0	47.8
Netherlands	−1.6	7.3	−5.2	1.5
New Zealand	—	12.6	0.9	6.4
Norway	−0.4	11.1	−1.2	3.1
Portugal	—	—	1.6	12.9
Spain	—	12.5	−1.9	6.7
Sweden	−1.8	11.1	0.2	5.6
Switzerland	−2.2	5.1	−4.2	3.3
Turkey[e]	—	—	46.8	62.3
United Kingdom	−1.0	9.7	−0.9	5.0
United States	0.2	8.4	—	3.2
Correlation with:[f]				
Total spending	0.05	0.40	−0.12	−0.09
Public sector deficit	−0.47	0.42	0.44	0.46
Capital tax rate	0.09	0.07	0.44	−0.03
Inflation		0.63	0.98	

[a]1985–93 average for annual outflows minus inflows of FDI (% GDP).
[b]1985–94 average for annual interest rates on ten-year government bonds, from OECD Historical Statistics, 1960–94.
[c]1985–93 average depreciation against the $US, from OECD Historical Statistics, 1960–94.
[d]1985–94 averages for annual GDP price deflator, from OECD Historical Statistics, 1960–94.
[e]Not used in correlations because of absence of economic policy data.
[f]Economic policy variables are averages from 1985 to the latest available year; correlations exclude all missing data.

In most analyses of policy credibility, inflation is the key link between fiscal policy and the behavior of international financial markets. The market's expectations about movements in exchange rates are the proximate determinant of differences in interest rates. In turn, differences in inflation rates are the best predictors of exchange-rate movements. These relationships are clearly demonstrated in Table 7. The correlation between deficits and inflation was quite strong but not nearly as strong as that between inflation and interest-rate premiums. Moreover, the correlation between higher inflation and currency depreciation was almost perfect.

Analyzing in detail the interrelationships among the size of the public economy, budget deficits, inflation, and interest rates is beyond the scope of this article. Here I will only sketch two possible approaches to the problem. The first is a path model that reflects the logic underpinning the conventional wisdom about the costs of big government in the global economy. The results based on post-1985 averages are[102]

$$\text{Spending} \rightarrow \text{Budget deficit} \rightarrow \text{Inflation} \rightarrow \text{Interest rates}$$
$$\quad\quad (.22) \quad\quad\quad\quad (.56) \quad\quad (.63)$$

These correlations are all in the expected direction—more spending was correlated with larger deficits, which were associated with higher inflation rates, which tended to result in higher interest rates. But note that the correlations increase in size along the path. A history of high inflation is certainly likely to lead the financial markets to impose an interest-rate premium on today's borrowing. Countries with larger public sector deficits are more likely to be inflationary, but this connection is less strong. Finally, although the correlation between the size of government and deficits is positive, it is even weaker.

The other basic approach to these relationships is to assume that spending, deficits, and inflation rates all have independent effects on interest rates. The following equation is a simple multivariate regression estimating these effects for the post-1985 period:[103]

$$\text{INTRATE} = 2.53 + 0.06\text{SPEND}* + 0.04\text{DEFICIT}* + 1.00\text{INFLATION}$$
$$\quad\quad (2.00) \quad (0.04) \quad\quad\quad (0.11) \quad\quad\quad\quad (0.26)$$

All the estimated parameters were in the expected direction, but only the effects of inflation were significant at traditional levels. This is not to say that spending and deficits were irrelevant—because of their impact on inflation. The path model suggests, however, that these effects are not very strong.

In summary, there is some evidence supporting the view that governments that have persisted with activist fiscal stances in recent years have paid a price in global capital markets. The causal pathways between fiscal policy and the propensity for capital flight, however, are quite diffuse. It is possible, of course, that the absence of globalization constraints on government spending and taxation only shows that financial markets are not yet sufficiently integrated for these effects to be apparent. There may be a threshold—not yet reached in the OECD—beyond which the policy race to the bottom will ensue. One preliminary way to test this argument is to examine the

---

102. Numbers in parentheses are Pearson's *r* correlations.

103. $n = 18$. The regression equation is based on the eighteen countries for which all the data were available (Australia, Austria, Belgium, Canada, Denmark, Finland, France, Germany, Ireland, Italy, Japan, the Netherlands, Norway, Spain, Sweden, Switzerland, the United Kingdom, and the United States). Adjusted $R^2 = .56$. Figures in parentheses are standard errors. $*p > .10$, two-tailed test.

TABLE 8. *Tax rates among U.S. states*

State	Average tax rate
Top five	
Minnesota	8.8
Hawaii	7.9
Michigan	7.0
District of Columbia	7.0
Utah	6.8
Bottom five	
Louisiana	2.0
Wyoming	1.9
Texas	1.7
North Dakota	1.6
Alaska	0
Coefficient of variation (for 50 states)	0.32

Note: Average rate of income and sales tax paid in 1983 by individuals with $20,000 income (1979 dollars). Data are from Feenberg and Rosen 1986, 175–76.

political economy of fiscally decentralized countries, where there are effectively no barriers to movement across state lines. The United States is a good example.

Table 8 presents data for the fifty U.S. states on combined rates of sales and income taxation (by far the largest two components of state-level revenues). The data do not indicate a race to the bottom. The relevant comparison with respect to the OECD is not overall tax rates (given the size of the federal government in the United States), but rather the dispersion of tax rates. The coefficient of variation for state taxes is .32. This is higher than the comparable OECD-wide coefficients for both capital taxation and government spending (see Table 3). The complete integration of the U.S. market has not resulted in convergence of tax rates around a minimal mean. Nor is it the case that the low-tax states are the best macroeconomic performers—Louisiana, North Dakota, and Wyoming are quite poor. Texas and Alaska can afford low taxes because of their wealth of natural resources. The data should give pause to those who believe that it is only a matter of time before market pressures force fiscal convergence on the OECD.

Governing in the Global Economy

In this article I have sought to paint in broad brush strokes the relationship between the globalization of markets and national autonomy in the OECD. I have made two basic points. First, there are strong parallels between recent arguments about the constraining effects of globalization on national autonomy and those all the way back to the eighteenth century about the domestic effects of market integration. With hindsight, we know that past predictions of the effective demise of the nation-state were unfounded. Are there signs that things will be different in the contemporary epoch?

My second point is that, up until the mid-1990s, globalization has not prompted a pervasive policy race to the neoliberal bottom among the OECD countries, nor have governments that have persisted with interventionist policies invariably been hamstrung by damaging capital flight. Governments wishing to expand the public economy for political reasons may do so (including increasing taxes on capital to pay for new spending) without adversely affecting their trade competitiveness or prompting multinational producers to exit. The reason is that governments provide economically important collective goods—ranging from the accumulation of human and physical capital, to social stability under conditions of high market uncertainty, to popular support for the market economy itself—that are undersupplied by markets and valued by actors who are interested in productivity. This is particularly the case in corporatist political economies where the potential costs of interventionist government are mitigated by coordination among business, government, and labor.

This is not to say, however, that no facet of globalization significantly constrains national policy options. In particular, the integration of financial markets is more constraining than either trade or the multinationalization of production. But even here, one must be very careful to differentiate among various potential causal mechanisms.

Talk of lost monetary autonomy only makes sense if one believes that the integration of financial markets forces governments to peg their exchange rates to external anchors of stability. On recent evidence, the credibility gains of doing so are far from overwhelming; indeed, noncredible pegs (that is, those not consistent with other political and economic conditions) have promoted the most debilitating cases of financial speculation and instability. On the other hand, the costs of giving up the exchange rate as a tool of economic adjustment are great, and economies that allow their currencies to float freely seem to benefit as a result. Governments simply should not feel any compunction to give up monetary autonomy in the era of global financial markets.

But even if countries float their exchange rates, the financial markets—fearing inflation—do impose interest-rate premiums on governments that persistently run large budget deficits. Some governments have been willing to pay this price in the name of other objectives. Others have sought domestic solutions to credibility problems in the markets, such as central banking reforms. Still others (especially in the developing world) apparently have been unable to attain reputations for fiscal responsibility. For these countries, fixing the exchange rate may be the only option, but there can be no guarantee that this will not just fuel even more financial speculation.

Finally, there is no evidence that the financial markets attach interest-rate premiums to the expansion of the public economy per se—that is, provided new tax revenues balance increased spending. This is even true if the taxation of capital is one source of new revenues. Moreover, the empirical connections between expansion of the public economy and deficits are quite weak and heavily mediated by domestic political conditions. Strong left-labor regimes, for example, have historically been able to increase government spending without incurring large debts. The financial markets are essentially disinterested in the size and scope of government. Their primary concern is whether the government balances it books.

My analysis is thus considerably more bullish about the future of the embedded liberalism compromise than some of its earlier advocates suggest. As a result, I do not believe that supporters of interventionist government must call for a dose of protectionism or the reimposition of capital controls to maintain the domestic balance between equity and efficiency. Nor must advocates look to international cooperation and institutions as the only attractive option for the future. As has been the case for more than two hundred years, the coupling of openness with domestic compensation remains a robust and desirable solution to the problem of reaping the efficiency benefits of capitalism while mitigating its costs in terms of social dislocations and inequality.

Economics and Security in Statecraft and Scholarship
Michael Mastanduno

In his classic essay on the works of Adam Smith, Alexander Hamilton, and Friedrich List, published in 1943, Edward Mead Earle asserted that the relationship between economics and security "is one of the most critical and absorbing problems of statesmanship."[1] Albert Hirschman echoed this sentiment in his pioneering study of economic statecraft, first published in 1945. He argued that in addition to Machiavelli's classic chapters, a textbook for the modern prince should contain "extensive new sections on the most efficient use of quotas, exchange controls, capital investment, and other instruments of economic warfare."[2] The suggestion of Hirschman and Earle that economics and security should be understood in an integrated fashion was also taken up by other prominent scholars writing during the 1930s and 1940s, including Jacob Viner, Frederick Dunn, E. H. Carr, and Eugene Staley.[3]

The successor generation of professional students of international relations (IR), however, was slow to heed this advice. Writing several decades after World War II, Klaus Knorr and Frank Trager found that the relationship between economic and national security issues had been a "neglected area of study" in IR scholarship.[4] An informal review of the first twenty-five years of *International Organization* confirms this finding: a remarkably small number of articles addressed, as a central theme, the link between security and economic issues in international affairs.[5] The editors of *International Studies Quarterly,* introducing a special issue in 1983 on the economic foundations of war, observed that even in the extensive new literature on interna-

The comments of Peter Katzenstein, Robert Keohane, and Stephen Krasner were invaluable in the drafting of this article. I also wish to thank the other participants in this project as well as Mlada Bukovansky, Robert Gilpin, Christopher Hill, Sean Kay, Gene Lyons, Jennifer Mitzen, Robert Paarlberg, Robert Pape, Brad Thayer, Alex Wendt, Howard Wriggins, participants in faculty seminars at Harvard University and Dartmouth College, and two anonymous reviewers from *International Organization* for reactions and suggestions.

1. Earle 1943, 117.
2. Hirschman [1945] 1980, xv.
3. See Viner 1948; Dunn 1949, 86–87; Carr 1939; and Staley 1935.
4. Knorr and Trager 1977, v.
5. Exceptions include Knorr 1948; Gordon 1956; Diebold 1960; and Rubenstein 1964.

International Organization 52, 4, Autumn 1998, pp. 825–854

tional political economy (IPE) that emerged in the 1970s, "the relationship between economic factors and the causes and occurrence of international conflict has seldom been considered or developed."[6]

The study of international relations and foreign policy as a social science discipline matured and flourished in the United States in the decades following World War II. In that context, the neglect of what an earlier generation of scholars considered one of the most critical and absorbing problems of statecraft is all the more striking.

Statecraft refers to the use of policy instruments to satisfy the core objectives of nation-states in the international system. As David Baldwin has emphasized, statecraft is most usefully thought of in broad and multidimensional terms. It involves the application and interplay of multiple instruments—military, economic, diplomatic, and informational—to achieve the multiple objectives of states, including national security, economic prosperity, and political prestige and influence.[7] During the 1950s and 1960s, however, students of IR came to conceive of statecraft fairly narrowly, primarily as a problem involving the relationship between military instruments and military objectives.[8] Economic statecraft and the link between economic and security issues were largely ignored.

By the 1970s and 1980s, specialists in IR became far more concerned with economic issues, and the study of IPE moved to the forefront of the discipline. However, the study of economic statecraft, and economic issues more generally, tended to be conducted separately from the study of military statecraft, and national security issues more generally. Rather than integrating these two concerns in the overall study of international politics, security studies and IPE progressed as separate scholarly activities.

A similar pattern eventually came to characterize the actual practice of statecraft in the United States. In the early years of the Cold War, U.S. officials consciously integrated economic and security concerns in U.S. foreign policy. Economic instruments and relationships were critical to launching the grand strategy of containing the expansion of Soviet power. But by the 1970s and 1980s, the economic and security components of U.S. foreign policy drifted apart. By the end of the 1980s, the economic and security agencies of the U.S. executive were in open conflict over which set of objectives should take priority in U.S. foreign policy.

The disjunction of security and economic policy in U.S. statecraft continued during the early years of the 1990s. By 1995, however, the Clinton administration moved to reintegrate the two concerns. In relations with other major powers, administration officials began to direct foreign economic policy to complement and reinforce their preferred national security strategies.

The division in IR scholarship between security studies and IPE persists after the end of the Cold War. But change in the direction of reintegration is observable in the academy as well. There is now a greater interest among IR scholars in issues and

---

6. Duvall et al. 1983, 379.
7. D. Baldwin 1985.
8. See Rosecrance and Stein 1993; and Baldwin 1995.

problems that lie at the intersection of economics and security, and research is being revitalized on the link between international trade and peace, between security relations and international economic cooperation, and between economics and security in the grand strategies of powerful states. The line dividing IPE and security studies is becoming less prominent and more permeable.

This article addresses the evolution of the relationship between economics and security in U.S. statecraft and scholarship over the past fifty years. My narrative moves back and forth, analyzing developments in the policy world and in the academy. I seek to explain how and why U.S. government officials have approached the relationship between economics and security in their conduct of foreign policy and to understand how IR scholars have treated the relationship in their writings. In my analysis of the integration of economics and security in U.S. statecraft, I emphasize the extent to which economic policies are subordinated to and supportive of security concerns. I place less emphasis on the extent to which security policies have been used to promote U.S. economic objectives.

I argue that three factors are critical in helping us to understand variations in the extent to which economic and security concerns are integrated in both statecraft and scholarship. One key variable is international structure. Different international structures provide different incentives for integration or separation. Multipolar world politics creates incentives for integration—great powers tend to be economically interdependent, they rely heavily on allies for their security, and the risk that allies will defect is relatively significant. Economics is a critical instrument of statecraft in this setting. Bipolar world politics encourages the separation of economics and security. Bipolar great powers tend to be economically independent, they rely less on allies, and the risk that allies will defect from more fixed, as opposed to more fluid, alliance structures is relatively low.[9]

The analysis of unipolar structures is not well established in IR theory. I develop the argument later, however, that unipolarity motivates the dominant state to integrate economic and security policies. A unipolar structure tempts the dominant state to try to preserve its privileged position; that effort, in turn, requires its international economic strategy to line up behind and reinforce its national security strategy in relations with potential challengers.

The structure of the international system provides incentives to separate or integrate economics and security, but by itself it does not determine behavior. Policymakers and scholars respond to the opportunities and constraints of the international structure, but not always immediately or in precisely the same way. In the narrative that follows, I emphasize two additional variables that help to account for the patterns observed and for how quickly or readily U.S. policymakers in particular responded to the incentives of the international security structure.

First, specific features of the strategic environment faced by policymakers can accentuate or weaken the incentives to integrate economics and security. The more pressing or immediate the challenges to their preferred national security strategy, the

---

9. The logic of these arguments is developed in Waltz 1979; and Gowa 1994.

more strongly U.S. policymakers have felt the need to integrate their instruments of statecraft.[10] The less threatening the strategic context, or, to put it differently, the more benign the international environment, the easier it has been for U.S. officials to pursue economic and security interests along separate tracks. During the early Cold War period, for example, the threat to the viability of the nascent U.S. containment strategy was profound, and economic statecraft was pressed into service to bolster U.S. security objectives. By the late 1960s, European and Asian alliance systems were firmly in place, and the stability of the bipolar world seemed assured, leaving U.S. officials freer to respond to structural incentives and pursue economic and security goals without necessarily integrating the two in statecraft.

The second factor concerns the position of the United States in international economic competition. The more the United States has dominated that competition, the easier it has been for policymakers to employ foreign economic policy as a complement to national security policy. The more the United States has found itself challenged by international competitors, the greater the domestic pressure has been on policymakers to use foreign policy in pursuit of particularistic or national economic interests. The United States began the postwar era in a position of overwhelming economic preponderance but experienced relative decline as other countries recovered.[11] The decline that actually took place during the 1950s and 1960s was perceived most clearly in the United States during the 1970s and 1980s, and that perception mobilized economic nationalists and encouraged the separate pursuit of economic and security objectives in U.S. statecraft. In contrast, the belief by the middle of the 1990s that the United States once again enjoyed a position of international economic superiority made it easier for U.S. officials to respond to the United States' unipolar security position and reintegrate economics and security in statecraft.

Two points that pertain to the overall argument are worthy of emphasis. One is that my conception of the international environment incorporates both material and nonmaterial factors. U.S. statecraft responds not only to the distribution of material capabilities emphasized by structural realists but also to considerations in the realm of ideas such as identification of threats, strategic uncertainty, and the perception of relative economic decline or renewal.[12] My analysis highlights the need to move beyond the purely material understanding of state strategy normally found in neorealism in any effort to develop effective explanations of state behavior.

The second point concerns the sociology of knowledge. Although it is fairly common, though not uncontroversial, to contend that the international system shapes the foreign policies of particular states, it is far less common to claim that the nature of

10. Skalnes highlights how the "strategic need" of policymakers in different circumstances helps to account for whether economic policies are used to reinforce the security strategies of great powers. Skalnes forthcoming.

11. The U.S. share of world economic output was 45 percent in the late 1940s. It dropped the 25 percent by the late 1960s and stayed roughly the same through the late 1980s. See Friedberg 1989; Kennedy 1987; and Nye 1990.

12. Analyses of foreign policy that emphasize these ideational factors include Johnson 1994; Friedberg 1988; and Walt 1987.

the international system has a strong impact on the way that IR scholars conduct their business. This article makes the latter claim. I try to show that scholarship responds to the particular features of the international environment, and that the resulting patterns become institutionalized in academic life. Security studies arose and became institutionalized in U.S. universities during the Cold War environment of the 1950s and 1960s, and in a similar way the division between security studies and IPE emerged and became entrenched in the context of U.S. economic decline during the 1970s and 1980s. Whether and when the systemic incentives currently inviting IR scholars to reintegrate economics and security will lead to the complete collapse of the established division of labor in IR scholarship remains to be seen.

The rest of this article unfolds in three sections, with each corresponding to a particular phase in the postwar era. The first section considers the early Cold War period, roughly 1947–68. The second takes up 1968–89, the later phase of the Cold War; and the third examines the post–Cold War years of 1989 to the present. For each phase, I explore connections among the international security environment, the international economic environment, and the links between economics and security in conceptions of statecraft held by scholars and in the practice of statecraft by U.S. policymakers. A concluding section summarizes the argument and implications.

Early Cold War Era

The difference in the international environments to which IR scholars and policymakers were responding in the decades before and after World War II is striking. Prior to the war the international system was multipolar. Diplomatic interactions among great powers were sustained and complex. Alliance commitments were relatively flexible, in part because statesmen believed that rigid alignments helped to precipitate the outbreak of World War I. The great powers were economically interdependent with important commercial and financial links to each other. Their mutual vulnerability was highlighted during the early 1930s as sharp contractions in global trade and finance damaged the economies of core as well as peripheral states.[13] War was a routine instrument of diplomacy, and the leading states engaged in conventional wars even though they sometimes escalated into protracted, exhausting struggles.

In this setting, with no clearly dominant power and with security alignments uncertain, great powers resorted to whatever means they could muster to press their advantage. The use of economic instruments to promote security goals was a matter of routine as the leading states sought to exploit asymmetries in their economic and strategic relationships with each other and with lesser powers. Germany's manipulation of trade expansion during the 1930s to extract resources from weaker East European states and inculcate their political dependence constitutes a classic example.[14] Britain used trade discrimination in an effort to coax the United States away from

13. Kindleberger 1973.
14. For treatment of this episode in detail, see Kaiser 1980; and Hirschman [1945] 1980.

neutrality and to assure strong relations with Commonwealth states who would be a source of income, critical raw materials, and food supplies in the event of war.[15]

In Asia during the 1930s, the United States and Britain used purchases of silver and other techniques of monetary manipulation to protect the Chinese currency and thereby forestall Japan's attempt to conquer China. Japan, for its part, sought to undermine the Chinese currency to encourage the fracture of China into autonomous regions that could be subdued more easily.[16] The United States turned the economic weapon against Japan later in the decade, resorting to economic sanctions to exploit Japanese dependence on imported raw materials in order to weaken Japan's war-making capacity and influence its political behavior in southeast Asia.[17]

A strong economic base was critical to military power and political influence. In peacetime, great powers sought to translate their national wealth into power in order to enhance their security and advance their relative position. In times of war, the size and quality of the national economy was an important determinant of the ability of a state to sustain its military effort. During World War II, the major combatants devoted up to 50 percent of their gross national product to the war effort.[18] In the "total" wars of the twentieth century, the economies of belligerent powers became attractive targets for embargoes and blockades, and economic warfare emerged as an important instrument of statecraft.[19]

In an environment in which economic power and relationships were central to political interaction among multiple great powers, it is not surprising that many scholars struggling to make sense of international relations during the 1930s and 1940s viewed close linkages between economics and security as necessary and normal. Hirschman, reflecting on the interwar experience, noted that "practice preceded theory" in that the extensive use of international economic relations as instruments of national power was a key feature that required the sustained attention of scholars.[20] His own contribution, a theoretical framework for understanding how states use asymmetrical interdependence, became a foundation for later scholarship on international economic sanctions. Other prominent economists, including J. B. Condliffe and John Maynard Keynes, sought to model the connections among economic interdependence, economic nationalism, and international political tensions in an effort to promote peace.[21] Similarly, and reflecting the sentiment of the League of Nations Covenant, students of international law and organization explored the potential for international economic sanctions to serve as a substitute for war.[22]

In the classic work he subtitled "An Introduction to the Study of International Relations," E. H. Carr pointed out that the nineteenth century "illusion of a separation between politics and economics has ceased to correspond to any aspect of cur-

---

15. Skalnes forthcoming, chap. 5.
16. Kirshner 1995, 51–62.
17. See Feis 1950, 227–50; and D. Baldwin 1985, 165–74.
18. Knorr 1975, 84.
19. See Medlicott 1952, 1959; and Milward 1977.
20. Hirschman [1945] 1980, xv.
21. See Condliffe 1938; and Keynes 1920. Excellent reviews are de Marchi 1991; and Barber 1991.
22. Mitrany 1925.

rent reality," and went on to assert that "power is indivisible" and that "the military and economic weapons are merely different instruments of power."[23] Earlier, Eugene Staley made a similar point, warning against the "fallacy" that economic issues could be usefully studied in isolation from political and military ones.[24] Herbert Feis argued that investment and finance were instruments of security policy for the major powers prior to World War I: "The struggle for power among nations left no economic action free."[25] Jacob Viner, in the inaugural issue of *World Politics,* saw fit to refresh readers' understanding of a long-standing intellectual tradition, mercantilism, that viewed economics and security as fully integrated and complementary aspects of statecraft.[26] Edward Mason argued that economic considerations were always critical to the attainment of a state's primary security objectives: the maintenance of peace and the maximization of military effort against enemies.[27] R. G. Hawtrey explored the economic aspects of sovereignty and war, and Wilhelm Röpke argued that the proper functioning of the world economy depended on political institutions and unwritten codes of behavior.[28]

By the 1950s, of course, the international environment and relations among great powers had changed dramatically, and a new international system consolidated itself. The dominant powers in this system were "super" powers; they were not traditional great powers and did not have traditional great power relationships. Instead of being economically interdependent, the United States and Soviet Union were large, relatively self-sufficient, and economically independent of each other. There were important changes in warfare as well: the two superpowers were nuclear powers that did not engage each other directly, much less fight long conventional wars, for fear of escalating to unacceptably destructive nuclear exchanges. Alliances became fixed rather than flexible, with each superpower leading its own bloc.

The position of the United States differed across the international security and international economic environments. In the former, the United States was one of two superpowers, competing with the Soviet Union politically, militarily, and ideologically. In the latter, the United States was the undisputed hegemonic power, and the Soviet Union was not even a player. This bifurcation in the United States' position in the international distribution of power proved important in shaping the study and practice of U.S. statecraft in the early Cold War period and beyond.

U.S. Statecraft

Commentators often point out that U.S. statecraft became more militarized after World War II, with increasing reliance on the covert and overt use of force.[29] While

23. Carr 1939, 117–20.
24. Staley 1935, x–xi.
25. Feis 1930, 192.
26. Viner 1948.
27. Mason 1949. See also Condliffe 1944.
28. See Röpke 1942; and Hawtrey 1930.
29. See Ullman 1983; and Nathan and Oliver 1987.

this is certainly true, U.S. officials were also extraordinarily active in international economic policy. The United States took the lead in creating the institutions of the Bretton Woods system—the International Monetary Fund, the General Agreement on Tariffs and Trade, and the International Bank for Reconstruction and Development. U.S. officials reorganized international trade and monetary systems and undertook the Marshall Plan in Europe, economic reconstruction programs in Japan and South Korea, and economic assistance programs in various parts of the world.

The key point is that these international economic initiatives were integrated with and subordinated to U.S. security objectives. As Melvin Leffler demonstrates in his exhaustive study, U.S. officials "gave primacy to geopolitical configurations of power" yet also understood that economic strength and stability were key factors in defending the United States' geopolitical position and core values.[30] Robert Pollard's recent account of early postwar policy reached a similar conclusion: U.S. officials used "economic power to achieve strategic aims."[31] The Marshall Plan was prompted by proximate and enduring security concerns, including the risk of internal communist subversion or external Soviet aggression against the fragile economic and political systems of Western Europe, and the need to solve the long-standing Franco–German problem by binding West Germany and France into a more integrated European and Atlantic community.

U.S. officials tolerated economic discrimination in an effort to cement security alliances in Western Europe and Northeast Asia.[32] The United States encouraged, indeed demanded, the integration of the West European economies and the formation of a European customs union, even though the latter discriminated against U.S. exports through a common external tariff. The asymmetries were even more profound in U.S. relations with Japan. In Europe, the ability of U.S. firms to establish wholly-owned subsidiaries helped to compensate for Europe's higher trade barriers. In the case of Japan, in addition to tolerating high tariff and nontariff barriers, U.S. officials accommodated the desire of the Japanese government to minimize U.S. foreign direct investment and thereby granted a significant edge to Japan in the "rivalry beyond trade."[33] At the same time, the U.S. government prodded U.S. firms to transfer technology that would enhance the productivity of their Japanese counterparts.[34]

Economic relations with the Soviet Union and its allies also were explicitly governed by political and security concerns. Immediately after the war, U.S. officials sought to employ positive economic sanctions—the promise of postwar reconstruction loans—to integrate the Soviet Union into a postwar order on terms advantageous to the United States. That effort failed by 1947, and U.S. officials promptly turned to a comprehensive trade and financial embargo to reinforce the emerging, confrontational strategy of containment. U.S. officials proved insensitive to the economic costs of their statecraft; they maintained the comprehensive embargo even as other West-

30. Leffler 1992, 2–3.
31. Pollard 1985, 244.
32. See Gilpin 1975; and Krasner 1982.
33. Encarnation 1992.
34. Mastanduno 1991.

ern states distanced themselves from U.S. policy and opened trade with communist countries.[35]

The dominant role of security concerns and the integration of security and economics were evident institutionally. The National Security Act of 1947 expanded the security establishment by creating the National Security Council, the Defense Department, and the CIA to complement the State Department. Defense and the CIA soon came to dwarf State in terms of size and institutional resources. Trade policy, consolidating a process that began in 1934, moved out of the hands of Congress and came to be controlled by the State Department with an emphasis on the United States' broad diplomatic interests as opposed to more particularistic economic interests. Societal pressures for protection certainly existed, but with few exceptions were channeled away from the political arena and into a system of administrative remedies that offered, at least until the 1970s, little meaningful relief.[36] The embargo of communist states was run by the Commerce Department, but with such zeal for trade denial that conflicts with the security bureaucracies were almost nonexistent.

The United States' position in the international security structure—one of two superpowers locked in what was perceived as a life or death struggle with an implacable adversary—was obviously critical in pushing U.S. officials to give priority to security concerns and adopt the grand strategy of containment. At the same time, the particular features of the early Cold War strategic environment encouraged U.S. officials to use economic statecraft to reinforce their preferred security strategy. The durability of the bipolar standoff and the success of the United States' global containment strategy, evident in retrospect, were by no means a foregone conclusion in the first postwar decade. The states of Western Europe and Japan had weak, vulnerable economies and uncertain political prospects. The commitment of the United States to engage in more permanent, "entangling alliances" was also uncertain, and West European governments in particular were anxious for signs that the United States was truly committed to their defense.[37] For its part, the United States "worried almost as much about the steadfastness of its European allies as it did about the threats posed by its enemy."[38] U.S. officials feared that a breakdown in morale in West European countries would be exploited by the Soviet Union. NATO was as much a response to this political and psychological concern as it was to the Soviet military threat.[39] U.S. fears may have been overstated, but as Arnold Wolfers suggested in 1962, a state that was suddenly thrust into danger after having enjoyed a long period of security was likely to be extremely sensitive to external threat.[40]

Economic statecraft played critical, multiple roles in this uncertain strategic context. U.S. trade and financial assistance helped to bolster West European and Japanese economic capacity and political stability, and their self-confidence and morale.

35. Mastanduno 1992.
36. Destler 1992.
37. Lake forthcoming.
38. Johnson 1994, 68.
39. See Osgood 1962; and Johnson 1994.
40. Wolfers 1962, 151.

The asymmetrical opening of the U.S. market, along with U.S. efforts to dismantle European colonial empires in Southeast Asia and prod European governments to admit Japan into the GATT helped to reorient Japanese commerce, and foreign policy, away from China and toward the West.[41] Access to the U.S. market and to the integrated European market similarly helped to redirect West German trade away from its traditional reliance on Eastern Europe and the Soviet Union. U.S. geopolitical influence assured that energy supplies would be available to the industrializing economies of its allies with predictability and at reasonable cost.[42]

Deepening economic ties between the United States and its security partners reinforced the U.S. security commitment and bolstered its credibility. They signaled to West Europeans that the United States was there to stay and helped to reassure the United States that Western Europe and Japan would not suffer the kind of political breakdown upon which the Soviet Union would prey. The United States' comprehensive embargoes against communist states eventually created friction in U.S. relations with its allies, but in the early Cold War they also signaled the lack of ambiguity in the U.S. commitment to engage in the Cold War struggle as a moral as well as strategic necessity. In short, the integration of U.S. economic and security policies during the strategic uncertainty of the 1950s was necessary to create the stability and predictability that characterized the bipolar order in subsequent decades.

The position of the United States in international economic competition helped to facilitate this integration of economics and security in U.S. statecraft. The United States enjoyed significant advantages over potential competitors in production, trade, finance, and technology, advantages that eroded only slowly as other economies recovered. Because the United States was so dominant economically, and so large and self-sufficient, the tendency of U.S. officials to subordinate international economic policy to national security concerns was politically manageable at home. The health of the domestic economy was surely important, but at least until the late 1960s, when the realization of relative decline began to set in, the United States could have its cake and eat it, too. Size, superior productivity, and relative insularity from the world economy meant that the United States could enjoy domestic economic prosperity and at the same time place its international economic strategy at the service of what were then more pressing geopolitical objectives.

IR Scholarship

Conceptions of the relationship between economics and security in IR scholarship also shifted in response to the new realities of the postwar international structure, though not in the same way as U.S. foreign policy. National security issues, narrowly defined, came to dominate the scholarly agenda to the extent that one political scientist has characterized 1955–65 as a "golden age" in security studies.[43] The priority

41. Schaller 1997.
42. Kapstein 1990.
43. Walt 1991. See also Betts 1997.

concern was to grasp the implications of the nuclear revolution as it affected the relationship between the new bipolar superpowers. Theoretical contributions centered on the elaboration of the logic of deterrence in arguments about mutual assured destruction and the use of nuclear weapons in political bargaining.[44] Analyses of the interplay between economics and security, however, so prominent in the scholarship of the previous era, were conspicuous by their absence.

In the immediate aftermath of the war, professional students of IR were still inclined to take a broad, integrative approach to statecraft. Arnold Wolfers pointed to the ambiguity and various meanings of "national security," and Bernard Brodie emphasized that national security policy dealt broadly with political, economic, and social as well as military matters.[45] But by the middle of the 1950s, as the U.S.–Soviet competition came to define international politics, the thrust of IR scholarship narrowed considerably to an examination of military instruments and statecraft.[46] The application of game theory and rational actor assumptions, which informed much of the early theoretical work in the field, reinforced the narrowing of the agenda by enabling scholars to represent U.S.–Soviet relations plausibly as a two-player, zero-sum contest under conditions of uncertainty and with high stakes.[47] And, as Stephen Walt has noted, the Cold War prompted U.S. scholars to take the Soviet desire to expand for granted. Consequently, they focused on how to deter that expansion while downplaying the sources of state behavior and nonmilitary dimensions of statecraft.[48]

Marc Trachtenberg noted recently that strategic studies "emerged in the United States as a new field with a distinct intellectual personality."[49] Hedley Bull, writing two decades earlier, noted similarly that this new literature was characterized by precision and sophistication. Scholars saw themselves "presiding over the birth of a new science, eliminating antiquated methods and replacing them with up-to-date ones." Bull observed that in developing elegant models of the superpower relationship, academic specialists were inclined "to think too readily in terms of military solutions to the problems of foreign policy and to lose sight of the other instruments that are available."[50]

Distinctive features of both the U.S.–Soviet relationship and nuclear weapons made it all the more plausible for security scholars to narrow the agenda and downplay economic dimensions of statecraft. The two dominant powers had no direct economic relationship to analyze and neither was especially dependent on the international economy.[51] And, as nuclear weapons took center stage in defense strategy, the connection between economic and military power became less proximate and direct.

44. Major works included Kissinger 1957b; Wohlstetter 1959; Brodie 1959; Snyder 1961; and Schelling 1960, 1966.
45. See Wolfers 1952; and Brodie 1949, 477.
46. Baldwin 1995.
47. Betts 1997, 14; and Mirowski 1991.
48. Walt 1991, 215.
49. Trachtenberg 1989, 301.
50. Bull 1968, 595, 600.
51. Waltz 1970.

Once superpowers possessed the hydrogen bomb, for example, it was no longer self-evident that the ability to mobilize economic resources for a long war or to destroy the economic capacity of an adversary were important national security objectives.[52] Nuclear capabilities were the "absolute" weapon; they enabled states to provide for their security without continually worrying, as traditional great powers had to, about their relative position in great power economic competition.[53]

Nevertheless, since U.S. officials were active in the international economic arena and conceived of economics and security issues as integrated, why did more of this conception not carry over into IR scholarship? A key reason is that although international economic policies were an important aspect of U.S. statecraft, they were not especially salient politically. The sense of political struggle and the higher stakes, domestically as well as internationally, that later came to characterize U.S. foreign economic relations, and that had characterized U.S. economic relations prior to World War II, were essentially absent in the era of U.S. economic hegemony. It was thus plausible for IR scholars to recognize a distinction between "high" and "low" politics, to focus attention on the more pressing security issues, and to leave the study of economic issues essentially to the economists.

There were scattered treatments of international economic problems and issues in the IR literature, but what later became the field of IPE did not exist. David Baldwin recounts a conversation in 1969 in which Susan Strange asked him which other scholars in the United States saw themselves working in IPE. He could name only Klaus Knorr.[54] Strange herself published a prescient article in 1970 that warned of a growing divergence between conceptions of the international system prevalent in scholarship and a real world in which the pace of international economic change was transforming that system.[55]

International economists, of course, did address the world economy. Yet, unlike their prewar and wartime predecessors, they generally proceeded without much concern for conceptualizing the political and strategic dimensions of international economic relations.[56] To be sure, a select group of economists did move from RAND to the Defense Department and eventually shaped U.S. national security policy at high levels. But for the economics profession as a whole, the economic dimensions of national security policy ceased to be a major concern. Perhaps it was because the economic analysis that proved so valuable during World War II in devising precision bombing campaigns against Germany were less essential in a era of nuclear armaments. Perhaps it was because war was "too simple" an economic problem—that is, the analysis of national security policy did not require the refined methodological techniques at the cutting edge of the discipline.[57] Whatever the reason, mainstream

52. Trachtenberg 1989, 302, 310.

53. See Brodie 1946; and Jervis 1993, 55.

54. D. Baldwin 1985, xii. Knorr's 1956 book addressed the relationship between economics and security, and his 1975 book was a systematic contribution to IPE.

55. Strange 1970.

56. Cooper 1968 was an important exception that was analytically sophisticated and sensitive to political considerations.

57. Leonard 1991.

academic economists devoted little energy to the economic aspects of national security as the Cold War progressed.

Economists working in the international area tended to produce either descriptive accounts of international economic processes[58] or, as professionalization advanced, sophisticated models of the workings of international trade and payments that relied on simplified assumptions about the international political environment. As Strange argued after examining both the IR and international economics literature: "we shall soon need to have rather urgently a *theory* of international economic relations, a political theory which is consistent with whatever other sort of theory of international relations we individually find most satisfactory."[59] Economists went their own way, and political scientists took up this challenge during the 1970s.

Later Cold War Era

Between 1968 and 1989, the United States and the Soviet Union remained the dominant powers in a bipolar world. They experimented during the 1970s with detente, reverted to a more confrontational stand-off during the early 1980s, and returned to a more cooperative relationship with the rise of Gorbachev in 1985. Nuclear diplomacy in the form of arms control negotiations and geopolitical competition in the form of proxy struggles in the developing world remained central features of the bipolar relationship until it collapsed at the end of the 1980s.

Although the international security structure remained stable, there was increased awareness in the United States of the transformation that had occurred in international economic affairs: the growth of interdependence and the relative decline of the United States. Seminal events such as the collapse of Bretton Woods, the energy crises of the 1970s, and the trade and budget deficits of the 1980s brought the shift in the United States' competitive position into sharper focus politically. As the perception of relative decline became widespread, international economic policies took on greater salience in U.S. domestic politics and in U.S. interactions with other major powers.

IR Scholarship

These developments had one crucial consequence in the U.S. academy—the emergence of IPE. But, the rise to prominence of international economic issues did not also lead to an integration of economics and security in IR scholarship. Instead, two distinctive subfields, IPE and security studies, developed along parallel paths.

IPE emerged in the context of a debate between liberalism and realism over how to explain the renewed salience of international economic issues. Liberals contended that IR scholars needed new tools and approaches. The international environment of

58. For example, Gardner 1956; and Patterson 1966.
59. Strange 1970, 310.

the 1970s had been transformed by interdependence and relative U.S. decline, and the realist-inspired, state-centric paradigm at the heart of security studies was no longer an adequate guide to international politics or U.S. foreign policy.[60] The realist slogan, in effect, was "old tools, old issues"—existing approaches to international politics were still useful in explaining the reemergence of past patterns of interdependence and international economic conflict.[61] This debate helped to motivate research programs in hegemonic stability theory,[62] regime theory and the role of institutions,[63] and the link between domestic politics and foreign economic policies.[64] Both liberals and realists were interested in the implications of their analyses for U.S. foreign policy; Robert Keohane and Joseph Nye, for example, devoted the final chapter of their book *Power and Interdependence* to the role of the United States in complex interdependence and argued that "an appropriate foreign policy for the most powerful state must rest on a clear analysis of changing world politics."[65]

For scholars working the security side of IR, economic issues, even international economic crises, remained matters of "low politics." But, by the 1970s, security studies found itself more on the defensive than at the forefront of the discipline. As U.S.–Soviet arms control progressed and their nuclear relationship stabilized, the study of nuclear weapons did not sustain the urgency it had taken on during the era of the Cuban Missile Crisis.[66] And the prolonged prominence of the Vietnam War exposed security studies to the criticism that it granted overwhelming attention to the least likely type of war and scant attention to more likely types.[67] Vietnam and the missile crisis prompted some scholars to relax the unitary-state-as-actor assumption and draw on bureaucratic politics models and psychological approaches to explain deviations from rational behavior in foreign policy decision making.[68]

Security studies was reinvigorated by the early 1980s as the Cold War entered a dangerous new phase and U.S.–Soviet nuclear and global competition once again took center stage. Funding at political science departments and university centers expanded as scholars revisited nuclear deterrence[69] and used the comparative analysis of historical cases to generate new insights about alliance strategy,[70] conventional deterrence,[71] and the sources of military doctrine.[72]

Scholars in both security studies and IPE thrived during the 1970s and 1980s. But why did they generally proceed along separate tracks rather than develop an inte-

---

60. See Keohane and Nye 1972 and 1977; and Morse 1970.

61. See Gilpin 1975, 1977; and Krasner 1976. Krasner's article title emphasized the point by recalling the title of Hirschman's wartime classic.

62. See Gilpin 1975; Krasner 1976; R. Keohane 1980, 1984; Stein 1984; Russett 1985; and Lake 1988.

63. See Krasner 1983b; and Keohane 1984.

64. See Katzenstein 1978; Krasner 1978; Milner 1988; and Ikenberry, Lake, and Mastanduno 1988.

65. Keohane and Nye 1977, 242.

66. Trachtenberg 1989, 332.

67. Betts 1997, 14–15.

68. See Allison 1971; Art 1973; Jervis 1976; and Janis 1982.

69. See Mandelbaum 1981; Jervis 1989c; and Sagan 1989.

70. Walt 1987.

71. Mearsheimer 1983.

72. See Posen 1984; and Snyder 1984.

grated conception of the relationship between economics and security? The international environment was the crucial factor. By the early 1970s bipolar world politics was clearly established and seemed likely to endure indefinitely.[73] Even though economic issues became more salient, bipolarity discouraged integration and encouraged scholars instead to pursue a division of labor that subsequently became institutionalized in U.S. political science departments and IR programs.

The 1970s fully exposed the peculiar, bifurcated character of international politics. The United States was competing against one state in international security affairs and interacting with and competing against a different set in international economic affairs. This duality was a challenge to scholars seeking to advance an integrated conception of international economics and security. Robert Gilpin, for example, developed a consistent account of hegemonic transitions through history but struggled to make sense of the "anomalous" contemporary situation characterized by "the multiple nature of the challenge to the dominant power in the system."[74] Aaron Friedberg reflected that "to a degree that appears unprecedented in recent history, the pattern of military power is now considerably out of alignment with the worldwide distribution of economic resources."[75] The principal security challenger was not an economic challenger, and the principal economic challengers were security allies. International economic and security relations seemed to be different games involving different major players.

One plausible conclusion for scholars to draw in this international setting was that different models or approaches should be applied to explain different issues or situations.[76] In one of the most influential works of the 1970s, Robert Keohane and Joseph Nye argued that "contemporary world politics is not a seamless web . . . one model cannot explain all situations."[77] They juxtaposed realism and complex interdependence as ideal types and sought to understand under what conditions, or within which "issue areas," each might usefully apply. In his subsequent work Keohane argued that "it is justifiable to focus principally on the political economy of the advanced industrial states without continually taking into account the politics of international security."[78] In a dual international structure, presumably one also could focus on the international security relations of the dominant actors without continually taking into account the politics of international economic relations.

Many IR scholars seemed to abide by this logic. A pattern of scholarship developed in which specialists in IPE turned to liberal or realist approaches to explain the outcomes of interest to them—at the system level, international economic cooperation and conflict; and at the unit level, foreign trade, investment, and monetary policies. As research progressed, IPE specialists became more systematic and self-

---

73. Waltz 1964, 1979.
74. Gilpin 1981, 239.
75. Friedberg 1989, 428.
76. Hoffmann 1978.
77. Keohane and Nye 1977, 4.
78. Keohane 1984, 137. The dominant IPE textbooks of the 1970s and 1980s approached the field in this spirit. See Spero 1981; and Blake and Walters 1976.

conscious in borrowing concepts and insights from economics.[79] Security scholars placed more emphasis on historical analogy (for example, the origins of World War I) and borrowed from psychology in seeking to explain a different set of outcomes: the incidence of war and peace, the formation and maintenance of alliances, and the sources of defense policies and doctrines.

There were some conscious attempts at integration. A special issue of *World Politics* published in 1986 brought together work by political economy and security specialists to suggest that game theoretic approaches could contribute meaningfully to explaining outcomes in both arenas.[80] The effort had potential to synthesize work across the two fields based on a common argument about the need to address problems of market failure through institutional arrangements and information sharing. The market failure argument, however, resonated more strongly in IPE than in security studies.[81] Marxism and its offshoot, dependency theory, constituted a more sustained attempt at integration. Scholars working in these traditions long accepted as natural the interaction of the capitalist world economy and political-military patterns.[82] But Marxism never moved into the mainstream of the U.S. IR discipline, and dependency theory, the subject of a special issue of *International Organization* during the 1970s, withered during the 1980s as it became apparent that linkages to the capitalist world system did not necessarily lead to the perpetuation of underdevelopment.[83]

Other examinations of economic and security issues tended to reinforce the division between the two fields. Charles Lipson explained how and why the prospects for cooperation among states varied across the very different arenas of international economic and international security affairs.[84] Richard Rosecrance distinguished territorial states (a product of the traditional security arena) from trading states (a product of the new economic arena) and argued that the contemporary trends were favoring the prospects for the latter.[85] These contributions and others that adopted a similar logic represented a plausible scholarly response to a bifurcated international environment.

Professional specialization and academic institutionalization reinforced the separate study of economic and security issues. By the 1980s, scholars in security studies and IPE identified themselves and each other as members of distinctive subcommunities within the broader IR scholarly community. Graduate students at major institutions oriented their training and dissertations in one direction or the other. *International Organization* came to be recognized as a leading journal for IPE contributions; *International Security,* introduced in 1976, quickly emerged as an important place for security scholars to publish. One of the most prestigious academic publishers,

79. See Gilpin 1981; Keohane 1984; and Rogowski 1989.
80. Oye 1986.
81. See Keohane 1984; Martin 1992a; and Mearsheimer 1994.
82. Lenin's 1916 classic linked imperialism, uneven development, and war. See also Wallerstein 1974; Kaldor 1978; and Halliday 1983.
83. See, for example, Evans 1979.
84. Lipson 1984.
85. Rosecrance 1986.

Cornell University Press, developed parallel book series in IPE and security studies, edited by leading scholars in the now well-established subfields.

U.S. Statecraft

National security concerns remained the highest priority of U.S. foreign policy during the 1970s and 1980s. Presidents Nixon through Reagan placed the management of the bipolar relationship at the top of their external agendas. Even the administration of Jimmy Carter, which sought initially to distance U.S. policy from an obsession with the East–West confrontation, found itself driven eventually to reaffirm its centrality. But U.S. officials also abandoned the integrated approach to economics and security that characterized U.S. statecraft during the early Cold War. Instead of foreign economic policy supporting and reinforcing national security policy, or security policy being used to promote economic objectives, economics and security drifted apart and were treated increasingly as separate problems of foreign policy. This approach represented a response to the incentives of both the international security environment and the changing perception of the United States in international economic competition.

By the end of the 1960s the bipolar world appeared highly stable to U.S. officials. The urgent challenges of the early Cold War period had been met successfully. Western Europe and Japan recovered economically and were secure politically.[86] Alliance structures were institutionalized and the risks of defection were low. France challenged U.S. hegemony and departed NATO's integrated command structure but was hardly prepared to exit the Atlantic alliance altogether or join the Warsaw Pact. Although alliance unrest on the other side of the bipolar divide met with a more forceful Soviet response, the United States acknowledged by its restrained behavior in 1956 and 1968 that Eastern Europe was properly in the Soviet sphere of influence. The risks of East–West military confrontation, which seemed high during the 1950s and early 1960s, appeared fairly remote by the 1970s. The nuclear balance was robust, and arms control helped to lock in strategic stability. Greater communication between the United States and Soviet Union helped to ensure crisis stability, leaving the bipolar powers free to compete for influence without seriously risking mutual annihilation.

With the early Cold War mission accomplished and the bipolar structure firmly in place, the strategic environment no longer imposed a pressing need on U.S. officials to place foreign economic policy at the service of national security strategy. And international economic competition now presented the United States with a very different set of incentives than it had during the 1950s. As the perception of relative economic decline spread, beleaguered segments of U.S. industry and their supporters in Congress expressed resentment at the unfair advantages still enjoyed by the United

---

86. Nordlinger makes the point even more forcefully: "If America's security did require a deep involvement in the defense of Western Europe in the late 1940s, it could have been phased out starting in the late 1950s." Nordlinger 1995, 14.

States' now recovered trading partners and pressed the executive to apply the machinery of foreign policy directly to the service of national economic objectives.

The key problem for economic nationalists was that economic interests could not be easily satisfied through the use of the traditional foreign policy machinery, because that machinery was developed during the early Cold War era and was dominated by agencies and officials who gave priority to the United States' security interests as traditionally defined. As Peter Peterson, who served as commerce secretary under President Nixon, recently reflected, "whenever 'economics' clashed directly with military 'security policy,' the United States instinctively opted to give precedence to the latter."[87] The national security establishment was generally unsympathetic to claims that foreign firms and governments were taking unfair economic advantage of the United States and generally unresponsive to the argument that the U.S. government needed to pursue U.S. economic interests more aggressively in the international arena.[88]

With the traditional national security establishment unresponsive, the solution for those in industry beset by international competition was to call on Congress to mobilize and strengthen the existing foreign economic policy apparatus within the U.S. executive branch. One key development was the renegotiation of authority between the executive branch and Congress over trade policy and the reassertion of congressional influence.[89] Members of Congress redrafted trade policy legislation during the 1970s and 1980s and exerted pressure on the executive branch to make it easier for firms to receive import protection from foreign competition. On the export side, Congress thrust upon the economic agencies of the executive branch controversial new tools such as 301, Super 301, and Special 301 to attack barriers to entry in foreign markets—in some cases the same barriers executive branch officials tolerated or even encouraged for security reasons during the 1950s and 1960s.[90]

Industry and congressional pressure forced the executive branch to shift adjudication of antidumping cases from the more internationally minded Treasury Department to the more nationalist-inclined Commerce Department, with a subsequent increase in "process protectionism."[91] The Export Control Act of 1949, which gave the executive broad, discretionary powers to use trade as an instrument of statecraft, was replaced in 1969 and 1979 by the Export Administration Act, which directed the executive to liberalize national security export controls and sought to constrain the use of economic sanctions for foreign policy purposes.[92] And, lodged institutionally in the White House, the Office of the U.S. Trade Representative (USTR) rose to prominence as a mediator between domestic pressures and international commitments and a politically credible defender of the United States' national economic interests in international negotiations.

With the backing of Congress and U.S. industry, Commerce and the USTR became the chief advocates within the executive branch for a more assertive defense of

87. Peterson and Sebenius 1992, 58.
88. Prestowitz 1990.
89. See Milner 1990; and Destler 1992.
90. See Bhagwati and Patrick 1990; and Tyson 1992.
91. Destler 1992.
92. Mastanduno 1992.

U.S. economic interests in foreign policy. The State and Defense Departments continued to support a foreign policy that placed security concerns above other objectives. But the traditional security establishment no longer controlled the initiative in foreign economic policy. This shift was even evident in East–West economic policy, which became highly contentious within the executive and between the executive and Congress during the 1970s and 1980s. In 1981, President Reagan succumbed to domestic economic pressure and lifted the grain embargo despite adopting a security strategy designed to isolate and confront the Soviet Union.

Thus, U.S. statecraft became less integrated as foreign economic policy and national security policy proceeded on separate diplomatic and institutional tracks. This was even the case during the years that Henry Kissinger moved the conduct of foreign policy under his direct personal control in order to maximize linkage across different aspects of policy.[93] As Mac Destler has noted, "U.S. foreign policy making in the seventies and eighties featured two semi-autonomous sub-governments, a security complex and an economic complex."[94] When direct conflicts emerged—for example, over how hard to push a recalcitrant trading partner who was simultaneously an important security ally—security concerns still tended to prevail. The Reagan administration was deemed notorious for "selling out" U.S. economic interests when trade negotiations reached the critical final stages at the highest levels.[95]

By the latter half of the 1980s, this pattern led to increasing frustration among economic nationalists in the United States. One result was the rise of "revisionists" in industry, government, and the academy calling for a balancing or reversal of U.S. priorities in relations with Japan in particular and in U.S. foreign policy more generally. This low-intensity conflict between the economic and security sides of the U.S. foreign policy establishment broke into open warfare over the FSX, as the economic agencies forced the national security agencies to reopen and revise a security arrangement with Japan, at considerable diplomatic cost, to assure that the United States' national economic interests were more effectively protected.[96] Since the FSX agreement had been negotiated by State and Defense to the exclusion of the economic side of the foreign policy house, Commerce and the USTR also demanded and obtained "a seat at the table" in future negotiations in which economic and security interests were intermingled. It was not a coincidence that the year of the FSX crisis, 1989, marked the beginning of the post–Cold War era.

Unipolar Politics and the Post–Cold War Era

Since 1989, the international environment has changed dramatically. The Cold War is over, and bipolarity has been replaced by a unipolar structure. Only the United States currently possesses a full range of great power attributes: size, military capa-

93. Kissinger had very limited influence on international economic issues. See Nathan and Oliver 1987, 66.
94. Destler 1994, 31.
95. Prestowitz 1990.
96. Mastanduno 1991.

bility and preparedness, economic and technological superiority, political stability, and "soft" power attributes such as cultural or ideological appeal.[97] Other potential great powers are limited or constrained in one or more crucial areas.

Neorealism typically treats unipolarity as an anomaly and views a unipolar "moment" as an inevitably brief transition to yet another era of multipolar balancing.[98] The main implication for U.S. policy is that U.S. officials have little choice but to accept the inevitable and prepare for a multipolar world. As I have argued elsewhere, however, if we accept that states respond to threats, and not just capabilities, then unipolarity has the potential to be more enduring and U.S. policy has more room to maneuver.[99] Whether, and how quickly, other states balance the United States depends in part on how threatening they perceive the international environment to be in general and U.S. behavior and ambitions to be in particular. U.S. foreign policy, in turn, has the potential to shape the perceptions and behavior of other major powers and discourage them from posing a challenge to the global status quo. In a unipolar world the dominant power faces risks rather than direct threats; we should expect it to dedicate its foreign policy to preventing risks from becoming threats.[100]

This logic suggests that a plausible U.S. response to the unipolar structure is a strategy of preponderance: an attempt to preserve an international environment in which the United States is the dominant power and world politics primarily reflects U.S. preferences. Bipolar and multipolar systems induce states to respond to external constraints, but a unipolar structure encourages the dominant state to try to maintain the system as it is.

Despite criticism that it has been indecisive or unguided, U.S. security policy since the end of the Cold War has in fact been largely consistent with an effort to preserve preponderance. The Defense Department articulated the idea most clearly in 1992: "our strategy must now refocus on precluding the emergence of any future global competitor by convincing potential competitors that they need not aspire to a greater role."[101] U.S. officials have sought to discourage Germany and Japan from becoming independent great powers by reaffirming and strengthening commitments to provide for their security. They have sought to engage Russia and China and integrate them into the practices and institutions of a U.S.-centered international order. They have intervened in regional conflicts in Europe, Asia, and the Middle East that have the potential to disrupt the security status quo or tempt other powers to aspire to a more independent role.[102]

U.S. Statecraft

The unipolar structure and the concomitant strategy of preserving preponderance provide incentives for a reintegration of economics and security in U.S. statecraft.

---

97. Nye 1990.
98. See Waltz 1993; and Layne 1993.
99. Mastanduno 1997.
100. The risk–threat distinction comes from Wallander 1998.
101. See *New York Times,* 8 March 1992, A14; and Jervis 1993, 53–64.
102. For an elaboration of this argument, see Mastanduno 1997.

We should expect foreign economic policy to complement and reinforce the national security policies of engagement, reassurance, and integration that the United States has adopted in relations with other major powers. In an interdependent world economy, positive economic relationships are an important instrument in any effort to engage or reassure other major powers. Economic conflicts or friction could lead to political conflicts and prompt others to reevaluate the extent to which they view the international environment and relations with the United States as threatening. U.S. foreign economic policy is thus potentially a key instrument in helping to assure that other powers are willing to accept, or at least tolerate, a U.S.-centered world order.

Although it is too soon to render any definitive judgment on the post–Cold War pattern, the available evidence suggests that U.S. policymakers have moved to reintegrate economics and security in U.S. statecraft. This was not true during the early years of the 1990s, during which U.S. economic and security policy toward other major powers seemed to work at cross purposes. More recently, however, U.S. officials have recognized and acted on the need for economic relations to reinforce, rather than contradict, the security strategy of preserving preponderance. This general shift is evident in U.S. relations with the European Union (EU) and, in Asia, with Japan and China.

Economic relations between the United States and the European Union were more a source of conflict than stability as the Cold War ended. Sharp transatlantic disagreements led to the collapse of the Uruguay Round in 1990. The round was completed three years later, but without resolving key disputes over agriculture, "cultural protection," and EU aircraft subsidies.[103] The United States subsequently announced that it would not abide by post–Uruguay Round agreements crafted by the EU in financial services and telecommunications because they did not provide sufficient advantages to U.S. firms in overseas markets. U.S. Trade Representative Charlene Barshefsky asserted that "with the Cold War over, trade agreements must stand or fall on their merits. They no longer have a security component."[104]

Yet, by mid-1995, it was apparent that the Clinton administration was moving away from the sentiment expressed by Barshefsky and toward an explicit link between trade and the United States' broader security relationship with key members of the EU. President Clinton visited Europe and launched a series of initiatives designed to "show Europe that the United States still cares."[105] The New Transatlantic Agenda (NTA) was intended as a confidence-building measure to give "new focus and direction to our political and economic partnership" in response to growing concern in Europe that the United States was losing interest in its long-standing trade and security partner after the Cold War.[106] The improvement and deepening of economic relations have been a centerpiece of this new initiative. The two sides committed to building a "new transatlantic marketplace," and by the middle of 1997 had resolved their differences over telecommunications and concluded agreements to liberalize trade in information technology, combat bribery in trade competition, and foster

103. Hoffmann 1997.
104. *New York Times,* 30 June 1995, D1.
105. *New York Times,* 3 December 1995, 20.
106. U.S. Department of State 1997.

mutual recognition of technical standards. The intent has been not simply to resolve outstanding disputes but also to restore confidence by searching proactively for opportunities to reach agreements in areas of mutual economic interest. U.S. officials depicted the NTA as a commemoration of the fiftieth anniversary of the Marshall Plan and have used it to deepen transatlantic engagement not only at the official level but also between U.S. and European firms and publics.[107]

The disjunction between the United States' economic and security policy toward Japan during the early 1990s was even more profound. The FSX crisis, the targeting of Japan under the controversial Super 301 provision, and the launching of the Structural Impediments Initiative assured that the bilateral economic relationship remained in an almost constant state of crisis management. In early 1992, the Bush administration transformed what had been conceived as a traditional head-of-state summit meeting to emphasize mutual security interests into a commercial sales mission, with President Bush thrust into the awkward role of chief sales representative for the U.S. auto industry.

This economic pressure intensified during the early years of the Clinton administration. Clinton initiated the U.S.–Japan Framework Talks to force Japan, on a short timetable, to make concessions on an array of outstanding trade disputes. Japan resisted, and in February 1994 both sides walked away without even reaching a cosmetic agreement to paper over their differences. Clinton escalated the pressure by reinstating Super 301. The next round of conflict focused on the automotive sector, with negotiations taking place under the threat of U.S. sanctions and a Japanese counterthreat to drag its closest ally through the new dispute settlement procedures of the World Trade Organization (WTO). U.S. diplomacy was working at cross purposes: while security officials were emphasizing the need to reaffirm and deepen the U.S. commitment to Japan's defense, economic officials were locked in an escalating series of confrontations.

By 1996, however, the United States clearly had shifted its course. The Clinton administration relaxed its economic pressure on Japan and emphasized the bilateral security relationship. The April 1996 summit between Clinton and Japanese Prime Minister Hashimoto was a turning point. Trade disputes remained unresolved, and in fact Japan's Ministry of International Trade and Industry (MITI) raised the stakes by refusing to negotiate with the United States in two areas of major concern, semiconductors and photographic film. Yet, instead of using the summit to press the Japanese negotiators from the highest level, Clinton deflected demands from the U.S. corporate sector and downplayed economic disputes in order to focus on the U.S.–Japan security relationship.

Foreign policy initiative within the U.S. government has shifted from the economic revisionists to the security traditionalists. Beginning in 1995, U.S. policy toward Japan has been guided by the so-called Nye Initiative, a Defense Department plan that halted U.S. force reductions and called for the maintenance of U.S. troop

---

107. Ibid., 1–3. In May 1997 the United States sponsored a Transatlantic Conference for Americans and Europeans to coordinate future transatlantic initiatives in the private and nonprofit sectors.

levels in the region at 100,000 for the foreseeable future.[108] The initiative articulated a strategy of "deep engagement" in which a forward-based military presence and the expansion of the U.S.–Japan security alliance are the principal features.[109] Winning trade battles has become a lower priority, and the administration instead has stressed the positive aspects of U.S.–Japanese economic interdependence and sought opportunities to use trade relations to reinforce security relations. The Technology for Technology Initiative, for example, linked economic and security policy explicitly by recognizing the contribution U.S. technology flows have made to Japan and by encouraging Japan to transfer advanced technology with military applications back to the United States.[110]

U.S. policy toward China since the end of the Cold War has been exceedingly complex, but even in this case we can discern the shift in emphasis described earlier. The initial approach to economic relations with China was confrontational. U.S. officials spoke openly of China as the "next Japan" and vowed not to make the "same mistake" of waiting too long before adopting an aggressive response.[111] The State Department fought during the 1950s to allow Japan into the GATT on preferential terms; in the early 1990s, U.S. officials surprised China by blocking its request to join the WTO as a developing state.[112] U.S. negotiators pressed China in 1992 to accept agreements on market access and intellectual property protection and subsequently threatened sanctions against China for failing to comply fully with the terms of those agreements.

Although U.S. officials have not completely relaxed the economic pressure, a gradual softening of the U.S. position is apparent. In 1994, the Clinton administration delinked China's most-favored-nation status from human rights conditionality. Subsequently, it stated officially that "we have adopted a policy of comprehensive engagement designed to integrate China into the international community as a responsible member and to foster bilateral cooperation in areas of common interest."[113] By 1996, U.S. officials were no longer blocking China and instead were focusing on defining terms and negotiating conditions for China's entry into the WTO.[114] In seeking to extract Chinese cooperation on proliferation problems, they minimized reliance on negative economic sanctions and focused instead on rewarding China for constructive behavior. Clinton and Chinese President Jiang Zemin met in 1997 in the first head-of-state summit since 1989, and their major summit agreement reflected the integration of economics and security. The Clinton administration lifted its ban on exports to China of nuclear reactors in exchange for a commitment from China to limit its own militarily sensitive trade with states seeking to develop nuclear weapons capabilities.

108. U.S. Department of Defense 1995.
109. Nye 1995.
110. National Research Council 1995.
111. Mastanduno 1997, 83.
112. Friedman 1997.
113. The White House 1996, 39.
114. Morici 1997.

What accounts first for the separation between U.S. economic and security policy and for the more recent turn to reintegration? The initial signal U.S. officials took from the end of the Cold War was that they were no longer constrained by the security imperatives of the bipolar struggle. In foreign policy, the pursuit of national economic interests could now be an equal, or perhaps even a greater, priority than the pursuit of traditional security interests. The fact that U.S. economic primacy appeared to be under challenge internationally as the Cold War ended—a perception that registered deeply in U.S. domestic politics—made it attractive for U.S. officials to elevate the pursuit of national economic interests. Clinton was determined to use foreign economic policy to contribute to domestic economic growth, and "the administration's drive was not going to spare America's main allies."[115]

As the 1990s wore on, however, the security opportunity of the new unipolar structure also became apparent to U.S. policymakers. As economic officials responded to the challenges of international economic competition with confrontational strategies, security officials reacted to the United States' position in the unipolar setting with strategies of engagement and integration designed to preserve U.S. preponderance. The resulting chasm between economic and security policies left both security traditionalists and economic revisionists dissatisfied. Henry Nau wrote in 1995 that "trade policy has been increasingly isolated from other U.S. foreign policy interests in a single-minded pursuit to capture exports and high-wage jobs for the American economy."[116] Chalmers Johnson expressed the opposite frustration: security agencies were constraining the pursuit of the national economic interest by focusing on anachronistic Cold War relationships.[117]

By the middle of the 1990s, two key factors, the perception of threat and of the position of the United States in international economic competition, helped to push U.S. policymakers to respond to the incentives of the unipolar structure by reintegrating economics and security. First, the intensification of security risks in both Europe and Asia brought into focus that the success of the U.S. "preponderance through engagement" strategy required, instead of business as usual, a conscious and sustained diplomatic effort across economic and security policy.[118] The protracted war in Bosnia and economic conflicts created political acrimony and, absent the Soviet threat, suggested the possibility that the United States and Europe would drift apart politically. As one U.S. official put it, without new economic and political "architecture" across the Atlantic, "natural economic juices may force us much farther apart than anyone conceives of right now."[119] The NTA was an initial attempt to provide the needed architecture, whereas the Dayton Accords placed the United States prominently at the center of the Bosnian conflict to remove the temptation for other major powers in the region to address the problem on their own.

---

115. Hoffmann 1997, 180.

116. Nau 1995, 1–2.

117. Johnson and Keehn 1995.

118. LaFeber stresses the dangers to U.S. security of taking the U.S.–Japan relationship for granted. LaFeber 1997.

119. *New York Times*, 29 May 1995, A3.

Security risks surfaced even more ominously in Asia. North Korea's defiance of nonproliferation norms in 1994 and China's military threat against Taiwan in early 1996 raised the prospect of direct U.S. military intervention, which, in turn, had the potential to shatter an unprepared U.S.–Japan alliance. Domestic politics in Japan precluded any meaningful Japanese assistance to U.S. forces, while domestic politics in the United States assured that there would be deep resentment if the United States absorbed casualties defending Japan's interests in Asia while Japan begged off from participation due to constitutional constraints. Clinton officials recognized an urgent need to modernize the security alliance for the post–Cold War environment and to remove the economic irritants that dominated the bilateral relationship. The April 1996 initiatives toward Japan reflected this dual concern, whereas the deeper engagement of China marked an effort to deflect at least one source of tension in a seemingly unstable region.

The U.S. response to the Asian financial crisis of 1997–98 reflected similar calculations. The Asian crisis was fraught with security risks: the potential for economic turmoil to lead to political instability, the collapse of the North Korean nuclear deal, or the inability of South Korea and Japan to bear the cost of bilateral security agreements with the United States. In the face of domestic opposition, U.S. officials fought for an expansion of International Monetary Fund (IMF) lending, emergency backup financing, and export credit guarantees. U.S. officials assured that the United States would remain at the center of crisis resolution by suppressing a Japanese proposal for an Asian bailout fund that had the potential to undermine the lead role of the U.S.-dominated IMF.[120]

Second, the international economic environment appeared far more accommodating to the United States by 1997 than it did in 1989. The "hegemonic decline" argument popular during the 1970s and 1980s depicted a United States hampered by declining productivity, diminished technological prowess, and huge budget deficits. The United States was trapped in a burdensome arms race with the Soviet Union while its economic competitors, in particular Japan, seemed to be taking full advantage and surging ahead.

By the late 1990s, this picture had changed dramatically. The United States enjoyed almost a decade of steady economic growth. Its budget deficits had disappeared, and U.S. firms were widely acknowledged to be at the cutting edge of international commercial and technological competition. For its part, Japan seemed incapable of pulling out of recession. Its supposedly omnipotent "Asian development model" was discredited, its financial sector was in deep crisis, and its most powerful firms seemed incapable of competing with their U.S. counterparts at the technological frontier. With the EU moving toward integration yet unable to generate sustained growth and employment, and with Asia's emerging tigers mired in financial crisis, the gap between the United States and its economic challengers seemed to be widening.

---

120. *Wall Street Journal*, 20 November 1997, A16; and *New York Times*, 22 February 1998, 3.

In this more advantageous setting, it was clearly easier for U.S. officials to forego confrontational economic demands on other major powers and place foreign economic policy at the service of national security strategy. In 1989, a majority of Americans believed that rising Japanese economic power posed a greater threat to U.S. security than Soviet military power.[121] A decade later, the United States faced neither the Soviet military threat nor the Japanese economic threat. Indeed, U.S. officials confronted a different and more delicate diplomatic problem: how to assure that the United States' seemingly overwhelming superiority in economic and military power did not provoke resentment and a backlash against the U.S. global presence and policies, thereby jeopardizing the U.S. effort to preserve preponderance.[122]

IR Scholarship

The end of the Cold War was a great transformation in the international system, and great transformations force IR scholars to rethink basic assumptions and reconsider enduring questions. The intensified disciplinary debate over the utility of realism relative to liberal and constructivist approaches is only the most visible manifestation of the reassessment taking place as scholars try to respond to the changing international context.

The collapse of bipolarity and the passing of the Cold War also provide incentives for scholars to reintegrate the study of economic and security issues. The bipolar world was an historical anomaly in terms of the nature of the dominant powers, the relationship between them, and their relations with other states in the system. Relations among the United States and other major powers in the emerging international environment are likely to return, at least to some extent, to more historically familiar patterns.[123] Major powers after the Cold War are likely to remain economically interdependent rather than independent. Alliance patterns over time are likely to become more fluid than fixed. Great powers may eventually return to the pre–Cold War practice of settling their differences through direct military conflict, although we obviously cannot know for certain at this point whether war among great powers is indeed obsolete. These features make it imperative for all major powers to calibrate the security implications of their economic relationships and the economic implications of their security relationships.

IR scholarship has begun to respond to the incentives of the new environment by redirecting attention to theoretical and substantive issues at the intersection of IPE and security studies.[124] These include work by younger scholars who now find it professionally profitable to straddle the two concerns, just as new graduates during the 1970s and 1980s found it profitable to identify themselves as either "IPE types"

---

121. Mastanduno 1991.

122. State Department officials have begun to refer to this as the "Hegemon Problem." *Washington Post National Weekly Edition*, 9 March 1998, 5.

123. Kirshner 1998.

124. For reviews, see Caporaso 1995, Moran 1996, and Kapstein 1992. Kapstein considers his text the first word rather than the last word, "given the paucity of recent books on the subject." Kapstein 1992, xv.

or "security types." Several research agendas, underdeveloped during the Cold War, have become and are likely to continue to be the subject of increased scholarly attention.

One research agenda concerns the classic question, long debated by realists and liberals, of the relationship between trade and peace. Rosecrance's statement of the liberal position and Barry Buzan's more skeptical assessment, among other work, kept this question in play during the 1980s.[125] The prospect of deep economic interdependence among major powers gives the question fresh political and theoretical significance after the Cold War. Recent contributions have introduced intervening variables to refine classic liberal and realist formulations.[126] Dale Copeland has shown that the propensity of interdependent states to go to war depends not on the degree of interdependence but on their expectations of future trade relations.[127] Paul Papayoanou has shown that the strength of economic ties among allies and between allies and adversaries influences the credibility of balancing efforts and thus the prospects for peace.[128]

A second research agenda reverses the causal arrow to examine the impact of security relationships on international economic cooperation and conflict. Gilpin's work during the 1970s underscored this link and helped to launch the hegemonic stability research program.[129] As that literature developed, however, it moved away from emphasizing the causal weight of security factors and instead emphasized the international distribution of economic power.[130] Although it was plausible during the 1970s and 1980s to analyze the international economic structure independently of the international security structure, it is harder to justify that approach after the Cold War, since economic and security relations among major powers are unlikely to play out in compartmentalized arenas. The relative gains debate, which has engaged scholars across IPE and security studies, is directly pertinent to the question of whether and how the international security environment affects the prospects for economic cooperation.[131] The same is true of Joanne Gowa's study establishing that allies trade more extensively in bipolarity than in multipolarity and more with each other than with adversaries.[132] Recent work by John Odell spells out hypotheses on how military conditions influence international economic bargaining.[133]

Third, there is renewed interest in the use of economic instruments to serve foreign policy objectives. Baldwin's seminal study argued that the economic, military, and diplomatic options available in any foreign policy situation had to be analyzed syn-

---

125. See Rosecrance 1986; and Buzan 1984.
126. McMillan provides a comprehensive review of recent work. McMillan 1997.
127. Copeland 1996.
128. Papayoanou 1996.
129. Gilpin 1975. Stein also emphasizes the link between geopolitics and economic cooperation. Stein 1984.
130. Lake, offering one of the most rigorous treatments, focuses on the causal power of the international *economic* structure to explain trade policy. Lake 1988.
131. See Grieco 1990; Baldwin 1993; and Liberman 1996.
132. Gowa 1994.
133. Odell 1997.

thetically within a common framework.[134] Subsequent work has focused on multilateral coordination of sanctions efforts and on the circumstances under which economic sanctions can complement or substitute for the use of military force.[135] Jonathan Kirshner takes the substantive focus beyond trade and finance to examine how monetary arrangements can be used to advance state security.[136]

Finally, the end of the Cold War has revived the study of grand strategy. Cold War conceptions were heavily influenced by the bipolar structure, and IR scholars tended to focus on grand strategy in narrow military terms.[137] During the 1980s, Gilpin and Paul Kennedy led the way in emphasizing more broadly the interplay of economic and security factors in sweeping assessments with implications for U.S. foreign policy.[138] After the Cold War, grand strategy has become significant not only for the United States but also for other potential great powers, such as Germany, Japan, and China, whose strategic choices were heavily conditioned by the bipolar structure.[139] Scholars have responded with studies of grand strategy in contemporary and historical perspective that develop links between economic and security factors in domestic and international politics. These include Jack Snyder's argument linking late industrialization to the strategy of overexpansion;[140] Mark Brawley's integrated account of liberal economic leadership and great power war;[141] David Lake's use of relational contracting theory to explain U.S. and Soviet grand strategies during the Cold War;[142] Lars Skalnes's work on how great power security needs drive their foreign economic policies;[143] and the ongoing debate over U.S. grand strategy after the Cold War.[144]

The new wave of work linking economics and security and illustrated by these research programs reflects the general advances in social science that have influenced IR scholarship over the course of the postwar era. Scholars have become increasingly self-conscious in sorting out and operationalizing variables, situating their research in the context of prior work and linking arguments with empirical evidence. It also reflects a response to Strange's urgent call of 1970 for IR specialists to "build their own bridges across the gulf" dividing international economics from IR by becoming more familiar with the literature and methods of economics.[145] As showcased in the work of Lake, Gowa, Edward Mansfield, and Robert Powell, IR

---

134. D. Baldwin 1985.
135. See, for example, Martin 1992a; Mastanduno 1992; and Pape 1997.
136. Kirshner 1995.
137. Rosecrance and Stein 1993.
138. See Gilpin 1981; and Kennedy 1987.
139. Kapstein and Mastanduno 1998.
140. Snyder 1991.
141. Brawley 1993.
142. Lake 1996 and forthcoming. He writes that "the theory developed above and the difference in relations it explains are not simply of academic or historical interest. The concerns central to the variation in superpower relations are central to every state's foreign policy—especially for those seeking to find their way in the post–Cold War world." Lake 1996, 29.
143. Skalnes forthcoming.
144. See Nordlinger 1995; Posen and Ross 1997; Ruggie 1997b; and Layne 1997.
145. Strange 1970, 314.

scholars working at the intersection of economics and security, as in IPE more generally, have shown greater sensitivity to the work of economists in constructing explanations.[146]

We should expect scholarship that links economics and security to become increasingly prominent in the post–Cold War IR literature. In a recent review, James Caporaso went further and asserted that "security studies and IPE are increasingly becoming one integrated literature rather than two."[147] That may overstate the case and underestimate the durability of the division of labor institutionalized during the Cold War. Nonetheless, Caporaso's assessment resonates with a growing number of calls for a closer connection between the two fields.[148] Joseph Nye and Sean Lynn-Jones termed the separation of political economy and security studies "one of the most serious problems within the discipline of political science."[149] Even scholars who are associated with the defense of "traditional" security studies against those who wish to broaden it recognize the need for closer links between the two fields. Stephen Walt, for example, highlights "economics and security" as an important area of new research for security scholars after the Cold War.[150]

Conclusion

In this article I have argued that three factors are crucial in understanding how U.S. policymakers and IR scholars have treated the relationship between economics and security over the past half-century. The international distribution of material capabilities provides important incentives for the integration or separation of economics and security. But by itself international structure is underdetermining. Perceptions of the international strategic environment and of the position of the United States in international economic competition also prove critical in accounting for the patterns observed in statecraft and scholarship.

In the prewar world of ordinary great powers interacting in a multipolar setting, scholars viewed linkages between economics and security as routine. But the scholarly treatment of economics and security changed dramatically in response to an international environment characterized by bipolarity, independent superpowers, the nuclear balance of terror, and the perception of U.S. economic hegemony. Instead of encouraging an understanding of economics and security as part of the "seamless web" of international relations, the bipolar world provided incentives for scholars

146. Theodore Moran observes that economists have been much slower to draw on the relevant work of political scientists. His overall assessment that the "analytical synergies" between the IR and international economics communities are "dramatically underexploited" is strikingly similar to the critique made by Strange twenty-five years earlier. See Moran 1996, 176, 191–92.

147. Caporaso 1995, 121.

148. See Baldwin 1995; Buzan 1991; Skalnes forthcoming; Krause and Williams 1996; Moran 1996; Kirshner 1998; and Caporaso 1995.

149. Lynn-Jones and Nye 1988, 25.

150. Walt 1991, 227. David Baldwin places Walt in the category of scholars who see little need to reform security studies. Baldwin 1995.

first to neglect international economic issues and later, with the realization of interdependence and relative U.S. decline, to pursue a division of labor strategy that resulted in the development and institutionalization of two separate subfields.

Since 1989 the external environment again has been transformed, and IR scholarship is responding to new challenges and opportunities. It is not surprising that the collapse of bipolarity and end of the Cold War have prompted renewed interest in the intersection of economics and security along with a critical reassessment of the scholarly pattern that considered the two as separate areas of inquiry. The sharp distinction between IPE and security studies that made sense during the Cold War is increasingly of questionable utility as we move away from that distinctive international context.

U.S. statecraft similarly has responded to the changing features, material and non-material, of the external environment. The strategic urgency and uncertainty perceived by U.S. officials in the early Cold War setting led them to integrate economic and security policies. U.S. officials sought to create an international order, and economic instruments and relationships were a vital part of that undertaking. The fact that the United States was dominant in and insulated from international economic competition made it easier for U.S. officials to place foreign economic policy at the service of national security strategy. But, by the latter half of the 1960s, the bipolar order was firmly established, the U.S. economy was less insulated, and the realization of relative economic decline had set in. U.S. officials responded by separating the pursuit of economic and security objectives in relations with security allies who were now economic competitors. The traditional security establishment within the U.S. government responded to the geopolitical imperatives of the Cold War, while a strengthened foreign economic policy apparatus responded to calls from domestic interest groups for a more assertive approach to international economic relations.

The end of the Cold War and the emergence of a unipolar structure once again afford U.S. officials with the opportunity to shape a new international order. The integration of economic and security policy is crucial in this context, as it was during the early years of the Cold War. As the initial shock of the end of the Cold War subsided, and as new security risks emerged in Europe and Asia, U.S. officials began to recognize that and to integrate foreign economic relations in pursuit of a grand strategy of preserving preponderance. Their future challenge will be to sustain that effort in the absence of a central strategic threat and in the face of forces in domestic society inclined either to disengage the United States from a global role or to mobilize its power in pursuit of more particularistic political and economic objectives.

What Makes the World Hang Together? Neo-utilitarianism and the Social Constructivist Challenge

John Gerard Ruggie

Edward Teller, the nuclear physicist, used to draw overflow crowds to his "physics for poets" course at Berkeley, despite his hawkish views on military matters and unwavering conservative politics. Through a thick Hungarian accent he would announce at the outset, "I will show you what makes the world hang together." And he did just that.

An analogous puzzle has occupied theorists of international relations right from the start: what makes *this* world hang together? Traditionally, the intellectual protagonists have been realism and liberalism—from Machiavelli or Hobbes versus Kant on down—with the liberal tradition attributing greater efficacy to ideational factors. The postwar academic aversion to idealism in the United States, however, resulted in a widespread discounting of, and thus a poor grasp on, the role of such factors in international life, be they identities, norms, aspirations, ideologies, or simply ideas about cause–effect relations.

Two subsequent developments have reinforced this state of affairs. The first was the ascendancy of neorealism and neoliberal institutionalism in the 1980s and their convergence around neo-utilitarian precepts and premises.[1] Within the ontology of neo-utilitarianism, ideational factors, when they are examined at all, are rendered in strictly instrumental terms, useful or not to self-regarding individuals (units) in the pursuit of typically material interests, including efficiency concerns. The second development has been the widespread embracing in the field of a model of social science that in certain epistemological respects has become almost Newtonian in character. As the physicist Gerald Feinberg put it, "Newtonian mechanics . . . did not attempt to explain what forces might exist in nature, but rather described how motion occurred when the force was known."[2] One obtains the essence of mainstream theo-

---

A longer and somewhat different version of this article appears in my book *Constructing the World Polity* (Routledge, 1998). I acknowledge with thanks helpful comments by Barry Buzan, Ernst Haas, Robert Jervis, Robert Keohane, Stephen Krasner, Cecilia Lynch, Art Stein, and Mark Zacher.

1. Baldwin 1993.
2. Feinberg 1978, 9.

International Organization 52, 4, Autumn 1998, pp. 855–885

rizing in international relations today merely by substituting the terms "interests" or "preferences" for "forces" in Feinberg's characterization.

The shift toward neo-utilitarianism has produced rigorous analytical results, some of which have been subjected to empirical tests. But it also has serious blind spots and silences, particularly regarding the ideational realm. The growing recognition of that fact has been most directly responsible for the blossoming in the 1990s of a very different approach to international relations theorizing, one that has come to be known as social constructivism.

Social constructivism rests on an irreducibly intersubjective dimension of human action. As Max Weber insisted at the turn of the century, "We are *cultural beings,* endowed with the capacity and the will to take a deliberate attitude towards the world and to lend it *significance.*"[3] This capacity gives rise to a class of facts that do not exist in the physical object world: social facts, or facts that, in the words of the linguistic philosopher John Searle, depend on human agreement that they exist and typically require human institutions for their existence.[4] Social facts include money, property rights, sovereignty, marriage, football, and Valentine's Day, in contrast to such brute observational facts as rivers, mountains, population size, bombs, bullets, and gravity, which exist whether or not there is agreement that they do.

In short, constructivism is about human consciousness and its role in international life. In contrast to neo-utilitarianism, constructivists contend that not only are identities and interests of actors socially constructed, but also that they must share the stage with a whole host of other ideational factors that emanate from the human capacity and will of which Weber wrote. The fact that human behavior at all levels of social aggregation is constrained is not in dispute. Nor is the likelihood that modal responses may exist to some types of structural constraints or situational exigencies. What social constructivists reject, however, is the presumption or pretense that their study constitutes the totality or even the main part of the social scientific enterprise.

My aim in this essay is to provide an analytical account of social constructivism in international relations today. No general theory of the social construction of reality is available to be borrowed from other fields, as is the case for neo-utilitarianism, and international relations constructivists have not as yet managed to formulate a fully fledged theory of their own. As a result, constructivism remains more of a philosophically and theoretically informed perspective on and approach to the empirical study of international relations. Hence, I present the constructivist project much as it has evolved in the field over the past fifteen years or so: as a critical reflection on the limits of neo-utilitarianism. I do so in three steps.

First, to gain a firmer grounding of what this approach is all about, I locate its roots in the sociology of Emile Durkheim and Max Weber, and I briefly note the analytical means whereby they resisted the ascending tide of utilitarianism and methodological individualism more generally in the late nineteenth century. Second, I inventory the increasingly extensive empirical results produced by constructivism in international

3. Weber 1949, 81, emphases in original.
4. Searle 1995, 2.

relations in recent years, as a result of which it is no longer possible to claim, as Judith Goldstein and Robert Keohane did in 1993, that constructivism "remains more an expression of understandable frustration than a working research program."[5] In addition, I explicate the philosophical bases informing this empirical work, showing how and why they differ from neo-utilitarianism. Third, I identify the common features of all constructivist approaches to the study of international relations and those that differentiate among the main variants. I conclude with a brief discussion of paradigmatic (ir)reconcilability between social constructivism and neo-utilitarianism, not to assert the primacy of the former, but to argue that the theoretical repertoire of our field must include it if we are to have a fuller understanding of the real world of international relations.

The Classical Roots

If neorealism and neoliberal institutionalism are contemporary theoretical branches that continue to draw sustenance from utilitarianism's nineteenth century roots, social constructivism in international relations today remains indebted to Durkheim and even more so to Weber.

Durkheim is perhaps best known to students of international relations as a result of being invoked by Kenneth Waltz to buttress his claim that the international system shapes and constrains the relations among its units.[6] Durkheim did propound such a perspective. But one would not know from Waltz's references that Durkheim's primary research concern was with moral phenomena in society. In his major empirical studies, Durkheim sought to demonstrate how a variety of social outcomes, ranging from patterns of social cooperation to individual feelings of anomie and differential suicide rates were influenced by the different interpersonal bonds of social order that are embodied within the reference groups to which individuals belong, from the family on up to society as a whole. Thus, in *Suicide* he attributed its lower incidence among Catholics to the fact that the practice of their faith makes more extensive use of integrative rituals within a stronger and more hierarchical moral community than does Protestantism.[7]

Durkheim's concern with moral phenomena is as interesting for our purposes as his attributing causality to forms of sociality. For it meant that he had to come to grips with two issues: the role of ideational factors in social life and how ideas, which can exist only in individuals' heads, become socially causative. On both issues, Durkheim differentiated himself from the utilitarians, on the one hand, and transcendentalists, on the other.

With regard to ideational factors, Durkheim wrote, "A third school is being born which is trying to explain [mental phenomena] without destroying their specificity."[8]

---

5. Goldstein and Keohane 1993a, 6.
6. Waltz 1979, 104, 115n, 121, 197.
7. Durkheim 1951.
8. Durkheim [1911] 1953b, 32.

For the Kantians and idealists, he stated, "mental life certainly had a nature of its own, but it was one that lifted the mental out of the world and above the ordinary methods of science."[9] For the utilitarians, on the other hand, mental life "was nothing in itself, and the role of the scientist was to pierce the superficial stratum in order to arrive at the underlying realities."[10] The third school, which he advocated, aimed to bring "the faculty of ideation . . . in its various forms into the sphere of nature, with its distinctive attributes unimpaired."[11] In short, Durkheim held that ideational factors have their own specificity and integrity as a result of which they cannot be reduced to other factors. But, at the same time, these ideational factors are no less "natural" than material reality and, therefore, are as susceptible to normal scientific modes of inquiry.

Durkheim's position on how ideas, of which individuals are carriers, come to express a social force is derived from his understanding of the nature of social order generally. Here, too, he differentiated himself vigorously from utilitarianism. If societies were based on its atomistic premises, he rebutted Herbert Spencer, "we could with justice doubt their stability."[12] And to the instrumental, contractarian view of social relations that Spencer represented he retorted, "Wherever a contract exists" it rests on "regulation which is the work of society and not that of individuals."[13]

But Durkheim also rejected organic conceptions of society and other forms of "substantial social realism," to use Ernest Wallwork's term,[14] notably that of Auguste Comte. Instead, Durkheim adopted what Wallwork describes as a "relational social realism," in which social facts are constituted by the combination of individual facts through social interaction. As Durkheim put it in an oft-cited formulation, "Whenever certain elements combine and thereby produce, by the fact of their combination, new phenomena, it is plain that these new phenomena reside not in the original elements but in the totality formed by their union."[15] Among the elements so transformed to become "social facts" are linguistic practices, religious beliefs, moral norms, and similar ideational factors. Once constituted as social facts, these ideational factors in turn influence subsequent social behavior.

Contemporary social constructivists in international relations remain indebted to Durkheim for his concept of social facts, the centrality of social ideas and beliefs ("*la conscience collective*") in them, and for an ontology that steered clear of both individualism and transcendentalism. But Durkheim did not actually study the concrete processes whereby individual elements, including ideas, are transformed to become social facts. Instead, he inferred them from the forms of social expression ("*représentations collective*") that he believed to be their products, ranging from liturgical practices to legal codes and similar expressions of civic morals. In other words,

9. Ibid.
10. Ibid.
11. Durkheim [1898] 1953a, 96.
12. Durkheim [1893] 1933, 203.
13. Ibid., 211.
14. Wallwork 1972, 16–26. On relational ontologies, also see Gilligan 1993.
15. Durkheim [1895] 1938, xlvii.

Durkheim "solved" a key methodological problem by means that are roughly analogous to stipulating "revealed preferences"—a problematic maneuver. However, doing so permitted him to use "objective" indicators and to adhere to positivist epistemological practices, which he believed necessary for establishing the scientific legitimacy of sociology. Weber's influence on social constructivism remains the greater for having tried to work this problem through.

Like Durkheim, Weber found himself amid disciplinary conflicts.[16] And, like Durkheim, Weber sought to avoid the pitfalls of the prevailing alternatives. The major methodological opposition he confronted was between the subjectivism of the German Historical School and the positivism of the Austrian Theoretical School (marginal utility theory) and Marxism. Although the latter two differed in many respects, both sought to reduce problems of social action and social order to material interests, and both embraced a naturalistic monism—that is, the belief that the natural sciences embody the only valid model of science to which the social sciences should, therefore, aspire.

Weber believed strongly in the possibility of a social science. But to be valid it had to give expression to the distinctive attributes of social action and social order, namely, the human capacity and will "to take a deliberate attitude towards the world and to lend it *significance.*"[17] Thus, the task of interpreting the significance that social actors attribute to actions and the shared meanings that make that attribution possible fundamentally differentiates the social and natural sciences. Weber's major methodological innovations followed from this premise.

The natural and social sciences both use concepts, and both seek causal knowledge, according to Weber. But they use different kinds of concepts, and the way in which concepts are ordered to provide explanations differ. Natural science aims at the general, seeks to establish universally valid laws, and identifies individual events as types to be subsumed under those laws. Its concepts are constructed accordingly, to facilitate generalizability. But in the study of social behavior, concepts in the first instance must aid in uncovering the meaning of specific actions and in demonstrating their social significance. That is to say, they must be capable of grasping the distinctiveness of the particular. In Weber's words, "We wish to understand on the one hand the relationships and the cultural significance of individual events in their contemporary manifestations and on the other the causes of their being historically *so* and not *otherwise.*"[18]

Meaning and significance are, of course, ideational phenomena, so the role of ideas is central to Weber's social science. He included not only their instrumental but also normative roles. "One thing is certain," he wrote, namely, "the broader [the] cultural significance [of a social phenomenon], the greater the role played [in it] by value-ideas."[19] Hence, when social scientists set out to attribute meaning to actions,

16. See Schluchter 1989, chap. 1. See also Ringer 1997; I became aware of this excellent study too late to incorporate it fully into this article.
17. Weber 1949, 81, emphases in original.
18. Ibid., 72, emphases in original.
19. Ibid., 56.

they must concern themselves with not merely the instrumental rationality of the means actors select but also the normative self-understanding of the ends held by the social groups in question. This premise implied, according to Wolfgang Schluchter, that Weber "had to go beyond the concept of utility."[20]

Weber proposed to uncover social meanings and significance by means of an analytic method he termed *Verstehen,* or, loosely, "understanding."[21] Somewhat simplified for our purposes here, Weber took this method to comprise three steps. The first is to discern a "direct" or an "empathetic" understanding of whatever act is being performed, from the vantage point of the actor. The second is to devise an "explanatory understanding" of that act by locating it in some set of social practices recognized as such by the relevant social collectivity—or identifying, as Searle puts it, what the act "counts as" within the intersubjective frameworks held by that collectivity.[22] The third is to unify these individualized experiences into a broader set of objectively valid truth statements or explanations—of "objectivating" *Verstehen,* as Schluchter depicts it.[23]

Weber accomplished this last task by a combination of probabilistic and counterfactual reasoning coupled with the use of ideal types. He described ideal types as "a conceptual construct which is neither historical reality nor even the 'true' [i.e., some underlying] reality. It is even less fitted to serve as a schema under which a real situation or action is to be subsumed as one *instance.* It [is] a purely ideal *limiting* concept with which the real situation or action is *compared* and surveyed for the explication of certain of its significant components."[24] Among the best-known ideal types devised by Weber are traditional, charismatic, and rational-legal forms of authority, the "modern Occidental type" of persons, and their distinctive institutions, including capitalism, bureaucracy, and the modern state.

In constructing his own causal explanations—whether of the impact of the distinctive spirit of Protestant asceticism on the rise of capitalism, or the growing pervasiveness in the West of a certain form of rationality and its positive as well as negative consequences for social order—Weber linked together multiple ideal types. Moreover, for analytical purposes, Weber had no objection to sequencing ideal types (for example, his concepts of authority). Lastly, he even accepted marginal utility theory (a precursor of rational choice theory) as an ideal type, defending it on that basis against claims that it needed a more robust psychological foundation.[25] But Weber warned that ideal types must not be confused either with social reality or (even in developmental sequences or axiomatic formulations) with causal explanation. They are selective and deliberately one-sided abstractions from social reality, and their methodological role is to serve as "heuristic" devices in the "imputation" of causal-

20. Schluchter 1989, 9.
21. For a summary with international relations examples, see Hollis and Smith 1990, 78–82.
22. Searle 1995, chap. 2.
23. Schluchter 1989, 19, according to whom Weber here built in part on Georg Simmel.
24. Weber 1949, 93, emphasis in original.
25. Weber 1975. I thank Guenther Roth for this reference.

ity[26]—for example, by helping to pinpoint differences between the logic of the ideal type and patterns of outcomes on the ground.

Actual causal knowledge of social action and social order, Weber insisted, remains concrete and is anchored in meaning, showing why things are historically *so* and not *otherwise.* The purpose of the various analytical tools that Weber used, then, was not to subsume specific social actions or events under putative deductive laws, of which he believed few existed, but to establish links between them and concrete antecedents that most plausibly had causal relevance within the social collectivity at hand. Though Weber gave it no name, today we would call his a "narrative explanatory protocol," in contrast to the deductive-nomological model that is favored by all forms of naturalistic monism, including neo-utilitarianism.[27]

It is not my aim to vindicate Durkheim or Weber, nor to suggest that social constructivists in international relations today directly apply or copy their insights or methods. It is their theoretical objectives that are of interest, and what they thought they had to do in order to achieve them, because these efforts illuminate the contemporary constructivist project. Both Durkheim and Weber held that the critical ties that connect, bond, and bind individuals within social collectivities are shared ideational ties, and they sought to establish these factors by rigorous social scientific means. In doing so, both rejected utilitarianism on the grounds of its methodological individualism and because it failed to encompass normative self-understandings of the ends of social action—without which, they believed, instrumental rationality was devoid of meaning.

For our purposes, the major difference between them is that Durkheim inferred ideational social facts from "objective" indicators represented by their institutionalized forms of expression and thereby was able to remain within a conventional positivist epistemological framework. In contrast, Weber explored actual processes whereby certain ideas had become social forces, as a result of which he felt the need to depart from several positivist precepts, in particular the influence of its naturalistic monism on concept formation, the study of meaning, and the character of causal explanation.

Searle is surely correct when he states that we—meaning contemporary social constructivists—"are much in debt to the great philosopher-sociologists of the nineteenth and early twentieth centuries—one thinks especially of Weber, Simmel, and Durkheim." Nevertheless, he adds, "they were not in a position to answer the questions that puzzle [us] because they did not have the necessary tools. That is, through no fault of their own, they lacked an adequate theory of speech acts, of performa-

26. Weber 1949, 90, 103.
27. For a fuller discussion of narrative explanatory protocols, see Ruggie 1998, chap. 3. Mainstream international relations theorizing is utterly confused on this point. Virtually no theoretical account in our field meets the formal criteria of the deductive-nomological model, and when challenged most theorists readily admit that fact. Yet so strong is the ideal of naturalistic monism that general methodological discussions and teachings systematically ignore actual practice and hold up the deductive-nomological model as the only valid model.

tives, of intentionality, of collective intentionality, or rule-governed behavior. . . ."[28] With these newer analytical tools in hand, and based on the classical foundations, what are the main features of constructivism in international relations today?

The Emergence of Social Constructivism

Neorealism and neoliberal institutionalism are drawn directly from microeconomics. Although social constructivism in international relations is strongly influenced by the sociological tradition, as we have just seen, no corresponding theory exists elsewhere for it simply to import. Consequently, it has had to be a relatively homegrown and heterodox theoretical creation. Among its antecedents, neofunctionalism embodied elements that we now recognize to be social constructivist in character, but it did so largely unconsciously.[29] And the so-called English school anticipated constructivist concerns, but one of its major aims was to resist the influence of American social scientific modes of analysis and less to firm up its own theoretical basis.[30] The actual label of social constructivism may not have been affixed to or by any international relations scholar prior to 1989, when it was featured in an analytical study by Nicholas Onuf[31]—although Anthony Giddens's closely related term, "structuration theory," was in use earlier, and Giddens's work profoundly affected the emerging constructivist project.[32]

Beginning at the margins of the field, scholarly interest in the social constructivist approach has grown steadily as certain analytical and empirical limitations of conventional theories have become better understood, most emphatically after their neoutilitarian turn. The constructivist project has sought to open up the relatively narrow theoretical confines of the field—by pushing them back to problematize the interests and identities of actors; deeper to incorporate the intersubjective bases of social action and social order; and into the dimensions of space and time to establish the "duality" of structure, in Giddens's terms, at once constraining social action but also being (re)created and, therefore, potentially transformed by it. I briefly summarize these efforts.

Interests and Identities

Neorealism and neoliberal institutionalism treat the identity and interests of actors as exogenous and given. Some neorealists claim to "derive" state interests from the condition of anarchy but, as Helen Milner has argued persuasively, anarchy is an

---

28. Searle 1995, xii.
29. See, for example, Haas 1958, 1961, 1964a.
30. See Butterfield and Wight 1968; James 1973; Wight 1977; Bull 1977; Bull and Watson 1984; and Watson 1992. Good surveys may be found in Buzan 1993; and Little 1995.
31. Onuf 1989.
32. Giddens 1979, 1981. For discussions in the context of international relations theory, see Ruggie 1983a; Dessler 1989; and Wendt 1987.

exceedingly slippery concept, and the propositions one can derive from it are almost entirely indeterminate.[33] Hence, interests are, in fact, handled by assumption, notwithstanding claims to the contrary. The power and elegance of the neo-utilitarian model rests on this point of departure. But so, too, do some of its limitations.

First, neo-utilitarianism provides no answer to the core foundational question: how the constituent actors—in international relations, territorial states—came to acquire their current identity and the interests that are assumed to go along with it. Similarly, any potential future change in this identity and in corresponding interests is beyond the scope of the theory. States and the system of states simply *are*: endowed with the ontological status of being, but not of becoming, to borrow a phrase from Nobel laureate Ilya Prigogine.[34] Addressing these foundational issues requires the concept of constitutive rules, which I take up in a subsequent section.

Second, not only does neo-utilitarianism have no analytical means for dealing with the generic identities and interests of states *qua* states, it also excludes consideration of how specific identities of specific states shape their interests and, thereby, patterns of international outcomes. This is true even of treatments of the United States—the century's central great power and yet so atypical in its advantageous geopolitical position and internal political and ethnic makeup. I have indicated elsewhere how the postwar international order would have differed if the Soviet Union or Nazi Germany had ended up as its hegemon instead of the United States; indeed, important things would have differed if Britain had become the leading power. Thus, contra neorealism, I argued that *American* hegemony was every bit as important as American *hegemony* in shaping the postwar order.[35] And, contra neoliberal institutionalism, I noted that America's choice of the specific features of the postwar institutional frameworks—be it the United Nations, indivisible security commitments in NATO, or nondiscriminatory norms in trade and monetary relations—cannot be rendered accurately merely in terms of marginal utility but also reflected America's sense of self as a nation.

What is more, the identity of the same state can change and pull its interests along. Thus, Thomas Berger argues that Germany and Japan today differ significantly from their pre–World War II predecessors. Antimilitarism, he maintains, has become integral to their sense of self as nations and is embedded in domestic norms and institutions.[36] Peter Katzenstein makes a similar case for the police and military in postwar Japan and Germany.[37] Robert Herman explains the Gorbachev revolution in the Soviet Union and its international aftermath in terms of an identity shift leading to a radical recalibration of interests.[38] It may be true that constraints and opportunities led initially to changes in behavior, but in all three cases, the authors contend, a transformation of identity has taken place. Although it is possible that these changes

33. Milner 1991.
34. Prigogine 1980.
35. Ruggie 1992, 1997b.
36. Berger 1996.
37. Katzenstein 1996a,c.
38. Herman 1996.

are not irreversible, Katzenstein in particular identifies the specific normative and institutional practices in Japan and Germany that any move toward a reversal would have to contend with and overcome.

Third, there is growing empirical evidence that normative factors in addition to states' identities shape their interests, or their behavior, directly, which neo-utilitarianism does not encompass. Some of these factors are international in origin, others domestic.

On the international side, the literature that Martha Finnemore depicts as "sociological institutionalism" has documented successive waves in the diffusion of identical cultural norms to developing countries, which differ radically among themselves in their specific circumstances but which come to express identical preferences for policies and institutional arrangements.[39] The norms diffused are those of rationalized bureaucratic structures and, more generally, standards of what it means to be a modern state. Finnemore has extended this research to include the emergence of norms among the core countries, such as the Geneva conventions on warfare and the evolution of humanitarian intervention.[40] Others have addressed normative taboos on the use of chemical weapons[41] and nuclear weapons.[42] In a completely different (and far more robust institutional context), the European Court of Justice has been shown to shape domestic legal practices within the member states of the European Union.[43] Each of these studies specifies logics that depart significantly from neo-utilitarianism, even as they fully appreciate that power and interests are deeply implicated.

On the domestic side, Elizabeth Kier and Alistair Johnston raise serious questions about neo-utilitarian renderings of the origins of strategic cultures and military doctrines, contending that—at least in the cases of France and China, respectively—they are not simply functionally determined either by external or internal factors, but reflect broader cultural and political forces.[44]

In a frequently cited remark, Waltz has stated that his theory does not pretend to explain everything, but what it does explain is important.[45] He is right on both counts. But the subjects addressed in the studies noted here (and others like them) are hardly unimportant either. Indeed, all are important for precisely those dependent variables that Waltz's theory claims to explain. The same point also holds, correspondingly, for neoliberal institutionalism. More empirical work in the social constructivist vein is necessary, and the origins of identities and other normative factors need to be better theorized. But it is not an undue stretch to conclude, even at this point, that neo-utilitarianism's assumptions that the identities and interests of states are exogenous and given (in contrast to being treated as endogenous and socially constructed) pose potentially serious distortions and omissions, even as they provide the basis on which neo-utilitarianism's theoretical payoff rests.

39. Finnemore 1996b.
40. Finnemore 1996a,c.
41. Price 1995.
42. Price and Tannenwald 1996.
43. Burley and Mattli 1993.
44. See Kier 1996 and 1997; and Johnston 1995a and 1996.
45. Waltz 1986, 329.

Ideational Causation

Neo-utilitarianism has a narrowly circumscribed view of the role of ideas in social life. But because neorealism and neoliberal institutionalism differ somewhat in this respect, I discuss them separately.

Waltz's neorealist model is physicalist in character. Hence, ideational factors make only cameo appearances in it. Take his reference to the recurrent normative element in U.S. foreign policy: "England claimed to bear the white man's burden; France spoke of her *mission civilisatrice*. In like spirit, we [the United States] say that we act to make and maintain world order. . . . For countries at the top, this is predictable behavior."[46] It is Waltz's *sole* reference to the role of norms. Ideational factors enter the picture again briefly in the form of socialization, one of the mechanisms by which states, according to Waltz, learn to conform to the dictates of the system.[47] Numerous critics have been puzzled by the presence of socialization in a physicalist model that disclaims any sociality on the part of its actors. But perhaps even more serious is the fact that Waltz, in this instance as elsewhere in his *Theory,* turns what is supposed to be a methodological principle into an ontological one: Waltz has *actual states* becoming socialized to *his model* of the international system, not to the more variegated world of actual international relations.[48]

Other neorealists have modestly modified Waltz's model. Krasner has explored the role of ideology in North–South economic negotiations,[49] and more recently he has made reference to states'"ideational interests."[50] But neither factor has been fully squared with his enduring neorealist premises. Following the collapse of the Soviet system, several neorealists discovered nationalism, which was previously black-boxed into domestic factors, said to have no role in systemic theory.[51] However, as Yosef Lapid and Friedrich Kratochwil note, neorealists' interest in nationalism is largely limited to its role as a source of conflict or in affecting the capability of existing or would-be states to wage conflicts, thus "making it difficult to conceive of a nontautological relationship between 'nation' and 'state'."[52]

Finally, Katzenstein has pointed out that neorealists who seek to add greater determinative content to the predictions of Waltz's sparse model often do so by importing into it unacknowledged ideational factors, such as the role of culture as an instrument of social mobilization or in generating threat perceptions.[53]

Generally speaking, neoliberal institutionalism also assigns a limited causal role to ideational factors. In strictly rationalist explanations, Goldstein and Keohane observe, "ideas are unimportant or epiphenomenal either because agents correctly an-

---

46. Waltz 1979, 200.
47. Ibid., 127.
48. For a discussion of the confusion between ontological and methodological principles in Waltz, see Ruggie 1983a.
49. Krasner 1978.
50. Krasner 1997, 3.
51. See Mearsheimer 1990; and Posen 1993a,b.
52. Lapid and Kratochwil 1996, 113.
53. Katzenstein 1996b, 26–27.

ticipate the results of their actions or because some selective process ensures that only agents who behave as if they were rational succeed."[54] Goldstein and Keohane believe otherwise, however, and present a framework for analyzing the impact of ideas on policy outcomes. It serves as a useful point of reference for our discussion because, even though the framework is posed as a challenge to both neo-utilitarianism and social constructivism, Goldstein and Keohane are quickly drawn back into the neo-utilitarian fold.

One part of the framework consists of three causal pathways for ideas to influence policy outcomes.[55] The first is by serving as "road maps," a role that "derives from the need of individuals to determine their own preferences or to understand the causal relationship between their goals and alternative political strategies by which to reach those goals." The second is as "focal points" in strategic situations of multiple equilibria, that is, several equally "efficient" outcomes. Here, ideas can help individuals select one from among the set of viable outcomes. The third causal pathway is through "institutionalization," whereby ideas, once they have become encrusted in institutions, continue to "specify policy in the absence of innovation."

Goldstein and Keohane also define three types of ideas that may do these things.[56] One they call "world views," which are "entwined with people's conceptions of their identities, evoking deep emotions and loyalties." Another is "principled beliefs," which "specify criteria for distinguishing right from wrong and just from unjust." The last is "causal beliefs," that is, beliefs about cause–effect relations, derived from the shared consensus of recognized authorities.

The framework holds promise, but the pull of neo-utilitarian precepts is stronger. Most significantly, what Goldstein and Keohane call world views are disposed of circumstantially: "Since all the subjects discussed in this volume [of which theirs is the introductory essay] have been profoundly affected by modern Western world views, and our authors all share this modernist outlook, we can say relatively little about the impact of broad world views on politics."[57] Set aside, thereby, are state identities and corresponding interests—the heart of the social constructivist project. Left unexplored, thereby, are ideas of the sort that John F. Kennedy had in mind when he honored Jean Monnet by saying: "you are transforming Europe by a constructive idea."[58] Nor is it clear where ideologies fit in, not merely those for which an instrumental rationalization can be claimed, like the resurgence of neo-laissez faire, but others, such as the American sense of exceptionalism,[59] Nazi doctrines of racial superiority, or Mao's Cultural Revolution.

But what of principled and causal beliefs? Do they not fare better? From a social constructivist vantage, not much. For the individuals featured in the Goldstein–Keohane story are not born into any system of social relationships that helps shape

54. Goldstein and Keohane 1993a, 4.
55. Ibid., 12–17.
56. Ibid., 8–10.
57. Ibid., 9.
58. Duchene 1994, 6.
59. See Lipset 1996; and Ruggie 1997b.

who they become. When we first encounter them, they are already fully constituted and poised in a problem-solving mode. As a result, neither principled beliefs nor ideas as road maps are intended to tell us much about those individuals, only about how they go about their business. By a process of elimination, then, the heavy lifting in the Goldstein–Keohane scheme ends up being done by principled and causal beliefs functioning as focal points in multiple equilibria situations and as sunk costs embedded in institutions—both fully consistent with neo-utilitarian precepts.

What is the social constructivist contribution to the ideational research program? Social constructivists have sought to understand the full array of roles that ideas play in world politics, rather than specifying a priori roles based on theoretical presuppositions and then testing for those specified roles, as neo-utilitarians do. Because there is no received theory of the social construction of international reality, constructivists have gone about their work partly in somewhat of a barefoot empiricist manner and partly by means of conceptual analysis and thick description. To briefly map constructivist research on ideational factors, I begin by using Goldstein and Keohane's own typology and then push beyond it.

As noted, a core constructivist research concern is what happens *before* the neo-utilitarian model kicks in. Accordingly, what Goldstein and Keohane call "world views" are of great interest: civilizational constructs, cultural factors, state identities, and the like, together with how they shape states' interests and patterns of international outcomes. I identified some of the empirical work on these subjects earlier. In addition, such world views include changing forms of nationalism in its constitutive and transformative roles, as Ernst Haas has studied it extensively, not merely as adjuncts to states and their power.[60] They include the globalization of market rationality and its effects, which has been of particular interest to constructivists who work in the tradition of Antonio Gramsci,[61] Karl Polanyi,[62] as well as the sociological institutionalists. And they include emerging bonds of "we-feeling" among nations, such as appear to have taken effect within the transatlantic security community—much as Karl Deutsch predicted forty years ago[63]—and, of course, in the European Union.

Constructivist empirical studies documenting the impact of principled beliefs on patterns of international outcomes include, among other subjects, decolonization,[64] international support for the termination of apartheid,[65] the growing significance of human rights,[66] the role of multilateral norms in stabilizing the consequences of rapid international change,[67] as well as the already-mentioned studies on increasingly nondiscriminatory humanitarian interventions and the emergence of weapons taboos.

60. Haas 1986 and 1997.
61. Gill 1995.
62. Ruggie 1995b.
63. Deutsch et al. 1957. For a useful update of Deutsch's concept of security communities, see Adler and Barnett 1996. For its application to the issue of NATO expansion, see Ruggie 1997a.
64. Jackson 1993.
65. Klotz 1995b.
66. See Forsythe 1991; and Sikkink 1993a.
67. Ruggie 1992.

The most important feature differentiating constructivist from other readings of these and similar phenomena is that they make the case that principled beliefs are not simply "theoretical fillers," to use Mark Blyth's apt term, employed to shore up instrumentalist accounts, but that in certain circumstances they lead states to redefine their interests or even their sense of self.[68]

One major route for constructivist explorations of the impact of causal beliefs has been through the roles played by transnational networks of knowledge-based experts, or "epistemic communities."[69] Here, the empirical research seeks to relate the impact of the shared beliefs held by such communities on resolving particular policy problems, such as ozone depletion;[70] specifying operational content to general and sometimes ambivalent state interests, as at Bretton Woods;[71] and helping to redefine states' interests, including in the case of the antiballistic missile treaty[72] as well as the Mediterranean pollution control regime.[73] Disentangling strictly ideational from institutional impacts is difficult in practice, but that problem is not unique to the epistemic community literature.[74]

The further up one climbs on this ideational impact ladder, the more is learning said to come into play.[75] At the upper rungs, learning no longer means adapting to constraints, imitating the successful, or undertaking bounded search processes until a viable solution is identified—its typical meaning in conventional theories. It progressively becomes second-order learning—or what Ernst Haas and his associates have termed "evolutionary epistemology."[76] This refers to the process whereby actors alter not only how they deal with particular policy problems but also their prevailing concept of problem solving, including in the direction of adopting what neo-utilitarians would describe as interdependent utility functions. That possibility takes us well beyond the Goldstein–Keohane typology.

Learning of this sort entails forms of communicative dynamics that are absent from neo-utilitarianism. Theoretical analysis along these lines is most advanced among German international relations scholars, more influenced by the work of Jürgen Habermas than their American counterparts.[77] One of the central questions they have posed is the extent to which Habermas' theory of communicative action can be reconciled with rational choice theory and neo-utilitarianism more generally.[78] The consensus is that to accommodate communicative action, including acts of deliberation and per-

68. Blyth 1997.

69. The concept of epistemic communities was introduced by Ruggie 1975; and productively elaborated by Haas 1992a.

70. See Haas 1992b; and Litfin 1994.

71. Ikenberry 1992.

72. Adler 1992.

73. P. Haas 1990.

74. See Yee 1996; and Blyth 1997.

75. For the most extensive discussion, see E. Haas 1990.

76. This perspective draws on the work of Toulmin 1972; and Campbell 1987. See E. Haas 1983, 1990; Adler 1991, 1992; and Adler and Haas 1992.

77. Habermas 1979, 1984, 1987.

78. See the debates in Müller 1994; Keck 1995; Risse-Kappen 1995a; Schmalz-Bruns 1995; and Müller 1995. Also consult Kratochwil 1989; and Alker 1990 and 1996.

suasion, one must devise a conception of actors who are not only strategically but also discursively competent, a feat that is unlikely to be achieved, at least within currently available neo-utilitarian formulations.[79]

A final major difference between social constructivism and neo-utilitarianism on the issue of ideational causation concerns how "causation" itself is understood. Some ideational factors simply do not function causally in the same way as brute facts or the agentive role that neo-utilitarianism attributes to interests. As a result, the efficacy of such ideational factors is easily underestimated. The role of aspirations is one instance, the impact of legitimacy is another, and the power of rights a third. This is too complex a problem to be fully explored here.[80] Suffice it to say that these factors fall into the category of *reasons for actions,* which are not the same as *causes of actions.* Thus, the *aspiration* for a united Europe has not *caused* European integration as such, but it is the *reason* the causal factors (which presumably include bipolarity and economic interests) have had their specific effect—in Weber's words, produced an outcome that is historically *so* and not *otherwise.* Absent those "reasons," however, and the same "causes" would not have the same causal capacity.[81]

Collective Intentionality

When all is said and done, the critical differences between the social constructivist and neo-utilitarian ideational research programs does not lie in empirical issues of the sort we have been looking at, as important as they are. They have to do with more fundamental, even philosophical, issues.

One such issue concerns the neo-utilitarian misspecification of certain kinds of ideas. For example, Goldstein and Keohane define ideas exclusively as "beliefs held by individuals."[82] It is, of course, true, physiologically speaking, that only individuals can have ideas or beliefs. But the reverse proposition, that all beliefs are individual beliefs or are reducible to individual beliefs, does not follow. It is the product of the methodological individualism on which neo-utilitarianism rests. Social constructivism, in contrast, also deals in the realm of "intersubjective beliefs," which cannot be reduced to the form "I believe that you believe that I believe," and so on. They are social facts and rest on what Searle calls "collective intentionality."[83] Searle stresses that the concept of collective intentionality does not require "the idea that there exists some Hegelian world spirit, a collective consciousness, or something equally implausible."[84] Why not? Because the intentionality remains in individual

79. Keohane seems to be entertaining moves in a similar direction, if I correctly understand his remarks on the desirability of a supplementary "extra-rationalistic research program." He specifically mentions wanting to accommodate acts of persuasion, for which, he notes, there is no need within the logic of what he calls "intra-rationalistic analysis." Keohane 1996b.
80. See Kratochwil 1989; and Ruggie 1998, chap. 3.
81. On the concept of causal capacity, see Yee 1996.
82. Goldstein and Keohane 1993a, 3.
83. Searle 1995, 24–25.
84. Searle 1995, 25.

heads. But within those individual heads it exists in the form of "we intend," and "I intend only as part of our intending."[85]

Constructivists have explored the impact of collective intentionality, so understood, at several levels in the international polity. At the deepest is the question of who counts as a constitutive unit of the international system. The mutual recognition of sovereignty, I have argued elsewhere, is a precondition for the normal functioning of a system of sovereign states.[86] Sovereignty, like money or property rights, exists only within a framework of shared meaning that recognizes it to be valid—that is, by virtue of collective intentionality. But its impact is not limited to a one-time designation, "you are in this game, and you are out." Over time, sovereignty has affected patterns of conflict between sovereign states and other types of political formations.[87] And it empowers and provides resources to some states irrespective of how dysfunctional they may be, states that might not survive except for such external recognition.[88] Though this is not the place to pursue the issue, constructivists also tend to believe, as a working hypothesis, that insofar as sovereignty is a matter of collective intentionality, in the final analysis, so, too, is its future.

In addition to this constitutive role, collective intentionality also has a deontic function within the system of states—that is, it creates new rights and responsibilities. The process that Inis Claude called collective legitimation includes an entire class of such functions that, if anything, has expanded since he wrote his classic article.[89] For example, Finnemore observes that humanitarian intervention is not only becoming more nondiscriminatory, but states are increasingly seeking endorsement by international organizations before undertaking such interventions.[90] Searle, viewing the subject through a philosopher's eyes, finds that human rights are "perhaps the most amazing" instance of creating rights through collective intentionality—amazing because it ascribes rights "solely by virtue of being a human being."[91] Equally amazing, from the vantage of conventional international relations theory, is the fact that it ascribes these rights to individuals vis-à-vis their own states.

At the most routine level, collective intentionality creates meaning. To cite one well-documented instance, the Bretton Woods negotiations and the corresponding efforts to establish an international trade regime produced more than external standards of behavior and rules of conduct in monetary and trade relations. They also established intersubjective frameworks of understanding that included a shared narrative about the conditions that had made the regimes necessary and the objectives they were intended to accomplish and generated a grammar, as it were, on the basis of which states agreed to interpret the appropriateness of future acts that they could not possibly foresee.[92]

85. Ibid., 26.
86. Ruggie 1993.
87. Strang 1991.
88. See Jackson 1990; and Ruggie 1993.
89. Claude 1966.
90. Finnemore 1996c.
91. Searle 1995, 93.
92. The original formulation in these terms was Ruggie 1993b. For an update, see Ruggie 1996b, chap. 5, 6. See also Ikenberry 1992.

Constitutive Rules

Perhaps the most consequential difference between neorealism and neoliberal institutionalism, on the one hand, and social constructivism, on the other, has to do with the distinction between constitutive and regulative rules. The distinction goes back to a seminal article by John Rawls.[93] Searle offers an easier point of entry.

Let us begin with a simple illustration. We can readily imagine the act of driving a car existing prior to the rule that specified "drive on the right(left)-hand side of the road." In an account perfectly consistent with neo-utilitarianism, the rule would have been instituted as a function of increased traffic and growing numbers of fender-benders. Specifying which side of the road to drive on is an example of a regulative rule; as the term implies, it regulates an antecedently existing activity. To this rule were soon added others, such as those requiring licenses, yielding at intersections, imposing speed limits, and forbidding driving while under the influence of alcohol.

Now imagine a quite different situation: playing the game of chess. "It is not the case," Searle notes sardonically, "that there were a lot of people pushing bits of wood around on boards, and in order to prevent them from bumping into each other all the time and creating traffic jams, we had to regulate the activity. Rather, the rules of chess create the very possibility of playing chess. The rules are constitutive of chess in the sense that playing chess is constituted in part by acting in accord with the rules."[94] Regulative rules are intended to have causal effects—getting people to approximate the speed limit, for example. Constitutive rules define the set of practices that make up a particular class of consciously organized social activity—that is to say, they specify *what counts as* that activity.

This basic distinction permits us to identify an utterly profound gap in neo-utilitarianism: it lacks any concept of constitutive rules. Its universe of discourse consists entirely of antecedently existing actors and their behavior, and its project is to explain the character and efficacy of regulative rules in coordinating them. This gap accounts for the fact that, within their theoretical terms, neorealism and neoliberal institutionalism are capable of explaining the origins of virtually nothing that is constitutive of the very possibility of international relations: not territorial states, not systems of states, not any concrete international order, nor the whole host of institutional forms that states use, ranging from the concept of contracts and treaties to multilateral organizing principles. All are assumed to exist already or are misspecified.

Why is this the case, and is it inherent to the enterprise? The reason is not difficult to decipher: neo-utilitarian models of international relations are imported from economics. It is universally acknowledged that the economy is embedded in broader social, political, and legal institutional frameworks that make it possible to conduct economic relations—which are constitutive of economic relations. Modern economic theory does not explain the origins of markets; it takes their existence for granted. The problem arises because, when neo-utilitarian models are imported into other fields, they leave those constitutive frameworks behind.

93. Rawls 1955.
94. Searle 1995, 28.

This problem appears not to matter for some (as yet unspecified) range of political phenomena, domestic and international, which has been explored by means of micro-economic models and the microfoundations of which are now far better understood than before. But there are certain things that these models are incapable of doing. Accounting for constitutive rules—which they were not responsible for in econom-ics—is among the most important.[95]

Nor can this defect be remedied within the neo-utilitarian apparatus. Alexander James Field has demonstrated from within the neoclassical tradition, and Robert Brenner the neo-Marxist, that marginal utility analysis cannot account for the consti-tutive rules that are required to generate market rationality and markets[96]—an insight that Weber had already established at the turn of the century[97] and Polanyi demon-strated powerfully a half century ago.[98] The terms of a theory cannot explain the conditions necessary for that theory to function, because no theory can explain any-thing until its necessary preconditions hold. So it is with modern economic theory.

Social constructivists in international relations have not yet managed to devise a theory of constitutive rules, but the phenomenon itself is of central concern to them.[99] Take first the states system. The very concept of the modern state was made possible only when a new rule for differentiating the constituent units within medieval Chris-tendom replaced the constitutive rule of heteronomy (interwoven and overlapping jurisdictions, moral and political). And the modern system of states became conceiv-able only when the constitutive rule of reciprocal sovereignty took hold.[100]

Moreover, Hedley Bull of the English school has argued that norms regarding promise keeping and contracting are constitutive of order in the international realm no less than the domestic.[101] But the *concept* of promises and the *institution* of con-tracts must be understood and enjoy legitimacy before there can be any talk of regu-lative rules designed to deal with problems of cheating on agreements or incomplete contracting. Kratochwil elaborates on these issues fruitfully in an explicitly construc-tivist vein.[102]

In addition, even as they acknowledge that the specific (as opposed to generic) identities of states are defined primarily internally, constructivists have shown that to some extent such identities are also interactively constituted. Alex Wendt draws on

95. Art Stein points out that economists create property rights in pollution and markets in emissions, for example, and he claims that these are constitutive acts. Art Stein, personal communication with the author, March 1998. But they represent specific instances of creating property rights and markets, whereas the concept of constitutive rules pertains to the class of actions of which they are an instance.

96. See Field 1979, 1981, 1984; and Brenner 1977. The reason the so-called new economic history does such a poor job at retrodicting actual outcomes in the origins of capitalist economies and territorial states stems from its practice of retrojecting actor responses to alleged incentives, which yield those responses only under modern market rationality, into the very differently constituted economies of pre-modern Europe. See, for example, North and Thomas 1973.

97. Weber 1958b.

98. Polanyi 1944, 1957b.

99. For general theoretical treatments, see Kratochwil 1989; Onuf 1989; and Wendt forthcoming.

100. See Ruggie 1983a, 1993.

101. Bull 1977.

102. Kratochwil 1989.

G. H. Meade's theory of symbolic interactionism to elucidate the process.[103] On the premise that every identity implies a difference, constructivist scholars have also explored the role of "the other"—denigrated, feared, or emulated—in the interactive constitution of identities: Ivar Neumann and Jennifer Welsh on the role of the Ottoman Empire, "the Turk," in consolidating the civilizational construct of Europe;[104] David Campbell on the "old world," the communist menace, as well as various internal "others" in forging America's sense of self;[105] and James Der Derian on the mediating role of diplomacy in sustaining relations among culturally estranged entities.[106]

Lastly, it is necessary to take note of an epistemological point: in some cases, constitutive rules themselves provide the desired explanation. If we are asked to "explain" the game of chess, the appropriate response consists of its constitutive rules. In Searle's simple formulation, constitutive rules are of the type "X [a move] counts as Y [checkmate] in context C [chess]."[107] Because X does not temporally precede and is not independent of Y, it follows that these are noncausal explanations. (A causal explanation is called for in response to questions like, "why do I keep losing at chess?") Precisely the same holds for "explaining" modern international politics in contrast to the medieval or classical Greek systems: the relevant answer is provided by their respective constitutive rules. Indeed, it also holds for social constructions that are closer to the surface level of the international system, such as the Cold War or the embedded liberalism compromise. The point to note is this: lacking a conception of constitutive rules makes it impossible to provide endogenously the noncausal explanations that constitutive rules embody and that are logically prior to the domain in which causal explanations take effect.[108]

Constitutive rules are the institutional foundation of all social life. No consciously organized realm of human activity is imaginable without them, including international politics—though they may be relatively more "thin" in this than in many other forms of social order. Some constitutive rules, like exclusive territoriality, are so deeply sedimented or reified that actors no longer think of them as rules at all. But their durability remains based in collective intentionality, even if they started with a brute physical act such as seizing a piece of land. The sudden and universally surprising collapse of the Soviet Union's East European empire illuminates vividly what can happen, Searle observes, "when the system of status-functions [assigned by constitutive rules] is no longer accepted"[109]—despite the fact that, in that instance,

103. Wendt 1992.
104. Neumann and Welsh 1991.
105. Campbell 1992.
106. Der Derian 1987.
107. Searle 1995.
108. This argument is not uncontroversial. For example, King, Keohane, and Verba find the whole notion of noncausal explanation "confusing," though the concept is hardly alien to the philosophy of social science. King, Keohane, and Verba 1994, 75. My point would not be compromised if these "accounts" were called something else so long as it is understood that they go well beyond even compound definitions, well beyond even very thick descriptions, and function in a logical domain that precedes the scope of causal relations as we normally understand that term.
109. Searle 1995, 92.

brute force remained *entirely* on the side of the status quo.[110] A similar erosion of collective intentionality, only partly related to shifts in brute force or material interests, was evidenced in the termination of colonialism and of the slave trade before it. Under certain circumstances, it seems, collective intentionality can "will" the rules of the game to change.

Constructivists do not claim to understand the extraordinarily complex processes regarding constitutive rules fully (or even mostly). But neorealists and neoliberal institutionalists lack even a place for them in their ontology. The scope of their theories, as a result, is confined to regulative rules that coordinate behavior in a preconstituted world.

Transformation

In light of the foregoing discussion, it follows almost axiomatically that neo-utilitarian models of international relations theory would have little to offer on the subject of systemic transformation: doing so would require them to have some concept of constitutive rules. Waltz's model, I have shown elsewhere, contains only a reproductive logic, but no transformative logic.[111] Neorealists have made some effort to respond by claiming, in essence, that no such logic is necessary. Neoliberal institutionalism has remained relatively silent on the subject.

The neorealist claim that no theory of transformation is necessary takes two forms. One argues that there is no decisive difference between medieval Europe and the modern system of states—the "case" on which this debate has focused—because conflict groups, striving for advantage, forging alliances, and using force to settle disputes existed in both and were not visibly affected by whatever common norms medieval Christendom may have embodied.[112] This realist historiography and the selection bias on which it rests have been ably challenged.[113] But even if the basic point were correct, it is irrelevant to the issue at hand because the identity of the constituent "conflict groups" was transformed: the personalized and parcelized structure of political authority relations in feudal society collapsed and was replaced by the entirely different institutional form of modern states.

The second neorealist argument is that not enough is happening in the world today to warrant a theory of transformation. This position has been elaborated most extensively by Krasner.[114] Krasner maintains that the "Westphalian baseline"—the Peace of Westphalia (1648), symbolizing the beginning of the modern state system—was never as clear-cut as some analysts have made it out to be, has been compromised from the start by recurrent forces, and with some exceptions (notably the European Union) it remains the rough approximation of the international polity that it has always been. Nevertheless, as Krasner acknowledges when he grapples with the

---

110. See also Koslowski and Kratochwil 1995.
111. Ruggie 1983a.
112. See Fischer 1992. See also Mearsheimer 1994.
113. Hall and Kratochwil 1993.
114. Krasner 1993, 1995a, 1997.

elusive concept of sovereignty, even the markers of international transformation are badly underspecified and ill-understood in the literature. A deeper theoretical grasp of transformation would go some way toward clarifying its indicators.

Here again, constructivists have not yet managed to devise a fully fledged theoretical formulation. But its general thrust has become evident. It consists of historicizing the concept of structure in international politics: that is to say, rescuing it from being treated as the reified residue left behind by long-ceased historical processes. Doing so involves addressing both macro and micro dimensions of international political life.

Giddens's theory of structuration has been found helpful at the macro level.[115] It expresses what he calls the "duality" of structure: at once constraining human action but also being (re)created by it. "Structural principles," Giddens states, "are principles of organization implicated in those practices most 'deeply' (in time) and 'pervasively' (in space) sedimented into society."[116] To understand system transformation, therefore, requires that the contingent nature of structure, conceived of as social practices situated in time and space, be made transparent.

Temporality plays little role in international relations theorizing, and when it does it denotes little more than "elapsed time." Pushing beyond that everyday meaning without giving way to Heideggerian flights of mysticism is not easy. The *Annales* school of historiography is suggestive, especially the works of Fernard Braudel and Jacques Le Goff.[117] The key, as they make clear, is to understand time not merely as duration but as comprising different temporal forms. Thus, the history of *la longue durée* differs from *l'histoire événementielle* not merely in its longer duration but, more importantly, in its deeper and wider framing of relevant causal factors. The implication for the study of international transformation is this: one is unlikely to fully grasp its potential if time is conceived merely as a succession of increments, rather than as different temporal forms that bring deeper and wider "presents" into view. Structure as constraining residue becomes structure as contingent practice only when it is located in its own "present," even though the sources of its contingency may not be subject to immediate volition.[118]

If structure is brought to life, as it were, through the dimension of time, its effects on social practices are inscribed in space: in the case of the modern international polity, the system of fixed, disjoint, and mutually exclusive territorial formations. But space is not given in nature. It is a social construct that people, somehow, invent. Moreover, space serves not merely as an inert container for the effects of structure. It generates emergent properties of its own—the need for open and secure diplomatic relations across mutually exclusive territorial formations, for example—that may lead states to modify the structural principles that had defined that space—such as the

115. Giddens 1979, 1981. For international relations applications, see Ruggie 1983a; Wendt 1987; and Dessler 1989.

116. Giddens 1981, 55.

117. See Braudel 1980; and Le Goff 1980. See also Koselleck 1985. For elaborations in the context of international relations, see Ruggie 1986, 1989, 1993.

118. See also Koselleck 1985; and Emory and Trist 1973.

236 The Social Constructivist Challenge

invention of the concept of extraterritoriality. Indeed, the "unbundling of territoriality" more generally has been shown to be a fruitful terrain in which to explore the possibility of postmodernity in international politics.[119]

And so the loop closes. The duality of structure is operationalized; it is made time–space contingent. And the possibility of transformation is not foreclosed as an artifact of theoretical presupposition; it remains an open empirical question, as indeed it should be.

Having identified the possibility of system transformation at the macro level, corresponding micro practices that may have transformative effects must be identified and inventoried. Recent examples in a constructivist vein include Saskia Sassen's work on the institutional mechanisms that are reconfiguring global economic geography today, ranging from legal practices and financial instruments to accounting rules and telecommunication standards.[120] Kathryn Sikkink's work on "advocacy networks" similarly exemplifies this genre.[121] So too does a host of studies on the growing role of nongovernmental actors and the emergence of transnational civil society.[122] Finally, even though there is little sign that the modern state is becoming irrelevant in the face of these and other global institutional developments, there is growing evidence that the state is, nevertheless, increasingly playing international roles that involve a degree of collective legitimation that is not traditionally associated with the Westphalian model—most notably in the European Union, but also in certain aspects of economic relations, the environment, and even security policy. In short, having been the political instantiation of single-point perspective, the expression of a single political subjectivity, the modern state may be becoming more of a "multiperspectival" political form.[123]

The Question of Agency

"Men [people] make their own history," Marx wrote in the *Eighteenth Brumaire,* "but they do not make it just as they please; they do not make it under circumstances chosen by themselves, but under circumstances directly found."[124] The two major international relations theories today, neorealism and neoliberal institutionalism, are mostly about "circumstances" that states "find" in the object world around them and that constrain their behavior. Based on particular renderings of those circumstances (such as polarities for neorealism and instances of market failure for neoliberalism), and by assuming the interests of states to be given and fixed, these theories seek to explain patterns of outcomes. The actors, in the context of these models, merely enact (or fail to) a prior script.

---

119. For a fuller discussion, see Ruggie 1993; and Kratochwil 1986.
120. Sassen 1996.
121. See Sikkink 1993a; and Keck and Sikkink 1998.
122. See, for example, Wapner 1995.
123. Ruggie 1993.
124. Tucker 1978, 595.

Constructivism, we have seen, is interested as much in the "making" of circumstances, to extend Marx's aphorism, as in their being "found"—without, however, lapsing into subjectivism or idealism. It takes "making" to have at least two meanings: What do people make of their circumstances in the sense of understanding them? And what do they make of them in the sense of acting on whatever understanding they hold? Here, the actors engage in "an active process of interpretation and construction of reality,"[125] as Frank Ninkovich has put it in his study of the domino theory in U.S. foreign policy.

The distinction between finding and making circumstances is especially critical at times of discontinuity such as the world has experienced since 1989. The core foreign policy problem for states then becomes precisely how to redefine their interests and preferences vis-à-vis the international order. It is not surprising that the mainstream theories have been so incoherent in the face of these discontinuities.[126]

For example, NATO features centrally in all "what now?" scenarios concerning European and transatlantic security relations. But highly regarded realists have argued with equal certitude and based on the same core premises that NATO has become irrelevant and is likely to collapse;[127] remains alive by dint of inertia but will wither away sooner rather than later;[128] and is as important as ever and should expand.[129] Neoliberal institutionalists, for their part, have said relatively little systematically about security relations. Concerning NATO, Robert Keohane and Lisa Martin claim that demand for its services remains high, including in Central and Eastern Europe.[130] But the countries that are "functionally" in greatest need of NATO's services (the Baltics, Ukraine, Belarus) are not even in the queue for future membership.

The constructivist approach has received a ringing (though presumably unintended) endorsement from Czech President Václav Havel, whose country has been invited to join NATO: "If we in 'postcommunist countries' call for a new order, if we appeal to the West not to close itself off to us, and if we demand a radical reevaluation of the new situation, then this is not because we are concerned about our own security and stability. . . . We are concerned about the destiny [in our countries] of the values and principles that communism denied, and in whose name we resisted communism and ultimately brought it down."[131] In short, according to Havel, the would-be NATO members are asking for affirmation that they belong to the West—an affirmation of identity *from which* concrete interests and preferences flow.[132]

---

125. Ninkovich 1994, xv.

126. See Lebow and Risse-Kappen 1995; and Koslowski and Kratochwil 1995.

127. Mearsheimer 1990.

128. Waltz 1993.

129. Henry Kissinger, "Expand NATO Now," *Washington Post,* 19 December 1994, A27.

130. Keohane and Martin 1995.

131. Havel 1994, 4.

132. It may be that Poland and Hungary are more concerned about their security situations, but their actions are not entirely consistent with that view. Well before they were invited to join NATO, both countries shortened the terms of military conscription, and the Polish army (along with the Czech) reduced some divisions and disbanded others; see Brown 1995, 37.

An outright concession by the master practitioner of realist statecraft affirms the same point from a different vantage. Without the Soviet threat, Henry Kissinger concludes ruefully in his book *Diplomacy,* realism by itself cannot suffice to frame U.S. foreign policy. In the new era, a foreign policy strategy based merely on interest calculations is simply too unreliable. Hence, realism, Kissinger contends, must be coupled with a "vision" that provides the American people with a sense of "hope and possibility that are, in their essence, conjectural."[133] To put it plainly, Kissinger now looks for salvation to the "idealism" that he spent his entire career mocking— but which is more properly described as the animating ideas and values that emerge out of America's own sense of self as a nation and which have always framed successful U.S. foreign policy, even during the era of strategic bipolarity. They include the desire to reform the international politics of the "old world" by moving beyond the system of bilateralist alliances, as well as to promote nondiscriminatory economic relations, democracy, and human rights as general milieu goals.[134]

In summary, "making history" in the new era is a matter not merely of defending the national interest but of defining it, nor merely enacting stable preferences but constructing them. These processes are constrained by forces in the object world, and instrumental rationality is ever present. But they also deeply implicate such ideational factors as identities and aspirations as well as leaders seeking to persuade their publics and one another through reasoned discourse while learning, or not, by trial and error. As a result, nothing makes it clearer than the question of agency at times such as ours why the constructivist approach needs to be part of the theoretical tools of the international relations field.

The Social Constructivist Project

Social constructivism in international relations has come into its own during the past decade, not only as a metatheoretical critique but also increasingly in the form of empirical findings and insights. Constructivism addresses many of the same issues that neo-utilitarianism has addressed, though typically from a different angle. But it also concerns itself with issues that neo-utilitarianism treats by assumption, discounts, ignores, or simply cannot apprehend within its ontology and/or epistemology. We are now in a position to specify more systematically the core elements of the constructivist approach. I first summarize the analytical features that are shared by all forms of social constructivism and then those that differentiate them.

Constructivism's Core Features

As noted at the outset, constructivism concerns the issue of human consciousness in international life: the role it plays and the implications for the logic and methods of

---

133. Kissinger 1994, 835.
134. Ruggie 1997b.

inquiry of taking it seriously. Constructivists hold the view that the building blocks of international reality are ideational as well as material; that ideational factors have normative as well as instrumental dimensions; that they express not only individual but also collective intentionality; and that the meaning and significance of ideational factors are not independent of time and place.

The most distinctive features of constructivism, then, are in the realm of ontology, the real-world phenomena that are posited by any theory and are invoked by its explanations.[135] As summarized in the previous section, at the level of individual actors constructivism seeks, first of all, to problematize the identities and interests of states and to show how they have been socially constructed. Neorealists come close to believing that states' identities and interests are, in fact, given and fixed. For neoliberal institutionalists, this premise is more likely to reflect a convenient assumption, intended to permit their analytical apparatus to function. When neoliberal institutionalists are pressed about the origins of either, however, they turn immediately to domestic politics.[136] Social constructivists, in contrast, argue and have shown that even identities are generated in part by international interaction—both the generic identities of states qua states and their specific identities, as in America's sense of difference from the Old World. Still at the level of individual units, constructivism also seeks to map the full array of additional ideational factors that shape actors' outlooks and behavior, ranging from culture and ideology to aspirations and principled beliefs, onto cause–effect knowledge of specific policy problems.

At the level of the international polity, the concept of structure in social constructivism is suffused with ideational factors. There can be no mutually comprehensible conduct of international relations, constructivists hold, without mutually recognized constitutive rules resting on collective intentionality. These rules may be more or less "thick" or "thin," depending on the issue area or the international grouping at hand. Similarly, they may be constitutive of conflict or cooperation. But in any event, these constitutive rules prestructure the domains of action within which regulative rules take effect. In some instances, collective intentionality includes an interpretive function—as in the case of international regimes, which limit strictly interest-based self-interpretation of appropriate behavior by their members. And in others collective intentionality also includes a deontic function—creating rights and responsibilities in a manner that is not simply determined by the material interests of the dominant power(s). In short, constructivists view international structure to be a social structure—the concept of "relational social realism" that Wallwork uses to describe Durkheim's ontology is apt—made up of socially knowledgeable and discursively competent actors who are subject to constraints that are in part material, in part institutional.

These ontological characteristics have implications for the logic and methods of constructivist inquiry. First, constructivism is not itself a theory of international relations, the way balance-of-power theory is, for example, but a theoretically informed

---

135. For a good discussion of ontology in the context of international relations theorizing, see Dessler 1989.

136. See, for example, Keohane 1993, 294.

approach to the study of international relations. Moreover, constructivism does not aspire to the hypothetico-deductive mode of theory construction. It is by necessity more "realistic," to use Weber's term, or inductive in orientation. Additionally, its concepts in the first instance are intended to tap into and help interpret the meaning and significance that actors ascribe to the collective situation in which they find themselves. It is unlikely that this function could be performed by concepts that represent a priori types derived from some universalizing theory-sketch or from purely nominal definitions.[137]

Finally, constructivism differs in its explanatory forms. As discussed earlier, for some purposes constitutive rules themselves provide appropriate and adequate, albeit noncausal, explanatory accounts. And in its causal explanations, constructivism adheres to narrative explanatory protocols, not the nomological-deductive (N-D) model prized by naturalistic monism. The N-D model establishes causality by subsuming the explanandum under a covering-law or lawlike generalization—of which there are relatively few valid ones at the level of the international system.[138] Causality in the narrative explanatory form is established through a process of successive interrogative reasoning between explanans and explanandum, anticipated by Weber with his heuristic use of ideal types and called "abduction" by the American pragmatist philosopher Charles Peirce.[139] At least in these respects, then, constructivism is non- or postpositivist in its epistemology.

These epistemological practices of constructivism have not been well received in the mainstream of the discipline. Part of the problem is that the mainstream has become so narrow in its understanding of what constitutes social science that on the dominant conception today Weber might no longer qualify—his approach to concept formation, method of theory construction, and model of explanation all fail to conform to the norm. The other part of the problem is that there are different strands of constructivism in international relations and they differ precisely on epistemological grounds, not surprisingly creating confusion thereby. I briefly summarize the main differences.

Variants of Constructivism

Any distinction ultimately is arbitrary, and so it is with constructivism. There are sociological variants, feminist variants, jurisprudential approaches, genealogical approaches, an emancipatory constructivism and a more strictly interpretive kind. What

137. On the theoretical as well as practical significance of the difference between nominal and principled definitions of multilateralism, see Ruggie 1992.
138. Lawlike generalizations can be established either statistically or by means of randomized experiments or quasi-experimental research designs. The former require reasonably large and robust sets of observational data, whereas the latter require that causal variables be subject to manipulation at least in principle. In the field of international relations, neither condition holds for the international system *as a whole*. How many cases have there been of nuclear bipolarity? Or of any other kind, for that matter? How many hegemons have there been "like" the United States in the twentieth century, or Britain in the nineteenth?
139. Peirce [1940] 1955, 151–52. See also Ruggie 1995c.

matters most for the purposes of this article is their underlying philosophical bases and how they relate to the possibility of a social science. Accordingly, I differentiate among three variants.[140]

I propose to call the first *neo-classical constructivism*—not to strive for parity with the two mainstream "neos" but to indicate that it remains rooted in the classical tradition. The analytical means by which this foundation is updated differs among scholars who work in this genre but typically includes an epistemological affinity with pragmatism; a set of analytical tools necessary to make sense of intersubjective meanings, be it speech act theory, the theory of communicative action, their generalization as in the work of Searle, or evolutionary epistemology; and a commitment to the idea of social science—albeit one more plural and more social than that espoused in the mainstream theories, while recognizing that its insights will be temporary and unstable. I put myself in this category—and also the work of Ernst and Peter Haas, Kratochwil, Onuf, Emanuel Adler, Finnemore, recently Katzenstein, as well as some feminist scholars, such as Jean Elshtain.[141]

A second variant may be termed *postmodernist constructivism*. Here the intellectual roots are more likely to lead back to Friedrich Nietzsche, and any updating to the writings of Michel Foucault and Jacques Derrida, marking a decisive epistemic break with the precepts and practices of modernism. Richard Ashley first drew the attention of the field to this constructivist genre.[142] Other contributors include Campbell, Der Derian, R. B. J. Walker, and such feminists as Spike Peterson.[143] Here the linguistic construction of subjects is stressed, as a result of which discursive practices constitute the ontological primitives, or the foundational units of reality and analysis. Little hope is held out for a legitimate social science. In its place, a "hegemonic discourse" is seen to impose a "regime of truth," instituted through disciplinary powers in both senses of that term.[144] Lastly, causality is considered chimerical: "I embrace a logic of interpretation that acknowledges the improbability of cataloging, calculating, and specifying the 'real causes'," Campbell proclaims, and which "concerns itself instead with considering the manifest political consequences of adopting one mode of representation over another."[145]

A third constructivist variant is located on the continuum between these two. It combines aspects of both: like the neoclassical variant, it also shares certain features with mainstream theorizing; but it is grounded in the philosophical doctrine of scientific realism, particularly the work of Roy Bhaskar.[146] The writings of Alexander Wendt and David Dessler exemplify this third genre. Scientific realism, according to Wendt, offers the possibility of a wholly new "naturalistic" social science.[147] On its basis, it is no longer necessary to choose between "insider" and "outsider" accounts

140. For a different, less philosophically grounded categorization, see Adler 1997.
141. Elshtain 1987 and 1996. The other authors were cited earlier.
142. Ashley 1984, 1987, 1988.
143. See Campbell 1992; Der Derian 1987; Walker 1989 and 1993; and Peterson and Runyan 1993.
144. Keeley 1990, 91.
145. Campbell 1992, 4.
146. Bhaskar 1979.
147. Wendt 1991, 391.

of social action and social order—not because social science is made to emulate the natural sciences, as it was under the old naturalistic monism, but because there is little difference in their respective ontologies to begin with. Scientific inquiry of both material and social worlds deals largely in nonobservables, be they quarks or international structures, and much of the time even the intersubjective aspects of social life exist independently of the mental states of most individuals that constitute it. I call this *naturalistic constructivism*.

As of yet, little empirical research has been informed by this perspective, so we do not know what difference it makes in practice. On theoretical grounds, the dilemma identified by Martin Hollis and Steve Smith poses a serious challenge: "To preserve naturalism, the scientific realist must either subordinate the interpreted social world to [the] external mechanisms and forces [that govern the physical world] or inject similarly hermeneutic elements into 'outsider' accounts of nature."[148] Bhaskar struggles heroically with this problem, but, Hollis and Smith conclude, "we do not believe that he has settled the matter, nor even that he would claim that honour."[149]

In summary, distinctive attributes differentiate constructivism from mainstream theorizing, especially the neo-utilitarian kind. But significant differences exist among the various strands of constructivism. As a result of the latter, Neufield observes astutely, "the debate within the camp of [constructivists] may prove to be as vigorous as that between [them] and their positivist critics."[150]

Paradigmatic (Ir)Reconcilability

The "great debates" that have swept through the field of international relations over the decades typically have been posed in terms of the alleged superiority of one approach over another. But the fact that these debates recur so regularly offers proof that no approach can sustain claims to monopoly on truth—or even on useful insights. The current encounter between neo-utilitarianism and social constructivism exhibits the additional feature that the strength of each approach is also the source of its major weakness. As a result, the issue of any possible relationship between them must be addressed.

The strength of neo-utilitarianism lies in its axiomatic structure, which permits a degree of analytical rigor, and in neoliberal institutionalism's case also of theoretical specification, that other approaches cannot match. This is not an aesthetic but a practical judgment. Rigor and specificity are desirable on self-evident intellectual as well as policy grounds. At the same time, neo-utilitarianism's major weakness lies in the

148. Hollis and Smith 1991, 407.
149. Ibid. Searle critiques a corresponding attempt by David Chalmers to bridge the brain–mind divide on similar grounds. Searle 1997.
150. Neufield 1993, 40. See, for example, Campbell's comment that Wendt and I "seem to be exhibiting a fear, a (Cartesian) anxiety" in the face of his and other postmodernist challenges, this after taking me to task for my criticism (in 1993) of what I regard as certain fetishist and nihilist tendencies in postmodern constructivism. Campbell 1996, 16–17.

foundations of its axiomatic structure, its ontology, which for some purposes is seriously flawed and leads to an incomplete or distorted view of international reality. That problem is particularly pronounced at a time, such as today, when states are struggling to redefine stable sets of interests and preferences regarding key aspects of the international order.

The obverse is true of constructivism. It rests on a deeper and broader ontology, thereby providing a richer understanding of some phenomena and shedding light on other aspects of international life that, quite literally, do not exist within the neo-utilitarian rendering of the world polity. At the same time, it lacks rigor and specification—indeed, it remains relatively poor at specifying its own scope conditions, the contexts within which its explanatory features can be expected to take effect. Improvements are inevitable as work in the constructivist vein continues to increase in quantity and quality, but given its nature there are inherent limits.

Where do we go from here? Can a systematic relationship between the two approaches be articulated, and if so, how? A sizable number of adherents to each is unlikely to be interested in any such effort. Hard-core rational choice theorists, postmodernist constructivists, and most neorealists will reject out of hand any need to do so. But even coalitions of the willing may find the going tough as they discover the analytical limits beyond which their respective approaches cannot be pushed.

The first instinct of willing neo-utilitarians is to expand their analytical foundation in the direction of greater sociality. For example, Keohane claims that his version of institutionalist theory "embeds it selectively in a larger framework of neoliberal thought," which includes commercial, republican, and sociological liberalism.[151] This provides a richer and more robust social context for neoliberal institutionalism, Keohane believes. He is right up to a point: the point defined by the boundaries of methodological individualism and instrumental rationality. Commercial liberalism poses few problems in this regard, nor does the transnational bureaucratic politics that comprises one aspect of what he calls sociological liberalism. But republican liberalism? It would be enormously surprising if the ties among democratic societies today, especially those in "the West," did not reflect an intersubjective cultural affinity, a sense of we-feeling, a shared belief of belonging to a common historical project, falling well beyond the "selectively" expanded foundation of neoliberalism that Keohane proposes.

Indeed, Keohane himself is obliged to concede that not even the most fundamental attribute of liberalism, that which distinguishes it from all other views on the nature of humanity, justice, and good government, can be accommodated within his version of neoliberalism. He writes, "the emphasis of liberalism on liberty and rights only suggests a general orientation toward the moral evaluation of world politics," but it does not lend itself to the analysis of choice under constraints that he wishes to employ. As a result, he finds it "useful" to put that "emphasis" aside for analytical purposes.[152] All deontic features of social life go with it.

---

151. Keohane 1993, 289.
152. Keohane 1990b, 174.

In short, a selective expansion of neo-utilitarianism's core is possible. But we should not expect it to carry us far toward a "social"—ideational and relational—ontology.

The first instinct of the willing constructivist is to incorporate norms, identities, and meaning into the study of international relations with minimum disruption to the field's prevailing epistemological stance, on which hopes for analytical rigor and cumulative knowledge are believed to rest. Typically, this takes the form of maintaining that constructivist concerns are a useful tool in the context of discovery, but that at the end of the day they do not affect the logic of explanation.[153] I view the methodological discussions in Katzenstein's important edited volume *The Culture of National Security* as an instance. The essays in that book, Jepperson, Wendt, and Katzenstein insist, neither advance nor depend on "any special methodology or epistemology. . . . When they attempt explanation, they engage in 'normal science,' with its usual desiderata in mind."[154]

Everything hinges, of course, on what is meant by "normal science." On my reading, normal science in international relations cannot grasp truly intersubjective meanings in social collectivities, as opposed to aggregations of meanings held by individual actors; it lacks the possibility that ideational factors relate to social action in the form of constitutive rules; it is exceedingly uncomfortable with the notion of noncausal explanation, which constitutive rules entail; and it doggedly aspires to the deductive-nomological model of causal explanation even though it is rarely achieved in practice, and at the level of the international system probably cannot be,[155] while dismissing the narrative mode as mere storytelling.

The sanguine view of normal science expressed by Katzenstein and his colleagues may have something to do with the fact that, as the self-criticism they include in their volume notes, "the essays that make up the body of this book tend to treat their own core concepts as exogenously given."[156] To underscore the importance of this point, let me relate it back to our earlier discussion of Durkheim and Weber. In a manner reminiscent of Durkheim, Katzenstein and his colleagues cut into the problem of ideational causation at the level of "collective representations" of ideational social facts and then trace the impact of these representations on behavior. They do not, as Weber tried, begin with the actual social construction of meanings and significance

153. For an extended criticism of this line of argument, see Neufield 1993.
154. Jepperson, Wendt, and Katzenstein 1996, 65.
155. Even a philosopher of science so firmly committed to scientific monism as Ernest Nagel conceded long ago that the N-D model is inappropriate in explaining "aggregative events." Nagel [1942] 1961, 568–75. He specifically mentions revolutions as an example: there are too few of them, they are highly complex, and there are bound to be important differences between them, all of which render problematic the necessary condition that they be instances of recurring "types." Nagel suggests that aggregative events and large-scale social structures be "analyzed"—that is, broken down into their component parts or aspects. The parts, Nagel believes, may still be susceptible to covering-law explanations even when the larger whole is not. Waltz rejects this "analytic" method, however, on the grounds that it is reductionist, and he clings to the (inappropriate, according to Nagel) N-D model for the "aggregative" phenomenon of the international system as a whole. Waltz 1979. Neither Nagel nor Waltz entertains the possibility that other explanatory protocols exist to account for such phenomena.
156. Kowert and Legro 1996, 469.

from the ground up. It will be recalled that Durkheim, too, felt no need to move beyond the normal science of his day as a result, whereas Weber did.

Having said all that, I nevertheless conclude with the conviction that both moves can be fruitful. In the hope of gaining at once a deeper and more precise understanding of the structure and functioning of the world polity, neo-utilitarians should strive to expand their analytical foundations, and constructivists should strive for greater analytical rigor and specification. The two approaches are not additive, and they are unlikely to meet and merge on some happy middle ground. But by pushing their respective limits in the direction of the other, we are more likely to discover precisely when one approach subsumes the other, when they represent competing explanations of the same phenomenon, when one complements or supplements the other, and when they simply describe different and incommensurate worlds.[157] The stakes are high enough, and the limits of the two approaches inherent and apparent enough, for claims of universal superiority at this point to be summarily dismissed as pretense or delusion.

157. For an excellent beginning, see Jepperson, Wendt, and Katzenstein 1996, 68–72.

International Norm Dynamics and Political Change

Martha Finnemore and Kathryn Sikkink

Normative and ideational concerns have always informed the study of international politics and are a consistent thread running through the life of *International Organization*. When *IO* was founded, dominant realist views of politics, while rejecting idealism, were very much concerned with issues of legitimacy and ideology. The early Cold War, after all, was not simply a positional conflict among anonymous great powers: it was a war for "hearts and minds." The coupling of power with "legitimate social purpose" was central to American foreign policy of this period.[1] At the same time, international relations scholars were busy studying two of the greatest social construction projects of the age: European integration and decolonization. Neofunctionalists, like the realists, were consciously trying to distance themselves from "idealist" predecessors (in this case, David Mitrany and his colleagues), but the complex web of technical tasks that they designed aimed at more than promoting material well-being; they aimed ultimately at ideational and social ends. Spillover was supposed to do more than create additional technical tasks; it was supposed to change attitudes, identity, and affect among participants. Likewise, scholars recognized that decolonization was driven by a profoundly normative agenda and that it explicitly sought to reconstitute the identities of both the new states and their former colonizers, as well as the relationships between them.

Attempts in the 1960s and 1970s to build a science of politics modeled on economics or natural science never displaced these normative and ideational concerns completely. They have surfaced consistently in the stream of critiques of the dominant state-centric paradigms that focused on material power. Scholars of transnational relations in the 1970s called attention to transnational actors who were sometimes influenced by norms and ideas.[2] The regimes scholarship of the early 1980s similarly

We would like to thank the three editors, two reviewers, and Emanuel Adler, Michael Barnett, Elizabeth Boyle, Audie Klotz, Jeff Legro, Richard Price, Thomas Risse, and Daniel Thomas for their very helpful comments on various drafts of the manuscript. We are also grateful to James Fearon, Kurt Gaubatz, and Jim Morrow for answering questions, sharing manuscripts, and making suggestions related to our work.

1. Ruggie 1983b.
2. Keohane and Nye 1971.

International Organization 52, 4, Autumn 1998, pp. 887–917

emphasized the role of principles and norms in ways that opened the door for a more sweeping "ideational turn" in the late 1980s.

Elsewhere in this issue John Ruggie, James March, and Johan Olsen explore the intellectual history of this recent "turn" and locate its proponents in the more abstract theoretical debates of social science. Building on their contributions, we address theoretical issues facing those of us interested in empirical research on social construction processes and norm influences in international politics. We are concerned with such questions as How do we know a norm when we see one? How do we know norms make a difference in politics? Where do norms come from? How do they change? We are particularly interested in the role norms play in political change—both the ways in which norms, themselves, change and the ways in which they change other features of the political landscape. Like other theoretical frameworks in international relations (IR), much of the macrotheoretical equipment of constructivism is better at explaining stability than change. Claims that actors conform to "logics of appropriateness"[3] say little about how standards of appropriateness might change. Such static approaches to IR are particularly unsatisfying during the current era of global transformation when questions about change motivate much of the empirical research we do. Lacking good macrotheoretic guidance, our approach to these questions relies heavily on induction from the extensive and growing body of norms research that has sprung up, not just in political science, but in law, economics, sociology, and psychology. This variety of conceptual and empirical material is useful for our inductive enterprise, but it also raises some important questions for macrotheory that we explore at the end of the article.

We use our review of scholarship on norms and related ideational phenomena in this article to make three arguments. First, the ideational "turn" of recent years is actually a *re*turn to some traditional concerns of the discipline, but it has not brought us back to precisely the same place we began. Standards for good empirical research have changed dramatically (and for the better) since the founding of *IO,* and applying these standards to long-standing normative issues has had real payoffs. Second, we generate some propositions about three aspects of norms—their origins, the mechanisms by which they exercise influence, and the conditions under which norms will be influential in world politics. Specifically, we argue that norms evolve in a patterned "life cycle" and that different behavioral logics dominate different segments of the life cycle. Third, we argue that the current tendency to oppose norms against rationality or rational choice is not helpful in explaining many of the most politically salient processes we see in empirical research—processes we call "strategic social construction," in which actors strategize rationally to reconfigure preferences, identities, or social context.[4] Rationality cannot be separated from any politically significant episode of normative influence or normative change, just as the normative context conditions any episode of rational choice. Norms and rationality are thus intimately connected, but scholars disagree about the precise nature of their relation-

---

3. March and Olsen, this issue.
4. See Kahler, this issue, for a history of debates over rationality in international relations.

ship. We identify four focal points of debate where the relationship between norms and rationality is least understood and most important, and we show how these debates cross-cut research traditions in potentially fruitful ways.

The Return to Norms

Norms and normative issues have been central to the study of politics for at least two millennia. Students of politics have struggled with questions not only about the meaning of justice and the good society but also about the influence on human behavior of ideas about justice and good. Our conclusions (or our assumptions) about these issues condition every form of political analysis. Aristotle and Plato understood this in the fourth century B.C.E. just as E. H. Carr did in the twentieth century. Carr has become canonized in the discipline as a debunker of Wilsonian idealism, but this simplification misrepresents his message: "Political action must be based on a coordination of morality and power." Realism fails, in Carr's analysis, precisely because it excludes essential features of politics like emotional appeal to a political goal and grounds for moral judgment.[5] This conviction that understanding social purpose and legitimacy was essential to understanding politics continued through the 1950s and 1960s and is evident in the pages of *IO*. Inis Claude's work on the legitimation function of the United Nations deals precisely with this issue.[6] Early IR scholarship on certain issues—decolonization, human rights, education—recognized that much UN activity involved establishing norms, but it often failed to theorize these normative processes.[7] Certainly the work of the integration theorists such as Ernst Haas was implicitly, and often explicitly, about creating shared social purpose.[8] Even realists like Hans Morgenthau wrote extensively about the way in which ideational and normative factors such as nationalism, morality, and international law limit states' exercise of power.[9]

The "turn" away from norms and normative concerns began with the behavioral revolution and its enthusiasm for measurement. Normative and ideational phenomena were difficult to measure and so tended to be pushed aside for methodological reasons. This tendency was reinforced by the emerging infatuation of political scientists with economic methods in the late 1970s and 1980s.[10] Realists began recasting the pursuit of power as "utility maximization" and, following the economists, tended to specify utility functions in material terms only. Liberals drew on microeconomic analyses of collective action games (Prisoners' Dilemma, Stag Hunt) to reinvigorate their long-standing debate with realists and show that cooperation, welfare improve-

---

5. Carr [1946] 1964, 97, 89.
6. Claude 1966.
7. See Kay 1967; Henkin 1965; Jacobson 1962; and Ball 1961.
8. Haas 1961, 1964a. For an argument related to some concerns of this article, see Haas 1993.
9. Morgenthau [1948] 1985, pt. 5, 6.
10. For a discussion about the causes and effects of the dominance of economic models and methods in the study of U.S. politics, see Lowi 1992; Simon 1993a; Lowi 1993a,b; and Simon 1993b.

ment, and "progress" were possible even given some of realism's pessimistic assumptions about self-seeking human nature. In fact, these "neos," both realist and liberal, might more appropriately be called "econorealists" and "econoliberals," since what was new in both cases was an injection of microeconomic insights.[11]

Although the move to rational choice in no way required a move to a material ontology, its proponents showed little interest in ideational or social phenomena, and study of these issues languished during this period. However, when interest in these matters revived in the 1980s, first with the regimes project[12] and later with the constructivists led by John Ruggie, Friedrich Kratochwil, Alexander Wendt, and others,[13] the discipline to which norms returned had changed in important ways. Although the behavioral revolution and the "economic turn" of the 1970s and 1980s may have neglected norms, they made important contributions by forcing scholars to think much more rigorously about issues of research design, theoretical clarity, disciplinary cumulation, and parsimony.

As contemporary researchers make their arguments about norms, culture, and ideas, they will need to specify ideational causal claims and mechanisms clearly, think seriously about the microfoundations on which theoretical claims about norms rest, and evaluate those claims in the context of carefully designed historical and empirical research.[14] David Lumsdaine's analysis of the role of morality in international politics, for example, is very different from Carr's. Carr uses evidence anecdotally to illustrate his arguments about the moral character of "the ordinary man" and the political consequences of that morality. The result is a brilliant piece of political thought but one vulnerable to charges of wishful thinking, since Carr provides no systematic evidence that human beings actually *do* behave as his "ordinary man" does and not according to some other conception of human nature. Lumsdaine, by contrast, offers systematic evidence that morality actually does play a significant role in foreign aid by examining predictions from alternative explanations and compiling extensive evidence, both quantitative and qualitative, to arbitrate among explanations.[15] The same attention to alternative explanations, rigorous standards of evidence, and social theoretic microfoundations has characterized the article-length research on norms in *IO* on such issues as the end of apartheid in South Africa, the end of the Cold War, prohibitions against certain kinds of weapons, the end of slavery, and other prohibition regimes.[16] In a wide variety of issue areas, norms researchers have made inroads precisely because they have been able to provide explanations substantiated by evidence for puzzles in international politics that other approaches had been unable to explain satisfactorily.

---

11. See also Ruggie, this issue.
12. Krasner 1983b.
13. See Kratochwil and Ruggie 1986; Wendt 1987; Dessler 1989; Kratochwil 1989; and Adler 1997.
14. Readers should note that we use ideational "causation" here in a way that recognizes that ideas and norms are often reasons for actions, not causes in the physical sense of the word. See Ruggie, this issue.
15. Lumsdaine 1993.
16. See Klotz 1995a; Risse-Kappen 1994; Price 1995; Ray 1989; and Nadelmann 1990.

Norms are no easier to measure today than they were in the 1930s or 1960s, but conceptual precision is essential for both meaningful theoretical debate and defensible empirical work. In the remainder of this section we take up three issues where conceptual clarification seems most pressing and most possible: definitions, the relationship between domestic and international norms, and whether norms are agents of stability or change.

Definitions

There is general agreement on the definition of a norm as a standard of appropriate behavior for actors with a given identity,[17] but a number of related conceptual issues still cause confusion and debate. First, whereas constructivists in political science talk a language of norms, sociologists talk a language of "institutions" to refer to these same behavioral rules. Thus, elsewhere in this issue March and Olsen define "institution" as "a relatively stable collection of practices and rules defining appropriate behavior for specific groups of actors in specific situations."[18] One difference between "norm" and "institution" (in the sociological sense) is aggregation: the norm definition isolates single standards of behavior, whereas institutions emphasize the way in which behavioral rules are structured together and interrelate (a "collection of practices and rules"). The danger in using the norm language is that it can obscure distinct and interrelated elements of social institutions if not used carefully. For example, political scientists tend to slip into discussions of "sovereignty" or "slavery" as if they were norms, when in fact they are (or were) collections of norms and the mix of rules and practices that structure these institutions has varied significantly over time.[19] Used carefully, however, norm language can help to steer scholars toward looking inside social institutions and considering the components of social institutions as well as the way these elements are renegotiated into new arrangements over time to create new patterns of politics.[20]

Scholars across disciplines have recognized different types or categories of norms. The most common distinction is between regulative norms, which order and constrain behavior, and constitutive norms, which create new actors, interests, or categories of action.[21] Some scholars have also discussed a category of norms called evaluative or prescriptive norms, but these have received much less attention and, indeed, are often explicitly omitted from analysis.[22] This lack of attention is puzzling, since it is precisely the prescriptive (or evaluative) quality of "oughtness" that sets norms apart from other kinds of rules. Because norms involve standards of "appropriate" or "proper" behavior, both the intersubjective and the evaluative dimensions are inescapable when discussing norms. We only know what is appropriate by reference to

17. See Katzenstein 1996b, 5; Finnemore 1996a, 22; and Klotz 1995b.
18. March and Olsen, this issue.
19. Krasner 1984, 1988, 1993; Thomson 1994; Strang 1991; Ruggie 1993; and Spruyt 1994.
20. For an excellent discussion of these issues, see Jepperson 1991.
21. Ruggie, this issue; Searle 1995; Katzenstein 1996b; and Wendt forthcoming.
22. Gelpi 1997. See, for example, the treatment in Katzenstein 1996b, 5, fn12.

the judgments of a community or a society. We recognize norm-breaking behavior because it generates disapproval or stigma and norm conforming behavior either because it produces praise, or, in the case of a highly internalized norm, because it is so taken for granted that it provokes no reaction whatsoever.[23] Thus, James Fearon argues that social norms take the generic form "Good people do (or do not do) X in situations A, B, C . . ." because "we typically do not consider a rule of conduct to be a social norm unless a shared moral assessment is attached to its observance or non-observance."[24]

One logical corollary to the prescriptive quality of norms is that, by definition, there are no bad norms from the vantage point of those who promote the norm. Norms most of us would consider "bad"—norms about racial superiority, divine right, imperialism—were once powerful because some groups believed in the appropriateness (that is, the "goodness") of the norm, and others either accepted it as obvious or inevitable or had no choice but to accept it. Slaveholders and many non-slaveholders believed that slavery was appropriate behavior; without that belief, the institution of slavery would not have been possible.

Given this discussion, we can begin to answer the essential research question: how do we know a norm when we see one? We can only have indirect evidence of norms just as we can only have indirect evidence of most other motivations for political action (interests or threats, for example). However, because norms by definition embody a quality of "oughtness" and shared moral assessment, norms prompt justifications for action and leave an extensive trail of communication among actors that we can study. For example, the United States' explanations about why it feels compelled to continue using land mines in South Korea reveal that it recognizes the emerging norm against the use of such mines. If not for the norm, there would be no need to mention, explain, or justify the use of mines in Korea at all. Note that we separate norm existence or strength from actual behavioral change in our operationalization. Because one central question of norms research is the effect of norms on state behavior, it is important to operationalize a norm in a way that is distinct from the state or nonstate behavior it is designed to explain.[25]

Norms as shared assessments raise the question of how many actors must share the assessment before we call it a norm. In part this is a question of empirical domain. Norms may be regional, for example, but not global. Even within a community, norms are "continuous, rather than dichotomous, entities. . . . [They] come in varying strengths" with different norms commanding different levels of agreement.[26] We argue that one way to understand the dynamics of this agreement process is by examining what we call the "life cycle" of norms. We show how agreement among a critical mass of actors on some emergent norm can create a tipping point after which

23. For a particularly good discussion of the way in which conventions produce judgments of social "oughtness" and morality, see Sugden 1989. See also Elster 1989a,c; and Sunstein 1997.
24. Fearon 1997, 25, fn18.
25. Legro 1997.
26. Ibid., 33.

agreement becomes widespread in many empirical cases, and we provide some suggestions about common features of "critical mass."

Connecting Domestic and International Norms

In this article we are concerned with international or regional norms that set standards for the appropriate behavior of states.[27] Domestic norms, however, are deeply entwined with the workings of international norms. Many international norms began as domestic norms and become international through the efforts of entrepreneurs of various kinds. Women's suffrage, for example, began as a demand for domestic change within a handful of countries and eventually became an international norm.[28] In addition, international norms must always work their influence through the filter of domestic structures and domestic norms, which can produce important variations in compliance and interpretation of these norms.[29] Even in situations where it might appear at first glance that international norms simply trump domestic norms, what we often see is a process by which domestic "norm entrepreneurs" advocating a minority position use international norms to strengthen their position in domestic debates. In other words, there is a two-level norm game occurring in which the domestic and the international norm tables are increasingly linked.[30] We argue later, however, that all these domestic influences are strongest at the early stage of a norm's life cycle, and domestic influences lessen significantly once a norm has become institutionalized in the international system.

Recent work in U.S. legal circles also suggests that there is more similarity in the way norms and law work domestically and internationally than IR scholars have thought. IR scholars have generally assumed that the existence of a coercive state able to enforce laws made domestic order very different from international order. A prominent group of legal scholars at the University of Chicago, however, now argue that, even within a domestic setting, making successful law and policy requires an understanding of the pervasive influence of social norms of behavior. This is a particularly compelling insight for IR scholars, since the international system is characterized by law and norms operating without direct punitive capacity. The processes through which these legal scholars claim that norms work domestically—involving norm entrepreneurs, imitation, "norm cascades," and "norm bandwagons"—are entirely consistent with the research done on norms by scholars in IR and suggest that IR norms research might also learn from domestic analogies. For example, the normative and legal process through which Southern gentlemen in the United States stopped dueling, examined by Lawrence Lessig, may be relevant for thinking about

---

27. For analyses of domestic norms and their influence on domestic politics, see Kier 1997; Johnston 1995a; Katzenstein 1996a, 1993; and Berger 1998. For a critique of this emphasis on international as opposed to domestic norms, see Checkel 1998.
28. Dubois 1994.
29. See Risse-Kappen 1995b; and Risse, Ropp, and Sikkink forthcoming.
30. See Putnam 1988; and Evans, Jacobson, and Putnam 1993.

what kinds of norms and rules could lead to a decrease in conflict in the international system.[31]

Stability Versus Change

Macro-level theorizing has provided good explanations of the way norms produce social order and stability. Norms channel and regularize behavior; they often limit the range of choice and constrain actions.[32] From a constructivist perspective, international structure is determined by the international distribution of ideas.[33] Shared ideas, expectations, and beliefs about appropriate behavior are what give the world structure, order, and stability. The problem for constructivists thus becomes the same problem facing realists—explaining change. In an ideational international structure, idea shifts and norm shifts are the main vehicles for system transformation. Norm shifts are to the ideational theorist what changes in the balance of power are to the realist.

John Ruggie argues in this issue that "having identified the possibility of system transformation in the macro level, corresponding micro practices that may have transformative effects must be identified and inventoried." The following section is an attempt to identify these practices.

Evolution and Influence of Norms

In this section we advance some propositions about (1) the origins or emergence of international norms, (2) the processes through which norms influence state and nonstate behavior, and (3) which norms will matter and under what conditions. We illustrate the arguments with material drawn from two major issue areas: women's rights, especially suffrage, and laws of war. International norms about women's rights often came into direct competition with strongly held domestic norms, and, typically, there was no self-evident state "interest" in the promotion of such norms. Although topics related to gender and women have been absent from the pages of *International Organization*,[34] the suffrage campaign led to the formal political participation of half of the world's population and therefore seems worthy of study. Laws of war allow us to discuss the impact of norms where we might least expect it—the traditional security

31. See Sunstein 1997; and Lessig 1995. For an interesting journalist's overview, see Rosen 1997.

32. See Katzenstein 1996a, 3; and Sunstein 1997, 40. Even Waltz, in his discussion of socialization, says that norms encourage conformity and that "socialization reduces variety." Waltz 1979, 76.

33. Wendt 1992 and forthcoming.

34. In its first fifty years *International Organization* has published only one article on any issue related to gender or women, Craig Murphy's review essay on gender and international relations; Murphy 1996. We suggest that there may have been a well-internalized norm (with a taken-for-granted quality) that research on gender and women did not constitute an appropriate topic for international relations scholarship. Note that as with any well-internalized norm, this does not imply that the editors self-consciously rejected articles on gender-related topics. To the contrary, we know a strong norm is in effect when it does not occur to authors to write on the topic or submit articles because it is not generally understood as an appropriate topic.

field, where such norms limit state discretion in an area perceived as essential to national sovereignty and security.

The Norm "Life Cycle"

Norm influence may be understood as a three-stage process. As shown in Figure 1, the first stage is "norm emergence"; the second stage involves broad norm acceptance, which we term, following Cass Sunstein,[35] a "norm cascade"; and the third stage involves internalization. The first two stages are divided by a threshold or "tipping" point, at which a critical mass of relevant state actors adopt the norm. This pattern of norm influence has been found independently in work on social norms in U.S. legal theory, quantitative research by sociology's institutionalists or "world polity" theorists, and various scholars of norms in IR.[36] The pattern is important for researchers to understand because different social processes and logics of action may be involved at different stages in a norm's "life cycle." Thus, theoretical debates about the degree to which norm-based behavior is driven by choice or habit, specification issues about the costs of norm-violation or benefits from norm adherence, and related research issues often turn out to hinge on the stage of the norm's evolution one examines. Change at each stage, we argue, is characterized by different actors, motives, and mechanisms of influence.

The characteristic mechanism of the first stage, norm emergence, is persuasion by norm entrepreneurs. Norm entrepreneurs attempt to convince a critical mass of states (norm leaders) to embrace new norms. The second stage is characterized more by a dynamic of imitation as the norm leaders attempt to socialize other states to become norm followers. The exact motivation for this second stage where the norm "cascades" through the rest of the population (in this case, of states) may vary, but we argue that a combination of pressure for conformity, desire to enhance international legitimation, and the desire of state leaders to enhance their self-esteem facilitate norm cascades. At the far end of the norm cascade, norm internalization occurs; norms acquire a taken-for-granted quality and are no longer a matter of broad public debate. For example, few people today discuss whether women should be allowed to vote, whether slavery is useful, or whether medical personnel should be granted immunity during war. Completion of the "life cycle" is not an inevitable process. Many emergent norms fail to reach a tipping point, and later we offer arguments about which norms are more likely to succeed. Internalized or cascading norms may eventually become the prevailing standard of appropriateness against which new norms emerge and compete for support.

Research on women's suffrage globally provides support for the idea of the life cycle of norms and the notion of a "tipping point" or threshold of normative change. Although many domestic suffrage organizations were active in the nineteenth cen-

35. Sunstein 1997.
36. See Sunstein 1997; Meyer and Hannan 1979; Bergesen 1980; Thomas et al. 1987; and Finnemore 1993.

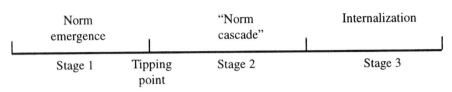

FIGURE 1. *Norm life cycle*

tury, it was not until 1904, when women's rights advocates founded the International Women's Suffrage Association (IWSA), that an international campaign for suffrage was launched. In fact, rather than a single international campaign for women's suffrage, there were three or four overlapping campaigns with different degrees of coordination.[37] A quantitative analysis of the cross-national acquisition of suffrage rights reveals a different dynamic at work for early and late adopters of women's suffrage.[38] Prior to a threshold point in 1930, no country had adopted women's suffrage without strong pressure from domestic suffrage organizations. Between 1890 and 1930, Western countries with strong national women's movements were most likely to grant female suffrage. Although some original norm entrepreneurs came from the United States and the United Kingdom, this was not a case of "hegemonic socialization," since the first states to grant women the right to vote (New Zealand, Australia, Finland) were not hegemons, and the United States and the United Kingdom lagged ten to twenty years behind. After 1930, international and transnational influences become far more important than domestic pressures for norm adoption, and countries adopted women's suffrage even though they faced no domestic pressures to do so. For women's suffrage, the first stage of norm emergence lasted over eighty years: it took from the Seneca Falls Conference in 1848 until 1930 for twenty states to adopt women's suffrage. In the twenty years that followed the tipping point, however, some forty-eight countries adopted women's suffrage norms.[39]

Stage 1: Origins or emergence of norms. Although little theoretical work has focused exclusively on the process of "norm building," the accounts of norm origins in most studies stress human agency, indeterminacy, chance occurrences, and favorable events, using process tracing or genealogy as a method.[40] Generalizing from these accounts, two elements seem common in the successful creation of most new norms: norm entrepreneurs and organizational platforms from which entrepreneurs act.

NORM ENTREPRENEURS. Norms do not appear out of thin air; they are actively built by agents having strong notions about appropriate or desirable behavior in their community. Prevailing norms that medical personnel and those wounded in war be treated as neutrals and noncombatants are clearly traceable to the efforts of one man, a Gen-

---

37. See Dubois 1994; and Berkovitch 1995.
38. Ramirez, Soysal, and Shanahan 1997.
39. Ibid.
40. See Kowert and Legro 1996; and Price 1995.

evese Swiss banker named Henry Dunant. Dunant had a transformative personal experience at the battle of Solferino in 1859 and helped found an organization to promote this cause (what became the International Committee of the Red Cross) through an international treaty (the first Geneva Convention). The international campaign for women's suffrage was similarly indebted to the initial leadership of such norm entrepreneurs as Elizabeth Cady Stanton and Susan B. Anthony in the United States and Millicent Garrett Fawcett and Emmeline Pankhurst in England. Both of these cases are consistent with the description Ethan Nadelmann gives of "transnational moral entrepreneurs" who engage in "moral proselytism."[41] Legal theorist Lessig uses the term "meaning managers" or "meaning architects" to describe the same kind of agency in the process of creating norms and larger contexts of social meaning.[42]

Norm entrepreneurs are critical for norm emergence because they call attention to issues or even "create" issues by using language that names, interprets, and dramatizes them. Social movement theorists refer to this reinterpretation or renaming process as "framing."[43] The construction of cognitive frames is an essential component of norm entrepreneurs' political strategies, since, when they are successful, the new frames resonate with broader public understandings and are adopted as new ways of talking about and understanding issues. In constructing their frames, norm entrepreneurs face firmly embedded alternative norms and frames that create alternative perceptions of both appropriateness and interest. In the case of the Red Cross, Dunant and his colleagues had to persuade military commanders not to treat valuable medical personnel and resources they captured as spoils of war, to be treated as they saw fit. In the case of women's suffrage and later women's rights, norm entrepreneurs encountered alternative norms about women's interests and the appropriate role for women. In other words, new norms never enter a normative vacuum but instead emerge in a highly contested normative space where they must compete with other norms and perceptions of interest.

This normative contestation has important implications for our understandings of the ways in which a "logic of appropriateness" relates to norms.[44] Efforts to promote a new norm take place within the standards of "appropriateness" defined by prior norms. To challenge existing logics of appropriateness, activists may need to be explicitly "inappropriate." Suffragettes chained themselves to fences, went on hunger strikes, broke windows of government buildings, and refused to pay taxes as ways of protesting their exclusion from political participation. Deliberately inappropriate acts (such as organized civil disobedience), especially those entailing social ostracism or legal punishment, can be powerful tools for norm entrepreneurs seeking to send a message and frame an issue. Thus, at this emergent stage of a norm's life

41. Nadelmann 1990.
42. Lessig 1995.
43. David Snow has called this strategic activity *frame alignment*—"by rendering events or occurrences meaningful, frames function to organize experience and guide action, whether individual or collective." Snow et al. 1986, 464.
44. March and Olsen 1989, and this issue.

TABLE 1. *Stages of norms*

	Stage 1 *Norm emergence*	*Stage 2* *Norm cascade*	*Stage 3* *Internalization*
Actors	Norm entrepreneurs with organizational platforms	States, international organizations, networks	Law, professions, bureaucracy
Motives	Altruism, empathy, ideational, commitment	Legitimacy, reputation, esteem	Conformity
Dominant mechanisms	Persuasion	Socialization, institutionalization, demonstration	Habit, institutionalization

cycle, invoking a logic of appropriateness to explain behavior is complicated by the fact that standards of appropriateness are precisely what is being contested.

Given the costs of inappropriate action and many of the persuasive tools they use, one has to wonder what could possibly motivate norm entrepreneurs (see Table 1). Obviously the answer varies with the norm and the entrepreneur, but for many of the social norms of interest to political scientists, it is very difficult to explain the motivations of norm entrepreneurs without reference to empathy, altruism, and ideational commitment. Empathy exists when actors have the capacity for participating in another's feelings or ideas. Such empathy may lead to empathetic interdependence, where actors "are interested in the welfare of others for its own sake, even if this has no effect on their own material well-being or security."[45] Altruism exists when actors actually take "action designed to benefit another even at the risk of significant harm to the actor's own well-being."[46] Kristen Monroe argues that the essence or "heart" of altruism is a "shared perception of common humanity. . . . a very simple but deeply felt recognition that we all share certain characteristics and are entitled to certain rights, merely by virtue of our common humanity."[47] Ideational commitment is the main motivation when entrepreneurs promote norms or ideas because they believe in the ideals and values embodied in the norms, even though the pursuit of the norms may have no effect on their well-being.

Of course, many norm entrepreneurs do not so much act against their interests as they act in accordance with a redefined understanding of their interests. Suffragists,

45. See Keohane 1984, chap. 7; Keohane 1990a; and Mansbridge 1990.
46. Monroe 1996. See also Oliner and Oliner 1988.
47. Monroe 1996, 206.

for example, were working on behalf of a coherent conception of women's political interests, but it was not an understanding initially shared by the great majority of women in the world. Women had to be persuaded that it was indeed in their interests to pursue suffrage. Similarly, the Red Cross had to persuade military leaders that protecting the wounded was compatible with their war aims.

ORGANIZATIONAL PLATFORMS. All norm promoters at the international level need some kind of organizational platform from and through which they promote their norms. Sometimes these platforms are constructed specifically for the purpose of promoting the norm, as are many nongovernmental organizations (NGOs) (such as Greenpeace, the Red Cross, and Transafrica) and the larger transnational advocacy networks of which these NGOs become a part (such as those promoting human rights, environmental norms, and a ban on land mines or those that opposed apartheid in South Africa).[48] Often, however, entrepreneurs work from standing international organizations that have purposes and agendas other than simply promoting one specific norm. Those other agendas may shape the content of norms promoted by the organization significantly.[49] The structure of the World Bank has been amply documented to effect the kinds of development norms promulgated from that institution; its organizational structure, the professions from which it recruits, and its relationship with member states and private finance all filter the kinds of norms emerging from it.[50] The UN, similarly, has distinctive structural features that influence the kinds of norms it promulgates about such matters as decolonization, sovereignty, and humanitarian relief.[51] The tripartite structure of the International Labor Organization, which includes labor and business as well as states, strongly influences the kinds of norms it promotes and the ways it promotes them.[52]

One prominent feature of modern organizations and an important source of influence for international organizations in particular is their use of expertise and information to change the behavior of other actors. Expertise, in turn, usually resides in professionals, and a number of empirical studies document the ways that professional training of bureaucrats in these organizations helps or blocks the promotion of new norms within standing organizations. Peter Haas's study of the cleanup of the Mediterranean shows how ecologists were successful in promoting their norms over others' in part because they were able to persuade governments to create new agencies to deal with the cleanup and to staff those posts with like-minded ecologists. Studies of the World Bank similarly document a strong role for professional training in filtering the norms that the bank promotes. In this case, the inability to quantify many costs and benefits associated with antipoverty and basic human needs norms

48. See Sikkink 1993a; Keck and Sikkink 1998; Klotz 1995a,b; and Price 1997.
49. See Strang and Chang 1993; Finnemore 1996a; Adler 1992; and Ikenberry and Kupchan 1990.
50. See Ascher 1983; Miller-Adams 1997; Wade 1996b; and Finnemore 1996a.
51. See Barnett 1995, 1997; McNeely 1995; and Weiss and Pasic 1997.
52. Strang and Chang 1993.

created resistance among the many economists staffing the bank, because projects promoting these norms could not be justified on the basis of "good economics."[53]

Whatever their platform, norm entrepreneurs and the organizations they inhabit usually need to secure the support of state actors to endorse their norms and make norm socialization a part of their agenda, and different organizational platforms provide different kinds of tools for entrepreneurs to do this.[54] International organizations like the UN and the World Bank, though not tailored to norm promotion, may have the advantage of resources and leverage over weak or developing states they seek to convert to their normative convictions. Networks of NGOs and intergovernmental organizations (IGOs) dealing with powerful states, however, are rarely able to "coerce" agreement to a norm—they must persuade. They must take what is seen as natural or appropriate and convert it into something perceived as wrong or inappropriate. This process is not necessarily or entirely in the realm of reason, though facts and information may be marshaled to support claims. Affect, empathy, and principled or moral beliefs may also be deeply involved, since the ultimate goal is not to challenge the "truth" of something, but to challenge whether it is good, appropriate, and deserving of praise.[55] In these cases, what the organizational network provides is information and access to important audiences for that information, especially media and decision makers.

In most cases, for an emergent norm to reach a threshold and move toward the second stage, it must become institutionalized in specific sets of international rules and organizations.[56] Since 1948, emergent norms have increasingly become institutionalized in international law, in the rules of multilateral organizations, and in bilateral foreign policies. Such institutionalization contributes strongly to the possibility for a norm cascade both by clarifying what, exactly, the norm is and what constitutes violation (often a matter of some disagreement among actors) and by spelling out specific procedures by which norm leaders coordinate disapproval and sanctions for norm breaking. Institutionalization of norms about biological and chemical weapons, for example, has been essential to coordinating the near universal sanctions on Iraq following the Gulf War and has enabled states to coordinate an invasive inspections regime aimed at securing compliance with those norms. Institutionalization is not a necessary condition for a norm cascade, however, and institutionalization may follow, rather than precede, the initiation of a norm cascade. Women's suffrage was not institutionalized in international rules or organizations prior to the beginning of the norm cascade. The first intergovernmental agency created to deal with women's issues was a regional organization, the Inter-American Commission of Women (CIM), established in 1928. Although scholars locate the tipping point on women's suffrage around 1930, the norm cascaded in similar ways both in Latin America (where it was

---

53. See Ascher 1983; Miller-Adams 1997; and Finnemore 1996a.

54. Paul Wapner points out that there are exceptions to the centrality of the state in these processes in environmental politics where activists lobby polluting corporations directly to bring about change (for example, the campaign against McDonald's clamshell containers for its sandwiches). Wapner 1996.

55. Fearon 1997.

56. See Goldstein and Keohane 1993b; and Katzenstein 1996b.

institutionalized) and in other places around the world where women's rights were not similarly institutionalized.

TIPPING OR THRESHOLD POINTS. After norm entrepreneurs have persuaded a critical mass of states to become norm leaders and adopt new norms, we can say the norm reaches a threshold or tipping point. Although scholars have provided convincing quantitative empirical support for the idea of a norm tipping point and norm cascades, they have not yet provided a theoretical account for why norm tipping occurs, nor criteria for specifying a priori where, when, and how we would expect it. We propose two tentative hypotheses about what constitutes a "critical mass" and when and where to expect norm tipping. First, although it is not possible to predict exactly how many states must accept a norm to "tip" the process, because states are not equal when it comes to normative weight, empirical studies suggest that norm tipping rarely occurs before one-third of the total states in the system adopt the norm.[57] In the case of women's suffrage, Francisco Ramirez, Yasemin Soysal, and Suzanne Shanahan place the threshold point in 1930, when twenty states (or approximately one-third of the total states in the system at that time) had accepted women's suffrage.[58] In case of land mines, by May 1997 the number of states supporting the ban on anti-personnel land mines reached 60, or approximately one-third of the total states in the system. After that point, a norm cascade occurred, and 124 states ratified the Ottawa land mine treaty in December 1997.

It also matters which states adopt the norm. Some states are critical to a norm's adoption; others are less so. What constitutes a "critical state" will vary from issue to issue, but one criterion is that critical states are those without which the achievement of the substantive norm goal is compromised. Thus, in the case of land mines, a state that did not produce or use land mines would not have been a critical state. By contrast, the decision in mid-1997 by France and Great Britain, both land mines producers, to support the treaty could well have contributed to the norm cascade that happened in late 1997.[59] Securing support of those same two states was simply essential to producing the norm cascade and near universal acceptance of the first Geneva Convention in Europe 130 years earlier. States may also be "critical" because they have a certain moral stature. For example, the decision of South Africa under Nelson Mandela to support the land mine treaty was very influential, especially with other states in Africa but also globally.[60] Although cascades require support from some critical states, unanimity among them is not essential. For example, after initially supporting the norm of banning land mines, the United States refused to support the treaty, but the norm cascaded nevertheless.

57. International law has had to wrestle with this problem repeatedly, since many modern international norms are embodied in treaties. Treaties implicitly recognize this concept of critical mass by specifying that a particular number of countries must ratify for the treaty to enter into force. Where treaties exist, the entry into force of the treaty may be a useful proxy for the critical mass necessary to say that a norm exists.
58. Ramirez, Soysal, and Shanahan 1997.
59. Price 1998.
60. Ibid.

Stage 2: Norm cascades.   Up to the tipping point, little normative change occurs without significant domestic movements supporting such change. After the tipping point has been reached, however, a different dynamic begins. More countries begin to adopt new norms more rapidly even without domestic pressure for such change. Empirical studies suggest that, at this point, often an international or regional demonstration effect or "contagion" occurs in which international and transnational norm influences become more important than domestic politics for effecting norm change.[61] Contagion, however, is too passive a metaphor; we argue that the primary mechanism for promoting norm cascades is an active process of international socialization intended to induce norm breakers to become norm followers.[62] Kenneth Waltz suggested some of the ways socialization in occurs: emulation (of heroes), praise (for behavior that conforms to group norms), and ridicule (for deviation).[63] In the context of international politics, socialization involves diplomatic praise or censure, either bilateral or multilateral, which is reinforced by material sanctions and incentives. States, however, are not the only agents of socialization. Networks of norm entrepreneurs and international organizations also act as agents of socialization by pressuring targeted actors to adopt new policies and laws and to ratify treaties and by monitoring compliance with international standards. The International Committee of the Red Cross (ICRC) certainly did not disappear with the signing of the first Geneva Convention. Instead, the ICRC became its chief socializing agent, helping states to teach the new rules of war to their soldiers, collecting information about violations, and publicizing them to pressure violators to conform.

Socialization is thus the dominant mechanism of a norm cascade—the mechanism through which norm leaders persuade others to adhere—but what makes socialization work? What are the motives that induce states opposed to the norm to adhere and adhere quickly? We argue that states comply with norms in stage 2 for reasons that relate to their identities as members of an international society. Recognition that state identity fundamentally shapes state behavior, and that state identity is, in turn, shaped by the cultural-institutional context within which states act, has been an important contribution of recent norms research.[64] James Fearon similarly argues that one's identity is as a member of a particular social category, and part of the definition of that category is that all members follow certain norms.[65] What happens at the tipping point is that enough states and enough critical states endorse the new norm to redefine appropriate behavior for the identity called "state" or some relevant subset of states (such as a "liberal" state or a European state).

To the degree that states and state elites fashion a political self or identity in relation to the international community, the concept of socialization suggests that the

61. See Ramirez, Soysal, and Shanahan 1997; and Whitehead 1996.
62. Socialization involves the "induction of new members . . . into the ways of behavior that are preferred in a society." Barnes, Carter, and Skidmore 1980, 35. Socialization can thus be seen as a mechanism through which new states are induced to change their behavior by adopting those norms preferred by an international society of states. See also Risse, Ropp, and Sikkink, forthcoming.
63. Waltz 1979, 75–76.
64. Katzenstein 1996b.
65. Fearon 1997.

cumulative effect of many countries in a region adopting new norms "may be analogous to 'peer pressure' among countries."[66] Three possible motivations for responding to such "peer pressure" are legitimation, conformity, and esteem.

Scholars have long understood that legitimation is important for states and have recognized the role of international sources of legitimation in shaping state behavior. Claude, for example, described international organizations as "custodians of the seals of international approval and disapproval," and emphasized their crucial role in establishing and assuring adherence to international norms.[67] Certainly there are costs that come with being labeled a "rogue state" in international interactions, since this entails loss of reputation, trust, and credibility, the presence of which have been amply documented to contribute to Pareto-improving effects from interstate interaction. We argue, though, that states also care about international legitimation because it has become an essential contributor to perceptions of domestic legitimacy held by a state's own citizens. Domestic legitimacy is the belief that existing political institutions are better than other alternatives and therefore deserve obedience.[68] Increasingly, citizens make judgments about whether their government is better than alternatives by looking at those alternatives (in the international and regional arena) and by seeing what other people and countries say about their country. Domestic legitimation is obviously important because it promotes compliance with government rules and laws; ruling by force alone is almost impossible. Thus, international legitimation is important insofar as it reflects back on a government's domestic basis of legitimation and consent and thus ultimately on its ability to stay in power. This dynamic was part of the explanation for regime transitions in South Africa, Latin America, and southern Europe.[69]

Conformity and esteem similarly involve evaluative relationships between states and their state "peers." Conformity involves what Robert Axelrod refers to as "social proof"—states comply with norms to demonstrate that they have adapted to the social environment—that they "belong." "By conforming to the actions of those around us, we fulfill a psychological need to be part of a group."[70] Esteem is related to both conformity and legitimacy, but it goes deeper, since it suggests that leaders of states sometimes follow norms because they want others to think well of them, and they want to think well of themselves.[71] Social norms are sustained, in part, by "feelings of embarrassment, anxiety, guilt, and shame that a person suffers at the prospect of violating them."[72] Fearon has argued that identity is based on those aspects of the self in which an individual has special pride or from which an individual gains self-esteem.[73] Thus, the desire to gain or defend one's pride or esteem can explain norm

---

66. Ramirez, Soysal, and Shanahan 1997.
67. Claude 1966. For more contemporary arguments that international organizations continue to play this role, see Barnett 1997, 1995; and Barnett and Finnemore 1997.
68. Linz 1978.
69. See Klotz 1995a,b; and Whitehead 1996.
70. Axelrod 1986, 1105.
71. Fearon 1997.
72. Elster 1989c.
73. Fearon 1997, 23.

following. In this sense, states care about following norms associated with liberalism because being "liberal states" is part of their identity in the sense of something they take pride in or from which they gain self-esteem.

The microfoundations of both the conformity and esteem arguments for individuals are psychological and rest on extensive research on the importance of self-esteem and conformity for individuals. The power of conformity to group norms is so strong in some experimental situations that individuals will make statements that are objectively wrong in order to avoid deviating from group judgments. In situations where the objective reality is ambiguous, individuals are even more likely to turn to "social reality" to form and evaluate their beliefs.[74] Theories of cognitive dissonance may also provide insights into the motivations for norm-conforming behavior. Studies suggest that cognitive dissonance is aroused primarily when people notice that their behavior leads to aversive consequences that cannot be easily rectified. The unpleasant experience of dissonance leads actors to reduce it by changing either their attitudes or their behavior.[75] We argue that an analog to this exists at the level of the state: state leaders conform to norms in order to avoid the disapproval aroused by norm violation and thus to enhance national esteem (and, as a result, their own self-esteem). It is difficult to generalize to the state level from research on esteem done at the individual level, but norm entrepreneurs frequently target individual state leaders for criticism. Because much norm advocacy involves pointing to discrepancies between words and actions and holding actors personally responsible for averse consequences of their actions, one way to think about norm entrepreneurs is that they provide the information and publicity that provoke cognitive dissonance among norm violators. In the area of human rights a body of empirical research is emerging that suggests that some state leaders care deeply about their international image as human rights violators and make significant policy changes in order to change that image.[76]

Stage 3: Internalization.   At the extreme of a norm cascade, norms may become so widely accepted that they are internalized by actors and achieve a "taken-for-granted" quality that makes conformance with the norm almost automatic. For this reason, internalized norms can be both extremely powerful (because behavior according to the norm is not questioned) and hard to discern (because actors do not seriously consider or discuss whether to conform). Precisely because they are not controversial, however, these norms are often not the centerpiece of political debate and for that reason tend to be ignored by political scientists. Institutionalists in sociology, however, have made many of these most internalized norms the centerpiece of their research program and have done us the service of problematizing and "denaturalizing" many of the most prominent Western norms that we take for granted—such as those about market exchange, sovereignty, and individualism. Instead of trying to explain variation in state behavior, these scholars are puzzled by the degree of simi-

---

74. For a survey of this literature, see Eagly and Chaiken 1993; on compliance with social norms, conformity in groups, and the normative origins of conformity, ibid., 630–34, 642–44; on self-esteem maintenance, ibid., 484; on ego defense, ibid., 480–81, 576–78; and on self-concept, ibid., 177–78.

75. Eagly and Chaiken 1993.

76. See Risse, Ropp, and Sikkink forthcoming, esp. chap. by Sieglinde Gränzer on Morocco.

larity or "isomorphism" among states and societies and how those similarities have increased in recent years. Their explanations for these similarities point to past norm cascades leading to states taking up new responsibilities or endowing individuals with new rights as a matter of course.[77]

Professions often serve as powerful and pervasive agents working to internalize norms among their members. Professional training does more than simply transfer technical knowledge; it actively socializes people to value certain things above others. Doctors are trained to value life above all else. Soldiers are trained to sacrifice life for certain strategic goals. Economists, ecologists, and lawyers all carry different normative biases systematically instilled by their professional training. As state bureaucracies and international organizations have become more and more professionalized over the twentieth century, we should expect to see policy increasingly reflecting the normative biases of the professions that staff decision-making agencies.[78] A number of empirical studies have already documented a role for highly internalized norms held by professionals determining policy. In addition to the role of economists at the World Bank mentioned earlier, Anne-Marie Burley's work shows a crucial role for legal professional norms in creating the post–World War II political order, and her work with Walter Mattli shows their importance in the European Union.[79]

Another powerful and related mechanism contributing to the consolidation and universalization of norms after a norm cascade may be iterated behavior and habit. Political scientists have understood the power of these mechanisms for years but have not connected them theoretically to norms and social construction debates. The core of the neofunctionalist argument about integration in Europe, after all, was that frequent interactions among people involving joint work on technical tasks would ultimately create predictability, stability, and habits of trust. As trust became habitual, it would become internalized and internalized trust would, in turn, change affect among the participants. Changed affect meant changed identity and changed norms as empathy and identification with others shifted. Thus, the engine of integration was indirect and evolutionary. Diplomatic tools such as confidence-building measures and track 2 diplomacy may follow a similar logic. Generalized, this argument suggests that routes to normative change may be similarly indirect and evolutionary: procedural changes that create new political processes can lead to gradual and inadvertent normative, ideational, and political convergence.[80]

Which Norms Matter Under What Conditions?

One of the common criticisms of norms research has been that it provides no substantive hypotheses about which norms will be influential in world politics and under

77. See Bergesen 1980; Thomas et al. 1987; Scott and Meyer 1994; McNeely 1995; Meyer et al. 1997; and Finnemore 1996b.

78. See Haas 1989; Ascher 1983; Adler 1992; Miller-Adams 1997; Finnemore 1995; and Barnett and Finnemore 1997.

79. See Burley 1993; and Burley and Mattli 1993. These empirical findings are consistent with theoretical arguments made by DiMaggio and Powell 1983.

80. See also Rosenau 1986.

what conditions they will be influential. Our review of the literature reveals a number of such hypotheses that could be tested and elaborated in future research.

Legitimation.   We argued earlier that an important condition for domestic receptiveness to international norms is a need for international legitimation. If legitimation is a main motivation for normative shifts, we might expect states to endorse international norms during periods of domestic turmoil in which the legitimacy of elites is threatened.[81] If states seek to enhance their reputation or esteem, we would expect states that are insecure about their international status or reputation to embrace new international norms most eagerly and thoroughly. Amy Gurowitz has argued, for example, that Japan has been more open to endorsing international norms about refugees than has Germany because Japan is "insecure" about its international political leadership role.[82] Dana Eyre and Mark Suchman similarly argue that developing states may adopt high-tech weaponry out of status concerns rather than from a utilitarian warfighting calculus.[83]

Prominence.   Some domestic norms appear more likely candidates for internationalization than others. This could be due either to the quality of the norm itself (discussed later) or to the quality of the states promoting the norm. Drawing on natural selection theory, Ann Florini has argued that "prominence" is an important characteristic of norms that are likely to spread through the system.[84] Norms held by states widely viewed as successful and desirable models are thus likely to become prominent and diffuse. The fact that Western norms are more likely to diffuse internationally would seem to follow from this observation. This fits the pattern of adoption of women's suffrage norms, since almost all the norm leaders were Western states (though the United States and Britain were latecomer norm leaders, not early ones). Jon Elster, however, suggests that prominence should be seen in cultural and economic as well as military terms since there are many examples of countries like Greece and China that were conquered but whose norms were assimilated by their conquerors.[85]

Intrinsic characteristics of the norm.   Within norms research, there are several sets of claims that intrinsic qualities of the norm itself determine its influence. We can divide these claims between those stressing the formulation of the norm (its clarity and specificity) and those stressing the substance of the norm and the issues it addresses (its content). Those stressing the form of the norm argue that norms that

---

81. See Ikenberry and Kupchan 1990; and Ron 1997.
82. Gurowitz 1997.
83. Eyre and Suchman 1996.
84. Florini 1996.
85. Elster 1989a. Some authors have discussed "hegemonic socialization" in which norms will be influential when they are embraced and espoused by the hegemon. Ikenberry and Kupchan 1990. This is clearly related to the prominence thesis but can only be a subset of prominence, since states may be viewed as successful without being hegemonic.

are clear and specific, rather than ambiguous and complex,[86] and those that have been around for awhile, surviving numerous challenges, are more likely to be effective.[87] Institutionalists in sociology have also argued that norms making universalistic claims about what is good for all people in all places (such as many Western norms) have more expansive potential than localized and particularistic normative frameworks like those in Bali described by Clifford Geertz.[88]

Arguments about which substantive normative claims will be more influential in world politics have varied widely. Work by sociology's institutionalists suggests that norms about issues congruent with capitalism and liberalism will be particularly powerful, but this formulation is too vague to be useful. Many norms (some of them conflicting) are congruent with liberalism and capitalism, but only a subset of such norms have powerful transnational effects. John Boli and George Thomas have refined this observation somewhat and argue that five principles are central to world culture: universalism, individualism, voluntaristic authority, rational progress, and world citizenship. By implication they suggest that norms underpinned by these principles will be more successful internationally.[89] Both James Lee Ray and Neta Crawford have argued in a similar vein that there is a long-term trend toward humanizing the "other," or "moral progress," that helps to explain both the end of slavery and the end of colonization and could predict the demise of international war in the future.[90] Margaret Keck and Kathryn Sikkink have advanced more specific claims. They argue that norms involving (1) bodily integrity and prevention of bodily harm for vulnerable or "innocent" groups, especially when a short causal chain exists between cause and effect, and (2) legal equality of opportunity are particularly effective transnationally and cross-culturally.[91] Norm entrepreneurs must speak to aspects of belief systems or life worlds that transcend a specific cultural or political context. Although notions of bodily harm are culturally interpreted, Keck and Sikkink argue, they also resonate with basic ideas of human dignity common to most cultures. The notion that norms about equality and protecting vulnerable groups from bodily harm will have more transnational resonance than other norms explains why norm campaigns around slavery and women's suffrage succeeded while a similar, powerful temperance campaign organized by many of the same people failed to reach a critical mass or tipping point. It might also explain why norms against drinking or smoking suddenly became more powerful when the effects on vulnerable or innocent bystanders of secondhand smoke or fetal alcohol syndrome became more widely known.

Arguments that the substantive content of a norm determines whether it will be successful imply that norm evolution has a clear direction if not a final endpoint and suggest that proponents of such arguments support some notion of "historical efficiency." It moves these norms researchers out of the "history-dependent institution-

---

86. See Chayes and Chayes 1993; Legro 1997; and Franck 1992.
87. See Legro 1997; and Franck 1992.
88. See Meyer, Boli, and Thomas 1987; and Geertz 1980.
89. Boli and Thomas 1998.
90. See Crawford 1993; and Ray 1989.
91. Keck and Sikkink 1998.

alism" box that James March and Johan Olsen discuss in this issue into some version of "functional institutionalism." Not all researchers accept functional arguments, however. In his work on the chemical weapons taboo, Richard Price rejects arguments about the intrinsic characteristics of the issue, arguing instead that chemical weapons are not any more terrible than other weapons, and yet they are the only weapons that have been the subject of such a prohibition.[92] Martha Finnemore has also emphasized contradictions among dominant global norms as a barrier to any sort of teleological argument about their effects.[93] Price's recent work on the prohibition of land mines, however, suggests that transnational norm entrepreneurs have successfully used graphic images of bodily harm as a means of mobilizing a powerful transnational campaign against these weapons.[94] The speed with which the ban on land mines moved from norm emergence to a norm cascade reinforces the idea that norms prohibiting bodily harm to innocent bystanders are among those most likely to find transnational support.

ADJACENCY CLAIMS OR PATH DEPENDENCE. The relationship of new normative claims to existing norms may also influence the likeliness of their influence. This is most clearly true for norms within international law, since the power or persuasiveness of a normative claim in law is explicitly tied to the "fit" of that claim within existing normative frameworks (discussed later). Robert Sugden makes a similar argument that "because prominence is largely a matter of common experience . . . the conventions that are best able to spread are those that are most susceptible to analogy. Thus we should find family relationships among conventions."[95] Political scientists also make arguments about adjacency, precedent, and fit. Price argues that the association of chemical weapons with poison, which had already been prohibited, was important for sustaining the prohibition on chemical weapons.[96] Yet, as Price and others recognize, the meanings of any particular norm and the linkages between existing norms and emergent norms are often not obvious and must be actively constructed by proponents of new norms. Activists work hard to frame their issues in ways that make persuasive connections between existing norms and emergent norms. Opponents of female genital mutilation made little headway, for example, when the practice was called "female circumcision," because male circumcision is often a positively valued practice. However, when they replaced the term *circumcision* with *mutilation* and campaigned under the banner of "violence against women," the issue resonated much more strongly, and the campaign gained adherents. These activists clearly recognized the power of adjacency claims and actively worked to situate their issue in such a way as to make it more difficult to dismiss by tying it to the better-established body of human rights norms.[97]

92. Price 1995, 1997.
93. Finnemore 1996a, chap. 5 and 1996b.
94. Price 1998.
95. Sugden 1989, 93.
96. Price 1995.
97. Keck and Sikkink 1998.

WORLD TIME–CONTEXT. World historical events such as wars or major depressions in the international system can lead to a search for new ideas and norms.[98] Ideas and norms most associated with the losing side of a war or perceived to have caused an economic failure should be at particular risk of being discredited, opening the field for alternatives.[99] This kind of explanation would suggest that the end of the Cold War would be such a period of major normative growth and consolidation, based on the principles of the winning coalition in the "war."

Notions of "world time" are also present in the arguments of those who see the current period of globalization as one that promotes dramatic expansion of new norms and creates new opportunities for norm entrepreneurs. Although norms have always been a part of international life, changes in communication and transportation technologies and increasing global interdependence have led to increased connectedness and, in a way, are leading to the homogenization of global norms. Although there is still inadequate information to make a conclusive argument, we suggest as an additional hypothesis that the speed of normative change has accelerated substantially in the later part of the twentieth century. If we compare the case of women's suffrage, where norm emergence took eighty years and the norm cascade another forty, to the issue of violence against women, which moved from norm emergence to cascade in less than twenty years, it appears that the speed of normative change is accelerating. The expansion of international organization (especially with the UN) is contributing to this acceleration process by providing more opportunities to address and negotiate on a broad range of normative issues.

Norms, Rationality, and Strategic Social Construction

The extensive body of empirical research on norms reveals an intimate relationship between norms and rationality. However, there is little good theoretical treatment of this relationship, partly because scholars have tended to counterpose norms to rationality in IR. The opposition of constructivist and "rationalist" arguments that has become widespread in the discipline implies that the issues constructivists study (norms, identities) are not rational and, similarly, that "rationalists" cannot or do not treat norms or identities in their research programs.[100] However, recent theoretical work in rational choice and empirical work on norm entrepreneurs make it abundantly clear that this fault line is untenable both empirically and theoretically.

Rational choice theorists have been working on problems related to norm-based behavior for more that two decades now and have begun working on identity prob-

---

98. Barkin and Cronin 1994. This is quite similar to explanations in the "ideas" literature about failure, crisis, and disappointment leading to changing ideas. See Odell 1982; and Hirschman 1982.
99. Hall makes this kind of argument about shifts in economic ideas. Hall 1989a.
100. For a related argument, see Fearon 1997, 28–29.

lems as well.[101] The fact that rational choice methods have been appropriated in the past by those with a material ontology has tended to obscure the fact that nothing about rational choice requires such an ontology. The utilities of actors could be specified as social or ideational as easily as they can be material. By making different assumptions about social relationships and ideational values, rational choice theorists provide interesting insights into the kinds of normative patterns that may develop and be stable. For example, B. Douglas Bernheim ascribes to actors concern about status and the opinions of others and shows how different patterns of social conformity result, including customs, fads, and subcultures.[102] Sugden examines the evolution of social conventions and shows how some Nash equilibria are evolutionarily stable in iterated games, whereas others are not, thus yielding certain kinds of social conventions. His analysis, however, finds a large role for "common experience" in determining the "focal points" around which particular conventions will emerge, an argument dovetailing nicely with constructivist arguments about the ways in which social structure and normative context shape the actions of agents and, again, suggesting the need for more theorizing about the connection between strategic choice and normative context.[103]

Similarly, empirical research on transnational norm entrepreneurs makes it abundantly clear that these actors are extremely rational and, indeed, very sophisticated in their means–ends calculations about how to achieve their goals.[104] They engage in something we would call "strategic social construction": these actors are making detailed means–ends calculations to maximize their utilities, but the utilities they want to maximize involve changing the other players' utility function in ways that reflect the normative commitments of the norm entrepreneurs. The first half of the process fits nicely in a rational game-theoretic framework. The second half does not. This suggests that instead of opposing instrumental rationality and social construction we need to find some way to link those processes theoretically.

Following Sugden, the editors of this volume make the important observation that what game theorists have called "common knowledge" provides an opening for conversation between rational choice scholars and constructivists, and they further suggest a two-stage division of labor between the frameworks: "Constructivists seek to understand how preferences are formed and knowledge generated, prior to the exercise of instrumental rationality."[105] Although this suggested division of labor captures one possible interaction of the two approaches, it does not exhaust the multiple ways in which norms and rationality interact. Specifically, this division ignores precisely what the empirical studies reveal—namely, that instrumental rationality and strategic interaction play a significant role in highly politicized social construc-

101. Akerlof 1980; Jones 1984; Axelrod 1986; Elster 1989a,c; Morrow 1994b; Laitin 1995; Fearon and Laitin 1996; and Fearon 1997.

102. Bernheim 1994.

103. Sugden 1989. For a discussion of common knowledge as "a point of complementarity" across theoretical perspectives, see Katzenstein, Keohane, and Krasner, this issue.

104. See Klotz 1995a,b; Price 1997; Sikkink 1993a; Keck and Sikkink 1998; Finnemore 1996a; Thomas 1997; and Nadelmann 1990.

105. Katzenstein, Keohane, and Krasner, this issue.

tion of norms, preferences, identities, and common knowledge by norm entrepreneurs in world politics. It ignores the "strategic" character of social construction. One of the consistent features of the empirical research reviewed here is that the common knowledge (or what constructivists would call intersubjective understandings) informing actors' calculations is not static nor is it just "out there" accreted by history and experience in some automatic way like the prominence of Grand Central Station (in Schelling's account) or driving on the left side of the road (in Sugden's account).[106] In many of the most politically salient strategic interactions, it is precisely the changing contours of common knowledge that are the object of the game, at least for some sets of players. Common knowledge about who is a political participant (suffrage), what the rules of war are, and even who is a person (slavery) has been created by strategic actors in highly contested processes that are central to our understanding of politics.

We realize that simply pointing out the complexity of this relationship between norms and rationality is not helpful by itself. We also understand that bracketing segments of a complex process like this one can be a useful way to understand a larger whole. After all, constructivists frequently bracket structure, then agency, to understand their mutual constitution. Our point is simply that processes of social construction and strategic bargaining are deeply intertwined, and pending a better theoretical treatment of this relationship we suggest that, at a minimum, a staged analysis of the relationship between rationality and social context could run either way: one could model rational choice as producing social knowledge as easily as one could model social context as a background for rational choice, depending on the empirical question being researched.

Rationality plays a role in virtually all research on norms. Even the institutionalists in sociology, whose work is perhaps most analytically distinct from rational choice, give rationality pride of place in the Weberian world culture that drives behavior and emphasize the ways in which rational action is prescribed and celebrated in that culture.[107] However, although all these research programs recognize rationality and link norms to rational behavior in important ways, they disagree strongly about the nature of that link. Our point is not that all scholars agree about how to research norms. They do not. Rather, our point is that the fights are not about (or should not be about) whether rationality plays a role in norm-based behavior. The fights are about the nature of the link between rationality and norm-based behavior. By unpacking that connection between rationality and norms we can see more clearly the issues at stake in contemporary research and understand better some of the debates driving it. Four issues stand out and create broad lines of cleavage and debate among scholars: materialism, utilitarianism, choice, and persuasion.

106. Architectural and social historians no doubt could provide an account of the active construction of these bits of common knowledge.

107. In fact, the institutionalists could make a subsuming argument: If we see something that looks like rational choosing going on in human affairs, institutionalists would argue, that is in large part an artifact of our culture that tells us that utility-maximization is the "right" way to act (as opposed to, for example, action according to duty or social hierarchy or divine will). In fact, the success of rational choice theory within the social sciences is, itself, a logical outgrowth of world culture, in institutionalist terms.

One problem with claims in empirical work that norms are a cause of behavior is that, in fact, such claims do not really tell us very much. There are lots of possible reasons to conform to a norm, and scholars disagree about the motivations they impute to actors in their analyses.[108] One set of disagreements involves the preferences we impute to actors and whether norm-based behavior can be explained by preferences that are entirely material. Certainly, some norm conformance may be driven by material self-interest. Neoliberal institutionalists and regimes scholars have been investigating norms flowing from this type of motivation for many years.[109] More recently, however, scholars have begun debating the adequacy of an entirely materialist ontology and have emphasized nonmaterial and even other-regarding preferences in their analyses of norm-based behavior. Note, however, that there are no obvious methodological consequences to this particular debate over the specification of preferences, since rational choice can specify a utility function that includes religious, ideological, or altruistic concerns, just as more interpretivist accounts could focus on material rather than social facts. Note, too, that frequently heard arguments about whether behavior is norm-based or interest-based miss the point that norm conformance can often be self-interested, depending on how one specifies interests and the nature of the norm.

Another debate among those studying norms that does, by contrast, have profound methodological and theoretical consequences involves the behavioral logic that scholars believe drives norm-conforming behavior. The behavioral logic underlying the economistic and rational choice approaches to norm analysis is utility maximization. Actors construct and conform to norms because norms help them get what they want. An alternative approach to understanding norm conformance is what March and Olsen call the "logic of appropriateness," in which actors internalize roles and rules as scripts to which they conform, not for instrumental reasons—to get what they want—but because they understand the behavior to be good, desirable, and appropriate. Habit, duty, sense of obligation and responsibility as well as principled belief may all be powerful motivators for people and underpin significant episodes of world politics.[110]

The debate over behavioral logics is the focus of both Ruggie's and March and Olsen's articles in this issue and does not require extended treatment here. As those articles make abundantly clear, which logic one invokes to explain behavior has significant methodological and theoretical consequences. Most obviously, the two logics lead one to different sides of the structure-agent debate that has been bubbling through the field for some time. The utilitarian and instrumental approach is entirely agent-driven. It is compatible with rational choice and methodological individual-

---

108. We are indebted to Fearon for helping us formulate this point succinctly.

109. See Keohane 1984; and Krasner 1983b.

110. On the logic of appropriateness and its contrast with a "logic of consequences," see March and Olsen 1989, chap. 2; and this issue. For more on the social psychological underpinnings of script and schemas and the ways these may override utility-maximizing choice, see Fiske and Taylor 1994; Nisbett and Ross 1980; Gilovich 1991; and Wilcox and Williams 1990. For a discussion of "habit-driven actors" in world politics, see Rosenau 1986.

ism, which, in turn, have long-standing relationships with realism and liberalism in the field of IR. The logic of appropriateness, however, necessarily has a structure-driven component. What channels and directs behavior in this view are components of social structure—norms of behavior, social institutions, and the values, roles, and rules they embody. Under a logic of appropriateness, notions of duty, responsibility, identity, and obligation (all social constructions) may drive behavior as well as self-interest and gain. Theoretically, this logic focuses attention on social construction processes that are not well explained by IR theories in their contemporary incarnations and has led scholars back into political theory writings dealing with the genealogy of morality (Price on Nietzsche), the social construction of rationality (Michael Barnett and Finnemore on Weber), the politics of communication and argumentation (Crawford and Thomas Risse on Aristotle and Habermas), symbolic interaction and the "presentation of self" (Wendt on Meade and Barnett on Goffman), and the origins of individualism and humanitarianism in liberal thought. Methodologically, this group has invoked different kinds of structuration, process tracing, text analysis, and *verstehen*. Unfortunately, debate in the field on this issue has not been over which logic applies to what kinds of actors under what circumstances. Rather, the debate has been over whether a "logic of appropriateness" exists at all or whether one can adequately capture all politically salient normative effects with a utilitarian and instrumental approach.

A third issue on which there is disagreement and, we think, some misunderstanding, is the role of choice and its converse, determinism, in norm-based behavior. For rational choice scholars, actors conform to norms (not surprisingly) out of choice; choices may be constrained, at times highly constrained, but the focus of the analysis is on the choice. Other researchers, however, focus almost exclusively on the way norms are "internalized" in actors, which raises important issues about the locus of causality in norms arguments. When norms become internalized in actors, actors are no longer choosing to conform to them in any meaningful way. For institutionalists in sociology, many norms, including some of the most powerful ones, have been so internalized that we no long think seriously about alternative behaviors. In this view, actors no longer think seriously about whether "the state" is the best or most efficient form of political organization (it almost certainly is not). They just set up more and more states to the exclusion of other political forms. They no longer think seriously about whether international institutions are the best way to solve international problems (again, a mixed bag). They just set up more and more international institutions.[111] Institutionalists might argue that "choice" is not a particularly robust analytic tool, since much of the most basic human behavior is not chosen in any meaningful sense. Rather, it is supplied to agents by the larger social and cultural environment. Social structure, not agent choice, institutionalists would argue, is where the real explanatory action lies.

In this understanding, norm conformance driven by a logic of appropriateness starts to look deterministic. Yet, as we survey the norms research that emphasizes

111. Barnett and Finnemore 1997.

appropriateness logic in IR, very little of it looks deterministic. Indeed, most of it emphasizes the highly contingent and contested nature of normative change and normative influence. We see two reasons for this. First, IR scholars applying a logic of appropriateness in their analysis have never been imperialistic in their claims. The argument has never been that other logics of action do not ever drive behavior; the argument has been that appropriateness is a powerful and important motor of political behavior worthy of investigation. Second, and more important, even within a logic of appropriateness there is often substantial room for agent choice. Actors may face varied and conflicting rules and norms all making claims for different courses of action. Indeed, most significant political choices are significant and difficult precisely because they involve two or more conflicting claims for action on a decision maker. Actors must choose which rules or norms to follow and which obligations to meet at the expense of others in a given situation, and doing so may involve sophisticated reasoning processes. These processes, however, involve a different kind of reasoning than that of utility maximization. Actors may ask themselves, "What kind of situation is this?" and "What am I supposed to do now?" rather than "How do I get what I want?" Actors often must choose between very different duties, obligations, rights, and responsibilities with huge social consequences, but understanding the choice depends on an understanding, not of utility maximization, but of social norms and rules that structure that choice.[112]

A final issue that separates different approaches to norms research is whether and how they treat persuasion. Persuasion is central to most of the empirical case studies about normative influence and change. It is the mission of norm entrepreneurs: they seek to change the utility functions of other players to reflect some new normative commitment. Persuasion is the process by which agent action becomes social structure, ideas become norms, and the subjective becomes the intersubjective. It is essential to much of the process tracing that scholars are currently doing, yet we have no good way of treating it theoretically. Rational choice can model the ways in which transfers of information may change actor strategies, but changes in underlying preferences cannot be endogenized. Institutionalists in sociology can talk about applying cultural models of action to new situations and the consequent unfolding or elaborating of global culture, but the process by which some models appear compelling and others do not, why some cultural innovations are persuasive and others are not, is not well explained. These approaches thus gloss over this problem in different ways, but persuasion is central to politics of all kinds, and we need a good theoretical apparatus for understanding it.

Looking to other disciplines, we see two types of arguments about persuasion that might be useful in political science: one structural and logical, the other psychological and affective. International legal scholars draw on a complex structure of rules to craft arguments about and adjudicate among competing normative claims. The persuasiveness of a normative claim in law is explicitly tied to the "fit" of that claim

---

112. March and Olsen emphasize choice within appropriateness much more than do Meyer and his colleagues in their work. March and Olsen 1989.

within existing normative frameworks; legal arguments are persuasive when they are grounded in precedent, and there are complex rules about the creation of precedent—such as which judgments trump which and how the accretion of judgments is to be aggregated over time. Since normative contestation in law is so explicit and well documented, and since much of contemporary norm politics in the world has a strong legal component, we believe an examination of legal mechanisms for norm selection and dissemination will be instructive for IR scholars.[113]

Approaches in psychology emphasize very different factors in bringing about persuasion. In these arguments both cognition and affect work synergistically to produce changes in attitudes, beliefs, and preferences. Most of this work stresses communicative processes that happen through argumentation, but, unlike the legal approach, logic alone does not dictate the result, since appeals to emotion may well be used to strengthen or undermine logical extensions of norms.[114] German IR scholars, for example, are beginning to apply Habermas's theory of communicative action (which requires empathy) as a means of understanding persuasion, accommodation, and arrival at mutual understandings in international politics.[115]

Debates over these four issues—materialism, utilitarianism, choice, and persuasion—will continue to shape the ways we understand normative influence and normative change in world politics. Our concern here has not been to settle these debates, but to clarify what, exactly, is being debated and what the stakes of the debates are. These are not debates about rationality, although rationality certainly plays a role in all of them. The debates also do not divide norms researchers into two tidy camps. Researchers may marry ideational ontologies with rational choice;[116] they may examine reasoned choice among conflicting "appropriate" behaviors;[117] they may examine highly instrumental and strategic interactions designed to construct new standards of appropriateness, as most studies of norm entrepreneurs do;[118] and they may generally find themselves cross-cut in ways that are refreshing and, we hope, stimulate new kinds of conversations.

Conclusions

The "return" to norms holds immense promise for shaking up the IR research agenda and opening up exciting new avenues for inquiry—and not just because it offers new (or previously forgotten) subject matter to study. More interesting, to our minds, is the way norms research opens up conversations with theoretical traditions that IR scholars have ignored in recent decades. The evaluative and prescriptive character of

113. See Franck 1990; Burley and Mattli 1993; and Burley 1993.
114. See Eagly and Chaiken 1993; and Chaiken, Wood, and Eagly 1996.
115. Risse 1997.
116. See Laitin 1995; Fearon and Laitin 1996; and Fearon 1997.
117. March and Olsen 1989.
118. See Klotz 1995a,b; Price 1997; Sikkink 1993a; Keck and Sikkink 1998; Finnemore 1996a; Thomas 1997; and Nadelmann 1990.

norms opens the way for a long-overdue conversation with political theory and ethics. For decades now IR research has been divorced from political theory on the grounds (implicitly, if not explicitly, articulated) that what "is" in the world and what "ought to be" are very different and must be kept separate, both intellectually and in policy. However, contemporary empirical research on norms is aimed precisely at showing how the "ought" becomes the "is." Empirical research documents again and again how people's ideas about what is good and what "should be" in the world become translated into political reality. People with principled commitments have made significant changes in the political landscape: slavery as a legal institution of property rights has been abolished everywhere on the planet for the first time in human history; women, more than half the world's population, have full formal political participation in most states of the world; and though war continues to be a horrible human practice, there is no doubt that it is less horrible as a result of efforts by humanitarians to curb the most awful weapons and practices. At the same time, principled commitments and notions of what "should be" have fueled xenophobic nationalism, fascism, and ethnic cleansing. Understanding where these "oughtness" claims come from, how they are related to one another, which ones will be powerful, and what their implications are for world politics is vital, but it is an inquiry that can only be undertaken at the nexus of political theory and IR.

Similar connections exist between norms research and other fields of study. International law, like philosophy and ethics, has been ignored by IR scholars for decades, yet customary international law *is* norms, and empirical research in IR is, again, demonstrating that these legal norms have powerful behavioral effects. Legal norms are also bound up inextricably with the workings of international institutions, which have been a central focus of virtually all types of IR research in recent years. Further, these legal norms are structured and channel behavior in ways that create precisely the types of patterns political scientists seek to explain. Understanding which norms will become law ("soft" law as well as "hard" law) and how, exactly, compliance with those laws comes about would seem, again, to be a crucial topic of inquiry that lies at the nexus of law and IR.

Microfoundations for norm-based behavior might be improved by paying more attention to studies in psychology, particularly work on the roles of affect, empathy, conformity, and esteem. Like law and philosophy, affect and empathy have been swept under the carpet in recent decades. Ideational phenomena have been treated as "information," which reduces uncertainty or provides new strategies to maximize utilities. The result is politics without passion or principles, which is hardly the politics of the world in which we live. Emotions can be politically dangerous and undesirable in politics; hate, after all, is affect, too. But to pretend that affect and empathy do not exist is to miss fundamental dynamics of political life, and we have tried to suggest how attempts in psychology to wrestle with these issues may be helpful.

Finally, we have tried to show how norms research cross-cuts our own discipline in ways that are refreshing and stimulate new conversations. Contrary to what we perceived to be the popular impression, rationality is not the issue that divides IR scholars. Rational choice theorists can and do have a great deal to say about ideational phenomena and how norms work, just as empirical studies of social construction and norm emergence repeatedly reveal highly rational strategic interaction. Scholars are divided, however, about the role that choice plays in norm-based behavior, about what motivates choice, and about the role persuasion plays in normative processes and how to treat it. No school of thought in the discipline is entirely comfortable with its answers to these questions at the moment. We believe this is a good state of affairs, one that will encourage scholars to venture beyond narrow methodological commitments to think more broadly about these issues.

Rationality in International Relations

Miles Kahler

The role of reason in international relations has been contested since the eighteenth century. The construction of a sphere of calculated state action, raison d'état, and an image of the balance of power suggested an Enlightenment equilibrium as comprehensible to human reason as a clockwork. Even at the time, however, the obsessive and often self-defeating war-making of Louis XIV and Frederick the Great illustrated the irrationality of collective outcomes and the failure of self-imposed limits in a world grounded in raison d'état.[1] During the nineteenth century, advancing industrial capitalism promised to overcome passions in the interest of human progress, and modern political economy reinforced the belief that individual calculations of interest could lead to beneficial social outcomes. International politics, however, was only partially captured by the force of reason.

The questioning of reason deepened in the twentieth century as modern psychology undermined the image of a unified and rational self. Democratic politics meant that the phantom of an elitist and state-centered rationality would remain elusive. Disastrous international outcomes—the failure of cooperation in the 1930s, the monumental carnage of two world wars—produced pessimism regarding the power of human reason to comprehend the realm of international competition and to contain the passions of ideology and nationalism.

Reason, Rationality, and American International Relations

As the study of international relations took shape in the United States after World War I, however, these shocks to reason in all of its guises—a model of individual psychology, an avenue for comprehending international reality, and an instrument of

The author wishes to thank Alexander Thompson and the other participants in the University of Chicago PIPES seminar, Arthur Stein, John McMillan, and the special editors of this issue for their comments on earlier drafts.

1. Kissinger 1994, 66.

International Organization 52, 4, Autumn 1998, pp. 919–941

progress—were felt only faintly. A perspective that was broadly liberal and materialist assumed a central place. Incorrectly labeled idealist, human reason in this view continued to offer the possibility of collective mastery over the forces that had precipitated world war.[2]

At the same time, international relations was defined in social scientific terms, as subject to the same regularities as other spheres of social life. By the 1930s, pioneers in the new field had begun to adopt the model of natural science for their research; like the liberal materialists, Charles Merriam, Harold Lasswell, and Quincy Wright assumed that human reason could illuminate international relations in the same way that it had comprehended the economy and political behavior. They embedded the study of world politics in a broader political analysis that stretched from individuals to national governments to the interaction among those governments.

Two events shook the rationalist faith of this liberal and nascent social scientific enterprise. The cataclysm of World War II produced progressive hopes for a world in which rational planning and institutional design would play a larger role. Those hopes were not entirely disappointed in the postwar management of international economic relations, but the onset of the Cold War undermined lingering hopes that collective reason could overcome the force of ideology. Political persecution and war also produced an emigration of European scholars whose realist tenets were far more pessimistic regarding the abilities of reason to comprehend and to curb the violent tendencies of world politics. Those beliefs were in sharp conflict with the prevailing consensus in American international relations.

The roots of realism lay in currents of European thought that had undermined the reign of reason. Realism injected an awareness drawn from European social theory and philosophy that the image of a unified and rational self had been overturned. Although these strands, particularly Freudian psychoanalysis, were not foreign to postwar American social science, the attack launched by realism against what it regarded as naive liberalism and a misconceived positivist scientific enterprise was deeper. At the time of its entry into American intellectual life, the relationship between realism and rationalism in politics was more confrontational than complementary.

In *Scientific Man Versus Power Politics*, published immediately after World War II, Hans Morgenthau drew intellectual ammunition from the European cataclysm for a realist attack on prevailing liberal ideology. He assailed the current intellectual consensus as "a repudiation of politics," offering a false hope of meliorating a social world driven by irrationality. Morgenthau declared that "our civilization assumes that the social world is susceptible to rational control conceived after the model of the natural sciences, while the experiences, domestic and international, of the age contradict this assumption."[3] He was not alone among realists in questioning the dominant liberal embrace of reason. In early formulations of the security dilemma, a core concept of realism, John Herz also pointed to an underlying irrationality in the

---

2. This account of interwar international relations in the United States is drawn from Kahler 1997.
3. Morgenthau 1946, 71, 2.

interdependence of human beings and the simultaneous "necessity for distrusting and possibly destroying" those same fellow beings.[4] Realists engaged in the practice of diplomacy, such as George Kennan, were intellectual allies, skeptical of claims for a scientific study of politics.[5]

Realist skepticism toward the power of reason, grounded in European intellectual life, was soon purged in its new American home. American policymakers may have deployed realist tenets in their contest with the Soviet Union, but domestic politics demanded a public attachment to liberal aspirations for international improvement. More important, international relations and realism absorbed what Dorothy Ross has called the "individualistic and ahistorical premises of liberal exceptionalism," best represented in neoclassical economics.[6] Running counter to this forceful but temporary European insertion in American international relations were more powerful countervailing tendencies that reinforced rationalist approaches to international relations: economic analysis exploited the assumption of utility maximization to construct a research program that was the envy of the other social sciences; strategic interaction began to yield to the power of game theory and its international relations offshoot, deterrence theory.

Rationality and Contemporary International Relations

Since the domestication of realism, the controversies surrounding rationality in postwar American international relations have been much more narrowly defined. The principal contenders have limited their disputation to the relative power of rational and nonrational models as behavioral foundations for international relations. On the one hand, rational and individualist models seem to fit the frequent delegation of authoritative foreign policy decisions to a relatively small elite, the smaller role of norms when compared to domestic politics, and the high costs of cognitive failure in international interaction. On the other hand, cognitive inadequacy, the barriers to a consistent pursuit of national interests imposed by domestic politics, and the intrusion of emotion-laden issues of identity suggest that rationalist models must be substantially modified or abandoned.

Other, larger controversies surrounding reason's powers and possibilities—whether constructing a science of international relations or serving as a progressive means for ameliorating the international realm—were set aside. Although some recent challenges to rationalist explanations call into question the social scientific enterprise and its philosophical underpinnings, this account will exclude those who seek to "dethrone" reason (using Jon Elster's term) and radically undermine the research enterprise in which most international relations scholars participate. Epistemological issues continue to divide the social sciences, but most of those considered

4. Herz 1951, 16.
5. Stephanson 1989, 180–81.
6. Ross 1991, 473.

here, from rational choice to social constructivist, pragmatically deploy their theories in order to understand the substance of international relations. Whether the field has reached agreement on the meaning of "understanding" is an issue too large to consider here; my own belief is that broad canons of evidence and argument in the social sciences are widely shared.[7]

On the narrower ground of whether rationality and rationalist models provide a basis for constructing (or reconstructing) the field of international relations, an alleged affinity between rational choice models and traditional state-centric views of international politics as well as a long-standing embrace of game theory has until recently insulated international relations from an increasingly acrimonious conflict between proponents of rational choice and their critics in other social sciences.[8] Nevertheless, the current tendency to set up rational choice models as imperialistic targets risks yet another fruitless and time-consuming "great debate" in international relations. Previous great debates, whether maxi- (realism versus idealism) or mini- (neorealism versus neoliberalism), have seldom advanced a coherent research program for the field.[9]

Another intellectual tournament of this kind might be preempted by demonstrating the value of a competitive exchange between those endorsing rationalist models and their critics, rather than an all-or-nothing contest producing victory or defeat for one side. Rationalist treatments have already been challenged to extend their scope and refine their modeling; those who are skeptical of such accounts (from a number of perspectives) have been pressed to reinforce the rigor of their arguments and to define domains in which rational choice and the proposed alternatives carry the most explanatory weight. Given the waves of "bashing" that too often occur on either side, it would be premature to argue for convergence between rational choice and its principal competitors. One feasible outcome, however, can already be discerned in particular fields of research: a willingness by either side to emphasize problem-focused research, permitting explanatory power rather than theoretical polemic to decide the contest.

Two additional and equally important observations serve to obscure the lines in the sand that are often drawn on either side. Rational and nonrational accounts share methodological shortcomings. One problem, considered at greater length later, is a too-easy aggregation from individual to collectivity. Confronting such shared methodological problems could also contribute to intellectual exchange between rational and nonrational modes of explanation.

Careful scrutiny of the criticisms leveled by either side also demonstrates that differences between rational and nonrational often revolve around questions of definition. In accepting the narrower terms of controversy, reason and rationality are defined here in broadly instrumental terms. Still, the variety of rationalist accounts is a target for critics, who see in diversity a slippery unwillingness to confront empirical

---

7. For a different view of the importance of epistemological concerns, see Smith, Booth, and Zalewski, 1996; and Ruggie, this issue.
8. See Green and Shapiro 1994; and Friedman 1996.
9. Kahler 1997.

shortcomings. For those employing rational choice frames, on the other hand, such variety undermines the allegations of some critics that they represent a monolithic intellectual tribe. Criticisms revolve around the distinction between what John Fere-john terms "thin" and "thick" rational accounts. To the former's assumption of simple instrumental rationality, the latter adds auxiliary assumptions regarding agent preferences and beliefs.[10] Many of these auxiliary assumptions—such as those concerning the possibility of other-regarding goals—lie at the core of many criticisms of rational choice.

Another important definitional misunderstanding that exaggerates the lines of disagreement is the common conflation of methodological individualism and rational choice, a reasonable linkage given the roots of both in economics. As the comparison of rationalist and constructivist accounts will suggest, individualist approaches need not imply rationality, and rationalist accounts can and do incorporate social content.[11]

Since the "thickness" and individualism of rationalist models is often at the center of disputes over their usefulness, Elster's definition of rational choice can serve as a useful benchmark. As an explanation of behavior,

> rational choice theory appeals to three distinct elements in the choice situation. The first element is the feasible set, i.e., the set of all courses of action which (are rationally believed to) satisfy various logical, physical, and economic constraints. The second is (a set of rational beliefs about) the causal structure of the situation, which determines what course of action will lead to what outcomes. The third is a subjective ranking of the feasible alternatives, usually derived from a ranking of the outcomes to which they (are expected to) lead. To act rationally, then, simply means to choose the highest-ranked element in the feasible set.[12]

Whether such a relatively "thin" definition remains empty or inaccurate, as some critics allege, or provides the basis for a far-reaching explanation of foreign policy and international outcomes has been central in controversies over the power of rationalist models in international relations.

Defining a benchmark for the nonrational side of this contemporary intellectual contest is even more contentious than establishing the meaning of rationality. The diverse critics of rational choice models in international relations either propose alternative nonrational explanations for behavior on the part of agents in international relations or call into question the scope and accuracy of a rationalist account for the behavior in question. Whether these alternatives modify, complement, or supplant rationalist accounts is another question of central importance.

Rationalist models have confronted four persistent sources of criticism as the research programs of international relations evolved after 1945. Realism has often been paired with the assumption of a rational and unitary state actor, but its relationship with rationalist theorizing has been uneasy, in both its classical, power-maximizing form and its neorealist and structural variants. Psychological assaults on

10. Ferejohn 1991, 282.
11. Arrow 1994, 2, 4; Sen 1995, 2, 14–18.
12. Elster 1986a, 4.

rational choice can be traced to Freud; contemporary criticisms share the individualist premises of rational choice models but dispute its claims regarding the information-processing powers of agents. Both rationalist and psychological models share a third hurdle in explaining international outcomes: constructing a plausible model of action for entities beyond the individual level, whether bureaucratic organizations, interest groups, or states. Finally, the rationality and the individualism of beliefs is questioned by theories that stress culture, identity, and norms as independent sources of action.

Reason and Neorealism

An elective affinity between international relations and rationalist models has often been based on the assumptions of realism, which has claimed a dominant place in the American study of international relations since 1945. The relationship of classical realism to rational models of state behavior is more tenuous than latter-day realists care to admit, however. The domestication of realism by the American study of international relations obscured the earlier history of realism and rendered it less subversive of rational choice models. In *Politics Among Nations*, Morgenthau himself adopted rational reconstruction from the viewpoint of actors as a means of comprehending foreign policy. This marriage of realist tenets and rationalist models took place most clearly in the evolution of deterrence theory, but taming realism and rendering it scientific has also been the program of structural realism (or neorealism).

Kenneth Waltz's neorealism represented the final domestication of realism by American social science.[13] Waltz self-consciously aimed to produce a social scientific version of realism far removed from the anti-scientific model of power politics endorsed by the younger Morgenthau. Whether Waltz's neorealism also represented a final incorporation of realism within a rational choice paradigm is far more uncertain. Although Robert O. Keohane attributed a rationality assumption to both classical realism and Waltz's structural variant, the microfoundations of both are unclear.[14] Morgenthau's critical stance toward rationalism has already been described. Normative prescriptions of calculation and prudence suggested that realism understood rational behavior as far from universal in international politics.

Waltz drew analogies between his enterprise and microeconomics, but his emphasis on structure seems to place neorealism in a different methodological camp. Elster notes that pure structuralist accounts deny the importance of rational choice in favor of structural constraints. A modified version of structuralism—which may approach Waltz's position—assumes uniformity in preferences and motivations and attributes differences in behavior to differences in the opportunity set, which could be defined by tighter or looser structural constraints.[15] This second variant can be accommo-

---

13. Waltz 1979, 1986.
14. Keohane 1986b, 165.
15. Elster 1984, 113–14.

dated within a rational choice framework, but whether structural realism relies on choice under structural constraints or two other adaptive mechanisms—selection along Darwinian lines and socialization—is uncertain. Waltz's own position seems to vary on this question. In *Theory of International Politics,* Waltz argues that structure affects behavior through socialization and competition.[16] In his treatment of both classical and structural realism, Keohane argues that the rationality assumption is one of three key assumptions that define the "hard core" of a realist research program; he includes Waltz within the rationalist camp as well.[17] In his response to Keohane, Waltz argues that selection carries most of the explanatory weight in structural realism, awarding it a position of "central importance"; he stipulates that political leaders cannot make "the nicely calculated decisions that the word 'rationality' suggests."[18] The realm of reason within neorealism remains ambiguous. Under tight structural constraints of international competition and selection, the rationality of agents seems superfluous. Waltz fails to demonstrate that structures have such consistent and predictable effects, however.

Psychology and Rationality: Individual Reason and Its Limitations

The inability of neorealism to demonstrate consistent behavioral or systemic outcomes from the structural constraints that it emphasizes—distribution of power or capabilities—may render the issue of its decision-making assumptions moot. To the degree that structural constraints are awarded less explanatory weight, however, other issues of rationality loom larger. The congruence between a rationalist model and the psychological and information-processing limitations of individual decision makers has preoccupied scholars. Given the apparent irrationality and destructiveness that pervades the international politics of this century—wars that appear to have served no state's interests, military technology whose use would destroy its user—the hypothesis that these outcomes resulted from the obstruction of human reasoning has often seemed powerful.

Psychoanalysis, another European import that was grounded in the irrational substructure of the human psyche, has been employed to examine decision-making behavior that appeared to violate the canons of rationality. In a classic study at the origins of psychobiography, Alexander and Juliette George plumbed the puzzling and recurrent leadership style of Woodrow Wilson, a style that gave evidence of a man "beset by great inner conflict which somehow led to self-defeat."[19] George and George confronted one criticism of psychological approaches—the weight attached to personality variables in explaining significant outcomes. In building their narrative to culminate in Wilson's central role in the unnecessary defeat of the Treaty of

16. Waltz 1979, 74.
17. Keohane 1986b, 164–65, 173.
18. Waltz 1986, 330–31.
19. George and George 1964, xix.

Versailles, George and George demonstrate that Wilson's behavior was critical to an important historical outcome. In demonstrating that his behavior in a complicated strategic setting was the result of nonrational influences of which he was unaware, however, two significant assertions must be confirmed: a counterfactual proposition that a more "reasonable" course would have resulted in a different outcome and the more difficult contention that his behavior was nonrational, if not when measured by short-term political ends, then by longer-term goals that he had set. These are difficult tests for those who argue that nonrational influences on behavior are strong.

Responding to such claims, Sidney Verba framed a telling response in defense of rational decision-making models.[20] Verba pointed to two important shortcomings in many psychological accounts that were critical of rationalist models. He noted unresolved issues of data: whether findings from experimental and clinical settings could be transferred to the far different environment of foreign policy and domestic politics. He also pointed to the problem of aggregation for any individualist model of choice: both rational and psychological models slipped too easily from individual attributions to those of organizations and bureaucracies.

Verba also clarified the methodological tests that should be applied to nonrational psychological explanations. He advanced a cost-benefit criterion for the inclusion of psychological variables: add psychological complexity only when it yielded greater explanatory power. Even more important, psychological explanations needed to move from important generalizations that were too broad in scope to contingent statements that would clarify when "nonlogical" influences on decision making would be significant. Finally, Verba pointed out that many psychological explanations or critiques incorporated, implicitly or explicitly, a rational benchmark. This benchmark was essential, whatever its limitations in particular cases, in order to permit "systematic consideration of deviations from rationality."[21] Each of the issues raised by Verba more than three decades ago remains significant in evaluating the psychological research agenda.

Cognitive psychology rapidly overtook psychoanalytic theory as the principal challenger to rational models of behavior. The proliferation of studies of foreign policy influenced by cognitive psychology also blurred the alternative research program. Philip Tetlock and Charles McGuire, Jr. discerned two key assumptions in this diverse literature: international politics imposes heavy information-processing demands on policymakers; in the face of those demands, policymakers—"limited capacity information processors"—employ "simplifying strategies" to comprehend their environment.[22] Those strategies may violate definitions of rational behavior and call into question the use of rational choice as a norm for individual decision making.

One widespread bias discovered by psychologists in foreign policy decisions is the reliance on cognitive structures (given a variety of labels—cognitive maps, operational codes, or schemas) deeply influenced by past experience and often resistant to

---

20. Verba 1961.
21. Ibid., 116.
22. Tetlock and McGuire, 1986, 149–50.

more recent data that might modify or overturn those structures. Yuen Foong Khong, for example, has carefully charted the persistent use of historical analogies as schemas for organizing incoming data, comparing a psychological interpretation of this widespread behavior to alternative explanations.[23]

The discovery of "theory-driven" behavior, the term that Tetlock and McGuire use to describe this mimicking by policymakers of scientific practice, poses difficult judgments for those evaluating its positive and normative effects on policy outcomes. Since reliance on preexisting beliefs is both widespread and necessary for the processing of new information, this research program must assess when such reliance becomes irrational and distorts policy outcomes. As Tetlock and McGuire, Khong, and others who argue for damaging cognitive rigidity are forced to admit, "reliance on prior beliefs and expectations is not irrational per se (one would expect it from a 'good Bayesian'); it becomes irrational only when perseverance and denial dominate openness and flexibility."[24] Assessing that point in other than a tautological way (by referring to a positive or negative outcome as evidence) is very difficult. In effect, the rationality of reliance on existing schemas or cognitive maps for interpreting the world is dependent on the desirability of updating beliefs more or less frequently in the face of discrepant information. No uniform answer to that dilemma is given in the psychological literature. Khong suggests a procedural strategy—forcing existing analogies to a rigorous and public "scientific" test of their validity. That kind of serious testing also imposes costs, however, and once again a sensitive comparison of the benefits (in terms of decision-making quality) would also be required. In cases where particular schemas seem to produce outcomes whose costs are uniformly high, avoiding the use of certain kinds of schemas or analogies might be a more efficient rule of thumb.

Other psychological alternatives to rationalist models of explanation emphasize the process by which decisions are made, particularly the use of information-processing shortcuts and heuristics; these alternatives are often portrayed as challenging rational choice models more directly. Prospect theory has evoked the most interest among students of foreign policymaking. Based on robust experimental evidence, prospect theory points to deviations from expected utility theory, the conventional means of explaining choice under conditions of risk. In barest outline, individuals systematically and frequently evaluate outcomes with respect to a reference point rather than using net losses or gains; individuals are risk-averse with respect to gains from that reference point and risk-acceptant with regard to losses; and preference ordering varies according to the framing of prospects (a clear violation of the criterion of invariance in rational choice).[25] Despite the difficulties in measuring these effects outside an experimental or laboratory setting, researchers using cases drawn from international politics have already begun to examine the explanatory power of prospect theory weighed against predictions based on expected utility.[26] To the de-

23. Khong 1992.
24. Tetlock and McGuire 1986, 160.
25. See Quattrone and Tversky 1988; Levy 1992; Levy 1997; and Pauly and Stein 1993.
26. See Pauly and Stein 1993; Farnham 1992; and McDermott 1992.

gree that convincing tests can be made using the data available, results appear mixed: expected utility theory is hardly without value in explaining many of the outcomes.

The rich psychological literature in international relations has produced many case studies demonstrating widespread cognitive and information processing distortions that deviate from the predictions of rational choice and expected utility theories. Psychological approaches often supplement rational choice explanations, however, rather than providing an alternative to them. In other cases, such as prospect theory, expected utility theorists are hard at work incorporating anomalous findings into broader and more inclusive theories of decision making.[27] Theory-building strategies among psychological critics of rationalist models confront the same issue of "thinness" as those using rational choice. Critics of rational choice voice dissatisfaction with the emptiness of those models in the absence of a theory of preferences. Psychological process models, such as prospect theory, remain equally empty without a theory of reference points or framing.

Psychological studies of foreign policymaking have produced important evidence that qualifies rational choice models, but they do not represent a single psychological alternative to rational choice. Mirroring the claims of rational choice theorists, psychological critics have argued wide scope for their findings. They have generally avoided a presentation of contingent theories or hypotheses that would stipulate the conditions under which psychological distortions of rational decision making are most likely. Even the most prolific and perceptive scholars who have mined historical and contemporary data find it difficult to claim more than the presence of systematic and widespread biases toward misperception across a wide range of cases.[28] The judgment of Tetlock and McGuire of a decade ago still stands: psychological approaches must work, not toward a single "cognitive portrait," but rather toward producing a "contingency theory of information processing," specifying more clearly the conditions under which particular cognitive strategies, rational and nonrational, are pursued.[29]

Unfortunately, the obstacles to that course are formidable. Critics of the psychological perspective on choice have long alleged that the transfer of experimental laboratory data, no matter how robust, to real-world choice situations is a flawed strategy: even the most ingenious experiments cannot capture the subjective perceptions of risk that are present in markets or international bargaining.[30] Even if one allows the validity of testing for such effects in historical or contemporary settings, the collection and evaluation of data that is aimed at reconstructing very refined, subjective estimates of risk and utility is difficult to accomplish. Alternative and equally convincing explanations based on different utility calculations (for example, those including domestic political goals) can often be constructed.

Given these difficulties, Verba's cost-benefit criterion of research efficiency must be taken seriously. Weighing the potential explanatory contribution of psychological

27. Machina 1987.
28. Jervis 1988.
29. Tetlock and McGuire 1986, 169–70.
30. For only one example, see Riker 1995.

approaches against more austere rationalist models becomes crucial in designing research strategy. As Arthur Stein has argued, even the direction of psychological effects on international outcomes is uncertain: plentiful and unbiased information may not lead to greater cooperation or to other desired outcomes.[31] Recent discussions of prospect theory have produced widely divergent conclusions regarding the overall effect of its decision heuristics on international politics. Timothy McKeown argues that prospect theory predicts "bland foreign policies"; Robert Jervis and Jack S. Levy perceive a status quo bias that might be upset by risk-acceptant propensities in the domain of losses.[32] A great deal hinges on the reference point deployed in a particular choice situation, and prospect theory provides no theory of reference points. If even the sign of these psychological effects is uncertain, then nonrational models of this kind may add little power to existing explanations.

Using an expected utility framework, Woosang Kim and Bruce Bueno de Mesquita have attempted to measure the importance of misperception—defined as *differences* in perception regarding the probability of crisis escalation.[33] This line of research sidesteps the methodological difficulty in demonstrating *mis*perception, a counterfactual that Kim and Bueno de Mesquita claim is unobservable in nearly all historical cases. Such a concentration on shared or dissimilar beliefs and the existence of common knowledge provides one rationalist response to the criticisms of psychologists. A second strategy in the face of evidence that rationalist models do not capture decision making in an array of cases is to relax the assumptions of the rationalist model. Evolutionary game theory and models incorporating bounded rationality have pursued this approach.

Both psychological and rational choice approaches share an individualist orientation. Both have tended to evade the crucial question of aggregation: whether assumptions regarding individual decision-making processes, rational or nonrational, can be transformed into plausible assumptions about the behavior of collectivities. That shared theoretical problem has been a stimulus to incorporating rational and nonrational models of organization and institutions into theories of national behavior.

Reason and Collectivities: The Issue of Aggregation

Deterrence theory represents one of the most sophisticated and highly elaborated uses of rational actor modeling in international relations. It has also been an intellectual testing ground for both rational actor (subjective expected utility) models and those deploying psychological models. Much of the debate has centered on methodological issues, particularly the use of deductive models rather than case studies. Participants on either side, however, have admitted that the contenders share an in-

---

31. Stein 1990, chap. 3.
32. See McKeown 1993, 217; Jervis 1992b, 190–91; and Levy 1992, 286.
33. Kim and Bueno de Mesquita 1995.

ability to offer convincing models that aggregate individual choices and behavior. Jervis has pointed out that units composed of many individuals appear more irrational than individual decision makers for several reasons: governments or coalitions that pursue contradictory goals, organizational or institutional incapacity in strategy choice, alternation of different groups (with different preference orderings) in power, and the possibility of cycling.[34] George Downs, who has urged a positive symbiosis between rationalist and psychological approaches to decision making in order to produce a "strong" model of deterrence, also remarks on a less positive attribute on the part of both rational deterrence theorists and psychological modelers to transfer their assumptions about individual choice to states and organizations.[35]

Elster notes that treating the polity "as a unitary actor, with coherent and stable values, well-grounded beliefs, and a capacity to carry out its decisions" is most widespread in international relations and in the theory of economic planning.[36] Given its unhappy consequences in economic planning, it is surprising that this assumption, which he labels potentially "treacherous and misleading," has been so easily accepted as an adequate microfoundation for much of international relations. Realist assumptions of state rationality depended on an implicit selection argument, as described in the case of Waltz: states that were unable to behave in at least a crudely rational manner would be selected out through intense international competition. Although a model of international selection may give some purchase on the differential survival of units, the link between rational action and survival has not been made. In fact, much of the psychological literature suggests precisely the opposite: that distortions in decision making and deviations from a rational model occur frequently in international politics, with mixed survival consequences for the units in question.

Building on early decision-making models, Graham Allison's *Essence of Decision* was one of the first efforts to challenge unitary and rational actor assumptions on the basis of political process.[37] Allison described a rational actor model of governmental decision making (model I) and then proposed two alternatives that heavily qualified the model. In choosing the Cuban Missile Crisis, the most threatening case of superpower crisis bargaining during the Cold War, Allison deliberately selected a case in which the international environment should have reinforced pressures toward unitary and rational decision making. Instead, Allison found substantial deviations from such a model, which he explained through two alternatives, an organizational process model (model II) and a bureaucratic politics model (model III).

Critics of Allison's approach focused initially on the descriptive accuracy of his account of the foreign policy process. More recently, however, his specification of the models and particularly his tilt against his candidate for a rational choice model have become a target. Jonathan Bendor and Thomas H. Hammond argue that Allison creates a rational actor model without a dimension of strategic behavior. Omitting a test of the insights of game theory is odd in a study of crisis bargaining. They contend

34. Jervis 1989b, 204–205.
35. Downs 1989, 236.
36. Elster 1989b, 177.
37. Allison 1971.

that Allison sets a benchmark for individual rationality that makes easier his promotion of boundedly rational or nonrational models.[38]

Allison's second and third models, whatever their shortcomings, trace two paths by which political and social units and organizations could be portrayed as rational. The first avenue is increasing circumscription of rationality as aggregation increases. Model II assumed that large organizations constrained individual rationality and behaved according to highly simplified decision rules. John Steinbruner's cybernetic theory of decision, published soon after Allison's work appeared, elaborated a similar model of simplified organizational behavior that relied on simple and nonrational decision-making processes.[39] In both cases, rationality was held to become more bounded and imperfect as one moved from individual choice to organizational routine. Despite the widely held view that organizations are less rational and "dumber" than the individuals who compose them, Bendor and Hammond argue that large organizations may, on the contrary, enhance the decision-making capacities of individuals rather than constrain them. Allison's view of institutional rationality is founded on an optimistic view of individual rationality embodied in model I.[40]

If limitations on rationality are one route toward aggregation (the whole is less rational than its parts), Allison's model of bureaucratic bargaining points toward another. Policy outcome may be seen as the equilibrium of two-level or linked games. In other words, bargaining among rational agents within an institutional setting adds a degree of specification and rigor missing in Allison's bureaucratic politics model, as well as captures the dimension of external bargaining. Helen Milner's contribution to this issue of *IO* describes at greater length the positive benefits of relaxing the assumption that states are units. She provides a particularly telling critique of the realist assumption that states are unitary actors. Less attention will be given here to the modeling of internal political processes. Aggregation conceived as bargaining among rational domestic actors in what Milner terms polyarchic settings has its own risks and limits, however. Allison's early bureaucratic politics model appears to assume that little hierarchy exists in foreign policy organizations.[41] Two-level game models sometimes evade this issue by positing a "chief of government" or other authoritative decision maker who bargains with other political actors, typically legislators (or the legislature). Whether that chief executive must also bargain with bureaucratic subordinates or cabinet colleagues (other than coalition partners in a parliamentary regime) can be unclear in simpler game-theoretic models of two-level games.

Modeling the influence and points of intervention of interest groups raises similar issues. Although on many international economic issues, a likely route for influencing foreign policy will be the legislature, many interest groups forge strong bonds with bureaucracies in order to influence policy implementation. How such influence filters into the preferences of the chief executive or head of government should also be incorporated in the modeling of foreign policymaking. Principal-agent models

38. Bendor and Hammond 1992, 313, 319.
39. Steinbruner 1974.
40. Bendor and Hammond 1992, 312.
41. Ibid., 316–17.

and delegation regimes provide one avenue of institutional analysis that can incorporate diverse domestic actors within hierarchical settings.[42]

Another potential weakness of rational institutionalist analysis is its treatment of the institutional rules of the game. Robert Bates's recent study of the International Coffee Organization is an excellent exemplar of building from rational social and economic actors toward institutions at the domestic and the international level.[43] His treatment of political institutions is squarely within the frame of positive political economy, "the study of rational decisions in a context of political and economic institutions," or, as Bates puts it, institutions "defining political games in which interests compete for influence over public policy."[44]

Building foreign policy actions from individual rational actors constrained by institutions leaves open the question of whether institutions are exogenous or endogenous, however. Positive political economy ultimately regards institutional change as explicable through the same rational choice means as equilibrium outcomes within a given institutional setting. However, most studies, like that of Bates, accept domestic institutions as fixed and play out the domestic political games (interacting with international strategic bargaining) within that context. In assessing the stability of national preferences in a more elaborated institutionalist analysis of foreign policy, as described by Milner, stability of domestic political institutions and the games that they define is crucial. Unfortunately, determining when political actors will opt for institutional change rather than change within institutions is rarely specified clearly. If one can assume relatively fixed preferences on the part of key individuals (or representatives of interests) and fixed institutional rules of the game, treating national preferences and behavior within a rationalist framework is far more convincing than under circumstances in which institutional rules change frequently and unpredictably.

Despite their weaknesses, Allison's alternative models stood at the beginning of two broad avenues for creating unified, if not unitary, rational actors from organizational and national collectivities. One route produces actors embedded in and constrained by organizational context. Whether that context bounds or amplifies their rational decision making remains open to argument. The second route carefully specifies domestic bargaining games that are then linked to international bargaining behavior and strategic interaction. Those games may vary according to domestic institutions, information environment, and type of international interaction.[45] This second avenue produces outcomes that may serve as proxies for a unified national interest. Both routes force close attention to the simple, conventional assumptions within international relations that have produced unitary and rational actors from the complexities of domestic political and bureaucratic competition.

---

42. For an introduction to agency problems and their solutions in a political context, see Kiewiet and McCubbins 1991, chap. 2.

43. Bates 1997a.

44. See Ibid., 164; and Alt and Shepsle 1990, 2.

45. For a representative and rigorous array of models linking international and domestic politics, see Pahre and Papayoanou 1997.

Culture, Norms, and Identity: Supplements and Alternatives to Rational Models

The insertion of norms and identity into the analysis of international relations has been taken by some as a direct assault on rationalist models of national policy and international interaction. That insertion has taken many different forms, however, and not all are incompatible with rational choice models. In part, the view that rationalist models are incompatible with the inclusion of norms or culture is the result of an unfortunate conflation of methodology and substance. Most cultural and normative treatments employ "thick description" or interpretive approaches to their subjects, in contrast to the deductive and parsimonious bent of rationalist models. The alternatives are critical of the methodological individualism that is coupled with rationality in these models of politics. Whether rationality and collective identity can be combined within a modified rational choice framework is one of the central questions posed by the recent turn toward identity and norms. To the degree that one can assemble common positions among a diverse group of theorists and researchers, four different criticisms have been leveled at rationalist models. These critical positions can be arrayed from those that complement modified rationalist models to those that suggest a much larger theoretical divide between rational and nonrational.

The treatment of preferences as exogenous and individualistic has been questioned by economists, social psychologists, and, within international relations, proponents of strategic culture as a determinant of behavior. For some, the absence of a theory of beliefs and preferences is simply a failure of explanation within rational choice models; if explanation occurs "when the mind is at rest," standard rational choice models often leave restless minds in their wake. Herbert Simon has argued that without strong auxiliary assumptions (such as those in public choice theory) rational choice models are nearly empty of explanatory or predictive content.[46] Others have questioned individualist assumptions regarding beliefs, preferences, and the information environment that seem to underlie many rationalist models. Kenneth Arrow has recently argued that both the rules of the game (in economic or strategic interaction) and much knowledge is irreducibly social.[47] Arrow's assertion can be tied to the assumption of common knowledge that underlies equilibrium analysis in game theory.[48] Norman Schofield situates this question at the heart of social (and by extension international) cooperation: "The theoretical problem underlying cooperation can be stated thus: what is the minimal amount that one agent must know in a given milieu about the beliefs and wants of other agents, to be able to form coherent notions about their behavior, and for this knowledge to be communicable to the others."[49] Schofield's language and the problem of common knowledge that he raises provide a link to those who propose including social and cultural content in rational models.

46. Simon 1995, 50.
47. Arrow 1994, 5–6.
48. For a summary, see Morrow 1994a, 307–308.
49. Schofield 1985.

Within international relations strategic culture is sometimes portrayed as an alternative to rational choice explanations. In fact, strategic culture is better seen as a modification or extension of those models, providing a source of organizational and national preferences. For example, Alastair Iain Johnston offers "a limited, ranked set of grand strategic preferences that is consistent across the objects of analysis . . . and persistent across time" as the "essential empirical referent of strategic culture." Strategic culture is proposed as a more powerful explanation for this ranking than variables such as "technology, threat, or organization."[50] Elizabeth Kier also presents a "culturalist" approach to the choice of military doctrine as a means of endogenizing preferences, in contrast to structural or functional explanations.[51] Jeffrey W. Legro, in another deployment of organizational culture (as an alternative to realist and institutionalist explanations), also uses the culture of military organizations as a means for explaining state preferences.[52] In each of these cases, cultural explanations are a means of enriching models of state choice, not an instrument for overturning them.

Even these efforts to explain the collective or social content of beliefs and preferences may with extension suggest a deeper conflict with rationalism. One point of disagreement concerns the nature of culture itself. To the degree that organizational and strategic culture is defined carefully, it is not seen as the result of individual interaction: through processes of socialization, organizational cultures are embedded in individuals and those individuals accept such cultures in a relatively unreflective way. Contrast this image with the rational and individualist model of corporate culture proposed by David M. Kreps. Although Kreps allows that corporate culture may be "rigid and immutable," he offers a definition of culture that is functional and evolutionary: a principle or set of principles that permit "relatively efficient transactions to take place and on which a viable reputation can be based."[53] Although both views of organizational culture employ the word *culture,* the means by which culture is created and transmitted is very different.

A second point of divergence links culturalist explanations to psychological critiques described earlier. If culture implies "culturally dictated schemas which guide individuals to see, do, and want what is required of them,"[54] one may arrive at a view of choice so constrained by culture that little choice remains: to return to Elster's original definition, the feasible set is sharply constrained by culture, collective beliefs largely guide interpretation of the choice situation, and in the most culturally driven account, choice can hardly be said to occur. If this interpretation is placed on strategic or organizational culture, we approach a nonrational, norm-driven behavior that is described later.

This first group of critics wishes to elaborate and "socialize" beliefs and preferences within reigning rationalist accounts. A second group is more concerned with

50. Johnston 1995b, 48.
51. Kier 1995, 67.
52. Legro 1995, 27–28.
53. Kreps 1990a, 127, 125.
54. Rosenberg 1995, 132.

anachronistic or inaccurate auxiliary assumptions that have characterized too many rational choice models of political behavior. If the first critics are concerned with the emptiness of rational choice models, the second set remarks that such models have been filled with particular assumptions about individual and state preferences, specifically the assumption of a self-interested *homo economicus.* Using Ferejohn's distinctions, the criticisms here are directed at "thick rationality" of the wrong kind (in the view of the critics) rather than the thin rationality that was the focus of the first criticisms.

The inclusion of other-regarding or altruistic motivations in rationalist models has been the source of considerable controversy, much of it without direct relevance to international relations. On one side, it is argued that by emptying rational choice of self-interest narrowly defined, the concept of rationality becomes so thin as to become a tautology.[55] The opposed view is in favor of "broad," not thin rationality, criticizing the narrow self-interest view of rationality as an unnecessary auxiliary assumption imposed by too many economists. Elster, for example, distinguishes between economic man "defined through continuous preferences and narrow self-interest," and rational man, "who may have non-Archimedean preferences and be moved by concern for others."[56]

Although less concerned with altruism, debates within international relations revolve around similar issues: does "broadening" rational models to incorporate different beliefs about the world and nonmaterial conceptions of interest render the model so "thin" as to undermine its explanatory usefulness? The introduction of ideational variables into explanations of foreign policy, widespread over the past decade, does not seem to have weakened the explanatory power of essentially rationalist models.[57] Ferejohn makes a convincing argument that even interpretivist accounts based on thick description of distant historical episodes, accounts that challenge some of the assumptions embedded in public choice and positive political economy models of political behavior, can be fruitfully incorporated into broader rational and purposive models of behavior. By drawing on both interpretivist and rationalist approaches the indeterminacies of each can be partially alleviated.[58] This apparently happy complementarity may reach its limits, however, when the beliefs and preferences of another culture or another time challenge rationalism itself. Some argue that the worldviews of other cultures, such as Islamic fundamentalism, cannot be melded with an approach derived from the European Enlightenment.[59] The reply to such arguments raises two questions: is this worldview, typically derived from the writings of intellectuals and clerics, shared widely by the population and reflected in its behavior? To the degree that action cannot be explained by a very thin rational model, how do these actors accomplish their political and religious ends (that is, are there costs or selective pressures imposed on nonrational operating codes)?

---

55. Monroe 1995, 5.
56. Elster 1984, 146. On less self-centered views of rationality, see also Sen 1994, 389.
57. See the contributions to Goldstein and Keohane 1993b.
58. Ferejohn 1991, 285.
59. Euben 1995, 157–78.

Rather than emphasizing the social and cultural content of beliefs and preferences, a third set of critics concentrates on the determinants of identity, which is held to be socially constructed and prior to any definition of preferences or behavior. Once again, the elevation of identity undermines methodological individualism rather than rationalist models per se, but some interpretations of identity call into question rational choice assumptions as well. Social constructivism, which incorporates a diverse body of scholarship, emphasizes socially constructed identity and its implications as a core constituent of its research program.[60] Sociological approaches to international relations also argue against a starting point of individual, rational agents. Instead, agents themselves, whether individuals or states, are shaped profoundly by a dense institutional environment. The environment can not only alter choices, it can also constitute the properties of actors and even their existence.[61] The sociological perspective accepts institutions as pervasive; although institutions "are certainly the product of human activity, they are not necessarily the products of conscious design." They represent "collective outcomes that are not the simple sum of individual interests."[62]

The social constructivist or sociological view of a highly institutionalized environment shaping or even determining the identity of its constituent actors need not be incompatible with rationalist models. One could argue that choices are simply highly constrained by social and cultural determinants (as earlier criticisms alleged) and that socially constituted identities are an ontological issue prior to behavioral modeling along rational choice lines.[63] As John Ruggie puts it, "a core constructivist research concern is what happens before the neo-utilitarian model purportedly kicks in."[64] In outlining the effects of identity on national security policy, for example, Ronald L. Jepperson, Peter J. Katzenstein, and Alexander Wendt point to two ways in which identity is prior to interests: states may develop interests linked to particular identities, or domestic identity politics may be reflected in foreign policy interests. In both cases, identity is prior to interests and may define those interests, but the pursuit of those interests could be incorporated in a rationalist model.[65]

Once again, however, extending or reinterpreting this concern with identity may produce conflict rather than complementarity with a rationalist approach. Identity may itself affect interests and behavior in a direct and unmediated way that is difficult to reconcile with rational choice models. Kristen Renwick Monroe's sphere of ethical action, for example, proceeds directly from identity: "Certain kinds of political action emanate primarily from one's perception of self in relation to others; this perception effectively delineates and sets the domain of choice options perceived as available to an actor, both in an empirical and moral sense." Or more radically:

60. See Adler 1997; and Ruggie, this issue.

61. Jepperson, Wendt, and Katzenstein 1996, 41.

62. DiMaggio and Powell 1991, 8–9.

63. Spruyt's excellent account of the emergence of the sovereign territorial state combines an analysis of the success of one identity with a rational choice explanation for the emergence of the initial competitors. Spruyt 1994.

64. Ruggie, this issue.

65. Jepperson, Wendt, and Katzenstein 1996, 60–61.

"ethical action does not result from conscious calculus."[66] Identity may also undermine a rationalist calculus if it can be attached to different forms of rationality. Shawn Rosenberg contends that individuals may exhibit different structures of reasoning and different rationalities; at the level of collectivities, cultural arguments (described earlier in the case of non-Western cultures) could ascribe the same variation.[67] Doubts remain, however: would selection produce some form of roughly similar rationality among individuals or collectivities; can the evidence of such radical variation in reasoning (drawn from experimental evidence) be transposed to social and political settings?

A final alternative to rational choice explanations of behavior, described by Elster as the only alternative that cannot be absorbed by even an expanded rationalist frame, is behavior driven by social norms.[68] Behavior driven by social norms defined in this way undermines both individualist and rationalist premises of rational choice models. The norms in question are social in two respects: they are shared by a population, and that population sustains them by enforcing them (through expressed approval and disapproval). Unlike rational action, which is determined by the instrumental pursuit of future outcomes, norm-driven behavior is not outcome-oriented. One easy guide to behavior governed by social norms (as compared to behavior driven by rational or optimizing behavior) is the response (when challenged) that a certain action "just isn't done." Norm-driven behavior is nonrational in a second sense, in its tie to the emotions: "Social norms have a grip on the mind that is due to the strong emotions their violations can trigger."[69]

Elster's conception of norm-driven behavior is contested from both the rationalist and the social constructivist positions. Those deploying rational choice models seek to incorporate this sphere of human behavior within a rationalist perspective as well. Russell Hardin, for example, challenges Elster's definition of norms as not outcome-oriented. For Hardin, following norms may combine elements of both rational self-interest and nonconsequentialist motivation. The fluid boundaries between norm-driven and rational choice can only be assessed empirically.[70] Social constructivists, on the other hand, would contest the methodological individualism of Elster's definition and seek to expand the scope of norm-driven behavior as against behavior explained through individual choice.[71] Two separable characteristics of norms are at issue then: to what degree norms can be regarded as based in individual beliefs and behavior and to what degree norms are sustained by rational self-interest (defined minimally as concern with the consequences of the behavior induced by norms).

More than in economic transactions (where there are strong norms regarding what money can buy), international relations has been portrayed as a setting of weak or nonexistent norms. Norm-driven behavior in the conventional or realist view is rare

66. Monroe 1995, 12–13.
67. Rosenberg 1995, 124–25.
68. The description here is drawn from Elster 1989c, chap. 3; and Elster 1989b, 32–35.
69. Elster 1989c, 100.
70. Hardin 1995, 108, 140.
71. On the individualism of Elster's conception of norms, see Elster 1989c, 105.

or absent. Social constructivists have expanded attention to outcomes that appear to be explained by the evolution of social norms in international relations—norms that are often closely tied to identity. Nevertheless, most case studies of the influence of norms in international relations, as responses to realist skepticism, have not been designed to establish norm-driven behavior as a nonrational alternative to rationalist, outcome-driven behavior described by Elster.[72] Although social constructivists would reject an individualist account for the origins of norms, as Martha Finnemore and Kathryn Sikkink make clear in this issue, they would not in every case reject a role for individual or state self-interest in sustaining norms. On further investigation, norms with a wholly nonrational basis may be discovered in international relations: the attachment to national sovereignty may be one example. In international relations, however, the ability to assign an instrumental explanation for the power of many norms and the absence of an apparent affective or emotional linkage that sustains compliance through social disapproval in domestic contexts may reduce the scope of wholly nonrational, norm-driven behavior.

Just as deterrence theory has served as the principal site of contest between rational choice and psychological approaches, identity- and norm-centered explanations on the one hand and rational choice models on the other have challenged each other on the field of ethnic or national identity since the end of the Cold War. In predicting the prevalence of ethnic conflict in particular, rational choice and cultural or eclectic models have competed for explanatory success. The competition is made more interesting by a mingling of normative and positive analysis. As Bernard Yack has argued, the familiar distinctions between civic and ethnic nationalism (good/bad, rational/ nonrational, peaceful/conflictual) combine unexamined assumptions about the sources of unfolding ethnic conflict as well as assumptions about desirable outcomes.[73]

Models of ethnic outbidding based on rational politicians have been widely employed; the instrumental view of ethnicity at the individual and the elite level is a powerful one. At the same time, those models appear incomplete or fail to "work" in the absence of a cultural (if not primordial) substrate that closely resembles Elster's norm-driven behavior: suffused with affect and often unconcerned with outcomes. All of the social and interpretive qualifications of rational choice models mentioned earlier are applicable here, as are the cautions regarding the easy leap from individual to group motivations and action.[74] Prevailing theoretical eclecticism in the study of ethnicity and ethnic conflict, combined with a rich and growing set of historical and contemporary cases, suggests that this arena will provide not only some clear tests of the limitations and strengths of rationalist models and their competitors but also a site for bridge building between the theoretical and methodological camps. Whether those bridges are illusory or real is the subject of the concluding section.

---

72. See the cases in Katzenstein 1996c.
73. Yack 1996, 7.
74. On this point, see Fearon and Laitin 1996, 731.

Reason and the Domain of International Politics

International relations has always been a realm of reason only in part, claimed by both passions and interests. Perhaps the long coexistence of those who have tried to capture its elements of calculation and prudence and those impressed by the irrationality of international outcomes and processes has spared the field from some of the battles that are underway between rational choice and its critics elsewhere in the social sciences. In the inconclusive great debates of international relations, those employing rational choice models could be found on either side, particularly in the most recent neorealist and neoliberal controversies. The image of rational and unitary state actors has been pervasive in the field; strategic interaction is a given. As a result, rational choice and game-theoretic approaches have been easier to accept.

A certain familiarity with models drawn from microeconomics has not meant an absence of critical scrutiny for those approaches, however. Critics from a number of psychological perspectives—depth psychology, cognitive psychology, prospect theory—have pointed out important deviations from austere models of subjective expected utility. Psychological approaches have confronted rational actor models on a level playing field: both accepted individualist premises. The long-standing exchanges between rational choice and its psychological critics demonstrate that arguments about scope must be framed precisely to move the field forward. The hegemonic aspirations of rationalist modelers have often confronted equally broad claims regarding the prevalence of psychological distortions in decision processes. Many of those at the center of psychological research programs, such as Robert Jervis, Philip Tetlock, and Janice Stein, have argued for context-dependent or contingent theories that would specify when rational choice or alternative psychological models of decision should be applied. Unfortunately, such a theory has not emerged on either side. Although the experimental results in support of prospect theory—the latest theoretical alternative championed by the psychologists—are robust, the translation of those findings into decision situations comparable to those in international politics remains problematic. Psychological critiques have elicited a significant response by rational choice modelers and game theorists, however. Expected utility models rely on a rationality that is increasingly constrained, reducing the heroic assumptions that provided such an easy target for the psychologists. The incorporation of bounded rationality into these models and the development of evolutionary game theory have permitted more realistic definitions of rational behavior and opened new research avenues.

In addition to the need for contingent statements of scope, rational choice and its individualist critics also share methodological shortcomings that could be explored together. Both rational choice and its micro-level critics have moved blithely from the individual to the organizational and governmental levels of analysis, accompanied by their rational and nonrational assumptions. The issue of appropriate aggregation or modification in order to preserve assumptions drawn from the individual level has seldom been broached explicitly. Under the influence of neorealism and moves to "bring the state back in," international relations, far more than the other social sciences, was willing to attribute a circumscribed rationality to states and other international actors. Typically, the issue is dealt with through simple pragmatism: unitary actors are a useful assumption until proven unrealistic. Only recently has institutional analysis provided a rigorous means for identifying the constraints on domestic political actors and modeling both the international and domestic bargaining in which they engage.

A diverse set of critics who emphasize culture and norms exemplify a third strategy that is necessary for fruitful theoretical exchange: clarifying points of complementarity and conflict through careful definition. Many of these critics have questioned the individualist assumptions of most rational choice models; their arguments have implications that are less clear for rational choice assumptions. By forcing implicit auxiliary assumptions to the surface, rational choice models have been broadened. By pressing for a theory of preference and belief formation and arguing for attention to the identity formation of actors, alternatives based on culture and norms opened questions that many rationalist models had mistakenly believed to be answered. As a result, new research agendas—driven by rationality, culture, and identity—have illuminated ethnic and identity politics and their influence on international relations, the character of units—as defined by themselves and by others—across time, and "knowledge politics," the construction of social knowledge within and across national boundaries.

Arguing for inevitable convergence or accommodation between rational choice and its critics would be as naive as proclaiming peace in our time. Nevertheless, the conditions described provide a basis for intellectual exchange that promises to advance research agendas on either side rather than promoting fruitless and grandiose claims and counterclaims. Careful stipulations of scope, acknowledgment of joint methodological shortcomings, and precise definition of perceived differences can be supplemented empirically by problem-centered research. If research agendas are largely theory-driven, selection biases will tend to favor research questions more tractable for rational choice or its critics. By accepting the "neutral" empirical ground of historical or contemporary issues whose importance is widely acknowledged, a level playing field for theoretical competition may be established. Deterrence served this purpose and illuminated the differences between rational deterrence theory and its critics. Nationalism and ethnicity provide a similar competitive research frontier for social constructivist and rational choice models.

Full-blown alternatives to rational choice may arise from each of these critical alternatives. An evolutionary or selective model, endorsed by Waltz, would render micro-level rationality otiose. Prospect theory or another model of psychological processes may yet offer the breadth of application that rational choice has enjoyed as a model of individual decision. Social constructivism could produce a unified, norm-driven model of international relations that will contend with the state-centric and rationalist predilections of both neorealists and liberal institutionalists.

What is more likely is further evolution of rationalist models in directions that accommodate at least some of these criticisms. Heroic and unrealistic assumptions regarding information and information processing will continue to be relaxed in favor of constrained or bounded rationality. Models of linked domestic and international bargaining will eliminate the need for another set of unrealistic assumptions concerning unitary and rational states. Finally, rational models will be "collectivized," as persistent cultural beliefs are incorporated into game-theoretic and institutionalist models.[75] In light of past experience, valuable complementarities between rational choice and its critics will be more rapidly exploited by rationalist models.

Assumptions of rationality and criticisms of those assumptions have defined research agendas in international relations; in the past they also defined a normative stance in international relations. Rational choice provided a means to explore the most efficient means to pursue national ends, to attain collectively desirable international outcomes, and to avoid disastrous ones. Military strategy, at least since Clausewitz, has been designed to impose reason on conflicts that threatened to spin out of control, to transform fights into games. Deterrence theory, with its applications to nuclear policy and arms control, was perhaps the most striking demonstration of reason in the service of particular national and international goals, but one that demonstrated in the eyes of some the irrationality of reason's offspring. Psychological dissents from rational choice were directed toward what was seen as the hubris of early deterrence theory, but the goal remained an undistorted set of rational beliefs and decision-making processes. The delicate balance of terror was rendered less delicate and less dangerous, but what many saw as the fundamental irrationality of mutual assured destruction remained.

The narrowing of reason's import to a criterion of decision-making efficiency may have eliminated its status as a normative standard. The effects of misperception and other nonrational distortions on international outcomes are ambiguous; theory-driven behavior can have both positive and negative consequences. Rational institutional design (from the point of view of individual agents) may produce governmental deadlock and foreign policy passivity at the national level. And nonrational influences, such as norms and national identity, may create both a community capable of forging a coherent and legitimate foreign policy and one that oppresses its own minorities and wages war against those outside the community's pale. Reason's role at the core of explanatory models continues to grow. Its status as a benchmark for judgment remains as uncertain as it was when Morgenthau attacked "scientific man."

---

75. For an important example of such a strategy, see Greif 1995.

The Institutional Dynamics
of International Political Orders

James G. March and Johan P. Olsen

Introduction

Students of international organization try to understand how and when international political orders are created, maintained, changed, and abandoned. Many of the key questions belong to a wider class of difficult questions about the dynamics of social order and development. How can order develop out of anarchy? What stabilizes an order? When and how does a stable order fall apart? How does peaceful change occur? Why do peaceful relations sometimes find themselves drawn into less peaceful confrontations? How is the search for order among collectivities linked to the search for order within them?

In this article we address such questions, though our ambitions are considerably less than might be imagined from such an agenda. We consider a few stylized ways of thinking about the history and possible future of international political organization and elaborate one of them, something that might be called an institutional approach to such thinking. The article is written from the perspective of students of organizations, thus with deference to, but without pretense of extensive knowledge of, the literature of international political relations.

Change and Continuity in International Orders

The history of political orders is written in terms of changes in domestic and international political relations.[1] At some periods in some areas, political life has been rather well organized around well-defined boundaries, common rules and practices, shared

The research for this article was supported by the Spencer Foundation and the ARENA program (Advanced Research on the Europeanisation of the Nation-State) financed by the Norwegian Research Council. We are grateful for the help provided by Peter Katzenstein, Robert O. Keohane, Stephen D. Krasner, Helene Sjursen, Arthur Stein, Bjørn Otto Sverdrup, and Arild Underdal in introducing us to the international relations literature and for constructive comments.
1. See Krasner 1983a; Smith 1996; and Remmer 1997.

International Organization 52, 4, Autumn 1998, pp. 943–969

causal and normative understandings, and resources adequate for collective action. At other times and places, the system has been relatively anarchic. Relations have been less orderly; boundaries less well-defined; and institutions less common, less adequately supported, and less involved. As political institutions experience their histories, political life achieves or loses structure, and the nature of order changes.[2]

The Westphalian Order of Nation-States

Although the history of international political order long antedates the seventeenth century, only in the last three or four hundred years has anything approximating a single world order developed. The Treaty of Westphalia (1648) reflected and proclaimed a conception of international political order that gradually extended itself from its European roots to encompass most of the world. It was a conception built around the central importance of a particular type of political actor—the territorial, sovereign state. By the end of the twentieth century, the idea of the nation-state and a world geography defined by national boundaries had evolved to a position of conceptual dominance, as had principles of international relations built upon them.[3] Such principles and the conceptions on which they were based were never all-encompassing. Indeed, states are still developing in some parts of the world as the twentieth century draws to its close,[4] and state authority and control have been weakened in other parts. Nevertheless, most contemporary writing portrays the world as partitioned into mutually exclusive and exhaustive territorial units called states.

This Westphalian nation-state order makes a fundamental distinction between domestic political spheres characterized by institutional density, hierarchical relationships, shared interests, and strong collective identities, and an international political sphere characterized by a lack of strong institutions, few rules, conflicting interests, and conflicting identities. The state imposes unity and coherence on domestic society,[5] a coherence based on a national identity that suppresses or subordinates competing identities and belongings and on an elaborate set of rules (laws) and institutions. National identity and other political identities are fundamental to structuring behavior, and rules of appropriate behavior and institutions associated with those identities both infuse the state with shared meaning and expectations and provide political legitimacy that facilitates mobilization of resources from society.

International political life, on the other hand, is seen as much less institutionalized, much more anarchical. Individual states are imagined to act rationally in the service of coherent goals, to form mutually beneficial coalitions with others, to seek understandings that are mutually satisfactory, and to use all available resources to maximize the attainment of separate national objectives. Such attainment is limited primarily not by explicit rules regulating international encounters but by the simultaneous competitive efforts of other states to maximize their own objectives. Although some

---

2. See Dewey 1927; Eisenstadt 1987; and March and Olsen 1995.
3. Hall 1996.
4. Mann 1993.
5. Habermas 1996, 1.

understandings are common within the international community and some rules are recognized, norms and institutions are weaker, less widely shared, and less taken for granted than they are within individual states. International institutions are generally seen as requiring explicit rationalization in terms of the current interests of current states in order to secure their force and effectiveness.

As a result, many contemporary theories of international politics (like many theories of economic systems of business firms) embrace a two-stage conception of organization. In the first stage, domestic political activities, including political socialization, participation, and discourse, create coherent state actors out of the conflicts and inconsistencies of multiple individuals and groups living within the boundaries of a single state. In the second stage, those coherent systems compete and cooperate, pursuing state interests in international spheres that recognize few elements of collective coherence beyond those that arise from the immediate self-interests of the actors. Political order is defined primarily in terms of negotiated connections among externally autonomous and internally integrated sovereigns. Although such a two-stage conception has frequently been questioned by writers who see domestic and international politics as richly interconnected, it remains the most common approach to thinking about international relations.

Contemporary Changes in the Nation-State Order

The nation-state order has never been static and is unlikely to become so.[6] According to most observers, in fact, change has accelerated in recent times. The possibility of the emergence of a distinctively different post-Westphalian order is a serious topic for contemporary discussion.[7] Moreover, traditional concerns with formal agreements reflected in treaties are being supplemented by attention to changes in a wide range of practices and relations.[8] In particular, three kinds of changes are commonly noted: First there have been relatively rapid changes in national boundaries, constituting and reconstituting the basic units of the international order. The disintegration of some states and the (re)integration of others are changing state borders. These splits and mergers do not directly challenge the Westphalian order. European nation-state history since 1648 is replete with border changes and state reconstitutions. Still, frequent changes are uncomfortably accommodated within theoretical approaches assuming stable and unitary actors.

Second, many contemporary states seem to be characterized by increasing fragmentation and disintegration. In the last decade, a number of developing countries have lost critical elements of statehood as their central governments have broken down.[9]

6. See Bendix 1968, 9; and Bull 1995, 21.
7. These were issues to be discussed at the International Conference to Celebrate the 350th Anniversary of the Peace of Westphalia 1648–1998: "From Pragmatic Solution to Global Structure," Münster, 16–19 July 1998. However, part of this conference was cancelled and part of it was moved to Twente, The Netherlands.
8. Stone 1994, 448.
9. See Jackson 1990; and World Bank 1997.

Internal (as well as external) processes of differentiation are making the state "centerless" or multicentered. Ethnic, religious, linguistic, regional, functional, and class identities have created solidarities that do not coincide with nation-state boundaries. The state seems to be evolving into a less coherent and less tightly coupled unit.[10] These resurgences of substate and supranational identities have renewed interest in concepts like culture and identity as fundamental to understanding international relations.[11] At the end of the twentieth century, many states show symptoms of incoherence and disintegration somewhat reminiscent of an earlier time when political life involved confusing, overlapping, and conflicting demands on individual allegiances; and when polities were organized around emperors, kings, feudal lords, churches, chartered towns, guilds, and families.[12]

Third, substantial increases in international and cross-national connections and institutions are challenging an international order dominated by monocentric, hierarchical, and unitary states.[13] State autonomy and sovereignty have been compromised in fundamental areas such as security, capital regulation, migration, ecology, health, culture, and language. Institutional barriers to interaction across nation-state boundaries have been weakened or removed, making integration based on voluntary exchange easier. This "negative integration"[14] includes relaxed borders and barriers to exchange. Numerous economic, cultural, and intellectual transnational networks have formed to link individuals across state boundaries,[15] responding to changes in the ease of communication, transactions, and travel across nation-state borders.[16]

At the same time, there has been considerable increase in the number and importance of international institutions, regimes, laws, organizations, and networks[17]; and the Westphalian principle of nonintervention in internal affairs has been eroded by interventions in the name of dispute resolution, economic stability, and human rights.[18] Some rudiments of an international polity seem to be emerging, including instruments of opinion and will formation[19] and institutions for applying rules, making and implementing policies, and *kompetenz-kompetenz*, or the ability to change the scope and character of one's own authority.

Intergovernmental and supranational institutions, including bureaucracies, courts, parliaments, and enduring committees, have elaborated to a point where they are creating their own systems of rules and identities. Institutional complexity and the coexistence of different partial orders, each considered legitimate in its sphere, seem

10. See Marin and Mayntz 1991; Luhmann 1982, 253–55; Teubner 1993; Habermas 1996, 393; Ladeur 1997; and Rhodes 1997.
11. Lapid 1996, 3, 5.
12. March and Olsen 1995, 70.
13. Ladeur 1997.
14. Scharpf 1996, 15.
15. See Risse-Kappen 1995b; and Joerges, Ladeur, and Vos 1997.
16. Deutsch et al. 1957.
17. See Krasner 1983a; Keohane 1983a, 1984, 5, 1996; Kratochwil and Ruggie 1986; Haggard and Simmons 1987; Young 1989, 13, 1994, 1996; Mayer, Rittberger, and Zürn 1995, 403; Levy, Young, and Zürn 1995; and Hasenclever, Mayer, and Rittberger 1996, 1997.
18. Checkel 1997.
19. Habermas 1996, 475.

to have become permanent features of the international scene.[20] These institutions link states (and their components) in structures of shared norms and expectations that impinge on nation-state autonomy and make it hard to maintain sharp distinctions between foreign and domestic politics.[21]

Understanding and Anticipating Change in Political Orders

Theories of political development are attempts to understand and anticipate such changes in political orders. In part, such theories presume that a political order is reformed by intentional design. Organization is seen as purposeful and the creation of organization as stemming directly from the desires of political actors. In part, the theories assume less intentional mechanisms by which changes in international environments lead to changes in a political order. They trace the organizational consequences of such things as economic and technological globalization, mass migration, changes in material or political power, or changing military capabilities. And, in part, theories of international political development assume that local processes of growth, adaptation, elaboration, cooperation, conflict, and competition within and among political units lead to new political orders. For example, they examine the international consequences of internal state dynamics associated with the long historical development of the West European state.

From the perspective of such theories, it is not at all clear how contemporary changes in the nation-state and relations among them will affect the Westphalian, territorial, nation-state order with which we are familiar. Are we observing only minor modifications of an international order based on sovereign states with exclusive authority over a population within territorial boundaries and interstate relations based on anarchy, intergovernmentalism, balance of power, and hegemony? Or are we witnessing a major transformation of the constitutive principles and practices of international political life and the beginnings of a new form of political order and governance?[22] Although there is no question that the nation-state political order has changed and will change,[23] a reading of recent studies in international relations and comparative government, politics, and law suggests that there is little agreement about the scope and significance of new elements of international order.

There is somewhat more agreement about the historical processes that will be involved in any changes that may occur. Nearly everyone agrees that wars, conquests, and foreign occupations will contribute significantly to the elaboration and modification of the international political order, as they have in the past.[24] And nearly everyone agrees that more peaceful, gradual changes will come about because such

---

20. Mayer, Rittberger, and Zürn 1995, 401, 405.
21. Lake 1996, 30.
22. See Krasner 1983b; Keohane 1983a, 1984, 5, 1989a, 9; Young 1986, 109, 1996; Rosenau and Czempiel 1992; Krasner 1995a, 150; Mayer, Rittberger, and Zürn 1995, 293–94, 397–98; Risse 1997, 18; Stokke 1997; and Olsen 1997a.
23. See Buzan 1993, 351; and Jepperson, Wendt, and Katzenstein 1996, 74.
24. See Tilly 1975, 1993; and Giddens 1985. But see also Kaysen 1990.

changes match the changing interests of powerful political actors and the changing demands of the environment. We do not disagree with such judgments, but we think that these intuitive notions of "interests," "power," and "environmental fitness" require considerable elaboration, qualification, and supplementation to provide much help in understanding international politics.

As a step in that direction, we wish to explore some ideas drawn from an institutional perspective. Research on international institutions became somewhat unfashionable during the 1970s, but recently it has become common to argue that a better understanding of how institutions are structured; how they work; and how they emerge, are maintained, and change may contribute to a better understanding of international political life.[25] In the course of this recent resurrection of a "new institutionalism," the term has acquired somewhat expanded and confusing definitions that strain its linkage with the "old institutionalism,"[26] but there is a core set of ideas that is fairly broadly shared. In the remainder of this article, we examine the main features of one variety of an institutional perspective and illustrate its application to interpreting the dynamics of international order.

An Institutional Perspective

The term *institutional* has come to mean rather different things in different contexts and disciplines in recent years.[27] In a general way, an "institution" can be viewed as a relatively stable collection of practices and rules defining appropriate behavior for specific groups of actors in specific situations. Such practices and rules are embedded in structures of meaning and schemes of interpretation that explain and legitimize particular identities and the practices and rules associated with them.[28] Practices and rules are also embedded in resources and the principles of their allocation that make it possible for individuals to enact roles in an appropriate way and for a collectivity to socialize individuals and sanction those who wander from proper behavior.[29]

Institutionalization refers to the emergence of institutions and individual behaviors within them.[30] The process involves the development of practices and rules in the context of using them and has earned a variety of labels, including structuration and routinization, which refer to the development of codes of meaning, ways of reasoning, and accounts in the context of acting on them.[31] An institutional approach is one that emphasizes the role of institutions and institutionalization in the understanding of human actions within an organization, social order, or society.

25. See Krasner 1983a, 1988, 1995a, 145; Keohane 1984, 1988, 380, 1989a, 2; Young 1986, 1994, 1996; Stone 1994, 464; and Goldmann 1996.
26. Stinchcombe 1997.
27. March and Olsen 1996, 260, n. 2.
28. DiMaggio 1997.
29. See March and Olsen 1984, 1989, 1995.
30. Olsen 1997a, 159–60.
31. See Weber 1978; and Giddens 1984.

Such definitions are consistent with the general terminology of current discussions in the literature, but they are broad enough to encompass things as varied as collections of contracts, legal rules, social norms, and moral precepts. To narrow the range somewhat, we define the perspective in terms of two grand issues that divide students of the dynamics of social and political action and structures.

Issue 1: Bases of Action

The first issue concerns the basic logic of action by which human behavior is interpreted.[32] On the one side are those who see action as driven by a logic of anticipated consequences and prior preferences. On the other side are those who see action as driven by a logic of appropriateness and senses of identity. As in most cases of arguments among students of decision making, the argument has both normative and descriptive elements. The normative question is whether one logic leads to a better society than the other. In this spirit, histories of Western democracies have been interpreted as reflecting a tension between the virtues of "bourgeois" calculating and taking care of personal interests and the virtues of "citoyen" service in the name of civic identity.[33] They reflect an argument between those who believe that an exclusively calculative, consequential approach undermines laws and institutions[34] and those who see the durability of laws and institutions as resting on their contribution to the calculated interests of rational actors.[35]

The descriptive question is whether (or when) one logic is more likely than the other to be observed as the basis for actual behavior. It is this descriptive question that primarily concerns us here. The two questions are, of course, not entirely separate, either objectively or in the mind of any particular discussant; but this article is addressed primarily to the descriptive value of two specific logics of action in interpreting the history of international orders.

Logic of expected consequences.   Those who see actions as driven by expectations of consequences imagine that human actors choose among alternatives by evaluating their likely consequences for personal or collective objectives, conscious that other actors are doing likewise. A consequential frame sees political order as arising from negotiation among rational actors pursuing personal preferences or interests in circumstances in which there may be gains to coordinated action. Political integration represents a collection of "contracts" negotiated among actors with conflicting interests and varying resources. Whether coordination is achieved and the terms of coordination (for example, who adopts whose system) depend on the bargaining positions of the actors.

In more complicated versions, the actors themselves are coalitions of rational actors and the negotiation goes on at several different levels simultaneously. Within the

32. See March and Olsen 1989; and March 1994a.
33. See Sabine 1952; and Friedrich 1963.
34. Habermas 1996, xi, 8, 26–29.
35. See North 1981; Shepsle 1989; and Coleman 1990.

consequentialist perspective, politics is seen as aggregating individual preferences into collective actions by some procedures of bargaining, negotiation, coalition formation, and exchange.[36] Society is constituted by individuals for the fulfillment of individual ends. The only obligations recognized by individuals are those created through consent and contracts grounded in calculated consequential advantage.

From this perspective, history is seen as the consequence of the interaction of willful actors and is fully understood when it is related to expectations of its consequences and to the interests (preferences) and resources of the actors. Individual actions are "explained" by identifying consequential reasons for them. Foreign policy is "explained" by providing an interpretation of the outcomes expected from it. The behavior of individuals or states is influenced by providing consequential incentives.

The idea that action by individuals, organizations, or states is driven by calculation of its consequences as measured against prior preferences has been subject to numerous criticisms.[37] In particular, presumptions of omniscience in anticipating consequences seem far from descriptive of actual human behavior in actual organized systems.[38] And presumptions of stable, consistent, and exogenous preferences seem to exclude from consideration the many ways in which interests are changing, inconsistent, and endogenous.[39] Theories of bounded rationality and ambiguity have resulted in significant modifications in the classical theory of rational instrumental action;[40] but like the theories they criticize, they assume, for the most part, a logic of consequences.

Theories of consequential calculation tend to ignore problems of exogenous uncertainties by using some variation on an assumption of rational expectations. In some versions, it is assumed that estimates about the future are on average accurate. In other versions, it is assumed that there are differences among actors in their abilities to predict, and competitive pressures eliminate those with lesser abilities until the population is reduced to those with the best abilities.

Similarly, theories of consequential action simplify problems of preference complexity and endogeneity by seeing politics as decomposing complex systems into relatively autonomous subsystems, most commonly by linking them hierarchically. In a hierarchical decomposition, many potential interactions are eliminated, and the problems of preference integration are restricted to relations among hierarchical equals. Thus, an engineering problem can be divided into subproblems, each of which is similarly divided. At each stage in the process, the solution to a prior problem is taken as given. It is a powerful device of problem solving, but one that is known for its failures as well as for its successes.

The equivalent hierarchical organization in international relations involves first integrating the relations of groups of people (for example, nations) and then integrat-

---

36. See Downs 1957; Riker 1962; Coleman 1966; March 1970; Niskanen 1971; and Hechter and Kanazawa 1997.
37. See Elster 1979, 1983; and March 1988, 1994a.
38. See Simon 1955, 1956.
39. See March 1978; and Elster 1986b, 1989c.
40. See March 1992, 1996.

ing across groups—what we have called earlier a "two-stage" conception of order. The constitution of the interests of a nation is taken as established before negotiations among nations begin.[41] Thus, the existence of coherent nations is taken as unproblematic in studying relations among states. However, the assumption of nation-state coherence, like the assumption of hierarchical problem structure, is a heroic one. It has been estimated, for instance, that over the last decades there have been more intrastate than interstate armed conflicts, and more people have been killed in such internal conflicts than have been killed in conflicts between states.[42]

A view of action as driven by expectations of its consequences constitutes the most conventional frame in interpretations of international political life. Stories built around such a frame are readily given credence as prima facie believable. Constructing stories of specific historical events within the frame is made easy by its flexibility in fitting events of the past into such an interpretation and by the familiarity and acceptability of such explanations to political actors. From this point of view, the coherence and significance of the nation-state in international relations is explained as the result of efforts of political actors to find structures favorable to their individual objectives. The major elements of the nation-state are assumed to thrive because they serve the interests of key actors. The interests of political actors come first; the interests of nation-states are derived from them. Within such an interpretation, changes in international institutions are the outcomes of local adaptation by political actors pursuing well-defined interests. For example, it is assumed that the European Union will prosper to the extent to which it increases the efficiency of collective decision making and strengthens national governments.[43]

Logic of appropriateness. Linking action exclusively to a logic of consequences seems to ignore the substantial role of identities, rules, and institutions in shaping human behavior. Within the tradition of a logic of appropriateness, actions are seen as rule-based. Human actors are imagined to follow rules that associate particular identities to particular situations, approaching individual opportunities for action by assessing similarities between current identities and choice dilemmas and more general concepts of self and situations. Action involves evoking an identity or role and matching the obligations of that identity or role to a specific situation. The pursuit of purpose is associated with identities more than with interests, and with the selection of rules more than with individual rational expectations.[44]

Appropriateness need not attend to consequences, but it involves cognitive and ethical dimensions, targets, and aspirations. As a cognitive matter, appropriate action is action that is essential to a particular conception of self. As an ethical matter, appropriate action is action that is virtuous. We "explain" foreign policy as the application of rules associated with particular identities to particular situations. We "explain" behavior by determining the identities that are evoked and the meaning given

41. See Moravcsik 1991, 1993, 1997.
42. See Heldt 1992; Rummel 1994, 1995; Holsti 1996; and Wallensteen and Sollenberg 1997.
43. See Milward 1992; and Moravcsik 1993.
44. See March and Olsen 1989, 1995.

to a situation. We influence behavior by providing alternative interpretations of the self and the situation.

Like the logic of consequences, the logic of appropriateness is explicitly a logic of individual action. It is specified as a mode of action or justification for an individual actor. Thus, it is as individualistic in structure as is the logic of consequences. In practice, however, the two traditions differ in their treatment of the relation between the premises of action and society. Scholars committed to a consequentialist position tend to see an international system of interacting autonomous, egoistic, self-interested maximizers. Preferences are usually taken as given, and expectations of consequences are taken as determined by the state of the external world and the biases (if any) of the individual.

Scholars committed to an identity position, on the other hand, see political actors as acting in accordance with rules and practices that are socially constructed, publicly known, anticipated, and accepted.[45] They portray an international society as a community of rule followers and role players with distinctive sociocultural ties, cultural connections, intersubjective understandings, and senses of belonging. Identities and rules are constitutive as well as regulative and are molded by social interaction and experience.[46]

Relationship between the two logics.   Although there is some tendency for society to be divided into separate spheres, each based primarily on either consequential calculation or rules,[47] the two logics are not mutually exclusive. As a result, political action generally cannot be explained exclusively in terms of a logic of either consequences or appropriateness. Any particular action probably involves elements of each. Political actors are constituted both by their interests, by which they evaluate their expected consequences, and by the rules embedded in their identities and political institutions. They calculate consequences and follow rules, and the relationship between the two is often subtle.

There are four major interpretations of the relationship between the two logics. The first assumes that a clear logic dominates an unclear logic. When preferences and consequences are precise and identities or their rules are ambiguous, a logic of consequences tends to be more important. When identities and their implications are clear but the implications of preferences or expected consequences are not, a logic of appropriateness tends to be more important. In this vein, Geoffrey Garrett and Barry Weingast suggest that ideational factors (such as norms and identities) will be important "the lesser the distributional asymmetries between contending cooperative equilibria and the smaller the disparities in the power resources of actors."[48] The impor-

45. Cerulo 1997.

46. See Ruggie 1983b; Kratochwil and Ruggie 1986; Wendt and Duvall 1989; Young 1989; Thomas et al. 1987; Kratochwil 1989; Buzan 1993; Wendt 1994; Risse-Kappen 1995b; Katzenstein 1996c; Chayes and Chayes 1995; Finnemore 1996a,b; Wæver 1997, 20; Risse 1997; and Hasenclever, Mayer, and Rittberger 1996, 220, 1997.

47. Habermas 1996.

48. Garrett and Weingast 1993, 186.

tance of rules may also increase when the consequences of agreements are unclear or relative capabilities difficult to determine.

The second interpretation distinguishes major decisions from minor refinements of them. The argument is that one logic is used to establish fundamental constraints for a decision, and the other logic is used to make refinements within the constraints. One version of this interpretation associates a logic of consequences with big decisions and a logic of appropriateness with refinements. In this version, rules are "weak causes" of human behavior. In order for institutions to affect macro issues, rather than the minor elaborations of them, decisions have to be shielded from "strong causes" of behavior such as personal interests and known consequences.[49] A second version, as might be expected, reverses the roles of the two logics. Rules are seen as the preconditions of calculation and the unfolding of consequential rationality. Only after important sources of contingency have been resolved by rules are the remaining (relatively minor) contingencies susceptible to resolution by deliberate rational calculation of alternatives.[50]

The third interpretation sees the relation between consequential action and rule-based action as a developmental one. As it is usually discussed, the distinction between consequence-based (instrumental) action and rule-based (identity) action is seen as reflecting a stable difference either among actors or among scholars. Alternatively, suppose that the basis of action changes over time in a predictable way. In particular, suppose that action becomes more rule-based in a specific situation the greater the accumulated experience in that situation. Rules and standard operating procedures supplant and constrain instrumental-calculative action in a given situation as result of experience. Actors enter into new relationships for instrumental reasons but develop identities and rules as a result of their experience, thus shifting increasingly toward rule-based action, which they then pass on to subsequent actors. By this mechanism, instrumental modes of action can be seen to be self-limiting, whereas rule-based modes are seen to be self-reinforcing.

The fourth interpretation sees either logic as a special case of the other.[51] Students of action who are wedded to a logic of consequences, for example, believe that all action is consequential. They picture rules as instruments resulting from prior consequential negotiation.[52] From this point of view, rules and identities are simply devices that minimize transaction costs in the implementation of consequential action. Students of action who are wedded to a logic of appropriateness, on the other hand, assume that all action involves rule following.[53] They see consequential logic and personal interest calculations simply as rules of a particular form that are associated with specific identities and situations.[54]

Despite these interconnections, we believe that the two logics are sufficiently distinct to be viewed as separate explanatory devices. They involve different explana-

49. Stinchcombe 1986, 158.
50. Offe 1996, 682.
51. March 1994a, 101–102.
52. See Coleman 1986; and Shepsle 1990.
53. Searing 1991.
54. See Taylor 1985; and Nauta 1992.

tions for action and different bases for institutional change. This is especially important in the modern era of international relations in which explanations based on a logic of consequences are ubiquitous and explanations based on a logic of appropriateness have been relegated to a considerably less significant role.

Issue 2: Historical Efficiency

The second grand issue that divides students of the dynamics of social and political action and structures is the question of historical efficiency. On the one side are those who see history as following a course that leads inexorably and relatively quickly to a unique equilibrium dictated by exogenously determined interests and resources. On the other side are those who see history as inefficient, as following a meandering path affected by multiple equilibria and endogenous transformations of interests and resources.

Efficient histories.   For those who see history as efficient, the primary postulated mechanism is competition for survival. Political actors compete for resources and primacy, and the resulting equilibrium eliminates actors who fail to achieve optimal resource allocations and strategies. In one version, mutually satisfactory trades are arranged until the system locates a position on the Pareto frontier. The point that is located depends critically on the initial preferences of the actors and on the initial distributions of resources, although it is not uniquely determined by them. In a second version, coercion is used by dominant actors to impose explicit or implicit agreements that are not (in a meaningful sense) voluntary for weaker actors but stem from differences in initial conditions. In both versions, history is determined by, and predictable from, prior conditions of the environment.

Efficient history perspectives see the outcomes of politics, including the dynamics of political order, as implicit in environmental constraints. Competition for survival is seen as compelling social structures to be consistent with environmental conditions. Different environments dictate different orders. Because optimality is required for survival, predicting the equilibrium order does not depend on any specific knowledge about the actors beyond the initial interests and resources that are imposed on them by the environment. The presumption is that political bargains adjust quickly and in a necessary way to exogenous changes, and changes in orders are explained as stemming from exogenous changes in interests and resources. As a consequence, there is little independent role for institutions. Institutions are simply products of a history that is exogenously determined.

Inefficient histories.   Those who see history as inefficient emphasize the slow pace of historical adaptation relative to the rate of environmental change, thus the low likelihood of reaching an equilibrium. Even more, they emphasize the existence of multiple equilibria and internal dynamics that make it difficult to escape local optima. Thus, a view of history as inefficient portrays the match between political institutions and their environments as less automatic, less continuous, and less precise than does a view of history as efficient. The pressures of survival are sporadic rather than constant, crude rather than precise, and environments vary in the extent to which they dictate outcomes. Institutions and identities are pictured as sometimes enduring in the face of apparent inconsistency with their environments, sometimes collapsing without obvious external cause. In short, neither competitive pressures nor current conditions uniquely determine institutional options or outcomes.[55] There are lags in matching an environment, multiple equilibria, path dependencies, and interconnected networks for the diffusion of forms and practices.

In such a world, institutional development depends not only on satisfying current environmental and political conditions but also on an institution's origin, history, and internal dynamics.[56] Inefficient history perspectives also place more emphasis on the interactive effects of an ecology of interacting locally adaptive actors. Consider in this regard the tradition of models of majority voting by rational actor citizens. A common focus of such studies is the way in which majority voting schemes lead to outcomes not uniquely determined by prior conditions but also dependent on procedural or institutional factors (for example, the order of voting on alternatives). In that spirit, for example, simple economic and majority vote models have been used to show how the institutions and procedures of a democratic political process might fail to achieve a system of nation-states and boundaries among them that is uniquely implicit in economic exchange considerations.[57]

Environments adapt to institutions at the same time as institutions adapt to environments. Institutions and their linkages coevolve. They are intertwined in ecologies of competition, cooperation, and other forms of interaction. Furthermore, institutions are nested, so that some adapting institutions are integral parts of other adapting institutions. Finally, ideas of inefficient history place a greater emphasis on the ways in which the unfolding results of history transform the premises of action. Identities, resources, values, norms, and rules guide action, but they are simultaneously shaped by the course of history.[58] From this point of view, individual identities and preferences are both premises of politics and products of it,[59] and the development of competencies makes institutions robust against external pressures for change. These features of action and its outcomes form a foundation for a variety of quite different stable equilibria.

The complications tend to convert history into a meander.[60] Rules and institutions become locally stable. Historical branches tend to be irreversible. The direction taken at any particular branch sometimes seems almost chancelike and subject to minor intentions, but the specific direction taken can be decisive in its effect on subsequent history.[61] As a result, the course of history can sometimes be changed by relatively

55. See North 1981, 1990.
56. See Berman 1983; March and Olsen 1989, 1996; and Olsen 1992.
57. See Alesina and Spolaore 1997; and Bolton and Roland 1997.
58. March 1994b.
59. Sandel 1982, 1984.
60. March 1994b.
61. See Brady 1988; and Lipset 1990.

small, timely interventions. The ability to create change, however, does not guarantee either that any arbitrary change can be made at any time, that changes will turn out to be consistent with prior intentions or interests,[62] or that the outcomes will be stable.

Four Perspectives

These two issues of the logic of action and the efficiency of history divide studies (and to a lesser extent students) of international political dynamics into four relatively distinct groups. The first group of studies emphasizes a view of action based on a logic of consequences and a view of history as efficient (upper-left quadrant of Figure 1). This is the most common perspective in international political studies. Scholars in this group see history as resulting from interactions among consequentialist individuals, groups, organizations, or states, each seeking to realize as much as possible in terms of individual preferences but collectively confronting the fact that not everyone can have everything desired. In the resulting conflict, negotiation, warfare, and debate, outcomes are largely implicit in the environmental conditions that produce them.

This group comprises a number of somewhat different categories of studies. For example, studies by neoliberal institutionalists define international institutions and regimes as stemming from attempts by individual actors to achieve control and counteract the inadequacy of their own resources. Fluctuations in the number or strength of international institutions and regimes reflect the calculations of self-interested actors (primarily states) trying to resolve collective-action problems and gain efficiency through voluntary exchanges, contracts, and treaties. Outcomes depend on the ability to find and implement Pareto improvements, counteract market failures, reduce transaction costs, and overcome conflicts of interest. A core question is how alternative institutions and regimes affect the chances of discovering mutual benefits.[63]

On the other hand, studies by realists portray states as less concerned with Pareto improvements and more concerned with clashing interests, strategic interaction, alliances, coercion, relative power, distributional aspects, and relative gains. States are the important actors, and international institutions are less likely and less important. Because such elements of order reflect the interests of powerful states, they are more likely when power is concentrated in the international system—for instance, when a hegemon or a stable coalition of dominant powers sees an institutional arrangement as maintaining or increasing the ability to exercise power. Changes in order result from changing powers and material capabilities.[64]

While studies in the (neo)liberal institutional tradition and the (neo)realist tradition are often characterized as being in opposition, their differences are relatively

---

62. See March 1981; and Rothstein 1992.
63. See Keohane 1983a, 1984; Stein 1983; and Young 1996.
64. See Strange 1983; Grieco 1988; Keohane 1989b, 8; Mearsheimer 1994, 7, 13; Stone 1994, 449; and Krasner 1995a, 115.

Assumed logic of action

		Logic of consequences	Logic of appropriateness
Conception of history	*Efficient history*	Functional rationality	Functional institutionalism
	Inefficient history	History-dependent rationality	History-dependent institutionalism

FIGURE 1. *Four-fold division of perspectives on the dynamics of international political order*

narrow. They place different emphases on the role of voluntary exchange and dominance, and they specify utility functions differently, that is, the relative importance of absolute and relative gains.[65] They also locate rationality at a different level. The realist assumption of states as unitary actors is different from the neoliberalist assumption of rational individuals calculating the personal benefits of alternative memberships and policies.

Nevertheless, the two approaches share consequentialist assumptions about action and conceptions of history as efficient. Both traditions account for changes in the international order by describing calculating egoists acting in a history-free world. Actors are opportunistic and always look for individual advantage. They never honor contracts out of a sense of obligation. There are no intrinsically valuable forms of association and cohesion.[66] And although there is some recognition of a possible role of institutions in creating the preference functions of egoists,[67] for the most part, the creation of preferences and interests is seen as exogenous to the politics they affect.

The second group of studies emphasizes a view of action based on a logic of consequences but within an inefficient historical process (lower-left quadrant of Figure 1). This group includes many economic and evolutionary studies of search and local feedback.[68] Outcomes of actions taken at one time depend on factors of attention allocation and probabilistic interaction that are not predictable from environmental conditions. Those outcomes, however, determine subsequent paths of history in a way that makes a consequential history path dependent. In addition, interests and resources evolve from the outcomes of history. The premises of history are not fixed but coevolve with their consequences.

65. See Hasenclever, Mayer, and Rittberger 1996, 196, 202, 205, and 1997; and Wæver 1997, 19.
66. Lake 1996, 12, 13.
67. Keohane 1989a, 6.
68. See North 1981, 1990; and Arthur 1989.

The third group of studies emphasizes a view of action based on a logic of appropriateness and history as efficient (upper-right quadrant of Figure 1). This group includes many works by institutional economists and some by institutional sociologists.[69] For them, action is rule-based. Institutions and norms are important. Individual actors seek to fulfill their identities. However, the rules, norms, identities, organizational forms, and institutions that exist are the inexorable products of an efficient history. The principles are the principles of comparative statics. Surviving institutions are seen as uniquely fit to the environment, thus predictable from that environment.

The fourth group includes those studies that emphasize a view of action based on a logic of appropriateness but see history as inefficient (lower-right quadrant of Figure 1). Much of the time, our own work is located within this group.[70] So also is the work of evolutionary economists who emphasize the process of evolution rather than any necessary outcome.[71] The rules, norms, institutions, and identities that drive human action are seen as developing in a way that cannot be predicted from prior environmental conditions. They coevolve with the worlds in which they act. They are subject to local positive feedback that traps them at local optima. Rules are understandable only by understanding their histories.

Studies of international political orders draw from all four of these scholarly traditions to make sense of international organizations and politics, but they do not draw equally from each. The overwhelming inclination of interpreters of international politics is to favor consequentialist, efficient history accounts over accounts that emphasize appropriateness and inefficient histories. This preference is hard to justify strictly from historical observations. Any of the interpretations can claim a certain amount of confirmation in the historical record, but none is unambiguously dominant over the others on that basis. It is not obvious that any one approach is superior to the others in capturing the complexities of change. There are several stories to be told and a necessary humility associated with the telling of any one of them.

Given, however, that recent efforts to understand political orders have emphasized consequential action and efficient histories, either jointly (the upper-left quadrant of Figure 1) or individually (the lower-left and upper-right quadrants), we believe a perspective based on the lower-right quadrant may be useful in identifying otherwise overlooked or underestimated phenomena. Consequently, in this article we emphasize the perspective of the fourth group of studies. We examine some aspects of the inefficient historical processes by which identities, rules, resources, capabilities, and institutions of international political orders develop over time. The approach is not remarkable and provides no extraordinary magic of interpretation, but it may not be entirely foolish.

69. See Meyer 1980; Thomas et al. 1987; Finnemore 1996a,b; and Jepperson, Wendt, and Katzenstein 1996.
70. See March and Olsen 1989, 1994, 1995, 1996.
71. Nelson and Winter 1982.

Coevolution of Politics and Institutions

If history were efficient, political practice would adjust immediately and uniquely to current, exogenously determined desires and capabilities. We have argued that history is not efficient in that sense; that, indeed, institutions are relatively robust against environmental change or deliberate reform and that desires and capabilities coevolve with the practices that reflect them. As a result, history is path dependent in the sense that the character of current institutions depends not only on current conditions but also on the historical path of institutional development.

Change and stability are linked to definitions and redefinitions of the self and the situation. Those definitions are partly the result of deliberate policies adopted by existing authorities. Our interest, however, is more in the consequences of the ordinary course of political history as individuals, groups, and states act with only incidental concern for grand issues of international organization. Identities and competencies are shaped by political activities and interactions. They arise partly in the context of politics and become embedded in rules, practices, beliefs, and institutions. As illustrations, we consider two mechanisms of historical path dependence in the evolution of political order. The effect of engagement in political activities on the shaping of identities and the effect of engagement on the development of competence and capability.

Illustration 1: Engagement and the Development of Identities

Students of international politics tell three different exaggerated stories about the effects of political interaction on the premises of politics. In story 1 political identities arise in ways unconnected to political life. They are social products of broader cultures of belief that are beyond the reach of politics.[72] Sociocultural bonds, preferences, identities, internalized principles, codes of appropriate behavior, and political resources are all important, but they are formed outside of politics and prior to political interaction.[73]

In story 2, in contrast, political actors are pictured as malleable within politics. The emergence, development, and spread of understandings, identities, interests, and institutions are shaped by interaction and involvement in political activities.[74] Interdependence, interaction, and communication lead to shared experiences and hence to shared meaning, to a convergence of expectations and policies, and to the development of common institutions. As a result of either calculated strategy, learning, or socialization, actors are induced to act differently from the way they would act in

---

72. Cerulo 1997.

73. This mainstream view is discussed and criticized by Wendt 1992, 1994; Risse-Kappen 1996a,b; Buzan 1996; and Wæver 1997. See also Mayer, Rittberger, and Zürn 1995, 424; and Hasenclever, Mayer, and Rittberger 1996, 181, 184.

74. See Mayer, Rittberger, and Zürn 1995; Hasenclever, Meyer, and Rittberger 1996, 211; and Wendt 1992, 1994.

one-time encounters.[75] Long-term contacts create habits of working together, friend-ships, group loyalties, and knowledge about others. They create convergence, mutual confidence, and positive trust spirals.[76] They alter political competencies, augment-ing skills at political compromise.

In story 3, as in story 2 but not in story 1, political actors are seen as created by their political interactions, but contact is portrayed as exacerbating international dif-ferences. Contact contributes to exposing and sharpening differences rather than elimi-nating them and to reinforcing antagonisms, contradictory world views, and stereo-types rather than extinguishing them.[77] Whereas ignorance of differences allows cooperation, knowledge of those differences stimulates actions that accentuate them and encourage hostility. Whereas inexperience in international political relations makes political actors cautious about political adventures, experience breeds risky adven-tures justified by a sense of competence and control. In this view, extensive political involvement, contact, and experience do not facilitate understanding, but rather make conflict more likely.

The mechanisms involved in each of the three stories are well-established ones. The outcomes of each are easily imaginable, and history provides numerous occa-sions interpretable as consistent with any of them. Each of the stories clearly captures part of observed histories. In particular, we think it is clear that story 2 describes a significant mechanism involved in the development of international orders. The idea that contact and involvement in joint political activities among the individuals of different states will lead to a more stable and inclusive political order needs to be qualified in significant ways to fit history; but understandings, identities, interests, and institutions can mold the behaviors of political actors and through them the outcomes of politics. The nation-state secures much of its coherence from a sense of belonging among citizens that translates into a set of obligations of citizenship. Indi-viduals within a state are sometimes capable of empathy, confidence, trust, goodwill, shared norms, and bonds of cohesion, that is, "civicness" or "social capital."[78] Nation-states secure their legitimacy and permanence from shared conceptions of an orderly rule-based life.[79]

Creating international identities deliberately.   Some proponents of international order believe that the processes that sustain national civic identities and thereby reconstitute nation-states can be used deliberately to create some kind of interna-tional civic identity. Advocates of the European Union have argued that a common market and federal legal order were "not sufficient to bind the member states and the peoples of Europe together as the EU began to impinge on key attributes of state authority."[80] Europeans are invited to "imagine" a number of different "Europes,"

75. See Axelrod 1984; Buzan 1993, 349; Mayer, Rittberger, and Zürn 1995, 394.
76. See Slaughter 1995, 530; and Tonra 1996.
77. Allport 1954.
78. Putnam 1993.
79. See Habermas 1996, 139; and Eriksen and Weigård 1997.
80. Laffan 1997a, 4.

to remember some identities and common ties, and to forget identities that tend to create cleavages and conflicts.[81] This emphasis on the importance of a European identity and constitutive belongings tends to be paired with a view of communication, joint reasoning, and argumentation as necessary conditions for international cooperation, civilized conflict resolution, and political order.[82] Hopes for such a transformation are buoyed by the observation that even if genuine identity-related discourse is rare in world politics,[83] pockets of such discourse can be found, for instance, around themes like human rights[84] and environmental sustainability.[85]

Enthusiasm for achieving new identities through political engagement cannot entirely negate either the pessimism about the political molding of human identities that typifies story 1 or the dangers of interaction highlighted by story 3. There are ample grounds for caution in anticipating a sudden burst of global definitions of self. The difficulties involved in trying to develop a European identity, citizenship, and culture deliberately are manifest. Attempts by EU authorities to use cultural and media policies to construct collective identities and a common European communicative space confront highly diverse and conflicting existing identities and allegiances.[86]

The world views, values, desires, commitments, and capabilities necessary for more inclusive political orders can be quite inaccessible to political experience and learning, but an elementary fact of the past two hundred years is that humans have civilized their lives within the nation-state context by developing institutions and rules that regulate their relations. They have created identities that often restrain passions and interests, inducing individuals to follow rules of conduct that are both taken for granted and oriented to collective obligations.[87] Whether a similar program can accomplish a similar integration at an international level is certainly in doubt, but when organizations such as the OECD call attention to differences between "leaders" and "laggards" among countries in terms of their willingness and ability to adopt what is defined as a modern, democratic, and economically efficient public sector, they modify the reference groups of national bureaucrats, their aspirations, and their behavior.[88]

Creating international identities unintentionally. The mechanisms of education, socialization, and participation that develop, maintain, and undermine shared identities are obviously more weakly developed at the international level than within individual nation-states.[89] That situation will not change quickly, but it can change

81. Schlesinger 1991, 178, 182.
82. Risse 1997.
83. Risse 1997, 19.
84. Eide and Hagtvet 1992.
85. World Commission 1987.
86. See Schlesinger 1993, 1994.
87. Elias [1939] 1994.
88. Olsen 1997b.
89. See Krasner 1995a, 117; and March and Olsen 1996, 259.

gradually without much in the way of conscious intention.[90] To explore how this might happen, consider two mechanisms that contribute to making international institutions and identities imaginable:

First, it is possible that international identities will evolve from a "spillover" of domestic democratic orientations and identities into international politics. The tendency of democratic states to deviate from strictly consequentialist international actions has been noted by students of international relations. Scholars have observed that democracies rarely go to war against each other.[91] In bilateral relations, democracies appear generally to treat each other in a somewhat more rule-based manner than do nondemocratic regimes. Rules of appropriateness are sometimes followed even in critical cases of societies living on "the security knife-edge."[92] For example, the (Norwegian, not British) historian Odd-Bjørn Fure observes that in a war involving an existential struggle, Britain refrained in 1940 from using its sea power against German transportation of iron ore from Northern Norway in Norwegian waters. Such attacks were seen to be against international law, and British authorities apparently acted less from a calculation of military or political consequences than out of concern for what could legitimately be done in international affairs. Fure also observes that similar concerns inhibited Britain from using force in disputes with Norway over sea territory and fishing rights in 1933–36.[93]

Moreover, although they also often calculate consequences, democratic states are likely to import democratic norms and decision-making rules into international encounters, for example, norms of transparency, consultation, and compromise. Since such internal norms and rules tend to be shared among democratic states, their generalization to international relations is unsurprising, although hardly assured in all instances. In turn, experience with shared rules facilitates the development of rule-based international institutions and makes the creation of a collective identity more likely.[94] At the same time, democratic norms are contagious. They spread through international contact to countries with less secure democratic traditions. For example, participation in the EU has been portrayed as contributing to the construction not only of a European identity but also of a domestic democratic political identity in countries such as Greece and Spain.[95]

In these ways, rule-based versions of democratic identities and action, negotiation, and collective behavior have been extended to international institutions. The extension is, however, neither reliable nor assured for the future. In addition to the complications already noted, it should be observed that the idea of political institutions based on democratic rules has been somewhat eroded in modern market-based societies by conceptions that place greater emphasis on consequence-based action and

---

90. See Wendt and Duvall 1989; Buzan 1996, 59; and Wæver 1997, 10.
91. See Doyle 1983a,b; and Gleditsch 1992. This phenomenon, as one might expect, has also been given an interest-based, consequential interpretation. See S. Chan 1997; and McMillan 1997.
92. Keohane 1996a, 470.
93. Fure 1996, 247, 349.
94. See Slaughter 1995; and Risse-Kappen 1996b, 397, 399.
95. See Pérez-Díaz 1993; and Katzenstein 1996c, 520.

market exchange mechanisms for collective choice, that is, by introducing into politics the basic rules and practices of markets. Thus, the spillover of democratic political identities from domestic politics to international politics is counterbalanced by the spillover of individualistic identities of competitive self-interest in the other direction.

Second, international identities may evolve from the practice of expert cooperation around specific tasks. The tension between expertise and politics has been a familiar theme of democratic political theory since the days of the Greek city-state. Those discussions are primarily concerned with the difficulties that expertise and specialized knowledge create for democratic control over public policy and the difficulties that democratic control create for intelligent use of expertise. Those issues remain in the international sphere, along with the difficulties of defining boundaries between expert and lay domains. Partly because modern democratic processes are primarily organized around and within the nation-state, international political issues tend to be defined as issues of nation-state interests, bargaining, negotiation, and conflict. Some issues are, however, defined as "nonpolitical" in the sense that national interests are not treated as overwhelmingly compelling. In particular, "modernization" emphasizes notions of instrumental performance and efficiency, rather than local traditions or interests. Such issues allow more room for experts, technical considerations, and professionalism. The boundary shifts with changing political pressures, but there is always a domain for expertise and technical problem solving, and this domain tends to be organized along transnational lines.

Concepts of expertise stimulate associations and collaborations that recognize national boundaries but tend to subordinate them to shared professional concerns. These "epistemic communities"[96] and international networks of experts and bureaucrats define problems, construct conceptions of causal knowledge, and create frames for action that integrate across nation-states.[97] Their activities and associations lead to bonds that can develop into international identities. Concepts and codes of appropriate behavior, traditionally the province of local schools and civic education, become a product of international contact, institutions, allegiances, and organizations. As international identities and contacts among experts become more dense and specialized, these linkages contribute to definitions of problems as international in scope and of identities and meaning as cutting across state boundaries.

This mutual reinforcement of associations, identities, and perceptions of problems leads to an elaboration of international connections, making them more pervasive, more overlapping, and more embedded in definitions of expertise.[98] The process can be described simply: stage 1: "non-political," technical issues create occasions for participation across borders; stage 2: frequent and long-term participation in discussing technical issues fosters more general familiarity, shared identities, and mutual trust; stage 3: trust, shared identities, and familiarity encourage further contact, fur-

96. Haas 1992a.
97. Hill and Wallace 1996, 11.
98. Young 1996, 1, 20.

ther integration, an expansion of the number of topics viewed as appropriate for discussion and the development of common definitions of problems and appropriate actions.[99]

The resulting order is characterized by functional networks of people often organized around representatives of "sister-institutions," like central banks, professional associations, courts, and bureaucracies operating at the national and international decision-making levels.[100] This pattern of organization stimulates and supports new transnational identities. This suggests that the institutions of expertise associated with the World Bank, UNESCO, OECD, the EU, and other similar organizations have to be seen as creators of meaning in general and more specifically of identities.[101] That is, they are not only decision-making institutions but also institutions for socializing individuals and creating meaning and for promoting specific concepts of the nature and role of the state, markets, human rights, and international organizations.

Illustration 2: Engagement and the Development of Capabilities

Political actors accumulate experience with existing institutions, practices, and rules as they try to track and adapt to their environments and to changes in them. Capabilities for using institutions, practices, and rules are refined through mundane processes of learning, interpretation, reasoning, education, imitation, and adaptation. As a result, involvement in political activities not only changes identities. It also builds and directs political capabilities.

Competency traps and multiple equilibria.   Political arrangements become more efficient as the rules are refined and as actors become more competent in operating within them. Efficiency, however, easily becomes the enemy of adaptiveness. As particular rules are used repeatedly, political actors become more familiar with them and more competent operating within them, thus encouraging their further use. This local positive feedback[102] produces what has been called a competency trap—the tendency for a system to become firmly locked into a particular rule-based structure by virtue of developing familiarity with the rules and capabilities for using them.[103] These refined capabilities strengthen a system in the short run and make it resistant to change. By developing competence with rules, institutions stabilize their norms, rules, meanings, and resources so that many different procedures can exhibit surprising durability.[104]

The accelerating development of competence with particular institutional arrangements and practices is a major feature of institutional history and is one of the more

---

99. Haas 1958.
100. See Egeberg and Trondal 1997; and Joerges, Ladeur, and Vos 1997.
101. See Finnemore 1993, 1996a,b; and Olsen 1997b.
102. See Arthur 1989.
103. See Levitt and March 1988; and March 1991.
104. See Stinchcombe 1965; and Starbuck, Greve, and Hedberg 1978.

obvious reasons why history is path dependent. The local optima produced by competence elaboration are resistant to new opportunities. For that reason, they are also potential precursors to long-run obsolescence[105] and to the discontinuous, contested, and problematic change[106] associated with "punctuated equilibria,"[107] "critical junctions,"[108] and "performance crises."[109]

The competency trap is a variation on a standard problem in adaptation: The exploitation and refinement of known technologies, practices, and rules tend to drive out the exploration of possible new ones. As competence grows with established rules and practices, the disadvantage of new rules and practices increases. As that disadvantage increases, experiments with new rules are decreased. And as experiments with new rules decrease, the chance of finding a good new alternative or gaining competence on one that might be superior becomes smaller.

Social, economic, and political systems are all prone to competency traps and to at least moderate jerkiness in fundamental transformations. They typically have difficulty sustaining experimentation. From any immediate perspective, this is not because they are stupidly rigid, but because they are intelligently efficient. For them to pursue new alternatives makes little apparent sense. The returns to exploration tend to be less certain and less immediate than the returns to exploitation. They also tend to be more distant, less localized in their realization to the immediate organizational neighborhood of the exploration. This is partly because new ideas tend to be poor ones, and it is partly because even good new ideas have returns that are more distant in time and space than those realized from current ideas. It is not easy for an organization to justify experimentation that, at least in the short run, does not make sense in terms of immediate local return. What is required is a willingness to engage in experimentation that is unlikely to succeed and particularly unlikely to be rewarding in the temporal and spatial neighborhood of the experiment. Unfortunately, although too little experimentation is likely to be disastrous in the longer run, too much experimentation is likely to be disastrous immediately.

Few organizations do well with the problems associated with balancing exploitation and exploration,[110] and there is little reason to think that international organizations will be particularly clever about it. There is an obvious difficulty in producing a requisite level of exploration in an organizational world dedicated to responding to short-run feedback or maximizing local expected return. It seems very likely that rather little of the experimentation in international organization occurs because of a conscious organizational intent to experiment. It occurs because of identities associated with experimentation, because of conflict, because of ideologies of experimentation, and as an unintended byproduct of instrumental action.[111] For example, some

105. Levinthal and March 1993.
106. See Skowronek 1982; and Orren and Skowronek 1994.
107. Krasner 1984.
108. Collier and Collier 1991.
109. March and Olsen 1989.
110. Levinthal and March 1993.
111. March 1994a, 40–54.

scholars have argued that core democratic identities require that citizens have a "hypothetical attitude" toward existing institutions and forms of life and should seek to restructure the institutions, rules, and manners of living together.[112] This tendency to legitimize change introduces a bias that often seems perverse in the way it overturns functioning practices. For example, democratic politics is sometimes an annoyance to experts in law, who seek coherent and unified legal hierarchies of norms and values.[113] To a limited extent, however, a bias for change is a way by which democracy becomes a source of experimentation in political relations,[114] making continuous processes of integration, disintegration, and reintegration more likely and less dependent on external pressures alone.

Not surprisingly, institutions are particularly likely to be changed when they are seen to fail. On the whole, people are less likely to follow institutional rules if they believe that the rules produce poor results.[115] If institutions miss their targets or aspiration levels, the failure creates a loss of confidence in existing rules and a search for new alternatives.[116] Since experience frequently improves performance, failure would not produce much experimentation in a highly competent system were it not for the fact that definitions of "success" and "failure" are notoriously subject to updating of aspirations, bias, and noise. If success and failure were reliably determined, the development of competence would make institutions more stable than they are. Unreliability in assessment of success and the insatiable character of aspirations are quite likely to lead political institutions to experiment at the right time for the wrong reasons.

Competence and the transformation of objectives.   The development of competence in the service of existing institutions and objectives is primarily a stabilizing force. But it also creates foundations for new institutions and new objectives. Organizations not only become better and better at what they do, they also see new things to do. Having the capability of doing new things leads, in turn, to seeing their desirability. Capabilities stimulate recognition of the salience of problems to which they can provide solutions.[117] By transforming capabilities, therefore, competence transforms agendas and goals.

Of particular relevance to present concerns is the way competence is developed in the context of concrete activities and then becomes the basis for expansion of objectives to a wider range of concerns. In their early stages, European states developed competencies as an artifact of solving immediate practical problems and taking care of local interests. Those competencies gradually were transformed into institutions and political practices that used them. Nation-state builders started with instrumental motives, such as winning a war or collecting taxes; over time they discovered that

112. Habermas 1996, 468.
113. Stone 1994, 442.
114. Shapiro and Hardin 1996, 5–6.
115. Stinchcombe 1986, 166.
116. Cyert and March 1963.
117. See Cyert and March 1963; and Cohen, March, and Olsen 1972.

they had built the foundations for strongly institutionalized states.[118] In a similar way, the development of military and economic competencies and institutions using them poses a persistent threat to nonmilitary and noneconomic political institutions. The existence of capabilities is converted into an inclination to discover goals the abilities might serve, perhaps in competition with the political system. Thus, the elaboration of tasks is as much a consequence of competence as a cause of it.

The EU has numerous arenas for interaction, argumentation, and collective problem solving and conflict resolution for bureaucrats, experts, representatives of organized interests, and elected politicians. The process of *engrenage* exposes participants to new arguments, new perspectives, and new identities.[119] More importantly perhaps, it develops capabilities for mutual engagement. Considerable experience with acting together is accumulated, and a significant amount of mutual influence between the EU and domestic institutions and actors is taking place, with no clear-cut borderline between the "national" and the "European."[120] The number of meetings in the context of the EU, together with meetings in the context of other international institutions, during some periods actually make ministers, bureaucrats, and experts interact as much with colleagues from other countries as with their domestic colleagues.[121]

The changes these contacts have produced were neither particularly well anticipated by, nor the result of the will of, any easily identifiable group of political actors.[122] The elaboration of international capabilities is part of a long historical transformation of the West European state, reflecting as well as contributing to the erosion of state autonomy.[123] That transformation continues, and predicting the direction it will take is not easy. For example, the EU is still an unsettled constitutional order, in terms of geographical reach, institutional balance, decision rules, and functional scope. Efforts to deepen European integration and create a European polity, or even society, are balanced against nation-states protecting their autonomy and the potential fragmentary tendencies of enlargement of the EU.[124] Even within expert domains, there are conditions that encourage a balkanization of expertise. Developments occur through learning in small (though not always consistent) ways in many places.

The resulting institutional structure more closely resembles a marble cake than a hierarchy,[125] but it is not the same as it used to be. Involvements in highly instrumental and technical activities in the EU have created organizational capabilities for international collaboration that translate into a more general international institution and make more elaborate international coordination possible. The EU has become the most highly institutionalized international organization in history, in terms of

---

118. Tilly 1975.
119. See Hill and Wallace 1996, 1; Rometsch and Wessels 1996; and Laffan 1997b, 9.
120. See Rometsch and Wessels 1996, 329; and Jachtenfuchs and Kohler-Koch 1996.
121. See Wessels 1990; and Hill and Wallace 1996, 7, 11.
122. Stone 1994, 425.
123. See Flora 1983; and Wessels 1997, 22–24.
124. Laffan 1997a.
125. Jachtenfuchs and Kohler-Koch 1996.

depth as well as breadth, yet without becoming a federal state.[126] Participation in the EU has, indeed, altered the nation-state itself. For example, EU citizens and corporations can, and do, invoke EU law against other individuals and their national governments. The Europeanization of law and the increased significance of norms in international politics[127] clearly have compromised the identity of territory and authority[128] in ways that owe much to the gradual accumulation of experience and the resulting gains in competence.

A Different Emphasis

The two examples illustrate some differences between a perspective (which we have called an institutional perspective) that assumes identity-based action and inefficient history and a more conventional perspective that attributes action to calculations of consequences and environmental constraints. The latter interprets changes in an international political order primarily in terms of exogenously specified interests and capabilities, rational actors, expectations of consequences, and environmental pressures. The former sees changes in a political order more as involving the construction and evocation of rules, institutions, and identities, the development of capabilities, and the path-dependent meanders of an inefficient history.

The illustrations are drawn from a universe that includes others, but they are not randomly drawn from that universe. Although the illustrations themselves are brief and incomplete, they are chosen not only to exemplify institutional modes of thinking in general but also to identify two of the more important specific contributions to the study of international relations that might be drawn from institutional perspectives. Understanding the ways in which political identities, rules, and capabilities evolve within a political order and the ways in which the evolution of identities, rules, and capabilities serves to create, sustain, or corrupt an order may be important to understanding histories of international political order.

Conclusion

The historical processes by which international political orders develop are complex enough to make any simple theory of them unsatisfactory. An interconnected and interdependent world produces histories in which changes in environmental conditions are not automatically or unambiguously reflected in changing political orders and institutional arrangements. Nor is it possible to describe the evolution of international political orders in terms of any simple notions of intentionality and design at the nation-state level. History is created by a complicated ecology of local events and locally adaptive actions. As individuals, groups, organizations, and institutions seek

126. See Hill and Wallace 1996, 12; Haas 1967, 331; Keohane 1996a, 467; and Laffan 1997b.
127. Stone 1994, 473.
128. Krasner 1995a, 134.

to act intelligently and learn in a changing world involving others similarly trying to adapt, they create connections that subordinate individual intentions to their interactions. The locally adaptive actions that constitute that ecology are themselves based on subtle intertwinings of rational action based on expectations of consequences and rule-based action seeking to fulfill identities within environments that influence but do not uniquely dictate actions. Expectations, preferences, identities, and meanings are affected by human interaction and experience. They coevolve with the actions they produce.

Such ideas do not encourage aspirations for applying standard experimental design or hypothesis testing in conventional form to the naturally occurring histories of international relations. Nor do they provide justification for expecting to predict specific events such as the end of the Cold War, the fall of the Wall, the ebbs and flows of European integration, or the renewed strength of ethnic nationalism. The study of international relations, like much of social science, is a branch of history, and the history of history discourages grandiose predictive hopes. Historical interpretations of the development of international orders are made difficult by the necessity of learning from small samples of uncontrolled conditions.

We accept the implications of that difficulty and thus the implausibility of proclaiming a bold new direction built on institutional representations of international political orders. Nevertheless, we think it may be useful to consider conceptions of history that build on the lower right-hand quadrant of Figure 1, supplementing ideas of consequential action, exogenous preferences, and efficient histories with ideas of rule- and identity-based action, inefficient histories, and institutional robustness. Used to interpret careful historical observations and descriptions of behavior and events, such a perspective provides a basis for intelligent compromises between simple renderings of history that are inconsistent with reality and complex renderings that are inconsistent with human capacities for comprehension.

Realism in the Study of World Politics

Robert Jervis

Fifty years of *International Organization* encompass both accomplishments and disappointments, as does this period of international history. The articles in this issue of *IO*, especially *"International Organization* and the Study of World Politics" by Peter J. Katzenstein, Robert O. Keohane, and Stephen D. Krasner, also give us a lot to think about, learn from, and criticize. I will not attempt a full review but, as befitting a commentator, will concentrate on questions that the other authors have downplayed or that I would pose or answer somewhat differently, perhaps because of my greater familiarity with the work in security studies than in international political economy (IPE), a field in which *IO* and most of the authors in this issue specialize.[1]

I begin by discussing some determinants of the fates of schools of thought and research programs, noting the relationships between scholarship and contemporary international politics. I then turn to the theme presented by Katzenstein, Keohane, and Krasner that rationalism and constructivism will be the two points of contestation in the coming years, which will lead into my claims for the continuing relevance of realism. In closing, I will comment on the field of IPE, about which the other authors in this issue have said surprisingly little.

Research Programs, Knowledge, and Politics

If the discipline is functioning well, each school of thought enriches others as powerful research of one kind strengthens, not weakens, the alternatives. No one approach

I am grateful for comments by Richard Betts, Judith Goldstein, Peter Katzenstein, Robert Keohane, Stephen Krasner, Helen Milner, Jack Snyder, and Arthur Stein.

1. Another good review concentrating on IPE broadly conceived is Kahler 1997. I should also join Katzenstein, Keohane, and Krasner and Wæver (articles in this issue) in noting that although our subject is international politics, the relevant community of scholars is almost entirely American, with a few contributors from the rest of the English-speaking world. We do not know the impact of this condition, but I suspect it is considerable. To take just one example, the fact that during the Cold War American security scholarship was centered more on realism than was European is not likely to have been unrelated to the different roles and policies of the United States and West Europe. For earlier discussions of different national scholarly perspectives, see Hoffmann 1977; Strange 1983; Alker and Biersteker 1984; and Holsti 1985.

consistently maintains a leading position: each of them catches important elements of international politics, and many of our arguments are about the relative importance of and the interrelationships among various factors. Thus, in their article in this issue, Katzenstein, Keohane, and Krasner usefully point to the dialectical nature of social science. Popular approaches inevitably are taken too far and call up opposing lines of argument; and if any important approach is ignored for too long, scholars will return to it as the picture of international politics becomes excessively imbalanced.[2]

Although it is easy to see that various kinds of research wax and wane, explaining the pattern is more difficult. Indeed, there is an element of circularity in determining what constitutes a successful research program. In the absence of some external and arguably objective measure, a research program succeeds when many scholars adopt it. Without claiming that initial incidents set off positive feedback to such an extent that success is accidental or arbitrary, we should not assume that those approaches currently most popular necessarily tell us more about international politics than do alternative approaches. Determining which research programs are "progressive" and which are "degenerating" is difficult because the relevant judgments are influenced by our perspectives and interests (in both senses of the term) and because all theories undergo change in light of empirical investigations.[3] Thus, though I would not dissent from the consensus that the democratic peace has been an extraordinarily fruitful area of scholarship, there are grounds for arguing that we have learned relatively little since the original investigations. Many of the findings hinge on definitions, debatable codings affect the results, the causal mechanisms remain unclear and have not proved readily amenable to empirical research, and it is questionable whether additional phenomena, such as the purported tendency of democracies to resolve differences short of war, can be fit under the same theoretical umbrella.

The other side of this coin is that the failure of a research program may not be primarily attributable to its lack of potential. For example, although I join many others in believing that there are great limitations to the utility of bureaucratic politics analysis because it is difficult to specify ex ante the actors' preferences and even harder to say what outcome is likely to emerge from the posited pushing and hauling among the diverse bureaucratic interests, these failings are hardly unique to this approach. Can one argue that bureaucratic politics yields fewer testable propositions than constructivism, for example? Thus, I would not dismiss four other sources of the approach's current lack of popularity. First, it resonates with, and indeed partly was developed by, those who had been in the government. As the political science discipline has separated from the practice of politics, fewer people move back and forth between the academy and the government, thereby reducing the ranks of those who are likely to produce this kind of work or find it intellectually satisfying. Second, the

---

2. Citing Goethe, Stephen Jay Gould notes that "some dichotomies must interpenetrate, and not struggle to the death of one side, because each of their opposite poles captures an essential property of any intelligible world"; Gould 1987, 19.

3. Lakatos 1970. For contrasting views of the status of realism in these terms, see the articles in the "Forum" section of the *American Political Science Review* 1997, 899–935.

only neighboring field that bureaucratic politics can draw on is organization theory from sociology, which, compared to the field of economics (which has lent so much weight to the rational choice school), is of little prestige or assistance. Third, although studies of foreign policymaking often produce explanations involving the details of bureaucratic perspectives and interests, the discipline now favors theories that, while admitting of many exceptions, are more parsimonious. Finally, unlike constructivism, bureaucratic politics does not hold out hope for drastic change. Although it is usually critical of the policies that have been adopted and, even more, of the way they are implemented, it does not question the decision makers' basic outlook and goals, let alone the prevailing pattern of international politics.

Both recent events and the contemporary political atmosphere influence the acceptability of theories, though this is usually clearer in retrospect than at the time. Thus, Jerald Combs has shown that interpretations of past events in American foreign policy were strongly marked by what was happening when scholars were writing.[4] In the same vein, the changing fortunes of Marxism in political science are better explained by such events as the Vietnam War (which fits Marxism badly[5]) and the disintegration of the Soviet Union coupled with the abandonment of communism in the People's Republic of China (which actually says nothing about the validity of Marxist theory) than by the ability or inability of Marxist approaches to generate propositions or account for evidence. So, not surprisingly, the relatively uncompelling nature of the international environment now facing the United States has renewed interest in how state interests are defined and in the domestic sources of foreign policy, not only currently but also in previous eras. Similarly, scholars often argue that a resurgence of violence between states would increase the popularity of realism. I have no doubt this is correct, but even if we were to accept the questionable equation of realism with violence, would we want current events to drive our research, rather than being concerned with explaining patterns over a longer span of history?[6] Contemporary events can of course be relevant here—and war among the developed countries would undermine some theories discussed later—but they usually tell us more about the popularity of various approaches than about their scholarly utility.

The kinds of theories we find attractive are influenced not only by events but also by our general political orientations. As usual, seeing these forces operating in others is easier than seeing them in one's self, and though I agree with the description of the evolution of the subfield of international organization presented here by Katzenstein, Keohane, and Krasner, I see normative considerations playing a larger role. To oversimplify, the field moved from analyzing the United Nations, to studying regional integration, to looking at the role of transnational and transgovernmental organizations, to examining the causes and effects of foreign economic policies and ac-

4. Combs 1983.

5. Krasner 1978.

6. During the Cold War, the field of security studies was criticized for being preoccupied with contemporary issues at the expense of more abstract arguments that would apply to a wider sweep of history. So it is a little odd to hear many of the same people now say that the end of the Cold War makes security studies less important.

tivities. The first three phenomena, and to a lesser extent the fourth, are ones in which the use or threat of force is in the background, if not absent, and each appeared to hold out hope for a more peaceful world, perhaps even a more humane and just one. The subfield has been guided by the beliefs that such changes are possible, that greater areas of world politics can be governed by law rather than by force, and that universalistic criteria should and can become increasingly important.

The normative agenda is even more apparent with social constructivism. The obvious desire is to see world politics transformed by the spread of appropriate norms, identities, and concepts of world politics. Intriguingly, constructivists pay little attention to norms and ideas that are both revolutionary and evil. This oversight has been at the cost of ignoring perhaps the strongest argument against materialist claims: one cannot understand Hitler's Germany and Stalin's Soviet Union, the two most destructive states of the twentieth century, without understanding the norms, identities, and ideas held by the dominant elites.[7] Both regimes were driven by the desire to remake first their societies and then the world. Neither took the state as the unit whose interests were to be served; no narrow self-interest or considerations of national security or even national gain could have led to such domestic slaughter and dangerous expansion.[8] Perhaps constructivists slight these cases because they indicate that realism can be a force for moderation, that new ideas can make the world worse, and that those who seek radical change may be monsters. Recent civil strife has increased constructivists' (and everyone else's) interest in nationalism, but it will be a challenge to deal with desired and undesired ideas in analytically similar ways.

Normative impulses also account for much of the passion in the attacks on realism. Robert Gilpin's claim that "no one loves a political realist"[9] is only a bit exaggerated: those who are committed to the need for and possibility of radical change in international politics find what they believe to be realism's deep pessimism on this score not only incorrect but also a major obstacle to progress.[10] Similarly, liberal reformers have long argued that those who describe the world in terms of the utility of the use, or even the threat, of force are teaching incorrect and dangerous lessons and that realism partly is a self-fulfilling prophecy.[11]

This is not to say that realists like war, although in earlier eras many intellectuals believed that armed conflict was the main motor of human progress—a proposition that should not be dismissed out of hand. Indeed, many realists study the causes of war in the hope of reducing the chances of future conflict. What I find interesting is

---

7. Lumsdaine 1994. See also Mearsheimer 1994, 42–44.

8. Relevant here is the general topic of passions and interests: Hirschman 1977. In this connection, the association between constructivism and "left" political preferences is significant. This commitment gives the work much of its drive and, for many, its appeal. But it also raises doubts as to whether the approach can produce answers—or even ask questions—that have unpalatable political implications.

9. Gilpin 1996.

10. Although realism sees the possibility of cooperation and peace, as I will discuss later, there is much to K. J. Holsti's comment that "many of the theoretical arguments about the fundamental contours of our discipline are really debates about optimism and pessimism, our very general outlooks toward the world in which we live"; Holsti 1986, 356.

11. See, for example, Rapoport 1973.

that nonrealists have been slow to develop and test arguments about the conditions they consider conducive to peace. A large literature exists on the effects of threats and arms increases, but even leaving aside the questionable relevance of the answers to these crucial questions for realism and its alternatives,[12] this research is plagued by almost insurmountable endogeneity problems, especially when decision making is not closely examined. Classical liberalism was founded on the idea that unfettered international intercourse would produce peace, but only recently have scholars reexamined the correlations between high levels of trade and conflict,[13] and neoliberal institutionalists have not looked at whether peace has historically been associated with a high density of international institutions. (Of course, we need to consider that causation can run both ways and that peace and its purported causes may be the products of third factors.[14]) Thus, I think it is the hope for a better world more than the results of investigations of the causes of conflicts that has led many scholars to reject realism.

In summary, then, we should not adopt the Whiggish stance that the fate of a research program is predominantly determined by the extent to which it produces propositions that anticipate and fit with empirical facts. Programs—and, even more, their first cousins, paradigms—are notoriously difficult to confirm or disconfirm. Not only do they shape what counts as a fact at all, but there are so many steps between the assumptions and outlooks on the one hand and empirical findings on the other that neither in social nor in natural science can the evidence ever be unambiguous. If this were not the case, competing theories of political life could not have survived over several centuries. Granted, they rise and fall and undergo permutations (and, we hope, improvements), but the basic schools of thought of realism, liberalism, Marxism, and constructivism have been around for a very long time. Any that could have been disconfirmed would have gone extinct long ago.

Constructivism and Rationalism: Necessarily Incomplete

Leaving for the next section the question of whether rationalism and constructivism will be the major points of contestation in the coming years, here I want to note that they are even less complete than realism, liberalism, and Marxism. As approaches or styles of thought they need to be filled with content in order to become theoretical statements, and much of their explanatory power must come from auxiliary assumptions about the identities of actors, their goals, and their beliefs. This is most obviously true for rationalism, which argues that behavior can be understood as the actors' attempts to maximize some consistent utility function. But this claim says nothing

---

12. The view that arms increases and deterrence can preserve the status quo is clearly realist, but the claim that these postures will set off a spiral of increasing conflict is not necessarily nonrealist: Jervis 1976, chap. 3.

13. See Oneal and Russett 1997; and Kim 1998. For more skeptical views, see Copeland 1996; and Ripsman and Blanchard 1996.

14. Blainey 1973, chap. 2.

about what actors value and what behaviors they believe will produce maximum benefit. To move beyond a "thin" version of rational choice, a great deal must be added, which means that there can be no single rational choice theory of politics.

Rationalism then should not be contrasted with liberalism or realism. Indeed, it needs theories like these to do any explanatory work. Debate over the merits of assuming utility maximization has obscured the crucial nature of the suppositions about what goals actors seek and how they believe they can best reach them. Glossing over these questions in IPE is perhaps easier than in security because both goals and understandings of means-ends relationships are more widely shared in the former area than in the latter. But even when applied to IPE, rationalism cannot successfully bracket people's ideas about how the economy functions: actors who believe the theory of mercantilism will behave very differently from those who have been schooled in neoclassical economics.

There are several affinities between rationalism and realism, however. Most formulations of the latter rely on an assumption of rationality,[15] though to a less demanding degree than does the former. Self-interest is usually seen as quite narrow, although rationalists are more prone than realists to see the interest being maximized as that of the individual rather than the country being led, a topic to which I will return. Neither approach pays much attention to differences among individuals or biases in the way people think, leaving them vulnerable to criticisms rooted in individual and cognitive psychology. Furthermore, both approaches are simultaneously normative and descriptive because they run together what actors should do to serve their interests and how they actually behave. Thus, rationalist accounts of institutions tend to resemble the functionalist approach that was originally a target of rationalism; that is, the institutional arrangements that have developed are seen as those that best serve the interests of powerful actors.[16] But when realists and rationalists confront policies they see as misguided, if not disastrous, their theories as well as the country are in trouble: Hans Morgenthau not only said that countries follow their national interests, he also lectured Americans on the need to do so—a task that would have been unnecessary had his descriptive argument been without flaws.

Constructivism, too, is an approach or a style. It is one thing to argue that material factors and the external environment do not determine a state's behavior and to point to the importance of regulative and constitutive norms, shared understandings, and common practices; it is quite another to say how norms are formed, how identities are shaped, and how interests become defined as they do. Leaving aside the question of what evidence would bear on the claims being made, my point is that although constructivism says something about the processes at work in political life, it does not, by itself, tell us anything about the expected content of foreign policies or international relations.

Constructivism does, however, have an important affinity with realism in its skepticism about the universality, if not the sincerity, of the ideas and rationales expressed

---

15. Morgenthau does not do so consistently, however; Morgenthau 1978.
16. Sometimes microfoundations can be developed for this account.

by national leaders. Realists are often accused of too readily adopting the perspectives of those in power, but scholars of this persuasion often argue that the beliefs articulated by statesmen (and other people as well) are reflections of their historical and personal circumstances, that elites tend to universalize the concepts and values that are particular to their own situation or era, and that leaders are likely to convince themselves that worldwide interests are served by policies that mainly benefit their countries and perhaps only themselves. There is a valuable cynicism to both constructivism and realism in the appreciation of the self-righteousness of powerful actors.[17] E. H. Carr's analysis is best known in this regard, but Morgenthau similarly stressed that liberal elites attributed objective and universal validity to the ideas that accompanied the rise to power of their countries and social strata.[18] Subsequent realists have also been quick to point out that the justifications offered by the dominant powers typically clothe national interests in broader terms; Kenneth Waltz continues this tradition when he argues that Americans fail to recognize that although inhibiting the spread of nuclear weapons is indeed good for the United States, it disadvantages nonnuclear countries that face threats, including threats from the United States.[19]

Interestingly, liberal IPE scholarship has less in common with constructivism on this score in that its arguments parallel those made by dominant elites who espouse the benefits of an open economic system. Because these scholars see greater common interests among actors and perhaps because they are less focused on the multiple effects of power, including its influence on the intellectual frameworks of powerholders, they tend to accept the claims of liberal leaders to be serving interests extending beyond those of the leading actors.

In many of their variants, rationalism and constructivism share a valuable focus on the importance of interaction. But, contrary to the claims of their proponents, the extent of their difference from realism is not clear. For rationalism, interaction is treated through game theory, which leads to an understanding that outcomes often diverge from intentions and that actors set their behavior on the basis of their expectation of how others are going to act and with the knowledge that others are doing likewise. This contrasts with the error common to much formal decision theory—that is, the assumption that although the actor that is the focus of attention will maximize his or her utility, others will not anticipate this and react accordingly. But the basic outlook of game theory does *not* contrast with realism and sophisticated diplomatic histories, which have been deeply concerned with interactions as well as with actors' anticipations, strategies, and estimates of others' strategies and anticipations.

Constructivism has a large place for the ways in which norms and practices not only restrict what actors can do but also enable them to act and, indeed, shape their identities and constitute the fundamental nature of the prevailing international relations. By contrast, constructivists argue, neorealism, if not realism, assumes the iden-

17. There is a tension in constructivism here: to argue that ideas largely are rationalizations is to locate major causality in preexisting interests, whose existence constructivists usually deny. If ideas are to have any autonomy, they cannot be mere reflections of actors' experiences and interests.
18. See Carr [1946] 1964; and Morgenthau 1946, 20–53, 153–67.
19. Waltz and Sagan 1995.

tities and existence of the states and does not see how the units and the international system mutually form each other. But Waltz's conception of the relations between the units and the system is not so different from theirs: "B's attributes and actions are affected by A, and vice versa. Each is not only influencing the other; both are being influenced by the situation their interaction creates. . . . The behavior of [a pair of units in a system] cannot . . . be resolved into a set of two-way relations because each element of behavior that contributes to the interaction is itself shaped by their being a pair."[20]

Although rationalism does not see the interactive process operating as profoundly as this, far from being starkly opposed to constructivism, in a related area the two need to be combined. Game theory rests on assumptions about each actor's expectations about how the other will behave—expectations that form socially, both through establishing conventions about the meaning of behavior and by actors trying to convince others to accept their explanations of their past behavior.[21] The centrality of interactions and anticipations leads actors to seek to shape their informational and interpretational environments; meanings and expectations are sources of influence and sites of cooperation and contestation. In understanding these processes, strategic rationality and deductive logic can be—indeed, need to be—coupled with an appreciation of how actors attribute meaning to behavior. Rationalism cannot supply this knowledge, but constructivism is one of the approaches that can guide the required empirical research.

Any diplomatic history or newspaper provides examples of these processes and shows that meanings are both central and problematic. Let me just mention three cases that occurred in a two-day period in January 1998 as I was drafting this article: the Ulster Protestants "wanted any concessions [from Britain and Ireland] to be part of the negotiating process rather than 'sweeties' passed out by the British and Irish governments outside the talks"; Iran's president proposed cultural exchanges with the United States, whereas the latter would accept only government-to-government talks; and the United States, Israel, and Turkey staged joint naval operations to improve their abilities to coordinate rescues at sea, an act that called up strong protests from Syria and Egypt.[22] People here are concerned with the political and psychological significances of these acts, not their physical consequences. Most behavior has influence only as it is interpreted by others who hold their own (often implicit) theories about how the world works and who are trying to discern the implications of acts for future behavior, while keeping in mind that the actor and other audiences are engaging in similar attributions and projections of meaning. There is no objective way of specifying the significance people will attach to these acts, and indeed they may be read differently by different audiences. The concerns are rational and fit well

20. Waltz 1979, 74–75.
21. See Jervis [1970] 1989a; and Kreps 1990b.
22. Warren Hoge, "Protestant Threat Imperils Peace Talks in Ulster," *New York Times*, 7 January 1998, 4; Elaine Sciolino, "Seeking to Open to U.S., Iranian Proposes Cultural Ties," *New York Times*, 8 January 1998, 1; and Serge Schmemann, "Unusual Naval Alliance Shows Off, and Arabs Glare," *New York Times*, 8 January, 3.

with strategic logic, but the crucial interpretations that people are making and trying to get others to make must come from elsewhere and can only be understood within frameworks that are social, psychological, and cultural.

Rationalism and Constructivism as Central?

Although I believe that constructivism and rationalism will play large roles in the future, to predict that they will be points of contestation may be an exaggeration. Much research is too eclectic to be readily classified, which I think is a sign of healthy diversity. I find it difficult to fit many of the articles in *IO* under the theoretical headings used in this issue. Looking at other journals, especially *International Studies Quarterly* and *Journal of Conflict Resolution*, reinforces this impression. Here we see empirical research using large-scale data sets that is less closely tied to strong theories. Put another way, the articles in this issue are strongly "bicoastal." Quite different work tends to be done in the rest of the country (Chicago is an honorary coastal university, perhaps by virtue of being on Lake Michigan). I do not want to exaggerate this distinction, but neither should it be dismissed. Without rehearsing the familiar arguments about induction versus deduction, the value and frequency of approaches that do less to elaborate general theories and more to detect patterns in events should not be underestimated.

It is also telling that two of the major debates in the field and one of the major points of focus have been only marginally influenced by rationalism and constructivism. To start with the latter, the past decade has seen a resurgence of attention to the domestic sources of foreign policy.[23] Many of the articles in this issue discuss this research, and I need only note that though some of it is grounded in rationalism or constructivism, most is not. Although constructivism attends to the role of domestic processes in forming identities, interests, and norms, much work with a domestic focus either brackets these subjects or analyzes them quite differently. Whereas rationalism linked to methodological individualism sees foreign policy as the product of the narrow self-interests of domestic actors and focuses on how domestic political institutions influence policy outcomes, much of the domestic sources literature is more diverse—and also shares with bureaucratic politics the difficulty of estimating how the domestic bargaining processes will work themselves out, which coalitions will form, and how the national leaders will balance internal and external pressures and values. Thus, the renewed attention to "second image"[24] should not be equated with the triumph of either constructivism or rationalism.

So it is not entirely surprising that the theory of the democratic peace, probably the most vibrant theory drawing on domestic sources, cannot be readily classified as either rationalist or constructivist. Both styles have contributed to this topic, but

---

23. For interesting discussions, see Sterling-Folker 1997; and Fearon 1998.
24. Waltz 1959. For recent statements of the liberal version of the domestic sources of foreign policy, see Doyle 1997 and Moravcsik 1997, neither of which presents a rationalist or a constructivist account.

neither has dominated it. What is arguably the most important challenge to one of realism's central precepts did not arise from a strong methodological vision but instead from a renewed sense of the validity of the liberal ideas that democracies are different from autocracies and that foreign policy reflects domestic habits and values, coupled with intensive analysis of data and case studies.

Similarly, the contending arguments concerning the purported rise of globalization are not dominated by rationalism and constructivism.[25] Instead, the range of analytical tools and approaches remains broad and the basic questions addressed fit well with traditional realism, particularly in the focus on the extent to which the external environment disciplines the behavior of states and other actors. The argument that high levels of economic interaction impose severe limits on states' abilities to choose their economic policies parallels Waltz's claim that states that do not conform to the necessary modes of international behavior will "fall by the wayside".[26] The causal mechanisms are a bit different with globalization and involve a greater role for nongovernmental actors, but the underlying relationships between competing actors and the resulting constraints are much the same.

Realism: Alive and Well

Related to my doubts about the centrality of constructivism and rationalism is my belief that realism is not likely to disappear. Neorealism may become less important not only because many people are becoming tired of it, but also because its concern with the differences between bipolar and multipolar systems, especially in terms of stability, appears less interesting with the declining fear of major war and the end of bipolarity.[27] As Waltz notes, realism, in contrast to neorealism, is more of an approach than a theory—it points to a set of actors that are important, makes claims about the considerations that decision makers weigh, and describes sets of outcomes that can result from particular combinations of national policies.[28] Although it does not readily yield specific propositions, it has continually generated new questions, insights, and arguments.

Realism has many versions, but the assumptions that states can be considered the main actors and that they focus in the first instance on their own security are central to most. They are, of course, descriptively inaccurate. But, as almost all social scientists agree, this is not the point. Rather, we ask whether these assumptions yield a wider array of better confirmed propositions than do alternative approaches. Without claiming that realism is appropriate for all questions, I would like to advance the

25. This subject has been treated extensively in the pages of *IO* and is examined in Garrett's essay in this issue.

26. Waltz 1979, 71, 91, 118–19.

27. For the differences between realism and neorealism, see Gilpin 1984; Waltz 1991; Shimko 1992; and Schweller and Priess 1997. For recent discussions of the utility of both, see the special issues of *Security Studies*, winter 1995 and spring 1996; and the "Forum" section of *American Political Science Review* 1997, 899–935.

28. Waltz 1991.

weaker but still not trivial argument that these assumptions are often of great utility and that it is unlikely that we will see highly productive theories that abandon all of them or that start from their opposites.

Let me begin with the assumption that states seek a high measure of security.[29] This is not to claim that security is unambiguous or that it is the only value.[30] Indeed, rather than pay the price of destruction in war, states have surrendered in the hope of regaining their autonomy later (partly through the efforts of others). They have also peacefully (and not so peacefully) submerged their political units into those of others or joined together to form larger units in the belief that doing so would better serve a variety of political, social, and ideological goals. But if security is rarely the only objective, even more rarely can it be ignored. Of course security has been defined differently by different actors, and the routes to it can be multiple and contested, but the desire for security is part of the bedrock explanation for why international politics exists at all. That is, though it is easy to take for granted the fact that no unit has come to dominate the entire international system, this outcome needs to be explained. The desire for security, coupled with the knowledge that one's current allies may be one's adversaries in the future and that current adversaries may provide future support generates many of the constraints that maintain the international system because self-protection dictates that states do not want their allies excessively aggrandized or their adversaries excessively diminished.

Is the security assumption relevant today? As the developed states fear each other much less and have come to form what Karl Deutsch called a pluralistic security community,[31] other values come to the fore. But these states still worry about security threats from elsewhere (including nonstate actors), and other countries remain deeply concerned about their neighbors. Nevertheless, if it is true that the most powerful states in the world no longer think they may have to fight each other, the change in world politics will be very great, a topic to which I will return. Note, however, that the importance of this development is apparent only when we see that throughout history states have focused on their security concerns.

This analysis assumes that states are the main actors, which is most appropriate when the values at stake are widely shared or, if they are not, when the top decision makers are motivated and able to support policies that will serve the country as a whole. But even in other circumstances the state is not likely to lack importance and autonomy. For all our discussion of the roles of bureaucracies, economic sectors, multinational corporations, and transnational interests, in most cases it is the state that is the target of their activities and it is mainly through national policies that these groups can have influence. For further evidence of the continuing centrality of states

---

29. One can, of course, talk of the security of individuals, societies, or of the international system as well as of states (Buzan 1991), but it is interesting to note that aggressive states are also likely to oppress their own populations.

30. Wolfers 1962, chap. 10.

31. Deutsch et al. 1957. The countries I have in mind are the United States, West Europe, Japan, Australia, and New Zealand. The question of why these states but not others are so included, important as it is for many analyses, fortunately can be put aside here.

we need only look to countries undergoing bloody internal struggles in which the objective is to gain control of whatever national machinery there is or to secede and establish an independent state. Even if states are never the only actors on the scene, can we write history or current analysis without them? Vulgar Marxists, pluralists, or transnationalists would see the state as merely registering and implementing the views of powerful societal actors. If these perspectives could be maintained, we should dispense with the names of the states and their leaders, which serve as ventriloquists' dummies, and write our accounts in terms of the groups and interests determining the behavior.

The state has proven remarkably resilient in the face of multiple social forces and the insistence of scholars that its importance is rapidly waning. Assertions to the contrary by realists are less important than the actions by national leaders to reassert their control, often supported by nongovernmental actors who see great value in central authority. Of course the fact that previous obituaries of the state were premature does not mean that they are not warranted now. In the 1960s the state was indeed obstinate rather than obsolete, as Stanley Hoffmann argued,[32] but the European Union may yet supplant its members—in which case it would form a state of its own, and though the process by which it formed may violate some realist assumptions, many of the constraints and incentives that it would face will be familiar. The claims that globalization has hollowed out states may be similarly overstated in part because they overestimate the implications of the economic flows and in part because they fail to appreciate the way in which new forces call up new incentives and instruments for state action.[33]

Arguing that states are the central actors does not tell us which interests and policies they pursue. This question looms particularly large in the security field: even though it may be true that all states want a high measure of security, some strive for others goals, especially expansion of various kinds, in addition to or even at the expense of security.[34] Furthermore, even if security is the prime objective, this does not tell us—or statesmen—what behavior will reach it.[35] For example, belligerent policies are likely to decrease rather than increase the state's security when other

---

32. Hoffmann 1966.

33. See Huntington 1973; Haskel 1980; Gilpin 1996; and Garrett 1998a. For a parallel discussion of the relations between states and transnational actors, see Krasner 1995b. For a strong claim that we are witnessing "the retreat of the state," see Strange 1996.

34. Disagreements over the prevalence of expansionism is perhaps the main issue between "offensive" and "defensive" realism; see, for example, Snyder 1991; Zakaria 1992; Glaser 1994; and Schweller 1996. See also Brooks 1997; Labs 1997; and Kydd 1997. For further discussion, see pp. 986–87.

35. See, for example, Snyder 1984; Van Evera 1984b; and Rhodes 1996. It is also worth noting that studies of the conduct of war, a topic that has been pushed to the margins of scholarship, have bitterly debated the extent to which the outcomes of battles and wars are determined by material forces (for example, equipment, firepower) as opposed to morale or moral factors (for example, faith in one's cause and comrades). Many military leaders have stressed the latter—and it is not without interest that they use the terms *moral* and *morale* interchangeably—which is contrary to the common academic view that the military regards anything nonmaterial as inconsequential, if not nonexistent. In fact, nations are rarely literally destroyed in a war, and victory does not automatically go to the side that inflicts more deaths than it suffers.

states are satisfied with the status quo; conciliatory policies, effective under those circumstances, will decrease the state's security if others are striving to expand.[36] This would not be a problem if statesmen could tell whether others were—or will become—expansionist. But they cannot, in part because realism and other theories of foreign policy offer insufficient guidelines on this score. It is therefore not surprising that students of security policy have been quick to see that realism needs to be supplemented by an understanding of the ideas that decision makers use to guide them to their goals.[37]

Subjective as some security interests are, realism argues that their importance means that they provide the crucial context for everything else. Although convenience often dictates bracketing security politics when they remain constant in a period when economic behavior changes,[38] I doubt if many foreign economic policies and outcomes are untouched by broad security concerns. Certainly it would be foolish to try to explain the economic relations among the advanced industrialized countries after 1945 without taking into account the Cold War.[39] Indeed, the need to bolster the strength of its allies required the United States to give much consideration to their economic needs, especially if it was to limit their trade with the Soviet Union or China. U.S. policies to alleviate poverty and increase stability in the Third World (misguided or not) also cannot be seen apart from the perceived fear that only economic progress could forestall revolutions and the establishment of anti-American if not pro-communist regimes.

American security policies also conditioned other countries' economic relations with each other. European economic integration was facilitated if not made possible by the American security guarantee that assuaged British and French fears of Germany and allowed these countries to develop an unprecedented division of labor. The expectation of a continued U.S. presence meant that they did not have to worry about going to war with each other in the foreseeable future and so did not have to behave in typical realist fashion. The other side of this coin is that economic relations are often set with at least one eye on their implications for security. Recent progress in European integration is not unrelated to the unification of Germany as all parties—including current German elites—want to see that Germany will not have the incentives or the easy ability to menace its neighbors in the future.[40] (This is not to say that

---

36. Jervis 1976, chap. 3.

37. The situation is different, at least in degree, in IPE: the pursuit of wealth, either by subnational actors or by states, involves less need to estimate how others will behave and fewer difficult choices about which instruments to employ. Differences over how to pursue wealth often are easier to trace to differences in interest, and the sources—and validity—of beliefs about how the economy functions tend to be taken for granted by actors and observers. Thus, the discovery of the importance of ideas comes as more of an innovation in IPE; see Odell 1982; Rothstein 1984; Goldstein 1993; Ikenberry 1993a; and Halpern 1993. For a cultural explanation of political and economic underdevelopment, see Harrison 1985. For an interesting discussion of economic cultures, see Rohrlich 1987.

38. See, for example, Keohane 1984, chap. 3, 137.

39. See, for example, Pollard 1985; Jentelson 1986; and Gowa 1994.

40. A high German official explained his country's support for an expanded NATO in similar terms: "We wanted to bind Germany into a structure which practically obliges Germany to take the interests of its neighbors into consideration. We wanted to give our neighbors assurances that we won't do what we don't

even an extremely high degree of economic integration guarantees continued unity and peace, as the division of Czechoslovakia, the disintegration of the Soviet Union, and the civil war in the former Yugoslavia remind us.)

Realism, Change, and Cooperation

Realism's assumptions lead to a focus on continuity, and John Ruggie has argued that this approach, particularly in security studies, has been egregious in its failure to recognize the possibilities for "epochal" change.[41] But this is not the whole picture. Much depends, of course, on the kind and degree of change that one is looking for. Realists have argued that the last half-century has witnessed as many as three enormous shifts in international politics—changes, furthermore, that most of them have seen as making the world more peaceful. First, realists argued that the shift from multipolarity to bipolarity in the aftermath of World War II was extremely important. Although disagreeing about the consequences of this change, they concluded that dangers, opportunities, and state policies were all effected by the new international structure. Ironically, it was Waltz, who placed great stress on continuity, who most persuasively argued that bipolarity was unprecedented (contrary to the previously prevailing view that the pre-1914 system was bipolar) and that it made the world, or at least the major states, much safer. To those who believed that the bipolarity made the world more war-prone because the great powers were tied to their smaller allies for whom they might have to fight,[42] Waltz and those who reasoned similarly replied that this dynamic actually characterized multipolarity and that under bipolarity small allies could defect at will because the superpowers relied on internally generated resources, thereby giving them unprecedented freedom of action.[43] The substance of the debate is important for theory and policy, but all that is crucial here is that both sides agreed that bipolarity significantly changed world politics.

Realists similarly differed on whether nuclear weapons made the world more or less safe, but again agreed that they brought important changes in state policies, bargaining tactics, alliance relationships, and opportunities to change the status quo. In the end, most scholars came to the conclusion that nuclear weapons decreased the chance of war and coercive change at the center of the international system (but not in the periphery). Bernard Brodie and his colleagues saw this as early as 1946, arguing that atomic bombs were "absolute weapons" that radically changed the fundamental character of military power, which had previously been relative.[44] With rea-

---

intend to do anyway" (quoted in Jane Perlez, "Blunt Reasoning for Enlarging NATO: Curbs on Germany," *New York Times*, 7 December 1997, 18; see also Feldstein 1997, 68–69). For the worries of British, French, and Soviet leaders at the time of German unification, see Zelikow and Rice 1995, 137–38, 345; Maier 1997, 249, 252; and Powell 1992, 235.

41. Ruggie 1993, 143.

42. See, for example, Deutsch and Singer 1964; and Hoffmann 1968, chap. 2.

43. See Waltz 1979; and Snyder and Diesing 1977, chap. 6.

44. Brodie 1946. This point of view never convinced decision makers, however. Some U.S. presidents felt that nuclear weapons had made their country less rather than more secure and sought to abolish them,

son, then, many realists referred to the "nuclear revolution." As with bipolarity, what changed here was the external situation: not what states sought, the prevailing normative principles, or the ideas people held, but rather incentives, especially the punishments that statesmen believed would be incurred by dangerous and expansionist policies.[45]

More than this is at work in the third candidate for major change that realists—as well and some nonrealists—have seen, which is the decline of war among the developed states and even the creation of a security community among them.[46] The fear of punishment operates here as well in that everyone realizes that a major war, even if it did not involve nuclear weapons, would be extraordinarily destructive. But rewards may be equally important, since states can gain much of what they want by peaceful means. Of course, high levels of economic interaction would be viewed with alarm if states feared that others would use their increased strength to menace the state or might threaten to sever the valuable ties in the event of a dispute. Thus, a reciprocal relationship exists between expectations of peace and the development of a high degree of economic integration. But this dynamic is not foreign to realism.

This cannot be said of the third element that many people, myself included, see as creating the current security community. This element involves a change in outlooks and even values among general populations, elites, and national leaders. Rabid and competitive nationalism has greatly declined, war is seen as a brutal necessity if not a crime rather than a glorious activity, and control of historically disputed territories such as Alsace and Lorraine is of greatly decreased concern, in part because the developed countries are democratic and share most values. Realism cannot readily explain these developments. It can argue that they were brought about at least in part by the increased costs of war, but the causal links involve psychological processes of attitude change outside the focus of most international politics theories. Realism is not alone in struggling here, however: changes in values are beyond the scope of rationalism; and though they are, in principle, central to constructivism, it is not clear whether this approach can provide more than a post hoc redescription. Classical liberalism might be more relevant.

Even if changes in values do not fit well with realism, the other shifts discussed in the previous paragraphs do. Although this analysis cuts against the most dramatic and far-reaching claims for continuity, it shows that realism not only is compatible with significant alterations in international politics but also points to the powerful motors of change in what states can do to help and, especially, to hurt others. A focus on the threat and use of force does not imply that behavior remains uniform.

---

albeit on terms that strongly favored their side. (Gorbachev and Reagan were abolitionists, which was one of the bonds between them.) Furthermore, almost no statesmen, with the exception of Gorbachev and at times Khrushchev and Eisenhower, thought that the weapons were absolute. Instead they felt it was necessary to seek greater capability than the other side and pursued targeting doctrines that were designed to gain military advantage or at least to deny such advantage to the adversary.

45. Some analysts argued that modern technology would have produced this result even without nuclear weapons; Mueller 1989.

46. See Mueller 1989; Van Evera 1990; Jervis 1991; and Singer and Wildavsky 1993. For dissents, see Mearsheimer 1990; and Layne 1993.

Realism similarly does not imply unremitting conflict. To conceive of international politics as a Hobbesian state of nature means not that warfare is constant, but only that it is always a possibility and that actors understand this. Although the anticipation of conflict may make it more likely, it can also lead actors to take measures to reduce the danger. Three facets of realist thought are particularly relevant here and lead to policy prescriptions. First, realism is well known for arguing that power must be mustered in order to reach the state's possible goals; Morgenthau's "interest defined in terms of power" is its most familiar formulation.[47] But for realists it is equally important that goals have to be trimmed to fit within the possibilities created by the configuration of power. Thus, the first edition of Carr's *Twenty Years' Crisis* applauded Britain's appeasement policy. We now know this to have been in error because Hitler could not have been satisfied short of world domination, but realist statesmen faced by more reasonable adversaries have been able to avoid conflict by appeasing them.[48]

Just as understanding the limits of the state's power can reduce conflict, so in protecting what is most important to them states must avoid the destructive disputes that will result from failing to respect the vital interests of others. Realists have long argued that diplomacy and empathy are vital tools of statecraft; conceptions of the national interest that leave no room for the aspirations and values of others will bring ruin to the state as well as to its neighbors.[49]

Realism also can speak to the conditions under which states are most likely to cooperate and the strategies that actors can employ to foster cooperation. This line of theorizing is sometimes associated with neoliberalism, but the two are hard to distinguish in this area.[50] Making a distinction would be easy if realism believed that conflict was zero-sum, that actors were always on the Pareto frontier. This conclusion perhaps flows from the view of neoclassical economics that all arrangements have evolved to be maximally efficient, but realists see that politics is often tragic in the sense of actors being unable to realize their common interests. Although "offensive realists" who see aggression and expansionism as omnipresent (or who believe that security requires expansion) stress the prevalence of extreme conflict of interest, "defensive realists" believe that much of international politics is a Prisoners' Dilemma or a more complex security dilemma.[51] The desire to gain mixes with the need for protection; much of statecraft consists of structuring situations so that states can maximize their common interests. The ever-present fear that others will take advantage of the state—and the knowledge that others have reciprocal worries—leads

47. Morgenthau 1978, 5–8.
48. See Kennedy 1983, chap. 1; and Schroeder 1976.
49. See Morgenthau 1978; Calleo 1978; Kennan 1967, 127–30; and Kennan 1968.
50. Keohane 1984, 67. This is not to say there are no disputes between these two schools of thought: most centrally, they disagree about the importance and fungibility of force, the typical balance between conflicting and common interests, and the extent to which cooperative arrangements among states can unintentionally alter their preferences; see, for example, Keohane and Nye 1977; Baldwin 1989, chap. 7; Baldwin 1993; Nye 1990, chap. 6; and Art 1996.
51. For the former, see, for example, Gray 1992; and Schweller 1996; for the latter, see Schelling and Halperin 1961; Jervis 1978; Waltz 1979; and Snyder and Jervis forthcoming.

diplomats to seek arrangements that will reduce if not neutralize these concerns. Even if international politics must remain a Prisoners' Dilemma, it can often be made into one that is more benign by altering the pay-offs to encourage cooperation, for example, by enhancing each state's ability to protect itself should the other seek to exploit it and increasing the transparency that allows each to see what the other side is doing and understand why it is doing it. The knowledge that even if others are benign today, they may become hostile in the future due to changes of mind, circumstances, and regimes can similarly lead decision makers to create arrangements that bind others—and themselves, as previously noted.

But, in parallel to the earlier discussion of the kinds of changes that realism cannot explain, deeper forms of cooperation exist that are more problematic from this perspective. Thus, though realism can account for the dramatic growth in cooperation when the balance of power (narrowly conceived) is transformed into a concert regime, the more profound alterations in attitudes, identities, and values that perhaps surrounded the original Concert of Europe in 1815 is beyond the reach of this approach.[52] The basis and forms of cooperation after the Napoleonic Wars may have rested on conceptions of common interests and shared responsibilities that are alien to realism, although realists would not be surprised that these beliefs and arrangements eventually decayed.

Extensions of Realism

Much criticism has been leveled at realism for the linked assumptions that states exist in a condition of anarchy and that they follow their narrow self-interests. Interestingly, rationalism as applied to international politics and the current work in American and comparative politics that inspired it adopt a similar approach. As Helen Milner's article in this issue shows, these studies see domestic actors as uninhibited by norms, worried (with good reason) that unenforceable promises and threats will prove empty, and seeking ways to avoid the suboptimal outcomes that can result from unnecessary conflict. Thus, many recent arguments about the U.S. Congress are more familiar to students of international politics than to those who had seen this institution as governed by rules serving the interest of the institution as a whole and populated by individuals seeking the good of the collectivity, if not of the country at large. Of course, this perspective is not entirely new in the fields of domestic politics and society. But the "amoral familism" that Edward Banfield saw as making life in an Italian village so miserable was considered pathological, and Richard Neustadt's discussion of presidential power in terms of the interests the president did *not* share with others was unsettling, if insightful.[53] Now this kind of behavior is taken as normative in one if not both senses of the term.

---

52. See Schroeder 1992 and 1994; and Jervis 1992a. For a realist view of the Concert, see Kagan 1997.

53. See Banfield 1958; and Neustadt 1960.

This perspective not only draws the subfields of political science together but also points to a basic tension in traditional realist thought. There, national leaders are ruthless for their states but selfless as individuals. The utilities they maximize are those of the country as a whole, not of themselves personally; they respect no restraints on the acts necessary for their countries but never put their own interests first. People of this type can exist and perhaps have come to power. Realists are fond of quoting Cavour's remark to a colleague that "if we were to do for ourselves what we have done for our country, we should indeed be very great rogues,"[54] but they have not explored why he did not advance his personal interests in this way. Although such behavior is compatible with "thin" rational choice theory that does not specify people's utility functions, rationalism does direct us to the idea that political leaders, like many people, will put their own interests first. This perspective leads us to expect that leaders are prone to exploit their societies for their material good and to adopt foreign policies that maximize their own power. Such behavior is antithetical to the precepts of realism, but follows from many realist assumptions and indeed can be seen as removing a major inconsistency in realism's conception of human nature.

Realists pay little attention to the formation and maintenance of ethnic and national identity, a topic crucial not only for current world politics but also for much of the past. This observation, however, does not mean that realism is of no use here. Indeed, consistent with the logic in the previous paragraph, many scholars are now stressing the extent to which identities are manipulated, if not created, by self-serving elites who see that power is to be gained by convincing a large segment of the population that they form a community—one, furthermore, that is threatened by people who are different from them. Realism points to the reciprocal relationship between identities and conflict, arguing that conflict both grows out of and stimulates the perception of differences among groups. Thus, a realist would not be surprised by the fact that the breakdown of the state is as much a cause as a consequence of ethnic conflict. Not only does the absence of central authority mean that people and groups are less protected against their neighbors, but, through a security dilemma, fear as well as rapaciousness and rationality as well as psychology lead to the strengthening of available group identities.[55]

The process, of course, is not entirely one of free choice. Identities are often forced on people, as in Northern Ireland when Catholics are attacked because they are Catholic and Protestants because they are Protestant. As a nineteen-year-old said recently in Sarajevo, "I was sitting in my classroom the other day and the teacher handed out a form where we had to write down whether we were a Serb, Muslim, or a Croat. We were told that we would be segregated into different classrooms according to our ethnicity. It's not what any of us asked for."[56] Social psychologists have long known that perceptions—and misperceptions—of what people have in common often grow

54. Quoted in Palmer and Palmer 1976, 37.
55. For the application of the security dilemma to civil conflicts, see Posen 1993a; Walter 1994; and Walter and Snyder forthcoming.
56. Quoted in Chris Hedges, "In Bosnia's Schools, Three Ways Never to Learn from History," *New York Times*, 11 November 1997, 4.

out of conflicts as internal unity is gained by seeing others as the Other.[57] Groups and identities can be created through such processes: the "Bosnians" did not exist until the recent war, which also led many "Muslims" to become Muslims by turning to Islam. Similarly, recent scholarship argues that the identity of Indians as having "red" skin came not from European colonialists but from Indians who were in conflict with them or who wanted to set themselves apart from black slaves. The Native Americans were not passive recipients of a color designation, but formed it through struggles with others.[58] Related processes of differentiation help to explain why black female high school students smoke much less than either their white female or their black male counterparts: they see smoking as white and male.

International Political Economy

Oddly, the articles in this issue say little about the state of the IPE subfield.[59] Striking by their absence are the old but still central topics of the existence and shape of mutual causation between economic intercourse and peaceful relations;[60] the linkages among economic and political issues; the determinants of the degree of openness of international economic systems;[61] the causes and prospects of the current consensus among less developed countries that economic development is positively associated with exposure to the international economy rather than negatively associated, as once believed; and the relationships between states, both rich and poor, on the one hand, and nonstate actors, especially labor and multinational corporations, on the other.

How much progress have we made in understanding the crucial questions of whether, when, and how economic frictions lead to political conflict and vice versa? It was once commonly accepted that economic competition drove allies apart and heightened, if not created, deadly enmities: "Nations which act as enemies in the marketplace cannot long be friends at the council table," as a high government official put it at the end of World War II when explaining why the United States needed to reconstruct the international economic system.[62] Is this correct? Is the relationship conditioned by people's economic and political beliefs? The sources of stability and

---

57. See Sherif and Sherif 1953; Sherif 1966; and Mercer 1995. The basic arguments from sociology are Simmel 1955; and Coser 1956.

58. Shoemaker 1997.

59. I am also struck by the claim of Katzenstein, Keohane, and Krasner in their article in this issue that "ideas originally developed in IPE have been redeployed to a wider range of issues, including questions of national security." Although this is true for some concepts recently borrowed from economics, to its credit IPE has learned much from other subfields of international politics. Thus, recent discussions of salient solutions, issue linkages, credibility, commitments, and reputation follow the treatments by students of diplomacy and security. Of course much of the credit here goes to an economist who supplied many of the key concepts: Schelling 1960 and 1966.

60. Much of what recent literature there is on some of these subjects is summarized in Mastanduno this issue. See also McMillan 1997.

61. Discussed in Webb and Krasner 1989; Lake 1993; and Keohane 1997.

62. Clayton 1945, 979.

change in the international political economic system also have received less atten-tion than was the case in the 1970s and 1980s.[63] Ruggie's important application of Karl Polanyi's "embedded liberalism," though often cited, has not been adequately developed despite some treatment in the context of globalization.[64]

It is also striking that we do not have many constructivist accounts of European integration, which is an obvious arena in which to explore the causes and effects of changing identities.[65] Similarly lacking are discussions of the implications for indi-vidual lives and national policies of the changing value and indeed the meaning of wealth. Ronald Inglehart's research on shifts in Europeans' values could be a good starting point,[66] but it has not attracted much attention from constructivists or the IPE community. More fundamentally, constructivist IPE theorists have not challenged economists on their own ground by exploring what it is that individuals and collec-tivities seek to maximize, how economic well-being is construed, and the interrela-tionships among capitalist ideas, individual identities, and the activities of economic actors.

To put it bluntly, the IPE subfield, after a marvelous period of development in the 1970s and 1980s, seems to be stagnating. At the start, realism, liberalism, and Marx-ism vigorously contended in the process of carrying out well-grounded empirical research.[67] This flow has slackened without being replaced by sustained constructiv-ist and rationalist accounts. Indeed, most applications of constructivism or rational-ism have been to security or general international politics, with less attention to IPE. The internal workings, incentives, self-identities, and cultures of the organizations involved in international political economy similarly have been studied less than those in diplomacy and security.[68] Also noteworthy is that economists more so than political scientists have shaped the public debate about international economic poli-cies.

The Future of IPE, War, and Realism

It will be hard to construct powerful theories of the international economy without keeping in mind the political relationships among countries, the ways economic ties can ameliorate conflict or create exploitable vulnerabilities, the actors' expectations about what alliances are likely to form and how long they are likely to last, and their beliefs about which technologies will be most useful if armed conflict occurs.[69] In

63. See, for example, Krasner 1983b; and Keohane 1984.
64. Ruggie 1983b. For Ruggie's more recent analysis, see Ruggie 1996b, chap. 5–6.
65. For work partially along these lines, see Englemann et al. 1997; and Spirtas 1998.
66. The most recent study is Inglehart 1997.
67. See, for example, Gilpin 1975 and 1987; Katzenstein 1984 and 1985; Krasner 1976, 1978, and 1985; Keohane and Nye 1977; and Keohane 1984.
68. For examples, see Demchak 1991; Posen 1984; Sagan 1993; Avant 1994; Rosen 1991 and 1996; Legro 1995; and Kier 1997.
69. Of course, the patterns here may not be constant, and we need to understand the changes. In many eras, for example, states sold arms to their potential enemies and carried on economic intercourse during warfare; see Stevenson 1996, chap. 1; and Kennedy 1983, chap. 3.

other words, the study of IPE must remain political, and international politics has always taken place in the shadow of war.

But, as noted earlier, I do not think this is any longer true for the developed countries. The consensus among scholars and, more importantly, elites is that the most powerful states will not fight each other. This situation represents a truly revolutionary change in world politics and makes particularly relevant the path-breaking analysis of Robert Keohane and Joseph Nye.[70] This does not mean the end of conflict and the struggle for advantage, let alone the end of the state.[71] Thus, I do not believe it means the end of realism; although, since this approach stressed the pervasive influence of the fear of inter-state war, it will have to be reshaped if it is to explain, let alone guide, a world in which security threats are of a very different nature and probably much less important.[72] It will also be a challenge for other schools of thought to explain and predict how states within the security community will manage their relations. Particularly interesting and important is the question of how and whether the security community will be transformed into a real community—for example, whether the European countries will seek or be able to maintain their separate identities if they are perceived to lose the ability to manage their individual economies and, conversely, whether the belief that one country is suffering so that another can prosper will decrease the EU's unity even if war remains unthinkable. We should not, however, neglect the relations among countries that are not in this community (that is, most of the world), the relations between states in the community and those outside it, and the possibility that armed conflict elsewhere will influence relations within the community. In all these areas the relations between wealth and power are likely to remain central.

I wonder what the next fifty years of international politics will bring; I also wonder what will appear in the centennial issue of *IO* and what the relationship between the two will be. The study of international politics will be impoverished if it is totally divorced from contemporary events and hopes and fears for the future, but if it is to mature, it will have to develop some distance from them.

---

70. Keohane and Nye 1977. See also Rosecrance 1986.
71. For the argument that the changed international environment will affect different kinds of states in different ways, see Desch 1996.
72. For a discussion of realism in such a world, see Kapstein and Mastanduno 1998; and Waltz 1998.

Dental Hygiene and Nuclear War: How International Relations Looks from Economics

Barry Eichengreen

Introduction

Economists are notorious for their intellectual imperialism, feeling no compulsion about applying their kit of tools to everything from dental hygiene to nuclear war. It is hardly a stretch, therefore, to adopt economics as a perspective from which to view scholarship in international relations.

I may have been offered (and accepted) this commission because my fields of specialization are economic history and international economics. The latter field shares with its political science counterpart an obvious preoccupation with international matters. Both international economics and international relations are concerned with such topics as international trade, the international monetary system, international financial markets, and the international debt crisis. The affinity between economic history and international relations is harder to define.[1] In part it derives from a shared inclination to treat parameters as variables. Specialists in both fields are unwilling to take as exogenous a variety of factors that their disciplinary colleagues are prepared to treat as fixed. In economic history this reflects the long time frame over which the relevant processes unfold; variables that are realistically regarded as predetermined in the short run cannot reasonably be taken as invariant over longer intervals. Although this long-run perspective is less central to international relations, there is a similar desire to relax the assumption that structure is impervious to change.[2] For example, international relations has in common with economic history a predilection to treat institutions as endogenous. Institutions being one source of positive feedback

This article was prepared for the fiftieth anniversary of *International Organization*. A first draft was written during a visit to the European Forum of the European University Institute, whose hospitality is acknowledged with thanks. I thank Jeffry Frieden, Peter Katzenstein, Robert Keohane, and especially Steve Krasner for helpful comments.

1. Although historically oriented economists have regularly strayed into the field, starting with Charles Kindleberger's 1951 article on foreign trade and international politics. Kindleberger 1951b.

2. There are exceptions, of course, to this generalization about lack of long-term perspective: Goldstein 1988 springs to mind.

International Organization 52, 4, Autumn 1998, pp. 993–1012

and lock in, it follows that the two subdisciplines share a fascination with path dependence.[3] At the same time, both subdisciplines pay a price from partaking of this unusually rich intellectual menu, namely, the difficulty of formalizing their models with the parsimony of other fields. That, of course, is what makes our chosen subjects so interesting and rewarding.

In organizing my discussion, I take as my starting point contributions to international relations that most closely parallel mainstream economics. I then describe other research in international relations that bears less resemblance to conventional economics. I do not, however, provide a chronological account of the development of the literature. Nor do I attempt to identify geopolitical events that worked to discredit popular approaches and encourage new ones.[4] And I do not focus on the special role, if any, of economic issues in international security questions.[5]

The most telling difference between international relations and economics, I argue, lies in the connection between theory and empirical work. The argument is not the common one that the strength of economics is the existence of a core of theoretical assumptions, most notably utility and profit maximization, that provide the basis for graduate instruction, serve as a common intellectual language, and are the point of departure for even the most unconventional research programs. Rather, I argue that the strength of economics is the complementary and mutually supporting character of theoretical and empirical work. The core of commonly accepted assumptions that unifies much research in modern economics did not descend like manna from heaven or spring full-blown from the brilliant minds of Marshalls and Samuelsons past. Rather, the assumptions and models that have survived and become part of this common theoretical core are those that deliver testable propositions and find systematic support in the data.

In international relations, in contrast, the connections between theory and empirical work are relatively loose. Theory-based propositions do not lend themselves comfortably to empirical verification and refutation. Empirical techniques do not develop to the same extent to facilitate tests of theory-based propositions. As a consequence, research in international relations has not converged on a core of common theoretical assumptions and an arsenal of commonly accepted empirical techniques. If this view is correct, then the task for scholars in international relations is to strengthen the connections between theory and empirics.

Theoretical Perspectives

To a surprising extent there are parallels in economics for even the most unconventional approaches in international relations, and vice versa. I make this point through

---

3. Other positive-feedback mechanisms include ideas and ideologies—even today economic historians invoke the Protestant ethic and the spirit of capitalism when teaching their graduate students about the Industrial Revolution.

4. Both of these tasks are discharged by Katzenstein, Keohane, and Krasner in their article in this issue.

5. A topic that is the subject of Mastanduno's article in this issue.

a review of the interest-, institution-, and idea-based theories of international relations.

Interest Group Models

For an economist, the natural point of departure for thinking about a country's foreign policy is the interests of constituencies.[6] Individuals will favor or oppose policies depending on how they perceive their welfare to be affected. The problem then becomes to identify interests. When the issue is foreign economic policy, the obvious basis is models of economic welfare in which interest groups are synonymous with factors of production (capital or labor) or with the sectors on which they depend for their livelihood (import competing versus export oriented, traded- or home-goods-producing). To explain a country's foreign trade policies, some political scientists have used the two-factor, two-sector Heckscher-Ohlin-Samuelson model, which predicts that a country's relatively abundant factor of production will favor a liberal trade policy (since that factor is used intensively in the export-oriented sector), whereas the scarce factor will favor a restrictive policy (since it is used intensively in the import-competing sector).[7] Others have used the three-factor, two-sector Jones-Mayer-Mussa model, which predicts that the factor used exclusively in the export-oriented (import-competing) sector will favor (oppose) free trade, whereas the attitude of the factor used in both sectors will depend on its consumption basket.[8] Other models provide other predictions, but the general approach—tracing policies to interest groups and interest groups to underlying structures—is fundamentally the same.[9]

The strength of this approach is its precision and parsimony. It has been used to conceptualize the political economy of issues like trade and currency policies and has provided the basis for empirical work attempting to verify or reject the theory's core predictions.[10] A corresponding difficulty is that it becomes harder to map interests into policies and to test the corresponding propositions when noneconomic issues are involved. It may be that international diplomacy has only oblique and diffuse impacts on economic outcomes narrowly defined. If one assumes that individuals care only about economic welfare, it is still possible to rely on off-the-shelf models of the factoral or sectoral distribution of income, however small the impact of policy on income distribution. But if one believes that individuals care about security policy because they value security, or that they care about power politics because they value power, then mapping from policy to interests, and conversely, is problematic.[11]

A further limitation of this approach is that it does not capture the nitty-gritty of politics. One simply counts the population in, say, the import-competing and export-

6. For example, R. Baldwin 1985.
7. For example, Rogowski 1989.
8. Frieden 1991.
9. A recent synthesis of this work is Milner 1988.
10. See Irwin and Krozner 1996; and Frieden 1997b.
11. A point recognized by Nagel 1975.

oriented sectors without worrying about the incentive to organize and lobby.[12] Finally, there is the problem that the model is essentially static and ahistorical. It does not capture the element of time, which implies learning and path dependence, issues that many political scientists believe should be at the center of their discipline.

Institutional Approaches

A second approach emphasizes the role of institutions—political, social, and economic. At one level these can be thought of as communication technologies transmitting the preferences of interest groups to the policy domain. Electoral institutions make it easier or harder for different interest groups to make their influence felt; for example, proportional representation with minimal thresholds for parliamentary representation tends to lead to party proliferation and to facilitate the representation of specialized interests. Political institutions like the committee system or the right of the lower house of the U.S. Congress to initiate budgetary legislation may allow those in a favorable institutional position to shape the policy agenda. Socioeconomic institutions like trade unions and industry associations allow factoral- and sectoral-based groups to organize and represent themselves more effectively than atomistic agents.[13]

One characterization of these institutions is that they aggregate preferences like an adding machine that makes due allowance for the concentration or dispersion of group interests and the intensity with which their particular policy preferences are held. The effect of institutions is then to amplify or mute the voices of different constituencies. Simply counting voters no longer suffices, but there remains a straightforward mapping from constituency preferences to public policies, except that the former must now be measured along several dimensions (quantity, concentration, intensity). In this spirit, Helen Milner defines institutions as "mechanisms of collective choice."[14]

A very different characterization portrays institutions as a source of principal-agent problems. The fact that constituents elect politicians who appoint officials who make policy allows multiple slips betwixt cup and lip. If it is costly for constituents to monitor and sanction politicians who pursue personal agendas, the preferences of elected leaders and appointed officials may affect outcomes. In this view, institutions

---

12. Newer work, like the common agency models of Grossman and Helpman 1994, go some way toward capturing these considerations, but whether they can be insightfully applied to international relations is not yet clear. Nor can this approach easily explain why policies develop discontinuously. Take the case of European integration, which has proceeded in fits and starts, with long periods of stasis punctuated by spurts of intense integrationist activity. Although the stance of policy has shifted dramatically, the sectoral composition and factor endowments of the European economy and the interest group pressures attributable to those structures have evolved only gradually. There was no obvious change in the balance of special interest influence between 1985 and 1987, for example, when the Single Act was passed, or between 1990 and 1992, when the Maastricht Treaty was signed. In other words, explaining the pivotal events in the evolution of the EU in terms of the interest group model strictly construed is difficult. I return to these issues later.

13. For example, Garrett and Lange 1995.

14. Milner, this issue.

are imperfect technologies for monitoring and sanctioning political agents. Indeed, they can serve as barriers to effective sanctioning and insulate policymakers from constituency pressures; central bank independence and lifetime appointment for judicial officials have been thought of in this way.

There is an obvious analogy here with the literature on corporate control. Many economists have analyzed the problem that investors face in directing the actions of managers to whom they delegate corporate control.[15] This problem is not easily solved in the presence of asymmetric information and costly monitoring; the same would seem to be true of domestic and international politics. At the same time, theorists of corporate control have shown how financial institutions (universal banks, for example) can act as delegated monitors to attenuate principal-agent problems and how financial engineering (the use of debt and equity in the firm's capital structure) can mitigate the incentive for managers to pursue personal agendas. Conversely, institutions like universal banks are sometimes seen as mechanisms for insulating managers from pressure to shorten their horizons, in that way enhancing efficiency (akin to the horizon-lengthening effect of central bank and judicial independence). Work in political science on recall elections, federalism, and divided government can be seen in this light.[16]

The notion that institutions attenuate incentive problems associated with delegation encourages a functionalist perspective on their evolution.[17] Institutions, in this view, exist to play an efficiency-enhancing role. For those schooled in economic theory, this conjures up the image of competition among rival political arrangements. Inefficient institutions that allow excessive principal-agent slack will be amended by dissatisfied publics. Those that allow inefficient outcomes to persist will be competed away by better systems, in the same way that inefficient firms will be competed out of business. However crude this formulation, a considerable literature on, among other things, the end of the Cold War and the collapse of the Soviet Union embraces this perspective.

It is easy to be sympathetic to functionalist interpretations, which provide a straightforward explanation for the evolution of political institutions. At the same time, there is reason to think that many social arrangements were created for reasons only remotely related to their current function. Once the die is cast, arrangements became locked in. Because they are resistant to change, they lend policy a strongly path-dependent cast. Even if strong functionalist pressures exist for the emergence of efficient institutions, there may still be more than one uniquely efficient institutional solution to a coordination problem, creating a role for ideology and history to select among them.

W. Brian Arthur identifies several circumstances under which market arrangements become locked in.[18] One circumstance is large setup costs, which agents must sink when altering exiting arrangements. Another is learning: society has learned

---

15. For example, Jensen and Meckling 1976.
16. Again, see Garrett and Lange 1995 and the references cited therein.
17. For example, Keohane 1984.
18. Arthur 1988.

how to work with existing institutions to the point where it becomes reluctant to abandon them. Most important in the present context may be that a core function of institutions is to coordinate the activities of agents. Because institutions, like any coordinating technology, are a source of network externalities, modifying their structure involves coordinating the wishes of a large number of different individuals, which can pose a formidable obstacle to change.[19]

Another possibility is that institutions are purposely structured to resist change. Their role is to serve as commitment technologies that prevent opportunistic behavior by those in power. Were it easy to modify a rule that certain policies could be adopted only by unanimity or super majority, for example, that rule would lose its force. Institutions are structured in such a way to make overturning such rules difficult, which works to lock them in. In turn, this increases the tendency for institutional arrangements that might have had efficiency-enhancing effects under the conditions that characterized their creation to outlive their usefulness.

Given the existence of so many competing interpretations of the role of institutions, not surprisingly, scholars widely disagree on their characterization. At a more fundamental level, scholars have difficulty deriving testable propositions from these alternative characterizations and confronting them with data. For all the earlier-mentioned reasons, institutional structures tend to evolve only slowly over time. A time-series investigation, even one with a considerable historical time frame, is unlikely to uncover sufficient variation along the relevant dimensions to yield robust correlations between institutional inputs and policy outputs. There may be more identifying variation across countries, but cross-country analysis requires a standardized measurement of institutional attributes as well as adequate controls for other characteristics of countries, which is no mean task. Thus, work along these lines has mostly been limited to issues like the political-economy effects of central bank independence, corporatist bargaining, and delegation in the formulation of trade policy, where relevant groundwork has already been done by economists.[20]

It is revealing in this connection to recall how the notion of institutions giving rise to path-dependence became an accepted concept in economics. Arthur and others had for some years undertaken analytical work on the subject but with little impact on the profession as a whole. Significant impact resulted only when Paul David used the model to study a particular empirical problem, namely, the design of the mechanical typewriter.[21] In painstaking detail he showed how the connections between a variety of institutions—secretarial schools, all of which had the incentive to teach the same typing skills as their competitors to maximize their market share; law and accountancy firms, all of which hired from a common pool of secretaries and none of which had an incentive to invest in their acquisition of firm-specific typing techniques; and manufacturers, who were forced to hire sales staffs similarly lacking specialized skills and therefore incapable of demonstrating the effectiveness of anything but a

19. David 1993.
20. For examples, see Simmons 1994; and Garrett 1998b.
21. David 1985.

standardized keyboard—caused one of many viable keyboard configurations to become locked in.[22] He did so by taking a standard problem in economics, the choice of technology, and modifying the canonical model in small but far-reaching ways. In doing so he demonstrated that institutions, time, learning, and lock-in could in fact be built onto an existing analytical infrastructure without forcing scholars to choose between pursuing these ideas and tossing out the entire corpus of accumulated knowledge. The key to the advance was that it was empirical and incremental—in other words, it was normal science. Abstract theorizing was progressive because it was linked to normal empirical work.

Endogenous Preferences and the Role of Ideas

The interest group and institutional approaches, as I have sketched them, assume that agents know their preferences and know the appropriate strategies for advancing them. For an economist, a striking feature of the international relations literature is the existence of a strand of work that rejects this fundamental assumption.

Contributions to this literature reject the notion that constituencies and their political agents know their self-interest. Self-interest is more difficult to define when the issue is power, security, and a country's place in the world rather than money in the bank; it is a socially constructed concept that has no existence outside its specific context. And even when individuals, interest groups, and institutionally empowered lobbies have a clear sense of their objectives, they may lack an understanding of the mechanisms for achieving them in a complex world. Thus, simple economic models of utility maximization in the presence of perfect information may not plausibly carry over to issues of international security and diplomacy.

If preferences are incompletely formed or means of achieving objectives are incompletely understood, there is scope for mechanisms to formulate social priorities and identify strategies for pursuing them. Simplifying strategies, historical analogies, cultural predispositions, epistemic communities, and policy elites have been offered to fill this void.[23] Philip Tetlock and Charles McGuire characterize policymakers as "limited capacity information processors" who use rules of thumb in lieu of full optimization.[24] Peter Haas similarly questions whether state actors understand the system in which they operate and whether rational choice is therefore the most appropriate framework for studying their actions. He highlights the role in policymaking of networks of professionals with recognized expertise and competence, who pro-

---

22. It is further revealing that David had been asked to demonstrate to the economics profession, in the Allied Social Sciences Association Meetings talk that was the basis for his article, the uses of history in economic analysis. Rather than giving an abstract talk, he chose to focus on a specific bit of empirical work. Leibowitz and Margolis have subsequently challenged the generality of the notion of path dependence by—revealingly—disputing David's empirical work. Leibowitz and Margolis 1990. This, too, illustrates the point: analytic concepts rise and fall not on the basis of the elegance of the underlying model but largely as a result of the normal scientific process of marshaling empirical evidence, which includes attempts to replicate the results of prior investigators.

23. Ikenberry 1993b.

24. Tetlock and McGuire 1986.

vide depictions of social processes and the likely consequences of actions.[25] Those who constitute these networks instruct officials about how to conceptualize their self-interest and how to enhance their welfare through strategy. G. John Ikenberry argues that, on technical issues in particular, experts can contribute to the development of a consensus about feasible and desirable social goals.[26] Peter Hall and his colleagues show how policy outcomes are shaped by the interaction of ideas—on the one hand, with the orientation of the governing party, the structure of the state, and state-society relations and, on the other, with the nature of political discourse.[27] Kathleen McNamara describes how an alliance of technical experts and policy entrepreneurs can create a policy consensus when inherited conceptions are ripe for rejection as a result of poor policy performance.[28] Judith Goldstein and Robert Keohane similarly argue that ideas shape outcomes when they take the form of world views ("principled or causal beliefs") that clarify actors' visions of goals and means–end relationships.[29]

Ideas, ideology, and elite consensus are not alternatives to the institutional approach, of course. They must be formulated, transmitted, received, and amplified by a socially constructed conveyance mechanism—an "institution" in the words of Ronald Jepperson, Alexander Wendt, and Peter Katzenstein.[30] As Geoffrey Garrett and Barry Weingast put it, "Shared belief systems and focal points . . . do not always emerge without conscious efforts on the part of interested actors. Rather, they must often be constructed."[31] To exercise influence, policy elites must be brought together and vested with authority. Institutions like the International Monetary Fund, the Group of Seven, and the Bank for International Settlements help those elites communicate their views and give those ideas their seal of approval. Institutions provide a venue for the ongoing, systematic exchange of information and ideas. They have an agenda-setting function that gives precedence to some conceptualizations above others. Background papers by in-house analysts inform their proceedings, defining the parameters of discourse and decision making. The written record and recollections of permanent staff allow these processes to endure beyond the terms in office of any particular set of elected officials.[32]

Obvious parallels exist between this literature and work in economics on bounded rationality.[33] It is revealing that the latter has never really taken off in the sense of being widely applied to concrete questions. In part the problem is that the conclusions derived from theoretical models are sensitive to small variations in specification, making it difficult to derive robust implications. A more fundamental problem is

---

25. Haas 1992a.
26. Ikenberry 1993b.
27. Hall 1989b.
28. McNamara 1996.
29. Goldstein and Keohane 1993a.
30. Jepperson, Wendt, and Katzenstein 1996.
31. Garrett and Weingast 1993, 176. "Ideas do not float freely," in the words of Risse-Kappen Risse-Kappen 1994. For a particularly clear statement of this view, see the introduction to Goldstein and Keohane 1993a.
32. There is an analogy with the way "cheap talk" (communication without commitment) can facilitate cooperation among firms in an imperfectly competitive market. Farrell and Rabin 1996.
33. For example, Simon 1986.

that work on bounded rationality has not generated testable, refutable propositions that can be systematically confronted with data.[34]

Similar criticisms can be levied against the international relations literature on "endogenous preferences." The "idea of ideas" is intriguing, but how to formulate it in a testable way is not clear. Is it rejectable? Can its explanatory power be systematically compared with that of alternative hypotheses? Can it be modeled formally with the goal of determining its internal consistency and drawing out its less obvious implications? Can it be synthesized with other literatures, like that on game theory, for example, so that not only can preferences be endogenized but their implications for strategic interaction can be systematically pursued?

Implications of the International Dimension

By definition, international relations differs from the rest of political science by its concern with the interaction of sovereign states. Even those scholars who are most heavily committed to the view that foreign policy outcomes are driven by domestic interests would admit a role for those same factors in foreign countries and therefore for interactions between them. The positions taken by governments in international negotiations depend in part on the positions of their foreign counterparts. How hard governments push for a particular objective will depend on how hard their foreign counterparts push back. In other words, bargaining among nation-states may be critically important for outcomes. For self-evident reasons, the literature in which these issues are emphasized is known as "intergovernmentalism."

Analyses of bargaining between governments typically use game-theoretic tools to model the choice of strategies. Modeling this interaction forces the analyst to think systematically about incentives and tactics and about the likely reaction of other states. The problem with game-theoretic models is that they generally admit to a multiplicity of solutions, requiring further assumptions to select an equilibrium. In addition, the institutions that aggregate interest group pressures at the national level drop from sight when attention turns to the strategic interaction of governments. The literature on two-level games seeks to combine the game between governments and their constituents with the game between countries, but the caveat in the preceding sentence continues to apply.[35]

In this view, interest groups and institutions matter mainly because they find reflection in the strategies pursued by national governments in international fora.[36] Sometimes scholars relax this strong assumption by positing a role for transnational inter-

---

34. For further discussion, see Kahler, this issue, who concludes, "what is most striking is not only the absence of a single psychological alternative to rational choice but also the absence of a clear set of theories or hypotheses about the importance of psychological distortions of rational decision making or the conditions under which those distortions are likely to be found." A partial exception to this generalization is work that has sought to contrast the predictions of utility theory with those of prospect theory. But, by my reading, this attempt to formulate a coherent, refutable alternative hypothesis has been less than convincing.

35. See Putnam 1988; and Evans, Jacobsen, and Putnam 1993.

36. I say "mainly" rather than "solely," because some scholars have attempted to extend the intergovernmental model to allow for international interactions through other channels, as I describe momentarily.

ests and institutions. Keohane, Joseph Nye, Robert Putnam, Wayne Sandholtz, and John Zysman all have highlighted the ability of transnational interest groups and coalitions to influence national policy.[37] There has been increasing interest, particularly in the literature on the EU, in the influence of transnational institutions.[38]

The weakness of transnational analysis lies in measurement: analysts appear to be particularly unable to agree on the political influence of transnational, as opposed to nation-bound, interests and institutions. The impression is that political scientists know a transnational interest when they see one but cannot identify it in a way that allows other investigators to independently verify their conclusions.[39] Once again, theorizing does not lend itself to systematic empirical verification, hindering the emergence of a strong analytical consensus.

The Level-of-Analysis Problem

Fifty years ago the parallels between the theorizing in international relations, on the one hand, and in microeconomics, on the other, were even more pronounced than today.[40] Realists argued that countries were the major actors in world affairs and that they could be treated as unitary actors. Members of the realist school argued that it was unnecessary, as Martin Hollis and Steve Smith put it, to "open the box" of the

---

37. See Keohane and Nye 1972; Putnam 1988; and Sandholtz and Zysman 1989.

38. To pursue this example, it is widely argued that the institutions of the EU possess sufficient autonomy to shape European policy outcomes; this is nothing more than a scholarly statement of popular complaints about the EU's "democracy deficit." And in the same way that principal-agent slack allows national politicians to do more than merely reflect the preferences of their domestic constituents, it can allow transnational institutions to do more than reflect the preferences of national governments. The Council of Ministers, it is true, is largely a venue for national government influence. But the European Commission and the European Court of Justice have considerable independence from the governments of member states (although the precise extent of this independence is debated).

39. The other place where institutions surface is in the neoliberal literature on international regimes. Economists think of regimes as tacit understandings about behavior. Many are inclined to restate the core points of this literature in game-theoretic terms, suggesting that tacit understandings about what is acceptable and likely can play a role in selecting among alternative equilibria. Institutions can play a role in shaping those understandings through the mechanisms described earlier. By transmitting information more or less smoothly and making it easier or harder for others (in the present context, other countries) to respond consistently, they can alter the incentives for individual players. Morrow 1994b. There is an analogy between these arguments and the literature in economics and economic history on trade in the absence of legal enforcement—see Greif 1994; and Milgrom, North, and Weingast 1990—that is, with the literature in which it is argued that "a dense social network leads to the development of informal structure with substantial stability," to quote North 1990, 38. The problem is ensuring conformance with the terms of a contract in the absence of an enforcement mechanism. Solutions are found in repeated interaction in the context of an institutional setting that encourages certain norms of behavior, takes recourse to impartial arbitrators to verify that those norms have been met, and encourages other traders to impose sanctions on those who fail to display the expected forms of behavior (such as by refusing to transact with them further, banishing them from the venue where transactions take place, or withholding certification of their wares). This work has helped to establish how traders can be encouraged to keep to the terms of an agreement in the absence of legal enforcement, with obvious implications for how countries can "cooperate under anarchy." Oye 1986.

40. Although the occasion for this symposium is the fiftieth anniversary of *International Organization*, for purposes of the paragraphs that follow, what is even more appropriate is that it will be published in 1998—the fiftieth anniversary of Morgenthau's *Politics Among Nations*.

state and view what went on inside.[41] There is a parallel with the theory of the firm as, say, Milton Friedman taught it at the University of Chicago, according to which it is enough to assume that firms behave "as if" they maximize profits; it is unnecessary to "open the box" and explore their inner workings.[42] Economists rationalized the assumption on the grounds that, in a competitive market, firms that do not maximize profits will be driven out of business, leaving a residual population whose behavior will satisfy the premise.

Subsequently, scholars devoted considerable effort to analyzing international relations at higher and lower levels. At a higher level this is the question posed by Kenneth Waltz of whether the system has its own dynamics.[43] The analogous question in economics is whether one can learn something about behavior or its consequences by studying the macroeconomy rather than individual households and firms. Economists in fact possess models in which one learns from aggregation—where the dynamics of the whole are more than the sum of its parts. An example is the paradox of thrift, in which individual households or firms, by attempting to save more, end up saving less because more saving means less demand and lower incomes in general equilibrium.

But these models, though confirming that gains may be made from studying dynamics at higher—systemic—levels, do not relieve the need for understanding the behavior of individual households and firms. Indeed, they require particular assumptions about household and firm behavior (a positive constant marginal propensity to save, for example), as well as assumptions about the structure of the system (the economy is closed to international transactions, wages are fixed, and so on), whose validity is an empirical question. The problem with the Waltzian formulation is that it poses the system level as an alternative to analysis of individual countries. In a sense, macroeconomics went through a similar phase in which model builders analyzed macroeconomic dynamics without much attention to microfoundations.[44] Today, in contrast, most macroeconomic models explicitly derive variables like economy-wide saving and investment by aggregating the decisions of individual households and firms. International relations has experienced a parallel—if less decisive—evolution in which the relatively sterile debate over the level-of-analysis problem has given way to a paradigm in which one must simultaneously analyze what goes on inside particular countries, on the one hand, and systemic dynamics, on the other.

International relations specialists concerned with lower levels of analysis have similarly questioned whether much can be learned using models based on the assumption that countries act as if they maximize the welfare of the median voter (as simple interest group models posit). They question the assumptions of rationality and maximizing behavior that undergird game-theoretic analyses.[45] Their qualms have coun-

41. Hollis and Smith 1986.
42. Friedman 1953.
43. Waltz 1979.
44. One is reminded of the first macro-model, built by Bill Phillips of Phillips-Curve fame, which consisted of a series of receptacles connected by pipes and filled with water to be used to analyze aggregate supply and demand hydraulically.
45. The relevant literature is surveyed by Smith 1988.

terparts in economics—in the literature on psychology and economics in particular. But although anecdotal evidence, studies of market efficiency, and results from experimental economics all provide some evidence of deviations from rationality, utility maximization, and productive efficiency, analysis has not pushed much beyond that point.[46] For purposes of illustration, consider the literature on international debt. Jack Guttentag and Richard Herring invoked the psychology-and-economics literature in arguing that disaster myopia leads commercial banks to lend excessively to developing countries.[47] Subsequent investigators, however, found it difficult to model that behavior and draw out its less obvious implications. In the end, the strand of work based on insights from psychology and economics stalled, and the literature on debt developed in other directions.[48] The same can be said of other attempts to apply the psychology-and-economics literature: speculation is fun, analysis is difficult. The approach has not lent itself to normal science.

Others question not the assumption of rationality but the commonality of motives within countries and the absence of transactions and communications costs. The literature on bureaucracy and foreign policy that explains outcomes in terms of bureaucratic interactions has relaxed these assumptions productively.[49] This is very much the spirit of developments in microeconomics over the last fifty years. At one time economists analyzed markets by assuming that firms act "as if" they maximize profits, but the discipline has devoted its attention in recent years almost entirely to incentive problems within firms and to how units of production organize themselves internally.[50] There is no question that, in principal, analyzing the internal organization of foreign-policymaking bureaucracies could be similarly productive. The problem, as Peter Katzenstein, Robert Keohane, and Stephen Krasner in this issue note, is that the bureaucratic-politics literature, like that based on cognitive psychology, has succeeded in developing few testable propositions.[51] The few hypotheses it has generated, such as the notion that bureaus are interested in maximizing the size of their budgets, have not withstood empirical scrutiny.

An Application to European Monetary Unification

In this section I apply the perspectives developed earlier to the case of economic and monetary unification in Europe (EMU). Not only is this a case with which I am familiar, but also the literature on it is part of a body of work with a long lineage in international relations. Describing how the various analytical approaches recounted in the second section have been used to understand a particular problem illustrates

---

46. On the evidence, see Hogarth and Reder 1986.

47. Guttentag and Herring 1985.

48. This occurred mostly toward game-theoretic models in which banks and governments each seek to maximize their own objective functions but where problems of commitment and collective action make the Nash equilibrium suboptimal.

49. See Snyder, Bruck, and Sapin 1954; and Allison 1971.

50. In addition to Jensen and Meckling 1976, in this connection one might mention Williamson 1975.

51. Katzenstein, Keohane, and Krasner, this issue.

both the strengths and the limitations of the case-study methodology that continues to dominate research in international relations.

Although I focus on the attempt to create a monetary union by 1 January 1999, I am necessarily concerned with the longer-term context, which can be traced to abortive late-1940s plans for a European monetary union. Discussions of European monetary integration took on new urgency with the impending collapse of the Bretton Woods system in the late 1960s. Early discussions led to the Werner Report in 1970, which envisaged a three-stage transition to monetary union over the subsequent decade. But the vehicle for navigating this course, the European Snake, failed to hold the road. The European Monetary System (EMS), created in 1979, eliminated the Snake's most serious deficiencies, although its early years were turbulent before it settled into normal operation after 1986. Then came the Single Act, which mandated the removal of capital controls, followed by the Delors Report and the Maastricht Treaty. The process continued to gather momentum before slowing significantly following the European currency crises of 1992–93. Since then, EMU has proceeded in fits and starts. Although the EU remains on course for monetary union on 1 January 1999, at the time of this writing the project's ultimate success remains uncertain.

Interest Group Models

The logical starting point for an analysis of these developments is interest group politics. Some interest groups are intrinsically more concerned than others with eliminating exchange-rate volatility and uncertainty. Firms with strong international ties evince a particular interest in exchange-rate stability. Banks and corporations that invest throughout the EU will be interested in intra-European exchange-rate stability in particular. More generally, producers of tradable goods with EU-wide markets should be averse to currency fluctuations in general and competitive devaluations in particular. Conversely, producers and consumers of nontraded goods will display relatively little interest in exchange-rate stability or monetary unification.

This perspective points to economic integration as the force behind the monetary-union project. As the post–World War II integration has proceeded, the number of companies and banks that value exchange-rate stability has climbed. The share of Europe's trade that stays within the continent has risen from 40 to 60 percent of the total since the mid-1960s. Although the explosion of cross-border direct foreign investment (DFI) was delayed (partly because controls on capital flows were maintained for longer than controls on trade), by the 1980s DFI was growing at impressive rates.

The argument, then, is that "the greater cross-border mobility of goods and capital within Europe made stabilizing exchange rates more attractive."[52] The number and political influence of those favoring exchange-rate stability were augmented by the same technological and institutional factors that caused trade to grow faster than

52. Frieden 1996, 211.

incomes over much of the industrial and developing world.[53] Empirical studies taking both case-study and cross-country econometric approaches have lent considerable support to the hypothesis.[54]

But the reference in the last paragraph to the rest of the world points to an uncomfortable fact: foreign trade and investment have been growing faster than incomes, not just in Europe but also globally.[55] Yet while Europe was attempting to reduce the variability of its exchange rates, countries elsewhere were accepting greater flexibility.[56] Part of the explanation may be that even though Europe's trade was growing relative to income, it was also becoming more regionalized. Because an increasing share of that trade stayed within Europe, EU member states seeking to peg their currencies no longer faced the decision of whether to peg to the deutsche mark, dollar, or yen, a dilemma that might have otherwise tempted them to peg to no one at all. Unfortunately, it is not hard to cite other countries that also grew increasingly dependent on a single trading partner or group of partners and yet moved away from exchange-rate pegging (Canada and Mexico vis-à-vis the United States spring to mind).

To the extent that reductions in transportation costs and improvements in communications and information technologies stimulated cross-border transactions, there is no reason to think that they should have lent the greatest impetus to trade over short distances (in this case, between neighboring European countries).[57] In fact, growth in the share of intra-European trade in the continent's total has reflected not so much technological progress as policy. The six founding members of the European Economic Community had completed their customs union by the early 1960s, ahead of the schedule in the Treaty of Rome, and extended that achievement to additional countries through successive rounds of enlargement. Intra-European trade liberalization encompassed nontariff barriers in the 1980s with the adoption of the Single Act. Although the GATT has taken important steps toward achieving reductions in tariff and nontariff barriers to trade among its contracting parties, its achievements pale in comparison with those of the EU. If the growth of trade reflects policy, rather than policy reflecting the growth of trade, then we hardly have here an autonomous explanation for the policy outcomes we seek to understand. The empirical work described

53. Some argue, echoing the literature on multinational enterprises dating from the early 1970s, that the development of transnational interest groups (transnational financial, business, and labor coalitions in particular) accelerated the translation of this interest into policy. Sandholtz and Zysman argue for the importance of these transnational interest groups, Moravcsik against. See Sandholtz and Zysman 1989; and Moravcsik 1991.

54. See, for example, Giavazzi and Giovannini 1989; Frieden 1996; Bayoumi and Eichengreen 1997; and de Boissieu and Pisani-Ferry 1998. An institutional variant of the interest group argument can be found in Garrett 1998b.

55. Furthermore, some economic models suggest that DFI will render multinational firms less concerned about currency fluctuations, not more. To the extent that a change in the exchange rate reduces the cost of producing in one country relative to another, a firm producing in both will be better hedged than one producing at only one site. Cushman 1988.

56. As documented in Eichengreen 1996.

57. Indeed, plausible reasons exist for assuming that the opposite is true. See the discussion in Frankel, Stein, and Wei 1996.

earlier may have simply uncovered a correlation between a pair of endogenous variables (political support for monetary integration, and dependence on international transactions) without identifying the exogenous factor behind their co-movement.

Neofunctionalist Spillovers

The interest group argument, with the driving force of the European Community appended, suggests that the customs union and the Single Market accelerated the process of monetary integration by shifting the political balance between producers of traded and nontraded goods. It altered the balance of power between those favoring and opposing exchange-rate stability. An appeal of this argument is that it illustrates the operation of Hassian neofunctionalist spillovers. It provides a mechanism by which the integration of goods and capital markets, achieved through the creation of a European customs union, spilled over to the monetary domain. It suggests a virtuous cycle of positive feedback: since currency stability encourages trade and factor mobility as well as the other way around, mutually reinforcing spillovers will occur in both directions, lending European integration a strongly path-dependent character.[58]

It is possible to point to several sources of spillover. One is the linkage between the Common Agricultural Policy (CAP) and monetary integration. The goal of the CAP, the European Community's first substantive achievement, was to stabilize the domestic currency prices of agricultural commodities through a system of variable levies and subsidies. Changes in intra-European exchange rates were highly disruptive to its operation. According to Francesco Giavazzi and Alberto Giovannini, the need to defend the CAP against the corrosive effect of currency fluctuations provided important impetus for the development of the EMS and for European monetary integration more generally.[59] It would, in principle, be possible to test this hypothesis directly by asking whether support for monetary integration was strongest in those countries with the greatest stake in the CAP, although this does not appear to have been done.

Another potential source of spillover is linkage with the Single Act. The Single Act did more than shift resources into the traded goods sector, augmenting the ranks of those engaged in international financial transactions and creating more groups with a vested interest in currency stability. By mandating the removal of capital controls, it "hollowed out" the middle ground between floating exchange rates and monetary unification. Whereas Frieden suggests that capital mobility mattered by increasing the number of special interests exposed to international transactions, this alternative emphasizes instead how capital mobility limited the range of feasible responses to

---

58. This argument is made in Bayoumi and Eichengreen 1997. Frankel and Rose provide another variation on the theme in which countries whose business cycles move together prefer stable currencies (on optimum currency area grounds), and stable currencies cause their business cycles to move together. Frankel and Rose 1996.

59. Giavazzi and Giovannini 1989. See also McNamara 1992.

their demands. Faced with no alternative to the extremes of floating and monetary union and given a strong aversion to floating, Europe chose unification.[60]

The empirical corollary is that countries that removed capital controls should have at the same time become stronger proponents of monetary unification, since proceeding as before (with the pegged-but-adjustable exchange rates of the EMS) was no longer feasible. The problem, of course, is that all members of the European Community ratified the Single Act at the same time, leaving little room for identifying variation. To be sure, countries phased out controls at different rates, providing some identifying variation, although this may reflect their comparative ease of running independent national monetary policies, which may itself be a function of structural features of their economies—structural features that could be correlated with preferences toward monetary integration for independent reasons. This empirical analysis does not appear to have been undertaken, which is revealing of its complexity.

Linkage Politics

Some have argued that the Single Market was important not just because it promoted trade but also because it was a stepping-stone to more important goals such as political integration. Germany was ready to accede to French pressure for monetary unification, the intergovernmentalist argument goes, only because France was prepared to agree to meaningful steps toward political integration, which Germany desired in order to obtain an expanded foreign policy role in the context of an EU foreign policy. The fact that EU member states had taken significant steps toward political integration by ratifying the Maastricht Treaty and scheduling another Intergovernmental Conference to elaborate the treaty's political pillar spilled over to the monetary domain.[61] The fact that Germany and France could credibly threaten to proceed without British support won British accession to the Maastricht bargain in the end.[62]

Arguing that monetary integration must be seen as a corollary of the EU's broader program of economic and political integration poses no logical problem for proponents of the interest group model. For them the analytical task then becomes identifying the interest group pressures that lie behind Europe's broader integration agenda. Unfortunately, as an empirical matter this is not straightforward. Once the relevant domain is economic and political integration, not just monetary integration, it becomes harder to recover the identity of the relevant interest groups from standard

60. For a variant of this view, see Webb 1991. A related argument is that the Single Market mattered not just by shifting additional pressure groups into the free trade camp and undermining the flexibility of narrow bands but also by heightening the sensitivity of sectoral interests to currency fluctuations. (These arguments are elaborated in Eichengreen and Ghironi 1996.) Currency instability (more specifically, the "competitive devaluations" problem) threatened to erode support for the Single Market by shifting the locus of competitive advantage and rewarding beggar-thy-neighbor policies. Insofar as the Single Market was a valued objective, exchange-rate stability was seen as necessary to solidify political support.

61. Creating deliberate linkages as a strategy for encouraging progress was a theme of Nye 1971.

62. Moravcsik calls this combination of intergovernmental bargaining and structural preconditions that allowed the Franco–German alliance to credibly threaten to proceed without Britain "intergovernmental institutionalism," following Keohane. Moravcsik 1991.

models of international trade and finance.[63] In the absence of strong theoretical guidance for identifying the relevant interest groups, there is a tendency to specify the model in a way that is irrefutable. Identifying interest groups that favored and opposed a particular initiative is always possible, and in the absence of strong theoretical pointers to the null hypothesis, it is tempting to simply assert that their influence must have been key.

Ideas, Ideology, and Policy Entrepreneurship

Political scientists were not slow to fill the gaps in the interest group model. Wayne Sandholtz and John Zysman argued that the relative decline of the United States and rise of East Asian economic power led Europeans to reassess the costs and benefits of regional integration.[64] The instability of the dollar, reflecting imbalances between U.S. monetary and fiscal policies, provided an incentive to create a zone of monetary stability in Europe. The perception that both the United States and Japan were creating commercial and financial blocs provided Europe with an incentive to do likewise, resulting in neofunctionalist spillovers into monetary affairs. The end of the Cold War eroded the EU–U.S. security alliance, removing restraints on Europe's pursuit of its regional strategy.

Although changes in the international balance of economic and political power may have triggered the revival of integrationist sentiment, translating sentiment into action, according to this story, required institutional intervention. This presupposed policy entrepreneurship on the part of the European Commission. Not even national political elites, in this view, had a clear sense of their policy priorities in the post–Cold War, post–American hegemony era. The Commission's role was to mobilize a coalition of governmental elites in support of regional integration. Effective entrepreneurship was made possible, in part, by changes in domestic structure (the decline or transformation of the left, and the failure of national economic strategies) that can be understood as the response of interest groups to integration. It only remained for policy entrepreneurs to capitalize on the opportunity.

In contrast to the assumptions underlying game-theoretic formulations, then, neither national leaders nor their constituencies "possessed the intellectual means to foresee alternative outcomes, much less rank them."[65] The preferences of national leaders and their constituencies were incompletely formed, providing scope for them

---

63. And there is the further problem that monetary integration in Europe has proceeded discontinuously, as emphasized in a similar context by Sandholtz and Zysman 1989. One might attempt to salvage the simple interest group model by arguing that it would have delivered monetary integration in a more linear fashion, with steadily increasing economic integration delivering progressively greater intra-EU exchange-rate stability, had exogenous disturbances like German economic and monetary unification not disrupted Europe's financial markets and efforts to achieve policy convergence. This attempt at salvation seems rather tortured; in particular, it seems strange to treat German unification as entirely exogenous to the integration process with which we are concerned.

64. Sandholtz and Zysman 1989.

65. Ibid., 107ff.

to be shaped by an entity like the Commission. The mechanism it used was a series of technical measures designed to create a fully unified internal market. The successful implementation of theses measures, in turn, created further integrationist momentum.

In their discussion of the structural conditions that opened the way for the Commission's policy entrepreneurship, Sandholtz and Zysman emphasize the policy failures of the 1970s and 1980s—in particular, the failure of national economic policy strategies that produced high inflation and unemployment. In France, the manifest failure of the macroeconomic strategy of the first Mitterand government (whose finance minister was, of course, none other than Jacques Delors) led, in the end, to a renewed commitment to European integration, partly as a way of providing a friendlier international environment for the kind of policies the French desired. If France could not reflate unilaterally without risking the collapse of the franc, perhaps she could reflate collectively in the context of a strengthened EMS (especially if the EMS provision requiring other countries to provide unlimited support for currencies that fell to the bottom of their fluctuation bands could be taken at face value).[66] Somehow, however, France's rededication to the EMS did more to alter French preferences than to reshape those of her partners in the Exchange Rate Mechanism (although Sandholtz and Zysman do not explain why).

The role of policy failure and reinterpretation is also evident in McNamara's analysis of European monetary integration.[67] According to McNamara, the solidification of the EMS and the agreement to strike out for monetary union reflected an emerging consensus about the goals and instruments of monetary policy. That consensus was the product of learning by national elites in the inflationary 1970s.[68] In the face of uncertainty about the connections between macroeconomic and regulatory policies, on the one hand, and currency stability and growth, on the other, elites were able to shape political actors' perceptions of the relevant relationships. David Cameron places particular stress on the role in this process of a transnational coalition of central bankers, a role that was strengthened by decades of EU institution building through which central bankers had gained access to the channels of influence.[69] These elites concluded that it was not feasible to pursue an activist monetary strategy in a world of integrated financial markets. Here European views may have been influenced by the successful record of the monetarist-oriented German Bundesbank, by the concurrent advent of monetarist monetary policy in the United States, and by developments in economic theory (the Friedman-Phelps expectations-augmented Phillips Curve and the Kydland-Prescott demonstration of the time inconsistency of optimal policy) that provided intellectual justification for the new policy stance. The development of this pan-European consensus rendered the EMS more stable and easier to manage. Cameron's transnational policy elite was similarly able to shape the Maas-

66. See Pauly 1991. As it turned out, this commitment was not worth the paper it was written on, although this was not fully appreciated until 1992. See Eichengreen and Wyplosz 1993.
67. McNamara 1996.
68. Hall makes the same argument for Britain. Hall 1993.
69. Cameron 1995.

tricht Treaty to its liking, removing one potential source of opposition to monetary unification.[70]

This approach emphasizing incompletely formed preferences or incompletely formed understandings of the strategic environment is widely applied by political scientists to the question of European monetary unification. Interests motivate decision making, but, when the issue is something as confusing and complex as monetary integration, they cannot be taken as fully formed from the start. Institutions transmit the influences that help nascent preferences to coalesce.[71]

However appealing this synthesis, without a methodology for calibrating its explanatory power relative to alternatives, operationalizing it is difficult. Those who advocate the interest group view can pose their arguments in a refutable way (formulating hypotheses of how, among other things, the magnitude of foreign trade and investment should be correlated with economic policy decisions) and offer formal statistical tests of their arguments, as Frieden has done in the context of European monetary unification.[72] Those who argue for the importance of institutions can and have done likewise. Those who emphasize the role of ideas continue to have considerably greater difficulty in operationalizing their approach.

Conclusion

Scholars in international relations possess a rich portfolio of theories, hypotheses, and interpretations of the factors shaping the interaction of nation-states. Some of these will be familiar to economists, including those approaches that take nations as unitary actors whose governments seek to advance the national interest and use game theory to study international interactions; those that disaggregate nation-states into interest groups who dictate governments' policy decisions according to the median voter or adding-machine models; and those that focus on institutions in shaping domestic and international interactions. Other approaches—such as those concerned with ideas, norms, or regimes—will appear more novel. Either way, few economists

---

70. It is tempting to appeal to this new policy consensus as a focal point for coordinating the strategies of policymakers in a situation of multiple equilibria. This analogy, developed by Goldstein and Keohane and by Garrett and Weingast, is not entirely satisfactory from the perspective of an economist. See Goldstein and Keohane 1993a; and Garrett and Weingast 1993. The problem is that game-theoretic models with multiple equilibria and focal points assume stable, well-defined preferences, where players do not know which strategy to pick only because they do not know which one will be picked by their opponents. But what these authors have in mind is something fundamentally different, namely, where agents do not even know their own preferences, or at least how to translate their preferences into actions given assumptions about the behavior of their rivals in the policy game. It seems wise therefore not to push the analogy too far.

71. Sandholtz provides a clear statement of this view: "Each member state tries to ensure that EC outcomes are as close as possible to its national interests, but the crucial point is that those national interests are defined in the context of the EC. . . . In other words, the national interests of EC states do not have independent existence; they are not formed in a vacuum and then brought to Brussels. Those interests are defined and redefined in an international and institutional context that includes the EC. States define their interests in a different way as members of the EC than they would without it." Sandholtz 1993.

72. Frieden 1996.

will question that research in international relations is now informed by a rich variety of suggestive analytical approaches—if anything, a richer menu of theories than in mainstream economics itself.

But what international relations lacks from the perspective of economics is close connections between theory and empirical work. It lacks systematic, standardized ways of bringing data to bear on those theories. It lacks a standard methodology for assessing their explanatory power. The case study remains the dominant testing ground for alternative approaches. As shown in the third section of this article, this tendency can be a weakness as well as a strength. Case studies are useful for illustrating the practical applicability of abstract reasoning, but they are crude instruments for discriminating among alternative hypotheses and rating their relative explanatory power. Because individual cases, in their richness, are complex, they can always be interpreted in terms of several alternative analytical approaches. And because explanatory variables are correlated, interpretations in terms of one that omit all reference to others will suffer from omitted-variables bias and run the risk of spurious correlation. This danger follows inevitably from the case-study approach, since the limited number of cases any one scholar has the energy to master offers limited degrees of freedom for systematic tests.

From the perspective of economics, the task for scholars in international relations is to develop other ways of more formally, systematically, and rigorously testing their theories, presumably by pooling cases across countries or over time and by taking advantage of the institutional variation in that expanded data set. Having said this, it is important to emphasize that a call for more empirical work should not encourage those who engage in the search for theory-free patterns in the data. Empirical work that degenerates into mindless empiricism will not be progressive, whereas empirical work that is theory-linked will push the field forward.

Scholars must avoid the tendency in economics to take this approach too far by disregarding hypotheses that are not easily quantified and tested and by neglecting one-of-a-kind events whose analysis is not conducive to the application of a general theory or a general test. It is hard to imagine a field of international relations in which unique situations (World War I, Nazi Germany, post–World War II European integration) were excluded because of the lack of an adequate, comparable group of situations on which to base cross-section analyses.

This, then, is not a plea to study classical statistics or the econometrics of panel data. Nor is it a plea for political scientists to engage in more large-scale empirical work (some would say "mindless data mining"). It is a suggestion that the field needs to move in the direction of formulating parsimonious models and clearly refutable null hypotheses, and toward developing empirical techniques that will allow those hypotheses to be more directly confronted by the data. This, admittedly, is easier said than done.

References

Adler, Emanuel. 1987. *The Power of Ideology: The Quest for Technological Autonomy in Argentina and Brazil*. Berkeley: University of California Press.

———. 1991. Cognitive Evolution: A Dynamic Approach for the Study of International Relations and Their Progress. In *Progress in Postwar International Relations,* edited by Emanuel Adler and Beverly Crawford, 43–88. New York: Columbia University Press.

———. 1992. The Emergence of Cooperation: National Epistemic Communities and the International Evolution of the Idea of Nuclear Arms Control. *International Organization* 46:101–45.

———. 1997. Seizing the Middle Ground: Constructivism in World Politics. *European Journal of International Relations* 3:319–63.

Adler, Emanuel, and Michael Barnett. 1996. Governing Anarchy: A Research Agenda for the Study of Security Communities. *Ethics and International Affairs* 10:63–98.

Adler, Emanuel, and Michael Barnett, eds. 1998. *Security Communities*. Cambridge: Cambridge University Press.

Adler, Emanuel, and Peter M. Haas. 1992. Conclusion: Epistemic Communities, World Order, and the Creation of a Reflective Research Program. *International Organization* 46:367–90.

Aggarwal, Vinod K. 1996. *Debt Games: Strategic Interaction in International Debt Rescheduling*. Cambridge: Cambridge University Press.

Akerlof, George A. 1970. The Market for "Lemons." *Quarterly Journal of Economics* 84:488–500.

———. 1980. A Theory of Social Custom, of Which Unemployment May Be One Consequence. *Quarterly Journal of Economics* 94:749–75.

Alesina, Alberto, and Roberto Perotti. 1996. Income Distribution, Political Instability and Investment. *European Economic Review* 40:1203–28.

Alesina, Alberto, and E. Spolaore. 1997. On the Number and Size of Nations. *Quarterly Journal of Economics* 112:1027–56.

Alger, Chadwick. 1965. Personal Contact in Intergovernmental Organizations. In *International Behavior: A Social-Psychological Analysis,* edited by Herbert C. Kelman, 523–47. New York: Holt, Rinehart and Winston.

———. 1970. Research on Research: A Decade of Quantitative and Field Research on International Organization. *International Organization* 23:414–50.

Alker, Hayward R. 1970. Computer Simulations, Conceptual Frameworks, and Coalition Behavior. In *The Study of Coalition Behavior,* edited by Sven Groennings, 369–95. New York: Rinehart and Winston.

———. 1990. Rescuing "Reason" from the "Rationalists": Reading Vico, Marx, and Weber as Reflective Institutionalists. *Millennium: Journal of International Studies* 19:161–84.

———. 1996. *Rediscoveries and Reformulations: Humanistic Methodologies for International Studies.* New York: Cambridge University Press.

Alker, Hayward R., and Thomas J. Biersteker. 1984. The Dialectics of World Order: Notes for a Future Archaeologist of International Savoir Faire. *International Studies Quarterly* 28:121–42.

Alker, Hayward R., and Bruce Russett. 1965. *World Politics in the General Assembly.* New Haven, Conn.: Yale University Press.

Allison, Graham T. 1971. *Essence of Decision: Explaining the Cuban Missile Crisis*. Boston: Little, Brown.

Allison, Graham, and Morton Halperin. 1972. Bureaucratic Politics: A Paradigm and Some Policy Implications. *World Politics* 24:40–79.

Allport, Gordon W. 1954. *The Nature of Prejudice*. Reading, Mass.: Addison-Wesley.

Almond, Gabriel. 1950. *The American People and Foreign Policy*. New York: Harcourt Brace.

Alt, James E., and Kenneth A. Shepsle, eds. 1990. *Perspectives on Positive Political Economy*. Cambridge: Cambridge University Press.

Alter, Karen. 1996. The European Court's Political Power. *West European Politics* 19:458–60.

Alvarez, R. Michael, Geoffrey Garrett, and Peter Lange. 1991. Government Partisanship, Labor Organization, and Macroeconomic Performance. *American Political Science Review* 85:541–56.

American Political Science Review. 1997. Forum (articles by John Vasquez, Kenneth Waltz, Thomas Christensen and Jack Snyder, Colin Elman and Miriam Fendius Elman, Randall Schweller, and Stephen Walt). *American Political Science Review* 91:899–935.

Andersen, Heine. 1997. *Forskere i Danmark—videnskabssyn, vurderinger og aktiviteter: En videnskabssociologisk undersøgelse med særlig vægt på samfundsvidenskaber.* Working Paper 97. Copenhagen: Copenhagen Business School, Department of Management, Politics, and Philosophy.

Andersen, Heine, and Lars Frode Frederiksen. 1995. Internationale Tidsskrifter i Samfundsvidenskaber— Myter og realiteter. *Samfundsøkonomen* 5:14–22.

Andrews, Bruce. 1975. Social Rules and the State as a Social Actor. *World Politics* 27:521–40.

Andrews, David M. 1994. Capital Mobility and State Autonomy. *International Studies Quarterly* 38:193–218.

Andrews, David M., and Thomas D. Willett. 1997. Financial Interdependence and the State. *International Organization* 51:479–511.

Angell, Norman. 1911. *The Great Illusion.* New York: Putnam and Sons.

Appadurai, Arjun. 1996. *Modernity at Large: Cultural Dimensions of Globalization.* Minneapolis: University of Minnesota Press.

Aron, Raymond. 1966. *Peace and War: A Theory of International Relations.* Translated by Richard Howard and Annette Baker Fox. New York: Doubleday.

Arrighi, Giovanni. 1994. *The Long Twentieth Century.* London: Verso.

Arrow, Kenneth J. 1994. Methodological Individualism and Social Knowledge. *American Economic Review* 84:1–9.

Art, Robert J. 1973. Bureaucratic Politics and American Foreign Policy: A Critique. *Policy Sciences* 4:467–90.

———. 1996. American Foreign Policy and the Fungibility of Force. *Security Studies* 5:7–42.

Arthur, W. Brian. 1988. Self-Reinforcing Mechanisms in Economics. In *The Economy as an Evolving Complex System,* edited by Philip W. Anderson, Kenneth J. Arrow, and David Pines, 9–32. Reading, Mass.: Addison-Wesley.

———. 1989. Competing Technologies, Increasing Returns, and Lock-in by Historical Events. *Economic Journal* 99:116–31.

Aschauer, David A. 1990. *Public Investment and Private Sector Growth.* Washington, D.C.: Economic Policy Institute.

Ascher, Charles A. 1952. Current Problems in the World Health Organization. *International Organization* 6:27–50.

Ascher, William. 1983. New Development Approaches and the Adaptability of International Agencies: The Case of the World Bank. *International Organization* 37:415–39.

Ashley, Richard K. 1984. The Poverty of Neorealism. *International Organization* 38:225–86.

———. 1987. The Geopolitics of Geopolitical Space: Toward a Critical Social Theory of International Relations. *Alternatives* 12:403–34.

———. 1988. Untying the Sovereign State: A Double Reading of the Anarchy Problematique. *Millennium: Journal of International Studies* 12:227–62.

Austin-Smith, David. 1995. Campaign Contributions and Access. *American Political Science Review* 89:566–81.

Austin-Smith, David, and John Wright. 1992. Competitive Lobbying for a Legislator's Vote. *Social Choice and Welfare* 9:229–57.

———. 1994. Counteractive Lobbying. *American Journal of Political Science* 38:25–44.

Avant, Deborah D. 1994. *Political Institutions and Military Change: Lessons from Peripheral Wars.* Ithaca, N.Y.: Cornell University Press.

Axelrod, Robert. 1981. The Emergence of Cooperation Among Egoists. *American Political Science Review* 75:306–18.

———. 1984. *The Evolution of Cooperation.* New York: Basic Books.

———. 1986. An Evolutionary Approach to Norms. *American Political Science Review* 80:1095–1111.

———. 1997. *The Complexity of Cooperation: Agent-Based Models of Competition and Collaboration.* Princeton, N.J.: Princeton University Press.

Badie, Bertrand, and Marie-Claude Smouts. 1992. *Le retournement du monde. Sociologie de la scène internationale*. Presses de la Fondation Nationale des Sciences Politiques and Dalloz.

Baldwin, David A. 1979. Power Analysis and World Politics: New Trends Versus Old Tendencies. *World Politics* 31:161–93.

———. 1985. *Economic Statecraft*. Princeton, N.J.: Princeton University Press.

———. 1989. *Paradoxes of Power*. New York: Blackwell.

———. 1995. Security Studies and the End of the Cold War. *World Politics* 48:117–41.

Baldwin, David A., ed. 1993. *Neorealism and Neoliberalism: The Contemporary Debate*. New York: Columbia University Press.

Baldwin, Robert E. 1985. *The Political Economy of U.S. Trade Policy*. Cambridge, Mass.: MIT Press.

Ball, M. Margaret. 1951. Bloc Voting in the General Assembly. *International Organization* 5:3–31.

———. 1961. Issue for the Americas: Human Rights and the Preservation of Democratic Institutions. *International Organization* 15:21–37.

Banfield, Edward. 1958. *The Moral Basis of a Backward Society*. New York: Free Press.

Banks, Michael. 1984. The Evolution of International Relations Theory. In *Conflict in World Society: A New Perspective on International Relations*, edited by Michael Banks, 1–21. Brighton, Sussex: Wheatsheaf.

Banuri, Tariq, and Juliet Schor, eds. 1992. *Financial Openness and National Autonomy*. New York: Oxford University Press.

Baran, Paul A., and Paul M. Sweezy. 1966. *Monopoly Capital: An Essay on the American Economic and Social Order*. New York: Monthly Review Press.

Barber, Benjamin. 1995. *Jihad Versus McWorld*. New York: Times Books.

Barber, William J. 1991. British and American Economists and Attempts to Comprehend the Nature of War, 1910–1920. In *Economics and National Security: A History of Their Interaction*, edited by Craufurd D. Goodwin, 61–86. Durham, N.C.: Duke University Press.

Barkin, J. Samuel, and Bruce Cronin. 1994. The State and the Nation: Changing Norms and Rules of Sovereignty in International Relations. *International Organization* 48:107–30.

Barnes, James, Marshall Carter, and Max Skidmore. 1980. *The World of Politics*. New York: St. Martin's Press.

Barnett, Michael. 1995. The New United Nations Politics of Peace: From Juridical Sovereignty to Empirical Sovereignty. *Global Governance* 1:79–97.

———. 1997. Bringing in the New World Order: Liberalism, Legitimacy, and the United Nations. *World Politics* 49:526–51.

Barnett, Michael, and Martha Finnemore. 1997. The Politics, Power, and Pathologies of International Organizations. Paper presented at the 93d Annual Meeting of the American Political Science Association, Washington, D.C.

Baron, David. 1991. A Spatial Bargaining Theory of Government Formation in Parliamentary Systems. *American Political Science Review* 85:137–65.

Baron, David, and John Ferejohn. 1989. Bargaining in Legislatures. *American Political Science Review* 83:1181–1206.

Barro, Robert, and Xavier Sala-I-Martin. 1995. *Economic Growth*. New York: Macmillan.

Bates, Robert H. 1997a. *Open-Economy Politics: The Political Economy of the World Coffee Trade*. Princeton, N.J.: Princeton University Press.

———. 1997b. Area Studies and the Discipline. *PS: Political Science and Politics* 30:166–70.

Bauer, Raymond A., Ithiel de Sola Pool, and Anthony Dexter. 1972. *American Business and Public Policy: The Politics of Foreign Trade*. 2d ed. Chicago: Aldine-Atherton.

Bayoumi, Tamim, and Barry Eichengreen. 1997. Ever Closer to Heaven? An Optimum Currency Area Index for European Countries. *European Economic Review* 41:761–70.

Beard, Charles. 1935. *The Open Door at Home*. New York: Random House.

Bendix, Reinhard. 1964. *Nation-Building and Citizenship*. New York: Wiley.

Bendix, Reinhard, ed. 1968. *State and Society*. Boston: Little, Brown.

Bendor, Jonathan, and Thomas H. Hammond. 1992. Rethinking Allison's Models. *American Political Science Review* 86:301–22.

Berger, Suzanne, and Ronald Dore, eds. 1996. *National Diversity and Global Capitalism*. Ithaca, N.Y.: Cornell University Press.

Berger, Thomas U. 1996. Norms, Identity, and National Security in Germany and Japan. In *The Culture of National Security*, edited by Peter J. Katzenstein, 317–56. New York: Columbia University Press.

———. 1998. *Cultures of Antimilitarism: National Security in Germany and Japan*. Ithaca, N.Y.: Cornell University Press.

Bergesen, Albert, ed. 1980. *Studies of the Modern World System*. New York: Academic Press.

Berkovitch, Nitza. 1995. From Motherhood to Citizenship: The Worldwide Incorporation of Women into the Public Sphere in the Twentieth Century. Ph.D. diss., Stanford University, Stanford, Calif.

Berman, Harold J. 1983. *Law and Revolution. The Formation of the Western Legal Tradition*. Cambridge, Mass.: Harvard University Press.

Bernauer, Thomas. 1995. The Effect of International Environmental Institutions: How We Might Learn More. *International Organization* 49:351–77.

Bernheim, B. Douglas. 1994. A Theory of Conformity. *Journal of Political Economy* 102:841–77.

Betts, Richard K. 1997. Should Strategic Studies Survive? *World Politics* 50:7–33.

Bhagwati, Jagdish, and Hugh Patrick. 1990. *Aggressive Unilateralism: America's 301 Policy and the World Trading System*. Ann Arbor: University of Michigan Press.

Bhaskar, Roy. 1979. *The Possibility of Naturalism*. Atlantic Highlands, N.J.: Humanities Press.

Bigo, Didier. 1996. *Polices en réseaux: l'expérience européenne*. Paris: Presses de la Fondation Nationale des Sciences Politiques.

Blainey, Geoffrey. 1973. *The Causes of War*. New York: Free Press.

Blake, David, and Robert Walters. 1976. *The Politics of Global Economic Relations*. Englewood Cliffs, N.J.: Prentice Hall.

Bloomfield, Lincoln P. 1960. *The United Nations and U.S. Foreign Policy*. Boston: Little, Brown.

Blyth, Mark. 1997. Any More Good Ideas? *Comparative Politics* 29:229–50.

Boli, John, and George Thomas. 1998. INGOs and the Organization of World Culture. In *Constructing World Culture: International Nongovernmental Organizations Since 1875*, edited by John Boli and George Thomas. Stanford, Calif.: Stanford University Press.

Bolton, P., and G. Roland. 1997. The Breakup of Nations: A Political Economy Analysis. *Quarterly Journal of Economics* 112:1057–90.

Bonham, G. Matthew. 1970. Participation in Regional Parliamentary Assemblies: Effects on Attitudes of Scandinavian Parliamentarians. *Journal of Common Market Studies* 8:325–36.

Brady, D. W. 1988. *Critical Elections and Congressional Policy Making*. Stanford, Calif.: Stanford University Press.

Braudel, Fernand. 1980. *On History*. Translated by Sarah Matthews. Chicago: University of Chicago Press.

Brawley, Mark. 1993. *Liberal Leadership: Great Powers and Their Challengers in Peace and War*. Ithaca, N.Y.: Cornell University Press.

Brenner, Robert. 1977. The Origins of Capitalist Development: A Critique of Neo-Smithian Marxism. *New Left Review* 104:25–92.

Brodie, Bernard. 1949. Strategy as a Science. *World Politics* 1:467–88.

———. 1959. *Strategy in the Missile Age*. Princeton, N.J.: Princeton University Press.

Brodie, Bernard, ed. 1946. *The Absolute Weapon: Atomic Power and World Order*. New York: Harcourt, Brace and Company.

Brooks, Stephen G. 1997. Dueling Realisms. *International Organization* 51:445–78.

Brown, Michael E. 1995. The Flawed Logic of NATO Expansion. *Survival* 37:34–52.

Brown, Seyom, and Larry L. Fabian. 1975. Toward Mutual Accountability in Non-Terrestrial Realms. *International Organization* 29:877–92.

Bryant, Ralph. 1987. *International Financial Integration*. Washington, D.C.: Brookings Institution.

Bueno de Mesquita, Bruce, and David Lalman. 1992. *War and Reason*. New Haven, Conn.: Yale University Press.

Bull, Hedley. 1968. Strategic Studies and Its Critics. *World Politics* 20:593–605.

————. 1972. The Theory of International Politics, 1919–1969. In *The Aberystwyth Papers: International Politics, 1919–1969,* edited by Brian Porter, 30–55. London: Oxford University Press.

————. 1977. *The Anarchical Society: A Study of Order in World Politics.* London: Macmillan.

————. 1995. *The Anarchical Society. A Study of Order in World Politics.* 2d ed. London: Macmillan.

Bull, Hedley, and Adam Watson, eds. 1984. *The Expansion of European Society.* London: Oxford University Press.

Burley, Anne-Marie. 1993. Regulating the World: Multilateralism, International Law, and the Projection of the New Deal Regulatory State. In *Multilateralism Matters,* edited by John Gerard Ruggie, 125–56. New York: Columbia University Press.

Burley, Anne-Marie, and Walter Mattli. 1993. Europe Before the Court: A Political Theory of Legal Integration. *International Organization* 47:41–76.

Butterfield, Herbert. 1959. *The Whig Interpretation of History.* London: G. Bells and Son.

Butterfield, Herbert, and Martin Wight. 1968. *Diplomatic Investigations: Essays in the Theory of International Politics.* London: Allen and Unwin.

Buzan, Barry. 1984. Economic Structure and International Security: The Limits of the Liberal Case. *International Organization* 38:597–624.

————. 1991. *People, States, and Fear: An Agenda for International Security Studies in the Post–Cold War Era.* Boulder, Colo.: Lynne Reinner.

————. 1993. From International System to International Society: Structural Realism and Regime Theory Meet the English School. *International Organization* 47:327–52.

————. 1996. The Timeless Wisdom of Realism? In *International Theory: Positivism and Beyond,* edited by S. Smith, K. Booth and M. Zalewski, 47–65. Cambridge: Cambridge University Press.

Buzan, Barry, and Richard Little. 1996. Reconceptualizing Anarchy: Structural Realism Meets World History. *European Journal of International Relations* 2:403–38.

Buzan, Barry, Ole Wæver, and Jaap de Wilde. 1997. *Security: A New Framework for Analysis.* Boulder, Colo.: Lynne Rienner.

Calleo, David. 1978. *The German Problem Reconsidered: Germany and the World Order, 1870 to the Present.* Cambridge: Cambridge University Press.

Cameron, David R. 1978. The Expansion of the Public Economy. *American Political Science Review* 72:1243—61.

————. 1995. Transnational Relations and the Development of European Economic and Monetary Union. In *Bringing Transnational Relations Back In,* edited by Thomas Risse-Kappen, 37–78. Cambridge: Cambridge University Press.

Campbell, David. 1992. *Writing Security: United States Foreign Policy and the Politics of Identity.* Minneapolis: University of Minnesota Press.

————. 1996. Political Prosaics, Transversal Politics, and the Anarchical World. In *Challenging the Boundaries,* edited by Michael J. Shapiro and Hayward R. Alker, Jr. Minneapolis: University of Minnesota Press.

Campbell, Donald T. 1987. Evolutionary Epistemology. In *Evolutionary Epistemology, Theory of Rationality, and the Sociology of Knowledge,* edited by G. Radnitsky and W. W. Bartley. La Salle, Ill.: Open Court.

Cantwell, John. 1989. *Technical Innovations in Multinational Corporations.* London: Blackwell.

Caporaso, James A. 1978a. Dependence, Dependency, and Power in the Global System: A Structural and Behavioral Analysis. *International Organization* 32:13–44.

————. 1995. False Divisions: Security Studies and Global Political Economy. *Mershon International Studies Review* 39:117–22.

Caporaso, James A., ed. 1978b. Dependence and Dependency in the Global System. *International Organization* 32 (1). Special issue.

Cardoso, Fernando Henrique, and Enzo Faletto. 1979. *Dependency and Development in Latin America.* Berkeley: University of California Press.

Carey, John. 1996. *The Politics of Term Limits.* New York: Cambridge University Press.

Carr, Edward Hallett. 1939. *The Twenty Years' Crisis: An Introduction to the Study of International Relations.* New York: Harper and Row.

————. [1946] 1962. *The Twenty Years' Crisis 1919–1939: An Introduction to the Study of International Relations.* 2d ed. Reprint, London: Macmillan.

————. [1946] 1964. *The Twenty Years' Crisis, 1919–1939: An Introduction to the Study of International Relations.* 2d ed. Reprint, New York: Harper and Row.

Carter, Gwendolen M. 1950. The Commonwealth in the United Nations. *International Organization* 4: 247–60.

Caves, Richard E. 1996. *Multinational Enterprise and Economic Analysis.* 2d ed. New York: Cambridge University Press.

Cederman, Lars-Erik. 1997. *Emergent Actors in World Politics: How States and Nations Develop and Dissolve.* Princeton, N.J.: Princeton University Press.

Cerny, Philip G. 1990. *The Changing Architecture of Politics.* London: Sage.

Cerulo, K. A. 1997. Identity Construction: New Issues, New Directions. *Annual Review of Sociology* 23:385–402.

Chaiken, Shelly, Wendy Wood, and Alice Eagly. 1996. Principles of Persuasion. In *Social Psychology: Handbook of Basic Principles,* edited by E. T. Higgins and A. Kruglanski, 702–42. New York: Guilford Press.

Chan, Gerald. 1997. International Studies in China: Origins and Development. *Issues and Studies* 33:40–64.

Chan, S. 1997. In Search of Democratic Peace: Problems and Promises. *Mershon International Studies Review* 41:59–91.

Chan, Stephen. 1994. Beyond the North-West: Africa and the Rest. In *Contemporary International Relations: A Guide to Theory,* edited by A. J. R. Groom and Margot Light, 237–54. London and New York: Pinter Publishers.

Chayes, Abram, and Antonia Handler Chayes. 1993. On Compliance. *International Organization* 47:175–205.

————. 1995. *The New Sovereignty. Compliance with International Regulatory Agreements.* Cambridge, Mass.: Harvard University Press.

Checkel, Jeffrey T. 1997. International Norms and Domestic Politics: Bridging the Rationalist-Constructivist Divide. *European Journal of International Relations* 3:473–95.

————. 1998. The Constructivist Turn in International Relations Theory. *World Politics* 50:324–48.

Clarida, Richard, and Mark Gertler. 1996. How the Bundesbank Conducts Monetary Policy. Unpublished manuscript, Columbia University, New York.

Claude, Inis L. 1956. *Swords into Plowshares.* New York: Random House.

————. 1963. The Political Framework of the United Nations' Financial Problems. *International Organization* 17:831–59.

————. 1966. Collective Legitimization as a Political Function of the United Nations. *International Organization* 20:367–79.

Clayton, William. 1945. The Foreign Economic Policy of the State Department. *Department of State Bulletin* 12:979–82.

Coase, Ronald. 1937. The Nature of the Firm. *Economica* 4:386–405.

————. 1960. The Problem of Social Cost. *Journal of Law and Economics* 3:1–44.

Cohen, Benjamin J. 1973. *The Question of Imperialism: The Political Economy of Dominance and Dependence.* New York: Basic Books.

————. 1991. *Crossing Frontiers.* Boulder, Colo.: Westview Press.

————. 1993. The Triad and the Unholy Trinity. In *Economic Relations in the 1990s,* edited by Richard Higgot, Richard Leaver, and John Ravenhill, 133–58. Boulder, Colo.: Lynne Rienner.

————. 1996. Phoenix Risen: The Resurrection of Global Finance. *World Politics* 48:268–96.

Cohen, Benjamin V. 1951. The Impact of the United Nations on United States Foreign Policy. *International Organization* 5:274–81.

Cohen, M. D., James G. March, and Johan P. Olsen. 1972. A Garbage Can Model of Organizational Choice. *Administrative Science Quarterly* 17:1–25.

Coleman, J. S. 1966. Foundations for a Theory of Collective Decisions. *American Journal of Sociology* 71:615–27.

———. 1986. *Individual Interests and Collective Action*. Cambridge: Cambridge University Press.

———. 1990. *Foundations of Social Theory*. Cambridge, Mass.: Harvard University Press.

Collier, R. B., and D. Collier. 1991. *Shaping the Political Arena: Critical Junctures, the Labor Movement, and Regime Dynamics in Latin America*. Princeton, N.J.: Princeton University Press.

Collini, Stefan, Donald Winch, and John Burrow. 1983. *That Noble Science of Politics: A Study in Nineteenth-Century Intellectual History*. Cambridge: Cambridge University Press.

Collins, Susan. 1988. Inflation and the European Monetary System. In *The European Monetary System*, edited by Francesco Giavazzi, Stefano Milosi, and Marcus Miller, 112–36. New York: Cambridge University Press.

Combs, Jerald. 1983. *American Diplomatic History: Two Centuries of Changing Interpretations*. Berkeley: University of California Press.

Comisso, Ellen, and Laura D'Andrea Tyson, eds. 1986. *Power, Purpose, and Collective Choice: Economic Strategy in Socialist States*. Ithaca, N.Y.: Cornell University Press.

Commission of the European Communities. 1990. One Market, One Money. *European Economy* 44: 63–68.

Condliffe, J. B. 1938. *Markets and the Problem of Peaceful Change*. Paris: League of Nations.

———. 1944. Economic Power as an Instrument of National Policy. *American Economic Review* 34: 305–14.

Conforti, Benedetto. 1993. *International Law and the Role of Domestic Legal Systems*. Dordrecht: Martinus Nijhoff.

Conybeare, John A. C. 1980. International Organization and the Theory of Property Rights. *International Organization* 34:307–34.

Cooper, Richard N. 1968. *The Economics of Interdependence: Economic Policy in the Atlantic Community*. New York: McGraw Hill.

Copeland, Dale C. 1996. Economic Interdependence and War: A Theory of Trade Expectations. *International Security* 20:5–41.

Corsetti, Giancarlo, and Nouriel Roubini. 1991. Fiscal Deficits, Public Debt, and Government Insolvency. *Journal of Japanese and International Economies* 5:354–380.

———. 1995. Political Biases in Fiscal Policy. In *Monetary and Fiscal Policy in an Integrated Europe*, edited by Barry Eichengreen, Jeffry Frieden, and Jürgen von Hagen, 118–37. New York: Springer.

Coser, Louis. 1956. *The Functions of Social Conflict*. New York: Free Press.

Cox, Gary W. 1987. *The Efficient Secret*. Cambridge: Cambridge University Press.

———. 1997. *Making Votes Count*. Cambridge: Cambridge University Press.

Cox, Robert W. 1969. The Executive Head. *International Organization* 23:205–30.

———. 1981. Social Forces, States, and World Orders: Beyond International Relations Theory. *Millennium: Journal of International Studies* 10:126–55.

———. 1983. Gramsci, Hegemony, and International Relations: An Essay in Method. *Millennium: Journal of International Studies* 12:162–75.

———. 1987. *Production, Power, and World Order: Social Forces in the Making of History*. New York: Columbia University Press.

Cox, Robert W., and Harold K. Jacobson. 1973. *The Anatomy of Influence: Decisionmaking in International Organization*. New Haven, Conn.: Yale University Press.

Crawford, Elisabeth T., and Albert D. Biderman. 1969. *Social Scientists and International Affairs: A Case for a Sociology of Social Science*. New York: John Wiley and Sons.

Crawford, Neta. 1993. Decolonization as an International Norm: The Evolution of Practices, Arguments, and Beliefs. In *Emerging Norms of Justified Intervention*, edited by Laura Reed and Carl Kaysen, 37–61. Cambridge, Mass.: American Academy of Arts and Sciences.

Cummins, Jason G., Kevin A. Hassett, and R. Glenn Hubbard. 1995. Tax Reforms and Investment: A Cross-Country Comparison. NBER Working Paper 5232. Cambridge, Mass: National Bureau of Economic Research.

Cushman, David. 1988. Exchange-Rate Uncertainty and Foreign Direct Investment in the United States. *Weltwirtschaftsliches Archiv* 124:322–36.

Cyert, R. M., and James G. March. 1963. *A Behavioral Theory of the Firm.* Englewood Cliffs, N.J.: Prentice-Hall.

Dahl, Robert A. 1961. *Who Governs? Democracy and Power in an American City.* New Haven, Conn.: Yale University Press.

———. 1984. *Modern Political Analysis.* 4th ed. Englewood Cliffs, N.J.: Prentice-Hall.

———. 1994. A Democratic Dilemma: System Effectiveness Versus Citizen Participation. *Political Science Quarterly* 109:23–34.

David, Paul. 1985. Clio and the Economics of Qwerty. *American Economic Review Papers and Proceedings* 75:332–37.

———. 1993. Institutions as the "Carriers of History"? Unpublished manuscript, Stanford University, Stanford, Calif.

de Boissieu, Christian, and Jean Pisani-Ferry. 1998. The Political Economy of French Economic Policy in the Perspective of EMU. In *Forging an Integrated Europe,* edited by Barry Eichengreen and Jeffry Frieden, 49–89. Ann Arbor: University of Michigan Press.

de Marchi, Neil. 1991. League of Nations Economists and the Idea of Peaceful Change in the Decade of the 1930s. In *Economics and National Security: A History of Their Interaction,* edited by Craufurd D. Goodwin, 143–78. Durham, N.C.: Duke University Press.

de Wilde, Jaap. 1991. *Saved from Oblivion: Interdependence Theory in the First Half of the Twentieth Century. A Study on the Causality Between War and Complex Interdependence.* Dartmouth, England: Aldershot.

Demchak, Chris. 1991. *Military Organizations, Complex Machines: Modernization in the U.S. Armed Services.* Ithaca, N.Y.: Cornell University Press.

Dennett, Raymond. 1949. Politics in the Security Council. *International Organization* 3:421–33.

Der Derian, James. 1987. *On Diplomacy.* Oxford: Blackwell.

Desch, Michael. 1996. War and Strong States, Peace and Weak States? *International Organization* 50:237–68.

Dessler, David. 1989. What's at Stake in the Agent-Structure Debate? *International Organization* 43:441–74.

Destler, I. M. 1992. *American Trade Politics: System Under Stress.* Washington, D.C.: Institute for International Economics.

———. 1994. Foreign Policy Making with the Economy at Center Stage. In *Beyond the Beltway,* edited by Daniel Yankelovich and I. M. Destler, 26–42. New York: Norton.

Deutsch, Karl W. 1953. *Nationalism and Social Communication: An Inquiry into the Foundations of Nationality.* Cambridge, Mass.: MIT Press.

Deutsch, Karl W., and J. David Singer. 1964. Multipolar Power Systems and International Stability. *World Politics* 16:390–406.

Deutsch, Karl W., Sidney A. Burrell, Robert A. Kann, Maurice Lee, Jr., Martin Lichterman, Raymond E. Lindgren, Francis L. Loewenheim, and Richard W. Van Wagenen. 1957. *Political Community and the North Atlantic Area: International Organization in the Light of Historical Experience.* Princeton, N.J.: Princeton University Press.

Dewey, J. 1927. *The Public and Its Problems.* Denver, Colo.: Alan Swallow.

Diebold, William, Jr. 1960. The Changed Economic Position of Western Europe: Some Implications for United States Policy and International Organization. *International Organization* 14:1–19.

Diez, Thomas. 1997. International Ethics and European Integration: Federal State or Network Horizon? *Alternatives* 22:287–312.

DiMaggio, Paul. 1997. Culture and Cognition. *Annual Review of Sociology* 23:263–87.

DiMaggio, Paul J., and Walter W. Powell. 1983. The Iron Cage Revisited: Institutional Isomorphism and Collective Rationality in Organizational Fields. *American Sociological Review* 48:147–60.

———. 1991. Introduction. In *The New Institutionalism in Organizational Analysis,* edited by Paul J. DiMaggio and Walter W. Powell, 1–38. Chicago: University of Chicago Press.

Donnelly, Jack. 1986. International Human Rights: A Regime Analysis. *International Organization* 40:599–642.

———. 1995. Realism and the Academic Study of International Relations. In *Political Science in History: Research Programs and Political Traditions*, edited by James Farr, John S. Dryzek, and Stephen T. Leonard, 175–97. Cambridge: Cambridge University Press.

Downs, Anthony. 1957. *An Economic Theory of Democracy*. New York: Harper and Row.

Downs, George W. 1989. The Rational Deterrence Debate. *World Politics* 41:225–38.

Downs, George W., and David Rocke. 1995. *Optimal Imperfection: Domestic Uncertainty and Institutions in International Relations*. Princeton, N.J.: Princeton University Press.

Doyle, Michael W. 1983a. Kant, Liberal Legacies, and Foreign Affairs. Part 1. *Philosophy and Public Affairs* 12:205–35.

———. 1983b. Kant, Liberal Legacies, and Foreign Affairs. Part 2. *Philosophy and Public Affairs* 12:323–53.

———. 1997. *Ways of War and Peace: Realism, Liberalism, and Socialism*. New York: Norton.

Dubois, Ellen Carol. 1994. Woman Suffrage Around the World: Three Phases of Suffragist Internationalism. In *Suffrage and Beyond: International Feminist Perspectives*, edited by Caroline Daley and Melanie Nolan, 252–74. New York: New York University Press.

Duchene, Francois. 1994. *Jean Monnet: The First Statesman of Interdependence*. New York: Norton.

Dunn, Frederick S. 1948. The Scope of International Relations. *World Politics* 1:142–46.

———. 1949. The Present Course of International Relations Research. *World Politics* 2:80–95.

Dunne, Timothy. 1994. The Genesis and the History of the "English School" of International Relations. In *The "English School" of International Relations: A Conference Report*, edited by Iver B. Neumann, 1–17. NUPI Report 179. Oslo: Norwegian Institute of International Affairs.

Dunning, John H. 1988. *Multinationals, Technology, and Competitiveness*. Boston: Unwin Hyman.

Dupont, Cedric. 1994. Domestic Politics and International Negotiations. In *Game Theory and International Relations,* edited by P. Allan and C. Schmidt, 156–90. Cambridge: Cambridge University Press.

Durkheim, Emile. 1933. The *Division of Labor in Society*. Translated by G. Simpson. New York: Macmillan.

———. 1938. The *Rules of Sociological Method*. 8th ed. Translated by Sarah A. Solovay and John H. Mueller. Edited by E. G. Catlin. New York: The Free Press.

———. 1951. *Suicide, A Study in Sociology*. Translated by John A. Spaulding and George Simpson. Edited by George Simpson. New York: Free Press.

———. 1953a. Individual and Collective Representations. In *Sociology and Philosophy,* translated by D. F. Pocock. London: Cohen and West.

———. 1953b. Value Judgments and Judgments of Reality. In *Sociology and Philosophy,* translated by D. F. Pocock. London: Cohen and West.

Duvall, Raymond D., P. Terrence Hoppmann, Brian L. Job, and Robert T. Kudrle. 1983. The Economic Foundations of War: Editor's Introduction. *International Studies Quarterly* 27:379.

Dyson, Kenneth H. F. 1980. *The State Tradition in Western Europe—A Study of an Idea and Institution*. Oxford: Martin Robertson.

Eagly, Alice, and Shelly Chaiken. 1993. *The Psychology of Attitudes*. Fort Worth, Tex.: Harcourt Brace Jovanovich.

Earle, Edward Mead. 1943. Adam Smith, Alexander Hamilton, Friedrich List: The Economic Foundations of Military Power. In *Makers of Modern Strategy: Military Thought from Machiavelli to Hitler*, edited by Edward Mead Earle, 117–54. Princeton, N.J.: Princeton University Press.

Easton, David, John G. Gunnell, and Luigi Graziano, eds. 1991. *The Development of Political Science: A Comparative Survey*. London and New York: Routledge.

Egeberg, M., and J. Trondal. 1997. An Organization Theory Perspective on Multi-level Governance in the EU: The Case of the EEA as a Norm of Affiliation. Working Paper Series 21. Oslo: ARENA.

Eggertsson, Thrainn. 1996. A Note on the Economics of Institutions. In *Empirical Studies of Institutional Change,* edited by L. Alston, T. Eggertsson, and D. North, 6–24. New York: Cambridge University Press.

Eichengreen, Barry. 1994. The Endogeneity of Exchange-Rate Regimes. In *Understanding Interdependence*, edited by Peter Kenen, 3–33. Princeton, N.J.: Princeton University Press.

———. 1996. *Globalizing Capital: A History of the International Monetary System.* Princeton, N.J.: Princeton University Press.

Eichengreen, Barry, and Fabio Ghironi. 1996. European Monetary Unification: The Challenges Ahead. In *Monetary Reform in Europe,* edited by Francisco Torres, 83–120. Lisbon: Universidade Catholica Editora.

Eichengreen, Barry, and Charles Wyplosz. 1993. The Unstable EMS. *Brookings Papers on Economic Activity* 1:51–143.

Eide, A., and B. Hagtvet, eds. 1992. *Human Rights in Perspective. A Global Assessment.* Oxford: Blackwell.

Eisenstadt, S. N. 1987. *European Civilization in Comparative Perspective.* Oslo: Norwegian University Press.

Elias, Norbert. 1994. *The Civilizing Process.* Translated by Edmund Jephcott. Oxford: Blackwell.

Elshtain, Jean. 1987. *Women and War.* New York: Basic Books.

———. 1996. Is There a Feminist Tradition on War and Peace? In *The Ethics of War and Peace,* edited by Terry Nardin. Princeton, N.J.: Princeton University Press.

Elster, Jon. 1979. *Ulysses and the Sirens: Studies in Rationality and Irrationality.* Cambridge: Cambridge University Press.

———. 1983. *Sour Grapes: Studies in Subversion of Rationality.* Cambridge: Cambridge University Press.

———. 1984. *Ulysses and the Sirens: Studies in Rationality and Irrationality.* Rev. ed. Cambridge: Cambridge University Press.

———. 1986a. Introduction. In *Rational Choice,* edited by Jon Elster, 1–33. Cambridge: Cambridge University Press.

———. 1989a. Social Norms and Economic Theory. *Journal of Economic Perspectives* 3:99–117.

———. 1989b. *Nuts and Bolts for the Social Sciences.* Cambridge: Cambridge University Press.

———. 1989c. *The Cement of Society: A Study of Social Order.* Cambridge: Cambridge University Press.

Elster, Jon, ed. 1986b. *The Multiple Self.* Cambridge: Cambridge University Press.

Emerson, Rupert, and Inis L. Claude. 1952. The Soviet Union and the United Nations: An Essay in Interpretation. *International Organization* 6:1–26.

Emory, F. E., and E. L. Trist. 1973. *Towards a Social Ecology: Contextual Appreciation of the Future in the Present.* London: Plenum.

Encarnation, Dennis. 1992. *Rivals Beyond Trade: America Versus Japan in Global Competition.* Ithaca, N.Y.: Cornell University Press.

Englemann, Daniela, Hans-Joachim Knopf, Klaus Rocher, and Thomas Risse-Kappen. 1997. Identity Politics in the European Union: The Case of Economic and Monetary Union. In *The Politics of Economic and Monetary Union,* edited by Petri Minkkinen and Heikki Patomäki, 105–32. Boston: Kluwer.

Epstein, David, and Sharyn O'Halloran. 1997. Choosing How to Decide: Efficient Policy Making Under Separate Powers. Unpublished manuscript, Columbia University, New York.

Eriksen, E. O., and J. Weigård. 1997. Conceptualizing Politics: Strategic or Communicative Action? *Scandinavian Political Studies* 20:219–41.

Ernst, Manfred. 1978. Attitudes of Diplomats at the United Nations: The Effects of Organization Participation on the Evaluation of the Organization. *International Organization* 32:1037–43.

Esping-Andersen, Gösta. 1985. *States Against Markets.* Princeton, N.J.: Princeton University Press.

Euben, Roxanne. 1995. When Worldviews Collide: Conflicting Assumptions About Human Behavior Held by Rational Actor Theory and Islamic Fundamentalism. *Political Psychology* 16:157–78.

Evans, Peter B. 1972. National Autonomy and Economic Development. In *Transnational Relations and World Politics,* edited by Robert O. Keohane and Joseph S. Nye, Jr., 325–42. Cambridge, Mass.: Harvard University Press.

———. 1979. *Dependent Development: The Alliance of Multinational, State, and Local Capital In Brazil.* Princeton, N.J.: Princeton University Press.

———. 1995. *Embedded Autonomy: States and Industrial Transformation.* Princeton, N.J.: Princeton University Press.

Evans, Peter B., Harold K. Jacobson, and Robert D. Putnam, eds. 1993. *Double-Edged Diplomacy: International Bargaining and Domestic Politics.* Berkeley: University of California Press.

Evans, Peter B., Dietrich Rueschemeyer, and Theda Skocpol, eds. 1985. *Bringing the State Back In.* Cambridge: Cambridge University Press.

Evans, Tony, and Peter Wilson. 1992. Regime Theory and the English School of International Relations: A Comparison. *Millennium: Journal of International Studies* 21:329–51.

Eyre, Dana P., and Mark C. Suchman. 1996. Status, Norms, and the Proliferation of Conventional Weapons: An Institutional Theory Approach. In *The Culture of National Security: Norms and Identity in World Politics,* edited by Peter J. Katzenstein, 79–113. New York: Columbia University Press.

Fagen, Richard. 1978. A Funny Thing Happened on the Way to the Market. *International Organization* 32:287–300.

Farnham, Barbara. 1992. Roosevelt and the Munich Crisis: Insights from Prospect Theory. *Political Psychology* 13:205–35.

Farr, James. 1988. The History of Political Science. *American Journal of Political Science* 32:1175–95.

Farr, James, John Gunnell, Raymond Seidelman, John S. Dryzek, and Stephen T. Leonard. 1990. Can Political Science History Be Neutral? *American Political Science Review* 84:587–607.

Farr, James, and Raymond Seidelman, eds. 1993. *Discipline and History. Political Science in the United States.* Ann Arbor: University of Michigan Press.

Farr, James, John S. Dryzek, and Stephen T. Leonard, eds. 1995. *Political Science in History: Research Programs and Political Traditions.* Cambridge: Cambridge University Press.

Farrell, Joseph, and Matthew Rabin. 1996. Cheap Talk. *Journal of Economic Perspectives* 10:103—18.

Fearon, James D. 1994a. Cooperation and Bargaining Under Anarchy. Unpublished manuscript, University of Chicago, Chicago, Ill.

———. 1994b. Domestic Political Audiences and the Escalation of International Disputes. *American Political Science Review* 88:577–92.

———. 1995. Rationalist Explanations for War. *International Organization* 49:379–414.

———. 1997. What Is Identity (As We Now Use the Word)? Unpublished manuscript, University of Chicago, Chicago, Ill.

———. 1998. Domestic Politics, Foreign Policy, and Theories of International Relations. In *Annual Review of Political Science* 1, edited by Nelson Polsby, 289–313. Palo Alto, Calif.: Annual Reviews.

Fearon, James D., and David D. Laitin. 1996. Explaining Interethnic Cooperation. *American Political Science Review* 90:715–35.

Feenberg, Daniel R., and Harvey S. Rosen. 1986. State Personal Income and Sales Taxes, 1977–1983. In *Studies in State and Local Public Finance,* edited by Harvey S. Rosen, 134–79. Chicago: University of Chicago Press.

Feinberg, Gerald. 1978. *What Is the World Made of? Atoms, Leptons, Quarks, and Other Tantalizing Particles.* Garden City, N.Y.: Anchor/Doubleday.

Feis, Herbert. 1930. *Europe, the World's Banker, 1870–1914.* New Haven, Conn.: Yale University Press.

———. 1950. *The Road to Pearl Harbor.* Princeton, N.J.: Princeton University Press.

Feldstein, Martin. 1997. EMU and International Conflict. *Foreign Affairs* 76:60–73.

Feldstein, Martin, and P. Bacchetta. 1991. National Savings and International Investment. In *National Savings and Economic Performance,* edited by Douglas Bernheim and John Shoven, 201–26. Chicago: University of Chicago Press.

Feldstein, Martin, and Charles Horioka. 1980. Domestic Savings and International Capital Flows. *The Economic Journal* 90:314–29.

Ferejohn, John. 1991. Rationality and Interpretation: Parliamentary Elections in Early Stuart England. In *The Economic Approach to Politics,* edited by Kristen Renwick Monroe, 279–305. New York: Harper-Collins.

———. 1993. Structure and Ideology. In *Ideas and Foreign Policy: Beliefs, Institutions, and Political Change,* edited by Judith Goldstein and Robert Keohane, 207–33. Ithaca, N.Y.: Cornell University Press.

———. 1995. Foreword. In *Positive Theories of Congressional Institutions,* edited by Kenneth Shepsle and Barry Weingast, ix–xiii. Ann Arbor: University of Michigan Press.

Ferejohn, John, and Charles Shipan. 1990. Congressional Influence on Bureaucracy. *Journal of Law, Economics, and Organization* 6:1–20.

Field, Alexander James. 1979. On the Explanation of Rules Using Rational Choice Models. *Journal of Economic Issues* 13:49–72.

———. 1981. The Problem with Neoclassical Institutional Economics: A Critique with Special Reference to the North/Thomas Model of Pre-1500 Europe. *Explorations in Economic History* 19:174–98.

———. 1984. Microeconomics, Norms, and Rationality. *Economic Development and Cultural Change* 32:683–711.

Finger, J. Michael, Merlinda Ingco, and Ulrich Reincke. 1996. *The Uruguay Round.* Washington, D.C.: World Bank.

Finnemore, Martha. 1993. International Organizations as Teachers of Norms: The United Nations Educational, Scientific, and Cultural Organization and Science Policy. *International Organization* 47: 565–97.

———. 1995. Sovereign Default and Military Intervention. Paper presented at the 91st Annual Meeting of the American Political Science Association, San Francisco.

———. 1996a. *National Interests in International Society.* Ithaca, N.Y.: Cornell University Press.

———. 1996b. Norms, Culture, and World Politics: Insights from Sociology's Institutionalism. *International Organization* 50:325–47.

———. 1996c. Constructing Norms of Humanitarian Intervention. In *The Culture of National Security: Norms and Identity in World Politics,* edited by Peter J. Katzenstein, 153–85. New York: Columbia University Press.

Fischer, Markus. 1992. Feudal Europe, 800–1300: Communal Discourse and Conflictual Practices. *International Organization* 46:427–66.

Fiske, Susan, and Shelly Taylor. 1994. *Social Cognition.* New York: Random House.

Flora, P. 1983. *State, Economy, and Society in Western Europe 1815–1975.* Frankfurt: Campus.

Florini, Ann. 1996. The Evolution of International Norms. *International Studies Quarterly* 40:363–89.

Forsythe, David P. 1991. *The Internationalization of Human Rights.* Lexington, Mass.: Lexington Books.

Fox, William T. 1949. Interwar International Relations Research: The American Experience. *World Politics* 2:67–79.

———. 1951. The United Nations in the Era of Total Diplomacy. *International Organization* 5:265–73.

Fox, William T., and Annette Baker Fox. 1961. The Teaching of International Relations in the U.S. *World Politics* 13:339–59.

Franck, Thomas. 1990. *The Power of Legitimacy Among Nations.* New York: Oxford University Press.

———. 1992. The Emerging Right to Democratic Governance. *American Journal of International Law* 86:46–91.

Frankel, Benjamin, ed. 1996. *Realism: Restatements and Renewal.* London: Frank Cass.

Frankel, Jeffrey A. 1993. *On Exchange Rates.* Cambridge, Mass.: MIT Press.

Frankel, Jeffrey A., and Andrew Rose. 1996. The Endogeneity of the Optimum Currency Area Criteria. Unpublished manuscript, University of California, Berkeley.

Frankel, Jeffrey A., Ernesto Stein, and Shang-Jin Wei. 1996. Regional Trading Arrangements: Natural or Super-natural? NBER Working Paper 5431. Cambridge, Mass.: National Bureau of Economic Research.

Fratianni, Michele, and Jürgen von Hagen. 1992. *The European Monetary System and European Monetary Union.* Boulder, Colo.: Westview Press.

French, Kenneth, and James Poterba. 1991. International Diversification and International Equity Markets. *American Economic Review (Papers and Proceedings)* 81:222—26.

Frey, Frederick. 1985. The Problem of Actor Designation in Political Analysis. *Comparative Politics* 127–52.

Friedberg, Aaron L. 1988. *The Weary Titan: Britain and the Experience of Relative Decline, 1895–1905.* Princeton, N.J.: Princeton University Press.

———. 1989. The Strategic Implications of Relative Economic Decline. *Political Science Quarterly* 104:401–32.

Frieden, Jeffry A. 1990. *Debt, Development, and Democracy*. Princeton, N.J.: Princeton University Press.

———. 1991. Invested Interests: The Politics of National Economic Policies in a World of Global Finance. *International Organization* 45:425–51.

———. 1996. The Impact of Goods and Capital Market Integration on European Monetary Politics. *Comparative Political Studies* 29:195–222.

———. 1997a. Actors and Preferences in International Politics. Unpublished manuscript, Harvard University, Cambridge, Mass.

———. 1997b. Monetary Populism in Nineteenth-Century America: An Open Economy Interpretation. *Journal of Economic History* 57:367–95.

Frieden, Jeffry A., and Ronald Rogowski. 1996. The Impact of the International Economy on National Policies. In *Internationalization and Domestic Politics*, edited by Robert O. Keohane and Helen V. Milner, 25–47. New York: Cambridge University Press.

Friedman, Edward. 1997. The Challenge of a Rising China: Another Germany? In *Eagle Adrift: American Foreign Policy at the End of the Century*, edited by Robert Lieber, 215–45. New York: Longman.

Friedman, J., ed. 1996. *The Rational Choice Controversy*. New Haven, Conn.: Yale University Press.

Friedman, Milton. 1953. *Essays in Positive Economics*. Chicago: University of Chicago Press.

———. 1968. The Role of Monetary Policy. *American Economic Review* 58:1–17.

Friedrich, C. J. 1963. *Man and His Government*. New York: McGraw-Hill.

Frohlich, Norman, Joe Oppenheimer, and Oran Young. 1971. *Political Leadership and Collective Goods*. Princeton, N.J.: Princeton University Press.

Fudenberg, Drew, and Jean Tirole. 1991. *Game Theory*. Cambridge, Mass.: MIT Press.

Fukuyama, Francis. 1992. *The End of History and the Last Man*. New York: Free Press.

Fure, Odd-Bjørn. 1996. *Mellomkrigstid 1920–1940*. Oslo: Universitetsforlaget.

Galtung, Johan. 1981. Structure, Culture, and Intellectual Style: An Essay Comparing Saxonic, Teutonic, Gallic, and Nipponic Approaches. *Social Science Information* 20:817–56.

Gardner, Richard M. 1956. *Sterling-Dollar Diplomacy: Anglo-American Collaboration in the Reconstruction of Multilateral Trade*. Oxford: Clarendon Press.

Gareau, Frederick H. 1970. Cold War Cleavages as Seen from the United Nations General Assembly: 1947–1967. *Journal of Politics* 32:929–68.

———. 1981. The Discipline of International Relations: A Multi-National Perspective. *Journal of Politics* 43:779–802.

Garrett, Geoffrey. 1995. Capital Mobility, Trade, and the Domestic Politics of Economic Policy. *International Organization* 49:657–87.

———. 1998a. *Partisan Politics in the Global Economy*. New York: Cambridge University Press.

———. 1998b. The Transition to Economic and Monetary Union. In *Forging an Integrated Europe*, edited by Barry Eichengreen and Jeffry Frieden, 21–47. Ann Arbor: University of Michigan Press.

———. 1998c. Capital Flows, Capital Mobility, and Capital Taxation. Unpublished manuscript, Yale University.

———. 1998d. Governing in the Global Economy. Paper presented at the 94th Annual Meeting of the American Political Science Association, September, Boston.

Garrett, Geoffrey, and Peter Lange. 1991. Political Responses to Interdependence: What's 'Left' for the Left? *International Organization* 45:539–64.

———. 1995. Internationalization, Institutions, and Political Change. *International Organization* 49:627–55.

———. 1996. Internationalization, Institutions, and Political Change. In *Internationalization and Domestic Politics*, edited by Robert O. Keohane and Helen Milner, 48–78. New York: Cambridge University Press.

Garrett, Geoffrey, and Deborah Mitchell. 1998. External Risk and Social Insurance: Reassessing the Globalization–Welfare State Nexus. Unpublished manuscript, Yale University, New Haven, Conn.

Garrett, Geoffrey, and George Tsebelis. 1996. An Institutional Critique of Intergovernmentalism. *International Organization* 50:269–99.

Garrett, Geoffrey, and Barry R. Weingast. 1993. Ideas, Interests, and Institutions: Constructing the European Community's Internal Market. In *Ideas and Foreign Policy: Beliefs, Institutions, and Political*

Change, edited by Judith Goldstein and Robert O. Keohane, 173–206. Ithaca, N.Y.: Cornell University Press.

Geertz, Clifford. 1980. *Negara: The Theater-State in Nineteenth-Century Bali*. Princeton, N.J.: Princeton University Press.

Gelpi, Christopher. 1997. Crime and Punishment: The Role of Norms in Crisis Bargaining. *American Political Science Review* 91:339–60.

George, Alexander L., and Juliette L. George. 1964. *Woodrow Wilson and Colonel House: A Personality Study*. New York: Dover Publications.

George, Jim. 1994. *Discourses of Global Politics: A Critical (Re)Introduction to International Relations*. Boulder, Colo.: Lynne Rienner.

Gerschenkron, Alexander. 1962. *Economic Backwardness in Historical Perspective*. Cambridge, Mass.: Harvard University Press.

Giavazzi, Francesco, and Alberto Giovannini. 1989. *Limiting Exchange Rate Variability: The European Monetary System*. Cambridge, Mass.: MIT Press.

Giddens, Anthony. 1979. *Central Problems in Social Theory: Action, Structure, and Contradiction in Social Analysis*. Berkeley: University of California Press.

———. 1981. *A Contemporary Critique of Historical Materialism*. Berkeley: University of California Press.

———. 1984. *The Constitution of Society: Outline of the Theory of Structuration*. Berkeley: University of California Press.

———. 1985. *The Nation State and Violence*. Oxford: Polity Press.

Giesen, Klaus-Gerd. 1995. French Cancan zwischen Positivismus, Enzyklopädismus, und Historismus. *Zeitschrift für internationale Beziehungen* 2:141–70.

Gill, Stephen. 1995. Globalisation, Market Civilisation, and Disciplinary Neoliberalism. *Millennium: Journal of International Studies* 24:399–424.

Gill, Stephen, ed. 1993. *Gramsci, Historical Materialism, and International Relations*. Cambridge: Cambridge University Press.

Gill, Stephen R., and David Law. 1989. Global Hegemony and the Structural Power of Capital. *International Studies Quarterly* 33:475–99.

Gilligan, Carol. 1993. *In a Different Voice: Psychological Theory and Women's Development*. Cambridge, Mass: Harvard University Press.

Gilligan, Michael J. 1997. *Empowering Exporters*. Ann Arbor: University of Michigan Press.

Gilligan, Thomas W., and Keith Krehbiel. 1990. Organization of Informative Committees by a Rational Legislature. *American Journal of Political Science* 34:531–64.

Gilovich, Thomas. 1991. *How We Know What Isn't So: The Fallibility of Reason in Everyday Life*. New York: Free Press.

Gilpin, Robert. 1972. The Politics of Transnational Economic Relations. In *Transnational Relations and World Politics*, edited by Robert O. Keohane and Joseph S. Nye, Jr., 48–69. Cambridge, Mass.: Harvard University Press.

———. 1975. *U.S. Power and the Multinational Corporation: The Political Economy of Foreign Direct Investment*. New York: Basic Books.

———. 1977. Economic Interdependence and National Security in Historical Perspective. In *Economic Issues and National Security*, edited by Klaus Knorr and Frank N. Trager, 19–66. Lawrence: University of Kansas Press.

———. 1981. *War and Change in World Politics*. Cambridge: Cambridge University Press.

———. 1984. The Richness of the Tradition of Political Realism. *International Organization* 38:287–304.

———. 1987. *The Political Economy of International Relations*. Princeton, N.J.: Princeton University Press.

———. 1996. No One Loves a Political Realist. *Security Studies* 5:3–26.

Glaser, Charles. 1994. Realists as Optimists: Cooperation as Self-Help. *International Security* 19:50–90.

Gleditsch, N. P. 1992. Democracy and Peace. *Journal of Peace Research* 29:369–76.

Golden, Miriam A. 1998. Economic Integration and Industrial Relations. Unpublished manuscript, University of California, Los Angeles.

Goldmann, Kjell. 1995. Im Westen nichts Neues: Seven International Relations Journals in 1972 and 1992. *European Journal of International Relations* 1:245–60.

———. 1996. International Relations: An Overview. In *A New Handbook of Political Science*, edited by Robert E. Goodin and Hans-Dieter Klingemann, 401–27. Oxford: Oxford University Press.

Goldstein, Joshua. 1988. *Long Cycles: Prosperity and War in the Modern Age.* New Haven, Conn.: Yale University Press.

Goldstein, Judith. 1993. *Ideas, Interests, and American Trade Policy.* Ithaca, N.Y.: Cornell University Press.

———. 1996. International Law and Domestic Institutions: Reconciling North American "Unfair" Trade Laws. *International Organization* 50:541–64.

Goldstein, Judith, and Robert O. Keohane. 1993a. Ideas and Foreign Policy: An Analytical Framework. In *Ideas and Foreign Policy: Beliefs, Institutions, and Political Change*, edited by Judith Goldstein and Robert O. Keohane, 3–30. Ithaca, N.Y.: Cornell University Press.

Goldstein, Judith, and Robert O. Keohane, eds. 1993b. *Ideas and Foreign Policy: Beliefs, Institutions, and Political Change* Ithaca, N.Y.: Cornell University Press.

Goldthorpe, John H., ed. 1984. *Order and Conflict in Contemporary Capitalism.* New York: Oxford University Press.

Goodman, John B., and Louis R. Pauly. 1993. The Obsolescence of Capital Controls? *World Politics* 46:50–82.

Goodrich, Leland M. 1947. From League of Nations to United Nations. *International Organization* 1:3–32.

———. 1956. *Korea: A Study of U.S. Policy in the United Nations.* New York: Council on Foreign Relations.

Gordon, Lincoln. 1956. Economic Aspects of Coalition Diplomacy—The NATO Experience. *International Organization* 10:529–43.

Gordon, Roger, and Lans Bovenberg. 1996. Why Is Capital so Immobile Internationally? *American Economic Review* 86:1057–75.

Gorter, Wytze. 1954. GATT After Six Years: An Appraisal. *International Organization* 8:1–18.

Gosovic, Branislav, and John Gerard Ruggie. 1976. On the Creation of a New International Economic Order: Issue Linkage and the Seventh Special Session of the UN General Assembly. *International Organization* 30:309–45.

Gould, Stephen Jay. 1987. *Time's Arrow, Time's Cycle.* Cambridge, Mass: Harvard University Press.

Gourevitch, Peter A. 1978. The Second Image Reversed: International Sources of Domestic Politics. *International Organization* 32:881–912.

———. 1986. *Politics in Hard Times: Comparative Responses to International Economic Crises.* Ithaca, N.Y.: Cornell University Press.

Gowa, Joanne S. 1989. Rational Hegemons, Excludable Goods, and Small Groups: An Epitaph for Hegemonic Stability Theory? *World Politics* 41:307–24.

———. 1994. *Allies, Adversaries, and International Trade.* Princeton, N.J.: Princeton University Press.

Gray, Colin. 1992. *House of Cards: Why Arms Control Must Fail.* Ithaca, N.Y.: Cornell University Press.

Green, Donald P., and Ian Shapiro. 1994. *Pathologies of Rational Choice Theory.* New Haven, Conn.: Yale University Press.

Gregg, Robert W. 1966. The UN Regional Economic Commissions and Integration in the Underdeveloped Region. *International Organization* 20:208–32.

Greider, William. 1997. *One World, Ready or Not.* New York: Simon and Schuster.

Greif, Avner. 1994. On the Political Foundations of the Late Medieval Commercial Revolution: Genoa in the 12th and 13th Centuries. *Journal of Economic History* 54:271–87.

———. 1995. Cultural Beliefs and the Organization of Society: A Historical and Theoretical Reflection on Collectivist and Individualist Societies. *Journal of Political Economy* 102:912–50.

Grieco, Joseph M. 1988. Anarchy and the Limits of Cooperation: A Realist Critique of the Newest Liberal Institutionalism. *International Organization* 42:485–507.

———. 1990. *Cooperation Among Nations: Europe, America, and Non-Tariff Barriers to Trade.* Ithaca, N.Y.: Cornell University Press.

Groom, A. J. R. n.d. The Study of International Relations in France: A View from Outside. Paper prepared for a seminar at the Université Pierre Mendès-France, Grenoble. *http://snipe.ukc.ac.uk/international/ papers.dir/groom4.html*

———. 1994. The World Beyond: The European Dimension. In *Contemporary International Relations: A Guide to Theory,* edited by A. J. R. Groom and Margot Light, 219–36. London and New York: Pinter Publishers.

Grossman, Gene M., and Elhanan Helpman. 1994. Protection by Sale. *American Economic Review* 84: 833–50.

Grubel, Herbert G., and P. J. Lloyd. 1975. *Intra-industry Trade: The Theory and Measurement of International Trade in Differentiated Products.* New York: Wiley.

Gruber, Lloyd. 1996. Ruling the World: Power Politics and the Rise of Supranational Institutions. Unpublished manuscript, University of Chicago, Chicago, Ill.

Gunnell, John G. 1991. In Search of the State: Political Science as an Emerging Discipline in the U.S. In *Sociology of the Sciences—A Yearbook.* Vol. 15, *Discourses on Society: The Shaping of the Social Sciences,* edited by P. Wagner, B. Wittrock, and R. Whitley, 123–61. Dordrecht: Kluwer.

———. 1993. *The Descent of Political Theory: The Genealogy of an American Vocation.* Chicago: University of Chicago Press.

———. 1995. The Declination of the "State" and the Origins of American Pluralism. In *Political Science in History: Research Programs and Political Traditions,* edited by James Farr, John S. Dryzek, and Stephen T. Leonard, 19–40. Cambridge: Cambridge University Press.

Gurowitz, Amy. 1997. International Society and State Inclusion of Non-Citizens: The Changing Debate in Japan and Germany. Paper prepared for the Annual Convention of the International Studies Association, 18–22 March, Toronto.

Guttentag, Jack M., and Richard Herring. 1985. Commercial Bank Lending to Developing Countries: From Overlending to Underlending to Structural Reform. In *International Debt and the Developing Countries,* edited by Gordon W. Smith and John T. Cuddington, 129–50. Washington, D.C.: The World Bank.

Guzzini, Stefano. 1998. *Realism in International Relations/International Political Economy: The Continuing Story of a Death Foretold.* London: Routledge.

Haas, Ernst B. 1958. *The Uniting of Europe: Political, Social, and Economic Forces, 1950–1957.* Stanford, Calif.: Stanford University Press.

———. 1961. International Integration: The European and the Universal Process. *International Organization* 15:366–92.

———. 1964a. *Beyond the Nation State: Functionalism and International Organization.* Stanford, Calif. Stanford University Press.

———. 1964b. Technocracy, Pluralism, and the New Europe. In *A New Europe?,* edited by Stephen Graubard. London: Oldbourne Press.

———. 1967. The Uniting of Europe and the Uniting of Latin America. *Journal of Common Market Studies* 5:315–33.

———. 1975. *The Obsolescence of Regional Integration Theory.* Berkeley: Institute of International Studies, University of California, Berkeley.

———. 1976. Turbulent Fields and the Theory of Regional Integration. *International Organization* 30:173–212.

———. 1983. Words Can Hurt You; or, Who Said What to Whom About Regimes. In *International Regimes,* edited by Stephen D. Krasner, 23–59. Ithaca, N.Y.: Cornell University Press.

———. 1986. What Is Nationalism and Why Should We Study It? *International Organization* 40:707–44.

———. 1990. *When Knowledge Is Power.* Berkeley: University of California Press.

————. 1993. Nationalism: An Instrumental Social Construction. *Millennium: Journal of International Studies* 22:1001–35.

————. 1997. *Nationalism, Liberalism, and Progress.* Ithaca, N.Y.: Cornell University Press.

Haas, Peter M. 1989. Do Regimes Matter? Epistemic Communities and Mediterranean Pollution Control. *International Organization* 43:377–405.

————. 1990. *Saving the Mediterranean.* New York: Columbia University Press.

————. 1992a. Introduction: Epistemic Communities and International Policy Coordination. *International Organization* 46:1–35.

————. 1992b. Banning Chlorofluorocarbons: Epistemic Community Efforts to Protect Stratospheric Ozone. *International Organization* 46:187–224.

Haas, Peter M., ed. 1992c. Knowledge, Power, and International Policy Coordination. *International Organization* 46. Special issue.

Habermas, Jürgen. 1979. *Communication and the Evolution of Society.* Boston: Beacon Press.

————. 1984. *Theory of Communicative Action.* Vol. 1. Boston: Beacon Press.

————. 1987. *Theory of Communicative Action.* Vol. 2. Boston: Beacon Press.

————. 1996. *Between Facts and Norms: Contributions to a Discourse Theory of Law and Democracy.* Translated by William Rehg. Cambridge, Mass.: MIT Press.

Haggard, Stephan. 1990. *Pathways from the Periphery: The Politics of Growth in the Newly Industrializing Countries.* Ithaca, N.Y.: Cornell University Press.

Haggard, Stephan, and Robert R. Kaufman. 1995. *The Political Economy of Democratic Transitions.* Princeton, N.J.: Princeton University Press.

Haggard, Stephan, and Robert R. Kaufman, eds. 1992. *The Politics of Economic Adjustment.* Princeton, N.J.: Princeton University Press.

Haggard, Stephan, and Beth A. Simmons. 1987. Theories of International Regimes. *International Organization* 41:491–517.

Hall, J. A. 1996. *International Orders.* Cambridge: Polity Press.

Hall, Peter A. 1989a. Conclusion: The Politics of Keynesian Ideas. In *The Political Power of Economic Ideas: Keynesianism Across Nations,* edited by Peter A. Hall, 361–391. Princeton, N.J.: Princeton University Press.

————. 1993. Policy Paradigms, Social Learning, and the States: The Case of Economic Policymaking in Britain. *Comparative Politics* 26:275–96.

Hall, Peter A., ed. 1989b. *The Political Power of Economic Ideas: Keynesianism Across Nations.* Princeton, N.J.: Princeton University Press.

Hall, Rodney Bruce, and Friedrich V. Kratochwil. 1993. Medieval Tales: Neorealist "Science" and the Abuse of History. *International Organization* 47:479–91.

Hallerberg, Mark, and Scott Basinger. 1998. Internationalization and Changes in Tax Policy in OECD Countries. *Comparative Political Studies* 31:321–52.

Hallerberg, Mark, and William Roberts Clark. 1997. How Should Political Scientists Measure Capital Mobility. Paper presented at the 93d Annual Meeting of the American Political Science Association, August, Washington, D.C.

Halliday, Fred. 1983. *The Making of the Second Cold War.* London: Verso.

Halperin, Morton. 1974. *Bureaucratic Politics and Foreign Policy.* Washington, D.C.: Brookings Institution.

Halpern, Nina P. 1993. Creating Socialist Economies: Stalinist Political Economy and the Impact of Ideas. In *Ideas and Foreign Policy: Beliefs, Institutions and Political Change,* edited by Judith Goldstein and Robert O. Keohane, 87–110. Ithaca, N.Y.: Cornell University Press.

Hanreider, Wolfram. 1968. International and Comparative Politics: Toward a Synthesis? *World Politics* 20:480–93.

Harbert, Joseph R. 1976. The Behavior of Mini-States in the United Nations. *International Organization* 30:109–27.

Hardin, Russell. 1995. *One for All: The Logic of Group Conflict*. Princeton, N.J.: Princeton University Press.

Hargens, Lowell L. 1988. Scholarly Consensus and Journal Rejection Rates. *American Sociological Review* 53:139–51.

Harrison, Lawrence. 1985. *Underdevelopment Is a State of Mind: The Latin American Case*. Boston: Madison Books.

Harsanyi, John. 1969. Rational Choice Models of Political Behavior Versus Functionalist and Conformist Theories. *World Politics* 21:513–38.

Hartz, Louis. 1955. *The Liberal Tradition in America: An Interpretation of American Political Thought Since the Revolution*. New York: Harcourt, Brace, and World.

Hasenclever, Andreas, Peter Mayer, and Volker Rittberger. 1996. Interests, Power, Knowledge: The Study of International Regimes. *Mershon International Studies Review* 40:177–228.

———. 1997. *Theories of International Regimes*. Cambridge: Cambridge University Press.

Haskel, Barbara. 1980. Access to Society: A Neglected Dimension of Power. *International Organization* 34:89–120.

Hassner, Pierre. 1997. *Violence and Peace: From the Atomic Bomb to Ethnic Cleansing*. Translated by Jane Brenton. Budapest and New York: Central European University Press.

Havel, Vaclav. 1994. A Call for Sacrifice. *Foreign Affairs* 73:2–7.

Hawtrey, Ralph G. 1930. *Economic Aspects of Sovereignty*. London: Longman, Greens and Company.

Hayward, J. E. S. 1983. *Governing France: The One and Indivisible Republic*. 2d ed. London: Weidenfeld and Nicolson.

———. 1991. Cultural and Contextual Constraints upon the Development of Political Science in Great Britain. In *The Development of Political Science: A Comparative Survey*, edited by David Easton, John G. Gunnell and Luigi Graziano, 93–107. London and New York: Routledge.

Hechter, M., and S. Kanazawa. 1997. Sociological Rational Choice Theory. *Annual Review of Sociology* 23:191–214.

Heilbron, Johan. 1991. The Tripartite Division of French Social Science: A Long-Term Perspective. In *Sociology of the Sciences—A Yearbook*. Vol. 15, *Discourses on Society: The Shaping of the Social Sciences,* edited by P. Wagner, B. Wittrock, and R. Whitley, 73–92. Dordrecht: Kluwer.

Heldt, B., ed. 1992. *States in Armed Conflict 1990–1991*. Report No. 35. Uppsala: Uppsala University, Department of Peace and Conflict Research.

Hellmann, Gunther. 1994. Für eine problemorientierte Grundlagenforschung: Kritik und Perspektiven der Disziplin "Internationale Beziehungen" in Deutschland. *Zeitschrift für Internationale Beziehungen* 1:65–90.

Henkin, Louis. 1965. The United Nations and Human Rights. *International Organization* 19:504–17.

Herman, Robert G. 1996. Identity, Norms, and National Security: The Soviet Foreign Policy Revolution and the End of the Cold War. In *The Culture of National Security: Norms and Identity in World Politics,* edited by Peter J. Katzenstein, 271–316. New York: Columbia University Press.

Hermann, Charles. 1968. The Comparative Study of Foreign Policy. *World Politics* 20:521–34.

Herz, John. 1951. *Political Realism and Political Idealism: A Study in Theories and Realities*. Chicago: University of Chicago Press.

Hill, Christopher. 1987. The Study of International Relations in the United Kingdom. *Millennium: Journal of International Studies* 16:301–308.

Hill, Christopher, and W. Wallace. 1996. Introduction: Actors and Actions. In *The Actors in Europe's Foreign Policy,* edited by Christopher Hill, 1–16. London: Routledge.

Hilsman, Roger. 1958. Congressional-Executive Relations and the Foreign Policy Consensus. *American Political Science Review* 52:725–44.

Hines, James R. 1997. Altered States: Taxes and the Location of Foreign Direct Investment in America. *American Economic Review* 86:1076–94.

Hirschman, Albert O. 1977. *The Passion and the Interests: Political Arguments for Capitalism Before Its Triumph*. Princeton, N.J.: Princeton University Press.

————. [1945] 1980. *National Power and the Structure of Foreign Trade*. Reprint, Berkeley: University of California Press.

————. 1981. *Essays in Trespassing*. New York: Cambridge University Press.

————. 1982. *Shifting Involvements*. Princeton, N.J.: Princeton University Press.

Hirst, Paul, and Grahame Thompson. 1996. *Globalization in Question*. Cambridge: Polity.

Hix, Simon. 1998. The Study of the European Union II; The "New Governance" Argument and Its Rivals. *European Journal of Public Policy* 5:386–402.

Hoffman, Mark. 1987. Critical Theory and the Inter-Paradigm Debate. *Millennium: Journal of International Studies*. 16:231–49.

Hoffmann, Stanley. 1956. The Role of International Organization: Limits and Possibilities. *International Organization* 10:357–72.

————. 1959. International Relations: The Long Road to Theory. *World Politics* 11:346–77.

————. 1960. *Contemporary Theory in International Relations*. Englewood Cliffs, N.J.: Prentice-Hall.

————. 1966. Obstinate or Obsolete? The Fate of the Nation-State and the Case of Western Europe. *Daedalus* 95:862–915.

————. 1968. *Gulliver's Troubles or the Setting of American Foreign Policy*. New York: McGraw-Hill.

————. 1977. An American Social Science: International Relations. *Daedalus* 106:41–60.

————. 1978. *Primacy or World Order—American Foreign Policy Since the Cold War*. New York: McGraw Hill.

————. 1986. Hedley Bull and His Contribution to International Relations. *International Affairs* (London) 62:179–96.

————. 1987. Raymond Aron and the Theory of International Relations. In *Janus and Minerva: Essays in the Theory and Practice of International Politics*, by Stanley Hoffman, 52–69. Boulder, Colo.: Westview Press.

————. 1997. The United States and Western Europe. In *Eagle Adrift: American Foreign Policy at the End of the Century*, edited by Robert Lieber, 178–92. New York: Longman.

Hoffmann, Stanley, ed. 1960. *Contemporary Theory in International Relations*. Englewood Cliffs, N.J.: Prentice-Hall.

Hogarth, R., and M. Reder, eds. 1986. The Behavioral Foundation of Economic Theory. *The Journal of Business* 59 (supplement).

Hollis, Martin, and Steve Smith. 1986. Roles and Reasons in Foreign Policy Decision Making. *British Journal of Political Science* 16:269–86.

————. 1990. *Explaining and Understanding International Relations*. Oxford: Clarendon Press.

————. 1991. Beware of Gurus: Structure and Action in International Relations. *Review of International Studies* 17:393–410.

Holsti, Kalevi J. 1985. *The Dividing Discipline: Hegemony and Diversity in International Theory*. Boston: Allen and Unwin.

————. 1986. The Horsemen of the Apocalypse: At the Gate, Detoured, or Retreating? *International Studies Quarterly* 30:355–72.

————. 1996. *The State, War, and the State of War*. Cambridge: Cambridge University Press.

Holsti, Ole. 1970. *Crisis, Escalation and War*. Montreal: McGill University Press.

Hoole, Francis W. 1977. Evaluating the Impact of International Organizations. *International Organization* 31:541–63.

Hopf, Ted. 1998. The Promise of Constructivism in International Relations Theory. *International Security* 22:171–200.

Hopkins, Raymond F., and Donald J. Puchala. 1978. Perspectives on the International Relations of Food. *International Organization* 32:581–616.

Hosli, Madeleine O. 1993. Admission of European Free Trade Association States to the European Community: Effects on Voting Power in the European Community Council of Ministers. *International Organization* 47:629–43.

Hovet, Thomas, Jr. 1958. *Bloc Votes in the United Nations*. Cambridge, Mass.: MIT Press.

Huber, John D. 1992. Restrictive Legislative Procedures in France and the United States. *American Political Science Review* 86:675–87.

———. 1996a. The Vote of Confidence In Parliamentary Democracies. *American Political Science Review* 90:269–82.

———. 1996b. *Rationalizing Parliament: Legislative Institutions and Party Politics in France.* New York: Cambridge University Press.

Huntington, Samuel P. 1968. *Political Order in Changing Societies.* New Haven, Conn., and London: Yale University Press.

———. 1973. Transnational Organizations in World Politics. *World Politics* 25:333–68.

———. 1996. *The Clash of Civilizations and the Remaking of the World Order.* New York: Simon and Schuster.

Huysmans, Jef. 1998. Revisiting Copenhagen or On the Creative Development of a Security Studies Agenda in Europe. *European Journal of International Relations* 4.

Ikenberry, G. John. 1992. A World Economy Restored: Expert Consensus and the Anglo-American Postwar Settlement. *International Organization* 46:289–321.

———. 1993a. Creating Yesterday's New World Order: Keynesian "New Thinking" and the Anglo-American Postwar Settlement. In *Ideas and Foreign Policy: Beliefs, Institutions, and Political Change,* edited by Judith Goldstein and Robert O. Keohane, 57–86. Ithaca, N.Y.: Cornell University Press.

———. 1993b. The Political Origins of Bretton Woods. In *A Retrospective on the Bretton Woods System,* edited by Michael D. Bordo and Barry Eichengreen, 155–200. Chicago: University of Chicago Press.

Ikenberry, G. John, and Charles Kupchan. 1990. Socialization and Hegemonic Power. *International Organization* 44:283–315.

Ikenberry, G. John, David Lake, and Michael Mastanduno, eds. 1988. *The State and American Foreign Economic Policy.* Ithaca, N.Y.: Cornell University Press.

IMF, Various years. *Balance-of Payments Statistics.* Washington, D.C.: IMF.

———. 1983. Exchange Rate Volatility and World Trade. Unpublished manuscript, International Monetary Fund, Washington, D.C.

———. 1991. *Determinants and Systematic Consequences of International Capital Flows.* Washington, D.C.: International Monetary Fund.

Inglehart, Ronald. 1997. *Modernization and Postmodernization: Cultural, Economic, and Political Change in 43 Societies.* Princeton, N.J.: Princeton University Press.

Irwin, Douglas, and Randall Krozner. 1996. Log-rolling and Economic Interests in the Passage of the Smoot-Hawley Tariff. NBER Working Paper 5510. Cambridge, Mass.: National Bureau of Economic Research.

Isaacson, Walter. 1992. *Kissinger: A Biography.* New York: Simon and Schuster.

Iversen, Torben. 1996. Power, Flexibility and the Breakdown of Centralized Wage Bargaining. *Comparative Politics* 28:399–436.

Jachtenfuchs, Markus, and Beate Kohler-Koch, eds. 1996. *Europäische Integration.* Opladen, Germany: Leske und Budrich.

Jackson, Robert H. 1990. *Quasi-States: Sovereignty, International Relations, and the Third World.* Cambridge: Cambridge University Press.

———. 1993. The Weight of Ideas in Decolonization: Normative Change in International Relations. In *Ideas and Foreign Policy: Beliefs, Institutions, and Political Change,* edited by Judith Goldstein and Robert O. Keohane, 111–38. Ithaca, N.Y.: Cornell University Press.

Jacobson, Harold. 1962. The United Nations and Colonialism: A Tentative Appraisal. *International Organization* 16:37–56.

———. 1967. Deriving Data from Delegates to International Assemblies. *International Organization* 21:592–613.

James, Allan, ed. 1973. *The Bases of International Order.* London: Oxford University Press.

Janis, Irving L. 1982. *Groupthink: Psychological Studies of Policy Decisions and Fiascoes.* 2d ed. Boston: Houghton Mifflin.

———. 1983. *Groupthink: Psychological Studies of Policy Decisions and Fiascoes.* 2d ed., rev. Boston: Houghton Mifflin.

Jebb, Sir Gladwyn. 1952. The Role of the United Nations. *International Organization* 6:509–20.

Jensen, Michael C., and William H. Meckling. 1976. Theory of the Firm: Managerial Behavior, Agency Costs, and Ownership Structure. *Journal of Financial Economics* 3:305–60.

Jentleson, Bruce. 1986. *Pipeline Politics: The Complex Political Economy of East-West Energy Trade.* Ithaca, N.Y.: Cornell University Press.

Jepperson, Ronald L. 1991. Institutions, Institutional Effects, and Institutionalism. In *The New Institutionalism in Organizational Analysis,* edited by Walter W. Powell and Paul J. DiMaggio, 143–63. Chicago: University of Chicago Press.

Jepperson, Ronald L., Alexander Wendt, and Peter J. Katzenstein. 1996. Norms, Identity, and Culture of National Security. In *The Culture of National Security: Norms and Identity in World Politics,* edited by Peter J. Katzenstein, 33–75. New York: Columbia University Press.

Jervis, Robert. 1976. *Perception and Misperception in International Politics.* Princeton, N.J.: Princeton University Press.

———. 1978. Cooperation Under the Security Dilemma. *World Politics* 30:167–214.

———. 1988. War and Misperception. In *The Origin and Prevention of Major Wars,* edited by Robert I. Rotberg and Theodore K. Rabb, 101–26. Cambridge: Cambridge University Press.

———. [1970] 1989a. *The Logic of Images in International Relations.* Reprint, New York: Columbia University Press.

———. 1989b. Rational Deterrence: Theory and Evidence. *World Politics* 41:183–207.

———. 1989c. *The Meaning of the Nuclear Revolution: Statecraft and the Prospect of Armageddon.* Ithaca, N.Y.: Cornell University Press.

———. 1991. The Future of World Politics: Will It Resemble the Past. *International Security* 16:39–73.

———. 1992a. A Political Science Perspective on the Balance of Power and the Concert. *American Historical Review* 97:716–24.

———. 1992b. Political Implications of Loss Aversion. *Political Psychology* 13:187–204.

———. 1993. International Primacy. Is the Game Worth the Candle? *International Security* 17:52–67.

Joerges, C., K-H. Ladeur, and E. Vos, eds. 1997. *Integrating Scientific Expertise into Regulatory Decision-Making. National Traditions and European Innovations.* Baden-Baden: Nomos.

Johnson, Chalmers, and E. B. Keehn. 1995. The Pentagon's Ossified Strategy. *Foreign Affairs* 74:103–14.

Johnson, Howard C., and Gerhart Niemeyer. 1954. Collective Security: The Validity of an Ideal. *International Organization* 8:19–35.

Johnson, Robert H. 1994. *Improbable Dangers: U.S. Conceptions of Threat in the Cold War and After.* New York: St. Martin's Press.

Johnston, Alastair I. 1995a. *Cultural Realism: Strategic Culture and Grand Strategy in Chinese History.* Princeton, N.J.: Princeton University Press.

———. 1995b. Thinking about Strategic Culture. *International Security* 19:32–64.

———. 1996. Cultural Realism and Strategy in Maoist China. In *The Culture of National Security: Norms and Identity in World Politics,* edited by Peter J. Katzenstein, 216–68. New York: Columbia University Press.

Jones, R. J. Barry. 1995. *Globalisation and Interdependence in the International Political Economy: Rhetoric and Reality.* London: Pinter Publishers.

Jones, Stephen R. G. 1984. *The Economics of Conformism.* Oxford: Blackwell.

Jönsson, Christer. 1993. International Politics: Scandinavian Identity Amidst American Hegemony? *Scandinavian Political Studies* 16:149–65.

Kagan, Korina. 1997. The Myth of the European Concert: The Realist-Institutionalist Debate and Great Power Behavior in the Eastern Question, 1821–41. *Security Studies* 7:1–57.

Kahler, Miles. 1993. International Relations: Still an American Social Science? In *Ideas and Ideals: Essays on Politics in Honor of Stanley Hoffmann,* edited by Linda B. Miller and Michael Joseph Smith, 395–414. Boulder, Colo: Westview.

———. 1997. Inventing International Relations: International Relations Theory Since 1945. In *New Thinking in International Relations Theory,* edited by Michael W. Doyle and G. John Ikenberry, 20–53. Boulder, Colo.: Westview Press.

Kaiser, David E. 1980. *Economic Diplomacy and the Origins of the Second World War.* Princeton, N.J.: Princeton University Press.

Kaldor, Mary. 1978. *The Disintegrating West.* New York: Hill and Wang.

Kaplan, Morton A. 1957. *System and Process in International Politics.* New York: Wiley.

Kapstein, Ethan B.. 1990. *The Insecure Alliance: Energy Crises and Western Politics Since 1944.* New York: Oxford University Press.

———. 1992. *The Political Economy of National Security.* New York: McGraw Hill.

———. 1996. Workers and the World Economy. *Foreign Affairs* 75:16–37.

Kapstein, Ethan, and Michael Mastanduno, eds. Forthcoming. *Unipolar Politics: Realism and State Strategies After the Cold War.* New York: Columbia University Press.

Karns, David A. 1977. The Effect of Interparliamentary Meetings on the Foreign Policy Attitudes of United States Congressmen. *International Organization* 31:515–39.

Kastendiek, Hans. 1991. Political Development and Political Science in West Germany. In *The Development of Political Science: A Comparative Survey,* edited by David Easton, John G. Gunnell, and Luigi Graziano. 108–26. London and New York: Routledge.

Katzenstein, Peter J. 1975. International Interdependence: Some Long-Term Trends and Recent Changes. *International Organization* 29:1021–34.

———. 1976. International Relations and Domestic Structures: Foreign Economic Policies of Advanced Industrial States. *International Organization* 30:1–45.

———. 1984. *Corporatism and Change: Austria, Switzerland, and the Politics of Industry.* Ithaca, N.Y.: Cornell University Press.

———. 1985. *Small States in World Markets: Industrial Policy in Europe.* Ithaca, N.Y.: Cornell University Press.

———. 1993. *Japan's National Security: Structures, Norms, and Policy Responses in a Changing World.* Ithaca, N.Y.: Cornell University Press.

———. 1996a. *Cultural Norms and National Security: Police and Military in Postwar Japan.* Ithaca, N.Y.: Cornell University Press.

———. 1996b. Introduction: Alternative Perspectives on National Security. In *The Culture of National Security: Norms and Identity in World Politics,* edited by Peter J. Katzenstein, 1–32. New York: Columbia University Press.

Katzenstein, Peter J., ed. 1978. *Between Power and Plenty: Foreign Economic Policies of Advanced Industrial States.* Madison: University of Wisconsin Press.

———. 1996c. *The Culture of National Security. Norms and Identity in World Politics.* New York: Columbia University Press.

———. 1997. *Tamed Power: Germany in Europe.* Ithaca, N.Y.: Cornell University Press.

Kay, David. 1967. The Politics of Decolonization: The New Nations and the United Nations Political Process. *International Organization* 21:786–811.

Kaysen, C. 1990. Is War Obsolete? A Review Essay. *International Security* 14:42–64.

Keck, Margaret, and Kathryn Sikkink. 1998. *Activists Beyond Borders: Advocacy Networks in International Politics.* Ithaca, N.Y.: Cornell University Press.

Keck, Otto. 1995. Rationales Kommunikatives Handeln in den Internationalen Beziehungen: Ist eine Verbindung von Rational-Choice-Theorie und Habermas' Theorie des Kommunikativen Handelns Möglich? *Zeitschrift Für Internationale Beziehungen* 1:5–48.

Keeley, James F. 1990. Toward a Foucauldian Analysis of International Regimes. *International Organization* 44:83–105.

Kelman, Herbert C. 1962. Changing Attitudes Through International Activities. *Journal of Social Issues* 18:67–87.

Kennan, George F. 1967. *Memoirs: 1925–1950.* Boston: Little, Brown.

———. 1968. *From Prague After Munich: Diplomatic Papers, 1938–1940.* Princeton, N.J.: Princeton University Press.

Kennedy, Paul. 1983. *Strategy and Diplomacy, 1870–1945.* London: Allen and Unwin.

———. 1987. *The Rise and Fall of the Great Powers: Economic Change and Military Conflict from 1500 to 2000.* New York: Random House.

Keohane, Nannerl. 1980. *Philosophy and the State in France: The Renaissance to the Enlightenment.* Princeton, N.J.: Princeton University Press.

Keohane, Robert O. 1967. The Study of Political Influence in the General Assembly. *International Organization* 21:221–37.

———. 1969. Who Cares About the General Assembly? *International Organization* 23:141–49.

———. 1978. The International Energy Agency: State Influence and Transgovernmental Politics. *International Organization* 32:929–51.

———. 1980. The Theory of Hegemonic Stability and Changes in International Economic Regimes, 1967–1977. In *Change in the International System*, edited by Ole Holsti, Randolph M. Siverson, and Alexander L. George, 131–62. Boulder, Colo.: Westview Press.

———. 1982. The Demand for International Regimes. *International Organization* 36:325–56.

———. 1983a. The Demand For International Regimes. In *International Regimes*, edited by Stephen D. Krasner, 141–71. Ithaca, N.Y.: Cornell University Press.

———. 1983b. Theory of World Politics: Structural Realism and Beyond. In *Political Science: The State of the Discipline*, edited by Ada W. Finifter, 503–40. Washington, D.C.: American Political Science Association.

———. 1984. *After Hegemony. Cooperation and Discord in the World Political Economy.* Princeton, N.J.: Princeton University Press.

———. 1986a. Realism, Neorealism, and the Study of World Politics. In *Neorealism and Its Critics*, edited by Robert O. Keohane, 1–26. New York: Columbia University Press.

———. 1986b. Theory of World Politics: Structural Realism and Beyond. In *Neorealism and Its Critics*, edited by Robert O. Keohane, 158–203. New York: Columbia University Press.

———. 1988. International Institutions: Two Approaches. *International Studies Quarterly* 32:379–96.

———. 1989a. Neoliberal Institutionalism: A Perspective on World Politics. In *International Institutions and State Power: Essays in International Relations Theory*, edited by Robert O. Keohane, 1–20. Boulder, Colo.: Westview Press.

———. 1990a. Empathy and International Regimes. In *Beyond Self-Interest,* edited by Jane Mansbridge, 227–36. Chicago: University of Chicago Press.

———. 1990b. International Liberalism Reconsidered. In *The Economic Limits to Modern Politics,* edited by John Dunn. New York: Cambridge University Press.

———. 1993. Institutional Theory and the Realist Challenge After the Cold War. In *Neorealism and Neoliberalism: The Contemporary Debate,* edited by David A. Baldwin, 269–300. New York: Columbia University Press.

———. 1996a. International Relations, Old and New. In *A New Handbook of Political Science,* edited by Robert E. Goodin and Hans-Dieter Klingemann, 462–76. Oxford: Oxford University Press.

———. 1996b. Remarks at the Annual Convention. American Political Science Association.

———. 1997. Problematic Lucidity: Stephen Krasner's "State Power and the Structure of International Trade." *World Politics* 50:150–70.

Keohane, Robert O., and Lisa Martin. 1995. The Promise of Institutionalist Theory. *International Security* 20:39–51.

Keohane, Robert O., and Joseph S. Nye, Jr. 1971. Transnational Relations and World Politics: An Introduction. *International Organization* 25:329–52.

———. 1974. Transgovernmental Relations and International Organizations. *World Politics* 27:39–62.

———. 1977. *Power and Interdependence: World Politics in Transition.* Boston: Little, Brown.

Keohane, Robert O., ed. 1989b. *International Institutions and State Power. Essays in International Relations Theory.* Boulder, Colo.: Westview Press.

Keohane, Robert O., and Stanley Hoffmann, eds. 1991. *The New European Community.* Boulder, Colo.: Westview Press.

Keohane, Robert O., and Helen Milner, eds. 1996. *Internationalization and Domestic Politics.* Cambridge: Cambridge University Press.

Keohane, Robert O., and Joseph S. Nye, Jr., eds. 1972. *Transnational Relations and World Politics.* Cambridge, Mass.: Harvard University Press.

Keohane, Robert O., Joseph S. Nye, Jr., and Stanley Hoffmann, eds. 1993. *After the Cold War: International Institutions and State Strategies in Europe, 1989–1991.* Cambridge, Mass.: Harvard University Press.

Kerr, Henry H., Jr. 1973. Changing Attitudes Through International Participation: European Parliamentarians and Integration. *International Organization* 27:45–83.

Keynes, John Maynard. 1920. *The Economic Consequences of the Peace.* New York: Harcourt, Brace, Howe.

Khong, Yuen Foong. 1992. *Analogies at War.* Princeton, N.J.: Princeton University Press.

Kier, Elizabeth. 1995. Culture and Military Doctrine: France Between the Wars. *International Security* 19:65–93.

———. 1996. Culture and French Military Doctrine Before World War II. In *The Culture of National Security: Norms and Identity in World Politics,* edited by Peter J. Katzenstein, 186–215. New York: Columbia University Press.

———. 1997. *Imagining War: French and British Military Doctrine Between the Wars.* Princeton, N.J.: Princeton University Press.

Kiewiet, D. Roderick, and Mathew D. McCubbins. 1991. *The Logic of Delegation.* Chicago: University of Chicago Press.

Kim, Soo Yeon. 1998. *Ties That Bind: The Role of Trade in International Conflict Processes, 1950–1992.* Ph.D. diss., Department of Political Science, Yale University, New Haven, Conn.

Kim, Woosang, and Bruce Bueno de Mesquita. 1995. How Perceptions Influence the Risk of War. *International Studies Quarterly* 39:51–66.

Kindleberger, Charles P. 1951a. Bretton Woods Reappraised. *International Organization* 5:32–47.

———. 1951b. Group Behavior and International Trade. *Journal of Political Economy* 59:30–46.

———. 1962. *Foreign Trade and the National Economy.* New Haven, Conn.: Yale University Press.

———. 1969. *American Business Abroad:Six Lectures on Direct Investment.* New Haven, Conn.: Yale University Press.

———. 1973. *The World in Depression, 1929–1939.* Berkeley: University of California Press.

———. 1978. *Economic Response: Comparative Studies in Trade, Finance, and Growth.* Cambridge, Mass.: Harvard University Press.

King, Garry, Robert O. Keohane, and Sidney Verba. 1994. *Designing Social Inquiry.* Princeton, N.J.: Princeton University Press.

Kirshner, Jonathan. 1995. *Currency and Coercion: The Political Economy of International Monetary Power.* Princeton, N.J.: Princeton University Press.

———. 1998. Political Economy in Security Studies After the Cold War. *Review of International Political Economy* 5:64–91.

Kissinger, Henry A. 1957a. *A World Restored: Castlereagh, Metternich, and the Restoration of Peace, 1812–1822.* Boston and London: Scott, Foresman.

———. 1957b. *Nuclear Weapons and Foreign Policy.* New York: Harper and Row.

———. 1965. *The Troubled Partnership.* New York: McGraw-Hill.

———. 1969. *American Foreign Policy: Three Essays.* New York: Norton.

———. 1994. *Diplomacy.* New York: Simon and Schuster.

Klotz, Audie. 1995a. Norms Reconstituting Interests: Global Racial Equality and U.S. Sanction Against South Africa. *International Organization* 49:451–78.

———. 1995b. *Norms in International Relations: The Struggle Against Apartheid.* Ithaca, N.Y.: Cornell University Press.

Knight, Jack. 1992. *Institutions and Social Conflict.* New York: Cambridge University Press.

Knorr, Klaus. 1948. The Bretton Woods Institutions in Transition. *International Organization* 2:19–38.

———. 1956. *The War Potential of Nations.* Princeton, N.J.:Princeton University Press.

———. 1975. *The Power of Nations: The Political Economy of International Relations.* New York: Basic Books.

Knorr, Klaus, and James Rosenau. 1961. *The International System.* Princeton, N.J.: Princeton University Press.

Knorr, Klaus, and Frank N. Trager. 1977. *Economic Issues and National Security.* Lawrence: University of Kansas Press.

Knutsen, Torbjörn L. 1992. *A History of International Relations Theory.* Manchester, England: Manchester University Press.

Koselleck, Reinhart. 1985. *Futures Past: On the Semantics of Historical Time.* Translated by Keith Tribe. Cambridge, Mass.: MIT Press.

Koslowski, Rey, and Friedrich V. Kratochwil. 1994. Understanding Change in International Politics: The Soviet Empire's Demise and the International System. *International Organization* 48:215–48.

———. 1995. Understanding Change in International Politics: The Soviet Empire's Demise and the International System. In *International Relations Theory and the End of the Cold War,* edited by Richard Ned Lebow and Thomas Risse-Kappen. New York: Columbia University Press.

Kowert, Paul, and Jeffrey Legro. 1996. Norms, Identity, and Their Limits: A Theoretical Reprise. In *The Culture of National Security: Norms and Identity in World Politics,* edited by Peter J. Katzenstein, 451–97. New York: Columbia University Press.

Krasner, Stephen D. 1976. State Power and the Structure of International Trade. *World Politics* 28:317–47.

———. 1977. United States Commercial and Monetary Policy: Unravelling the Paradox of External Strength and Internal Weakness. *International Organization* 31:635–72.

———. 1978. *Defending the National Interest: Raw Materials Investments and U.S. Foreign Policy.* Princeton, N.J.: Princeton University Press.

———. 1982. American Policy and Global Economic Stability. In *America in a Changing World Political Economy,* edited by William P. Avery and David P. Rapkin, 29–48. New York: Longman.

———. 1983a. Regimes and the Limits of Realism: Regimes as Autonomous Variables. In *International Regimes,* edited by Stephen D. Krasner, 355–68. Ithaca, N.Y.: Cornell University Press.

———. 1984. Approaches to the State: Alternative Conceptions and Historical Dynamics. *Comparative Politics* 16:223–46.

———. 1985. *Structural Conflict: The Third World Against Global Liberalism.* Berkeley: University of California Press.

———. 1988. Sovereignty: An Institutional Perspective. *Comparative Political Studies* 21:66–94.

———. 1991. Global Communications and National Power: Life on the Pareto Frontier. *World Politics* 43:336–66.

———. 1993. Westphalia and All That. In *Ideas and Foreign Policy: Beliefs, Institutions, and Political Change,* edited by Judith Goldstein and Robert O. Keohane, 235–64. Ithaca, N.Y.: Cornell University Press.

———. 1995a. Compromising Westphalia. *International Security* 20:115–51.

———. 1995b. Power Politics, Institutions, and Transnational Relations. In *Bringing Transnational Relations Back In: Non-state Actors, Domestic Structures, and International Institutions,* edited by Thomas Risse-Kappen, 257–79. New York: Cambridge University Press.

———. 1997. Sovereignty and Its Discontents. Unpublished manuscript, Stanford University, Stanford, California.

———. Forthcoming. *Sovereignty: Organized Hypocrisy.* Princeton, N.J.: Princeton University Press.

Krasner, Stephen D., ed. 1983b. *International Regimes.* Ithaca, N.Y.: Cornell University Press.

Kratochwil, Friedrich V. 1986. Of Systems, Boundaries, and Territoriality: An Inquiry into the Formation of the State System. *World Politics* 39:27–52.

———. 1989. *Rules, Norms and Decisions. On the Conditions of Practical and Legal Reasoning in International Relations and Domestic Affairs.* Cambridge: Cambridge University Press.

Kratochwil, Friedrich V., and John Gerard Ruggie. 1986. International Organization: A State of the Art on an Art of the State. *International Organization* 40:753–75.

Krause, Keith, and Michael C. Williams. 1996. Broadening the Agenda of Security Studies: Politics and Methods. *Mershon International Studies Review* 40:229–54.

Krause, Lawrence. 1972. Private International Finance. In *Transnational Relations and World Politics,* edited by Robert O. Keohane and Joseph S. Nye, Jr., 173–90. Cambridge, Mass.: Harvard University Press.

Krehbiel, Keith. 1991. *Information and Legislative Organization.* Ann Arbor: University of Michigan Press.

Kreps, David M. 1990a. Corporate Culture and Economic Theory. In *Perspectives on Positive Political Economy,* edited by James E. Alt and Kenneth A. Shepsle, 90–143. Cambridge: Cambridge University Press.

———. 1990b. *Game Theory and Economic Modeling.* New York and Oxford: Oxford University Press.

Krugman, Paul R. 1996. *Pop Internationalism.* Cambridge, Mass.: MIT Press.

Krugman, Paul R., ed. 1986. *Strategic Trade Policy and the New International Economics.* Cambridge, Mass.: MIT Press.

Kuhn, Thomas. 1962. *The Structure of Scientific Revolutions.* Chicago: University of Chicago Press.

Kupchan, Charles A. 1994. *The Vulnerability of Empire.* Ithaca, N.Y.: Cornell University Press.

Kurth, James. 1979. The Political Consequences of the Product Cycle: Industrial History and Political Outcomes. *International Organization* 33:1–34.

Kurzer, Paulette. 1993. *Business and Banking.* Ithaca, N.Y.: Cornell University Press.

Kydd, Andrew. 1997. Why Security Seekers Do Not Fight Each Other. *Security Studies* 7:114–55.

Labs, Eric. 1997. Beyond Victory: Offensive Realism and the Expansion of War Aims. *Security Studies* 6:1–49.

Ladeur, K-H. 1997. Towards a Legal Theory of Supranationality—The Viability of the Network Concept. *European Law Journal* 3:33–54.

LaFeber, Walter. 1997. *The Clash: A History of U.S.–Japan Relations.* New York: Norton.

Laffan, B. 1997a. The IGC as Constitution-building—What's New at Amsterdam. Unpublished manuscript, University College Dublin, Dublin, Ireland.

———. 1997b. The European Union: A Distinctive Model of Internationalization? *European Integration Online Papers* 1(018):*http://eiop.or.at/eiop.texte/1997018a.htm*

Laitin, David D. 1995. Identity in Formation: The Russian-Speaking Nationality in the Post-Soviet Diaspora. *Archives Europeenes de Sociologie* 36:281–316.

Lakatos, Imre. 1970. Falsification and the Methodology of Scientific Research Programmes. In *Criticism and the Growth of Knowledge,* edited by Imre Lakatos and Alan Musgrave, 91–195. Cambridge: Cambridge University Press.

Lake, David A. 1984. Beneath the Commerce of Nations: A Theory of International Economic Structures. *International Studies Quarterly* 28:143–70.

———. 1988. *Power, Protection, and Free Trade: International Sources of U.S. Commercial Policy, 1887–1939.* Ithaca, N.Y.: Cornell University Press.

———. 1993. Leadership, Hegemony, and the International Economy: Naked Emperor or Tattered Monarch with Potential? *International Studies Quarterly* 37:459–89.

———. 1996. Anarchy, Hierarchy, and the Variety of International Relations. *International Organization* 50:1–33.

———. Forthcoming. *Entangling Relations: American Foreign Policy in Its Century.* Princeton, N.J.: Princeton University Press.

Lakoff, George. 1996. *Moral Politics: What Conservatives Know that Liberals Don't.* Chicago: Chicago University Press.

Landes, David S. 1969. *The Unbound Prometheus: Technological Change and Industrial Development in Western Europe from 1750 to the Present.* Cambridge: Cambridge University Press.

Lange, Peter, and Geoffrey Garrett. 1985. The Politics of Growth. *Journal of Politics* 47:792–827.

Lange, Peter, and Lyle Scruggs. 1997. Where Have All the Members Gone? Paper presented at the 93d Annual Meeting of the American Political Science Association, August, Washington, D.C.

Lange, Peter, Michael Wallerstein, and Miriam Golden. 1995. The End of Corporatism? Wage Setting in the Nordic and Germanic Countries. In *The Workers of Nations,* edited by Sanford Jacoby, 76–100. New York: Oxford University Press.

Lapid, Yosef. 1996. Culture's Ship: Returns and Departures in International Relations Theory. In *The Return of Culture and Identity in IR Theory,* edited by Yosef Lapid and Friedrich V. Kratochwil, 3–20. Boulder, Colo.: Lynne Rienner.

Lapid, Yosef, and Friedrich V. Kratochwil. 1996. Revisiting the "National": Toward an Identity Agenda in Neorealism? In *The Return of Culture and Identity in IR Theory*, edited by Yosef Lapid and Friedrich V. Kratochwil, 105–26. Boulder, Colo: Lynne Rienner.

Lasswell, Harold. 1930. *Psychopathology and Politics*. Chicago: University of Chicago Press.

Laver, Michael, and Kenneth Shepsle. 1995. *Making and Breaking Governments*. New York: Cambridge University Press.

Layne, Christopher. 1993. The Unipolar Illusion: Why New Great Powers Will Rise. *International Security* 17:5–51.

———. 1997. From Preponderance to Offshore Balancing: America's Future Grand Strategy. *International Security* 22:86–124.

Le Gloannec, Anne-Marie, ed. 1998. *Entre Union et Nations: L'État en Europe*. Paris: Presses de la Fondation Nationale des Sciences Politiques.

Le Goff, Jacques. 1980. *Time, Work, and Culture in the Middle Ages*. Translated by Arthur Goldhammer. Chicago: University of Chicago Press.

Leamer, Edward E. 1996. Wage Inequality from International Competition and Technological Change: Theory and Country Experience. *American Economic Review (Papers and Proceedings)* 86:309–14.

Leander, Anna. 1997. Bertrand Badie: Cultural Diversity Changing International Relations? In *The Future of International Relations: Masters in the Making?*, edited by Iver B. Neumann and Ole Wæver, 145–69. London: Routledge.

Lebow, Richard Ned. 1994. The Long Peace, the End of the Cold War, and the Failure of Realism. *International Organization* 48:249–77.

Lebow, Richard Ned, and Thomas Risse-Kappen. 1995. Introduction: International Relations Theory and the End of the Cold War. In *International Relations Theory and the End of the Cold War*, edited by Richard Ned Lebow and Thomas Risse-Kappen. New York: Columbia University Press.

Leffler, Melvyn P. 1992. *A Preponderance of Power: National Security, the Truman Administration, and the Cold War*. Stanford, Calif.: Stanford University Press.

Legro, Jeffrey W. 1995. *Cooperation Under Fire: Anglo-German Restraint During World War II*. Ithaca, N.Y.: Cornell University Press.

———. 1997. Which Norms Matter? Revisiting the Failure of Internationalism. *International Organization* 51:31–63.

Leibowitz, S. J., and Stephen Margolis. 1990. The Fable of the Keys. *Journal of Law and Economics* 33:1–25.

Leites, Nathan. 1953. *A Study of Bolshevism*. Glencoe, Ill.: Free Press.

Lenin, V. I. 1916. *Imperialism: The Highest Stage of Capitalism*. New York: International Publishers.

Leonard, Robert J. 1991. War as a "Simple Economic Problem": The Rise of an Economics of Defense. In *Economics and National Security: A History of Their Interaction*, edited by Craufurd D. Goodwin, 261–83. Durham, N.C.: Duke University Press.

Lessig, Lawrence. 1995. The Regulation of Social Meaning, *University of Chicago Law Review* 62: 968–73.

Levinthal, D. A., and James G. March. 1993. The Myopia of Learning. *Strategic Management Journal* 14:95–112.

Levitt, B., and James G. March. 1988. Organizational Learning. *Annual Review of Sociology* 14:319–40.

Levy, Brian, and Pablo Spiller. 1996. *Regulations, Institutions, and Commitment*. Cambridge: Cambridge University Press.

Levy, Jack S. 1992. An Introduction to Prospect Theory. *Political Psychology* 13:171–86.

———. 1997. Prospect Theory, Rational Choice, and International Relations. *International Studies Quarterly* 41:87–112.

Levy, Marc A. 1993. European Acid Rain: The Power of Tote-Board Diplomacy. In *Institutions for the Earth: Sources of Effective International Environmental Protection*, edited by Peter M. Haas, Robert O. Keohane, and Marc A. Levy, 75–132. Cambridge, Mass.: MIT Press.

Levy, Marc A., Oran R. Young, and Michael Zürn. 1995. The Study of International Regimes. *European Journal of International Relations* 1:267–330.

Liberman, Peter. 1996. Trading with the Enemy: Security and Relative Economic Gains. *International Security* 21:147–75.

Lindberg, Leon N., and Stuart A. Scheingold. 1970. *Europe's Would-Be Polity: Patterns of Change in the European Community.* Englewood Cliffs, N.J.: Prentice-Hall.

———. 1971. *Regional Integration: Theory and Research.* Cambridge, Mass.: Harvard University Press.

Lindberg, Leon N., and Charles Maier, eds. 1985. *The Politics of Inflation and Economic Stagnation.* Washington, D.C.: Brookings Institution.

Linz, Juan. 1978. *The Breakdown of Democratic Regimes: Crisis, Breakdown, and Reequilibration.* Baltimore, Md.: Johns Hopkins University Press.

Lipset, Seymour Martin. 1990. *Continental Divide.* New York: Routledge.

———. 1996. *American Exceptionalism: A Double-Edged Sword.* New York: Norton.

Lipsey, Robert E. 1998. Internationalized Production in Developed and Developing Countries and in Industry Sectors. NBER Working Paper 6405. Cambridge, Mass.: National Bureau of Economic Research.

Lipson, Charles. 1984. International Cooperation in Economic and Security Affairs. *World Politics* 37: 1–23.

———. 1991. Why Are Some International Agreements Informal? *International Organization* 45:495–538.

Liska, George. 1957. *International Equilibrium.* Cambridge, Mass.: Harvard University Press.

Litfin, Karen. 1994. *Ozone Discourses.* New York: Columbia University Press.

Little, Richard. 1995. Neorealism and the English School: A Methodological, Ontological, and Theoretical Reassessment. *European Journal of International Relations* 1:14–27.

Little, Virginia. 1949. Control of International Air Transport. *International Organization* 3:29–40.

Lohmann, Susanne. 1998. Federalism and Central Bank Autonomy: The Politics of German Monetary Policy, 1957–1992. *World Politics* 50:401–46.

Lohmann, Susanne, and Sharyn O'Halloran. 1994. Divided Government and U.S. Trade Policy: Theory and Evidence. *International Organization* 48:595–632.

Loveday, A. 1953. Suggestions for the Reform of the United Nations Economic and Social Machinery. *International Organization* 7:325–41.

Lowi, Theodore J. 1992. The State in Political Science: How We Become What We Study. *American Political Science Review* 86:1–7.

———. 1993a. A Review of Herbert Simon's Review of My View of the Discipline. *PS: Political Science and Politics* 26:51–52.

———. 1993b. Response to Critiques of Presidential Address. *PS: Political Science and Politics* 26:539.

Lucas, Robert E. 1972. Expectations and the Neutrality of Money. *Journal of Economic Theory* 4:103–24.

Luhmann, N. 1982. *The Differentiation of Society.* New York: Columbia University Press.

Lumsdaine, David Halloran. 1993. *Moral Vision: The Foreign Aid Regime, 1949–1989.* Princeton, N.J.: Princeton University Press.

———. 1994. The Centrality of Worldviews and Normative Ideas in Twentieth Century International Politics. Paper delivered at the 90th Annual Meeting of the American Political Science Association, August, New York.

Lupia, Arthur, and Mathew D. McCubbins. 1994. Who Controls? Information and the Structure of Legislative Decision Making. *Legislative Studies Quarterly* 19:361–84.

Lynn-Jones, Sean, and Joseph S. Nye, Jr. 1988. International Security Studies: A Report of a Conference on the State of the Field. *International Security* 12:5–27.

Lyons, Gene M. 1982. Expanding the Study of International Relations: The French Connection. *World Politics* 35:135–49.

———. 1986. The Study of International Relations in Great Britain: Further Connections. *World Politics* 38:626–45.

Machina, Mark J. 1987. Choice Under Uncertainty: Problems Solved and Unsolved. *Journal of Economic Perspectives* 1:121–54.

MacRae, Duncan. 1958. *Dimensions of Congressional Voting.* Berkeley and Los Angeles: University of California Press.

Maddison, Angus. 1995. *Monitoring the World Economy.* Paris: OECD.

Magdoff, Harry. 1969. *The Age of Imperialism.* New York: Monthly Review Press.

Maier, Charles. 1997. *Dissolution: The Crisis of Communism and the End of East Germany.* Princeton, N.J.: Princeton University Press.

Majone, Giandomenico. 1996. A European Regulatory State? In *European Union: Power and Policymaking,* edited by Jeremy J. Richardson, 262–77. London and New York: Routledge.

Malin, Patrick Murphy. 1947. The Refugee: A Problem for International Organization. *International Organization* 1:443–459.

Mandel, Ernest. 1976. *Late Capitalism.* London: New Left Books.

Mandelbaum, Michael. 1981. *The Nuclear Revolution.* Cambridge: Cambridge University Press.

Manicas, Peter T. 1991. The Social Science Disciplines: The American Model. In *Sociology of the Sciences—A Yearbook.* Vol. 15, *Discourses on Society: The Shaping of the Social Sciences,* edited by P. Wagner, B. Wittrock and R. Whitley, 45–72. Dordrecht: Kluwer.

Mann, M. 1993. Nation-States in Europe and Other Continents: Diversifying, Developing, Not Dying. *Daedalus* 122:115–40.

Mansbach, Richard W., and John A. Vasquez. 1981. *In Search of Theory—A New Paradigm for Global Politics.* New York: Columbia University Press.

Mansbridge, Jane J. 1990. The Rise and Fall of Self-Interest in the Explanation of Political Life. In *Beyond Self Interest,* edited by Jane J. Mansbridge, 3–22. Chicago: University of Chicago Press.

March, James G. 1955. An Introduction to the Theory and Measurement of Influence. *American Political Science Review* 49:431–51.

———. 1970. Politics and the City. In *Urban Processes as Viewed by the Social Sciences,* edited by K. Arrow, J. S. Coleman, A. Downs, and James G. March, 23–37. Washington, D.C.: The Urban Institute Press.

———. 1978. Bounded Rationality, Ambiguity, and the Engineering of Choice. *Bell Journal of Economics* 9:587–608.

———. 1981. Footnotes to Organizational Change. *Administrative Science Quarterly* 26:563–77.

———. 1988. *Decisions and Organizations.* Oxford: Blackwell.

———. 1991. Exploration and Exploitation in Organizational Learning. *Organizational Science* 2:71–87.

———. 1992. The War Is Over and the Victors Have Lost. *Journal of Socio-Economics* 21:261–67.

———. 1994a. *A Primer on Decision Making.* New York: Free Press.

———. 1994b. The Evolution of Evolution. In *Evolutionary Dynamics of Organizations,* edited by J. Baum and J. Singh, 39–49. New York: Oxford University Press.

———. 1996. Continuity and Change in Theories of Organizational Action. *Administrative Science Quarterly* 41:278–87.

March, James G., and Johan P. Olsen. 1984. The New Institutionalism: Organizational Factors in Political Life. *American Political Science Review* 78:734–49.

———. 1989. *Rediscovering Institutions: The Organizational Basis of Politics.* New York: Free Press.

———. 1994. Institutional Perspectives on Governance. In *Systemrationalität und Partialinteresse,* edited by H. U. Derlien, U. Gerhardt, and F. W. Scharpf, 249–70. Baden-Baden: Nomos.

———. 1995. *Democratic Governance.* New York: Free Press.

———. 1996. Institutional Perspectives on Political Institutions. *Governance* 9:247–64.

Marin, B., and R. Mayntz, eds. 1991. *Policy Networks.* Frankfurt am Main: Campus.

Marks, Gary. 1993. Structural Policy and Multilevel Governance in the EC. In *The State of the European Community.* Vol. 2, *The Maastricht Debate and Beyond,* edited by Alan W. Cafruny and Glenda G. Rosenthal, 391–410. Boulder, Colo.: Lynne Rienner and Harlow, England: Longman.

Marston, Richard. 1995. *International Financial Integration*. New York: Cambridge University Press.

Martin, Lisa L. 1992a. *Coercive Cooperation: Explaining Multilateral Economic Sanctions*. Princeton, N.J.: Princeton University Press.

———. 1992b. Interests, Power, and Multilateralism. *International Organization* 46:765–92.

———. 1992c. Institutions and Cooperation: Sanctions During the Falkland Islands Conflict. *International Security* 16:143–77.

———. 1997. Democratic Commitments: Legislatures and International Cooperation. Unpublished manuscript, Harvard University, Cambridge, Mass.

Mason, Edward. 1949. American Security and Access to Raw Materials. *World Politics* 1:147–60.

Mastanduno, Michael. 1991. Do Relative Gains Matter? America's Response to Japanese Industrial Policy. *International Security* 16:73–113.

———. 1992. *Economic Containment: CoCom and the Politics of East–West Trade*. Ithaca, N.Y.: Cornell University Press.

———. 1997. Preserving the Unipolar Moment: Realist Theories and U.S. Grand Strategy After the Cold War. *International Security* 21:49–88.

Matecki, B. E. 1956. Establishment of the International Finance Corporation: A Case Study. *International Organization* 10:261–75.

Mathiason, John R. 1972. Old Boys, Alumni, and Consensus at ECLA Meetings. In *Communications in International Politics,* edited by Richard L. Merritt, 387–404. Urbana: University of Illinois Press.

Maxfield, Sylvia. 1997. *Gatekeepers of Growth*. Princeton, N.J.: Princeton University Press.

Mayer, Peter, Volker Rittberger, and Michael Zürn. 1995. Regime Theory: State of the Art and Perspectives. In *Regime Theory and International Relations*, edited by Volker Rittberger, with Peter Mayer, 392–430. Oxford: Oxford University Press.

McCloskey, Donald N. 1994. *Knowledge and Persuasion in Economics*. Cambridge: Cambridge University Press.

McDermott, Rose. 1992. Prospect Theory in International Relations: The Iranian Hostage Rescue Mission. *Political Psychology* 13:237–63.

McKay, David. 1988. Why Is There a European Political Science. *PS: Political Science and Politics* 21:1051–55.

McKenzie, Richard, and Dwight R. Lee. 1991. *Quicksilver Capital: How the Rapid Movement of Wealth Has Changed the World*. New York: Free Press.

McKeown, Timothy J. 1983. Hegemonic Stability Theory and 19th Century Tariff Levels in Europe. *International Organization* 37:73–92.

———. 1993. Decision Processes and Co-operation in Foreign Policy. In *Choosing to Cooperate*, edited by Louis Pauly and Janice Gross Stein, 202–19. Baltimore, Md.: Johns Hopkins University Press.

McLin, Jon. 1979. Surrogate International Organization and the Case of World Food Security. *International Organization* 33:35–55.

McMillan, Susan M. 1997. Interdependence and Conflict. *Mershon International Studies Review* 41: 33–58.

McNamara, Kathleen R. 1992. Common Markets, Uncommon Currencies: System Effects and the European Community. In *Coping with Complexity in the International System*, edited by Robert Jervis and Jack Snyder, 303–27. Boulder, Colo.: Westview Press.

———. 1996. Consensus and Constraint: The Politics of Monetary Cooperation in Europe. Unpublished manuscript, Princeton University, Princeton, N.J.

McNeely, Connie. 1995. *Constructing the Nation State: International Organization and Prescriptive Action*. Westport, Conn.: Greenwood Press.

McSweeney, Bill. 1996. Identity and Security: Buzan and the Copenhagen School. *Review of International Studies* 22:81–93.

Mearsheimer, John J. 1983. *Conventional Deterrence*. Ithaca, N.Y.: Cornell University Press.

———. 1990. Back to the Future: Instability in Europe After the Cold War. *International Security* 15:5–56.

———. 1994. The False Promise of International Institutions. *International Security* 19:5–49.

Medlicott, W. M. 1952–1959. *The Economic Blockade*, 2 vols. London: HMSO.

Meier-Walser, Reinhard. 1994. Neorealismus ist mehr als Waltz. Der Synoptische Realismus der Münchner Ansatzes. *Zeitschrift für Internationale Beziehungen* 1:115–26.

Meinecke, Friedrich. [1924] 1976. *Die Idee der Staatsräson in der neuren Geschichte.* Werke Bd. 1. Vienna and Munich: R. Oldenbourg.

Mendoza, Enrique, Giancarlo Milesi-Ferreti, and P. Asea. 1997. On the Effectiveness of Tax Policy in Altering Long-Run Growth. *Journal of Public Economics* 66:99–126.

Mercer, Jonathan. 1995. Anarchy and Identity. *International Organization* 49:229–52.

Merle, Marcel. 1987. *The Sociology of International Relations.* Translated by Dorothy Parkin. Leamington Spa, England: Berg.

Merritt, Richard L. 1966. *Symbols of American Community 1735–1775.* New Haven, Conn.: Yale University Press.

Merton, R. K. 1942. Science and Technology in a Democratic Order. *Journal of Legal and Political Sociology* 1:115–26.

Meyer, John W. 1980. The World Polity and the Authority of the Nation-State. In *Studies of the Modern World-System,* edited by A. Bergesen, 109–58. New York: Academic Press.

Meyer, John W., John Boli, and George M. Thomas. 1987. Ontology and Rationalization in the Western Cultural Account. In *Institutional Structure: Constituting State, Society, and Individual,* edited by George M. Thomas, John W. Meyer, Francsico Ramirez, and John Boli, 12–37. Newbury Park, Calif.: Sage Publications.

Meyer, John W., John Boli, George M. Thomas, and Francisco O. Ramirez. 1997. World Society and the Nation-State. *American Journal of Sociology* 103:144–81.

Meyer, John, and Michael T. Hannan, eds. 1979. *National Development and the World-System: Educational, Economic, and Political Change, 1950–1970.* Chicago: University of Chicago Press.

Meyers, Reinhard. 1990. Metatheoretische und methodologische Betrachtungen. In *Theorie der Internationalen Beziehungen: Bestandsaufnahme und Forschungsperspektiven,* edited by Volker Rittberger, (Politiche Vierteljahresschrift, Sonderheft 21):48–68. Opladen, Germany: Westdeutscher Verlag.

Milgrom, Paul, Douglass North, and Barry Weingast. 1990. The Role of Institutions in the Revival of Trade: The Law Merchant, Private Judges, and the Campagne Fairs. *Economics and Politics* 2:1–23.

Millar, Thomas B. 1962. The Commonwealth and the United Nations. *International Organization* 16: 736–57.

Miller-Adams, Michelle. 1997. The World Bank in the 1990s: Understanding Institutional Change. Ph.D. diss., Columbia University, New York.

Milner, Helen V. 1987. Resisting the Protectionist Temptation: Industry and the Making of Trade Policy in France and the United States During the 1970s. *International Organization* 41:639–66.

———. 1988. *Resisting Protectionism: Global Industries and the Politics of International Trade.* Princeton, N.J.: Princeton University Press.

———. 1990. The Political Economy of U.S. Trade Policy: A Study of the Super 301 Provision. In *Aggressive Unilateralism: America's 301 Trade Policy and the World Trading System,* edited by Jagdish Bhagwati and Hugh T. Patrick, 163–80. Ann Arbor: University of Michigan Press.

———. 1991. The Assumption of Anarchy in International Politics: A Critique. *Review of International Studies* 17:67–85.

———. 1997. *Interests, Institutions, and Information: Domestic Politics and International Relations.* Princeton, N.J.: Princeton University Press.

Milner, Helen V., and B. Peter Rosendorff. 1996. Trade Negotiations, Information, and Domestic Politics. *Economics and Politics* 8:145–89.

———. 1997. Elections and International Cooperation. *Journal of Conflict Resolution* 41:117–46.

Milward, Alan. 1977. *War, Economy, and Society, 1939–1945.* Berkeley: University of California Press.

———. 1992. *The European Rescue of the Nation-State.* Berkeley: University of California Press.

Mirowski, Philip. 1991. When Games Grow Deadly Serious: The Military Influence on the Evolution of Game Theory. In *Economics and National Security: A History of Their Interaction,* edited by Craufurd D. Goodwin. Durham, N.C.: Duke University Press.

Mitrany, David. 1925. *The Problem of International Sanctions.* London: Oxford University Press.

———. 1966. *A Working Peace System.* Chicago: Quadrangle Books.

Monroe, Kristen Renwick. 1995. Psychology and Rational Actor Theory. *Political Psychology* 16:1–21.

———. 1996. *The Heart of Altruism: Perceptions of a Common Humanity.* Princeton, N.J.: Princeton University Press.

Moore, Barrington, Jr. 1966. *Social Origins of Dictatorship and Democracy: Lord and Peasant in the Making of the Modern World.* Boston: Beacon Press.

Moran, Theodore H. 1996. Grand Strategy: The Pursuit of Power and the Pursuit of Plenty. *International Organization* 50:175–205.

Moravcsik, Andrew. 1991. Negotiating the Single European Act: National Interests and Conventional Statecraft in the European Community. *International Organization* 45:19–56.

———. 1993. Preferences and Power in the European Community: A Liberal Intergovernmentalist Approach. *Journal of Common Market Studies* 31:473–524.

———. 1995. Explaining International Human Rights Regimes: Liberal Theory and Western Europe. *European Journal of International Relations* 1:157–89.

———. 1997. Taking Preferences Seriously: A Liberal Theory of International Politics. *International Organization* 51:513–53.

———. 1998. *The Choice for Europe: Social Purpose and State Power from Messina to Maastricht.* Ithaca, N.Y.: Cornell University Press.

Morgenthau, Hans J. 1946. *Scientific Man Versus Power Politics.* Chicago: University of Chicago Press.

———. 1948. *Politics Among Nations: The Struggle for Power and Peace.* New York: Knopf.

———. 1962. The Trouble with Kennedy. *Commentary* 33:51–55.

———. 1978. *Politics Among Nations: The Struggle for Power and Peace,* 5th ed. New York: Knopf.

———. 1985. *Politics Among Nations: The Struggle for Power and Peace.* 6th ed., revised by Kenneth Thompson. New York: McGraw-Hill.

Morici, Peter. 1997. Barring Entry? China and the WTO. *Current History* 96:274–77.

Morrow, James D. 1994a. *Game Theory for Political Scientists.* Princeton, N.J.: Princeton University Press.

———. 1994b. Modeling the Forms of International Cooperation: Distribution Versus Information. *International Organization* 48:387–423.

Morse, Edward L. 1970. The Transformation of Foreign Policies: Modernization, Interdependence, and Externalization. *World Politics* 22:371–92.

———. 1972. Transnational Economic Processes. In *Transnational Relations and World Politics*, edited by Robert O. Keohane and Joseph S. Nye, Jr., 23–47. Cambridge, Mass.: Harvard University Press.

———. 1976. *Modernization and the Transformation of International Relations.* New York: Free Press.

Moses, Jonathan. 1994. Abdication from National Policy Autonomy: What's Left to Leave? *Politics and Society* 22:125–148.

Mowers, A. Glenn. 1964. The Official Pressure Group of the Council of Europe's Consultative Assembly. *International Organization* 18:292–306.

Mueller, John. 1989. *Retreat from Doomsday: The Obsolescence of Major War.* New York: Basic Books.

Müller, Harald. 1994. Internationale Beziehungen als Kommunikativen Handeln: Zur Kritik der Utilitarischen Handlungstheorien. *Zeitschrift für Internationale Beziehungen* 1:15–44.

———. 1995. Spielen Hilft Nicht Immer: Die Grenzen des Rational-Choice-Ansatzens Under der Platz der Theorie Kommunikativen Handelns in der Analyse International Beziehungen. *Zeitschrift für Internationale Beziehungen* 2:371–91.

Mundell, Robert. 1962. A Theory of Optimal Currency Areas. *American Economic Review* 51:657–65.

Murphy, Craig. 1996. Seeing Women, Recognizing Gender, Recasting International Relations. *International Organization* 50:513–38.

Nadelmann, Ethan. 1990. Global Prohibition Regimes: The Evolution of Norms in International Society. *International Organization* 44:479–526.

Nagel, Ernest. [1942] 1961. *The Structure of Science.* New York: Harcourt, Brace and World.

Nagel, Jack. 1975. *The Descriptive Analysis of Power.* New Haven, Conn.: Yale University Press.

Nathan, James A., and James K. Oliver. 1987. *Foreign Policy Making and the American Political System.* Boston: Little, Brown.

National Research Council. 1995. *Maximizing U.S. Interests in Science and Technology Relations with Japan. Report of the Defense Task Force*. Washington, D.C.: National Academy Press.

Nau, Henry R. 1990. *The Myth of America's Decline: Leading the World Economy into the 1990s*. Oxford: Oxford University Press.

———. 1995. *Trade and Security: U.S. Policy at Cross-Purposes*. Washington, D.C.: AEI Press.

———. 1997. Power and Legitimacy: Combining Realist and Constructivist Perspectives. Unpublished paper, George Washington University, Washington, D.C.

Nauta, L. 1992. Changing Conceptions of Citizenship. *Praxis International* 12:20–34.

Nelson, R. R., and S. G. Winter. 1982. *An Evolutionary Theory of Economic Change*. Cambridge, Mass.: Harvard University Press.

Nettl, J. P. 1968. The State as a Conceptual Variable. *World Politics* 20:559–92.

Neufield, Mark. 1993. Interpretation and the "Science" of International Relations. *Review of International Studies* 19:39–61.

Neumann, Iver B. 1997. Conclusion. In *The Future of International Relations: Masters in the Making?*, edited by Iver B. Neumann and Ole Wæver, 359–70. London: Routledge.

Neumann, Iver B., and Jennifer M. Welsh. 1991. The "Other" in European Self-Definition: An Addendum to the Literature on International Society. *Review of International Studies* 17:327–48.

Neumann, Iver B., and Ole Wæver, eds. 1997. *The Future of International Relations: Masters in the Making?* London: Routledge.

Neustadt, Richard. 1960. *Presidential Power*. New York: Wiley.

Niemeyer, Gerhart. 1952. The Balance Sheet of the League Experiment. *International Organization* 6:537–58.

Ninkovich, Frank. 1994. *Modernity and Power: A History of the Domino Theory in the Twentieth Century*. Chicago: University of Chicago Press.

Nisbett, R. E., and L. Ross. 1980. *Human Inference: Strategies and Shortcomings of Human Judgment*. Englewood Cliffs, N.J.: Prentice Hall.

Niskanen, W. A. 1971. *Bureaucracy and Representative Government*. Chicago: Rand McNally.

Nordlinger, Eric A. 1995. *Isolationism Reconfigured: American Foreign Policy for a New Century*. Princeton, N.J.: Princeton University Press.

North, Douglass C. 1981. *Structure and Change in Economic History*. New York: Norton.

———. 1990. *Institutions, Institutional Change, and Economic Performance*. Cambridge: Cambridge University Press.

North, Douglass C., and Robert Paul Thomas. 1973. *The Rise of the Western World: A New Economic History*. Cambridge: Cambridge University Press.

North, Douglass C., and Barry Weingast. 1989. Constitutions and Credible Commitments. *Journal of Economic History* 49:803–32.

Nowotny, Helga, and Klaus Taschwer. 1996. *The Sociology of the Sciences*. Vol. 1. Cheltenham, U.K.: Edward Elgar.

Nye, Joseph S., Jr. 1971. *Peace in Parts: Integration and Conflict in Regional Organization*. Boston: Little, Brown.

———. 1990. *Bound to Lead: The Changing Nature of American Power*. New York: Basic Books.

———. 1995. The Case for Deep Engagement. *Foreign Affairs* 74:90–102.

O'Halloran, Sharyn. 1994. *Politics, Process, and American Trade Policy*. Ann Arbor: University of Michigan Press.

Obstfeld, Maurice. 1997. Open-Economy Macroeconomics, Developments in Theory and Policy. NBER Working Paper 6319. Cambridge, Mass.: National Bureau of Economic Research.

Obstfeld, Maurice, and Alan M. Taylor. 1997. The Great Depression as a Watershed: International Capital Mobility over the Long Run. NBER Working Paper 5960. Cambridge, Mass.: National Bureau of Economic Research.

Odell, John S. 1982. *U.S. International Monetary Policy: Markets, Power, and Ideas as Sources of Changes*. Princeton, N.J.: Princeton University Press.

———. 1997. Military-Political Conditions and International Economic Negotiations. Unpublished manuscript, University of Southern California, Los Angeles.

OECD. Various years. *Trade Statistics*. Paris: OECD.

———. 1995. *Historical Statistics, 1960–1994*. Paris: OECD.

———. 1996. *Indicators of Tariff and Non-Tariff Barriers*. Paris: OECD.

Offe, C. 1996. Political Economy: Sociological Perspectives. In *A New Handbook of Political Science*, edited by R. E. Goodin and H-D. Klingemann, 675–90. Oxford: Oxford University Press.

Ohmae, Kenichi. 1995. *The End of the Nation State*. New York: Free Press.

Oliner, Samuel P., and Pearl M. Oliner. 1988. *The Altruistic Personality: Rescuers of Jews in Nazi Europe*. New York: Free Press.

Olsen, Johan P. 1992. Analyzing Institutional Dynamics. *Staatswissenschaften und Staatspraxis* 3:247–71.

———. 1997a. European Challenges to the Nation State. In *Political Institutions and Public Policy*, edited by B. Steunenberg and F. van Vught, 157–88. Dordrecht: Kluwer.

———. 1997b. Civil Service in Transition—Dilemmas and Lessons Learned. In *The European Yearbook of Comparative Government and Public Administration*, Vol. III/1996, edited by J. J. Hesse and T. A. J. Toonen, 225–50. Baden-Baden and Boulder, Colo.: Nomos/Westview.

Olson, Mancur. 1965. *The Logic of Collective Action: Public Goods and the Theory of Groups*. Cambridge, Mass.: Harvard University Press.

Olson, William C. 1972. The Growth of a Discipline. In *The Aberystwyth Papers: International Politics 1919–1969*, edited by Brian Porter, 3–29. London: Oxford University Press.

Olson, William C., and A. J. R. Groom. 1991. *International Relations Then and Now: Origins and Trends in Interpretation*. London: HarperCollins.

Olson, William C., and Nicholas Onuf. 1985. The Growth of a Discipline: Reviewed. In *International Relations: British and American Perspectives*, edited by Steve Smith, 1–28. Oxford: Basil Blackwell.

Oman, Charles. 1994. *Globalisation and Regionalisation: The Challenge for Developing Countries*. Paris: OECD, Development Centre.

Oneal, John, and Bruce Russett. 1997. The Classical Liberals Were Right: Democracy, Interdependence, and Conflict, 1950–1985. *International Studies Quarterly* 41:267–94.

Onuf, Nicholas Greenwood. 1989. *World of Our Making: Rules and Rule in Social Theory and International Relations*. Columbia: University of South Carolina Press.

Orren, K., and S. Skowronek. 1994. Beyond the Iconography of Order: Notes for a "New Institutionalism." In *The Dynamics of American Politics*, edited by L. C. Dodd and C. Jillson, 311–30. Boulder, Colo.: Westview Press.

Osgood, Robert E. 1962. *NATO: The Entangling Alliance*. Chicago: University of Chicago Press.

Oye, Kenneth. 1986. *Cooperation Under Anarchy*. Princeton, N.J.: Princeton University Press.

———. 1992. *Economic Discrimination and Political Exchange: World Political Economy in the 1930s and 1980s*. Princeton, N.J.: Princeton University Press.

Packenham, Robert. 1992. *The Dependency Movement*. Cambridge, Mass: Harvard University Press.

Pahre, Robert, and Paul A. Papayanou, eds. 1997. New Games: Modeling Domestic-International Linkages. *Journal of Conflict Resolution* 41 (1). Special issue.

Palmer, Alan, and Veronica Palmer. 1976. *Quotations in History*. Sussex, U.K.: Harvester Press.

Palmer, Norman D. 1980. The Study of International Relations in the United States. *International Studies Quarterly* 24:343–64.

Papayoanou, Paul A. 1996. Interdependence, Institutions, and the Balance of Power. *International Security* 20:42–76.

Pape, Robert. 1997. Why Economic Sanctions Do Not Work. *International Security* 22:90–136.

Patterson, Gardner. 1966. *Discriminating in International Trade: The Policy Issues, 1945–65*. Princeton, N.J.: Princeton University Press.

Pauly, Louis W. 1991. The Politics of European Monetary Union: National Strategies, International Implications. *International Journal* 57:93–111.

———. 1995. Capital Mobility, State Autonomy, and Political Legitimacy. *Journal of International Affairs* 48:369–388.

———. 1997. *Who Elected the Bankers?* Ithaca, N.Y.: Cornell University Press.

Pauly, Louis W., and Simon Reich. 1997. National Structures and Multinational Corporate Behavior: Enduring Differences in the Age of Globalization. *International Organization* 51:1–30.

Pauly, Louis W., and Janice Gross Stein, eds. 1993. *Choosing to Cooperate: How States Avoid Loss.* Baltimore, Md.: Johns Hopkins University Press.

Peck, Connie. 1996. *The United Nations as a Dispute Settlement System.* The Hague: Kluwer Law International.

Peck, Richard. 1979. Socialization of Permanent Representatives in the United Nations: Some Evidence. *International Organization* 33:365–90.

Peirce, Charles S. [1940] 1955. *Philosophical Writings of Peirce.* Edited by Justus Buchler. Reprint, New York: Dover.

Pendergast, William R. 1976. Roles and Attitudes of French and Italian Delegates to the European Community. *International Organization* 30:669–67.

Pentland, C. 1973. *International Theory and European Integration.* London: Faber and Faber.

Pérez-Díaz, V. M. 1993. *The Return of Civil Society.* Cambridge, Mass.: Harvard University Press.

Perkins, Whitney. 1958. Sanctions For Political Change—The Indonesian Case. *International Organization* 12:26–42.

Persson, Torsten, and Guido Tabellini. 1994. Is Inequality Harmful for Growth? *American Economic Review* 84:600–21.

Peterson, Peter G., and James Sebenius. 1992. The Primacy of the Domestic Agenda. In *Rethinking America's Security: Beyond Cold War to New World Order*, edited by Graham Allison and Gregory Treverton, 57–93. New York: Norton.

Peterson, V. Spike, and Anne S. Runyan. 1993. *Global Gender Issues.* Boulder, Colo.: Westview Press.

Pfaller, Alfred, Ian Gough, and Göran Therborn, eds. 1991. *Can the Welfare State Compete?* London: Macmillan.

Pfetsch, Frank R., ed. 1993. *International Relations and Pan-Europe—Theoretical Approaches and Empirical Findings.* Münster and Hamburg: Lit Verlag.

Pierson, Christopher. 1991. *Beyond the Welfare State?* Cambridge: Polity Press.

Pierson, Paul. 1996a. The New Politics of the Welfare State. *World Politics* 48:143–79.

———. 1996b. The Path to European Integration: A Historical Institutionalist Analysis. *Comparative Political Studies* 29:123–63.

Polanyi, Karl. 1944. *The Great Transformation.* New York: Farrar and Rinehart.

———. [1944] 1957a. *The Great Transformation.* Boston: Beacon Press.

———. 1957b. Aristotle Discovers the Economy. In *Trade and Markets in the Early Empires,* edited by Karl Polanyi, Conrad M. Arensberg, and Harry W. Pearson. Glencoe, Ill.: Free Press.

Pollack, Mark A. 1997. Delegation, Agency, and Agenda Setting in the European Community. *International Organization* 51:99–134

Pollard, Robert A. 1985. *Economic Security and the Origins of the Cold War, 1945–1950.* New York: Columbia University Press.

Pontusson, Jonas, and Peter Swenson. 1996. Labor Markets, Production Strategies, and Wage-Bargaining Institutions. *Comparative Political Studies* 29:223–50.

Porter, Tony. Forthcoming. Can There Be National Perspectives on International Relations? In *International Relations: Still an American Social Science? Towards Diversity in International Thought*, edited by Robert M. A. Crawford and Darryl S. L. Jarvis. Albany, N.Y.: SUNY Press.

Posen, Barry R. 1984. *The Sources of Military Doctrine: France, Britain, and Germany Between the World Wars.* Ithaca, N.Y.: Cornell University Press.

———. 1993. The Security Dilemma and Ethnic Conflict. In *Ethnic Conflict and International Security*, edited by M. Brown, 103–24. Princeton, N.J.: Princeton University Press.

———. 1993c. Nationalism, the Mass Army, and Military Power. *International Security* 18:80–124.

Posen, Barry R., and Andrew L. Ross. 1997. Competing U.S. Grand Strategies. In *Eagle Adrift: American Foreign Policy at the End of the Century*, edited by Robert J. Lieber, 100–34. New York: Longman.

Powell, Charles. 1992. What the PM Learnt About the Germans. In *When the Wall Came Down: Reactions to German Unification*, edited by Harold James and Marla Stone, 233–39. New York: Routledge.

Powell, Robert. 1990. *Nuclear Deterrence Theory.* Cambridge: Cambridge University Press.

———. 1991. Absolute and Relative Gains in International Relations Theory. *American Political Science Review* 85:1303–20.

———. 1996. Bargaining in the Shadow of Power. *Games and Economic Behavior*:255–89.

Powell, Walter W., and Paul J. DiMaggio, eds. 1991. *The New Institutionalism in Organizational Analysis.* Chicago: University of Chicago Press.

Prebisch, Raul. 1959. Commercial Policy in the Underdeveloped Countries. *American Economic Review* 49:251–73.

Prestowitz, Clyde, Jr. 1990. *Trading Places: How We Are Giving Our Future to Japan and How to Reclaim It.* 2d ed. New York: Basic Books.

Price, Richard. 1995. A Genealogy of the Chemical Weapons Taboo. *International Organization* 49:73–103.

———. 1997. *The Chemical Weapons Taboo.* Ithaca, N.Y.: Cornell University Press.

———. 1998. Reversing the Gun Sights: Transnational Civil Society Targets Land Mines. *International Organization* 52:613–44.

Price, Richard M., and Christian Reus-Smit. 1998. Constructivism and Critical International Theory. *European Journal of International Relations* 4.

Price, Richard M., and Nina Tannenwald. 1996. Norms and Deterrence: The Nuclear and Chemical Weapons Taboos. In *The Culture of National Security: Norms and Identity in World Politics,* edited by Peter J. Katzenstein, 114–52. New York: Columbia University Press.

Prigogine, Ilya. 1980. *From Being to Becoming: Time and Complexity in the Physical Sciences.* New York: W. H. Freeman.

Przeworski, Adam. 1991. *Democracy and the Market.* New York: Cambridge University Press.

Przeworski, Adam, and Michael Wallerstein. 1982. The Structure of Class Conflict in Democratic Capitalist Societies. *American Political Science Review* 76:215–38.

Putnam, Robert D. 1988. Diplomacy and Domestic Politics: The Logic of Two-Level Games. *International Organization* 42:427–60.

———. 1993. *Making Democracy Work: Civic Traditions in Modern Italy.* Princeton, N.J.: Princeton University Press.

Quattrone, George A., and Amos Tversky. 1988. Contrasting Rational and Psychological Analyses of Political Choice. *American Political Science Review* 82:719–36.

Quinn, Dennis. 1997. The Correlates of Changes in International Financial Regulation. *American Political Science Review* 91:531–52.

Quinn, Dennis, and Carla Inclan. 1997. The Origins of Financial Openness. *American Journal of Political Science* 41:771–813.

Ra'anan, Gavriel. 1983. *International Policy Formation in the USSR.* Hamden, Conn.: Archon Books.

Ramirez, Francisco, Yasemin Soysal, and Suzanne Shanahan. 1997. The Changing Logic of Political Citizenship: Cross-National Acquisition of Women's Suffrage Rights, 1890–1990. *American Sociological Review* 62:735–45.

Ramseyer, J. Mark, and Frances McCall Rosenbluth. 1993. *Japan's Political Marketplace.* Cambridge, Mass.: Harvard University Press.

Rapoport, Anatol. 1973. Games Nations Play. *Semiotica* 9:272–86.

Rapoport, Anatol, and Albert M. Chammah. 1965. *Prisoners' Dilemma.* Ann Arbor: University of Michigan Press.

Rawls, John. 1955. Two Concepts of Justice. *Philosophical Review* 64:3–33.

Ray, James Lee. 1989. The Abolition of Slavery and the End of International War. *International Organization* 43:405–39.

Reich, Robert B. 1990. Who Is Us? *Harvard Business Review* 68:53–64.

———. 1991. Who Is Them? *Harvard Business Review* 69:77–88.

Remmer, Karen L. 1997. Theoretical Decay and Theoretical Development: Resurgence of Institutional Analysis. *Comparative Politics* 50:34–61.

Rengger, Nick. 1988. Going Critical (and reply by Mark Hoffman, Conversation on Critical International Relations Theory). *Millennium: Journal of International Studies* 17: 81–96.

Renouvin, Pierre, ed. 1954. *Histoire des relations internationales.* 8 vols. Paris: Hachette.

Renouvin, Pierre, and Jean-Baptiste Duroselle. 1964. *Introduction à l'histoire des relations internationales.* Paris: A. Colin.

Restivo, Sal. 1994. The Theory Landscape. In *Handbook of Science and Technology Studies*, edited by Sheila Jasanoff, Gerald E. Markle, James C. Peterson, and Trevor Pinch, 95–110. Thousand Oaks, Calif.: Sage.

Reus-Smit, Christian. Forthcoming. *The Moral Purpose of the State: Culture, Institutional Rationality, and International Relations*. Princeton, N.J.: Princeton University Press.

Rhodes, Edward. 1996. Sea Change: Interest-based Versus Cultural-Cognitive Accounts of Strategic Choice in the 1890s. *Security Studies* 5:43–72.

Rhodes, R. A. W. 1997. *Understanding Governance. Policy Networks, Governance, Reflexivity, and Accountability*. Buckingham: Open University Press.

Rieselbach, Leroy N. 1960. Quantitative Techniques for Studying Voting Behavior in the United Nations General Assembly. *International Organization* 14:291–306.

Riggs, Robert. 1958. *Politics in the United Nations: A Study of United States Influence in the General Assembly*. Champaign: University of Illinois Press.

———. 1977. One Small Step for Functionalism: UN Participation and Congressional Attitude Change. *International Organization* 31:515–39.

Riggs, Robert E., Karen Hanson, Mary Heinz, Barry Huges, and Thomas Volgy. 1970. Behavioralism in the Study of the United Nations. *World Politics* 22:197–236.

Riker, William H. 1962. *The Theory of Political Coalitions*. New Haven, Conn.: Yale University Press.

———. 1995. The Political Psychology of Rational Choice Theory. *Political Psychology* 16:23–44.

Ringer, Fritz. 1997. *Max Weber's Methodology: The Unification of the Cultural and Social Sciences*. Cambridge, Mass.: Harvard University Press.

Ripsman, Norrin, and Jean-Marc Blanchard. 1996. Commercial Liberalism Under Fire: Evidence from 1914 and 1936. *Security Studies* 6:4–50.

Risse, Thomas. 1997. Let's Talk! Insights from the German Debate on Communicative Behavior and International Relations. Paper presented at the 93d Annual Convention of the American Political Science Association, 27–31 August, Washington D.C.

Risse, Thomas, Stephen Ropp, and Kathryn Sikkink, eds. Forthcoming. *The Power of Human Rights: International Norms and Domestic Change*. Cambridge: Cambridge University Press.

Risse-Kappen, Thomas. 1994. Ideas Do Not Float Freely: Transnational Coalitions, Domestic Structures, and the End of the Cold War. *International Organization* 48:185–214.

———. 1995a. Reden Ist Nicht Bilig: Zur Debate Um Kommunkation Und Rationalität. *Zeitschrift für Internationale Beziehungen* 2:171–84.

———. 1996a. Exploring the Nature of the Beast: International Relations Theory and Comparative Policy Analysis Meet the European Union. *Journal of Common Market Studies* 34:53–80.

———. 1996b. Collective Identity in a Democratic Community. In *The Culture of National Security: Norms and Identity in World Politics*, edited by Peter J. Katzenstein, 357–99. New York: Columbia University Press.

Risse-Kappen, Thomas, ed. 1995b. *Bringing Transnational Relations Back In: Non-State Actors, Domestic Structures, and International Institutions*. New York: Cambridge University Press.

Rittberger, Volker, and Hartwig Hummel. 1990. Die Disziplin ''Internationale Beziehungen'' im deutschsprachigen Raum auf der Suche nach ihrer Identität: Entwicklung und Perspektiven. In *Theorie der Internationalen Beziehungen: Bestandsaufnahme und Forschungsperspektiven*, edited by Volker Rittberger, (Politiche Vierteljahresschrift, Sonderheft 21):17–47. Opladen, Germany: Westdeutscher Verlag.

Rittberger, Volker, ed., with Peter Mayer. 1993. *Regime Theory and International Relations*. Oxford: Oxford University Press.

Robles, Alfredo C., Jr. 1993. How ''International'' Are International Relations Syllabi? *PS: Political Science and Politics* 26:526–28.

Rochester, J. Martin. 1986. The Rise and Fall of International Organization as a Field of Study. *International Organization* 40:777–814.

Rodrik, Dani. 1997. *Has Globalization Gone Too Far?* Washington, D.C.: Institute for International Economics.

Rogoff, Kenneth. 1985. The Optimal Degree of Commitment to an Intermediate Monetary Target. *Quarterly Journal of Economics* 100:1169–89.

Rogowski, Ronald. 1987. Trade and the Variety of Democratic Institutions. *International Organization* 41:203–24.

——. 1989. *Commerce and Coalitions: How Trade Affects Domestic Political Alignments.* Princeton, N.J.: Princeton University Press.

——. Forthcoming. Institutions as Constraints on Strategic Choices. In *Strategic Choice and International Relations*, edited by David A. Lake and Robert Powell. Princeton, N.J.: Princeton University Press.

Rohrlich, Paul E. 1987. Economic Culture and Foreign Policy: The Cognitive Analysis of Economic Policymaking. *International Organization* 41:61–92.

Rometsch, D., and W. Wessels. 1996. Conclusion: European Union and National Institutions. In *The European Union and Member States*, edited by D. Rometsch and W. Wessels, 328–65. Manchester: Manchester University Press.

Ron, James. 1997. Varying Methods of State Violence. *International Organization* 51:275–300.

Röpke, Wilhelm. 1942. *International Economic Disintegration.* London: William Hodge.

Rosecrance, Richard. 1963. *Action and Reaction in World Politics.* Boston: Little, Brown.

——. 1986. *The Rise of the Trading State.* New York: Basic Books.

Rosecrance, Richard, and Arthur A. Stein. 1973. Interdependence: Myth or Reality? *World Politics* 26: 1–27.

Rosecrance, Richard, and Arthur A. Stein, eds. 1993. *The Domestic Bases of Grand Strategy.* Ithaca, N.Y.: Cornell University Press.

Rosen, Jeffrey. 1997. The Social Police: Following the Law Because You'd Be Too Embarrassed Not To. *The New Yorker,* 20 October, 170–81.

Rosen, Stephen Peter. 1991. *Winning the Next War: Innovation and the Modern Military.* Ithaca, N.Y.: Cornell University Press.

——. 1996. *Societies and Military Power: India and Its Armies.* Ithaca, N.Y.: Cornell University Press.

Rosenau, James N. 1966. Pre-Theories and Theories of Foreign Policy. In *Approaches to Comparative and International Politics*, edited by R. Barry Farrell, 27–92. Evanston, Ill.: Northwestern University Press.

——. 1969a. *Linkage Politics.* New York: Free Press.

——. 1969b. Toward the Study of National-International Linkages. In *Linkage Politics*, edited by James N. Rosenau, 44–63. New York: Free Press.

——. 1986. Before Cooperation: Hegemons, Regimes, and Habit-Driven Actors in World Politics. *International Organization* 40:849–94.

——. 1990. *Turbulence in World Politics: A Theory of Change and Continuity.* Princeton, N.J.: Princeton University Press.

——. 1997. *Along the Domestic-Foreign Frontier: Exploring Governance in a Turbulent World.* Cambridge: Cambridge University Press.

Rosenau, James N., Gary Gartin, Edwin P. McClain, Dona Stinziano, Richard Stoddard, and Dean Swanson. 1977. Of Syllabi, Texts, Students, and Scholarship in International Relations. *World Politics* 29:263–340.

Rosenau, James N., and Ernst-Otto Czempiel, eds. 1992. *Governance Without Government. Order and Change in World Politics.* Cambridge: Cambridge University Press.

Rosenberg, Shawn W. 1995. Against Neoclassical Political Economy: A Political Psychological Critique. *Political Psychology* 16:99–136.

Ross, Dorothy. 1991. *The Origins of American Social Science.* Cambridge: Cambridge University Press.

Rothstein, B. 1992. Labor-Market Institutions and Working-Class Strength. In *Structuring Politics. Historical Institutionalism in Comparative Analysis*, edited by S. Steinmo, K. Thelen, and F. Longstreeth, 33–56. Cambridge: Cambridge University Press.

Rothstein, Robert L. 1984. Consensual Knowledge and International Collaboration: Some Lessons from the Commodity Negotiations. *International Organization* 38:733–62.

Rothwell, Charles Eaton. 1949. International Organization in World Politics. *International Organization* 3:605–19.

Rubinstein, Alvin Z. 1964. Soviet and American Policies in International Economic Organizations. *International Organization* 18:29–52.

Rudzinski, Alexander W. 1951. The Influence of the United Nations on Soviet Policy. *International Organization* 5:282–99.

Ruggie, John Gerard. 1972. Collective Goods and Future International Collaboration. *American Political Science Review* 66:874–93.

———. 1975. International Responses to Technology: Concepts and Trends. *International Organization* 29 (3):557–83.

———. 1983a. Continuity and Transformation in the World Polity: Toward a Neorealist Synthesis. *World Politics* 35:261–385.

———. 1983b. International Regimes, Transactions, and Change: Embedded Liberalism in the Postwar Economic Order. In *International Regimes*, edited by Stephen D. Krasner, 195–231. Ithaca, N.Y.: Cornell University Press.

———. 1986. Social Time and International Policy: Conceptualizing Global Population and Resource Issues. In *Persistent Patterns and Emergent Structures in a Waning Century,* edited by Margaret P. Karns, 211–36. New York: Praeger.

———. 1989. International Structure and International Transformation: Space, Time, and Method. In *Global Changes and Theoretical Challenges: Approaches To World Politics for the 1990s,* edited by Ernst-Otto Czempiel and James N. Rosenau, 21–35. Lexington, Mass.: Lexington Books.

———. 1992. Multilateralism: The Anatomy of an Institution. *International Organization* 46:561–98.

———. 1993. Territoriality and Beyond: Problematizing Modernity in International Relations. *International Organization* 47:139–74.

———. 1995a. The False Premise of Realism. *International Security* 20:62–70.

———. 1995b. At Home Abroad, Abroad at Home: International Liberalization and Domestic Stability in the New World Economy. *Millennium: Journal of International Studies* 24:507–26.

———. 1995c. Peace in Our Time? Causality, Social Facts, and Narrative Knowing. *American Society of International Law Proceedings* 89th Annual Meeting: 93–100.

———. 1996a. Globalization and the Embedded Liberalism Compromise: The End of an Era? Working Paper 97/1. Cologne: Max Planck Institut für Gesellschaftsforschung.

———. 1996b. *Winning the Peace: America and World Order in the New Era.* New York: Columbia University Press.

———. 1997a. Consolidating the European Pillar: The Key to NATO's Future. *Washington Quarterly* 20:109–24.

———. 1997b. The Past as Prologue? Interests, Identity, and American Foreign Policy. *International Security* 21:89–125.

———. 1998. *Constructing the World Polity: Essays on International Institutionalization.* London/New York: Routledge.

Rummel, R. J. 1994. Power, Genocide, and Mass Murder. *Journal of Peace Research* 31:1–10.

———. 1995. Democracy, Power, Genocide, and Mass Murder. *Journal of Conflict Resolution* 39:3–26.

Russell, Robert W. 1973. Transgovernmental Interaction in the International Monetary System, 1960–1972. *International Organization* 27:431–64.

Russett, Bruce M. 1963. *Community and Contention: Britain and America in the Twentieth Century.* Cambridge, Mass.: MIT Press.

———. 1985. The Mysterious Case of Vanishing Hegemony. *International Organization* 39:207–31.

———. 1993. *Grasping the Democratic Peace.* Princeton, N.J.: Princeton University Press.

Sabine, G. H. 1952. The Two Democratic Traditions. *The Philosophical Review* 61:493–511.

Sagan, Scott. 1989. *Moving Targets: Nuclear Strategy and National Security.* Princeton, N.J.: Princeton University Press.

———. 1993. *The Limits of Safety: Organizations, Accidents, and Nuclear Weapons.* Princeton, N.J.: Princeton University Press.

Samuels, Richard J. 1994. *Rich Nation, Strong Army: National Security, Ideology, and the Transformation of Japan.* Ithaca, N.Y.: Cornell University Press.

Sandel, M. J. 1982. *Liberalism and the Limits of Justice.* Cambridge: Cambridge University Press.

———. 1984. The Procedural Republic and the Unencumbered Self. *Political Theory* 12:81–96.

Sandholtz, Wayne. 1993. Choosing Union: Monetary Politics and Maastricht. *International Organization* 47:1–39.

Sandholtz, Wayne, and John Zysman. 1989. 1992: Recasting the European Bargain. *World Politics* 42:95–128.

Sassen, Saskia. 1996. *Losing Control? Sovereignty in an Age of Globalization.* New York: Columbia University Press.

———. 1997. The Urban Complex in a World Economy. *International Social Science Journal* 46:43–62.

Sbragia, Alberta M., ed. 1992. *Europolitics: Institutions and Policymaking in the "New" European Community.* Washington, D.C.: Brookings Institution.

Schaller, Michael. 1997. *Altered States: The United States and Japan Since the Occupation.* New York: Oxford University Press.

Scharpf, Fritz W. 1991. *Crisis and Choice in European Social Democracy.* Translated by Ruth Corwley and Fred Thompson. Ithaca, N.Y.: Cornell University Press.

———. 1996. Negative and Positive Integration in the Political Economy of European Welfare States. In *Governance in the European Union,* edited by Gary Marks, Fritz W. Scharpf, P. C. Schmitter, and W. Streeck, 15–39. London: Sage.

Schelling, Thomas C. 1960. *The Strategy of Conflict.* Cambridge, Mass.: Harvard University Press.

———. 1966. *Arms and Influence.* New Haven, Conn.: Yale University Press.

Schelling, Thomas C., and Morton Halperin. 1961. *Strategy and Arms Control.* New York: Twentieth Century Fund.

Schlesinger, P. R. 1991. *Media, State, and Nation.* London: Sage.

———. 1993. Wishful Thinking: Cultural Politics, Media, and Collective Identities in Europe. *Journal of Communication* 43:6–17.

———. 1994. Europe's Contradictory Communicative Space. *Daedalus* 123:25–52.

Schluchter, Wolfgang. 1989. *Rationalism, Religion, and Domination: A Weberian Perspective.* Berkeley: University of California Press.

Schmalz-Bruns, Rainer. 1995. Die Theorie Kommunikativen Handelns: Eine Flaschenpost? *Zeitschrift für Internationale Beziehungen* 2:347–70.

Schmidt, Brian C. 1998. *The Political Discourse of Anarchy: A Disciplinary History of International Relations.* Albany, N.Y.: SUNY Press.

Schneider, Gerald. 1994. Getting Closer at Different Speeds. In *Game Theory and International Relations,* edited by P. Allan and C. Schmidt, 125–55. Cambridge: Cambridge University Press.

Schneider, Gerald, Patricia Weitsman, and Thomas Bernauer. 1995. *Towards a New Europe: Stops and Starts in Regional Integration.* Westport, Conn.: Praeger.

Schofield, Norman. 1985. Anarchy, Altruism, and Cooperation. *Social Choice and Welfare* 2:207–19.

Schroeder, Paul. 1976. Munich and the British Tradition. *Historical Journal* 19:223–43.

———. 1992. Did the Vienna Settlement Rest on a Balance of Power? *American Historical Review* 97:683–706.

———. 1994. *The Transformation of European Politics, 1763–1848.* Oxford: Clarendon Press.

Schultz, Kenneth A. 1996. Domestic Political Competition and Bargaining in International Crises. Ph.D. diss., Stanford University, Stanford, California.

Schwartz, Herman. 1994. Small States in Big Trouble. *World Politics* 46:527–55.

Schweller, Randall L. 1996. Neorealism's Status-Quo Bias: What Security Dilemma? *Security Studies* 5:90–121.

Schweller, Randall L., and David Priess. 1997. A Tale of Two Realisms: Expanding the Institutions Debate. *Mershon International Studies Review* 41:1–32.

Scott, James C., and David A. Lake. 1989. The Second Face of Hegemony: Britain's Repeal of the Corn Laws and the American Walker Tariff of 1846. *International Organization* 43:1–29.

Scott, W. Richard, and John W. Meyer, eds. 1994. *Institutional Environment and Organizations: Structural Complexity and Individualism.* Thousand Oaks, Calif.: Sage.

Searing, D. D. 1991. Roles, Rules, and Rationality in the New Institutionalism. *American Political Science Review* 85:1239–60.

Searle, John R. 1995. *The Construction of Social Reality*. New York: Free Press.

———. 1997. Consciousness and the Philosophers. *New York Review of Books*, 6 March, 43–50.

Sen, Amartya. 1994. The Formulation of Rational Choice. *American Economic Review* 84:385–90.

———. 1995. Rationality and Social Choice. *American Economic Review* 85:1–24.

Senghaas, Dieter. 1969. *Abschreckung und Frieden: Studien zur Kritik organisierter Friedlosigkeit*. Frankfurt am Main: Europäische Verlagsanstatt.

Shapiro, I., and R. Hardin. 1996. Introduction. In *Political Order*, edited by I. Shapiro and R. Hardin, 1–15. New York: New York University Press.

Sharp, Walter R. 1953. The Institutional Framework for Technical Assistance. *International Organization* 7:342–79.

Shaw, Martin. 1994. *Global Society and International Relations*. Cambridge: Polity Press.

Shepherd, William F. 1994. *International Financial Integration*. Aldershot: Avebury.

Shepsle, Kenneth A. 1979. Institutional Arrangements and Equilibria in Multidimensional Voting Models. *American Journal of Political Science* 23:27–59.

———. 1986. Institutional Equilibrium and Equilibrium Institutions. In *Political Science: The Science of Politics*, edited by Herbert Weisberg. New York: Agathon Press.

———. 1989. Studying Institutions: Some Lessons from the Rational Choice Approach. *Journal of Theoretical Politics* 1:131–47.

———. 1990. *Perspectives on Positive Economy*. Cambridge: Cambridge University Press.

Shepsle, Kenneth A., and Barry R. Weingast, eds. 1995. *Positive Theories of Congressional Institutions*. Ann Arbor: University of Michigan Press.

Sherif, Muzafer. 1966. *Group Conflict and Cooperation: Their Social Psychology*. London: Routledge and Kegan Paul.

Sherif, Muzafer, and Carolyn Sherif. 1953. *Groups in Harmony and Tension*. New York: Harper and Row.

Shimko, Keith. 1992. Realism, Neorealism, and American Liberalism. *Review of Politics* 54:281–301.

Shoemaker, Nancy. 1997. How Indians Got to Be Red. *American Historical Review* 102:625–44.

Shonfield, Andrew. 1965. *Modern Capitalism*. New York: Oxford University Press.

Shugart, Matthew, and John Carey. 1992. *Presidents and Assemblies: Constitutional Design and Electoral Dynamics*. New York: Cambridge University Press.

Sikkink, Kathryn. 1991. *Ideas and Institutions: Developmentalism in Brazil and Argentina*. Ithaca, N.Y.: Cornell University Press.

———. 1993a. Human Rights, Principled Issue-Networks, and Sovereignty in Latin America. *International Organization* 47:411–41.

———. 1993b. The Power of Principled Ideas: Human Rights Policies in the United States and Western Europe. In *Ideas and Foreign Policy: Beliefs, Institutions, and Political Change*, edited by Judith Goldstein and Robert O. Keohane, 139–170. Ithaca, N.Y.: Cornell University Press.

Simmel, George. 1955. *Conflict and the Web of Group Affiliations*. New York: Free Press.

Simmons, Beth A. 1993. Why Innovate? Founding the Bank for International Settlements. *World Politics* 45:361–405.

———. 1994. *Who Adjusts? Domestic Sources of Foreign Economic Policy During the Interwar Years, 1924–1939*. Princeton, N.J.: Princeton University Press.

———. 1998. See You in "Court?" The Appeal to Quasi-Judicial Legal Processes in the Settlement of Territorial Disputes. In *A Roadmap to War: Territorial Dimensions of International Conflict*, edited by Paul F. Diehl, chap. 8. Nashville, Tenn.: Vanderbilt University Press.

Simon, H. A. 1955. A Behavioral Model of Rational Choice. *Quarterly Journal of Economics* 69:99–118.

———. 1956. Rational Choice and the Structure of the Environment. *Psychological Review* 63:129–38.

Simon, Herbert A. 1986. Rationality in Psychology and Economics. *Journal of Business* 59:S209–S224.

———. 1993a. The State of American Political Science: Professor Lowi's View of Our Discipline. *PS: Political Science and Politics* 26:49–51.

———. 1993b. Reply to the Letter Professor Lowi Kindly Wrote Me. *PS: Political Science and Politics* 26:539.

————. 1995. Rationality in Political Behavior. *Political Psychology* 16:45–61.

Singer, J. David. 1972. The "Correlates of War" Project. *World Politics* 24:243–70.

Singer, Marshall, and Barton Sensenig, III. 1963. Elections Within the UN: An Experimental Study Using Statistical Analysis. *International Organization* 17:901–25.

Singer, Max, and Aaron Wildavsky. 1973. *The Real World Order: Zones of Peace/Zones of Turmoil.* Chatham, N.J.: Chatham House.

Siverson, Randolph. 1973. Role and Perception in International Crisis: The Case of Israeli and Egyptian Decisionmakers in National Capitals and the United Nations. *International Organization* 27:329–45.

Sivertsen, Gunnar. 1994. Når er et tidsshrift internasjonalt? In *Det Vitenskapelige Tidsskrift*, edited by Nils Petter Gleditsch, Pehr H. Enckell, and Jørgen Burchardt, 37–51. Copenhagen: Nordisk Ministerråd (TemaNord 574).

Skalnes, Lars. Forthcoming. *When International Politics Matters: Grand Strategy and Economic Discrimination.* Ann Arbor: University of Michigan Press.

Skocpol, Theda. 1979. *States and Social Revolutions: A Comparative Analysis of France, Russia, and China.* Cambridge: Cambridge University Press.

Skowronek, Stephen. 1982. *Building a New American State.* Cambridge: Cambridge University Press.

Slaughter, Anne-Marie. 1995. International Law in a World of Liberal States. *European Journal of International Law* 6:203–38.

Smith, Keith A. 1973. The European Economic Community and National Civil Servants of the Member States—A Comment. *International Organization* 27:564–68.

Smith, M. 1996. The European Union and a Changing Europe: Establishing the Boundaries of Order. *Journal of Common Market Studies* 34:5–28.

Smith, Steve. 1985. Introduction. In *International Relations: British and American Perspectives*, edited by Steve Smith, ix–xiv. Oxford: Basil Blackwell.

————. 1987. Paradigm Dominance in International Relations: The Development of International Relations as a Social Science. *Millennium: Journal of International Studies* 16:189–206.

————. 1988. Belief Systems and the Study of International Relations. In *Belief Systems and International Relations*, edited by Richard Little and Steve Smith, 11–36. Oxford: Blackwell.

————. 1993. Hegemonic Power, Hegemonic Discipline? The Superpower Status of International Relations. In *Global Voices: Dialogues in International Relations*, edited by James N. Rosenau, 55–82. Boulder, Colo.: Westview Press.

————. 1995. The Self-Images of a Discipline: A Genealogy of International Relations Theory. In *International Relations Theory Today*, edited by Ken Booth and Steve Smith, 1–37. Cambridge: Polity.

Smith, Steve, Ken Booth, and Marysia Zalewski, eds. 1996. *International Theory: Positivism and Beyond.* Cambridge: Cambridge University Press.

Smouts, Marie-Claude. 1987. The Study of International Relations in France. *Millennium: Journal of International Studies* 16:281–86.

Smouts, Marie-Claude, ed. 1998. *Les nouvelles relations internationales. Théories et Pratiques.* Paris: Presses de Sciences Politiques.

Snidal, Duncan. 1985a. Coordination Versus Prisoners'Dilemma: Implications for International Cooperation and Regimes. *American Political Science Review* 79:923–42.

————. 1985b. The Limits of Hegemonic Stability Theory. *International Organization* 39:579–614.

————. 1991. Relative Gains and the Pattern of International Cooperation. *American Political Science Review* 85:701–26.

Snow, David A., E. Burke Rochford, Steven K. Worden, and Robert D. Benford. 1986. Frame Alignment Processes, Micromobilization, and Movement Participation. *American Sociological Review* 51: 464–81.

Snyder, Glenn. 1961. *Deterrence or Defense.* Princeton, N.J.: Princeton University Press.

Snyder, Glenn C., and Paul Diesing. 1977. *Conflict Among Nations: Bargaining, Decision Making, and System Structure in International Crises.* Princeton, N.J.: Princeton University Press.

Snyder, Glenn H. 1996. Process Variables in Neorealist Theory. In *Realism: Restatements and Renewal*, edited by Benjamin Frankel, 170–71. London: Frank Cass.

Snyder, Jack. 1984. *The Ideology of the Offensive: Military Decisionmaking and the Disasters of 1914.* Ithaca, N.Y.: Cornell University Press.

———. 1991. *Myths of Empire: Domestic Politics and International Ambition.* Ithaca, N.Y.: Cornell University Press.

Snyder, Jack, and Robert Jervis. Forthcoming. Civil War and the Security Dilemma. In *Civil War, Insecurity, and Intervention*, edited by Barbara Walter and Jack Snyder. New York: Columbia University Press.

Snyder, Richard. 1955. Toward Greater Order in the Study of World Politics. *World Politics* 7:461–78.

Snyder, Richard C., H. W. Bruck, and Burton Sapin. 1954. Decision-Making as an Approach to the Study of International Politics. Foreign Policy Analysis Series, 3. Princeton, N.J.: Princeton University.

———. 1962. *Foreign Policy Decision-Making.* New York: Free Press.

Sobel, Andrew. 1994. *Domestic Choices, International Markets.* Ann Arbor: University of Michigan Press.

Soskice, David. 1990. Wage Determination: The Changing Role of Institutions in Advanced Industrialized Countries. *Oxford Review of Economic Policy* 6:36–61.

Spero, Joan. 1981. *The Politics of International Economic Relations.* New York: St. Martin's.

Spirtas, Michael. 1998. With or Without: British and French Policies Toward Economic and Military Cooperation. Ph.D. diss., Department of Political Science, Columbia University, New York.

Spruyt, Hendrik. 1994. *The Sovereign State and Its Competitors: An Analysis of System Change.* Princeton, N.J.: Princeton University Press.

Staley, Eugene. 1935. *War and the Private Investor.* Chicago: University of Chicago Press.

———. 1939. *World Economy in Transition. Technology Versus Politics, Laissez-faire Versus Planning, Power Versus Welfare.* New York: Council on Foreign Relations.

Starbuck, W. H., A. Greve, and B. L. Hedberg. 1978. Responding to Crises. *Journal of Business Administration* 9:111–37.

Stein, Arthur A. 1980. The Politics of Linkage. *World Politics* 33:62–81.

———. 1983. Coordination and Collaboration: Regimes in an Anarchic World. In *International Regimes*, edited by Stephen D. Krasner, 115–40. Ithaca, N.Y.: Cornell University Press.

———. 1984. The Hegemon's Dilemma: Great Britain, the United States, and the International Economic Order. *International Organization* 38:355–86.

———. 1990. *Why Nations Cooperate: Circumstance and Choice in International Relations.* Ithaca, N.Y.: Cornell University Press.

———. 1993. Governments, Economic Interdependence, and International Cooperation. In *Behavior, Society, and Nuclear War.* Vol. 3, *Behavior, Society, and International Conflict.*, edited by Philip E. Tetlock, Jo L. Husbands, Robert Jervis, Paul C. Stern, and Charles Tilly, 241–324. New York: Oxford University Press.

Stein, Janice Gross. 1994. Political Learning By Doing: Gorbachev as an Uncommitted Thinker and a Motivated Learner. *International Organization* 48:155–83.

Steinbruner, John D. 1974. *The Cybernetic Theory of Decision.* Princeton, N.J.: Princeton University Press.

Steinmo, Sven. 1993. *Taxation and Democracy.* New Haven, Conn.: Yale University Press.

Steinmo, Sven, Kathleen Thelen, and Frank Longstreth. 1992. *Structuring Politics: Historical Institutionalism in Comparative Analysis.* New York: Cambridge University Press.

Stephanson, Anders. 1989. *Kennan and the Art of Foreign Policy.* Cambridge, Mass.: Harvard University Press.

Sterling-Folker, Jennifer. 1997. Realist Environment, Liberal Process, and Domestic-Level Variables. *International Studies Quarterly* 41:1–26.

Stevenson, David. 1996. *Armaments and the Coming of War: Europe, 1904–1914.* Oxford: Clarendon Press.

Stinchcombe, A. L. 1965. Social Structure and Organizations. In *Handbook of Organizations*, edited by James G. March, 142–93. Chicago: Rand McNally.

———. 1986. Reason and Rationality. *Sociological Theory* 4:151–66.

———. 1997. On the Virtues of the Old Institutionalism. *Annual Review of Sociology* 23:1–18.

Stokke, O. S. 1997. Regimes as Governance Systems. In *Global Governance: Drawing Insights from the Environmental Experience*, edited by Oran R. Young, 27–63. Cambridge, Mass.: MIT Press.

Stone, A. 1994. What Is a Supranational Constitution? An Essay in International Relations Theory. *The Review of Politics* 56:441–74.

Strang, David. 1991. Anomaly and Commonplace in European Political Expansion: Realist and Institutionalist Accounts. *International Organization* 45:143–62.

Strang, David, and Patricia Mei Yin Chang. 1993. The International Labor Organization and the Welfare State: Institutional Effects on National Welfare Spending, 1960–1980. *International Organization* 47: 235–62.

Strange, Susan. 1970. International Economics and International Relations: A Case of Mutual Neglect. *International Affairs* 46:304–315.

———. 1976. International Monetary Relations. In *International Economic Relations of the Western World 1959–1971*, edited by Andrew Shonfield, vol. 2, 3–359. London: Oxford University Press.

———. 1979. The Management of Surplus Capacity: Or How Does Theory Stand Up to Protectionism 1970s Style? *International Organization* 33:303–334.

———. 1983. *Cave! hic Dragones*: A Critique of Regime Analysis. In *International Regimes*, edited by Stephen D. Krasner, 337–54. Ithaca, N.Y.: Cornell University Press.

———. 1986. *Casino Capitalism*. Oxford: Blackwell.

———. 1988. *States and Markets*. London: Frances Pinter.

———. 1995. 1995 Presidential Address: ISA as a Microcosm. *International Studies Quarterly* 39: 289–95.

———. 1996. *The Retreat of the State: The Diffusion of Power in the World Economy*. Cambridge: Cambridge University Press.

Sugden, Robert. 1989. Spontaneous Order. *Journal of Economic Perspectives* 3:85–97.

Suhr, Michael. 1997. Robert O. Keohane: A Contemporary Classic. In *The Future of International Relations: Masters in the Making?*, edited by Iver B. Neumann and Ole Wæver, 90–120. London: Routledge.

Sunstein, Cass. 1997. *Free Markets and Social Justice*. New York: Oxford University Press.

Swank, Duane. 1998. Funding the Welfare State. *Political Studies* 46: 671–92.

Swedberg, Richard. 1991. "The Battle of the Methods": Toward a Paradigm Shift? In *Socio-Economic Trends: Toward a New Synthesis*, edited by Amitai Etzioni and Paul R. Lawrence, 13–33. Armonk, N.Y.: M. E. Sharpe.

Swenson, Peter. 1991. Bringing Capital Back In, or Social Democracy Reconsidered. *World Politics* 43:513–34.

Taylor, C. 1985. *Philosophy and the Human Sciences*. Cambridge: Cambridge University Press.

Taylor, Michael. 1967. *Anarchy and Cooperation*. Cambridge: Cambridge University Press.

Tetlock, Philip E., and Charles McGuire, Jr. 1986. Cognitive Perspectives on Foreign Policy. In *Political Behavior Annual*, edited by Samuel Long, 147–79. Boulder, Colo.: Westview Press.

Teubner, G. 1993. *Law as an Autopoietic System*. Oxford: Blackwell.

Thomas, Daniel C. 1997. Norms and Change in World Politics: Human Rights, the Helsinki Accords, and the Demise of Communism, 1975–1990. Ph.D. diss., Cornell University, Ithaca, N.Y.

Thomas, George M., John W. Meyer, Francisco O. Ramirez, and John Boli, eds. 1987. *Institutional Structure: Constituting State, Society, and Individual*. Newbury Park, Calif.: Sage Publications.

Thomson, Janice E. 1994. *Mercenaries, Pirates, and Sovereigns: State-Building and Extraterritorial Violence in Early Modern Europe*. Princeton, N.J.: Princeton University Press.

Tickner, J. Ann. 1992. *Gender in International Relations*. New York: Columbia University Press.

Tilly, Charles. 1990. *Coercion, Capital, and European States, A.D. 990–1990*. Cambridge: Basil Blackwell.

———. 1993. *Coercion, Capital, and European States, A.D. 990–1990*. Rev. ed. Cambridge: Blackwell.

Tilly, Charles, ed. 1975. *The Formation of National States in Western Europe*. Princeton, N.J.: Princeton University Press.

Tirole, Jean. 1989. *The Theory of Industrial Organization*. Cambridge, Mass.: MIT Press.

Tonra, B. 1996. Dutch, Danish, and Irish Foreign Policy in the EPC/CFSP 1970–1996. Ph.D. diss., University of Dublin, Trinity College.

Toulmin, Stephen. 1972. *Human Understanding*. Princeton, N.J.: Princeton University Press.

Trachtenberg, Marc. 1989. Strategic Thought in America, 1952–1966. *Political Science Quarterly* 104: 301–44.

Tsebelis, George. 1990. *Nested Games*. Berkeley: University of California Press.

———. 1994. The Power of the European Parliament as a Conditional Agenda-Setter. *American Political Science Review* 88:128–47.

———. 1995. Decision Making in Political Systems: Veto Players in Presidentialism, Parliamentarianism, Multicameralism, and Mutlipartyism. *British Journal of Political Science* 25:289–325.

Tsebelis, George, and Jeannette Money. 1995. Bicameral Negotiations: The Navette System in France. *British Journal of Political Science* 25:101–29.

———. 1997. *Bicameralism*. New York: Cambridge University Press.

Tucker, Robert C. 1978. *The Marx–Engels Reader.* 2d ed. New York: Norton.

Tully, James, ed. 1988. *Meaning and Context: Quentin Skinner and His Critics*. Princeton, N.J.: Princeton University Press.

Tyson, Laura D'Andrea. 1992. *Who's Bashing Whom? Trade Conflict in High Technology Industries*. Washington, D.C.: Institute for International Economics.

Ullman, Richard. 1983. Redefining Security. *International Security* 8:129–53.

U.S. Department of Defense. 1995. Report, Assistant Secretary of Defense for United States Security Strategy for the East Asia–Pacific Region. Office of International Security Affairs, February. Washington, D.C.: U.S. Government Printing Office.

U.S. Department of State. 1997. Office of European Union and Regional Affairs. New Transatlantic Agenda. Senior Level Group Report to the U.S.–E.U. Summit, The Hague, 28 May.

Van Evera, Stephen. 1984a. Causes of War. Ph.D diss., University of California, Berkeley.

———. 1984b. The Cult of the Offensive and the Origins of the First World War. *International Security* 9:58–107.

———. 1990. Primed for Peace: Europe After the Cold War. *International Security* 15:7–57.

Vasquez, John A. 1997. The Realist Paradigm and Degenerative Versus Progressive Research Programs: An Appraisal of Neotraditional Research on Waltz's Balancing Proposition. *American Political Science Review* 91:899–913. Followed by reactions from Kenneth N. Waltz, Thomas J. Christensen and Jack Snyder, Colin and Miriam Fendius Elman, Randall L. Schweller, and Stephen M. Walt.

Vaubel, Roland. 1986. A Public Choice Approach to International Organization. *Public Choice* 51:39–57.

Verba, Sidney. 1961. Assumptions of Rationality and Non-Rationality in Models of the International System. In *The International System: Theoretical Essays*, edited by Klaus Knorr and Sidney Verba, 93–117. Princeton, N.J.: Princeton University Press.

Vernon, Raymond. 1971. *Sovereignty at Bay*. New York: Basic Books.

Viner, Jacob. 1948. Power Versus Plenty as Objectives of Foreign Policy in the Seventeenth and Eighteenth Centuries. *World Politics* 1:1–29.

Vogel, David. 1995. *Trading Up: Consumer and Environmental Regulation in a Global Economy*. Cambridge, Mass.: Harvard University Press.

Volgy, Thomas. 1973. The Role of the Outsider in Quasi-Legislative Systems: The Potential Utility of a Legislative Model. *International Organization* 27:85–98.

Volgy, Thomas J., and Jon E. Quistgard. 1974. Correlates of Organizational Rewards in the United Nations: An Analysis of Environmental and Legislative Variables. *International Organization* 28:179–205.

———. 1975. Learning About the Value of Global Cooperation: Role-Taking in the United Nations as a Predictor of World-Mindedness. *Journal of Conflict Resolution* 19:349–76.

Vout, Malcolm. 1991. Oxford and the Emergence of Political Science in England 1945–1960. In *Sociology of the Sciences—A Yearbook*. Vol. 15, *Discourses on Society: The Shaping of the Social Sciences,* edited by P. Wagner, B. Wittrock, and R. Whitley, 163–194. Dordrecht: Kluwer.

Wade, Robert. 1990. *Governing the Market: Economic Theory and the Role of Government in East Asian Industrialization*. Princeton, N.J.: Princeton University Press.

———. 1996a. Globalization and Its Limits. In *National Diversity and Global Capitalism*, edited by Suzanne Berger and Ronald Dore, 60–88. Ithaca, N.Y.: Cornell University Press.

———. 1996b. Japan, The World Bank, and the Art of Paradigm Maintenance. *New Left Review* 217: 3–36.

Wæver, Ole. 1992. *Introduktion til Studiet af International Politik*. Copenhagen: Forlaget Politiske Studier.

———. 1996. The Rise and Fall of the Inter-Paradigm Debate. In *International Theory: Positivism and Beyond*, edited by Steve Smith, Ken Booth, and Marysia Zalewski, 149–85. Cambridge: Cambridge University Press.

———. 1997. Figures of International Thought: Introducing Persons Instead of Paradigms. In *The Future of International Relations. Masters in the Making?*, edited by Iver B. Neumann and Ole Wæver, 1–37. London: Routledge.

Wagner, Peter. 1989. Social Science and the State in Continental Western Europe: The Political Structuration of Disciplinary Discourse. *International Social Science Journal* 122:509–28.

———. 1990a. *Sozialwissenschaften und Staat: Frankreich, Italien, Deutschland 1870–1980*. Frankfurt and New York: Campus Verlag.

———. 1990b. The Place of the Discourse on Politics Among the Social Sciences: Political Science in Turn-of-the-Century Europe. In *Texts, Contexts, Concepts: Studies in Politics and Power in Language*, edited by Sakari Hänninen and Kari Palonen, 262–281. Jyväskylä, Finnland: Finnish Political Science Association.

Wagner, Peter, and Björn Wittrock. 1991. Analyzing Social Science: On the Possiblity of a Sociology of the Social Sciences and States, Institutions, and Discourses: A Comparative Perspective on the Structuration of the Social Sciences. In *Sociology of the Sciences—A Yearbook*. Vol. 15, *Discourses on Society: The Shaping of the Social Sciences,* edited by P. Wagner, B. Wittrock, and R. Whitley, 3–22, 331–58. Dordrecht: Kluwer.

Wagner, Peter, Carol H. Weiss, Björn Wittrock, and Hellmut Wollmann, eds. 1991. *Social Sciences and Modern States*. Cambridge: Cambridge University Press.

Wagner, R. Harrison. 1974. Dissolving the State: Three Recent Perspectives on International Relations. *International Organization* 28:435–66.

Walker, R. B. J. 1989. History and Structure in the Theory of International Studies. *Millennium: Journal of International Studies* 18:163–83.

———. 1993. *Inside/Outside: International Relations as Political Theory*. New York: Cambridge University Press.

Wallace, William, ed. 1990. *The Dynamics of European Integration*. London: Pinter, for the Royal Institute of International Affairs.

Wallander, Celeste. 1998. *Balancing Acts: Security, Institutions, and German–Russian Relations After the Cold War*. Ithaca, N.Y.: Cornell University Press.

Wallensteen, P., and M. Sollenberg. 1997. Armed Conflicts, Conflict Termination, and Peace Agreements, 1989–1996. *Journal of Peace Research* 34:339–58.

Wallerstein, Immanuel. 1974. *The Modern World System: Capitalist Agriculture and the Origins of the European World-Economy in the Sixteenth Century*. New York: Academic Press.

———. 1979. *The Capitalist World-Economy*. Cambridge: Cambridge University Press.

———. 1991. *Geopolitics and Geoculture: Essays on the Changing World System*. Cambridge: Cambridge University Press.

Wallwork, Ernest. 1972. *Durkheim: Morality and Milieu*. Cambridge, Mass.: Harvard University Press.

Walt, Stephen M. 1987. *The Origins of Alliances*. Ithaca, N.Y.: Cornell University Press.

———. 1991. The Renaissance of Security Studies. *International Studies Quarterly* 35:211–39.

Walter, Barbara. 1994. The Resolution of Civil Wars: Why Negotiations Fail. Ph.D. diss., Department of Political Science, University of Chicago, Chicago, Ill.

Walter, Barbara, and Jack Snyder, eds. Forthcoming. *Civil War, Insecurity, and Intervention*. New York: Columbia University Press.

Waltz, Kenneth N. 1959. *Man, the State, and War*. New York: Columbia University Press.

———. 1964. The Stability of a Bipolar World. *Daedalus* 93:881–909.

———. 1967. *Foreign Policy and Democratic Politics: The American and British Experience.* Boston: Little, Brown.

———. 1970. The Myth of National Interdependence. In *The International Corporation*, edited by Charles P. Kindleberger, 205–23. Cambridge, Mass.: MIT Press.

———. 1979. *Theory of International Politics.* Reading, Mass: Addison-Wesley.

———. 1986. Reflections on *Theory of International Politics*: A Response to My Critics. In *Neorealism and Its Critics*, edited by Robert O. Keohane, 322–45. New York: Columbia University Press.

———. 1990. Nuclear Myths and Political Realities. *American Political Science Review* 84:731–46.

———. 1991. Realist Thought and Neorealist Theory. In *The Evolution of Theory in International Relations*, edited by Robert Rothstein, 21–38. Columbia: University of South Carolina Press.

———. 1993. The Emerging Structure of International Politics. *International Security* 18:45–80.

———. 1998. Realism After the Cold War. Paper delivered at the 94th Annual Meeting of American Political Science Association, August, Boston.

Waltz, Kenneth N., and Scott D. Sagan. 1995. *The Spread of Nuclear Weapons: A Debate.* New York: Norton.

Wapner, Paul. 1995. Politics Beyond the State: Environmental Activism and World Civic Politics. *World Politics* 47:311–40.

———. 1996. *Environmental Activism and World Civic Politics.* Albany, N.Y.: SUNY Press.

Watson, Adam. 1992. *The Evolution of International Society.* London: Routledge.

Webb, Michael C. 1991. International Economic Structures, Government Interests, and International Co-ordination of Macroeconomic Adjustment Policies. *International Organization* 45:307–42.

Webb, Michael, and Stephen Krasner. 1989. Hegemonic Stability Theory: An Empirical Assessment. *Review of International Studies* 15:183–98.

Weber, Axel. 1991. Reputation and Credibility in the European Monetary System. *Economic Policy* 12:57–102.

Weber, Max. 1949. "Objectivity" in Social Science and Social Policy. In *The Methodology of the Social Sciences,* by Max Weber, translated and edited by Edward A. Shils and Henry A. Finch. Glencoe, Ill.: Free Press.

———. [1919] 1958a. Science as a Vocation. In *From Max Weber: Essays in Sociology*, edited and translated by H. H. Gerth and C. Wright Mills, 129–156. New York: Oxford University Press.

———. 1958b. The *Protestant Ethic and the Spirit of Capitalism.* Translated by Talcott Parsons. New York: Scribners.

———. 1975. Marginal Utility Theory and "the Fundamental Law of Psychophysics." *Social Science Quarterly*:21–36.

———. 1978. *Economy and Society: An Outline of Interpretive Sociology.* Edited by Guenther Roth and Claus Wittich. Translated by Ephraim Fishoff et al. Berkeley: University of California Press.

Weigert, Kathleen, and Robert E. Riggs. 1969. Africa and the United Nations Elections: An Aggregate Data Analysis. *International Organization* 23:1–19.

Weingast, Barry R. 1995. The Economic Role of Political Institutions. *Journal of Law, Economics, and Organization* 11:1–31.

———. 1997. The Political Foundations of Democracy and the Rule of Law. *American Political Science Review* 91:245–63.

Weingast, Barry R., and William Marshall. 1988. The Industrial Organization of Congress. *Journal of Political Economy* 96:132–63.

Weiss, Thomas G., and Amir Pasic. 1997. Reinventing UNHCR: Enterprising Humanitarians in the Former Yugoslavia, 1991–1995. *Global Governance* 3:41–57.

Wells, Louis T., Jr. 1972. The Multinational Business Enterprise. In *Transnational Relations and World Politics*, edited by Robert O. Keohane and Joseph S. Nye, Jr., 97–114. Cambridge, Mass.: Harvard University Press.

Wendt, Alexander. 1987. The Agent-Structure Problem in International Relations Theory. *International Organization.* 41:335–70.

———. 1991. Bridging the Theory/Meta-Theory Gap in International Relations. *Review of International Studies* 17:383–92.

———. 1992. Anarchy Is What States Make of It: The Social Construction of Power Politics. *International Organization* 46:391–425.

———. 1994. Collective Identity Formation and the International State. *American Political Science Review* 88:384–96.

———. 1995. Constructing International Politics. *International Security* 20:71–81.

———. Forthcoming. *Social Theory and International Politics*. New York: Cambridge University Press.

Wendt, Alexander, and R. Duvall 1989. Institutions and International Order. In *Global Changes and Theoretical Challenges: Approaches to World Politics for the 1990s*, edited by Ernst-Otto Czempiel and James N. Rosenau, 51–73. Lexington, Mass.: Lexington Books.

Wessels, W. 1990. Administrative Interaction. In *Dynamics of European Integration*, edited by W. Wallace, 229–41. London: Pinter.

———. 1997. An Ever Closer Fusion. Unpublished manuscript, Universität zu Köln.

Whitehead, Laurence. 1996. Three International Dimensions of Democratization. In *The International Dimensions of Democratization: Europe and the Americas*, edited by Laurence Whitehead, 3–25. Oxford: Oxford University Press.

The White House. 1996. *Report: A National Security Strategy of Engagement and Enlargement*. Washington, D.C.: Government Printing Office.

Whitley, Richard. 1984. *The Intellectual and Social Organization of the Sciences*. Oxford: Clarendon Press.

———. 1986. The Structure and Context of Economics as a Scientific Field. In *Research in the History of Economic Thought and* Methodology: A Research Annual, edited by Warren J. Samuels, 4:179–209. Greenwich, Conn., and London: JAI Press.

Wight, Martin. 1977. *Systems of States*. Leicester: Leicester University Press.

Wilcox, Clyde, and Leonard Williams. 1990. Taking Stock of Schema Theory. *Social Science Journal* 27:373–93.

Williamson, Oliver E. 1975. *Markets and Hierarchies: Analysis and Antitrust Implications*. New York: Free Press.

———. 1985. *The Economic Institutions of Capitalism*. New York: Free Press.

———. 1996. *The Mechanisms of Governance*. New York: Oxford University Press.

Winters, Jeffrey. 1996. *Power in Motion: Capital Mobility and the Indonesian State*. Ithaca, N.Y.: Cornell University Press.

Wittrock, Björn. 1992. Discourse and Discipline: Political Science as Project and Profession. In *European Social Science in Transition: Assessment and Outlook*, edited by Meinolf Dierkes and Bernd Biervert, 268–308. Frankfurt am Main: Campus Verlag and Boulder Colo.: Westview Press.

———. 1993. The Modern University: The Three Transformations. In *The European and American University Since 1800: Historical and Sociological Essays*, edited by Sheldon Rothblatt and Björn Wittrock, 303–62. Cambridge: Cambridge University Press.

Wohlforth, William C. 1994. Realism and the End of the Cold War. *International Security* 19:96–100.

Wohlstetter, Albert. 1959. The Delicate Balance of Terror. *Foreign Affairs* 37:211–34.

Wolf, Peter. 1974. International Organization and Attitude Change: A Re-Examination of the Functionalist Approach. *International Organization* 28:352–53.

Wolfers, Arnold. 1952. National Security as an Ambiguous Symbol. *Political Science Quarterly* 67: 481–502.

———. 1956. Introduction. In *The Anglo-American Tradition in Foreign Affairs*, edited by Arnold Wolfers and Laurence W. Martin. New Haven, Conn.: Yale University Press. Reprinted in Wolfers, *Discord and Collaboration*, 233–51.

———. 1962. *Discord and Collaboration: Essays on International Politics*. Baltimore, Md.: Johns Hopkins University Press.

Wood, Adrian. 1994. *North-South Trade, Employment, and Inequality*. New York: Oxford University Press.

Wood, Robert J. 1952. The First Year of Shape. *International Organization* 6:175–91.

Wooley, John. 1984. *Monetary Politics: The Federal Reserve and the Politics of Monetary Policy*. New York: Cambridge University Press.

World Bank. 1997. *World Development Report 1997: The State in a Changing World*. Oxford: Oxford University Press.

World Commission on Environment and Development. 1987. *Our Common Future*. Oxford: Oxford University Press.

Wright, Quincy. 1952. Realism and Idealism in International Politics. *World Politics* 5:116–28.

Yack, Bernard. 1996. The Myth of the Civic Nation. *Critical Review* 10:193–211.

Yarbrough, Beth, and Robert Yarbrough 1992. *Cooperation and Governance in International Trade*. Princeton, N.J.: Princeton University Press.

Yee, Albert S. 1996. The Causal Effects of Ideas on Policies. *International Organization* 50:69–108.

Young, Oran R. 1972. The Perils of Odysseus: On Constructing Theories of International Relations. *World Politics* 24:179–203.

———. 1979. *Compliance with Public Authority: A Theory with International Applications*. Baltimore, Md.: Johns Hopkins University Press.

———. 1986. International Regimes: Toward a New Theory of Institutions. *World Politics* 39:104–22.

———. 1989. *International Cooperation: Building Regimes for Natural Resources and the Environment*. Ithaca, N.Y.: Cornell University Press.

———. 1994. *International Governance: Protecting the Environment in a Stateless Society*. Ithaca, N.Y.: Cornell University Press.

———. 1996. Institutional Linkages in International Society: Polar Perspectives. *Global Governance* 2:1–24.

Young, Oran R., ed. 1997. *Global Governance: Drawing Insights from the Environmental Experience*. Cambridge, Mass.: MIT Press.

Zakaria, Fareed. 1992. Realism and Domestic Politics. *International Security* 17:177–98.

Zelikow, Philip, and Condoleezza Rice. 1995. *Germany Unified and Europe Transformed*. Cambridge, Mass: Harvard University Press.

Zuckerman, Harriet. 1989. The Sociology of Science. In *Handbook of Sociology*, edited by Neil Smelser, 511–74. Newbury Park, Calif: Sage.

Zürn, Michael. 1994. We Can Do Much Better! Aber Muss es auf amerikanisch sein? *Zeitschrift für Internationale Beziehungen* 1:91–114.

Zysman, John. 1977. *Political Strategies for Industrial Order: State, Market, and Industry in France*. Berkeley: University of California Press.

———. 1983. *Governments, Markets, and Growth: Financial Systems and the Politics of Industrial Change*. Ithaca, N.Y.: Cornell University Press.